THE PAPERS

of

JOHN C. CALHOUN

John C. Calhoun

This bust by an unknown sculptor is in the collections of the Gibbes Museum of Art/Carolina Art Association, Charleston. Unlike the more familiar busts by Hiram Powers and Clark Mills, it portrays Calhoun as a modern rather than a Roman.

THE PAPERS

of

JOHN C. CALHOUN

Volume XXI, 1845

Edited by

CLYDE N. WILSON

Shirley Bright Cook, *Associate Editor*

Alexander Moore, *Assistant Editor*

UNIVERSITY OF SOUTH CAROLINA PRESS, 1993

*Publication of this book was made possible
by a grant from the National Historical Publications
and Records Commission.*

*International Standard Book Number: 0–87249–889–1
Library of Congress Catalog Card Number: 59–10351*

Manufactured in the United States of America

CONTENTS

◫

PREFACE

◫

Two decades ago, a kind reviewer of an early volume of *The Papers of John C. Calhoun* remarked in the *London Times Literary Supplement*: "The great enterprise of publishing the Calhoun papers moves majestically on, and the standards of near perfection . . . are maintained . . . ." Seventeen volumes later, we would like to think that the compliment still applies. Seventeen volumes in a little over twenty years, without any compromise of the edition's high scholarly standards or retreat from its original comprehensive plan. And with material resources generally in the range of the barely adequate.

Documentary editing occupies a fairly anomalous position in the larger scholarly enterprise, perhaps more so now than when the encomium quoted above was written. Whether done well or not, it tends to be under-recognized by the historical profession. Possibly we have made it seem too easy. We take consolation in the expectation that these volumes will be in use among the historically-minded of future generations and other lands when most of the fashionable monographs of today are long forgotten.

It is gratifying that our edition is appearing continually and increasingly in the footnotes of scholarly articles, books, and theses. We hope scholars (and not professional scholars alone) will make full use of the documents and everything that arises from them. On the other hand, there are cases of scholars having appropriated some of the historical insights in the Introductions to these volumes as their own, without feeling any need for due acknowledgment. We do not take gratification from this.

The book in hand completes the documentary accounting of Calhoun's tour in the State Department, carries him through a few months of private life that followed, and brings the edition to a point less than five years from the end of his career, though those five years are the most heavily documented of all.

We have received support from the following, support that was generous, substantial, and indispensable: the National Endowment for the Humanities, the National Historical Publications and Records

Commission, and the University of South Carolina. The University South Caroliniana Society has also come to our assistance with timely aid, as it has in the past.

Clyde N. Wilson

Columbia, January, 1990

INTRODUCTION

⬚

Calhoun in Early 1845

Young Jabez L.M. Curry, recently from the University of Georgia and the Harvard Law School and later a U.S. and Confederate Representative from Alabama, encountered John C. Calhoun in Washington in early March, 1845, among the throngs present for President Polk's inauguration. Curry witnessed what he described as "an interview" which took place at Brown's Hotel between Calhoun and Mike Walsh, radical leader of the hard-fisted working men of New York City:

> Alike thoroughly honest, no two men could have been more unlike, physically, socially, mentally. Walsh was a radical, a "subterranean" politician from New York city; Calhoun was a profound and philosophical statesman, with a trained intellect, and his mental characteristic was a tenacious grasp of abstract principle, with a tendency to metaphysical subtlety. A number of visitors were assembled in the parlor, but for half an hour or more only these two men shared in the conversation. Calhoun talked of the Albany regency, of the defalcations in the New York Custom House, of the infamous spoils system with its necessary corruptions, and of the ways, dark and crooked, by which Van Buren won office.

These recollections were published after Curry had been a significant participant in some of the major scenes of the Civil War and antebellum and postbellum strife, yet he described Calhoun as, in conversation, "fascinating and bright, more suggestive and interesting, than any one I ever heard." He applied to Calhoun what was said of Edmund Burke: "He is a wonderfully wise man, but he is wise too soon."[1]

In early March, 1845, Calhoun was at a point of transition—about to complete nearly a year as Secretary of State and to enter on a six-month's period as a private citizen.

Not every observer then or since agreed, but Calhoun considered

[1] J.L.M. Curry, *Civil History of the Government of the Confederate States With Some Personal Reminiscences* (Richmond: B.F. Johnson, 1901), pp. 19–20.

himself to have been a successful Secretary of State. Within the last few days, the admission of Texas to the Union, which had been his first objective, had been irrevocably determined. In the three-day period from February 27 to March 1, both houses of Congress had passed and the President had approved a joint resolution determining upon that goal, which had been a subject of conflict and doubt for the past ten months. And the administration, at Calhoun's urging, had taken immediate steps to win the agreement of Texas to the proposition that had been offered. The role that Calhoun played in the Cabinet deliberations at the end, and in arranging agreement between President Tyler and President-elect Polk for immediate action, does not appear fully in his own papers, but was important.[2]

On that other great matter, Oregon, Calhoun had carried negotiations with the British as far as they could be carried given the fact that the American elections had made Oregon an issue and that the Tyler administration was reluctant to tie the hands of its successor. A British offer of arbitration, submitted in early 1845, was refused. Throughout the negotiations Calhoun had maintained a firm defence of American rights, coupled with a temperate and constructive approach. He had shown the same spirit toward the issue earlier in the Senate and would again the next year at a critical time. In regard to Oregon, he had won and would continue to hold respect and credit on both sides of the Atlantic as a constructive statesman.[3]

As Secretary of State, Calhoun had been at pains to expose to the public in America and Europe what he considered to be the disguised designs of the British Empire to interfere with African slavery in the Americas—and the cynical self-interest and mistaken philanthropy that motivated those designs. While this had hardly been a universally popular effort, he considered that it had been a success. He had brought to light and created a counterweight to a threatening situation. Many then and later found his explicit confrontation of antislavery provocative, but there were also a great many, from di-

---

[2] A concise summary of the events of these three days, with sources, is given in Oliver Perry Chitwood, *John Tyler: Champion of the Old South* (New York and London: D. Appleton-Century Co., 1939), pp. 360–362. See also Calhoun's letter herein of March 3, 1845, to the U.S. representative in Texas, Andrew J. Donelson.

[3] A good statement of the achievement of the Oregon negotiations, from Calhoun's viewpoint, is given by Richard K. Crallé in his prefatory remarks, "The Oregon Negotiation," in Crallé, ed., *The Works of John C. Calhoun* (6 vols. Columbia, S.C.: printed by A.S. Johnston, 1851, and New York: D. Appleton & Co., 1853–1857), 5:414–415.

verse quarters, as is indicated by Calhoun's correspondence, who approved.[4]

A fairly tangential and minor but interesting aspect of Calhoun's anti-abolition efforts concerns United States dealings with the emergent Dominican Republic, whose Spanish whites and free mulattoes were maintaining by force of arms their independence from the government of black Haiti. Dr. José M. Caminero, representative of the Dominicans, visited Washington and wrote a series of letters to Calhoun which appear herein.

In 1858 Edmund Ruffin recorded in his diary that Calhoun's friend Robert M.T. Hunter had told him that Calhoun, as Secretary of State, had "used the secret service fund to supply arms" to the Dominicans.[5] If so, assiduous search has not revealed any documentary record, though, given the nature of the case, there may be no such record. Such a decision would almost surely have been one of the President rather than of the Secretary of State. What is clear from the documents herein is that a Special Agent was sent to the scene to observe first-hand. Chosen for this purpose was John Hogan, an Irish-American politician from Utica, New York, who had been friendly to President Tyler and to Calhoun. Hogan's report could not have been delivered until after Calhoun left office. No official dealings were had with the Dominican Republic until 1856, and it was not recognized until 1866.

After he left office on March 10, and returned home, the major question for Calhoun (setting aside a host of personal matters) was the relationship of himself and the public men, interests, and ideas that he led to President Polk and the Democratic party. Throughout 1845 there was a great deal of uncertainty. Among the many diverse groups that made up the party, Calhoun's was by no means the only one enjoying an ambiguous relationship with the President. The barely victorious party was, in some respects, in considerable disarray.

Calhoun's relationship to Polk in 1845 and as it would unfold the

---

[4] Quite a few letters in this and the previous volume approve of Calhoun's course and report accrued benefits in public opinion, especially on the Continent. The Charleston, S.C., *Mercury*, April 26, 1845, p. 2, found that a Parliamentary speech of Sir Robert Peel, on February 26, revealed the salutary influence of Calhoun's efforts.

[5] Entry for January 22, 1858, in William K. Scarborough, ed., *The Diary of Edmund Ruffin. Volume I: Toward Independence, October, 1856–April, 1861* (Baton Rouge: Louisiana State University Press, 1972), p. 149.

next year when he returned to the Senate is a complex and interesting story. Calhoun's friends had been led to believe by Polk's friends that he would be continued as Secretary of State, though Calhoun had predicted otherwise.[6] It is clear from the press and Calhoun's correspondence that much of the public considered that this would be a natural thing, recognizing Calhoun's services both to the country and the party and adding strength to a fairly anonymous administration.

There was a sense of betrayal, then, when, a few days before the inauguration, Polk informed Calhoun that he intended to appoint an entirely new Cabinet. He offered Calhoun the mission to England, which he almost certainly knew would be refused. Calhoun professed to be neither surprised nor disappointed. Though he would have been willing to stay under the right conditions, he had expected as much from Polk and fully acknowledged the President's right to select his own advisors.[7]

It makes for an interesting but fruitless speculation to consider what changes might have occurred in Calhoun's career and the immediate course of American history if he had agreed to go abroad for the first time. Calhoun was hardly the most popular of American statesmen, yet his capacities were widely recognized, sometimes grudgingly. This had led to widespread approval of his original appointment as Secretary of State.

The New York *Herald*, an outspoken press by no means friendly to Calhoun, observed (later in the year, when it was again rumored that Calhoun might be appointed Minister Extraordinary to Great Britain to settle the Oregon question and make a commercial treaty):

> Mr. Calhoun is peculiarly fitted for this great mission. His sentiments on the Oregon question are known, and command confidence at the North and among the commercial classes. His opinions on the tariff and the principles of reciprocity, carry the whole South. The selection of this great statesman for such a mission would seem to indicate that a new light has broken over the councils of Mr. Polk.[8]

Clearly many people took the Democratic victory in the same way that Calhoun did: as an opportunity for tariff reform and a return to

---

[6] Crallé, "Oregon Negotiation," in *The Works of John C. Calhoun*, 5:415.

[7] *Ibid.*, p. 415. See herein Calhoun to Robert M.T. Hunter, February 14, 1845; to James Edward Colhoun, February 16, 1845; and to James K. Polk, February 28, 1845.

[8] New York, N.Y., *Herald*, as quoted in the Charleston, S.C., *Mercury*, May 17, 1845, p. 2.

Jeffersonian principles. An Ohio Democrat wrote to Calhoun: "The result of the election has been to establish for the present, your opinions of the nature and policy of the general government." He added: "He who is competent to interpret great events, must see in Mr. Polk's election, the decided ascendancy" of Calhoun's 1843 campaign platform: free trade, retrenchment, and strict construction.[9]

For most of 1845 Calhoun's relations with the administration remained friendly but not intimate. What conclusion was to be drawn from the limited patronage that Calhoun's friends sought and were allowed was uncertain. Calhoun, as always, emphasized principles. The administration would receive his support in accordance with how it conducted itself on the tariff and Oregon.

A new administration brought changes in the Washington press establishment. The *Constitution,* the last in a series of struggling Calhoun newspapers in the capital, folded in December, 1845. More significant, *The Globe* of Francis P. Blair published its last issue on April 30, 1845. It had long enjoyed the Congressional printing and spoken authoritatively for the Jackson and Van Buren Democrats. Its plant was sold to the new *Union,* which would be edited by Thomas Ritchie and enjoy the patronage of the Polk administration. The *Union* would remain a leading paper of the capital until 1859. The *Madisonian,* organ of the Tyler administration, shut down at the same time as did *The Globe.* The Whig organ, the *Daily National Intelligencer* of Gales & Seaton, survived until 1870, but its great days were past, as were those of its thrice-defeated hero, Henry Clay. During 1844–1845 Duff Green published the New York *Republic* as a Calhoun organ, but that paper soon faded away from the same inadequate support that had killed other Calhoun papers.

Calhoun's most compelling reason for declining the British mission was undoubtedly a mistrust of the Polk administration, whose short-sighted and ambiguous maneuverings would have left him in an untenable position. There were also sufficient personal reasons. The family fortunes needed urgent attention.

Then there was the question of health. In late January, 1845, Calhoun was taken by pneumonia, a fact widely reported in the press. He recovered, but Calhoun was an experienced and keen observer of the human constitution. He must have had, from early 1845 onward, a sense of borrowed time. While most of the press minimized the illness and emphasized the recovery, one friendly paper forthrightly observed that this was "an attack of disease of the

---

[9] From William M. Corry, February 14, 1845, herein.

lungs, which, sooner or later, will prove fatal . . . . He will, probably, recover from the attack in a few days; but the disease is seated."[10] The lungs were a family weakness which would fell Calhoun in little more than five years, as well as cause the death of four of his five sons in their twenties and thirties.

For those caught up in the moment, the South was triumphant. Florida a State; Texas soon to be; the Presidency, the Cabinet, the Congress, and both political parties led by the South. Calhoun did not, in the terms of the moment or in effective political terms, putting aside prophecy, speak for the South. He merely led an advance party. The two recent Presidential candidates, Polk and Clay, were much more typical of Southern opinion of the moment.

The South was, for the most part, relaxed and confident. In regard to slavery it was where it had been since the seventeenth century, in regard to politics where it had been since Calhoun's youth. The North, except for a brief period of New England militancy in the early Republic, had docilely followed the lead of the South in politics.

But there was a new volatility in the politics of the North. A modernizing economy that looked to an integrated and protected national market; a hardening utilitarian ethics that scorned Constitutional scruples and cynically manipulated electoral blocks; a population beginning to be massively altered by the inrush of new immigrants with European notions of government.

As a correspondent of Calhoun, a North Carolinian, who made his living as a journalist in New York City and wandered all regions of the Union, wrote:

> The progress of fanaticism, every year at the North is becoming more alarming and dangerous to the peace of the country. All ranks of citizens, and especially the wealthy and influential classes, are tinctured with the spirit of abolitionism. The whigs, openly courted their support, and we now find the *Wright wing* of the Democracy approximating, and almost fraternizing with abolition, whig men & Journalls!![11]

In 1845 most Southerners did not share Calhoun's alarm at these new phenomena. They either did not notice or considered them temporary eruptions. Texas, after all, had been annexed. The new world which had been revealed by the election campaign just closed would not be noticed for two more years—until it became inescapably apparent under the name of "Wilmot."

[10] Mobile, Ala., *Register and Journal*, February 10, 1845, p. 2.
[11] From Alexander Jones, January 9, 1845, herein.

The State Department, 1844–1845

Omitted Subjects

Although we have devoted three and one-half volumes to documents arising from Calhoun's service as Secretary of State, that publication amounts to only an approximate thirty-five per cent of the materials we have collected—though we have we hope published the most active and pertinent part.[12]

We have made what we believe is an unprecedentedly exhaustive exploration of the State Department records in the National Archives, though for a limited time period of a little over a year in 1844–1845. It may be worthwhile to record some of the subject areas that do not appear or appear only slightly in the documents that we have been able to publish in Volumes XVIII through XXI of *The Papers of John C. Calhoun.* These records offer a rich source for historians of all sorts, as yet largely untapped, as far as we are able to determine, despite the fact that most, if not all, are available in National Archives published microcopies.

The reader should first study the careful description of included and omitted materials in Volume XVIII, pp. xii–xxiv, and should regard what follows as a supplement to that. It should be remembered that this discussion is far from exhaustive and that, for many of the subjects and many of the diplomats and Consuls who appear in the published volumes, there is much additional material that has not been published.

A great deal of omitted material concerns the routine administration of the local affairs of the District of Columbia, of U.S. Marshals and District Attorneys, and of the territorial governments.[13] Also the publication and distribution of the laws of the United States and other public documents and the use of the State Department library. Such correspondence is found in RG 59 (State Department), in Miscellaneous Letters, incoming correspondence (M-179), and Domestic Letters, outgoing correspondence (M-40).

Another large portion of omissions concerns financial transactions.

---

[12] It is intended to preserve the reproductions of mss. and the editorial transcriptions or abstracts of all omitted documents as a permanent archive at the end of the editorial project.

[13] Some omitted correspondence about Florida citrus culture is printed in Clarence E. Carter and John Porter Bloom, eds., *The Territorial Papers of the United States* (28 vols. to date. Washington: U.S. Government Printing Office, 1934–), vol. 26.

There is much in these records that might be of interest to historians of various sorts, including, perhaps, the relationship of the United States government to the Baring Brothers banking concern of London. Such materials are found in two series of RG 59 (State Department), Accounting Records: Miscellaneous Letters Sent, 1832–1916, and Letters Received from the Fifth Auditor and Comptroller, 1829–1862. Neither file has been filmed.

Another large category of omitted correspondence is found in the file of Passport Applications, 1795–1905 (M-1372). While not of major significance, these records do reveal a good deal about American tourists, students, missionaries, and others, as well as containing occasional unexpected items of humor and criminal activity.

Most correspondence with foreign Ministers and Consuls in the U.S. is omitted, only the most important matters being covered. The largest amount of such papers concerns Great Britain, with which the United States had the most frequent contact about the largest number of matters—territorial, commercial, naval, and cultural. This correspondence with the British Minister, Richard Pakenham, is found in RG 59 (State Department), Notes to Foreign Legations, Great Britain (M-99), and Notes from Foreign Legations, Great Britain (M-50), with much related matter in the Domestic Letters and Miscellaneous Letters.

Three British-American subjects, only slightly represented in the published documents but much more extensively documented in the unpublished ones, are perhaps worth mentioning: early cases of implementation of the criminal extradition clause of the Treaty of Washington of 1842; the fate of the American or former American citizens imprisoned in Tasmania for participation in the abortive Canadian rebellion of 1839; and the "Disputed Territories Fund," that is, the settlement of private land claims between residents of Maine and New Brunswick under the implementation of the Northeastern boundary survey called for by the Treaty of Washington. Many other matters appear in the same correspondence files.

Two subject areas of major interest that run through many different files are commerce and literature. There is a vast amount of material about American commerce in every corner of the world, as well as about the U.S. Navy and the merchant and whaling fleets. Among much else, there is a great deal of material about American seamen, a class which included a substantial number of free black men—material about adventures, illness and death, mistreatment, and crime.

Less tangible but fascinating is the role of diplomatic and Consular posts as a source of livelihood for American scholars and literary men. Besides the well-known case of Washington Irving, Minister to Spain, the U.S. Ministers to Great Britain, Edward Everett, and Prussia, Henry Wheaton, were well-known and much published scholars.

Calhoun appointed Robert Walsh, a prolific author and also a proslavery writer, as Consul at Paris. John Howard Payne, author of the immortal lines of sentimental Americana in "Home, Sweet Home" and much else, was U.S. Consul at Tunis. C. Edwards Lester, U.S. Consul at Genoa, was a prolific economist, and George Washington Greene, at Rome, was a good minor historian. Other cases could be cited, including at a later period Nathaniel Hawthorne and Herman Melville.

The published documents in this edition contain only a fraction of the despatches received from American Ministers and Chargés abroad, except for Mexico and Texas. Such despatches are often frequent and full but do not concern immediately vital matters. There is, nevertheless, a great deal of material about commerce, politics, and the activities of individual Americans. Four such posts for which there are large and conspicuous omissions, despite the publication of a good many despatches, are described below.

—Great Britain. Edward Everett, Minister to Great Britain, wrote frequently, fully, and informatively about a host of matters, involving a vast range of contact between the United States and Britain as well as his comments on other areas of the world. RG 59 (State Department), Diplomatic Despatches, Great Britain (M-30). Study of British-American relations could be usefully supplemented by the records of the busiest American Consulates: London (T-168), Liverpool (M-141), Glasgow (T-207), and many other Consulates in the British Isles.

—Spain. Only a few of Washington Irving's despatches are included. There is a large correspondence which is perhaps not vital to American history, though interesting. Fortunately, Irving's most important letters to the Secretaries of State have been published.[14]

—China. The important Chinese mission of Caleb Cushing, commissioned earlier but carried out and consummated almost entirely during Calhoun's term in the State Department, is represented in our publication by only a few of the most decisive documents. However, this event, fraught with large historical consequences, is very abun-

---

[14] Ralph M. Aderman, and others, eds., *Letters [of Washington Irving]* (4 vols. Boston: Twayne, 1978–1982), comprising vols. 23–26 of *The Complete Works of Washington Irving.*

dantly documented in Diplomatic Despatches, China (M-92), and has been the subject of several documentary publications. A facsimile edition of its records has been produced,[15] and most of the important papers were printed at the time or soon after by the Congress.[16] These papers can be usefully supplemented by the Consular Despatches (in RG 59) of Paul S. Forbes at Canton (M-101), and Thomas W. Waldron at Hong Kong (M-108).

—Hawaii. Despite the publication herein of a number of documents, there is much more available material about American relations with this future State in the despatches of Commissioner George Brown. RG 59 (State Department), Diplomatic Despatches, Hawaii (T-30). See also the Consular Despatches from William Hooper at Honolulu (M-144).

Another vast area of omissions is the business of the approximately 170 U.S. Consuls and Commercial Agents abroad. Despite the inclusion of a large number of documents, our publication has only scratched the surface of this material. Each post has its own file in RG 59 and its own Microcopy for letters incoming to the State Department. Letters outgoing from the Department are contained in RG 59 (State Department), Consular Instructions, in volumes 10–12 for the Calhoun period. Consular Instructions have not been reproduced in Microcopy.

There is a vast amount of material about the activities and interests of Americans abroad in these records, which cover every part of the inhabited world except Japan and the interior of Asia and Africa. Most voluminous are the files from dozens of the old ports of Britain and the European Continent. The same is true to an only slightly lesser degree of the ports of South America and the West Indies.

A few substantial matters in the Consular despatches not included in the published documents are described below, although it should be remembered that the accounting is not exhaustive.

—Puerto Rico. In this Spanish colony and future American possession were four Consuls, at San Juan, Ponce, Mayaguez, and Guayama. Their despatches (M-76) contain much information about trade, tariffs, conditions, and postal arrangements.

—Montevideo. The despatches of Consul Robert M. Hamilton

[15] Jules Davids, ed., *American Diplomatic and Public Papers: The United States and China*, Series I [1842–1860] (2 vols. Wilmington, Del.: Scholarly Resources, Inc., 1973).

[16] See Senate Documents No. 3 (Confidential) and No. 67, 28th Congress, 2nd Session.

(M-71) give a fuller account of the war between Argentina and Uruguay than could be published.

—Buenos Aires. Consul Amory Edwards, a nephew of the Ohio Free Soil Senator Benjamin Tappan, was involved in considerable difficulties with charges of misbehavior in regard to the large estate of an American who had died in Argentina (M-70).

—St. Helena. This remote post, where former Governor of Tennessee William Carroll was U.S. Commercial Agent, contains an abundant documentary record that is perhaps of interest to maritime history (T-428).

—Genoa. Consul C. Edwards Lester was an able observer and commentator on European economic conditions whose interests ranged far beyond his immediate duties (T-64).

—Gibraltar. The despatches of Consul Horatio Sprague concern extensive attempts to raise the wrecked U.S.S. *Missouri*, health quarantine regulations affecting American commerce with the Mediterranean, and other matters (T-206).

—North Africa. There were three American Consuls west of Egypt: John Howard Payne at Tunis (T-303), John F. Mullowny at Tangier (T-61), and Daniel S. Macauley at Tripoli (M-77). All were keen observers of the imperial maneuverings of France and other European powers in this region at the time.

—Tahiti. The despatches of Samuel R. Blackler, U.S. Consul, relate the extension of French authority over this interesting place and American activities there, including the strange case of the disappearance of a young man from Connecticut, Henry E. Dwight (M-465).

—Australia. Elisha Hathaway, Jr., Consul at Hobart Town, Van Diemen's Land, and James H. Williams, Consul at Sydney, New South Wales, reported on the visits of American whalers and the gradually increasing American interchange with that portion of the world (T-127 and M-173).

THE PAPERS

of

JOHN C. CALHOUN

Volume XXI

JANUARY 1–15, 1845

◫

January of the year 1845 was Calhoun's tenth month in charge of the State Department and as busy as any he had yet encountered. The calls of Congress in regard to a host of matters were unceasing, as were the importunities of office-seekers who evidently felt that Calhoun had influence with the Polk administration that would come in next March as well as with the expiring government of John Tyler.

On January 4 Caleb Cushing reported his arrival in Washington from a long and successful mission to China. And on the same day, the representative of Texas officially reported the installation of a new President, Anson Jones, the previous month in the Republic of Texas, while assuring Calhoun of that Republic's continuing desire for juncture with the Union of the States. On the 7th Calhoun issued instructions for an American agent to Ecuador, an effort to settle long-standing claims. And the next day he received a report from Dr. Caminero, the representative of the Spanish portion of Santo Domingo, who was seeking American support for the independence of his people from black Haiti.

As always, of course, Texas and Mexico were on the top of the agenda. On the 9th Calhoun wrote to the U.S. Minister in Texas rather pessimistically about the ongoing struggle over annexation in Congress. On the same day, the U.S. Minister in Mexico City wrote (though his despatch was not received for a month) to warn of "the settled policy of the English Government to acquire possession of the two Californias."

The Oregon negotiations had occupied much of the past fall and then taken a recess. On January 15 the British Minister re-opened them with a new twist—an offer to submit the matter to arbitration.

There was much public speculation as to whether Calhoun would continue in his present post under the new administration. "As to myself," the Secretary wrote to an old friend, "I was forced into my present position, greatly ag[ai]nst my inclination, by a sense of duty. Nothing else could have induced me to accept it, and nothing can induce me to hold it for a single day, whenever I can retire consistently with duty & propriety." Meanwhile, the Washington Con-

3

stitution *of January 4 reported Calhoun as one of about a hundred citizens, from public and private life, who had been enlisted as "managers" of an "Inauguration Ball" planned for next March 4.*

𝕀

From RICHARD GARDNER

Coleman's Hotel [Washington]
Sunday Ev[enin]g [1845?]

My dear Sir, As my sole object in visiting this country is Political information I am very anxious to have the honour of another interview with you, and if your engagements permit you to name a time, I w[oul]d endeavour not to let any thing interfere with y[ou]r convenience. It is certainly remarkable that in the two best regulated states of the North and South respectively[,] Massachusetts & S. Carolina[,] regard is had to the element of taxation as well as population. I think an accurate analysis of the various governments of the Union w[oul]d tend to throw light upon the working of the system ([Friedrich] Von Raumer by the way, has done the thing on a small scale) though I am not able to see clearly the existence of the check of which you spoke[,] at least in the great majority of instances; and certainly the experience of the organization of the new States goes to show that the Progressive Democracy (or whatever you please to call it) of the day is not very sollicitous [*sic*] to provide them. With much respect D[ea]r Sir Very faithfully Y[ou]rs, Richard Gardner.

ALS in ScCleA. NOTE: Richard Gardner was an English political pamphleteer and a Member of Parliament from Leicester during 1847 and 1852–1856. The year of this undated letter is conjectural.

From "A Virginian," [Samuel M. Janney?], published 1845. In a public letter published in a 13-pp. pamphlet, "A Virginian" writes Calhoun to demonstrate the immorality of slavery and the cruelty of the institution as regulated by the laws of Va. "When we seriously and impartially reflect upon the character of these laws, for whom they were intended, their hardness, severity, and we might properly say cruelty, the cause of injured humanity irresistibly forces itself upon the mind and demands instant consideration." The author finds it "remarkable that a gentleman of his [Calhoun's] transcendent abilities and long experience, who has studied the human character with so critical an eye, and knows so well what should be the rule of action for the human family in our intercourse with subordinates, should, in the retirement of his closet, publish to the world a letter, in which he states that *slavery is an institution right in the abstract, and that the prosperity of the South depends upon its existence.*" "A Virginian" believes that the rights of slave owner-ship are found in customary, not natural, law and that, as a form of property, slaves cannot be involuntarily emancipated without compensation. He proposes no remedy to end slavery in the U.S. but believes that the progress of humanity, the growing unprofitability of the institution, and the enlightened self-interest of slaveowners will lead them voluntarily to emancipate their slaves. [The most likely author of this letter is Samuel M. Janney (1801–1880), a Quaker and native of Loudoun County, Va. He used the pseudonym "A Virgin-ian" in anti-slavery newspaper essays in 1844 and 1845.] PC in "A Virginian," *Letter Addressed to the Hon. John C. Calhoun, on the Law Relating to Slaves, Free Negroes, and Mulattoes* (Washington: J. & G.S. Gideon, 1845).

From George Ditson, [U.S.] Vice-Consul, Nuevitas, Cuba, 1/1. "I have the honour of complying with the wishes of my Government by forwarding specimens of the mineral wealth of this District. The box containing them I send to the care of the Collector of the port of New York; they are from my mines & I hope that some of them will be worthy a place in the Natural History Rooms at Washington." ALS in DNA, RG 59 (State Department), Consular Despatches, Nuevitas (T-588:1), received 1/15.

From JOHN W. FISHER

Consulate of the United States of America
Island Guadeloupe
Pointe à Pitre, 1st of January 1845
Sir, I have the honor at this time to forward you my half yearly Re-turns from 1st of July to 31st December 1844.

At the same time it becomes my duty to inform the Department of the existence in this place of rather a jealous feeling towards the American Commerce, which appears to me to be the case on account of the augmentation of the different charges. American Manufac-tures are admitted under a duty of 15 p[er] Ct. ad valorum and it often happens that the Officers of the Customs add 25 p[er] Ct. to the Invoice prices. The [French] Government opened the Ports of this Island to all Vessels, laden with building Materials, free of Charges; but on arrival of vessels, who are trying the Market and who find it impossible to dispose of their cargo without a great loss, they are compelled to pay the full Amount of tonnage money and other Port charges.

Vessels anchoring outside the Bar of Pointe à Pitre are liable to a Fine, although Pilots & Revenue Cutters are outside of the Anchorage; our American Citizens approaching Harbour whilst night is coming on, are under the necessity of going to an anchor outside, they are in consequence of this seased, process verbal issued and a Fine of 1000 to 2000 francs imposed on them: I have repeatedly called on the Authorities to redress these grievances, but I am sorry to say nothing satisfactory has be[en] done. The last vessel that found herself in this predicament was the Schooner Mary H. Tillet of North Carolina; she was in a leaky condition, anchored outside the Bar and had to pay a fine of 1000 fr[an]cs. I have represented the Case to Government and trust to be refunded.

I am under a full conviction at this time if one of our National Ships was to visit my Station, it would be of great benefit to the American Commerce. If the Department should think it proper to publish the enclosed Statement, it might have the effect of cautioning many of our Citizens from being imposed upon. I remain with great Respect Sir your very obedient Servant, John W. Fisher.

LS (No. 8) with Ens in DNA, RG 59 (State Department), Consular Despatches, Guadeloupe, vol. 2 (T-208:2), received 2/21. NOTE: Fisher's "Statement" was a draft public announcement that American ships lying outside Point à Pitre bar were subject to seizure and that building materials entering that port were obliged to pay full tonnage and port dues.

From JOHN MCLEAN, [Associate Justice of the U.S. Supreme Court]

Washington, 1 Jan[uar]y 1844 [*sic*; 1845]
Sir, The enclosed letter recommending Joseph W. Chapman for the appointment of District Attorney, of the United States, for Indiana, is signed by the judges of the Supreme Court of the State; and I ["take pleasure in saying" *interlined*] that they are gentlemen of the highest respectability, and distinguished for their ability and learning. Hav-

ing said thus much I will add, that I know of no reason why Mr. [Courtland] Cushing, the present incumbent should not be reappointed. He has discharged his duties ably and faithfully, and is a man of irreproachable character. His father was an officer in the army and lost his life in the public service, during the late War. And he has, by a ["most" *canceled*] continued and meritorious effort risen to great respectability in his profession.

Mr. Chapman, I have no doubt, will make a good officer; but being made the instrument of communicating the enclosed letter, I have supposed it is not improper to bear my testimony to the the [*sic*] faithfulness and ability of the present incumbent. With great respect Your ob[edien]t Ser[van]t, John McLean.

ALS with En in DNA, RG 59 (State Department), Applications and Recommendations, 1845–1853, Chapman (M-873:15, frames 73–77). NOTE: The En, dated 12/26/1844, was signed by Charles Dewey, Isaac Blackford, and Jer[emiah] Sullivan and addressed to McLean.

From S[ETH] T. OTIS

United States Consulate
Basel, Switzerland, January 1st 1845
Sir, In the matter of Gerard Koster, which I had the Honor to lay before You in my Communication No. 7 [of 6/26/1844], I beg leave to state at considerable length, the circumstances attending, & the situation of the same. Your reply upon this subject—under date of July 23rd last—was duly received, as briefly acknowledged in my Communication No. 8 [of 9/12/1844].

Some Three Weeks previous to its receipt—Koster having been driven by myself from one Canton to another in this Confederacy—left Switzerland for parts unknown.

Messrs. [Jon D.] Bugbee & [Thomas G.] Casey, despairing of arresting him in Europe, advised me from "Vevey" (Switz.), under date of Sept. 10/44, that they had entered into a Compromise with a Brother-in-law of his, residing at that place, by which all the process for K[oster]'s arrest was to be discontinued & he discharged from all the liabilities in question, & requested me to so discontinue them and notify the Swiss Authorities accordingly. I also learned from them a few days afterwards—in a hasty personal interview, that the payment of this Compromise depended *Entirely* upon the concurrence of of [*sic*] all parties interested—which were several Institutions & Individuals besides those they Represented, & Whose opinions could not be Known for many months. I need scarcely add that I found myself in a very Embarrassing Position. I had—as You are well aware—represented to the Swiss Authorities that K[oster] was a *Criminal* & had requested his deliverance to the authorities of the United States, & gave assurances of Reciprocity on the part of my Government, in case of K[oster]'s delivery, all of which You are aware they met most cordial[l]y, upon the conditions Expressed in my Communication No. 7, & which Conditions were promptly acceded to by my Government. The question arose, first—Can I consistently consent to *Compromise* what I have termed a *Criminal offence?* Secondly—Am I the mere Agent of Messrs. B[ugbee] & C[asey]—in the absence of a Treaty, & must I abide their instructions? I thought both extremely doubtful, & if so in *Reality*, the fact, would be very likely to bring my Government into disrepute with the Swiss Authorities. And particularly when I remembered the additional frauds of K[oster]'s—And which I had stated in my applications here. I thought I ["should" *canceled*] could not, abide ["their" *altered to* "the"] instructions of Messrs. B[ugbee] & C[asey]. Upon mature reflection, I deemed the questions of much importance, & resolved upon Visiting Paris, & laying the whole subject with the many various documents (amounting to nearly 200) before our Minister Mr. [William R.] King. This I done on the 1st Oct. last. Mr. [Henry] Wheaton (our Minister from Prus[s]ia) happened also to be present; & the whole subject ["was" *interlined*] fully discussed. The Conclusion was, that it was only *proper* for me to *suspend* proceedings. This fact I immediately advised Messrs. B[ugbee] & C[asey] of at Liverpool, stating my Views, & asking theirs in return; Mr. B[ugbee], in his reply (rec[eive]d Oct. 25/44) says "If You think it better to make a suspension, do so." I was preparing my papers accordingly—(but still in doubt) when I rec[eive]d an additional Letter from Mr. Casey dated New York Oct. 31/44, saying "You have done right to suspend operations against Koster & not withdraw them Entirely, as I Expect parties will not be satisfied." I then supposed it best to not make a suspension at all, but learning afterwards ["that" *altered to* "from"] the Agents of K[oster] that he was desirous of returning to Switzerland I thought perhaps his doing so would aid me in any future Efforts to arrest him, & accordingly on the 17th December Ultimo, I addressed a Letter to the high Governm[en]t of Switzerland, requesting a suspension of proceedings until further notice—a copy of which, with their Reply, I herewith Enclose to You. I need not Comment upon this reply, and will only say that it *pleased me.*

Thus Sir, stands this affair; my opinion now is this—When all the Parties interested in these extensive frauds shall unanimously agree upon a Settlement with Koster, I may then Entirely withdraw all proceedings, and allow them to take what they can get from this most Consummate *Swiss Robber.*

Should Your opinion be adverse to this, I have Earnestly to request that you advise me accordingly, at the Earliest day; directing Your Communication "Via Liverpool Steamer & Paris." I am Sir Very Truly Your Ob[edien]t Serv[an]t, S.T. Otis, Consul.

ALS (No. 14) with Ens in DNA, RG 59 (State Department), Consular Despatches, Basle, vol. 1 (T-364:1), received 1/27. NOTE: According to the Ens, Bugbee and Casey had agreed to a compromise with Koster that would recover *"one fifth"* of the funds Koster had embezzled.

From W[ILLIAM] H. ROANE, [former Senator from Va.]

Tree Hill near Richmond Va., Jan[uar]y 1st 1845

My D[ea]r Sir, I cannot more agreeably to myself, appropriate a portion of this great day—the first of ["a" *interlined*] new and in all probability eventful year, than by tendering to you personally the kindest wishes it can inspire for your long continued happiness & prosperity—and offering my fervent hope that through your instrumentality our beloved country may be rescued from the the [*sic*] dangers with which she is now environed by Domestic Cupidity, and forreign jealousy. I also desire to make my too long omitted acknowledgement of the rec[ei]pt under your Frank of the message & Doc[u]m[en]ts—(the latter of which I read with deep interest, and for the most part high satisfaction. I need not say that I allude to your letter [of 8/12/1844] to Mr. [William R.] King—) and thus avail myself of the occasion to assure you of my pleasing remembrance of our long standing uninterrupted personal friendship & regard. I might ["perhaps" *interlined*] solicit an occasional line from you, but for my knowledge that every moment of your time is more profitably employed—and of my own habitual & incurable indolence as a correspondent. In addition to all this—I had another inducement to write to you—and hope that I may make you my debtor, by introducing to your acquaintaince Mr. James T. ["Ship" *canceled*] Ship of Madison Co[unty,] Virg[ini]a, who will hand you this. My own acquaintaince with this young gentleman is recent & limited. Those who know

9

him more intimately speak highly of him. *I* only *know* that he was zealous and did good service in our late stirring campaign—that he is amiable & gentlemanly in his deportment & manners, and intelligent in conversation. He is *your* devoted admirer—as he is a proud member of that school, which the foul mouthed unscrupulous "Whigs" hereabouts have y'clept the *"chivalry"*; I must however refer you to his more intimate friends [Robert M.T.] Hunter and others as to his qualifications, wishes, Views &c.

Here I should stop—but I feel it difficult to restrain my pen from the vain effort to say how strongly I participate in the deep interest felt by every intelligent *thinking* Patriot not only in America, but throughout Christendom in regard to the present posture of affairs at *Washington* city. The word "Crisis" we must all admit has been much hackneyed; but I do solemnly ["declare" *interlined*] that I consider the present, the most *critical* and awful moment of public affairs, that I have witnessed, or read of, since the Declaration of American Independence. The "Texas question" as now presented, concerns the whole ["world," *interlined*] and is inseperably blended with the immediate & ultimate freedom of all its nations. Those who oppose it, oppose all *Declarations of* ["Indepence" *changed to* "Independence"], and Desecrate the temple of Liberty founded by our noble men of '76. *They* would have thought their ["work" *interlined*] incomplete if ["it" *interlined*] only served the then 13 colonies and their attached territories. *Their* far seeing vision and philanthropic hearts—intended a plan of ["political" *interlined*] salvation for this compact *continent*—the genial influence of which would ultimately extend to every nation—["although" *canceled and* "even though" *interlined*] *we* ["through" *interlined*] indulgence in satiety might (Jerusalem like) be consigned to darkness & infidelity. It surely cannot be that vile low party spirit—the spirit of abolitionism—and, that undying and undefineable love for Brittain and monarchy, will override the great principles of American liberty which lay at the *root* of this question of "annexation"! Great as may be our interest as regards the productions, population, position, boundaries &c of Texas, it is in my estimation small when compared with the *denial* of our *right* to own it—with the bold and infamous doctrine that nations who *will* it, and dare *do it*, can never shake off a Tyrant[']s yoke, and take their "equal stand amongst the nations of the earth." This doctrine extinguishes the brightest light of our Revolution & consigns to despair & darkness the fairest portions of the globe. I am inexpressibly indignant and horrified, when I think that Brittain is conspiring and plotting, to consign to servile Bondage, our own *Anglo Saxon*

10

brethren & children—occupying our own conterminous soil, acquired by their own honorable valour—under the base, *hypocritical* pretence of giving *freedom* & *liberty* to the woolly headed sons of Affrica!!

Taking the objections urged against annexation—in connexion with nativeism—the revived child of old Federalism—and ["aboliti" *canceled*] *Hell born* abolitionism, there will little remain worth preserving, of the rich inheritance bequeathed to us by the noble founders of our wonderful republic. Is it not "passing strange" that every American—and especially all those *south* of "Mason's & Dixon[']s line"—if blind to the great principles involved in this question, does not sufficiently understand his own interest, to strain every nerve, to rescue from the clutch of Brittain and abolitionism, the only *real cotton growing* country in the world—except our own!!! The devolopements of the Brittish press—especially the [London] Times newspaper—should tinge the cheeks of the American "Whigs," and arouse to energy and action every dormant or misguided emotion of Patriotism—but whither has my pen led me on a subject which you understand 100,000 times better than I can! But my paper is not out, & in my deep solitude I think ["at times," *interlined*] too much of public affairs to with[h]old my feelings when ["I" *canceled*] (very seldom) I see a friend or grasp a pen.

I presume annexation in some shape will pass the H[ouse of] Rep[resentatives], and I hardly suppose it can in any form get through the Senate. I have but little Hope that [William C.] Rives or [William S.] Archer [Senators from Va.] can be brought to its support! Saying nothing of *instructions*, it is certainly a bad sign when Represe[nta]t[i]v[e]s entirely disregard the *deliberately* expressed will of their constituents—and I do assure you, that but for the Texas question our late majority in Va. could not have been swelled to any thing like 6000—and [Thomas H.] Benton! writhing under false calculations & disappointed hopes, will perhaps ["take" *interlined*] any course to defeat the measure, unless he can strike out one of *annexation*, which he *thinks* may "save his Bacon," feed his vanity, and supply his *Egotism*. The Baltimore nomination fell heavily on *his* ear. It was "gall & wormwood" to his palate, and shewed him too plainly that his "cake was all Dough"—poor man! He is now, "step'd in so far, that, should he wade no more, returning were as tedious as go o'er." He has joined so fiercely with the Mexican pack in the Texas chase, and "given mouth" so freely, that he cannot now if he wishes it, "run with the Hound & hold with the Hare."

I cannot but feel much interest in *your* action in this great drama—especially as regards the time & manner of your exit from the stage.

11

The peculiar and honorable circumstances under which you made your entrance, and became one and certainly the chief one of its "Dramatis personae" turned all eyes towards you and made you ["at once" *interlined*] the "observed of all observers." Your letter to Mr. King of itself, has fully sustained your long standing and acknowledged reputation for high talent—and at the same time given you a just claim, which your past vocations had not allowed you praccitically to assert—as a Diplomatist. Your own future course of action is no doubt, under contingencies, resolved & fixed, and were it not, I could not volunteer my advice—the result of limitted views—but as I have run thus far, I trust that our long standing friendship and free intercourse, will exempt me from the semblance of presumption, when I say that it is a matter of much anxiety to your friends. That I have conversed unreservedly with several of the most ardent and talented of them in these parts, whose views were entirely concurrent with my own, & that they entreated me to communicate them to you, which for the reason above assigned I declined to do—and at this moment, I regret that my hasty pen has led me too near to them, to decline the advance. They are simply & briefly thus. That you owe it to the *country*, considering that you came into your present responsible office for the sole object of forwarding to an honorable close the great subjects of Texas & Orregon & their mighty consequences, to remain in it (provided you can do so on terms *fully* & *exactly agreeable* to *feelings*, of even fastidious delicacy) until your objects are all accomplished, or put in such a train, for weal, or for woe, as will render your longer continuance *for their* advancement unnecessary—when, in duty to *yourself*, you should make your respectful Bow, and resume the dignified retirement from which you were called "*pro hac vice*," [that is, for this occasion,] and be ready to fill any station or render any service which may at a future time make a proper appeal to your patriotism. But enough—enough. I am sure *you* will echo the word—["&" *interlined*] I beg that you will pardon all that I have said, that is too much. When I commenced, I only intended to write a short open letter of introduction to Mr. Ship & enclose it to him (by his request) in Washington—but as I have ran into matters which should not meet every eye—I will run off a hasty line ["of him" *canceled and* "for his" *interlined*] and send it herewith.

I am in great solitude and will be at all times thankful to receive under y[ou]r frank any *spare* Doc[u]m[en]t of interest or value. As ever very truly y[ou]r friend &c, W.H. Roane.

P.S. On reading over I find that my hasty & careless pen made so many blunders as to make me almost ashamed to send so "foul a sheet"—but I cannot begin anew—& again beg you to excuse my boring you at this rate.

ALS in ScCleA; slightly variant ALS (retained copy) in ViHi, Harrison Family Papers.

From G[EORGE] F. USHER

Commercial Agency of the U. States
Cape Haytien, Jan[uar]y 1st, 1845

Sir, I have the honor to transmit, herewith, my semi-annual returns up to this date.

Altho there is no actual outbreak here, yet this Island is far from being tranquil; Soldiers are constantly being collected & moved in bodies, generally towards Port-au-Prince, and the popular understanding is, that an attack will soon be made on the Spanish part of the Island; but those residing in this, the French part, are far from being satisfied with the proceedings of the existing authorities, and the dominant party is ready to offer any excuse for collecting troops around it. And it is difficult to predict, if general tranquility will soon prevail, under present circumstances. I have the honor, Sir, to be, with the highest consideration, Your Very Ob[edien]t S[er]v[an]t,

G.F. Usher, U.S. C[ommercial] Ag[en]t.

ALS (No. 20) with Ens in DNA, RG 59 (State Department), Consular Despatches, Cap Haitien, vol. 7 (M-9:7, frames 165–169), received 1/27.

From FRANCIS WHARTON

Philadelphia, Jan. 1, 1845

My dear Sir, I cannot refrain from addressing you once more on the subject of Judge [George W.] Woodward's confirmation, though I know the engrossing character of your public duties leaves little margin for general correspondence. From what Mr. [Simon] Cameron announces to his friends here, & from the whig indications, we very much fear his confirmation is ["perilled"(?) *canceled and* "doubtful" *interlined*]. *Here,* he is attacked solely on account of his *free trade* and *strict construction tendencies.* He is as pure a man as ever breathed; and the only personal charge against him is that his rigour of character even approaches to haughtiness. But he has been, when all others failed, a faithful advocate of old republican principles; and, with the exception of Mr. [David] Wilmot [Representative from Pa.] & Judge [George] Sharswood, is the only Pennsylvania politician who has been uniformly anti-bank & anti-tariff. If he is to be sacrificed for such views, it ought not to be without a hard fight. I have just heard from Judge W[oodward], &, if it would be necessary, I believe a powerful effort would be made by our best public men on his ["ef" *canceled*] behalf. The only question is whether, in the present Constitution of the Senate, such an effort would be advisable. Is it probable the Judiciary committee will report in his favour? I cannot forbear pressing the subject on your attention as it is one of such great importance not only to the country, but to ["the cause of" *interlined*] just Constitutional views. With great respect, I am yours, Francis Wharton.

ALS in ScCleA. NOTE: An AEU by Calhoun reads: "Mr. Wharton[,] relates to Judge Woodward[']s case." Woodward had been nominated to a seat in the U.S. Supreme Court after the nomination of Edward King had not been confirmed. Woodward also failed to win confirmation.

From H[enry] L. Ellsworth, [Commissioner of the] Patent Office, 1/2. "I have the honor to transmit herewith a list of Persons employed in this office during the year 1844 with the compensation of each—agreeably to your request of the 19th November." LS in DNA, RG 59 (State Department), Accounting Records, Letters Received from Departments and Bureaus.

From EDWARD EVERETT

London, 2 January, 1845

Sir, I forward herewith the last circular of the Messrs. [G. & H.] Davis relative to the state of the Tobacco trade. It is not in my power to add any thing to what is contained in my despatch Nro. 207 of the 11th November last, relative to the prospect of a reduction of the duty on this article.

Not the least injurious operation of the enormous duty on tobacco and the consequent temptation to smuggling is the embarrassment and loss caused to our Ship-masters and ship-owners in the British ports by the seizure of their vessels and the penalty inflicted upon them when attempts at smuggling are detected on the part of any of the Ship's Company. These attempts are continually made by the seamen and Steerage-passengers, to many of whom the profit on even a small quantity of Tobacco holds out an irresistible temptation. The seizure of the "St. George," which formed the subject of my despatch Nro. 215, was a case of the kind. The attempt at smuggling, which caused that vessel to be seized, was the act of the Stewart [*sic*] who immediately absconded. The "St. George" was promptly released on my representing the case at the Treasury, and as appears by a letter from our Consul at Liverpool [Joel W. White], of which I enclose a copy, on favorable terms.

I was lately informed by the Commander of one of the regular Newyork traders, that a large proportion of the vessels arriving at Liverpool from the United States are subjected to penalties varying from five to one hundred pounds, for these attempts at smuggling Tobacco. I did not understand him to complain that the law is administered with rigor in this respect. I rather suppose that the contrary is the case; but we have great reason to complain of the law itself, by which a duty is imposed so enormously disproportioned to the value of the Article and thereby unavoidably producing so serious an inconvenience to the honest trader. I am, Sir, with great respect, Your obedient Servant, Edward Everett.

Transmitted with despatch Nro. 233.

1. Mr. White to Mr. Everett, 2 December, 1844.
2. Circular of Messrs. G. & H. Davis & Co. 1 January, 1845 (Printed).

LS (No. 233) with En in DNA, RG 59 (State Department), Diplomatic Despatches, Great Britain, vol. 54 (M-30:50), received 1/27; FC in DNA, RG 84 (Foreign Posts), Great Britain, Despatches, 9:108–111; FC in MHi, Edward Everett Papers, 51:37–39 (published microfilm, reel 23, frames 572–573).

To C[harles] J. Ingersoll, Chairman [of the House Committee on Foreign Affairs], 1/2. Calhoun acknowledges receipt of Ingersoll's note of 12/26/1844 and in reply to its inquiry whether [Cornelius P.] Van Ness and [John H.] Eaton received reimbursement for "Office Rent and Expences and for profits in exchange on London," he encloses a communication [dated 12/28/1844] to himself from [Stephen Pleasonton] the Fifth Auditor, which explains the State Department's policy in regard to Van Ness and Eaton. LS with Ens in DNA, RG 233 (U.S. House of Representatives), 28A-D12.2; FC (dated 12/31/-1844) in DNA, RG 59 (State Department), Reports of the Secretary of State to the President and Congress, 6:131; FC (dated 12/31/1844) in DNA, RG 59 (State Department), Domestic Letters, 35:64 (M-40: 33); PC with Ens in House Report No. 50, 28th Cong., 2nd Sess., pp. 2–5.

From John McKeon, [former Representative from N.Y.], N[ew] York [City], 1/2. McKeon recommends Robert Hutton, "a merchant of standing in this section of the country," to be U.S. Consul at Maracaibo, Venezuela. Hutton is connected with a mercantile house doing business there and intends to reside at that place. ALS in DNA, RG 59 (State Department), Applications and Recommendations, 1845–1853, Hutton (M-873:44, frames 237–238).

From G. C. F. MORHARD

Geneva, 2 January, 1844 [*sic*; 1845]

Sir, Desiring to render myself useful to the cause of humanity, I have left my country and travelled last year in the West, for the purpose of finding in the U.S. an asylum for the unfortunate workmen of Europe. These men who ask only for a livelihood would soon populate the uncultivated regions of the West. The memorial which I submit herewith for your perusal would be the manner in which they would make their living.

To put an end to the abuses which have their sources from the negligence with which the governments of the Old and New Worlds have, up to the present day, looked upon the transportation and placing of Emigrants, a society will be formed in Paris, consisting of all the illustrious men who take an interest in the amelioration of the destinies of their equals. This society will have agents in all the principal Sea ports, and will send only such men who are worthy and capable to undertake a useful work. A society established at New York would devote its time in sending the workmen to different places in the U.S. where they will be the most needed.

The most appropriate manner, according to my views to make of emigration a source of prosperity for both hemispheres, and to render thousands happy, would be to employ the Emigrants at the public works such as Railroads, Canals, etc. which would keep an immense number in constant employment who would be contented with a small salary; or else receive as their reward lands in the West, and, for themselves and their children the rights and privileges of American citizens.

Confident of the great and noble cause which I am now pleading before the citizens of the U.S., I hope from you a speedy an[d] satisfactory answer. With respect etc., G.C.F. Morhard, Citizen of Geneva (Switzerland).

[P.S.] References[,]

Every one in the city of Geneva.

New York:

    Messrs. Albert Gallatin

    Orville Dewey

    Mac Daniel

    P. Maroncelli Prof[essor]

    [Louis P.] De Luze, Consul [from] Switzerland.

[Enclosure]

To be read before Congress.

Railroad from Milwaukie (Wisconsin) and from Jefferson (Missouri) to the Oregon territory.

A quick and easy communication established between the Western frontier of the U.S. and Oregon territory would be of a great political and commercial importance to America. Commercial intercourse between the Pacific and Atlantic would soon become for the inhabitants a fertile source of riches and prosperity. The passess of the Rocky Mountains would guarantie for ever the U.S. ["of" *altered to* "on"] the Western Side from the invasions and encroachments of a foreign power.

This colossal enterprise could never be executed alone by american laborers, with the exception of enormous expenses and many years labour.

In case a Railroad company should be formed between the above mentioned places, we would undertake to procure, from the year 1846, at little expense, workmen and engineers in sufficient numbers so that the work could be completed in two or three years at the farthest.

At the present day, amongst the European population, there are ten million of honest and laborious families who are in want of bread, and who look for their children to a future independance. From these, we would select the workmen necessary to the Construction of the above mentioned railroad.

Our Workmen would be paid in lands. The work of 100 men during one year to be paid by the Company at the rate of 2000 acres government lands.

Our workmen would be boarded and Clothed at the Company's expense as long as they are in its employ. The Company would besides engage itself to defray their expenses from Havre to New York. All in all, each workman, at the termination of the enterprise, would not have cost more than $350 to the Company and the Union would have acquired a useful citizen.

We hope that the inhabitants of the U.S. will easily perceive the immense advantage which would result to them from such an enterprise, and will entertain our proposition favorably.

All persons desirous to become stockholders [of?] the Oregon Railroad Company, and who would be willing to favor us with their confidence will please communicate their intentions in writing before the 1st of August next by address to G.C.F. Morhard, No. 15, Quai des Bergues, Geneva (Switzerland).

N.B. *The draining of the immense swamps* of Mississip[p]i and Missouri would render the Climate more healthy and considerably increase the value of the western lands; We would also engage to furnish workmen in sufficient numbers to any company which might be formed with the view of such an enterprise *or any other project of importance.* They would be remunerated in the same manner as those which we intend to procure for the Oregon Railroad Company. New York, 12 IXber, 1844.

ALS with En in DNA, RG 59 (State Department), Miscellaneous Letters (M-179:107, frames 2–5), received 2/10. NOTE: An AEU by Calhoun on the ALS reads "Relates to emigration."

From ROBERT B. CAMPBELL

Consulate of the United States of America
Havana, Jan[uar]y 3d 1845

Dear Sir, I have this moment received your communication of the 23d Nov[embe]r 1844 enclosing certain memoranda from Mr. [Richard S.] Coxe which shall be attended to promptly. The sailing of the Oregon only leaves me time for this acknowledgement, and to say that I forwarded you a Spanish paper containing important intelligence from Mexico. [Gen. Antonio Lopez de] Santa Anna is expected to arrive here in the British Steamer on the 6th inst., at all events she will bring confirmation or refutation of previous reports and all authentic information shall be immediately sent you. I have the honor to be with great respect & esteem Y[ou]r Mo[st] Ob[edien]t Serv[an]t, Robert B. Campbell.

ALS in DNA, RG 59 (State Department), Consular Despatches, Havana, vol. 21 (T-20:21), received 1/13.

From T. HARTLEY CRAWFORD

War Department
Office [of] Indian Affairs, Jan[uar]y 3d 1845
Sir, By direction of the Secretary of War [William Wilkins] I have the honor to enclose herewith a copy of a letter from Colo[nel] James Logan, agent for the Creek Indians, on the subject of the interferance of Indians ["with Citizens of the United States or Texas" *interlined*] on the frontier at the instance of any other government. Very respectfully Your mo[st] Ob[edient] S[ervan]t, T. Hartley Crawford.
[Enclosure]
James Logan to T. Hartley Crawford, Comm[issione]r [of] Indian Affairs

Creek Agency, [Indian Territory,] November 9, 1844
Sir, Your communication of the 17th Sept., owing to a severe attack of sickness while at Fort Smith [Ark.], whither I had gone after the Creek annuity, I did not receive until a late period. In reply to it I have to state, that as far as I can learn, there are no grounds for believing that any attempts are being made at the present time, on the part of Mexico or her citizens, to induce any of the Indian tribes on this frontier to acts of hostility against the United States or Texas. As regards the Creeks, their integrity is proof against all attempts, and I doubt not if there were any made they would be immediately reported by them to the proper authorities.

That such attempts have been made, and that lately too, upon the wild tribes of the prairies there is in my mind not a vestige of doubt, for the particulars of a council held for that ostensible purpose, near the head of the San Antonio river by seven Mexican military officers and a large concourse of Indians, of various tribes, comprising Tahcoockenies[?], Caddos, Kechies, Cheyens & many others, I beg leave to refer you to a communication made by me to your office in 1842. My informant, a Shawnee chief, named La-ne, tha, is a man of undoubted integrity on such subjects which I can vouch for from an acquaintance of over thirty years. He informed me that such councils were held annually but at different points and I doubt not but what they still continue.

From the fact that fourteen years of my early life were spent among the Shawnees, Delawares and Piankeshaws and from having consequently formed intimacies with their principal men, their language, customs and manners, I possess every facility of obtaining accurate and detailed information from them, probably to a greater extent than any other man on the frontier. These tribes are now about the only ones settled on the frontier who make distant excursions into the prairies, often obtain[in]g information of a varied and interesting nature; but from their naturally reserved disposition are unwilling to communicate to any persons unless intimately known to them.

I have not as yet met with any of them returning from their hunt on the prairies. Should I do so, and obtain any information from them upon the subject my first duty will be to report promptly to your office. Very &c &c, James Logan, Creek agent.

LS with En in DNA, RG 59 (State Department), Miscellaneous Letters (M-179:107, frames 8–10); FC in DNA, RG 75 (Bureau of Indian Affairs), Letters Sent by the Office of Indian Affairs, 36:133 (M-21:36).

From EDWARD EVERETT

London, 3d January 1845

Sir, I transmit herewith a copy of a note addressed by me to Lord Aberdeen on the 27th December last upon the subject of the duties improperly levied on the importation of "Rough Rice" from the United States. Having occasion to see Lord Aberdeen on other business the day following, he voluntarily alluded to this long standing controversy, and in a more satisfactory manner than when it last formed the subject of conversation between us.

Without entering again into the general argument, I have confined myself to insisting on the necessity of bringing the question to a settlement by some fair mode of adjustment, and I have urged upon Lord Aberdeen, in a manner I think not easily to be resisted, the duty of either acceding to the proposal of the claimants to raise an issue in a Court of Law or of suggesting some other equally reasonable method of deciding the point in dispute between the two Governments.

Lord Aberdeen did not pledge himself that this should be done, but gave me to understand that he was himself in favor of it, and that he would endeavor to overcome the repugnance of the Treasury. The general result of our conversation gave me greater encourage-

ment of final success, than I have at any time entertained since the receipt of Lord Aberdeen's note of the 11th August 1842. I am, Sir, with great respect, Your obedient Servant, Edward Everett.
Transmitted with despatch Nro. 235,
Mr. Everett to the Earl of Aberdeen, 27th December, 1844.

LS (No. 235) with En in DNA, RG 59 (State Department), Diplomatic Despatches, Great Britain, vol. 54 (M-30:50), received 1/27; FC in DNA, RG 84 (Foreign Posts), Great Britain, Despatches, 9:116–118; FC in MHi, Edward Everett Papers, 51:45–47 (published microfilm, reel 23, frames 576–577); PC with En in House Executive Document No. 38, 30th Cong., 1st Sess., pp. 3–8.

From Geo[rge] W[illia]m Gordon

Consulate of the United States
Rio de Janeiro, 3d Jan[uar]y 1845
Sir, On board the brig "Oriole" Barstow, Master, bound for New York, by which vessel this despatch is forwarded, has shipped a Dutchman, named Gerrit Ruig. This man shipped on board the brig "Montevideo" [Jason L.] Pendleton, Master, at this port on the 8th February 1844, as a seaman—and proceeded in that vessel to the Coast of Africa, returned in her to Victoria in this Empire, was attached to her when a slave deck was fitted at that place—returned in said vessel to Cabinda in Africa, where she was delivered to a slave dealer at that place in pursuance of a sale made previously by her owner, Captain Alexander Riddell, of New York—was on board of her when Captain Pendleton and crew left her, and saw the slave deck previously laid and other fixtures prepared for the reception of Negroes; was then discharged by Pendleton, and continued on board said brig on her return voyage to this Coast, when she brought and landed upwards of 800 Negroes.

The testimony of this man is very full, giving all the particulars of the voyage and fully sustaining the charges against Pendleton and his officers for aiding and abetting and *being engaged in* the slave trade.

By this vessel the "Oriole" I have written the Marshall of the United States for the Southern district of New York, and requested him on arrival of said vessel to detain and hold in safe custody the said Gerrit Ruig as a witness for the Governm[en]t against said Pendleton and others, until he shall receive instructions in regard to his disposure from the proper department at Washington.

Ruig has been detained here by me, as a witness for the Govern-m[en]t since the 19th December last until the 2nd instant, and I presume is entitled to pay as a witness for that time, 14 days. A certificate to that effect is enclosed. He has now shipped for wages on board the "Oriole" as aforesaid, and has promised to present himself again as a witness for the Government to the Marshall of the United States on arrival at New York. I have the honor to be, Sir, With great respect, Your Obedient Servant, Geo. Wm. Gordon, Consul of the United States.

LS (No. 21) with En in DNA, RG 59 (State Department), Consular Despatches, Rio de Janeiro, vol. 8 (T-172:9), received 2/24. NOTE: A Clerk's EU reads "Copy sent Dist. Att[orne]y N. York." An AES by State Department Clerk R[obert] S. Chew reads "Will Mr. Crallé let me know what to do in regard to the witness ment[ione]d." In an AEU Richard K. Crallé replied "Inform the District Attorney of the facts and tell him to take the proper steps to secure the attendance of the Witness."

From Ja[me]s M. Hughes, [Representative from Mo.], Washington, 1/3. "A friend of mine writes me that [Archibald M. Green] the Consul at Galveston Texas has recently died, and that the Consulship is vacant. If this should be the case I would recommend Edward Fitzgerald (a friend of yours and who has resided in Texas) as a suitable person to fill the vacancy. I know him personally and know that he is qualified. I would take it as a great favor would you assist Mr. Fitzgerald in procuring the appointment of Consul at Galveston." ALS in DNA, RG 59 (State Department), Applications and Recommendations, 1845–1853, Fitzgerald (M-873:28, frames 243–244).

From STEWART NEWELL

Consulate of the United States
Sabine, Texas
Jan[uar]y 3d 1845
Now in New Orleans

Sir, Leave of Abscence, having been granted me, for a short time, by Hon. A[ndrew] J. Donelson, I beg leave to inform the Department, of my arrival in this City, three days since, with a view of arrangeing some matters of private buissiness [*sic*], delayed by my detention on duty, during the prevalence of the Epidemic, the past Summer at

Galveston, and under the then existing circumstances, of Disease, and Death, I deemed my remaining at Galveston, would be required by the Department, but much of great, pecuniary interest to myself, have been lost by it.

I beg leave most respectfully, to ask of the Department, *if*, under the peculiar, and alarming state of affairs, caused by the ravages of the Epidemic at Galveston, I am entitled to any compensation for my services, during the time mentioned, if so, in what manner, and to whom, to present the same for allowance, the risk of Life, during the existence of the Epidemic, was much greater, than ever known of, in the Country, and although perhaps, I, would have been excused, by the Department, had I deserted the place, among others, yet a stronger sense of duty, impell'd me, to remain, and protect those interests, and property, of my Country, which by the Decease of the Consul Mr. [Archibald M.] Green, and the Chargés of the U. States, Gen[era]ls [William S.] Murphy and [Tilghman A.] Howard, were left entirely unprotected, and liable to total loss, no Public interest, during the whole time, was neglected, and had any other matter, of importance, claimed attention, it should have been as promptly given.

I am aware, that other Consuls abroad, have been allowed for services, during the abscence of, or, decease of our Chargés or Ministers[;] what those particular services, may have been, I have no knowledge of, but in my case, I cannot think my services, and attention to the interest of the Government, have been less valuable, under the circumstances, than those, which it has pleased the Congress of my Country, to allow for, and have deem'd it, proper to bring the matter, to the notice of the Hon. Secretary, and ask most respectfully, that liberal consideration of it, as may be deem'd just and equitable.

Cap[tai]n John R. Crane, to whom my Draft for *$106*, was transferred (for transcribing &C. records of Consulate at Galveston) having this day informed me, that said Draft was forwarded by him, to the Hon. Secretary of Treasury [George M. Bibb], at Washington and that the proceeds of which Draft, have not yet been received by his Son, Russell Crane, No. 71 Eldridge Street ["New York" *interlined*] to whom it was requested to be forwarded.

I had the honor to receive notice, of said Draft, being paid, p[e]r Letter from Departm[en]t of State, under date of Nov. 20th, 1844, of which I informed Cap[tai]n Crane, and who now desires, through me, to be informed from the Department, to whom, and how said Draft, was paid, and if forwarded to New York, when the same was

Mailed at Washington, that he may be enabled to trace it. I have the honor to be Most Respectfully Your Ob[edien]t Servant, Stewart Newell.

ALS (No. 34) and duplicate ALS (No. 33) in DNA, RG 59 (State Department), Consular Despatches, Texas, vol. 1 (T-153:1), received 1/15.

From A[BRAHAM] RENCHER

Legation of United States
of America in Portugal
Lisbon, Jan[uar]y 3rd 1845

Sir, Since my Despatch (No. 7 [*sic*]) nothing has occurred in the political condition of Portugal worthy of communication. The [Antonio Bernardo de Costa-]Cabral ministry continue to maintain their hold upon power with a very firm hand. Their measures for the suppression of the revolution and for the support of public credit underwent a protracted discussion in both Chambers of the Cortes at the last session, and were sustained by a large majority in the Chamber of deputies, and by a firm though less numerous majority in the Chamber of Peers. The session was closed on the 14th day of december last by the Queen [Maria II] in person. Her Speech upon the occasion, with a translation thereof, is herewith transmitted, (marked A).

The regular session of the Cortes was commenced on the 2nd instant. It was opened by commission and without any speech from the Throne. No election of new members having intervened, the strength of Parties remain the same as at the last session. In the interval the Government has strengthened itself somewhat in the Chamber of Peers by the creation ["of" *interlined*] some new members, among whom are Costa Cabral the Minister of the Interior, and Gomes de Castro the Minister of Foreign Affaires.

The firm support given to ministers by the representatives of the people, and the consequent tranquility which seems to pervade the Kingdom justifies the hope that this tranquility will not be disturbed for some time to come by any new revolution. One of the beneficial results of this political tranquility is the strength given to public credit at home and the appreciation of the stocks of Portugal in the foreign market. If this tranquility is permitted to last, still more important results may be hoped for in the improved condition of the arts and agriculture of the Kingdom, and in the moral and intellectual improvement of the people, which during the civil wars have been much neglected, and in which Portugal is behind the spirit of the age.

In a former Despatch I had occasion to mention a recent decree of this Government imposing additional burthens upon commerce, under which two American ships had been put in rigourous quarantine and heavy fees exacted. I am happy to state that since the date of that despatch most of these fees have been remitted, and the American ships which have since arrived at this port have been admitted to *free practique*. Their port regulations are still very stringent. They require all ships bound for the ports of Portugal to take out ["a" canceled] bills of Health from their Consuls residing abroad, and they even go so far as to require all ships leaving the ports of Portugal to take similar bills contrary to the usage of all other nations. These regulations tend to cripple commerce, but while the law is applied equally to the ships of Portugal as to those of other nations, I do not feel that we have just cause of complaint. The embarrassed condition of the Treasury makes it necessary for ministers to ava[i]l themselves of every source of revenue within their power. With all their means, they are barely able to make the revenue equal the current expenses of the Government.

I received by the last steamer from England under Cover from the State Department, the President's Message with the documents which accompany it relative to the annexation of Texas to the United States. I have read them with an interest and pleasure to which their value & importance entitle them ["to" canceled]. These advices, with the result of the late elections in the United States have created much interest in this Capital where there are many English residents, and where different results were anticipated. I am very sure that in the diplomatic circle here, as well as among others, a very general opinion prevailed that there existed an *entente Cordiale* between the Governments of England and France in opposition to the annexation of Texas to the United States. Certainly great efforts have been made to produce this result, and for this single purpose more than any other. No wonder therefore the English are very bitter in their denunciation of French duplicity. I have never entertained but one opinion on this subject and which I have ventured to express upon all suitable occasions, that whatever party might come into power in the United States that sooner or later Texas would be annexed to the Union. The bold and able manner in which the negotiation has been conducted is likely to accomplish this great result much earlier than

I had anticipated, and without collision with any European power. Without the Co-operation of France, England will adopt "the better part of valour," and judging from the sentiments expressed by their representatives here, some of the great continental powers desire the success of the United States, not from any love they have for free institutions, but because they see in her a power which is destined at no distant day to rival successfully Great Brittain in arts and in commerce, as well as in arms. In this point of view your despatch to Mr. [William R.] King has come most opportunely. It is just such a paper as was wanted in Europe and will doubtless produce good fruits.

I have not been able to obtain any decision in the case of the ship Miles, though I have more than once shown some impatience on the subject. I find among the papers of the Legation some other claims upon this Government but which have been so repeatedly rejected that I think it useless to renew them, and shall not feel it my duty to do so un[l]ess instructed to do it by the Department.

The accouch[e]ment of the Queen is expected during the latter part of this month or early in February. I have the honour to be with the highest respect y[ou]r ob[edien]t Servant, A. Rencher.

LS (No. 7) with Ens in DNA, RG 59 (State Department), Diplomatic Despatches, Portugal, vol. 14 (M-43:13, frames 408–413), received 2/22; FC in DNA, RG 84 (Foreign Posts), Portugal, Despatches.

[James Wishart], St. Clairsville, [Ohio], to [Richard K. Crallé], "Confidential," 1/3. Wishart expresses regret that he was able to visit only briefly with Calhoun during his trip to Washington in December. After a long encomium upon Calhoun's political virtues, Wishart states that, as a long-time sufferer for his allegiance to Calhoun, he will share in Calhoun's coming triumph. Wishart's "persecutions, which are a min[i]ature of his, will terminate." He asks that Calhoun and others in Washington work for the appointment of W.P. Simpson to be a U.S. Marshal in Ohio. Supporters of Martin Van Buren oppose Simpson and their opposition "ought to consign every man of them to the tomb of the Capulets." ALU (incomplete) in ScCleA.

From W[illia]m L. Brent, *"Private & confidential"*

Steam Boat Eagle, Mississippi river
4th Jan. 1844 [*sic*; 1845]

My dear Sir, I am so far on my way, to resume my residence among my old friends and former constituents in Louisiana. I omitted to call upon you, before I left Washington City and I avail myself of this mode, to say to you, what I had intended to do in person. From the commencement of our acquaintance in 1823 to this time, I have ever been a political and personal friend of yours, altho' from peculiar circumstances we have belonged to different political parties. It is unnecessary to explain those circumstances, at this time. Whilst I resided in the District of Columbia, I could be of little service to any one, from our disfranchised position. It will, now, be a different case and my position will enable me to use an influence, which I hope may be of service. I ever have been and ever will be a southern man in feelings and in principles and as such I cannot do otherwise than support those principles of government, so ably advocated by you. It is a source of the greatest pleasure to me, to reflect, that I have *always* and consistently opposed the Tariff, as a protective measure, and also the Bank of the United States. My votes in Congress, from 1823, for eight years, will shew this. Now, my dear Sir, I will be much obliged to you, if you would send me, the best and clearest exposition of the Doctrine of nullification, which I am satisfied has not been correctly understood, by the large portion of the American people, and also the document containing all the correspondence relative to Texas and any other matters that you may think, would enlighten me and enable me to properly explain to the people, when occasion might require your views and opinions, correctly understood, upon the great questions of our Country. They will be used with caution and with prudence. Our Louisianians, are warm hearted, open to conviction and to truth, ["and" *canceled*] Patriotic and disposed to persue the right tract [*sic*], if they are correctly informed and properly directed. No man understands their character and their interests, better than myself, and the unshrinking attachment, which they have ever shewn me, induces me to beleive [*sic*] that my influence there will be felt.

From these hasty remarks, written in a great hurry, you will at once see the motive that induces me, to make them and I deem it unnecessary to say more upon the subject. At all times, consider me as your friend and as such command my services in any way I can serve you. I hope, you will do it, without restraint. I shall, in a few days, see our mutual friend Gen[era]l [Walter H.] Overton [former Representative from La.]. His health has been so bad, for some years, that he has taken but little part, in the politics of the day, but he yet remains your steadfast friend and has great influence, should ["his" *altered to* "he"] exert it. Yours ever Sincerely, Wm. L. Brent.

P.S. My Post-office is St. Martinsville[,] Attakapas[,] Louisiana.

ALS in ScCleA. Note: An AEU by Calhoun reads "Mr. Brent." This letter was postmarked at Helena, Ark., on 1/7. Since it is addressed to Calhoun as Secretary of State in Washington, its correct year is almost certainly 1845. Brent (1784–1848), a native of Md., had been Representative from La. during 1823–1829.

From A[ngel] Calderon de la Barca, [Spanish Minister to the U.S.], 1/4. Calderon de la Barca reminds Calhoun that on 6/14/1844 he informed [Fidericio] Bourman, then Spanish Chargé d'Affaires, that the matter of excess duties collected on wines from the Great Canary islands had been referred to Congress with a favorable recommendation. Much time has passed and Calderon de la Barca has heard nothing of a resolution of the issue. LS (in Spanish) and State Department translation in DNA, RG 59 (State Department), Notes from Foreign Legations, Spain, vol. 11 (M-59:13, frames 1027–1029).

From S. F. Chapman

Washington, Jan[uar]y 4, 1845

Dear Sir: I very much regret, that I was so unfortunate, as to ask and to receive the favor at the hands of my friend Dr. Brockenborough [*sic*; John Brockenbrough], to present a note to you [*not found*], from the President of the Un[ited] States [John Tyler], in reference to a little office in your Department—And I regret it more deeply, as it seems, it was a matter of some sensibility, with you.

Amongst the earliest of my political friendships, & amongst the earliest of my votes, for any man, was that cast for you, for the Vice Pres[idenc]y in 1824. The reasons for that vote, at that early day, were good then, and have been and are still justified, by the principles of your private & public life, your fine abilities[,] your exalted patriotism, and the untiring zeal, with which you have ever advocated the great measures, so closely connected as they have been, with the interests and happiness of the country. I have stood by your side, with little variation, during all this time, & amidst the persecutions and denunciations of portions of the press, and of publick opinion, I may truly say, as I have often declared, I would have prefer[r]ed you for the first office, in the country, during the last canvass, and it was with me, a subject of constant regret and mortification, that the public mind & Judgement had been so lowered, as to pass by, so distinguished an individual, and fix itself upon a man [James K. Polk], good enough it is true, but compared with another, he certainly stood, as Hyperion to a Satyr.

Now Sir, I refer to these things, as an apology for troubling you at all, upon a late occasion. I know, they constituted no claim upon you, for any thing, for in all of them, I consulted my own principles and exercised my own independent opinions, regardless of any influence they might exert upon ["others" *canceled*] any body. I looked to my duty to the country, rather than to you, and have been happy to believe, that I have, with the best intentions, faithfully performed it, to both.

I certainly never expect or intend to ask you again, for any favor, and therefore, I shall not expect to receive any ["from you" *interlined*]; but I beg to assure you, that if, by the favor of the country, you shall be presented, for its suffrages in 1849, ["if then" *canceled*] and I shall be alive, it may be among my chee[r]ful gratifications to vote for you. With distinguished respect, I have the honor to be y[ou]r f[rien]d, S.F. Chapman.

ALS in ScCleA.

From C[aleb] Cushing

Washington, January 4th 1845
Sir: I have the honor to report to you my arrival in this city by the way of Mexico, and to place in your hands a duplicate original of the Treaty with China concluded at Wang-Hiya on the 3rd of July last. I am Very respectfully Your ob[edien]t ser[van]t, C. Cushing.

ALS (No. 99) in DNA, RG 59 (State Department), Diplomatic Despatches, China, vol. 2 (M-92:3).

From JOHN HASTINGS, [former Representative from Ohio]

New Garden, Columbiana C[ount]y Ohio
Jan. 4, 1845

Dear Sir, What I have to say at this moment is in the way of an old friend, who I believe you do not estimate otherwise than kindly. Were I addressing you in your official capacity, the manner would, of course, be appropriate.

Tax your time as I may, I cannot help expressing to you my heartfelt gratifications on reading your powerful letter [of 8/12/1844] to Mr. [William R.] King, which I have just studiously done for the second time. Any eulogy from me of the most friendly impartial character, (for he is no true friend who is not frankly impartial) appreciating ever so highly the talents, motives, and patriotism evinced in its fearless development of universally interesting circumstances, would be but a faint attempt to signalize its merits. It will be effective with all candid minds at home—with all who love their Country, who value the Union. And it speaks impressive truths to the nations of the old world, it vividly portrays their interests; and to conserve them, it proves the fitness and necessity of maintaining their individual sovereignties inviolate from the designs and graspings of a mammoth power among themselves, and that their true policy in such reference[?] where we are involved, is to discountenance and oppose operations against us of a similar character; and it shows the independencies on our own continent, that the preservation of their existence as Republics depends on that of ours. And it evidences to all, as clear as light, that the peaceful interests, and commercial intercourse and trade of the world, and balance of power among its nations, are deeply concerned in the conservative progress of our Union; and rightfully, as well as essentially and necessitously opposed to the extension and encroachment of British influence and power in the western hemisphere.

It is deeply to be regretted that the acquisition of Texas, vitally necessary as it is, should have conjured up such adverse conduct among the democracy. Every fresh occurrence at home and abroad in relation to this subject, increases my anxiety for the immediate consummation of a measure which is to determine the strength, the stability perhaps, of the Union. The great effort of the present session of Congress should be the introduction of Texas; waiving for once, tortuous subtleties, casuistries, and sophistries, the all-important measure should be passed upon without further demur.

It seems that Mr. [Caleb] Cushing has made a commercial arrangement with China which places our trade on an equal footing at least, with that of Britain in that region—so far right. In speaking of Britain: would it not have been well for Mr. Cushing to have embraced the idea of suggesting and enforcing to the Chinese authorities, as prudently as he might, the policy of employing American Engineers and Officers to improve to practicable effectiveness their militant [*sic*] forces, that they might be the better enabled to cope with Britain or other power[s] in any future contest? Through such improvement, the Chinese might not merely confine themselves to the defensive but become so far formidable as to present the possibility of a retaliatory presence to British India. Thus, it might not be among the impossibilities that the circumstance of the late British invasion of China might lead, ultimately, to the dismemberment of the East India possessions of the former. However, this induction would, as far as it might go, be a species of lex talionis in self defence against her project of disrupting our Union; a project she will hardly [*one word canceled*] relinquish until she is revolutionized herself, or until our power becomes so formidable that the success of the design will appear palpably hopeless. The motives for her proposition of abolishing slave labor throughout the world—while in the actual practice herself, hideously oppressive too under the informality of feature alone—are now so well understood, that to undermine the Union through that simulation is in no way possible. In truth, every right thinking ["man" *interlined*] must feel sensible that the chief circumstance that can jeopard the integrity of the Union, is the general government persevering in exercising the taxing power unjustly— there is the great danger: machinations from without and within can be exposed and disempowered, but the taxing power enforced in partiality, gangrenes the fundamental elements—the equal rights of the States and the federative equal rights of the People—which originated and must continue the Union.

In consonance with these brief reflections—measurably estimated—should not the commercial agent or diplomatic character we may have resident in China, be made to understand the policy I have suggested?

As there is nothing in my whole political being that I have so much at heart as the perpetuity of the integrity of the Union in its fullest amplitude of prosperity and happiness, you will make allowances, my dear Sir, for thus communing with you, rather intrusively perhaps, considering the arduous duties of the State Department in addition to the cares and anxieties you have ever underwent for your Country. With the highest esteem yours as ever, John Hastings.

ALS in ScCleA.

From ELIZABETH A. R. LINN

St. Louis, Jan[uar]y 4, 1845
Most highly Esteemed Sir, Will you permit me to solicit, your powerful influence, with Mr. [James K.] Polk, to obtain the Post Master[']s place, in this City, for my Son, Mr. J. Relfe Sprigg, if our most Worthy Friend, Col. [Samuel B.] Churchill, is to be removed from it. If you think it proper, & that my own chance would be better, than my Son[']s, in getting the Office, as Post Mistress, I would be sincerely grateful for it, and I do assure you, my dear Sir, that there is scarcely a Missourian, that would not rejoice to see me, in a situation, (without sacrificing our Property,) that would enable me, to Educate the Children of their Model Senator, as they unanimously called my blessed Husband [Lewis F. Linn]. My ever to be lamented Husband, left us a fine Estate, but it is so embarrassed, with Debts, incur[r]ed to relieve Friends, that to save it from being sacrificed, we are compel[l]ed to let *all* the proceeds of our Property go for several Years, to discharge those *cruel Debts.* Therefore I am without the Means to finish the Education of my Children, and had it not been, for the untyr'ing [*sic*] goodness, of my Brother Doctor [James H.] Relfe, I scarcely know, what would have become of us. My only hope of being able, to serve my Children, in preparing them, to enter the World, in a proper manner, is in my Son, or myself obtaining the Post Office, in this place. Yet far be [it] from me, to desire the removal of Col. Churchill, for he has most faithfully done his duty but from all I can learn, he has no hope, of keeping his present situation. Col. [Thomas H.] Benton has so cruelly persecuted me, and my family, since our dreadful bereav'ment, that I suppose he will use his influence against any thing, that would be of benefit to Dr. Linn[']s family. But to you, dear Mr. Calhoun I can look with a holy confidence, of receiv'ing aid. The noble integrity of your truly exalted mind, has ever made profession, & principle the same thing with you. How often, my most highly valued Friend, when I have felt heart sick in meeting with so much cold hypocrisy, from the great Men, of this World, have I turned with sincere delight, to the contemplation of

your pure, & intellectual Character, where wonderful [*one or more pages missing*] to dear Mrs. [Anna Maria Calhoun] Clemson, will you please to remember me kindly to her. My Children join me in many Respectful Regards to you. With sentiments of the highest Regard, I am Most truely your Friend, Elizabeth A.R. Linn.

ALS (incomplete) in ScCleA.

From EUSTIS PRESCOTT, "Private"

New Orleans, 4th Jan[ua]ry 1845
Dear Sir, Altho I am aware that you must be at this moment much engrossed with public affairs, still you doubtless think of your Cotton interest, and it is on that subject principally that I have now ventured to intrude upon you. The rapid decline in price within two months in Liverpool has awakened the South from a sleep of security which had nearly proved fatal to the Cotton growers—but it is not too late— a remedy can be provided; overproduction—the cause of all their disasters, can be arrested, but to do so, the pen of a powerful & influential mind must be exerted, and from no man in the country can a plan emanate which will command the attention of those interested so fully as from yourself. I do hope therefore that you will find time to suggest some plan by which the apprehended evil may be averted.

In this section a great reformation ought to take place in many things—first, the Planter should make his own food—which he does not now do; then, all the clothing possible for his negroes; next, it has occurred to me that a limitation of hours for work might be introduced, say *nine hours.* These would reduce the production in a small degree, but there must be something more, and I feel that my mind is not sufficiently capacious and that I have not sufficient knowledge of the subject to suggest it. I think that an over-estimate of the present crop is made, from my information I doubt whether it will reach 2250,000 bales, and many Planters will keep back their crops at the present price 4½ c[en]ts for good middlings. Indeed if a half million of bales could be held in this country for six months it would enhance the value in Europe at least one cent, perhaps more per lb. Southern interests ought to be represented in Liverpool, and I have the vanity to believe that if the Executive had conferred the Consulship upon me, it would have been in my power to ["have" *interlined*] obtained much valuable information, and such as an old practical Merchant is more likely to discover than persons of other occupations.

33

I have placed my business here in such a position that I can leave it on very short notice, if my services can be made available to the Government—in a position sufficiently lucrative, & respectable, and indeed—if encouraged by you, I will be an applicant to Mr. [James K.] Polk—after his inauguration, for the Consulship at Liverpool or Havre, but should prefer the former, as I could there be more useful to my southern friends.

Our Legislature commences its session on monday and an effort will be made to induce them (altho a whig majority) to pass resolutions instructing our Senators to vote for the annexation of Texas. We however entertain strong hopes that after the receipt of the late news from Mexico, that you will be able to carry the measure thro Congress on 8th Janu[ar]y.

Gen[era]l [George W.] Terrell [of Texas] was in the city several days *en route* to France & England on a special mission. I had several conversations with him, he avowed himself strenuously opposed to annexation, but acknowledged that *nine tenths* of the people of Texas were in favor of it. Major Donaldson [*sic*; Andrew J. Donelson] (whom I also had the pleasure of conversing with on the subject) is of the same opinion, but fears that if postponed again, the people will be discouraged and form foreign alliances from which it will be difficult to recede. The people of Louisiana are heartily with you.

You may possibly have discovered that we [have] succeeded in uniting the two Democratic [*mutilated*; morn]ing papers, and I beg leave to recommend [the] "Jeffersonian Republican" to the Departments for any advertising they may be enabled to bestow. The Editors and Proprietors are *our* friends, and when the time arrives, we can command its columns.

W[illia]m A. Elmore Esq[uir]e will be an Applicant for the office of District Attorney, and Mr. Tho[ma]s B. Eastland for that of Marshal; the offices could not be filled by more competent persons or those who would be more generally acceptable to this community— they are warm friends of yours. I remain my Dear Sir Very sincerely yours, Eustis Prescott.

ALS in ScCleA; PEx in Boucher and Brooks, eds., *Correspondence*, pp. 275–276.

From Cha[rle]s H. Raymond

Legation of Texas
Washington D.C., January 4th 1845
The Undersigned, Acting Chargé d'Affaires of Texas, by direction of his Government, has the honor to inform Mr. Calhoun, Secretary of State of the United States, that a new Administration of the Government of the Republic of Texas, in pursuance of the requirements of the constitution, commenced on the 9th ultimo, consisting as follows,
Anson Jones,   President.
Kenneth L. Anderson, Vice President.
Cabinet Officers.
Ebenezer Allen, Attorney General, and charged, *ad interim*, with the
    direction of the Department of State.
William B. Ochiltree, Secretary of the Treasury.
M[organ] C. Hamilton, Acting Secretary of War and Marine.
The Undersigned is further directed to make known to the Government of the United States the friendly feelings entertained by the President of Texas towards the United States, and his sincere desire to foster, preserve and strengthen that peace and amity which have so long and happily prevailed between the two nations, and also to present to His Excellency the President of the United States [John Tyler], through the Honorable Secretary of State, assurances of distinguished consideration on the part of His Excellency, the President of the Republic of Texas.
The Undersigned avails himself of this occasion to offer Mr. Calhoun renewed assurances of his very high consideration. Chas. H. Raymond.

ALS in DNA, RG 59 (State Department), Notes from Foreign Legations, Texas, vol. 1 (T-809:1); FC in Tx, Records of the Texas Republic Department of State, Letters and Dispatches Sent by the Texas Legation in Washington, 2:22–23; FC in Tx, Records of the Texas Republic Department of State, Copybooks of Letters Received from Texan and Foreign Representatives, vol. 2–1/103, p. 38; CC in Tx, Records of the Texas Republic Department of State, U.S. Diplomatic Correspondence. NOTE: Raymond (b. 1816) was a native of N.Y. who had emigrated to Texas about 1839. He came to Washington as a despatch bearer in 1842 and remained as Secretary of the Legation. James Reily was appointed by President Samuel Houston to succeed Isaac Van Zandt as the Texan Chargé d'Affaires in the U.S. but was not confirmed by the Texas Senate and never took up his post. Raymond was thus the chief Texas representative in Washington at this time.

From BENJAMIN H. WRIGHT

[*Ms. torn*; New Y]ork [City, January] 4 [1845]
Sir: Not having seen a confirmation of the nomination of Mr. [J.B.]
Lacey as Consul for the port of Nuevitas in the island of Cuba leads
me to suppose that he has declined. I should esteem it a favor to be
informed if he has proceeded to take his post or intends so to do.
Altho the emoluments are insufficient to sustain a representative of
our government there, it seems very desirable to have one, as american interests engaged in [coal] mining operations are increasing.

I may be permitted to avail of the opportunity to say, after having
resided several years in the island, that there is a strong bias in favor
of the people of the U.S. on the part of the native population of the
island—particularly in the Central province, which embraces Puerto
Principe a City of some 50,000 souls. It would not be amiss that a
vessel of our navy should occasional[l]y drop in at Nuevitas where
one is seldom or never seen. There will be a considerable number
of the principal inhabitants of Puerto Principe down at Nuevitas during the holy days which occur the last of March and it would add
much to the importance of our country if one could be seen at that
time; and moreover tend to the strengthening of friendly relations.
I am about to embark for the island & shall be at Nuevitas where I
shall be happy to render any assistance to any representative of the
gover[nment; *ms. torn*; *several words missing*] Respectfully Your
ob[edien]t Serv[an]t, Benjamin H. Wright.

ALS in DNA, RG 59 (State Department), Applications and Recommendations,
1845–1853, Wright (M-873:97, frames 394–397). NOTE: A Clerk's EU reads
"Respectfully referred to the Hon. Secretary of the Navy for perusal." Another
EU reads "read & returned."

From BARNARD E. BEE

Pendleton So. Ca., Jan[uar]y 5th[?]/45
My dear Sir, I believe you are aware that at the death of Com: Ed-
ward R. Shubrick, Mr. [Clement W.] Stevens['s] son *Clement* [H.
Stevens], was attached to the U.S. Ship Columbia in the capacity of
Clerk! Mr. Stevens has recently returned from the Mediterranean,
and so favorable an impression has he made, that immediately upon
Capt. Irvine Shubricks being ordered to the Saratoga he invited him

36

to accompany him. In the present dearth of occupation, Mr. Stevens feels he had better accept this act of attention, than remain in idleness, but is sensible that at the expiration of the cruise (three years) he will not have advanced a step—hence, he is solicitous (as the sea seems to be his destiny—his Father was an officer in the Navy) to procure a *permanent* appointment—that of *Purser!* Nor does he deem it presumptuous in seeking this office, as he has been thoroughly bred to business, having commenced as a youth with Gen[era]l [James] Hamilton[']s son James, at whose death, he was placed in one of the leading Houses in Charleston. Thus much as to qualification. As regards Character no young man stands higher. Col. [James] Gadsden and Com. W[illia]m Brandford [*sic*; Bradford] Shubrick will be his sponsors on this score. Mr. Stevens['s] name is now before the Dept., but in an interview with Judge [John Y.] Mason [Secretary of the Navy] as he passed through Washington that Gentleman very frankly told him, he consider[e]d the *gift* with the Presid[en]t [John Tyler]. Mr. Stevens was however informed by his friends in Washington, that if he really wished the appointment, he had only to obtain your "say so," and that on the first vacancy he would receive it.

I have said to Mr. Stevens that I was aware of your influence, but that I was equally so of your aversion to exercising it out of your immediate Dept., but that I could[n]'t doubt from your respect for his Mother [Sarah Fayssoux Stevens], and your very high estimate of Col. Gadsden and Com[mo]d[or]e Wm. B. Shubrick you would cheerfully have an interview with the President.

Mr. [Isaac E.?] Holmes [Representative from S.C.] will communicate with you on this application, and if it will at all comport with your your [*sic*] views, I assure you My dear Sir, this Gentleman will prove worthy of your recommendation. I am My d[ea]r Sir with great esteem respectfully Yours, Barnard E. Bee.

[P.S.] Col. [Edward] Harleston leaves us in the brig[?] for Texas! I rather think he will will [*sic*] meet Gen[era]l Hamilton at [New] Orleans, which will be pleasant for him.

As to annexation—I despair of it—and if Mexico could only be persuaded to recognize us, I think I should not deplore it, tho, one or the other I deem indispensable.

Our best regards to Mrs. [Floride Colhoun] Calhoun and your Daughter [Martha Cornelia Calhoun].

I tried to find Willie [William Lowndes Calhoun] to eat his Christmas dinner with us, but heard he had gone to Abbeville. Yours, B.E. Bee.

ALS in ScU-SC, John C. Calhoun Papers. NOTE: An EU, probably by a Clerk in the Navy Department, reads "file and inform Mr. Calhoun that it will be considered. Mr. Stevens's application will not be prejudiced by his being in employment as Capt. Shubrick's clerk." Bee (1787–1853) had moved from S.C. to Texas in 1836 and served as Texan Secretary of the Treasury, War, and State. From 1838 through 1841 he was the Texan Minister to the U.S. He was the father of Barnard Elliott Bee (1824–1861), the Confederate Brig. Gen. who is known for having given the name "Stonewall" to Thomas J. Jackson shortly before being killed in battle. Clement Hoffman Stevens (1821–1864) was related to the Bee family by marriage. He, too, was later killed in action while a Brig. Gen. of the Confederate States Army.

From Jos[eph] J. Singleton

Dahlonega [Ga.], 5th Jan[uar]y 1845

My Dear Sir, I have endeavored to refrain from exercising a right which emphatically belongs to me, and allowed myself ample time for reflection; the result still turns on the side of self preservation; and without the aid of my own exertions how can I expect to acquire the object in persuit [*sic*]. It is my right no doubt, (which no one will deny) to endeavor to restore to myself that which has been taken from me by the hand of power only—that hand has been withered long since, and another substituted for the time being, upon which I had my scruples of relyance, until perhaps it was too late to put in my claim, it having been confer[r]ed on one equally meritorious, and much higher in the natural ties of relationship.

Things have recently changed, and I hope the result will be satisfactory to all; consequently, a powerful effort will be made without regard to political feelings to restore me to an office in which I was orriginaly [*sic*] placed, and I may say by all the authorities of Georgia; Legislative, Executive, Judiciary, and I am proud to add her *Alma Mater*; besides a large number of those from whom all those powers are derived—all of which I presume are now among the archives at Washington.

Now my dear sir, with due respect to the President [John Tyler], and his appointment of Maj. [James F.] Cooper (who I highly respect) to the office of superintendent of our Br[anch] Mint, am I blamable in aiding my restoration to the said office[?] I respectfully ask your advice in this matter, as a friend, upon which I shall greatly rely. Will you therefore be so kind as to allow yourself a few moments of reflection apart from your arduous and valuable services to make me such a reply as you may think I deserve[?] I beg this favor of you the more readily because you were kind enough the last time I had the honor of your company at my house to voluntarily tender your services to me in any event which might occur in which you would have it in your power to aid me in the restoration to an office which I obtained under many sacrafices [*sic*], and one which I filled to the entire satisfaction of all concerned, which will be declared by thousands, including many of the first characters of the State, together with many other cogent reasons which will be given in a petition now under way to the President Elect [James K. Polk], and which I desire you may see. The Incumbent Maj. Cooper stands high in my estimation as a Gentleman, hence arrises [*sic*] my doubts with regard to the propriety of seeking an office which he now occupies; and but for the circumstance of my not being consulted by my successor, and the major's not consulting *His* predecessor, I predicate my right of restoration if it can be obtained by fair and honorable means. Maj. Cooper in my estimation is worthy of a better office, at least one more profitable to him, and it would afford me great pleasure to render him any aid in my power in the acquisition of such an office. Would it not be in the power of the President to find such an one for him, or would it be asking too much of you sir, to suggest something of the kind to His Excellency mainly in my behalf, as well as in behalf of Maj. Cooper; which, if successful it would supercede the contemplated effort for my restoration before *his* successors. You would be surprised sir to know the extent of interest manifested in this community for my restoration, and you will be more so should you see the Petition above alluded to, and the reasons therein given. I am confident that there will be thousands of Petitioners without regard to Political feelings, amongst whom will be found very many of the most respectable characters in the State, besides a number of private letters to the same effect. All of the foregoing sir, is respectfully submitted for your kind consideration, and should it be in your power to render me any service, of course it will never be forgotten by your friend and humble Servant, Jos. J. Singleton.

ALS in ScCleA. NOTE: Singleton (died 1854) had been a judge and a member of the Ga. legislature. He was an early settler in the Ga. gold mining region and had been Superintendent of the Dahlonega Branch Mint during 1837–1841.

From JAMES DAVIS

Enon Grove[,] Heard County Georgia, Jan. 6th 1845
Dear Sir, I am fearful I shall become rather trouble to you, but I hope
you will bear with ["me" *interlined*] while I communicate to you
some facts and make some enquirys on the subject of Gold mines. In
1843 I embarked in the business of Gold Mineing in Taliposa Co[un-
ty] Alabama near a little place called goldville[.] I obtained an
interest in eight entrey's which at the time I believed to be very valuable, as the ore when beat up, pan[n]ed finely. I raised in one small
pit on one, entry about two thousand bushells of gold ore; which was
thought to be worth from three to five dollars per bushel. This ore
I had washed out at the gold mill, which made almost an entire
failure. I did not realize more than fifty dollars out of this ammount
of ore. I then as I wished to obtain certain information as to the extent of the Richness of my ore, carryed a piece of it to Mr. Bucking
of Lagrange Georgia who *smelted* it, and found it to be ["not more
than" *canceled*] worth, 15 c[en]ts.

The piece was not larger than my fist or the hand of a common
man. According ["to this" *interlined*] a bushell would be worth,
about ten dollars, and I am confident the small piece of ore, was not
more than a sample of the ore gencral[l]y. I can with six hands per
diem raise from fifty to one hundred bushels of the ore, and some
days as much as two hundred, on this eighty, there are six or seven
["veins" *interlined*] developed, all panning about the same. The gold
is exce[e]ding fine, and makes a be[a]utiful circule around a pan,
and I am fulley satisfyed that it ["is" *interlined*] the most extensive
mineing region in the U.S. yet discovered, and if there could be any
plan devised for saving the gold the working would no doubt be as
valuable as any place in the union[.] The special object I have then
in writting to you at this time is to gain information on the subject of
"smelting" the ore, upon some general system by which the gold could
be saved. I am fulley apprisyed that ["there" *interlined*] are other
departements of the gover[n]ment to which this bussiness more properly belongs[.] But I hope you will take an interest so far as to communicate to me when you have leasure, all the information you have
on the subject which may be of considerable advantage in bringing
this extensive gold region into public notice. Also I was informed by
Gov[ernor James] Hamilton [Jr.] in [18]43 that you had a Son-in-law
[Thomas G. Clemson] who was a *Scientificate Miner*[.] His name
and address I have no knowledge of and it may be he would be interested in visiting this region the ensuing summer. If so I would ac-

company him and give him all the information in my power. The gold region extends from the Hilabee Creek in Talliposa County to the Muckfau [*sic;* Emuckfau] in Randolph, a distance of fifteen miles and about two or three miles in breadth on most of which lands there are large and extensive veins of gold ore, and on the Mountain, near the Herlibee Creek, There is gold ore in shuch great abundance, that six hands would be able to raise, from 4 to 5 hundred bushels per diem—and I am fully impres[s]ed with ["the" *interlined*] opinion from all *"the lights before me"* that upon the *smelting* process this ore would average from one to five and ten dollars per bushel. At this time the bussiness is rather under the we[a]ther, in consequence of the general failure in saving the gold by the usual, process of quick silver—Though there are some five or six that are still operating on the mines and are said to be doing good bussiness. I have not been engaged in the bussiness the last year nor do I contemplate engaging again in the bussiness unless a better plan of saving can be obtained. But as I have an extensive knowledge of the country, I am willing to unite with any company that may be formed, and I have no doubt at this time most of the mining land could be obtained at gover[n]ment price, and no doubt, many would now take half price for their lands, and if a process of saving could be, obtained that would save the gold I have no doubt of the richness of the Ore. But this matter can be fulley tested by sending specimens of the Ore to some point where the smelting operation is already in progress.

I was told the other day by Dr. [James H.?] Rogers of Carroll County in this State that two men from Habersham Co[unty] in this State, stayed with him all night and gave him information of a smelting operation [*one word canceled and* "which is" *interlined*] succes[s]ful[l]y saving the gold in that Region from veins, that they had not been able to save any by the ordinary process. If this be true I have no doubt, of the success of a simmelar operation about goldville. I shall write to some gentleman in that county for the truth of this report, at the same time with[h]olding all information of the extent [of] the region about goldville, untill I can hear something from you on the subject. Gen. Hamilton visited this region in [18]43, and after cearful examination was fully convinced of the Richness of the Ore, but doubted the practi[ca]bility of working it succes[s]ful[l]y, in the ordinary way and if it is practicable to work it on any plan now is a much more propentios time to obtain the ground than ["then" *interlined*]; for at that time the gold fever was raging, and every man believed that could obtain any interest at all, that he had a fortune. This state of things has died away and at this time things have gone

41

to the opposite extreame. I have myself ["obtained" *canceled*] sur-
stained an heavey loss unless I can regain it by the developement of
some new process of saving. But my faith has never for one moment
been shaken in the richness of the Ore; nor in the extent of the gold
Region; I am happy sir in conclusion to congratulate you on the very
able manner in which you have conducted our national affairs, on
the various and important subjects that has claimed your attention.
Never since the foundation of the gover[n]ment has the subjects
been more important and to my mind never has the gover[n]ment
been more faithful[l]y and honestly adminestered[.] Wishing you
he[a]lth and p[r]osperity I subscribe myself your obedient Servant,
James Davis.

N.B. Remember me to our excellent Chief Magristate [John
Tyler] if convenient. J.D.

ALS in ScCleA.

From W[illia]m L. Dayton, [Senator from N.J.]

Sen[ate] Chamber, 6 Jan[uar]y 1845

Sir, Enclosed is a Copy of a Joint Res[olutio]n which has passed the
House of Rep[resentative]s & is here refer[r]ed to Com[mitt]ee on
Pub[lic] Buildings.

Will, or will not its final passage be a source of great labor upon
the Depart[ment]s, much expense & little service? Stating any facts
bearing upon the question. Your Ob[edien]t ser[van]t, Wm. L. Dayton, Chair[ma]n of Com[mitt]ee on pub[lic] Buildings.

ALS with En in DNA, RG 59 (State Department), Miscellaneous Letters
(M-179:107, frames 25–27). Note: Dayton enclosed a PC of House Resolution
No. 53, submitted to the Senate on 12/31 and referred to the Senate Committee
on Public Buildings as a proposed joint resolution "To secure a more perfect
accountability for the public property." The proposed resolution called upon
the Secretaries of State, Treasury, War, and Navy, the Postmaster General, and
the Commissioner of Public Buildings to make a comprehensive inventory of all of
the real estate, public buildings, and moveable property belonging to the U.S. to
be presented to the next Congress and that the inventory should be maintained
and reported to successive Congresses. The resolution also called for inventories
of the library of the House of Representatives and of the furnishings of the
White House.

From John Lorimer Graham, [Postmaster], New York [City], 1/6.
Graham recommends Robert Hutton for appointment to be U.S. Con-

sul at Maracaibo, Venezuela, chiefly on the grounds of Hutton's mercantile experience in the Venezuela trade and his knowledge of the Spanish language. ALS in DNA, RG 59 (State Department), Applications and Recommendations, 1845–1853, Hutton (M-873:44, frame 239).

From Horn R. Kneass, Philadelphia, 1/6. Kneass recommends Dr. Jesse W. Griffiths for an appointment to be U.S. Consul at Matanzas, Cuba, "or some other equally important place from which the present incumbent is about to be removed." He praises Griffiths as a physician, lawyer, Pa. State legislator, a faithful and admired Democrat, and a man of integrity and ability. ALS in DNA, RG 59 (State Department), Applications and Recommendations, 1845–1853, Griffiths (M-873:35, frames 286–288).

From ENEAS MCFAUL, JR.

United States Consulate
Laguna [de Terminos, Mexico] January 6th 1845
Sir, On 20th Nov[embe]r last I had this pleasure, from New York previous to my departure for this Consulate; and I have now to inform you of my arrival here, on 17th ult[im]o, on which day I advised [Wilson Shannon] the U.S. Minister at Mexico of my being here; and I am in hopes of soon receiving my Exequatur from him— if the reports, of his having returned home, which abound here, should be untrue.

The Archives of the Consulate, have not as yet been received from N. Orleans, when they come to hand I will advise the department.

I have obtained from the authorities of this place permission to act as U.S. Commercial agent till the receipt of the usual exequatur.

The trade with the United States, of this port, tho' very Considerable, is principally carried on in foreign vessels. Logwood is the principal export, of which the best kind is found on the Coast.

Yucatan being independent of Mexico in her right to levy imposts and duties; and in the regulation of her Commerce, the Mexican Consuls in the ports of the United States can give no advice or guarrantee to shippers and ship owners there, as to the actual state of ["her" *canceled*] the tarrif [*sic*] laws in this state, and as they are changed very frequently, the U.S. trader has no Security; that his cargo, is not prohibited when he arrives here, and the whole made liable to confiscation. I have used the precaution of procuring from the Secretary of State of Yucatan a Certified Copy of the existing Tarrif laws and shall prepare a translation of the same at the earliest moment for the information of the department. I am Sir very Respectfully Your very obedient Servant, Eneas McFaul Jr., Consul.

P.S. I take the liberty of enclosing the annexed package for the U.S. in this communication. E. McF. Jr.

ALS in DNA, RG 59 (State Department), Consular Despatches, Ciudad del Carmen (M-308:1), received 2/9.

To SETH SWEETSER, U.S. Consul, Guayaquil, [Ecuador]

Department of State
Washington, January 6, 1845

Sir, Your communication dated 29th of August last has been received at this Department; and I am not a little surprised at the announcement it contains that you had deemed it your "duty to go up to Quito to carry out the views of our Government" in regard to the claims of certain Citizens of the United States on the Government of Ecuador; and that, "to this end, you had drawn on this Department for Five Hundred Dollars."

On an examination of the files of the Department of State, I do not find any instructions which authorize you to undertake this service in the name, or on behalf of the Government of the United States; and I have been compelled, in consequence, to suspend the payment of your Draft. Should you have received, however, any authority from the Government to adjust these claims, the amount may be paid hereafter, on receiving copies of the instructions under which you have acted, (if any such there be;) and you are requested to forward the same forthwith to this Department. If you have no such instructions or powers, you will immediately return to your Consulate as Mr. Delanzon [*sic*; Delazon] Smith, who will hand you this, has been fully authorized by the President to adjust all the claims of our Citizens on the Government of Ecuador. He has been instructed to communicate freely with you in regard to these claims, and to ascertain the actual condition in which they may be, before he presents his credentials; and you will accordingly give him such information in regard to your proceedings in the cases, as may enable him to avoid any difficulties or embarrassments in carrying out his Instructions. I am, Sir, Very Respectfully Your obedient Servant, J.C. Calhoun.

LS in PHarH, Samuel W. Pennypacker Papers, Scrapbook; FC in DNA, RG 59 (State Department), Consular Instructions, 11:320–321.

C[harles] A. Wickliffe, [Postmaster General], to [John Tyler], 1/6. Wickliffe requests Tyler to schedule a Cabinet meeting for "to day" in order to get the opinion of the Cabinet on the "R[aleigh] & W[ilmington] Rail Road." [This involved a controversy over the location of the main Southern mail route.] An AEI by Tyler, probably directed to Calhoun, reads: "This letter would seem to require a meeting of the Cabinet. The Members sh[oul]d be notified. J.T." ALS in ScCleA.

Ch[arles] H. Winder, Department of State, to R[ichard] K. Crallé, [Chief Clerk], 1/6. Winder encloses a list in tabular form of instructions sent by the Department of State to [George W.] Erving in 1816–1819, which list was requested in a House of Representatives resolution [of 6/14/1844]. The table indicates which instructions have been previously published and where they may be found. "I hope the Hon. the Sec[retar]y will not imagine, from what has transpired in relation to these books, that there has been any lack of zeal on my part. I could not know of the existence of these books—although upon referring to them now, I recollect to have seen them once before." ALS in DNA, RG 59 (State Department), Miscellaneous Letters (M-179:107, frames 28–29).

From J A M E S M. B U C H A N A N, *"Private and Confidential"*

Balt[imore,] Jan[uar]y 7th 1845

My Dear Sir, Judge Legrand [*sic*; John C. Le Grand] informed me on his return from Washington of a conversation which he had held with you in relation to myself. Although the conversation was not authorised by me it gave me great pleasure to hear from him that I was not overlooked by one who (pardon me) has ever had my sincerest regards. I feel that I owe it to myself to explain myself to you. My desire *was* to have gone abroad. My health is feeble and I wished to travel. Last summer I was absent for a short time from home and during my absence I lost by death my only daughter—this distressing event has *checked* my desire to leave my home and family again if indeed it has not wholly extinguished it. A number of my kind friends who I know have my welfare at heart have suggested to me the appointment which has been mentioned to you. At first I declined to have any thing to do with it but on reflection and on consultation I have thought that it would be advisable for me to accept it if it were offered to me.

It is not improbable that I may be nominated for Governor of Maryland and in that ["evet" *canceled*] event the emoluments arising from the office with my professional receip[t]s would enable me comfortably to go into the Contest. If you think me worthy of an effort *on your part* for me—you will I am sure make it. If you do not I shall not complain of *you* but consider *myself* unworthy of it. With great respect your S[ervan]t, James M. Buchanan.

[P.S.] I have not said as much to my most intimate friend as I have said above to you. I must therefore beg of you to consider this confidential. J.M.B.

[P.S.] I have been invited on to the great 8th of January [battle of New Orleans] dinner which is to take place in Philadelphia tomorrow. You will understand my Sentiment if you should read it.

I am not able to go in person but have written. J.M.B.

ALS in ScCleA.

From ROBERT B. CAMPBELL

Consulate of the United States of America
Havana, Jan[uar]y 7, 1845

Dear Sir, By the British steamer this day arrived from Vera Cruz bringing dates to 1 P.M. of the 2nd inst., intelligence apparently authentic is received of [José J. de] Herrera being proclaimed President of Mexico, [Nicolás] Bravo commanding Gen[era]l of the City, Pedro José Echeverría minister of the Treasury, [Pedro] García de Conde of foreign relations & Moriano Riba Palacios [*sic*; Mariano Riva Palacio] of Grace & Justice. [Gen. Valentín] Canalizo was besieged in Mexico [City], and has surrendered on terms personal to himself. [Mariano] Paredes is at the head of an army estimated at twenty thousand. [Gen. Antonio Lopez de] Santa Anna at the head of six thousand infantry & artillery & three thousand horse is on the road between Pueblo [*sic*] & Mexico [City,] one account representing him as determined to beseige [*sic*] Mexico. Another and most credited states that he is endeavoring to reach Vera Cruz.

Public opinion in all the Country against him, his enemies daily growing in strength, and his army lessening by desertion. The troops & City of Vera Cruz have declared against ["him" *interlined*], his likenesses taken from the palace & private houses torn and publicly burned. The garrison of San Juan de Ulloa are as yet true to the Ex Pres[iden]t and it is supposed if he can reach it (which is doubted) he may regain Vera Cruz and hold out some months. The best informed think Santa Anna has despaired of regaining his power and the show of resistance is kept up to enable him to make such terms as will secure his property and safe departure from the country, which if accomplished may redound to his own honor & the good of his Country. Provided the United States become his place of residence, for he is capable of observation, & learning, and familiarity with our institutions and witnessing their tendency to secure the happiness and foster the industry & enterprise of the many and protection of all; may have a happy influence upon his own and his country's destiny, when he is recalled which to judge the future by the past will happen should his life be spared. It would however be better for his Country to shoot him at once than that he should reside in any of the States of Europe where he could learn nothing liberal & only add experience to his cruelty & cunning. I shall not be surprised to see him here in some Spanish Vessel, as opportunities frequently offer from Vera Cruz. I have the honor to be with great respect & esteem, Robert B. Campbell.

ALS in ScCleA. NOTE: An AEU by Calhoun reads "G[e]n[era]l Campbell[,] Consul at Havannah [*sic*]."

From E. DE VENDEL

Mobile (Ala.) Jan[uar]y 7th 1845
Honored Sir, I trust that You will not deem impertinent the favor I beg leave to solicit at your hands.

Whilst I was in France last summer, a Young Parisian Lady, a relative of mine, was engaged in collecting the autographs of the most eminent and illustrious personages of the day, embracing all classes of distinction from the highest crowned head to the more humble, but

47

no less distinguished person who daily contributes to enlighten and adorn the age in which we live.

After an examination of this interesting and already numerous collection I expressed some surprise at finding none of our distinguished American names, upon which the Young Lady evinced much regret, saying that distance alone deprived her of autographs which she would have left no means untried to procure. I then made her a promise, a rash one perhaps, that I would, on my return to the U.S., use my best endeavors to increase the value of her collection by soliciting from some of our most eminent men the favor of contributing to her laudable enterprise. Have I been then, Sir, too presuming and dare I flatter myself that Your kindness will, by merely acknowledging the present, enable me to redeem my promise. I have the honor to be most respectfully Sir, Your most obed[ien]t Serv[an]t, E. De Vendel, Mobile (Ala.).

ALS in ScCleA. NOTE: An AEU by Calhoun reads "Desires my Autograph."

From W[illia]m Duncan, Philad[elphi]a, 1/7. Duncan highly recommends Dr. J[esse] W. Griffiths for appointment to a Consulship "to some foreign port." ALS in DNA, RG 59 (State Department), Applications and Recommendations, 1845–1853, Griffiths (M-873:35, frames 289–290).

From EDWARD EVERETT

London, 7th January, 1845

Sir, I transmit herewith a note from Lord Aberdeen of the 31st of December, in answer to mine of the 1st of November respecting the Act of the 6th and 7th Victoria Cap. 98 "for the more effectual suppression of the Slave Trade," together with a copy of my note of this day acknowledging the receipt of Lord Aberdeen's.

Lord Aberdeen's note, though dated the 31st of December did not reach me till a late hour on the evening of the 3d of January. It was consequently out of my power to forward it by the steamer of the 4th. I am, Sir, with great respect, Your obedient Servant, Edward Everett.

Transmitted with despatch Nro. 237;

1. The Earl of Aberdeen to Mr. Everett, 31 December, 1844.
2. Mr. Everett to the Earl of Aberdeen, 7 January, 1845.

[Enclosure]

Lord Aberdeen to Edward Everett

Foreign Office, December 31, 1844

The Undersigned, Her Majesty's principal Secretary of State for foreign Affairs has the honour to acknowledge the receipt of the note addressed to him by Mr. Everett, Envoy Extraordinary and minister Plenipotentiary of the United States of America, on the 1st Ultimo, respecting the Act of the 6th and 7th Victoria Cap: 98, entituled [*sic*] "An Act for the more effectual Suppression of the Slave Trade."

In that note Mr. Everett enquires, "whether British Subjects in the United States are intended to be embraced within the provisions of the Act; and if so, whether it is to be restricted to those who may be temporarily sojourning in the United States without intending to become naturalized Citizens, or whether it will be extended to all persons in the Union born within the limits of Her Majesty's Dominions, including as well those who have become naturalized Citizens, as those who have not."

The note of Mr. Everett has been submitted to Her Majesty's Law Advisers for their opinion on the Construction to be put upon the Act: And, in accordance with their official report, the Undersigned has the honour to state to Mr. Everett that the Act of the 6th and 7th Victoria Cap. 98, is applicable to all British Subjects without Exception, wherever they may be resident; but that it cannot be carried into effect against them unless they are found within the British Territory.

The latter part of this Opinion contains in itself a Reply to the further Enquiry proposed by Mr. Everett, whether, if such a Construction as is above cited be given to the Statute, any, and, if any, what measures have been adopted or are proposed to carry the Provisions of the Law into effect, as far as concerns the United States.

But Mr. Everett in his note requests moreover and in particular to know for the Information of his Government what Instructions, if any, have been given to Her Majesty's Consuls in the United States concerning the Acts of the 5th George IV Cap: 113, and of the 6th and 7th Victoria, Cap: 98.

The Undersigned, therefore, herewith transmits to Mr. Everett a Copy of the Instructions with which Her Majesty's Consuls are furnished with reference to the Act of the 5th George IV Cap: 113; And also a Copy of the Instruction addressed to Her Majesty's Consuls in all Slave holding Countries, with reference to the Act of the 6th and 7th Victoria Cap: 98.

And the Undersigned trusts that the Information now Communicated will be satisfactory to the United States Government.

The Undersigned avails himself of this occasion to renew to Mr. Everett the assurance of his distinguished Consideration. Aberdeen.

[Enclosure]

"Instructions with which Her Britannic Majesty's Consuls abroad are furnished, under the Act of the 5th George 4 Cap: 113, Entitled; 'An Act to amend and Consolidate the Laws relating to the Abolition of the Slave Trade.'"

§ 26 of the General Instructions for Her Majesty's Consuls.

"The Copy of an Act of Parliament amending and consolidating the Laws relating to the Abolition of the Slave Trade is annexed. The Consul will keep a Watchful Eye upon all undertakings for Trading in Slaves, within the district of his Consulate, and whenever he has reason to suspect that British Subjects or British Capital are engaged or concerned in the carrying on of this traffic, he will forthwith report the same to the Secretary of State, in order that steps may be taken for putting a Stop to such Criminal Acts, and for bringing to punishment the Offenders against the Laws of their Country."

LS (No. 237) with Ens in DNA, RG 59 (State Department), Diplomatic Despatches, Great Britain, vol. 54 (M-30:50), received 2/22; FC in DNA, RG 84 (Foreign Posts), Great Britain, Despatches, 9:121–122; FC in MHi, Edward Everett Papers, 51:56–57 (published microfilm, reel 23, frames 582–583).

From Jesse W. Griffiths, Philadelphia, 1/7. Griffiths applies for appointment to be U.S. Consul at Matanzas, [Cuba], "or some other equally important place, the returns of which would be adequate to the support of a family." He states that Gen. William Duncan and Horn R. Kneass support his application and that his friend Col. R[ichard] M. Johnson [former Vice-President] "has kindly patronized my application." ALS in DNA, RG 59 (State Department), Applications and Recommendations, 1845–1853, Griffiths (M-873:35, frames 291–293).

From HENRY W. HILLIARD, [former U.S. Chargé d'Affaires in Belgium]

Montgomery Ala., 7th Jan[uar]y 1845

My dear Sir, I regret that I had not the honor of an interview with you when I visited Washington upon my return home, that I might give you my views of some peculiarities affecting our relations with Belgium, and at the same time express to you in person my thanks for the kind terms in which you were good enough to address me in taking leave of my mission.

I hope that Mr. [Thomas G.] Clemson finds Brussels an agreeable residence; before leaving I endeavoured to put every thing in a train to make his public and private relations pleasant to him during his stay there. I hope at some future day to be fortunate enough to meet you, and I cannot deny myself the satisfaction of assuring you of the very high regard which I entertain for you, and which I have never permitted my political relations to disturb.

Be good enough to forward the enclosed letter to the [Fifth Auditor's] office of Mr. [Stephen] Pleasonton, and believe me to be Very respectfully & very faithfully Your's [*sic*], Henry W. Hilliard.

ALS in ScCleA.

To Rich[ar]d Pakenham

Department of State
Washington, 7th Jan[uar]y, 1845

With reference to the previous correspondence between this Department and Her Britannic Majesty's Legation at Washington, on the subject of the complaints of certain British merchants engaged in the woollen trade with the United States, who consider themselves aggrieved by the proceedings instituted against them by the custom-house authorities of the port of New York, the Undersigned has the honor to transmit to the Right Honorable Mr. Pakenham a copy of a letter [of 12/27], with accompanying papers, recently addressed to this Department by the Secretary of the Treasury [George M. Bibb], to whom the subject had been referred, containing his decision in regard to the application preferred to this Government in behalf of the parties interested.

The Undersigned avails himself of this occasion to offer to the Right Honorable Mr. Pakenham renewed assurances of his distinguished consideration. J.C. Calhoun.

FC in DNA, RG 59 (State Department), Notes to Foreign Legations, Great Britain, 7:59–60 (M-99:36).

To W[ILLIAM] H. ROANE, [near Richmond, Va.]

Washington, 7th Jan[uar]y 1845

My dear Sir, I have read your letter [of 1/1] with attention and interest. You needed no apology for writing me fully & frankly on any subject, however delicate. Our long and intimate acquaintance gave you the right, and I always hear you with pleasure.

I agree with you, substantially, in all your views, both as it relates to the publick & myself.

We have, indeed, at last reached a crisis. It has been long coming, but come it has. It remains to be seen whether our institutions & liberty will survive it. It has not come unexpectedly to me. Of one thing I feel assured, they will not survive, unless we shall return, in good faith & honesty, to the good old doctrines of '98, & that, that can only be done by Virginia taking the lead, at the head of the Southern States. To a departure from them, in many & important instances, the present dangerous condition of our affairs are to be attributed, and it is only by such a return to them, that impending dangers can be averted. No President, however, patriotick, segacious [*sic*] & energetick, can reform ["this" *changed to* "the"] Govt., without the united support of the South, & that can only be had through the lead of Virginia.

As to myself, I was forced into my present position, greatly ag[ai]nst my inclination, by a sense of duty. Nothing else could have induced me to accept it, and nothing can induce me to hold it for a single day, whenever I can retire consistently with duty & propriety. Your's truly & sincerely, J.C. Calhoun.

ALS in ScU-SC, John C. Calhoun Papers; PC in Jameson, ed., *Correspondence*, p. 637.

To ALBERT SMITH, [Commissioner, Northeastern Boundary]

Department of State
Washington, 7th Jan[uar]y 1845

Sir, An account of Lt. W[illiam] H. Emery [*sic*; Emory], for the transportation of his baggage from Boston to [*blank space*], and thence to this city, amounting to $101 has been presented to this Department through the Secretary [of] War.

Lt. Emery having been employed to aid in the survey of the Boundary line between the United States and Great Britain, his claim is payable out of the appropriation made for that object; and as the whole of that appropriation has been placed at your disposal, he has been directed to transmit the account to you for payment. You will, therefore, pay it.

You are requested, to report to this Department, as soon as practicable, the progress made in the work under your charge, and how much remains to be performed: And also to transmit your account of disbursements, and a statement of the amount of claims outstanding with the balance remaining in your hands. I am, Sir, Very respectfully, Your Ob[edien]t Servant, J.C. Calhoun.

Letterpress copy in DNA, RG 59 (State Department), Accounting Records: Miscellaneous Letters Sent, vol. for 10/3/1844–5/29/1845, p. 154; LS (fragment) in DLC, Albert Smith Papers.

To DELAZON SMITH

Department of State
Washington, 7th January, 1845

Sir: The President having appointed you Special Agent of the United States to the Republic of Ecuador, you will herewith receive a sealed letter to the Minister for Foreign Affairs of that Republic, introducing you in your official character, and an open copy of the same. As soon as may be convenient after your arrival at Quito, you will address a note to the Minister, informing him thereof, and requesting him to appoint a time for you to present your letter of introduction. You will embrace the opportunity which will thereby be afforded you to assure him of the anxious desire of the President to maintain the most friendly relations with the Republic of Ecuador, and that to promote this end is one of the objects of your mission.

The state of our relations and the commerce between the two countries, do not, it is considered, warrant either the establishment, on our part, of a formal mission at Quito or the employment there of a formal diplomatic agent of any grade. It is believed that the objects contemplated in your mission may be as well accomplished by means of a Special Agent as by a Chargé d'Affaires; and in expressing a desire on the part of our government to cultivate the most friendly relations, you will endeavor, by proper explanations, to allay any dissatisfaction which may be entertained on account of the informal character of your appointment.

Ecuador was one of the three States which composed the Republic of Colombia, and is consequently bound by the liabilities contracted by that Confederacy previous to its dissolution in 1830. On the 23d of December, 1834, a Convention between those States was signed and subsequently duly ratified, which provided for the adjustment of all the debts of Colombia. By this Convention, New Granada assumed fifty per cent of the debts, Venezuela twenty eight and a half and Ecuador, twenty one and a half per cent. Soon after the ratification of the Convention, Mr. [Robert B.] McAfee, the Chargé d'Affaires of the United States at Bogotá addressed a note to the Minister for Foreign Affairs of Ecuador, in which he stated that our government considered the several States which constituted the Republic of Colombia as jointly and severally liable for the claims of citizens of the United States, but that we would release any one of those States from further liability on account of the claims upon the payment of its share agreeably to the treaty between the States above referred to. The Ecuadorian minister replied that the diplomatic agent of his government who was about to proceed to Bogotá, would be instructed to treat with Mr. McAfee upon the subject. The arrival of this functionary was so long delayed that, on the 18th of July, 1836, Mr. McAfee was instructed to proceed to Quito himself for the purpose of negotiating with that government upon the subjects of commerce and claims. The messenger who was dispatched from this department with the instructions, failed to reach Bogotá in consequence of the vessel in which he embarked having been burnt at sea, and the instructions to Mr. McAfee were not renewed.

Mr. J[ames] C. Pickett, late Chargé d'Affaires of the United States to Peru, who set out upon his mission in the summer of 1838, was directed to proceed by the way of Quito and to enter upon the negotiation of a commercial treaty with the government of Ecuador. He complied with the instruction, and a treaty between the two governments was signed on the 13th of June, 1839. This treaty has since been duly ratified and is now in operation. A copy of the instrument and of the correspondence which led to it accompanies this letter.

Among the claims of citizens of the United States upon the Republic of Colombia for which Ecuador is responsible, those in the cases of the brig Josephine and schooner Ranger are considered to have been adjusted by the Convention of the 25th of November, 1829, between Mr. [Thomas P.] Moore, the Minister of the United States at Bogotá and Mr. Vergara, the Minister for Foreign Affairs of that

Republic. You will herewith receive an authenticated copy of that Convention in Spanish and English. Its sixth article required that it should be approved by President [Simon] Bolivar. The evidence of that approbation is contained in the extract from a despatch of Mr. Moore to this department and in the note of Mr. Caycedo to him which accompanied it. You will herewith receive an attested copy of these papers.

Pursuant to instructions to that effect, after the Treaty of Commerce with Ecuador was signed, Mr. Pickett, in a note of the 19th of June, 1839, presented to that government the claims in the cases of the Josephine and Ranger. The Minister for Foreign Affairs replied in a note of the same date that his government would not hesitate to recognize and pay those claims whenever Mr. Pickett would state the amount which New Granada had bound itself to pay. Mr. Pickett left Quito on his way to Lima immediately afterwards without complying with the requisition of the Minister. His correspondence with the Department does not afford any further information upon the subject.

Herewith you will receive an authenticated copy and a translation of a note from the Minister for Foreign Affairs of New Granada to Mr. McAfee, stating the amount appropriated by the Congress of that Republic in discharge of these claims. That amount has been received by the parties interested. Venezuela, also, has since paid her share, in proof of which you are herewith furnished with a certified extract from a despatch addressed to this department by Mr. [John G.A.] Williamson, the Chargé d'Affaires of the United States at Caracas at the time the payment was made. There is therefore every reason to expect that the Government of Ecuador will at once pay its proportion of the amount due in those cases, and you will accordingly apply for it at the earliest convenient opportunity after your arrival at Quito. The terms of the Convention between Mr. Moore and Mr. Vergara are sufficiently explicit to enable you to ascertain that amount with precision.

You will require any payments which that government may consent to make, to be made in gold or silver, or if it should prefer to make them in orders on the Custom Houses of the Republic, you will require an amount of those orders sufficient, when converted into cash, to make good any depreciation to which they may be subject. If the payments should in fact be made in such orders it would be advisable to convert them immediately into cash, to be remitted to this country by the first safe opportunity, and deposited to the credit of this Department at the port where the vessel may arrive. You will have insurance effected on the amount of the remittance, provided that can be done at a moderate premium by underwriters worthy of confidence, and you will deduct the premium and other incidental expenses from that amount. If, however, it would be preferable to make the remittance by good bills, you will adopt that course, being careful that the bills are made payable to the order of this Department.

Your attention is directed to a clause in the Convention between Mr. Moore and Mr. Vergara which adverts to the claim in the case of the brig Morris. This case has been the subject of repeated instructions from this Department to the Legations of the United States at Bogotá and Caracas, and of a voluminous correspondence between those Legations and the Ministers for Foreign Affairs of New Granada and Venezuela, respectively. The last mentioned State has recently acknowledged the claim and paid eighteen thousand dollars in discharge of its liability in the case. There is reason to expect that New Granada, also, will not much longer withhold her share of the indemnification. You will herewith receive a copy of the material parts of the correspondence relating to the claim. This will enable you to anticipate and to answer any objections to its merits which may be urged by the government of Ecuador.

The other claims of citizens of the United States upon the late Republic of Colombia for which Ecuador is in part responsible, are mentioned in the accompanying extract from the instructions, bearing date 9th January, 1838, which were given to Mr. [James] Semple on his departure as Chargé d'Affaires of the United States to New Granada. You will also receive, herewith, a copy of the previous instructions referred to in the extract, and of such of the documentary proof as is on file in this department. The originals of much of this however have been from time to time transmitted to to [*sic*] Bogotá, which will render it necessary for you to proceed to Quito by the way of that City, in order that you may obtain a transcript of them. Leave of absence to visit the United States has been granted to Mr. [William M.] Blackford, the Chargé d'Affaires to New Granada, and it is probable that he will have availed himself of it before you arrive at Bogotá. It will not, however be difficult for you to ascertain in whose custody he has lodged the archives of the Legation. You will herewith receive a written permission to examine them, and you can have the necessary copies made with all convenient despatch and upon as reasonable terms as may be practicable, to be charged in your account.

Perhaps the most eligible plan for adjusting all the claims, including those in the cases of the Josephine, Ranger, and Morris, would be by a Convention similar to that between the United States and Peru of which you will herewith receive a copy. The main features of this are stipulations by Peru to pay by instalments a round sum in discharge of the claims, this government assuming the distribution of the money amongst the claimants. So far as it can be ascertained, the amount of the claims on Colombia is about one million two hundred and fifty thousand dollars. Twenty one and a half per cent of this would be two hundred and sixty eight thousand seven hundred and fifty dollars. Under all the circumstances, however, it may be expedient for you to accept two hundred and fifty thousand dollars, payable as above mentioned, and you are authorized to conclude a Convention on this basis. A full power, authorizing you to sign the Convention is one of the accompanying papers.

If the government should decisively reject your overture for a Convention of the tenor adverted to, you are instructed to insist upon the prompt payment of the money in the cases of the Josephine, Ranger and Morris, and if, after waiting a reasonable time at Quito, say six months, for a final answer, you shall have cause to believe that the government of Ecuador is not disposed to acknowledge and pay the claims, you will return home.

It will be your duty from time to time to transmit to the department an account of your proceedings. Accurate information respecting the public affairs and the condition of that country and books and documents illustrative thereof, would be particularly acceptable.

Your compensation will be at the rate of eight dollars a day from the time of your departure until your return to your residence in Ohio, exclusive of your necessary travelling expenses, of which you will keep an account, supported by such vouchers as you may be able to obtain. It is to be understood, however, that the expenses consequent upon your sojourn in the City of Quito are not to be considered as travelling expenses.

The sum of [*blank space*] is now advanced to you on account, and you will receive herewith a letter of credit, authorizing you to draw on this department for the further sum of [*blank space*] if your necessities should require it.

Postscript. Since your instructions as above were written, information has been received at the department which makes it necessary to modify them. It seems that Mr. Sweetzer [*sic*; Seth Sweetser], our Consul at Guayaquil, has left his Consulate for Quito with the view of settling with the authorities of Ecuador the claims of our citizens in the cases of the Josephine and Ranger, and it may be, he purposes an adjustment of all other claims. By what authority he has thus undertaken to act, the Department is unable to determine. He may, however, have been empowered by private letters, and in virtue of such authority, have adjusted, by Convention or otherwise, the subjects of controversy referred to in your instructions, either in whole or in part.

It will therefore be your duty, as soon as you reach Quito, to call on Mr. Sweetzer (should he still be in that City) and after presenting the letter herewith enclosed (an open copy of which is enclosed for your perusal) to enter into a full and free conversation with him in order to ascertain what has been done in relation to the claims pending. If he shall have made a final adjustment of them on terms which, on a full view of all the circumstances of the case, may appear just and advantageous, you will not present your letter of credence at all, but return immediately home and report the facts to this Department. If the claims in the cases of the Josephine and Ranger, only, be adjusted, and on such terms as you approve, you will allow the settlement to stand and direct your attention to those which may remain unadjusted. With high respect, I am, Sir, your obedient servant, J.C. Calhoun.

FC in DNA, RG 59 (State Department), Diplomatic Instructions, Special Missions, 1:202–209 (M-77:152).

From Stephen Smith, Balt[im]o[re], 1/7. Smith encloses two letters written to him by Richard Pollard while Pollard was U.S. Chargé d'Affaires in Chile. They concern Smith's claim for $1,704 against the Chilean government for detention of Smith's property by an embargo in 1836. He seeks the aid of the Secretary of State to liquidate this claim. As Smith is soon to leave for Monterey, California, he offers to bear any communications to that place. ALS in DNA, RG 76 (Records of Boundary and Claims Commissions and Arbitrations), Miscellaneous Claims Records: Chile, 1819–1872.

From ROBERT WALSH, "Private"

Paris, 7 Jan[uar]y 1845

Dear Sir, The letter of the 12th ult[im]o [*not found*], with which you favored me, did not come into my hands until the day after the departure of the last mail for the Liverpool steamer of the 4 inst. Otherwise, you would have been immediately thanked for it. The packet conveyance must be tardy at this Season of the year. You will fully credit my assurance that I am grateful for what you have done & that I would not have obtruded my private Consular concerns on your attention, if I had not seen them in connexion with the public interests. The revenue of the United States suffers a considerable, increasing loss by the present law and practice in regard to invoices and oaths. But the Subject is before the Committee of Commerce in the House of Representatives and I have contributed Some pages for their judgment, in the shape of a letter to my neighbor, Mr. G[eorge] W. Erving [former U.S. Minister to Spain] who requested my ideas for the Chairman. If the Department Should, at any time, undertake the amendment & reorganization of the whole Consular system, I Shall have ready, ample information of the nature, history and machinery of the institution, throughout the world. The copies of the correspondence with Texas & Mexico, which you intended for Mr. [Adolphe] Jollivet and myself, did not accompany your letter. I found, in a London paper, a neat reprint of your despatch to Mr. [William R.] King, which I lost no time in taking to Mr. Jollivet. He engaged, at once, to translate and diffuse it in the pamphlet form. Yesterday, I received from him the following note; "Very luckily, there is a translation of Mr. Calhoun's letter, in my *Courrier des Etats Unis*, & it is already in the hands of my printer. I mean to issue with it, my own version of Governor [James H.] Hammond's answer to the Free Church of Scotland; The Title of the small pamphlet will be— 'American Documents: Annexation of Texas; Abolition Schemes. British Policy.['] Send me if you can a copy of your notes given to M. [Alexis] de Tocqueville. They would be exceedingly useful to me for my Preface." You see that the matter is in good way. I Shall cause the letter to Mr. King to be inserted in Some of the daily papers. It is an able, cogent production, indeed, & as an appeal to the Continent of Europe against British plans of monopoly & aggrandizement, cannot fail to have an extensive efficiency. I have in preparation, a Statistical synopsis (of the U.S.) with a prefatory Discourse addressed to an intimate friend Baron Charles Dupin, wherein I mean to exhibit the American Slavery question side by side, with the European; & especially with the British pauper and labor Statistics: the whole in good French. Enclosed is a specimen of the kind of article which I am able to get into the Paris journals. Mr. de Tocqueville made but an imperfect slender use of my copious notes. I am, Dear Sir, with great respect, your Serv[an]t, Robert Walsh.

ALS with En in ScCleA. Note: The enclosure is a clipping from an unnamed French newspaper dated Paris, 1/5, in which the writer presents statistical and political information that he has obtained from an American citizen living in Paris. The article is aimed at correcting errors in the French official newspapers concerning the election of [James K.] Polk, the character of the Democratic party and of the Northern abolitionists, and the U.S. political state in general. Jollivet, a French West Indian and the leading French opponent of emancipation, published *Documents Américains, Annexion du Texas, Emancipation des Noirs, Politique de l'Angleterre* (Paris: de l'Imprimerie de Bruneau, 1845).

From J[osé] M. Caminero

Washington, January 8th 1845

Sir, In order to comply with the wishes of the Government ["of the United States" *interlined*] for information on various points, connected with the actual condition and organisation of the New Dominican Republic, as expressed in the first interview on the 6th inst., I have the honour to submit the following to your consideration.

The former Spanish portion of the Island of St. Domingo, remained under the dominion of Spain, until the beginning of 1822; when from one of those fatalities, to which nations are subject, in consequence of factions formed in times of political changes, and from having natural enemies as their neighbours, the country was united *de facto* to the Republic of Hayti, which then occupied the western part of the island formerly belonging to France; and this union, together with the abolition of slavery at the same time, occasioned a general unsettlement of habits, as well as of the principles of social life, to which the Spanish inhabitants had been originally subjected ["subjected" *erased*].

After enduring for twenty years, the heavy yoke of Haytian despotism, the white Dominicans, in order to put an end to their sufferings, by another act of a contrary nature, availed themselves of the opportunity offered by the revolution which led to the fall of [Jean Pierre] Boyer; and on the night of the 27th of february 1844, they raised the cry of independance, to which all classes responded; and taking possession of the Capital of St. Domingo, and of other fortified points in its vicinity, they succeeded on the following day, the 28th, in effecting the surrender, on capitulation, of the General commanding the district, and the Haytian forces, who a few days afterwards embarked for Port au Prince.

The new Dominican flag was then raised, and a provisional Government was formed in the capital, under the name of *Central Junta of Government*, composed of eleven individuals, from the various

60

districts; whose authority was voluntarily recognised by the other cities and places, all rising, animated by the same enthusiasm and patriotism, and taking up arms, to defend the just and noble cause of their beloved country.

The Dominican territory was then invaded through its eastern and northern frontiers, by two Haytian armies of more than ten thousand men; that of the west commanded by President Riviere Herard, arrived at Azua, where was posted the advance guard of the Dominicans, under General Pedro Santana, consisting of about three thousand men, with three cannons. The fire was opened, and the battle begun, on the 19th of march, when the Spanish Dominicans gained the victory, preserving possession of the place, and repelling their enemy, with the loss of only two killed, and three wounded, whilst more than a thousand Haytians, remained dead on the field.

After this complete victory, the Dominicans withdrew their headquarters to the River Ocoa, and the valleys of Bani, where their cavalry and lancers could operate; and in this way they restrained the march of the aggressors, who could not advance beyond Azua; and having then attempted to open a way through the passes of the Maniel, they were in every rencounter driven back with loss.

The other Haytian army in the north, commanded by General Pierrot, appeared on the 30th of march near the city of Santiago de los Caballeros, where the Haytiens were also repulsed, with loss as great as at Azua, while only one was wounded on our side; these great advantages being due to the fire of our artillery, and to the zeal of our volunteers, protected by divine providence. This army abandoned the field of battle on the following day, and during its retreat was incessantly harrassed and pursued experiencing in this way additional losses. The Army at Azua, having failed in all its attempts to penetrate through the mountain passes, and suffering constant losses, likewise retreated to Port au Prince; committing before its departure the infamous and inhuman act of burning the houses at Azua. Since that time, no farther aggressions have been committed.

The territory being thus freed by the evacuation and retreat of the Haytian troops, whose usurpation and invasion was repelled by force of arms, the liberty and independance of the Dominican Republic were considered as established *de facto*; and the Central Junta of Government engaged in calling on the people to elect deputies, and to form a Constituent Congress which should ordain and establish the Fundamental law of the land; and accordingly on the 6th of november last, this fundamental law was decreed, of which I had the honour to present you a copy, and by which you you [*sic*] will see, consecrated, those social principles which secure liberty, property, equality, and the admission of foreigners to civil and political rights, under certain rules, rendered necessary by our situation at present, in order to preserve union and internal tranquillity.

On the formation of the Social Compact, in the same month of november, Senor Don Pedro Santana was appointed and installed as President of the Republic, with four Secretaries of State—namely— Don Thomas Bobadilla Secretary of Foreign Relations and Justice; Don Manuel Cabral Bernal of the Interior and Police; Don Ricardo Miura of Finance and Commerce; and General Don Manuel Gimenes of War and Marine.

The people were invited to hold elections of members of the *Conservative Council*, (like your Senate) and of the *tribunate*, (like your House of Representatives) for the next meeting of the Congress.

The Presidency of the Republic, the high functions of the members of Congress, and the Magistracies for the administration of justice, are all elective, and held during a fixed term, by the votes of the people; the right to vote is conceded by the Constitution (article 160) to those citizens who being in the full enjoyment of civil and political rights, are moreover owners of real property, or holding political employments, or officers in the army or navy, or licensed to carry on some industrial pursuit or profession, or professors of some liberal art or science, or lessees for at least six years, of a rural establishment actually under cultivation.

All these persons however have a direct vote only, on the appointment of their own parochial electors; these parochial electors meeting in an electoral college (or assembly) at the chief place of each province, elect the Executive Power; each Province voting in favour of one of its own citizens, and of some other citizen not belonging to that province; and if there be no absolute majority, Congress then elects the Executive power. The same Electoral colleges also appoint the members of Congress; and then form lists of candidates from among whom, Congress appoints the Judges of the Court, and tribunals of justice. So that by this mode of election, and by the sentiments, which animate the principal class, conducting the general administration, it is indubitable, that the high functions and magistracies must always be held by the persons most capable, and worthy to figure in the civilized world.

The Governors or Superior political chiefs of each province, are likewise appointed for four years, but by the Executive Power, which will certainly be able to choose proven individuals for these important places.

The territory of the Dominican Republic comprehends two thirds or more of the Island; its limits being the same which in 1793 divided it from the French portion; extending from the River Laxabon or Massacre river, which empties into the Sea on the north side, to the River Pedernales which falls into the Sea on the South, leeward (west) of Beata Island. It can contain many millions of inhabitants.

Its territory is mountainous, very fertile, and capable of yielding all the productions of the West Indies; with vallies and Savannahs for feeding and watering cattle. It contains many mines of copper[,] gold[,] iron and coal; two great bays which formidable squadrons can enter and anchor in security, namely the Bay of Ocoa on the South, and the Bay of the Peninsula of Samana on the northwest, the latter admitting the whale as well as pearl fishery; together with various other smaller bays as for instance those of Monte Cristi or Isabella, and Matanzas on the north, and numerous ports and large rivers on the south.

The principal places and ports for trade, are the Capital City of Santo Domingo, and the City of Puerto de Plata; and in order to encourage the increase and prosperity of our commerce, the ports of Azua, Samana, and Monte Cristi, have since the establishment of our independance, been opened to foreign vessels.

A constant trade is kept up with the islands of St. Thomas and Curaçao; with the United States, principally with New York; with France through the ports of Havre, Bordeaux and Marseilles; with England through London and Liverpool; and with various places in the German Confederacy, whither are transported, the greater part of our mahogany, and nearly two thirds of our tobacco, the cultivation of which is increasing constantly.

Although our agriculture decayed in consequence of the union with the Haytian Republic and the abolition of slavery in 1822, the cultivation of the cane has been partially kept up; and sugar enough is made for the supply of the people, and an equal quantity for exportation.

The principal articles of export are mahogany of the finest quality, espinillos?, fustic, lignum-vitae, logwood, tobacco in leaf in great quantities and cigars, cattle hides, yellow and white wax, gum guiacum, honey, and woods for building.

The City of Santo Domingo, the capital of the Republic, is surrounded by walls and fortifications, with the requisite artillery. The city of Santiago de los Caballeros the second in size, has been well fortified since the declaration of our independance. The cities of Puerto Plata, and Samana, are also fortified sufficiently. The fortifications of the city of Azua, are now in progress; and fortifications will also be made at those points on the frontier, towards our enemies the Haytians, at which the nature of the ground renders passage most difficult; and there will be kept forces, sufficient to prevent all aggression on the part of the blacks.

The Republic possesses cannon, ammunition, and other articles for war enough; with an arsenal well provided with all necessary materials; and it can easily obtain a greater number of musquets and cartouche boxes, to arm if necessary, all the men capable of bearing arms; the number of whom amounts to about sixteen thousand, one half of them now on duty. It has also for its defense, four armed vessels of large size; viz. one brig, and three schooners, all built in Curaçao, which have proved very useful in the service against the Haytian negroes.

The revenues of the Government are the custom house duties on imports and exports; mole and tonnage duties; the produce of the rents of various properties, and employments belonging to the State; stamp duties, license duties, and others from territorial or Communal revenues, sufficient to cover the ordinary expenses. These revenues must necessarily increase, so soon as the Government can itself place ["the mines" *interlined*] in operation or contract with some company to do so; and after the cessation of the present state of things, which obliges us to maintain an imposing armed force; this force may then be dismissed, and all our citizens may devote themselves to the cultivation of their property or the exercise of their professions.

* The population [*The following AES by R(ichard) K. Crallé was interpolated here*: "The population amounts to more than 200,000 souls, half of which are white, who hold the general administration— And two thirds of the other half, are *mulattoes*, a great portion of whom are Landed Proprietors, or else exercising mechanic arts in profitable professions. They are well-disposed, and are fond of order and subordination. The remainder are negroes, the greater part of whom are free-born and, consequently the number of ancient slaves is small. Slavery has been forever abolished in the Republic.

Mr. Calhoun: Dr. Caminero has just come over and informs me that the above paragraph was accidentally omitted in his Memoir, on the Sixth page of the original; and should be inserted after the paragraph in which the number of armed vessels, and the public Revenues, are spoken of."]

One of the chief objects now occupying the attention of the Government, is to effect immediately, the immigration of foreign agriculturists, who by increasing the white population, will not only produce greater security, but also by attracting and augmenting trade, will tend to the prosperity of the Republic, by the increase of its resources and revenues, and enable it to protect at the same time, and encourage, the advance of public instruction the great engine of civilisation.

With the same view, the Government has recalled (and no doubt they will come) all the white Dominicans, who emigrated in 1822. To those persons, the property which they left, and which was not alienated by the Haytian Government, shall be restored; ["to them" *canceled*]; that Government having without regard to right and order of succession, sequestrated these properties, in favour of the State, to the injury of the present heirs, and and [*sic*] united them to its dominions, in defiance of the most sacred principles of the Law of Nations.

The New Dominican Republic, under these circumstances, from the orderly character of the institutions, as set forth in its political Constitution, sworn to and put in execution, from the union and spirit reigning among its members, presents not only actual capacity to fulfil the obligations of an independant nation, but also the power to defend its sovereignty and to enter into relations with those nations which may grant it their sympathies; and with which, it promises to act, under the principles of justice[,] equity and impartiality and on the same footing, to maintain the integrity of its territory and the equal consideration of all.

It moreover presents to the world, an exemplary and interesting case. Its cause is noble, just, and worthy of the friendship[,] the assistence and the interference of civilized and Christian Nations; especially of those of the American Continent; as it is the interest of humanity, to place in shelter, from all new oppression, ["that" *altered to* "this"] portion of the great society of nations, which has by its heroic efforts, succeeded in throwing off the yoke imposed upon it by the shameful usurpation of the Haytians, from whom alone, can be expected or feared a new and unlawful invasion. This expectation or fear is founded on the innate and constitutional hatred of the Haytians to all of the white race, to whom the right of holding property is denied throughout the whole of the Republic; to their thirst for vengeance, and their interest in preventing the progress of prosperity, and the increase of the white population in the other portion of the island.

The Haytian population is much greater, amounting to more than half a million of persons; and it may consequently prepare and execute another plan of usurpation, by means of its greater forces: and though the Dominican territory has natural defences, and the patriotic fervor of its citizens will lead them to fight and defend themselves to the sacrifice of their lives, should fortune which favored them in march last, turn against them; yet the soil of the primary portion of the Indies, of the first settlement made by its discoverer the honoured Christopher Columbus, in the immediate vicinity of so many Christian Republics and civilized States, may present the horrible scene, the fearful spectacle of the destruction of its ["white" *interlined*] inhabitants, and even of those of colour, and of its cities and villages by conflagration[,] pillage and murder on the part of the intruding faithless Haytian usurpers.

This fear, and expectation of a new invasion, should not prove an obstacle to prevent the intervention of the nearest nations, as the right of protecting nations unjustly oppressed, enters into their general policy, and humanity moreover dictates, in our case, the redemption of the new Dominican State, as an act sanctioned by the philanthropy of the other nations.

This is an exact and true sketch, so far as circumstances allow, of the organisation and state of the new Dominican Republic, which considers itself entitled to take a place in the family of nations, in virtue of the recognition which it solicits, from the magnanimous and Christian nation of the Confederated States of the American Union, to which it has addressed itself, in preference as the founder of real liberty in the New World.

Upon the recognition of our country, as an independant State, and the establishment of relations of amity and commerce, the Dominican Republic will be properly respected; for by this identification of its interests, the vigour of its forces and institutions will be increased, the confidence necessary to attract immigration will be established, and science, arts and commerce will flourish. Finally it will be thus soon placed in a condition to advance rapidly and to secure its stability.

The question of its recognition as an independant State, may be resolved affirmatively, and in its favour, the more easily, as it involves no responsability whatever, like those of the other States which have hitherto presented themselves, for recognition in this hemisphere. For with respect to the Haytian Republic, neither has its political existence been ever recognised by the United States, nor has it nor could it ever have had, legitimate dominion over the Spanish portion, the shameful occupation of which, was a real usurpation; and with regard to Spain, which held dominion over it, and of which the Dominicans were originally subjects, the indolence and indifference of that nation, and her active abandonment of us, for twenty years, under the oppressions and vexations of the negroes of Hayti, shew and establish most positively, the right of the Dominicans, to reassume their own sovereignty, and to enjoy it in freedom, and to constitute themselves an independant State; it being unquestionable, that when protection on the part of the Sovereign ceases, with it also ceases the duty of obedience in the subject: and the inhabitants of the Spanish portion, should not be left in a worse condition than the other Republics of the South which have been recognised by Spain. I have the honour &c, Doctor J.M. Caminero.

State Department translation of ALS (in Spanish) in DNA, RG 59 (State Department), Notes from Foreign Legations, Dominican Republic, vol. 1 (T-801:1); PC in Senate Executive Document No. 17, 41st Cong., 3rd Sess., pp. 27–32; variant PC in the New York, N.Y., *Herald*, December 29, 1845, p. 2.

From R. Glover, New York [City], 1/8. Glover wishes to learn "if it will be in time to lodge in the Department a claim against the Mexican Government for a vessel which was unlawfull seized in the Port of Matamoros in the Republic of Mexico some time in the winter of 1831." Glover is concerned that this claim might be debarred by its not having been made prior to the Mexican convention of 1839. ALS in DNA, RG 59 (State Department), Miscellaneous Letters (M-179:107, frames 34–35).

From J[abez] W. Huntington, [Senator from Conn.], 1/8. "I will thank you to furnish me with such information as the Department may possess, relating to the [*one word altered to* "qualifications"] of Joseph Graham of Ohio, & Alex[ande]r G. Abell of Michigan, nominated to be Consuls." ALS in DNA, RG 59 (State Department), Applications and Recommendations, 1845–1853, Graham (M-873:34, frames 275–276).

To Charles J. Ingersoll, Ch[airma]n of the Committee on Foreign Affairs, House of Representatives, 1/8. "I have the honor to transmit for the information of the Committee on Foreign Affairs, a copy of a letter [of today] addressed to [James I. McKay] the Chairman of the [House] Committee of Ways and means, stating the necessity of providing for Outfits of Ministers to Great Britain, Russia, Prussia, Austria and Spain." Letterpress copy in DNA, RG 59 (State Department), Accounting Records: Miscellaneous Letters Sent, vol. for 10/3/1844–5/29/1845, p. [156].

To [JOHN W. JONES], Speaker of the House of Representatives

Department of State
January 8th 1845

Sir: In answer to a resolution of the House of Representatives of the 4th Inst., directing the Secretary of State to "report to this House the number of volumes of the manuscript papers of the Confederation and of Washington, in the Department of State, to which indices are being prepared, the progress which has been made, at what time the work may probably be completed, and the probable additional expense of completion," I have the honor to reply, that there are in this Department four hundred & four volumes of the Confederation, and two hundred and ninety-nine of the Washington papers; making Seven hundred and three volumes. Of these, the Washington papers, with the exception of the "Army returns," (which are now being fully indexed,) have indices to the names, only, of the authors of letters or communications embraced in them, without designating subjects.

Since the first appropriation for this object in 1842, full indices to their contents have been prepared to 72 volumes, and there will be completed by the end of the present session of Congress 60 additional volumes, making the number of 132 volumes, which will then be fully indexed. There will then remain to be indexed two hundred & seventy-two volumes. These volumes are of sizes varying from 100 to 900 pages.

The first appropriation for this object was made in ["an" *interlined*] act approved 26th Aug. 1842,* [*Interpolation*: "2nd Session 27th Congress, page 135."] being an item "For purchasing and preparing indices to the manuscript papers of the Confederation and to the Washington papers deposited in the Department of State, one thousand Dollars." $450 of which was applied to the purchase of Mr. [Jared] Spark[s]'s index to a portion of the letters to Washington, leaving $550, applicable to this work. No appointment was made, however, until towards the close of the session of Congress of 1843, and this small sum was all expended in July of that year, Mr. [Abel P.] Upshur, then Secretary of State, fully satisfied of the importance of the work, and of the inconvenience attending its suspension at that time, continued the gentleman employed upon it, relying upon an appropriation when Congress should again meet. An appropriation was accordingly made at the last session of Congress to cover arrearages, and for the present fiscal year, amounting to $2360, making the sum of $2910 heretofore appropriated to this work.

From the increased facilities which a practical acquaintance with the work and the manner of its execution affords, it is presumed that the remaining 272 volumes can be completed in about three years, though of this there can be no certainty, as from the nature of the work, it is necessarily slow and tedious.

Should the work be completed within the time specified the additional expense required would be $3756, at the rate of four dollars per day, for each day actually employed, as allowed under the act above referred to, page 132. I have the honor to be, Sir, Very Respectfully Your Ob[edien]t Serv[an]t, J.C. Calhoun.

LS in DNA, RG 233 (U.S. House of Representatives), 28A-F1; FC in DNA, RG 59 (State Department), Reports of the Secretary of State to the President and Congress, 6:120–121; PC in House Document No. 63, 28th Cong., 2nd Sess., pp. 1–2. NOTE: The resolution to which this is a response can be found in DNA, RG 59 (State Department), Miscellaneous Letters (M-179:107, frame 15) and in *House Journal*, 28th Cong., 2nd Sess ., p. 169.

To JAMES I. McKAY, Chairman of the Committee of Ways & Means, House of Representatives

Department of State
Washington, 8th Jan[uar]y 1845

Sir, I have the honor to state for the information of the Committee of Ways and Means that it will be necessary during the present session of Congress, to make provision for outfits of Ministers Plenipotentiary to Great Britain, Russia, Prussia, Austria and Spain; and to request that an appropriation of $45,000 may be made for that purpose. I have the honor to be, Sir, Very respectfully, Your Obedient Servant, J.C. Calhoun.

LS in DNA, RG 233 (U.S. House of Representatives), 28A-D30.6; FC in DNA, RG 59 (State Department), Accounting Records: Miscellaneous Letters Sent, vol. for 10/3/1844–5/29/1845, p. 155.

To [CHARLES H. RAYMOND]

Department of State
Washington, 8th January, 1845
The Undersigned, Secretary of State of the United States, has the honor to acknowledge the receipt of the note of the 4th instant of Mr. Raymond, Chargé d'Affaires *ad interim* of the Republic of Texas, communicating intelligence of the commencement, on the 9th ult:, of a new administration of the government of that Republic, mentioning the names of the persons composing it and the friendly feelings entertained by the President of Texas [Anson Jones] towards the United States.

The Undersigned has the honor to acquaint Mr. Raymond in reply, that the President of the United States [John Tyler] reciprocates the friendly feelings of the President of Texas, and hopes that nothing may occur which will disturb the existing relations of concord and good understanding between the two countries.

The Undersigned avails himself of this occasion to offer Mr. Raymond the assurance of his very distinguished consideration. J.C. Calhoun.

LS in Tx, Andrew Jackson Houston Papers; FC in DNA, RG 59 (State Department), Notes to Foreign Legations, Texas, 6:79 (M 99:95); FC in Tx, Records of the Texas Republic Department of State, Copybooks of Letters Received from Texan and Foreign Representatives, vol. 2-1/103, p. 42; CC in Tx, Records of the Texas Republic Department of State, U.S. Diplomatic Correspondence.

To W[ILLIA]M L. DAYTON, Chairman [of the Senate Committee on Public Buildings]

Department of State
Washington, 9th January 1845
Sir, I have the honor to acknowledge the receipt of your note of the 6th Inst. enclosing a copy of a joint resolution which has passed the House of Representatives, and been referred to the Committee on Public Buildings of the Senate; and inquiry whether its final passage will not be a source of great labour upon the Departments, much expence and little service.

In reply I have the honor to state that, in order to prepare the Statements and reports called for by the Resolution great labour and expense must necessarily be incurred by the Departments. As to the benefits to be secured, I am at a loss to express any opinion; as I do not know what final object is contemplated by the Resolution. So far as the proposed Statements and Report from this Department is concerned, I cannot conceive of any advantage which would counterbalance the costs and labour which their preparation would require. I am Sir with high respect Your obedient Servant, J.C. Calhoun.

FC in DNA, RG 59 (State Department), Reports of the Secretary of State to the President and Congress, 6:122.

To A[ndrew] J. Donelson

Washington, 9th Jan[uar]y 1845

My dear Sir, I regret to learn by your's of the 26th Dec[embe]r, that the cause to which you alluded, should have taken you back to Galveston. The dispatch contained nothing but documents; the President['s, John Tyler's,] Message with the accompanying reports from the Departments. There has, indeed, been nothing of importance to communicate since the dispatch, which conveyed your appointment.

I am happy to inform you, that the course you have pursued has met the entire approbation of the executive. The important points were to secure the confidence of the Government of Texas and to keep open the question of annexation, in both of which your efforts have been entirely successful.

That question is now under discussion in the House of Representatives, and by a judicious devision of the question, the first vote, will be on the naked question of annexing Texas, free from all details. I can hardly doubt, but it will be carried by a large majority; and if it should, that it will contribute much to its final success. But I fear the fate of the measure is very doubtful at this session; and that if it should fail *now*, there is great danger of its ultimate failure. That such a measure, at so favourable a moment for its accomplishment, should ["be" *interlined*] seriously opposed, is, indeed, wonderful, and can only be accounted for, to speak plainly, on the assumption, that the sperit of faction & opposition to the south on the ground of slavery are stronger than the love of country. I regret to say, that the assumption would embrace a portion of our party, not very numerous, indeed, but active, artful & incessant in their efforts. I fear nothing can conciliate them, and that they will agree to no terms, but such

71

as Texas will reject: and the South & West will be compelled, in self defence, to oppose.

This may be a dark picture, but I fear it will prove too true. But we must not dispair, nor even show distrust. The discussion has been able & animated on our side. By keeping it up, & thereby enlightening the people & rousing their feelings, combined with well timed & judicious concessions to weak friends, & stern resistance and exposure of the motives of secret enemies, I trust it may yet be carried, during the present session.

I rejoice to learn by your last letter, that the whigs of Louisiana begin to indicate a better disposition, and that there is hope that the Tennessee Senators [Ephraim H. Foster and Spencer Jarnagin, Whigs] may be brought to vote for it. It would be a great point & do much to ensure its success. I hope when I write next, I shall be able to present a more favourable state of things here.

I am instructed by the President to grant you the leave of absence you request, leaving it to you to decide at what time you can best leave consistently with the duties of your mission. The duration is also left to your discretion, with the single condition, that it will not be longer than the emergency which requires it may demand. With great respect yours truly, J.C. Calhoun.

ALS in DLC, Andrew Jackson Donelson Papers; PC in St. George L. Sioussat, ed., "Selected Letters, 1844–1845, from the Donelson Papers," in *Tennessee Historical Magazine*, vol. III (June, 1917), pp. 147–148.

From A[NDREW] J. DONELSON

Washington Texas, January 9th 1845

Sir, I have the honor to transmit herewith, a letter addressed to me on the 4th Inst. by this Government and my reply to it of the 6th Inst.—in relation to certain objectionable conduct imputed to Duff Green Esq[ui]r[e] and which resulted before my ar[r]ival here, in the revocation of his Exequatur as Consul for the port of Galveston.

Since the writing of those letters I have had an interview with his Excellency the President [Anson Jones], and have every reason to believe that all personal misunderstanding between him and Gen[era]l Green, will be removed and their relations will be placed on as friendly a footing as they were before this event happened.

The correspondence proper to shew this, has been defer[r]ed on account of my sickness and the absence of the President from town today, but will be forwarded as soon as practicable. I am verry Respectfully Your Ob[edien]t Serv[an]t, A.J. Donelson.

[Enclosure]

Eb[e]n[eze]r Allen to A[ndrew] J. Donelson

Department of State

Washington [Texas], January 4th 1844 [*sic*; 1845]

The undersigned, Attorney General of the Republic of Texas, charged, ad interim, with the direction of the Department of State, has the honor to congratulate Mr. Donelson, Chargé d'Affaires of the United States &c &c, on his return, after a temporary absence, to his residence near this Government; and avails himself of the occasion, to transmit to Mr. D[onelson], the enclosed copy of a Proclamation recently issued by His Excellency, the President of the Republic of Texas, revoking the *Exequatur* of Duff Green, Esq., as Consul of the United States for Galveston. For the satisfaction of Mr. D[onelson], and to enable him to present the matter with its incidents, to the consideration of his Government, should he deem it expedient so to do, the undersigned subjoins a statement of the causes and circumstances, which induced a revocation of the recognition by this Government of Mr. Green's authority as Consul.

Early during the present session of our national legislature, Mr. Green fixed his residence at this place, and has ever since been industriously occupied, in endeavoring to procure the sanction of Congress to certain projected measures, in the consummation of which, he has manifested strong personal interest; by availing himself of frequent private interviews with members of that body, to influence their public and legislative course, in aid of his favorite schemes. One of the projects thus originated and prepared by Mr. Green, was brought before the Senate, in the form of a bill for the incorporation of an institution, to be styled "The Texas Land Company," among the powers of which, under a perpetual charter; was that of acquiring, holding and disposing of real estate to an unlimited amount—connected with those privileges and rights usually enjoyed by Insurance, Rail Road, Life-Insurance and Trust Companies, and which constitute the peculiar and distinguishing features of such corporations; together with the power and capacity to monopolize the exclusive and perpetual use of all our navigable streams.

Another was a plan for the charter of the "Del Norte Company," so to be called, also projected by Mr. Green and designed to become a law by the action of the Legislature, but which has not as yet been presented to Congress; having in part, for its object, the conquest and occupancy in behalf of Texas, of the Calafornias [*sic*] and the Northern Provinces of Mexico by means of an army aided by some sixty thousand Indian warriors, to be introduced from the United States upon our western frontier.

In furtherance of these schemes, and to obtain for them the formalities and color of legislative sanction, Mr. Green solicited the aid and influence of the Executive; and, at an interview which he sought with the President at the Executive Department, on the 30th ultimo, as well as on some previous occasions, he endeavored to induce, His Excellency, to exert his influence to effect the objects specified; first, by an offer of portions of the corporate stock of the projected companies; and, secondly, by a threat to revolutionize the country, and overthrow the existing government, in the event of His Excellency's refusing to accede to the proposal.

Coupled with this threat, Mr. Green, took occasion, to boast of the ease with which he could execute it; observing, that the excitement among our citizens on the subject of Annexation, manifested by the mass meetings of Matagorda and Brazoria, together with the alarm, which could be readily aroused by exhibiting to their minds the dangers to which our republican institutions would be exposed, in consequence of the great influx of Europeans into our territory, and the facility, with which they would become entitled to the privileges of Citizenship; presented an inviting field for revolutionary operations.

In consequence of these circumstances, the confidence before that time entertained by the President in the fitness of Mr. Green for the station assigned to him as Consul, was necessarily destroyed; and His Excellency, however regretting the emergency, was compelled in justice to his own convictions, to withdraw the *Exequatur* referred to; believing that its continuance, not required by the principles of amity or courtesy which have ever distinguished the intercourse and relations of the two governments, would serve only as a false manifestation of Executive confidence, the existence of which had ceased; and that its revocation, not being inconsistant with any of those principles, presented in the present instance the mildest form for the expression of Executive disapprobation.

The President, being impressed with the belief, that the mode of proceeding adopted by him in this case, in reference to Mr. Greene [*sic*], is not susceptible of such a construction, as to render it in any degree objectionable to the Government of the United States, directs the Undersigned to express to Mr. Donelson, the continued and earnest desire of His Excellency, to preserve and promote the mutual relations of concord and friendship, which subsist between the two governments, and the harmony which characterizes the intercourse of the citizens of each with those of the other, and his high personal esteem and regard for Mr. D[onelson]; in commencing which, the undersigned avails himself of the occasion, to renew to Mr. Donelson the assurance of the distinguished consideration, with which the undersigned has the honor to remain His Obedient Servant, Ebnr. Allen.

[Enclosure]

"Proclamation, By the President of the Republic of Texas"

[Washington, Texas, December 31, 1844]

Whereas, on the 5th day of October, A.D. 1844, Duff Green, Esquire, having, before that time, been duly appointed "Consul of the United States, for Galveston," was, by an *Exequatur* of that date, issued by His Excellency, Sam Houston then President of the Republic of Texas, recognized as such Consul, and thereby authorized to exercise and enjoy such functions, powers and privileges as are allowed to Consuls of the most favored nations in the Republic of Texas—in which office the said Duff Green is still acting;

And whereas, owing to circumstances, known to the Executive, the *interest*[,] *honor* and *safety* of the Republic require that the authority, so extended, as aforesaid, to the said Duff Green be revoked:

Therefore, be it known, that I, Anson Jones President of the Republic of Texas, by virtue of the power, by law in me vested, do, hereby, solemnly revoke the *exequatur*, aforesaid, and the same is accordingly revoked, with all the powers, immunities[,] privileges and rights therein, or thereby, conceded, granted or extended to the said Duff Green, as Consul as aforesaid.

In testimony whereof, I have hereunto set my hand and caused the Great Seal of the Republic to be affixed. Done at Washington, the thirty-first day of December, in the year of our Lord, one thousand eight hundred and forty four, and of the Independence of the Republic, the ninth.

By the President: (Signed) Anson Jones.

(Signed) Ebenr. Allen, Attorney General & Secretary of State ad interim.

[Enclosure]

A[ndrew] J. Donelson to [Ebenezer Allen]

Legation of the United States

Washington [Texas], Jan[uar]y 6th 1845

The undersigned, chargé d'Affaires of the United States, has had the honor to receive the communication addressed to him on the 4th Inst., by the Hon[ora]bl[e] Mr. Allen, charged *ad interim* with the direction of the Department of State of Texas, congratulating him on his return to his residence near this Government, and stating the circumstances which led to the revocation of the Exequatur granted to Duff Green Esq[ui]r[e] on the 5th October 1844, as consul of the United States for the port of Galveston.

The undersigned will avail himself of the earliest occasion to transmit to his Government the explanation which has been furnished by the Hon[ora]bl[e] Mr. Allen of the transaction referred to, and is glad to perceive that it rests on causes, which, much as they are to be regretted, do not interrupt the friendly relations existing between the Governments of the two Countries. Mr. Green, soon after his ar[r]ival here, as bearer of despatches from Mexico, when questioned by the undersigned, as to the state of his consular duties, remarked that he was about to become a citizen of Texas, and having appointed a Vice Consul at Galveston, had informed his Government that he did not wish his name to be presented to the Senate of the United States for confirmation in the office, and that he would perform no further official act. Under these circumstances the undersigned did not feel it his duty to take cognizance of Mr. Green[']s absence from Galveston, particularly as he knew that the duties pertaining to his office, in the present state of the trade between the two countries were very light even for a Vice Consul. It will be recollected also that previous to his late departure for New Orleans, the undersigned mentioned verbally to his Excellency the President of Texas that Mr. Green had no authority in any manner to represent the Government of the United States.

These facts are stated for the purpose of shewing that Mr. Green, although within the range of the responsibility imposed by an *Exequatur* from this Government, was practically only a new comer into Texas with the intention of acquiring the rights of citizenship. In this light then, the objectionable conduct imputed to him, ceases to have any higher importance than what belongs to his individual, private character; and the undersigned is happy to be assured that his Excellency the President regards it as involving no interruption of those relations of amity and courtesy which in the intercourse of the Government and people of the two Republics, are so necessary to their reciprocal interest and welfare.

As to the measures sought to be accomplished by Mr. Green, under the authority and sanction of this Government, the undersigned feels it to be his duty to say that he had no knowledge of them, and participated in them in no wise, directly, or indirectly, either as a public officer or as a private individual. Indeed those measures conflict essentially with the course of policy which the undersigned if consulted, would have suggested as the most expedient for Texas at the present period. As the friend of reannexation he certainly could not have thought of a step, the effect of which would be to countenance the idea that the country between the Rio del Norte and the Pacific ocean was to be invaded and severed by another Revolution from Mexico. To check such speculations—to give a more safe direction to the spirit of adventure already too much aroused by the weakness and short sighted sighted [sic] policy of Mexico—and above all to seccure [sic] to the people of Texas the blessings of peace and independence, under the guarantee of incorporation into the American union, have been the aim and scope of all the counsel which the Undersigned has ventured to offer.

Any policy which would raise new issues—which would entangle Texas in new enterprizes calling for further aid in money or munitions of war—would be contrary to what the undersigned has supposed to be the wish and interest of Texas, because it would add new impediments to the success of the measures yet necessary to secure re-annexation to the United States, and jeopard in other respects her ability to maintain her present elevated position.

The undersigned having felt it his duty to make these observations, begs leave to add that he will submit to Mr. Green the reasons for the revocation of the *Exequatur*, under the hope that some explanation consistent with his honor and acceptable to his Excellency the President, will be made by him, not on the public account, but that imputations so deeply affecting his standing may be removed if they appear not to be meritted.

Appreciating highly the personal regard expressed for him by the President, the Undersigned begs leave to say in reply to the Hon[ora]bl[e] Mr. Allen that it is most sincerely reciprocated, and he trusts will continue to uphold him in the performance of all his duties near this Government and the Undersigned begs Mr. Allen to accept for himself also assurances of his high consideration and regard. He has the honor to be very respectfully his ob[edien]t Ser[van]t, A.J. Donelson.

LS (No. 9) with Ens in DNA, RG 59 (State Department), Diplomatic Despatches, Texas, vol. 2 (T-728:2, frames 447–471), received 1/31.

To J[esse] W. Griffiths, Philadelphia, 1/9. "I have to reply to your letter of the 7th inst., that there is, at present, no vacancy in the class of Consulates to which you therein refer, but should one occur, that your application will be favorably Considered." FC in DNA, RG 59 (State Department), Domestic Letters, 35:69 (M-40:33).

To J[abez] W. Huntington, Chairman of the Committee on Commerce of the Senate, 1/9. "I have the honor to reply to your letter of the 8th instant, so far as it respects the case of Mr. [Alexander G.] Abell, nominated to the Senate for the Consulate at Hawaii, that the Department is not in possession of any papers in reference to him, but that it is understood, the Senators from Michigan are well acquainted with his qualifications." FC in DNA, RG 59 (State Department), Reports of the Secretary of State to the President and Congress, 6:122.

To C[HARLES] J. INGERSOLL, [House Committee on Foreign Relations]

Department of State
Washington, 9th January 1845

Sir, On the 30th of March last the President transmitted a message to the House of Representatives, communicating a note from A[l-phonse] Pageot, Minister Plenipotentiary *ad interim* of the King of the French to the Secretary of State in relation to the tonnage duties levied on French vessels coming into the Ports of the United States from the Island[s] of St. Pierre and Miquelon; and proposing to place our Commercial intercourse with these islands upon the same footing as exists with the islands of Martinique and Guadaloupe, as regulated by the act of the 9th of May 1828, and the 13th of July 1832.

The President in his message suggested the propriety of extending the provisions of these laws to the commerce of the Islands in question, but Congress adjourned without having acted on the subject.

Under these circumstances, and at the instance of the French Minister, I beg leave to call your attention to the subject, and to suggest the expediency of some final action on the part of Congress during the present session. I have the honor to be with high respect Sir Your obedient Servant, J.C. Calhoun.

FC in DNA, RG 59 (State Department), Reports of the Secretary of State to the President and Congress, 6:123; PC in Jameson, ed., *Correspondence*, p. 638.

From ALEX[ANDE]R JONES

241 8th Avenue[,] New York [City]
Jan[uar]y 9th 1845

Dear Sir, If convenient, will you do me the favour of informing me of Gen[era]l [Duff] Green's present residence[?] I understood that he was probably at Galveston. I am interested in a case in New York, in reference to which it is important if practicable to obtain his evidence.

You will before this have received Gov. [Silas] Wright[']s message [to the N.Y. Legislature on 1/8]. Its extraordinary length, has not excited less public attention ["more" *interlined*], than ["the" *interlined*] vague and indefinite allusion towards the close, in relation to the question of annexation. The fact is, ["his" *interlined*] position and sentiments are equivocal. The recent movement in reference to annexation by a portion of the *so called*, Democratic party in this state, adds another proof, to the conclusion, that the leaders of this party at the North, cannot be trusted.

In the present instance the leaders are behind the sentiments of the great body, or mass of the party, and especially in this city. Never were issues more fairly made than in the late campaign. In every Democratic meeting in this city, in every procession, or other demonstration, was heard the cry for *immediate* Annexation. "[James K.] Polk[,] [George M.] Dallas and Texas" were the watchwords. Now the voice of the people is unheeded. Their decision is attempted to be evaded or set aside or grossly misrepresented. To say annexation was not a test question and especially in New York, is a gross absurdity. On the night before the Presidential election in this state the Whigs thrust a handbill under the door of every dwelling in this city, with the following sentiments printed in large letters:

"Citizens of the North, which do you prefer[,] Union without Texas, or ["disuion" *canceled*] disunion with Texas[?] Do you prefer, peace & prosperity, or adversity, with a large Texas debt saddled upon the Treasury, and a foreign war[?] If you love the honor, peace and happiness of your beloved country vote the Whig Ticket. &C."

Notwithstanding these exciting appeals made to the fears of the people, they met the issue and emphatically decided in favour of Annexation.

What can the Wright Democracy mean? The course of the [New York] Morning News and [the New York] Evening Post evidently harmonizes, with the views of ["righ" *canceled*] Wright and his friends on the floor of Congress. There is evidently a concert of action. There clearly exist[s] a combination or plan for some purpose? The desire for office under Col. Polk is supposed by some, (I see), ["as the main" *canceled*] to be the main spring of ["this" *interlined*] extraordinary conduct. This may influence them, and no doubt does; but I fear motives of even a less pure character, than a wish to control the appointments of Col. Polk, actuates their movements.

The Albany political tactics are based upon the principle of ruling the party, or overthrowing it. Whether the overthrow or defeat is designed in the event of failing to control ["or not" *canceled*] I do not undertake to say; but such has generally been the result.

They resorted to the most extraordinary means to force the nomination of Mr. [Martin] Van Buren upon the party, and when they failed in doing so, a portion of them meanly attempted to organize a cabal, to prevent Col. Polk's election. Van Buren[']s friends became excessively lukewarm and at first, were undecided what way to vote. And, if it had not been for the extraordinary zeal of the young Democracy including your friends, with the unpopularity of Van Burenism in the Lake or north western part of the State, and the adherence of the Abolitionist[s] to [James G.] Birney [Presidential candidate of the Liberty Party], we should have lost the State and Polk's election. Now forsooth, they set up as the exclusive friends of Col. Polk, misrepresent the voice of the people and will attempt ["by" *canceled*] through the agency of a self constituted committee in Tam[m]any Hall to control all Gov. Polk[']s appointments in this quarter!!

I shall always believe that Gov. Wright[']s refusal to run with Gov. Polk arose simply from his belief at the time, that the latter could not succeed.

To your immediate friends, in this city more than to any other cause, except Annexation[,] was owing the final abandonment of Van Buren and the nomination of Governor Polk. We formed a Calhoun or Congressional District Committee, composed of 52 persons, ["in w" *canceled*] among whom were found representatives from every ward in the city. We circulated documents in favour of the District plan of appointing Delegates to the Baltimore [Democratic National] Convention, and against the resolutions of the Syracuse [N.Y. Democratic] convention, and also against Van Buren and the expediency of his nomination.

These documents were sent into every section of the state; ["and" *canceled*] aroused powerful and strong opposition, ["&" *canceled*] which alarmed the Albany regency with the old Hunkers. The brief existence of the [New York Daily] Gazette, also, had its influence. His chances of receiving the nomination, became much ["weaked" *altered to* "weaken(e)d"], till his Texas Letter completed the work so auspiciously commenced & prosecuted in this city.

Finding they could not prevent Col. Polk[']s election, they came in at the eleventh hour to his support, and ["not" *canceled and* "now" *interlined*] set up for the rule, or ruin of his administration!!

They have marked every one who composed that association of 52 among whom are many of the most honorable and ["woth" *canceled*] worthy persons in this city. It is true we had a few among the number unworthy of trust or confidence, & who have since deserted us, & gone over to the Hunkers. No set of men ever fought harder in the late election than we did. Yet, we are proscribed. We are all still your warm and devoted friends, and are ready to stand by you in every extremity. We go for the *immediate Annexation of Texas, untram[m]elled by the mystifying conditions* proposed by its false friends with a view of indefinitely postponing or defeating its success.

We have a small private meeting tomorrow evening to determine by consultation upon the course we shall deem best to adopt.

If we find, the state of the public mind, in the pause of a calm after the late excitement[,] will bear us out in the movement, and give promise of a large meeting, it will be our ["pup" *canceled*] purpose to pave the way for one. We want it to be large, and if it cannot be so, we will be in doubt whether to call it at all.

We feel anxious, should your feelings and views, be not strongly repugnant ["to it" *interlined*], for you to continue as Secretary of State under Col. Polk. At least until Texas ["be" *canceled*] is annexed, or forever and finally ["lost" *interlined*] to our confederacy.

The progress of fanaticism, ["is" *canceled*] every year at the North is becoming more alarming and dangerous to the peace of the country. All ranks of citizens, and especially the wealthy and influential classes, are tinctured with the spirit of abolitionism. The whigs, openly courted their support, and we now find the *Wright wing* of the Democracy approximating, and almost fraternizing with abolition, ["and" *canceled*] Whig men & Journals!!

What does all this mean? May it not be the design of the ["wr" *and* "Wh" *canceled*] Wright Democrats; if they cannot mould and rule Gov. Polk's administration, to join with the Whigs and abolitionist[s] to make a candidate for the succession? The whigs have no

81

prominent man, they can bring forward with the least hope of success. Gov. Wright is the least objectionable to them of any prominent candidate I know any thing of. The whigs stand no chance; but, by taking up *a deserter* from Democracy, or ["a" *interlined*] man professing Democracy. And Gov. Wright seems to be made of plastic materials, just such, as would ["yield" *interlined*] to the forceable appeals of ["his" *interlined*] self interest.

What can the political Abolitionist[s] be aiming at? They evidently aspire to the dissolution of the Union. Who prompted or now prompts this, but Great Britain, or the Abolitionist[s] of England? Suppose the designs of the Abolitionist[s] accomplished, what follows? The Government of the north would look to England for support, for supplies of cotton and other tropical productions, in preference to the Southern States, and, if the South yiel[d]ed not to dictation, they would unite to force emancipation, and ruin the country!!

I should not be surprized, if some plan for the future has already been carved out between the English and American Abolitionist[s].

At all events, I think it high time the people of the South ["should more closely" *interlined*] watch, this *infernal spirit of fanaticism at the North*, and begin to look ["to look" *canceled*] to resources and means within themselves for their own future safety and protection.

What are we to think, when we see an Abolitionist [William Slade], in ["the" *interlined*] Governor's of [*sic*] chair of Vermont, another ([George N.] Briggs,) in that of Massachusetts, and read the open avowal and declaration of Abolitionism in the late letter of *ex-Governor* [of N.Y., William H.] *Seward*!!

The time has been in New York, when such a letter would have drawn down the indignation of a mob upon him, but, now such a letter excites no surprize, or censure especially among the upper class, to any great extent, many of whom no doubt approve of its sentiments!!

Of all instruments with which to work harm, and overthrow sound and established forms of Government, ["is" *interlined*] *fanaticism*"[.] What crime is it, that has not, and cannot be committed, in God[']s name (assumed) & under God[']s authority? Fanaticism never stops to reason. It is blind to truth, and deaf to all appeals made to the understanding. In their false view, God commands, and ["it" *canceled*] fanatics must obey. It makes no difference if unutterable evils, infinitely greater than any they imagine to exist, are inflicted. God bids and they must perform.

The scenes of St. Domingo supply no lessons for them. The

cruelties and massacres which desolated that ill fated Island, leaving it under the control of a black population, which, has given conclusive evidence within 52 years, of its total incapacity for self Government, and which, has been greatly diminished by the combined results of idleness, famine and disease, teaches nothing to them.

The early crusade with the rise of Oliver Cromwell at a later period, clearly show the strength and blind fury of *fanaticism.* And, I much fear another display of its fearful and ruinous effects ["in" *canceled*] sooner or later in this ["this" *canceled*] country. *Let the South be ready for the crisis.* It will quail and withdraw before the firm and united action of the South, the only thing which can save them.

Division and disunion among themselves, will only invite aggression and end in their overthrow.

I am running wild. I must recollect I am writing to one, who has already penetrated widely and deeply into the future, far beyond the utmost stretch of my ability to comprehend.

I was highly delighted with your able letter of instructions to Mr. [William R.] King. It was a ["state" *canceled*] patriotic state paper of the right kind and much wanted. Its contents are creditable & honorable both to yourself and the country; and cannot fail ["of" *interlined*] exercising a salutary influence on the foreign relations of the Government. I was also highly gratified with your instructions to Mr. [Wilson] Shannon. The object of the Wright *news papers* in this city has been ["made ac" *canceled and* "rather" *interlined*] to *entangle* the *negotiators,* ["rather" *canceled and* "than" *interlined*] to establish any tanglement of the negotiations with Mexico. Verily, I trust they will receive their reward.

Gen[era]l [Mirabeau B.] Lamar and Commodore [Edwin W.] Moore [of Texas] received their friends to day at the city Hall.

A large and respectable concourse of Ladies and gentlemen waited upon them; being introduced by his Honor [James Harper] the Mayor of the city. I observed *no* whigs were among the visitors and very few, if any, of the *"Bento-Wright"* Democrats. All passed ["off" *interlined*], however, well and in good taste.

I am glad this public interview has taken place between the citizens of New York and those worthy and distinguished officials of Texas. The result cannot be otherwise than favourable. Mr. [George M.] Dallas [Vice-President-elect] and C[harles] J. Ingersoll [Representative from Pa.] are still in the city. I understand the former made a speech at a dinner party last evening in favour of Annexation.

The winter is mild in New York.

If abolitionism increases much more, or gets much stronger at the North, I will quit the free states and find a residence some where south of "Mason & Dixon[']s line[.]"

If you see Col. D[ixon] H. Lewis [Senator from Ala.] be pleased to present him with my best compliments.

Please excuse the hasty and random manner in which I have written an epistle as much too long for a letter (for one of your constant occupation to read) as Gov. Wright[']s Message is too long for a state paper.

With every wish for your prolonged health and happiness I have the Honor to Remain as Ever Yours Very Truly & Sincerely, Alexr. Jones.

ALS in ScCleA; PEx in Jameson, ed., *Correspondence,* p. 1018.

From Gust[af] de Nordin, [Swedish Chargé d'Affaires to the U.S.], 1/9. At the request of Jorgen Flood, a merchant of Porsgrund, he recommends Flood to be U.S. Consul for the Norwegian ports of Porsgrund, Skien, Brevig, and Langesund, "all situated very near each other." "About 10 to 12 vessels leave yearly these ports for the United States with Iron and with Emigrants to this country. As no American Consul resides nearer than at Christiania, at a distance of about 150 miles, there are great difficulties and expenses occasioned by the necessity of sending ships documents far off for obtaining the necessary attestations of the said American Officer." (Nordin addressed this letter to "P.M.," meaning presumably Calhoun as "prime minister.") ALS in DNA, RG 59 (State Department), Applications and Recommendations, 1845–1853, Flood (M-873:28, frames 756–757).

From Wilson Shannon

Legation of the U.S. of A.
Mexico, Jan. 9th 1845

Sir, Since the date of my last dispatch the new Government has been busily engaged in the fortification of this city and it is now in a good state of defense considering the natural weakness of its position. Deep ditches are cut across all the streets except one or two and breast works thrown up in front of the ditches some six feet high. The roads leading from the city are fortified in the same way. The churches are used as fortifications for the defense of the city and the militia are stationed on the roofs of the houses. As was expected, President Santa Anna, immediately on learning the news of the revolutionary movements in this city and Puebla, changed his direction, and marched upon this place, with his whole force, amounting according to his own statement to twelve thousand men. About two weeks since[,] he appeared before Mexico [City] and all expected an attack but after remaining some four or five days before the place; deeming it too strong to be taken; he marched upon Puebla. He appeared before that city on the 3d Inst. and immediately commenced his attack and has kept it up ever since. Our last advices from the seat of war state, he had made five different assaults on the city but had been repulsed each time and driven back from the great central public square. He was, however, in possession of the outer parts of the place and was redoubling his efforts to get the entire possession of it. The loss is said to be great on both sides; the forces of the ex-president, however have sustained much the most injury. It is admitted on both sides that this is the best fought, as well as the most bloody battle, Mexico has ever witnessed. My information leaves the result doubtful. The contest however cannot last much longer. Should Santa Anna fail before Puebla his cause will be entirely hopeless, if he should succeed he may be able to agitate the country for some time to come but I do not believe he will be able, again to place himself in possession of the Government. I think the opinion may be relied on that those now in power will be able to hold possession of the Government as against Santa Anna. There are many however who fear that so soon as he is put down new strifes will spring up among the different military leaders and that this country is doomed to undergo all the evils of civil war for years to come. It is to be hoped that these unfavourable anticipations may not be realized, yet looking at things in the most favourable point of view, it must be some months before order is restored and the Government permanently settled. Gen[era]l [Nicolás] Bravo at the head of four thousand men has advanced forty miles towards Puebla. Gen[era]l [Mariano] Paredes at the head of six thousand men arrived in this city a few days since and has left with all the Government forces to join Gen[era]l Bravo. They march for the relief of Puebla and it is said that the Government will be able to concentrate at that place some sixteen thousand men, in the course of a few days. Many of these, however are new recruits, while those under Gen[era]l Santa Anna are the best in the Republic.

While Gen[era]l Santa Anna was at Queretaro his correspondence with the late Government was intercepted and a large portion of it has been published by the present Government, and it has all been laid before congress in secret session. From a portion of this correspondence, the fact has been disclosed, that a negociation was going on between President Santa Anna and the English Minister [Charles Bankhead] for the sale and purchase of the two Californias. That portion of the correspondence relating to this subject has not been published in the papers, but it has been laid before congress in secret session and the pendency of such a negociation may be relied on as true. The English Minister has no doubt, in this matter acted under instructions from his government; it may therefore be assumed that it is the settled policy of the English Government to acquire the possession of the two Californias. You are aware that the English creditors have now a mortgage on them for twenty six millions. The overthrow of Santa Anna has defeated this object for the present and it is not likely that the present powers will favour the measure as it is urged by them as a grave charge against the late administration. The very active part the English have taken in favour of President Santa Anna, and the well known advice which some of them gave him, to put congress down and declare himself dictator, has deprived them and their Government of all influence with the party now in power.

The American citizens residing in Puebla have all united in requesting the appointment of a consul at that place and have recommended James W. Angus Esqr. as a suitable person to receive the appointment. He is a very compotent [*sic*] man and I hope the President [John Tyler] will appoint him. I have the honor to be Yours with great respect, Wilson Shannon.

LS (No. 7) in DNA, RG 59 (State Department), Diplomatic Despatches, Mexico, vol. 12 (M-97:13), received 2/17; FC in DNA, RG 84 (Foreign Posts), Mexico, Despatches.

From R[ICHARD] F. SIMPSON, [Representative from S.C.]

[Washington] Jan[uar]y 9, 1845

I rec[eive]d this evening the enclosed letter [*not found*] from Mr. [Henry P.] Brewster, who removed from Laurens Dist. several years ago for Texas. He is the grandson of old Col. [Jonathan] Downs and was, when he left, thought to possess considerable sagacity.

Knowing from the full information in your possession you will at once be able to put the true value on his communication which I cannot, I enclose it for your perusal.

I learned to day from a Whig member that 8 or 10 of them had come to the conclusion (and among them a Tennessee Senator) to vote for annexing Texas as a State provided these stipulations were added towit [*sic*]—Texas to keep her territory and pay her ["own" *interlined*] debts—and that the line of the Missouri compromise should be the only line of boundary for Slavery in the Territory.

If this was acceptable to Texas I think there is a growing disposition in our House to favour that view. Your ob[edien]t Serv[an]t, R.F. Simpson.

ALS in ScCleA. NOTE: Ephraim H. Foster and Spencer Jarnagin, both Whigs, were Senators from Tenn. at this time.

To Stephen Smith, Baltimore, 1/9. "I have to acknowledge the receipt of your letter of the 7th inst. relative to your claim against the Chilian Government for ["the" *interlined*] illegal detention of a vessel at the port of Talc[a]huano. In reply, I have to state, that William Crump Esquire who recently embarked for that Country, as Chargé d'Affaires of the United States, was fully instructed by this Department upon the subject." FC in DNA, RG 59 (State Department), Domestic Letters, 35:77 (M-40:33).

To President [JOHN TYLER]

Department of State
Washington, 9th January, 1845

To the President of the United States:

The Secretary of State to whom has been referred the Resolution of the House of Representatives of the 14th of June last, requesting the President to "cause to be communicated to that House a copy of all the instructions to George W. Erving, upon his appointment as Minister Plenipotentiary to Spain in the year 1814, and afterwards, during his mission to that Court, which have not been heretofore made public"—has the honor to report to the President, in answer to that Resolution, the accompanying papers. Respectfully submitted, J.C. Calhoun.

LS in DNA, RG 233 (U.S. House of Representatives), 28A-E1; FC in DNA, RG 59 (State Department), Reports of the Secretary of State to the President and

Congress, 6:131–132; PC with Ens in House Document No. 42, 28th Cong., 2nd Sess., pp. 1–17. NOTE: Tyler transmitted this report to the House of Representatives on 1/9. The resolution to which the above letter is a reply can be found in DNA, RG 59 (State Department), Miscellaneous Letters (M-179:104, frame 539) and *House Journal*, 28th Cong., 1st Sess., p. 1121. Enclosed with the PC were approximately 20 documents dated between October 6, 1814 and November 28, 1818 dealing with U.S.-Spanish affairs.

To R. Glover, New York [City], 1/10. "I have to acknowledge the receipt of your letter of the 8th inst. and to inform you in reply, that the claim against the Mexican Government to which you refer will not be debarred or impaired in consequence of the Omission to ask the interposition of this Government. It would however be advisable to Communicate the papers to this Department without unnecessary delay." FC in DNA, RG 59 (State Department), Domestic Letters, 35:70 (M-40:33).

From Cha[rles] M. Leupp & Co. and twenty-one other companies, [New York City, *ca.* 1/10]. Leupp and other merchants engaged in the export of American hides and leathers recommend James Fiora to be appointed U.S. Consul at Manchester, England. Fiora is active in promoting the introduction of American sole leather into English markets. An AES, dated 1/16, by Z[adock] Pratt, [Representative from N.Y.], reads "I can with perfect Confidence recommend the appointment of James Fiora." An AEI by J[ohn] T[yler] reads: "The Secretary of State will look into this and if a consulate sh[oul]d be established the gentleman recommended is suited to the place." DS in DNA, RG 59 (State Department), Applications and Recommendations, 1845–1853, Fiora (M-873:28, frames 117–120).

From STEWART NEWELL

Consulate of the United States
Sabine, Texas
(Now in New Orleans)
Jan[uar]y 10th 1845

Sir, I beg leave to communicate a report, that has just reached this City, this morning, p[e]r St[eam] P[ac]k[e]t New York, from Galveston, which is, that owing to some misunderstanding between

Gen[era]l Duff Green, and his Excellency, the President of Texas [Anson Jones], the exequator of the former, has been withdrawn, by the latter, and I am informed, the recall of Gen[era]l Green, has been requested from Texas.

Should the above report, prove to be well founded, the Consulate being vacant, I beg leave to ask, that the honor of that Appointment, be confer[r]ed upon me, and which will, in no wise, interfere ["with" *interlined*] a proper and efficient, discharge of the duties of the Consulate, at Sabine, the latter, requireing attention, only about four months in the year, should his Excellency, be pleased to confer the honor upon me, I trust, that my past course, in discharge of my duties, and which the Department done me, honor to approbate, in Letter of Oct. 10th ult[im]o, shall be a guarrantee, that the honor of my Country, and the interests of her Citizens, are strictly guarded, and preserved, and that I shall endeavour, to merit a continuance of approbation, from the Department. I have the honor, to be, Most Resp[ectfull]y Your Ob[edien]t Servant, Stewart Newell.

ALS (No. 35) in DNA, RG 59 (State Department), Consular Despatches, Texas, vol. 1 (T-153:1), received 1/23.

[Richard K. Crallé, Chief Clerk, State Department, to McClintock Young, Chief Clerk, Treasury Department], 1/10. Crallé informs Young that Ashbel Smith, Texan Minister to France, has shipped his personal effects through the port of New York City. "He does not wished [*sic*] them opened. Cannot instructions be given to the Custom House to allow them to pass unexamined? This, I beleive, is done in all cases where Foreign Ministers are concerned— as an act of National Courtesy." ALU in DNA, RG 56 (Secretary of the Treasury), Letters Received from Executive Officers, Series AB, 1845, No. 12.

From Geo[rge] M. Bibb, Secretary of the Treasury, 1/10. Bibb informs Calhoun that instructions have been given to the Collector of Customs at New York City to allow the trunks and boxes containing the clothing and books of Ashbel Smith, Texan Minister to France, "to pass the Custom house unexamined & free of duty or other Custom house charges, in conformity with the usual courtesy extended in such cases." LS in DNA, RG 59 (State Department), Miscellaneous Letters (M-179:107, frame 41); FC in DNA, RG 56 (Secretary of the Treasury), Letters to Cabinet and Bureau Officers, Series B, 5:4.

From FRANKLIN CHASE

Consulate of the United States of
America, Tampico, January 11th 1845
Sir, I have the honor to acknowledge the receipt of your communication of the 12nd July last, and also a copy of the "acts & resolutions passed at the first session of the twenty-eighth Congress of the United States.["]

Before this reaches you, news of the radical change in political affairs of this country, will no doubt have been communicated to you. The result however is still rather doubtful. The mail which should have arrived here this day from the City of Mexico, has been detained beyond "Huajutla," and fears are entertained that it has been intercepted by Santa Anna.

The Garrison of this place declared in favor of the Congress, about the 18th Ult[im]o but as the principal Military Officers are in favor of Santa Anna but little reliance can be placed in their stability.

I enclose to you under separate cover, a file of papers containing the latest news received here from the City of Mexico, which I trust will be acceptable.

Herewith I have the honor to hand you the Gross Return of American and Foreign Trade, at this Port during the year 1844. I have the honor to be, with great respect, Sir, Your very Obedient Servant, Franklin Chase.

ALS (No. 59) with En in DNA, RG 59 (State Department), Consular Despatches, Tampico, vol. 3 (M-304:2, frames 95–97), received 1/29.

From John Fairfield, [Senator from Maine], 1/11. Fairfield reminds Calhoun of an earlier letter [of 5/2/1844] requesting that the claims of S[amuel] S. Thomas and J[oseph] R. Curtis, "Master & Mate of the Brig Zebra," be given attention by the Department of State. Their claims are for "unlawful detention & imprisonment at Gonaives [Haiti in] 1843." Fairfield requests information on the progress of the claims and encloses a letter of 1/4 from Hill and Thomas, agents of the claimants, to himself. ALS with En in DNA, RG 59 (State Department), Miscellaneous Letters (M-179:107, frames 42–44).

From JAMES H. FORSYTH, "Private"

Columbus O[hio,] Jan[uar]y 11, 1845
Sir, I arrived in this city a few days since and have not been an inattentive observer of the exertions that has been and is continued to be made to manufacture public opinion in favor of Gen[era]l [Lewis] Cass.

The efforts now making in this State to commit our party to the Support of Gen[era]l Cass in 1848 proceeds upon the supposition that Mr. [James K.] Polk[']s Administration will be greatly under his influence & that he will control Executive appointments in Ohio.

This assumption may or it may not be true[;] it is however a fact that a large majority of the Democracy of the State have not entire confidence in Gen[era]l Cass and unless this new movement effects his popularity favorably he will find us where we always have been[,] against him.

The efforts however is very ungracious and ought in some way to be rebuked first because the object is to commit men in advance to a course which upon reflection ["that"(?) *altered to* "they"] might not approve and second because the favors of Mr. Polk[']s administration are to be sold or offered in exchange for political services to be rendered Gen[era]l Cass and finally the efforts is made to a great extent in secret conventions. Now conventions at ["best" *interlined*] are bad enough but from secret political conventions the Lord deliver us.

I expect in a short time to be in Washington City where I shall be glad to confer personally with you upon the details of this new system of dictation.

I have heard of political Anti-masonry but this is the first political masonry with which I have ever come in contact.

I corresponded with you in 1840, and wrote you a letter in 1843 at a time when I was making efforts for you in the District where I reside which is Maumee City[,] Lucas Co.[,] Ohio.

I am this particular lest you may have forgotten my name.

I know that your time must necessarily be occupied therefore I do not wish to intrude upon it, and if it is your desire to see me while ["I am" *interlined*] in Washington upon your receipt of this you will please drop a note to that effect in the P.O. and I will avail myself of the priviledge [*sic*]. I have the honor of subscribing myself Truly Your Friend, James H. Forsyth.

ALS in ScCleA. NOTE: An AEU by Calhoun reads "Mr. Forsyth[,] relates to the effort making in reference to the next Presidency."

To J[abez] W. Huntington, Chairman of the Committee on Commerce of the Senate, 1/11. "I have the honor herewith to enclose certain papers relative to the qualifications of Joseph Graham, whose nomination is before the Senate to the office of Consul of the U.S. at Buenos Ayres. Should other evidence in his case be desirable, it is understood that reference may be made to Judge McClean [*sic*; John McLean], of the Supreme Court, and Messrs. [John J.] Crittenden, [James T.] Morehead, [William C.] Rives & [James] Semple of the Senate." FC in DNA, RG 59 (State Department), Reports of the Secretary of State to the President and Congress, 6:123.

To [CHARLES J. INGERSOLL and JAMES I. McKAY]

Department of State
Washington, January 11th 1845

Sir, I have the honor to transmit herewith a copy of a note addressed to me by [Angel Calderon de la Barca] the Spanish Minister in relation to the indemnity claimed by his Government in the case of the Schooner Armistead [*sic*; Amistad]; the facts and circumstances of which are fully set forth in a Report of the Committee on Foreign Relations of the House of Representatives (28th Congress, 1st Session, R. 426) to which I respectfully refer you.

The case is regarded by the Executive as one which strongly addresses itself to the honor, faith, and justice of the Country; and I consider it my duty to bring the subject to the notice of Congress, with a view to its prompt and final adjustment. I have the honor to be with high respect Sir, Your Obedient Servant, J.C. Calhoun.

FC in DNA, RG 59 (State Department), Reports of the Secretary of State to the President and Congress, 6:124. NOTE: Ingersoll was Chairman of the House Foreign Relations Committee and McKay of the House Ways and Means Committee.

To J[OHN] Y. MASON, Secretary of the Navy

Department of State
Washington, 11th January, 1845

Sir: The Secretary of State [Gerrit P. Judd] of the government of the Sandwich Islands has said in a recent note to Mr. [George] Brown, the United States Commissioner there, that the late Mr. [Abel P.] Upshur, had acknowledged that this government could not claim for our citizens in those Islands the privilege of being tried by a Jury of foreigners. No such acknowledgement is contained nor is the subject in any way alluded to in any letter or record in this Department whilst Mr. Upshur was Secretary of State. I will consequently thank you to inform me if it is mentioned in any order or other communication from your Department whilst he was Secretary of the Navy, and, if so, to send me a copy of or extract from the letter relating to it. I have the honor to be, Sir, Your obedient servant, J.C. Calhoun.

LS in DNA, RG 45 (Naval Records), Letters from Federal Executive Agents, 8:22–23 (M-517:3, frames 40–41); FC in DNA, RG 59 (State Department), Domestic Letters, 35:70–71 (M-40:33); PC in Jameson, ed., *Correspondence*, pp. 638–639. NOTE: An AEI by Mason on the LS reads "Examine carefully & give the information."

Ashbel Smith, [former Texan Minister to France and Great Britain], Washington, to Miss —— Hudson, 1/12. Smith informs his correspondent that he has obtained Calhoun's signature for her autograph collection, the signature being Calhoun's frank for mailing the letter. He describes his visits with Calhoun and President John Tyler. "Mr. Calhoun is no great favorite of the politicians of [my native] New England I believe; I have been personally acquainted with him from my boyhood, slightly of course for the first few years. I regard him as incapable of a mean, narrow or sordid thought—all is lofty and generous. He is in this respect as I believe his great competitor Mr. [Henry] Clay to be. I have had during my present stay in Washington two very long full talks with Mr. Calhoun; they were on business chiefly, about matters of great moment. Each of us had a great deal to say; it is a pleasure to talk with one so copious and rapid. Previously to entering on business last evening, we had a discursive[?] conversation on soils and agriculture, a favorite subject of his, I believe." ALS (retained copy) in TxU, Ashbel Smith Papers, Letterpress Book, pp. 282–285.

From HENRY A. WISE

Legation of the U. States
Rio de Janeiro, January 12th 1845

Sir, Since my last Mr. [Hamilton] Hamilton, the English Minister, has replied to the letter addressed to him by me on the subject of the

African slave-trade, and the part taken in it by English merchants & brokers in Brazil. Inclosed is a copy, marked No. 1, of his reply. My object in opening this correspondence with him was to show that England cannot, in the first place, pretend to assume the morale on this subject over the U. States; and to test, in the second place, the sincerity of English professions, and to demonstrate their real designs, if their professions be insincere. There is no question but that both the Minister & Consul of Great Britain at Rio de Janeiro, now know of the participation of English subjects in the slave-trade, and that they are fully informed of the direct and indirect mode & means of carrying it on by British Capital, goods & credit, from both English & foreign ports. And we will see what steps will be taken to punish their own subjects, whilst they are assuming the right of visit & search over the vessels and citizens of other countries. Our merchants here hesitate not to say, and to adduce many proofs, that the whole struggle on the part of England has been & is to monopolize the trade of Africa. Certainly many manifestations wear that appearance. But Mr. Hamilton seemed gratified at the tone of my letter to him, & is evidently himself sincere in earnest efforts to strike at the slave trade though it be at the risk of English Commerce. The prisoners arrested for aiding & abetting this traffic in the charter, fitting out & sale of the Brig Montevideo, will be sent home in the Frigate Congress. I regret to be compelled in duty to say to the Department, that there should be an immediate & prompt inquiry of the District Attorney of the U. States for New York [Ogden Hoffman] as to the manner of obtaining bail by Capt[ai]n [Cornelius F.] Driscoll, indicted for piracy, in a case where the evidence of guilt on the commitment was too strong, I suppose, to admit of bail in a capital case. In the midst of the examination of Capt[ai]n [Jason L.] Pendleton & his crew in this harbor, Capt[ai]n Driscoll arrived with a Commission to take depositions, on bail which he boasts, as I am informed by Mr. Jno. S. Wright of the firm of Maxwell, Wright & Co. was *"bought bail."* The appearance of that man here whilst his trial is pending for the capital crime of directly aiding & abetting the slave-trade, on evidence hardly doubtful, with such a boast in his mouth, & evidently with no intention of ever returning to the U. States, to stand his trial, had a very bad effect, you may be sure, upon the proceedings of U. States' officers who were in the act of endeavoring to do their duty in the suppression of the Slave trade by our citizens & vessels, & for the protection of the honor of our flag. The moment he came, the slave-traders exulted openly in a triumph over the U. States' laws & those who were trying to execute them faithfully; & not the least provoking feature of this triumph is that the Commission is directed to "*Geo. W. Slacum*, or whoever may be Consul" &c., and to a young Mr. Warner, a clerk in the House of Maxwell, Wright & Co., and to Mr. James Birckhead; and ["to" *canceled*] the firm of Maxwell, Wright & Co. or of Mr. James Birckhead is in almost every case, & the former was in Driscoll's very case, the *Consignees* who, through English brokers generally, negotiate these very charters & sales of our vessels to the Brazilian slave-traders!! This is exceedingly offensive to my views of administering the laws & especially of administering justice. I venture to go no further than to describe to you the facts of this—disgrace it must be, if I am rightly informed. I wish not to be understood as casting any reflection on Mr. Hoffman. I have known him too well & too long to suppose for a moment that he has been culpable even, much less criminal, in the discharge of his duty, but I trust that he will be made fully aware of the fact that it is feared there has been, in some way unknown to him, very great neglect, if not something worse, in the procuring of this bail and this Commission for Driscoll. Is the offense bailable in New York, where there is strong probability of guilt? In what way was the bail procured? Was it resisted? Who are the bail? What is the amount of the bond? Is it good, or what the lawyers call "straw-bail"? Did not the Dist. Attorney of the U. States know who was the Consul of the U. States at Rio de Janeiro? Was he or not informed that Mr. Birckhead, named as one of the Commissioners to take depositions, was inculpated in the correspondence of Ex-Consul Slacum with the State Department, and published by Congress as early as in the spring of 1844, on the charge of aiding & abetting the sales of American vessels for the uses and purposes of the slave-trade? Did he know that Mr. Warner, the other Commissioner, was a clerk in the very House to which Driscoll was consigned, or which had negotiated the business of his charter-party & sale deliverable on the coast? This Mr. Warner was absent when the Commission arrived, and Mr. Gordon & Mr. Birckhead only act, but Mr. Slacum, who whilst Consul, had caused Driscoll's arrest, was so disgusted by the bail & the commission & every thing connected with the proceedings & it was so evidently useless for him to trouble himself to see *mock*-justice done to the U. States, that he declined to act in any capacity whatever touching the matter. [*Interpolated*: "Note: Since writing the above Mr. Slacum has furnished me a copy of his letter to Mr. Hoffman, which I inclose."] The slave traders are rich enough to purchase any amount & any kind of evidence, and any sort can be easily got here for money; & if Driscoll gets enough to suit his purpose he may return, if not, he will save himself that trouble &

expense by raising the funds to pay his bail bonds in case they be worth anything at all. I beg that this case may be narrowly & sternly looked into.

In immediate connexion with this subject of the slave-trade is that of interference by Great Britain with the domestic slavery of the U. States. My intimacy with Mr. Slacum enabled me, through him, to procure from Mr. Sams, the English Commissary judge of the mixed commission here, a Document printed by the British Parliament, containing the correspondence of the Earl of Aberdeen with all the Consulates of Gt. Britain in countries not parties to treaties yielding the right of visit & search &c., such as Central America, the Barbary States, the U. States &c. &c. Lest the Department of State might not be in possession of this correspondence, and you might never have seen it, I caused my little son to copy so much of it as relates to the U. States, and it is inclosed, marked No. 2. Whatever doubt may have existed in the minds of many respecting the improper interference of Gt. Britain with our most delicate of domestic institutions, the most sensitive to foreign intrusion, there can be no doubt of it hereafter with this proof of the fact in hand. You will observe by the letter of "Aberdeen" No. 1 that the information is sought for "Her *Majesty's Government*"; that it is not only statistical information proper for Consuls to obtain & to transmit from their residence to their Govts.—such as the census of population, statements of trade &c. &c. to be furnished by *"public documents"*; but the inquiries of the British Govt. relate even to matters of *private household economy*, and to answers to be drawn *from "private information."* They not only inquire about population, about the importation of slaves against our own laws in our own jurisdiction, about the laws for the protection of slaves, about the civil capacities & disabilities of slaves by law, about their relative increase or decrease, about the melioration of laws in respect to them, about their general relative condition; but they pry into *the treatment of the slaves by their private owners, into their food and raiment, into the disposition of masters to manumit them, and into the existence, extent & influence of private societies or parties favorable to the abolition of slavery among us.* Now what can this mean? I beg to call your attention particularly to the Consular letter from Mobile which answers in relation to the abolition party, that there is no *"known party"*—these words *"known party"* printed in Italics—in the State of Alabama. I repeat, what does this mean? What use for, what title to, this kind of information has the British Govt. in respect to our private conduct & private property in the U. States? Is this a permissible function of a British Consul in the U. States? Ought it to be suffered at a time when insurrection & massacre are set on foot in the neighboring island of Cuba by [David Turnbull] a British Consul? If it were known at Norfolk, at Charleston, at Savannah, or Mobile, or New Orleans, that British Consuls there were spies upon the very privacy of our families & reporting the condition of our domestic & private relations daily to the British Govt., would it not bring down the just indignation of our best citizens upon these British authorities & expel them by force from among us, & endanger at once our peace with Gt. Britain? Ought not our Govt. to protest solemnly against such impudent & dangerous intrusion, & to notify the Earl of Aberdeen that it will not be tolerated? It is true that the answers generally are very fair & ["very" *interlined*] favorable to the nature & condition of our institution of slavery; but that does neither justify nor palliate the unauthorized assumption to take official cognizance & make official report of our domestic concerns. As a citizen of Virginia I certainly would not consent that our national Govt. should permit so gross a foreign invasion of the very sanctity of our private lives & of our private rights as well as of our public jurisdiction; & I am clear in the opinion that not only the President & Congress ought to be informed of this, but official notice of it ought to be sent to the Governors & Legislatures of the States, & to the Mayors & Magistrates of every City, in order that they may take decisive measures of preventing future interference of the kind, & the fatal consequences which may ensue when it becomes known to our Southern & Slave-holding people. They would not, I fear, wait long in such a case for protection by the Federal Govt., for it is of that class of imminent cases which belongs to the law of self-preservation. But you can fully appreciate & best judge of the action to be taken on such a subject.

In contrast with this painful subject of improper interference with our affairs by Gt. Britain, it gives me much pleasure to inform you of an instance of another kind of interference by her naval authorities on this station, very much to their credit & to the benefit of our Commerce. The accompanying copies marked No. 3, will exhibit a correspondence which Mr. Hamilton had the goodness to send to me, for my information; respecting the generous interposition of Commodore [John B.] Purvis, of H.B.M. frigate "Alfred," for the protection of the American Brig Columbus at Mangaratiba; and acknowledging the kind assistance furnished him by our ships of war in saving the "Gorgon" Steam frigate, grounded in the River Platte. I append to it my letter in reply to Mr. Hamilton, and I beg that the President will cause some proper acknowledgment to be made by our Govt. to Commodore Purvis.

In relation to the prospect & progress of the English negotiations for a new treaty with Brazil, I am confirmed in the impressions which I communicated in my last despatch—that there will be no treaty, unless England yields the most important objects she aims at. Brazil will not trammel her powers of revenue by any treaty regulations of a tariff again; she will leave herself free to meet British measures hostile to "slave sugar"; and she will not yield a jot or tittle of her sovereignty touching the slave-trade. On these points I feel authoritatively assured, & on these points I am convinced England will be obstinately exacting. Indeed it is no secret that the English Minister is already disgusted ad nauseam: he can get them to do nothing—has had an open rupture with Mr. [Ernesto F.] França, the Secretary for Foreign Affairs, and threatens to make, or has made, a demand for an audience of the Emperor himself. But though nothing is done with England, & nothing is likely to be done, yet the attempt at negotiation with her keeps all other business with the Foreign Department of Brazil in suspense. For my own part, I think that our policy is to stand aloof and remain watchful only for a while, until the teasing for treaties by other Powers has wearied Brazil a little more, & then she will listen more favorably to overtures from the only nation which has not obtruded its propositions both hastily & harshly upon her consideration. Indeed England seems to act as if she had a right to demand a treaty on her own terms & on her own time from this country, & the contempt with which this Govt. & its people are viewed by almost every European power, except Spain, is so illy concealed that the prejudice on the part of Brazilians against England & France, particularly, is becoming more & more inveterate. You may judge of the antipathy on the part of some against any treaty whatever with England, by the inclosed pamphlet published at Bahia. I have endeavored to remain silent but not inactive. I find the Secretary of State too embarrassed by his position to expect his attention to the minor business of our claims, though I continue gently to press them forward; & he assures me so directly & unambiguously that I need be under no apprehension in respect to our general relations with Brazil, come what may of the English negotiation, that I am content to "bide our time." Brazil, too, is embarrassed in her fisc very much, & could not immediately pay much money if she would. And, perhaps, too, we may better provide for our claims in gross by a general treaty stipulation for a convention or commission than in any other way. In this posture of waiting & watching, I have endeavored to extend my acquaintance with Brazilian persons & influences, & have made some progress in the acquisition of a knowledge of men & things. You can effect nothing, in public or private affairs, by direct approaches. Every thing must be done by the intervention of what here is called a "Compadre-ship." No man's father, but every man's god-father can influence him; & without knowing who stood sponsor at the baptismal font, you never know your man. The Emperor [Pedro II] is himself too young to control state-affairs, & the problem is who can influence those who influence him. His present Cabinet is decidedly liberal, not to say constitutional, or republican, or democratic, in its sentiment & feeling, and well disposed towards us; but the Emperor is suspicious of the jealousy of those who are of the old regime, and the Cabinet has to be cautious not to alarm ancient prejudices too much by manifesting any extraordinary zeal to favor the U. States. An *American* policy is a favorite topic with those whom I meet. That means with them what I would have it mean. The U. States & Brazil are the two elder states of North & South America, and are in a moral sense responsible for the whole family of States in the New World. They urge upon me the interposition of the U. States in the affairs of Monte Video & Buenos Ayres—my invariable reply is, that Brazil has precedence of friendly offices or of interposition in South America; the U. States has enough to do to protect American policy in the North American continent. Then, the understanding the U. States should have with Brazil is, that each will preserve its complete independence of Europe; neither should yield any thing unequal in commerce or navigation, or in taxation for revenue, and both should firmly defend their institutions from foreign interference. They seem to comprehend this, & especially that it is in all respects to their interest, if not to favor, not to impair the good understanding with us. The present ministry seems to be very unpopular with the whole diplomatic corps; and various complaints of Mr. França, & various rumors of his retirement, are heard from day to day; but the elections went in their favor, and, I think, they are likely to remain in some time—a liberal party in the Brazilian sense, or, in other words, strongly anti-European, & freely inclined to American policy & to American constitutional forms. I attended the opening of the Legislature Chambers on the first of the month, and inclose a printed copy of the Emperor's speech. It is of no importance, nor is the response of the Senate.

Two serious questions have arisen lately between the Brazilian authorities & some of the powers whose treaties have expired, which may arise also with the U. States. A citizen of Denmark died in Rio de Janeiro, & the Brazilian authorities immediately denied the right of the Danish Consul to administer upon his personal assets. The Danish Consul, however, did administer, and the Authorities are now demanding the delivery of the assets or the proceeds of their sale. The delivery was refused with due notice that its demand would be resisted, if necessary, by force. The Corps diplomatic seemed much disturbed, & our own citizens were somewhat alarmed on the subject. When referred to, I gave the opinion decidedly that no such question could arise between Brazil & the U. States, in as much as the parts of our treaty in relation to peace & amity were expressly perpetual, & such a question would come under the perpetual clauses. But, even if our treaty had expired in that respect, still the law of nations is clear on the point of consular administration on a decedent's personal effects. But this & some questions respecting taxation of our citizens, & especially one of our Consuls, leads me to request of the State Department to examine our treaty with Brazil, critically, with the view to instruct me as to which of its clauses, specifically, I must insist upon as still continuing in force. It is difficult to distinguish in some of the parts of that treaty, the subjects of commerce & navigation from those of peace and amity.

The other question is one of still more importance. The Spanish Minister informed me that several Spanish subjects had just been impressed for the naval Service of Brazil. To his surprize, when he called upon the Minister of Marine, Mr. [Antonio Francisco] Cavalcanti, to prevail on him as a friend to release them, the Minister informed him that, as his personal friend, he would cause them to be released, but that he must distinctly understand *that the right to impress foreign seamen* within the limits was claimed, & was not waived by the release in that case. When remonstrated with & warned that the exercise of such a pretension would at this day be resisted & resented by every power in Christendom, he replied that Brazil would exercise it, that he should submit that as a part of their plan for the increase of their navy to the Legislative Assembly in session, & if they sustained his recommendation, he would attempt to maintain the principle & practice against the world. In case such a pretension be set up in respect to our seamen or other citizens of the U. States, I shall not wait for instructions from home. Singular enough, however, just as this question arose here, the Brazilian Chargé at Monte Video demanded his passports for reason of the impressment of a Brazilian citizen there, whose release was not granted as promptly as his demand for it was made. We will see how they will get along with the exercise of the very pretension at home, for the exercise of which abroad their diplomatic functionaries are demanding their passports.

The affairs of Monte Video and Buenos Ayres remain in statu quo—not ante bellum, but in the same state they have been in ever since the war began. I trust that our Govt. will attach no blame whatever to Captain [Philip F.] Voorhees for his conduct in the La Platte; & that the reply to [Juan M.] Rosas will be that Com[mo]d[o]re [Daniel] Turner has, by restoring every thing to B. Ayres with proper explanations, made ample atonement. It is absurd to talk to those near the scene of that war, of further reparation to belligerents who deserve the name rather of buccaneers banded for murder & piracy under civilized forms. I repeat, that war ought to be arrested. Our Consul [at Montevideo], Mr. [Robert M.] Hamilton, has justified Capt[ai]n Voorhees. The action of Com[mo]d[o]re Turner was taken under my advice. My view was that *Capt[ai]n Voorhees* had treated Capt[ai]n [Juan] *Fitton* & *Gen[era]l* [Manuel] *Oribe* as they deserved, but *Com[mo]d[o]re Turner* had to deal amicably with *B. Ayres.* This he has done, & they should be satisfied.

To illustrate the true state of things at this Court, I deem it of sufficient importance to relate that, on the 28th of Dec[embe]r last, a circular was issued from the palace informing the members of the Corps diplomatic that the Emperor would receive them on the 1st of January, at the palace in the city, on the occasion of the anniversary festivities of the New Year, & on the 9th of the same month *"the day on which O[ur] Sen[ho]r Dom Pedro 1st, of illustrious memory, declared to remain in Brazil"*—(Declarou ficar no Brazil.) The decision of Dom Pedro I, then Prince Regent, to remain in Brazil, notwithstanding he was ordered home by his father [John VI], the King of Portugal, is regarded as in fact the declaration of Brazilian Independence; and the day of that declaration is kept as a national fête-day. On the 8th I received a note from [Johann Bernard,] Count Rechberg, the Minister of Austria, who has precedence by seniority immediately before me, saying that *"for grave reasons"* he could not attend Court on the occasion of the 9th, & notified me, if it was my intention to attend, to prepare myself to address the Emperor in behalf of the Corps Diplomatic. In fact, it seems that [Gregory XVI] the Pope's Nuncio, the English Minister, the Russian, the Monte Videan, the Buenos Ayrean, the Austrian, all having precedence, declined. Count [Eugene] Ney of France, was absent—& when I arrived in the saloon of the palace, I found Monsieur [José] Delavat, of Spain, alone, and he & I, with a suite of our Com[mo]d[o]re & navy officers & my secretary, honored the ceremonies by our presence. I was thrown into a difficulty by having to congratulate the Emperor, in the name of the Diplomatic corps, on an occasion which none of them, except the Minister of Spain & of the U. States, approved. A copy of my address I inclose. The next evening, Friday the 10th, the Pope's Nuncio waited on me, and said that one of the objects of his visit was to make me understand that the Corps Diplomatic did not approve of so many fête-days, & they wished to make the Court feel it— he pleaded the thermometer at 90° & the trouble & heat of preparation so often in such a climate. I simply bowed, & abstained from replying that I was not consulted about any such understanding, & that notwithstanding the heat & frequency of *Saints' Days,* or days of *Imperialism* &c. &c. all the members of the Corps are on those days in attendance upon Court. Our flag is up, & the guns of our men of war salute on all the properly *national days,* but the flag is down & the guns are mute on the days of *Legitimacy* or *Mummery.* I shall especially avoid uniting in any such *understandings* of the Corps Diplomatic as those intended to "*make the Court feel*" their joint displeasure on any occasion, except such as may really affect the *esprit de corps.* As the Nuncio was retiring, I received the visit of the Minister of Marine, Mr. Cavalcanti, who remained conversing for hours upon our institutions & those of Brazil; and he took occasion to thank me for my attendance & address on the "Fico" day. He seems to be "intus et cute" an American, and gave me many valuable hints. He is the most energetic man of the Cabinet, and is very actively promoting every kind of improvement in his Department, & in the Naval Marine. He will send to the U. States, in the frigate Congress, some officers of the Brazilian Navy to inspect & become thoroughly acquainted with our naval establishment. I beg that every facility may be tendered and afforded to them by our Govt. He inquired whether he could be allowed to place his own son at the Military Academy at West Point. I told him that I presumed the Govt. would cheerfully accept a compliment of the kind to its institution, but as a special law would probably be necessary, I recommended him to place his son either at the Virginia Military institute, or at that of Capt[ai]n [Alden] Partridge [at Norwich, Vt.]. They need & desire very much American mechanics for their Navy Yards, arsenals & all their public works; and I should be glad to be enabled to answer their inquiries whether a number of various kinds of workmen, such as ship-carpenters, sail makers, blacksmiths and steam-engineers, can be procured to come out here with the assurance of at least $1.50 c[en]ts p[e]r day, and wages higher in proportion to the grade of skill &c. &c.

Through this Minister of Marine, I hope to effect some useful end for the U. States. He fully concurred with me in the sentiment that as Brazil & the U. States strengthened themselves, they strengthened each other, ipso facto, without any alliance.

Inclosed also is a mercantile circular containing a more full view of the manner in which our trade is affected by the late Brazilian tariff. You will see that it is not injurious to our flour-trade, and none of our articles are seriously affected. I continue to urge upon them the differential clause of which I spoke in a former despatch; to tax the products of other countries in proportion as their own products are relatively taxed abroad. This would at once give us the advantage over every nation in this market, inasmuch as we tax the products of Brazil less than any other. This, I am confident, they will accede to, as it would necessarily compel England & France to reduce their duties on the products of Brazil, or drive many of their manufactures entirely out of the Brazilian market. With the highest regard and esteem, I have the honor to remain, Your ob[edien]t Servant, Henry A. Wise.

ALS (No. 10) with Ens in DNA, RG 59 (State Department), Diplomatic Despatches, Brazil, vol. 13 (M-121:15), received 3/14; FC with En in DNA, RG 84 (Foreign Posts), Brazil, Despatches, vol. 11; PEx in House Document No. 61, 30th Cong., 2nd Sess., pp. 44–46. NOTE: The above despatch from Wise to Calhoun has been included herein although it was received in the State Department a few days after Calhoun had left office. Two subsequent copious despatches on the same subjects, dated 2/18 and 2/25, were not received in the State Department until April and have been omitted from publication. They may be found in the same file as the ALS cited above.

From W[illia]m M. Blackford

Legation of U.S.
Carthagena, Jan. 13, [18]45

Sir, I have the honor to inform you that I arrived in this city on the 11th Inst.

The Oregon having, for reasons which seemed imperative to her commander, sailed on the 20th Ultimo, I have taken passage in the Brig Chaires, which will sail for New York, on Wednesday next.

It is with much regret that I announce the death of Thomas W. Robeson, Consul of the United States at Santa Martha, on the 4th of last month.

The news was communicated to me by H.B.M. Vice Consul for that port, Edward W. Mark, Esq[ui]r[e] whose kind attentions to Mr. Robeson during his long imprisonment deserve the grateful acknowledgment of his friends.

Mr. Mark informs me that he had put his seal on the effects of the Consulate as well as on the books & papers of the deceased. The authorities intimated an intention to appoint as administrators two persons of bad character, & who were moreover the largest debtors to the Estate. Mr. Mark protested against their being appointed and notified the Judge that he would not deliver the effects to them, if named, until he heard from me. I have written to thank Mr. Mark for his spirited intervention and to request that he will not deliver the books & papers to the these [*sic*] individuals.

I had procured the release of Mr. Robeson, but the letter, announcing the fact did not arrive until two hours after his death.

Hoping to have the pleasure of seeing you in a short time, I remain, with high respect, your Ob[edien]t S[ervan]t, Wm. M. Blackford.

ALS (No. 30) with En in DNA, RG 59 (State Department), Diplomatic Despatches, Colombia, vol. 10 (T-33:10, frames 308–312), received 2/14. NOTE: Blackford enclosed a protocol of a conference on 12/20/1844 between himself and Joaquin Acosta relating to tariff issues between the U.S. and New Granada.

From W[illia]m P. Buell

Petersburg, Va., Jan. 13th 1845

Sir, I have just returned from the kingdom of Siam, in Asia; and while living there, I became intimately acquainted with His Royal Highness, *Prince T. Momfanoi*, as he is called in this Country and Great Britain. His Highness has an only son, whom he has, of his own accord, named *"George Washington"* in honour of the venerable father of our country. His Highness is extremely anxious to have an accurate and good likeness or engraving of Gen. Washington. I thought that the compliment paid our American people and country, by a heathen prince, was one that should be returned by them, in the presentation of *a handsome* and *accurate Portrait* of *Washington* to the royal father and the General's Siamese name sake.

If your honour and our congress shall deem this subject worthy of your notice, and shall decide in favor of presenting His Royal Highness with [a] portrait, in the name of our American people, I shall feel myself honoured in being instrumental in the gratification of one of the strongest desires of my Royal, Siamese friend and acquaintance.

It is a remarkable circumstance that a heathen and despotic Prince, the heir to a despotic throne, should so much admire the character of our *republican* father and countryman, as to name his only son after him.

The young Siamese Washington is destined, in the hereditary succession to the throne, to sit, one day, at the head of that kingdom, and rule that people.

The character of our great General has been learned from our American Missionaries, and a history of our country published in the Siamese language. If you desire any references to satisfy yourself as to me and the genuineness of the foregoing statement, I would respectfully beg leave to refer you to—

Hon. Wa[l]ter Lowrie, New York [City,] Rev. R[obert] J. Breckenridge [*sic*] D.D. Baltimore, Rev. W[illia]m S. Plumer D.D. Richmond Va. If a Portrait be presented, it may be left with Hon. Walter Lowrie, Presbyterian For[eign] Mission Rooms, Corner of Centre and Reade Streets, New York, and he will forward it with great pleasure.

I will simply suggest that it be handsomely framed.

In replying, please address me at this place. I am a minister of the gospel, and a returned missionary of the Board, of which Mr. Lowrie is Secretary. I have, Sir, the honour to be your most obedient servant, Wm. P. Buell.

ALS in DNA, RG 59 (State Department), Miscellaneous Letters (M-179:107, frames 45–47).

To E[dward] G.W. Butler, Dun boyne Plantation near Bayou Goula P.O., La., 1/13. "Your letter of the 9th of October last, on the subject of the degeneration of our Sugar Canes &c was duly received. With a view to the accomplishment of your desire, and that of other planters, to try the effect of importations, I have addressed a Circular letter [dated 11/14/1844] to the United States Consuls and Commercial Agents in the various Islands and Countries in which the Cane is grown, a copy of which, is enclosed, requesting them to send specimens to you and it is hoped that it may be productive of highly beneficial results." FC in DNA, RG 59 (State Department), Consular Instructions, 12:108–109.

F L O R I D E [C O L H O U N] C A L H O U N to James
Ed[ward] Calhoun, University of Virginia

Washington, January 13th 1845
My Dear Son, Allow me to wish you the compliments of the season,
and may you live to enjoy many years of happiness and prosperity is
the earnest prayer of your ever devoted mother. I hope you will
commence the new year with hard study, you have no time to loose.
Your father and myself, are exce[e]dingly anxious you, should study
a profession, and acquit, yourself with honour, as none of your brothers have done so, which is a little strange. You are endowed with
tallenents, all that is required of you, is to apply yourself with vigour.
Read none but books of information. Trifling reading takes up too
much of your precious time, and unfits you for more sollid reading.
I was delighted with your letter. I think you will surpass all your
brothers in that line.

Your Uncle James [Edward Colhoun] surprised us all very much
a few days since, as we did not know of his coming on. William
Lowndes [Calhoun] wrote me he, and James [H.] Rion, were spending Christmas at Millwood with him, and enjoying themselves, very
much. He came on business.

[Martha] Cornelia [Calhoun] received a letter from Cudy [Mar-
tha Maria Colhoun], mentioning they had been very busy getting
[William] Ransome [Colhoun], ready to go to the Virginia University. I hope he will pass through here, on his way. I should like to
see him in Washington. You must be sure to bring him to the Inogu-
ration. I understand there is to be great parade here on that day.
It will soon be here now. Mr. [James K.] Polk[']s brother [William
H. Polk] was here three weeks. He came to engage rooms at Corl-
rans [*sic*; Cochran's] for the President, and family. We tease Eugenia [Calhoun], about him. He was very attentive to her, while
here, and engaged her to dance the first dance with him, at the Inogu-
ration ball.

I received a letter from John [C. Calhoun, Jr.], by the last mail
he says his cough is better, and he is delighted with Maringo [that is,
Marengo County, Ala.], he says they have the finest society in the
world. They had a number of invitations to spend Christmas. He
did not say one word about Eliza [M.] Green. It would be strange
if he should fall in love with her. She is a very fine Girl. He says
not one word about Margaret [Green Calhoun], or the Children
[Duff Green Calhoun and John Caldwell Calhoun], just says all the

family were well. I was in hopes he would have said something about the Children, whether they were interesting, or not.

I wish Cudy, had come on with your Uncle James. I think she would be delighted with Washington, it has been very gay, Eugenia goes out almost every evening in the week, and is perfectly enchanted with every thing she sees. She is quite a bell[e] here.

The weather has been remarkably fine all winter, but I expect we will pay for it next month. I can scarcely realise we will leave here in 7 weeks, time has passed so rapidly. Cudy says every thing is going on well at home, and that Mrs. [Margaret Hunter] Rion, is a treasure, she feels such an interest in every thing. She is really a very good Woman. I shall take on either a handsome dress for her, or a cap, she deserves it. If you have leisure I wish you would write her, she would be so much pleased at it. Do write your sister Anna [Maria Calhoun Clemson], as soon as possible. She appears hurt that none of you have written her. When you write inclose the letter to your father and he will send it on, with his package. Little [John] Calhoun [Clemson] has been very ill, and I do not now think him out of danger. Anna says he has no appetite, and is nothing but a skeleton. I dread to hear again. Do write some of us often, as we are always uneasy, when we do not hear once a fortnight. Patrick [Calhoun] is enjoying himself very much, he almost lives a[t the?] Wilken's ses, Miss Kate, is as fascinating as ever. All join [me in] much love to you[,] your affectionate mother, Floride Calhoun.

ALS in ScU-SC, John C. Calhoun Papers. Note: This letter was addressed by John C. Calhoun. An endorsement indicates that the letter was received on 1/16. Eugenia Calhoun was the daughter of John C. Calhoun's brother, William Calhoun. "Miss Kate" was Kate Wilkins, daughter of Secretary of War William Wilkins of Pa.

To [Caleb Cushing], 1/13. "Mr. Calhoun's compliments to Mr. Cushing and requests the honor of his company to dinner on Friday next [1/17] at 5 O'Clock. The favor of an answer is requested." LU in ScU-SC, John C. Calhoun Papers.

To John Fairfield, [Senator from Maine], 1/13. "I have the honor to acknowledge the receipt of your letter of 11th inst., accompanied by one addressed to you by Messrs. Hill & Thomas of North Yarmouth relative to the claim against the Government of Haiti in the Case of the Brig Zebra. In reply I have the honor to inform you, that Circumstances have not yet permitted this Department to take any further step towards obtaining for the aggrieved parties the reparation to which they are entitled." FC in DNA, RG 59 (State Department), Domestic Letters, 35:71–72 (M-40:33).

To C[harles] J. Ingersoll, Chairman of the Committee of Foreign Relations, House of Representatives, 1/13. "I had the honor on the 14th June last to transmit to you a communication from the Chev[alier Fidericio] Bourman on the subject of the Duties imposed upon the Wines of the Grand Canary, by the tariff of 1842, and in connection therewith I now enclose a copy of translation of a note, referring to the foregoing, addressed to this Department on the 4th inst. by M. [Angel] Calderon de la Barca, the Spanish Envoy near this Government." FC in DNA, RG 59 (State Department), Reports of the Secretary of State to the President and Congress, 6:124.

To JAMES I. MCKAY, Chairman, [House] Committee [on Ways and Means]

Department of State
Washington, 13th January 1845
Sir, The President, in his Annual Message, communicated to Congress copies of a correspondence between this Department and the Texan Chargé d'Affaires [Isaac Van Zandt], in reference to the disarming a body of Texan troops under the command of Col. [Jacob] Snively, by the order of Capt. [Philip St. George] Cooke of the U.S. Dragoons, and recommended an appropriation to pay the estimated value of the Arms seized, agreeably to an arrangement made with the Texan Minister.

In order that Congress may be informed of the amount required, I transmit herewith a copy of a note received from the Secretary of War [William Wilkins], with the enclosures accompanying it; and respectfully request your early attention to the subject, in order that the appropriation may be made during the present Session of Congress. I have the honor to be, with high respect, Sir, Your obedient Servant, J.C. Calhoun.

FC in DNA, RG 59 (State Department), Reports of the Secretary of State to the President and Congress, 6:125.

To W[illie] P. Mangum, President [Pro Tempore] of the Senate, and J[ohn] W. Jones, Speaker of the House of Representatives, 1/13.

In response to various Acts of Congress concerning Clerks, their compensation, and incidental State Department expenses, Calhoun reports that 15 regular Clerks have been employed at the State Department in 1844 with compensation ranging from $200 to $1709.89. Under the law of May 26, 1824 concerning "the employment of additional Clerks, and certain messengers and assistants, and other persons," a messenger, assistant messenger, and 28 others have been employed for such duties as packing laws and documents, proofreading, indexing, preparing and copying statements for Congressional resolutions, and translating. During 1844 the Patent Office employed 20 regular and eleven temporary Clerks with compensation ranging from $4.98 to $1500. Calhoun concludes that the number of permanent Clerks allowed by law "is insufficient to a prompt discharge of the public business." LS (to Mangum) in DNA, RG 46 (U.S. Senate), 28A-F1; FC in DNA, RG 59 (State Department), Accounting Records: Miscellaneous Letters Sent, vol. for 10/3/1844–5/29/-1845, pp. 162–165; variant PC (to Jones) with En in House Document No. 59, 28th Cong., 2nd Sess., pp. 1–5.

From C H A [R L E] S H. P O N D

Milford (Con[n].), Jan[uar]y 13th 1845
My dear Sir, I hope you will pardon me for withdrawing your attention from your arduous duties—but after consulting a few mutual friends, I take leave to write you respecting the Collector of the port of New Haven. And our long personal & political sympathies lead me to write with that frankness which marks confiding friendship. The matter in hand seems to be taking this shape. Our friend Royal R. Hinman Esq[ui]r[e] has been nominated Collector & is acting as such. But report says that it is doubtful whether he will be confirmed by the Senate. If confirmed he will remain until President [James K.] Polk makes a nomination. And if he is not confirmed it is thought that President [John] Tyler will not name any other person. Probably it will so turn out, for the office has not been worth much since Mr. H[inman] has had it. I would not place any block in his way: but report says that neither great party support him, & of course other candidates will be strongly urged by their friends. I say not these things disparagingly: but state facts.

There will be sundry candidates & among others Norris Wilcox Esq[ui]r[e] who was [U.S.] Marshall during Mr. [Martin] V[an]

Buren's Administration & now County Sheriff. Also Ira Merwin Esq[ui]r[e] both respectable men & will be well recommended. The former by men in office & by others: & the latter by a long list of good names. Other gentlemen are named for the station: so there will be plenty of candidates. I object to none personally, for all are good men.

I also learn that my name will be presented & I add, for various reasons, that any kind word you may speak or any kind act you may render will be duly appreciated by me & my friends. About the 20th of Febr[uar]y a friend expects to bear my testimonials to Washington; they will be headed by our friend the Hon. Ralph I. Ingersoll [former Representative from Conn.] & backed by other good men & true. To your right understanding [of] this case, I say, without meaning to injure any one, you may remember that the Hon. John Stewart & myself were candidates at the Congressional district convention two years ago & from 90 delegates he got 4 votes more than I did. My friends expected my nomination. But I lost it because I was stated to be your warm friend & therefore not as friendly to a high tariff as my competitor. So it worked. Probably Mr. [John M.] Niles [Senator from Conn.] will support Mr. Wilcox; the Senator is a fine man & a good democrat, & a warm friend of Mr. Van Buren. Mr. [Edmund T.] Bridge, a Post Office agent, now in W[ashington] is said to be active for Mr. W[ilcox]. I know little of Mr. B[ridge] but when in this State he affiliates closely with Mr. V[an] B[uren]'s old friends. These gentlemen's right to their political preferences is not questioned: but it is proper to know what their preferences are & how they have operated on their possessors as well as on me & my friends. They all united in placing me on the State ticket for two years past; for it happened that I got as many votes as my associates. But to be frank, *we* think it about time to place me where I can not only be a candidate but one of the *elect*. I have never been a U. States officer; for 12 years I was a Merchant & promptly paid on imports more than $75,000 into the Treasury: but have not traded for 8 years.

President Tyler did right in naming Jon[atha]n Stoddard Esq[ui]r[e] as District Attorney for this State. He was a delegate to our State convention last year when we tried to stop the convention from expressing any preference for any Presidential candidate & also from choosing delegates to the Baltimore convention, but leave their election to the districts.

Both of us know the importance of having friends stationed in such positions as will enable them to see passing events & also the whole field of operations. For signs plainly show that there will be some skirmishing during the next three years. And the past course of men pretty plainly shows their future course, & all should be willing to be judged by their actions.

I know that you are not President *now*; nor yet a member of President Polk's Cabinet; nor are you invested with the appointing power; but I know that splendid talents; great public services; an exemplary life; a kind Providence & friends concur to give your advice much weight. And so it is thought best to write this letter now that you may fully understand the tendencies of men & things & thus be prepared when the subject does come up for consideration & decision. I know that you do not intermeddle with others' business: but I also know that President Polk, nor no other President can be personally acquainted with most candidates & must necessarily depend on others for facts & circumstances to guide to right results.

You may think this a delicate task in me; & so it is; but, My dear Sir, did you know all the circumstances of the last few years you would see my justification; did you know how gratifying to my friends & how important to my interesting family a snug place for me would be; I know the kindness of your heart so well that I am sure you would remember the words of "Joseph to Pharaoh's Butler," & at this *propitious* time give the aid wanted by an old friend. But whether our wishes are gratified or not I shall ever rejoice to hear of your happiness & success in your private & public movements. I remain, dear Sir Very respectfully Your friend, Chas. H. Pond.

ALS in ScCleA. NOTE: Charles Hobby Pond (1781–1861) had perhaps crossed paths with Calhoun at Yale College, from which he graduated in 1802. During 1819–1837 he was either a judge or sheriff of New Haven County and in 1851–1852 he was Governor of Conn.

From ALBERT SMITH

Portland, Maine, Jan[uar]y 13th 1845

Sir, I have this moment rec[eive]d your letter of the 7th Inst. directing me to pay the account of Lt. [William H.] Emory for his transportation &c while in the employ of the [Northeastern] boundary commission—the same having been rejected by the War Department. Lt. Emory's account I suppose, is made out, under the rule of the *War Department*, at a *certain rate per mile*, for travel. The rule established by your Department, by which I was directed to be governed,

& which has prevailed in making out all accounts for transportation, is, to pay the sum *actually* expended by the applicant, & certified upon his honor.

By which of these regulations am I to be governed in settling with Lt. Emory?

My report of the progress of the survey—with my account of disbursements—I will make in a few days. It would have been done before, but that I have a party still in the woods, upon the Line. The account for their compensation, I am desirous to pay & include in my general statement before it is submitted for examination—& the progress of their work I wish to embrace in my report. There will then, I trust be no claims outstanding against the Commission—& the balance of the appropriation ["remaining" *interlined*] very little if any. The survey has been completed to the head of ["Hall's" *canceled*] Arnold's river—& the exploring line *cut out* to the Head of Hall's Stream (Connecticut river). If it be the intention of the Government to Complete the field operations the next season, seventy five thousand dollars will be required. The work would be as well done, if a less sum were appropriated, & a longer period taken to complete it. I have the honor to be Most respectfully Your ob[edien]t & hum[bl]e Serv[an]t, Albert Smith, U.S. Com[missione]r.

ALS in DNA, RG 59 (State Department), Accounting Records: Letters and Accounts from Despatch Agents at New York and Boston, vol. for 8/1840–11/1847.

BENJAMIN W. BARLOW to John Tyler

Washington, Jan[uar]y 14, 1845

Sir, I have in contemplation to take out a Colony of Young Men to the North of the Columbia River, Oregon Territory. I have visited the Seat of Government for the purpose of procuring the aid and encouragement of the administration. But as it is impolitic under the existing treaty with England for the Government to render me Any direct aid I humbly ask of you an appointment as the Corresponding Agent for the Government, to report upon the State of of [*sic*] the Colonies[,] the Resources of that Country And all other matters of interest to the United States.

I am actuated not so much by Any hope of immediate pecuniary advantage as I am by a wish to be honoured with a Confidence of a

Government of which I am proud to be a subject, And by a wish to place myself And those with whom I Am connected in such a position in that Country as will enable us to secure a post of honour after it is brought under the Jurisdiction of the United States.

I have been favoured by an interview with the Hon: Secretary of State and have the hope that he has approved of my plans and will reccommend my appointment.

I take the liberty to enclose to your Excellency a few letters that will doubtless prove to you that I am not wholly unworthy of your Confidence And of the honour I ask. I have the honour to remain Respectfully Your Ob[edien]t Servant, Benjamin W. Barlow.

ALS in DNA, RG 59 (State Department), Miscellaneous Letters (M-179:107, frames 51–53).

From John Macpherson Berrien, Ch[airman, Senate] Jud[iciary] Comm[ittee], 1/14. "I am instructed by the Committee of the Judiciary of the U.S. Senate, to ask for any information which your Department may afford of the qualifications of Andrew S. Pond, who is nominated to the office of Marshal of the Northern District of New York." LS in DNA, RG 59 (State Department), Applications and Recommendations, 1845–1853, Pond (M-873:69, frames 242–243).

From R[ichard] Brodhead, [Representative from Pa.], 1/14. Brodhead encloses a letter to himself [dated 1/7] from one of his constituents [Thomas Clark], seeking the appointment of his son, Dr. [Francis V.] Clark, to be U.S. Consul at San Juan de Nicaragua. ALS with En in DNA, RG 59 (State Department), Applications and Recommendations, 1845–1853, Clark (M-873:16, frames 26–30).

To Richard Brodhead, [Representative from Pa.], 1/14. "In answer to your letter of today, enclosing one from Thomas Clark, asking that his Son [Francis V. Clark] may be appointed Consul of the United States at San Juan de Nicaragua, I have to inform you that the commerce of the United States, with that port, is too limited, to warrant the appointment of a Consul there, and that the President declines making such appointments, unless they are demanded by the public service." FC in DNA, RG 59 (State Department), Consular Instructions, 11:323.

From ROB[ER]T R. HUNTER, "Private"

New York [City,] Jan[uar]y 14th 1845
Dear Sir, It is now openly asserted and generally believed here, that an agreement has been entered into between [Henry] Clay & [Martin] Van Buren to the effect that their friends in Congress shall unite in opposition to the annexation of Texas in order to defeat it, and the late movements of certain individuals in the interest of Van Buren here and in Albany are well calculated to confirm that belief.

It appears that Van Buren was the first mover of this plan, to form a coalition of Whigs, Van Burenites, & abolitionists in order to vanquish you on the Texas question; and I am somewhat apprehensive that Silas Wright will allow himself unwittingly to be used by Van Buren as an instrument for the accomplishment of this base design.

I presume you have seen a very sneering Commentary which appeared a few days ago Editorially in the [New York] "Evening Post" on the late letter of Gen[era]l [Andrew] Jackson to [Francis P.] "Blair." The article is intended and well calculated to ridicule Gen[era]l Jackson and destroy the effect of his letter with the public to the great injury of the cause of Annexation, for who can refute a sneer? or sufficiently oppose the disparaging insinuations which a newspaper writer may crowd into an Article[?]

The information I received from Albany to day leads me to believe that Van Buren procured the introduction of the Resolutions relative to Texas, by Gen[era]l Clarke [*sic*; Orville Clark] in the [New York] Senate last week, for the purpose of *defeating their passage*, and in relation to this subject and the appointment of two United States Senators, Silas Wright is playing a part which has great partiality for Van Buren, which prevents him from discerning the danger into which it will lead him. Respectfully & truly yours, Robt. R. Hunter.

[P.S.] Our mutual friend W[illia]m Lynn Brown Esq[ui]r[e] of Philadelphia is about to proceed to Washington, and will communicate to you some private information from me which may serve your interest as well as mine. R.R.H.

ALS in ScCleA; variant PC in Boucher and Brooks, eds., *Correspondence*, p. 277.

To W[illiam] W. Irwin, [U.S. Minister to Denmark], Copenhagen, 1/14. "I transmit, at the request of Mr. George L. Lowden, of Charleston, South Carolina, who represents the claim of the late Commodore John Paul Jones, upon the Danish Government, certain papers respecting it, which have been sent hither for that purpose.

Your despatch No. 32, has been received." FC (No. 15) in DNA, RG 59 (State Department), Diplomatic Instructions, Denmark, 14: 47 (M-77:50).

From James Larned, "W[ashington] City," 1/14. "I beg leave to submit this communication [to me from F. Banqe, dated 1/11], with the remark, that without any personal acquaintance with Mr. [Davis] Hatch; I have known Mr. Banqe, for many years, as a gentleman of character & good standing, & as one of our most enterprising merchants, being at this time largely engaged in the trade with Matamoros, where he has established a house." (Hatch sought appointment to be U.S. Consul at Ponce, Puerto Rico.) ALS with En in DNA, RG 59 (State Department), Applications and Recommendations, 1845–1853, Hatch (M-873:38, frames 482–484).

From DELAZON SMITH

Norfolk Va., Jan[uar]y 14th, 1845
Sir! On my arrival at this Port, I addressed a note ["to" *interlined*] John B. Montgomery Esq[ui]r[e], Commander of the United States Sloop-of-War "Portsmouth," apprising him of my mission to South America [as Special Agent to Ecuador] and expressing my desire to take passage in the ship under his command.

Commander Montgomery replies that "he is not yet apprised by the Navy Department of the purpose of the Government to send a passenger in the U.S. Ship 'Portsmouth' under his Command, to South America or elsewhere," &c. Will the Secretary of State be pleased to notify the Secretary of the Navy of my appointment and request that officer to send me a permission to sail either in the "Portsmouth" or the U.S. Schooner "Flirt"? This latter vessel is expected to leave this port for South America very soon: possibly before I can receive returns from Washington.

The "Portsmouth" goes round Cape Horn. Should I obtain a passage in her I desire that on my arrival in the Pacific the Commander of Squadron on that coast may be instructed to afford me means of conveyance to the port of my destination.

The Honorable Secretary will readily perceive that prompt action on the part of the Secretary of the Navy is important, otherwise I may be obliged to remain here a month or more. I have the honor to be, very respectfully Your obedient Servant, Delazon Smith.

ALS in DNA, RG 59 (State Department), Diplomatic Despatches, Special Agents, vol. 13 (M-37:13, frames 86–88). NOTE: A Clerk's EU reads "Respectfully referred for perusal to the Hon. Secretary of the Navy." An AEI by John Y. Mason, Secretary of the Navy, reads "Orders have been given conformably to the wishes of Mr. Calhoun."

To the U. S. SENATE

Department of State
Washington, Jan[uar]y 14 1845

The Secretary of State in compliance with the Resolutions of the Senate of the 23d Ult[im]o, directing him "to communicate to the Senate such information as may be in possession of the Department of State as to the practice of foreign Governments in transferring their criminals and paupers into the United States; and that he also communicate copies of such instructions, if any, as may have been given by the Government of the United States to its Consuls and other agents in foreign Governments upon this subject; and copies of such reports, if any, as may have been received from such Consuls and agents in relation thereto." And, also, "that he be instructed to communicate to the Senate, any information in his Department, of arrangements made by any foreign Governments, or Government, for the removal to the United States of foreign paupers or convicts—specifying, if the information in the Department will enable him to do so, the number of persons of the above descriptions, who have, within any given time, to which such information may extend, migrated to the United States—and any information in possession of the Department of the average number of foreigners of every description, annually arriving within the United States"; has the honor to transmit the accompanying documents, which contain all the information on the files of this Department in relation to the Subject except what may be found in the Report of Mr. [John] Forsyth to the [then] President of the United States [Martin Van Buren], dated 10th May 1838, (House doc. No. 370, 25th Congress 2d Session.) to which he respectfully refers.

The table accompanying this, Shewing the average number of persons annually arriving in the United States—is compiled from returns to this Department for the last eight years; and embraces as far as practicable, the information called for by the Resolution in regard to the description of the emmigrants [*sic*]. Respectfully Submitted, J.C. Calhoun.

LS with En in DNA, RG 46 (U.S. Senate), 28A-F1; variant FC (incomplete) in DNA, RG 59 (State Department), Reports of the Secretary of State to the President and Congress, 6:116; PC with Ens in Senate Document No. 42, 28th Cong., 2nd Sess., pp. 1–8. Note: Enclosed with the LS is a list of eight accompanying documents. The resolutions to which this is a reply can be found in DNA, RG 59 (State Department), Miscellaneous Letters (M-179:107, frames 337–338) and in *Senate Journal*, 28th Cong., 2nd Sess., pp. 50 and 54.

From CATHERINE AUBOYNEAU

La Rochelle [France,] Jan[ua]ry 15, 1845
Sir, I should really condemn myself as wanting in gratitude if I did not make an attempt to express to you the very great obligation I am under, for your very ready, and prompt compliance to the petition I had the honour of addressing to the American Government in behalf of my son [Francis M. Auboyneau]. You may be assured Sir, that this special favor was received by us with truly heartfelt satisfaction—and I feel convinced that my son will fulfil this trust reposed in him with all the devotedness of a true born american and as the grand son of one of the most zealous patriots of our Country.

Sir if my recollection does not mislead—I have some reason to believe that I had the pleasure of being acquainted with you at Newport [R.I.] with a widowed lady Mrs. [Floride Bonneau] Calhoon [*sic*] and a Miss Vendross [*sic*; Van der Horst] with whom I was intimate. There is now a long lapse of years—and since that happy period I have undergone many sad changes. My father (Mr. [Francis] Malbone) died very suddenly at Washington at the time he was serving his country as Senator. Some years after this melancholy event, I was obliged to leave my Country with an orphan boy—and now exiled as it were forever from the land of my father, you will easily believe with what delight I see my son invested in the honorable office of Consul of the United States [at La Rochelle]. It will be the means of keeping up an intercourse with my beloved country—for the prosperity and happiness of which I most ardently invoke the blessing and protection of Heaven.

To you Sir in particular I beg to reiterate my heart[']s warmest thanks and be pleased to accept my best wishes for your happiness. Your Ob[edien]t and devoted Servant, Catherine Auboyneau.

ALS in ScCleA. Note: An AEU by Calhoun reads "Mrs. Auboyneau."

From MARK A. COOPER, [former Representative from Ga.], "Confidential"

Mount Hope
Murray Co[unty] Geo[rgia]
15th Jan[uar]y [18]45

Dear Sir, After some weeks absence from home I had the satisfaction on my return to receive your letter [*not found*] in reply to mine dated at Athens. In regard to the vacancy in the marine Corps. Dr. [William C.] Daniel[l] was my informant. He has been misled by supposing that the Lieutenant [Ferdinand Piper, U.S.N.] who died belonged to that Corps.

I am pleased to hear you say Carolina & Georgia are one, expressing a hope also that they may remain one. If your Friends in Georgia can have influence to effect it, it shall be so. And for this purpose they are endeavouring to fortify. They look to you as the only sure reliance, to establish the ascendency of Democratic Faith, by Republican *Acts*. To realize their expectations so far as Georgia is concerned they must strive to strengthen themselves.

You speak as you are wont to speak in regard to the New Cabinet. It is manifest that public opinion clearly indicates, what should be its Complexion. And whilst you are silent as to men, & especially as to yourself, I am happy to feel permitted to anticipate that you may consent to remain. If that be so Georgia asks no more. You will represent her in common with Carolina. This has been our Hope & expectation. I have observed however that indications are given, & from Carolina too, authorizing the the belief that a Friend from South Carolina will go in. From which arises the apprehension that you may not remain. If you go out we shall have only one consideration to console us. It is that you will have done it because, it better serves the Country[']s good.

But, let me speak in all Frankness to one who I know can appreciate Frankness[;] in the event you do not remain, your Friends in Georgia, will think that the wisest arrang[e]ment has not been made, by placing a friend of yours from Carolina in. You & your friends, in Carolina, need no strengthening at home.

The Name of [Franklin H.] Elmore is presented. He is my Favourite Class mate [at South Carolina College], & if the question be what *man* shall be honoured—the man lives not, who I would sooner see honoured & I would say amen. But the Land & the People of his home enter into the question, for the ends to be consummated, so soon as you are out of the question.

We are all looking with great interest to the Action of Congress on the Texas question. We fear the worst. With highest respect I remain sincerely your Friend & obed[ien]t Serv[an]t, Mark A. Cooper.

ALS in ScCleA; PEx in Boucher and Brooks, eds., *Correspondence*, pp. 277–278.

From DAVID HAYDEN

Surveyor[']s Office
New Orleans, Jan[uar]y 15th 1845

Sir, The enclosed Extracts [*not found*] published in the [New Orleans] Jeffersonian Republican which I send you Enclosed, is from a private Correspondent of that Paper and is later news than any received by the ship Herman[?] except this. The information is from a merchant of Vera Cruz and is *reliable*. Although the Ship arrived day before yesterday, this letter did not come into the possession of the Editors of the Jeffersonian until last Evening, hence the delay. The Resolution of our Legislature in favor of the Annexation of Texas passed yesterday by the vote of 38 to 16. Eight of the most devoted friends of *immediate* annexation voting against the Resolutions on a/c of the proviso. The vote under other circumstances would have been 46 to 8—A *strong Expression* amounting almost to *unanimity*.

There is no doubt of the fact, that 9/10ths of the people of Louisiana are in favor of the immediate annexation of Texas, and none are more sensible of this fact than our Senators [Alexander Barrow and Henry Johnson, Whigs]. Will they then disregard the voice of the public will so clearly Expressed?

The conviction with me is abiding that Texas will be annexed this session, and this great National Measure of our honored Chief Magistrate [John Tyler], under your guidance, be finished.

May God grant to this people and nation this result! I am Sir as Ever Devotedly Your friend, David Hayden.

ALS in ScCleA.

From R O B [E R] T R. H U N T E R, "Private"

New York [City,] 15 Jan[uar]y 1845

Dear Sir, I wrote you yesterday in relation to some of the political movements in embryo here, Since which I have received intelligence from Albany that the choice of the U.S. Senators would be made on Saturday next.

A Canvass has been made in Albany on the subject, and it appears that the result, was favorable, for [John A.] Dix & Dickason [*sic*; Daniel S. Dickinson], who would probably be elected. At the Canvass it was found that the "Barn Burners," in the Senate, would have in that body, a majority of One. In that canvass however [George D.] Beers and [John C.] *Wright* of *Schoharie*, tho' declared in favor of that party, are thought to be rather doubtful.

The friends of [Henry A.] Foster it is said would be much exasperated against the choice of Dickason, and might vote against him & in that event, [Michael] Hoffman of Herkimer or [Samuel] Young of Saratoga might be chosen in his stead.

I believe these conflicting movements here, if properly and prudently managed, might be turned greatly to y[ou]r interest. Faithfully yours, Robt. R. Hunter.

ALS in ScCleA. Note: An AEU by Calhoun reads "Mr. Hunter. Relates to the state of the parties in N. York."

To J A M E S I. M c K A Y, Chairman of the Committee of Ways and Means, House of Representatives

Department of State

Washington, 15th Jan[uar]y 1845

Sir, I have the honor to state, for the information of the Committee of Ways and Means, that the balance in the Treasury, of the appropriation for the Relief and protection of American Seamen in foreign countries, will be wholly inadequate to the demands of the residue of the present fiscal year.

This Department, in December 1843, pending the appropriation of $50,000, for the fiscal year ending on the 30th of June 1844, nearly exhausted, was under the necessity of asking for an additional one of $40,500; which was made by the act of the 22nd of Jan[uar]y 1844; and, of estimating for the current fiscal year, at the sum of $75,000.

The appropriation for the latter object, was reduced to $30,000 which, with a balance remaining of the former one, of   7,394 made an amount of $37,394 applicable to the demands of the year. The payments from the 1st of July 1844, to the 9th of January 1845, inclusive, amounted to $32,120; leaving a balance in the Treasury, on the 10th instant, of $5274.

Should the demands of the ensuing six months be in the same ratio, as were those of the preceding, (and they may exceed it,) they will require nearly $30,000. I have the honor therefore to request, that an appropriation of that amount may be made, in order that the Department may be able to save from protest the drafts of the Consuls of the United States, for reimbursement of moneys advanced by them for the Relief of American Seamen.

I have the honor to inform you, that in compliance with its resolution of the 6th instant, a report will, in a few days, be made to the House of Representatives, containing all the information in the possession of this Department, or, attainable by it, on the causes of increased expenditure for the Relief of American Seamen in foreign countries. I have the honor to be, very respectfully, Your Ob[edien]t Servant, J.C. Calhoun.

Letterpress copy in DNA, RG 59 (State Department), Accounting Records: Miscellaneous Letters Sent, vol. for 10/3/1844–5/29/1845, pp. 167–168.

To [WILLIE P. MANGUM], President Pro Tempore of the Senate, and [JOHN W. JONES], Speaker of the House of Representatives

Department of State
Washington, Jan[uar]y 15 1845

Sir, I have the honor to transmit herewith, a Statement Shewing the number of passengers who have arrived in the Port of New Orleans during the 1st Quarter of last year.

This Statement Should have been embraced in the Annual Report of this Department transmitted to Congress on the 9th Ult[im]o; but it was not received until a few days ago. I now transmit it, in order to complete the passenger returns in obedience to the Act of Congress of 2d March 1819. I am respectfully Your ob[edien]t Ser[van]t, J.C. Calhoun.

LS (to Mangum) in DNA, RG 46 (U.S. Senate), 28A-F1; LS (to Jones) in DNA, RG 233 (U.S. House of Representatives), 28A-F1; FC in DNA, RG 59 (State Department), Reports of the Secretary of State to the President and Congress, 6:125; PC (to Jones) with En in House Document No. 60, 28th Cong., 2nd Sess., pp. 1–3.

From J[OHN] Y. MASON

Navy Department, 15 January, 1845

Sir, I have the honor to acknowledge the receipt of your letter of the 11th inst. in relation to a statement of the Secretary of State of the government of the Sandwich Islands that the late Mr. [Abel P.] Upshur had acknowledged that this government could not claim for our citizens in those Islands the privilege of being tried by a Jury of foreigners.

Upon a careful examination of all the instructions given to Commodore [Alexander J.] Dallas, the Officer appointed by Mr. Secretary Upshur to the command of the U.S.' Naval forces in the Pacific, it does not appear therefrom that there is any evidence in this Department in corroboration of the statement. The instructions to that Officer are silent on the point. I have the honor to be, very respectfully, Y[ou]r ob[edien]t ser[van]t, J.Y. Mason.

LS in DNA, RG 59 (State Department), Miscellaneous Letters (M-179:107, frame 60); FC in DNA, RG 45 (Naval Records), Letters Sent by the Secretary of the Navy to the President and Executive Agencies, 5:86–87 (M-472:3, frame 85).

From J[ohn] Y. Mason, Navy Department, 1/15. "I have the honor to acknowledge receipt of Rev. Abel McEwen's letter to you of 8th inst. [*not found*] recommending the Rev. Israel T. Otis for the appointment of Chaplain, and have ordered it to be filed with other testimonials in his favor for consideration when a vacancy shall occur." LS in DNA, RG 59 (State Department), Miscellaneous Letters (M-179:107, frame 59); FC in DNA, RG 45 (Naval Records), Miscellaneous Letters Sent by the Secretary of the Navy, 34:356 (M-209:13).

From A[lphonse] Pageot, [French Minister to the U.S.], Washington, 1/15. Pageot encloses to Calhoun a copy of a claim from F[ranç]ois Durand of Perpignan, for reimbursement of excess duties charged him for a shipment of French wines. According to Durand, the New York customs house has refunded excess duties on Portuguese wine but has refused to do so for Durand's imported Roussillon variety which is similar in character according to the 1842 tariff. LS with En (both in French) in DNA, RG 59 (State Department), Notes from Foreign Legations, France, vol. 12 (M-53:8, frames 732–735); CC with En (State Department translations) in DNA, RG 56 (Secretary of the Treasury), Letters Received from Executive Officers, Series AB, 1845, no. 13; CC with En (State Department translations) in DNA, RG 46 (U.S. Senate), 29A-D5.

From R[ICHARD] PAKENHAM

Washington, 15 January 1845

Sir, I did not fail to communicate to Her Majesty's Government all that had passed between us, with reference to the question of the Oregon Boundary, up to the end of last September, as detailed in the written statements interchanged by us, and in the Protocols of our Conferences.

Those papers remain under the consideration of Her Majesty's Government, and I have reason to believe that, at no distant period, I shall be put in possession of the views of Her Majesty's Government on the several points which became most prominent in the course of the discussion.

But considering on the one hand the impatience which is manifested in the United States for a settlement of this question, and on the other, the length of time which would probably be still required to effect a satisfactory adjustment of it between the two Governments, it has occurred to Her Majesty's Government that under such circumstances no more fair or honorable mode of settling the question could be adopted than that of arbitration.

This proposition I am accordingly authorized to offer for the consideration of the Government of the United States, and under the supposition that it may be found acceptable, further to suggest that the consent of both Parties to such a course of proceeding being recorded by an interchange of notes, the choice of an Arbiter and the mode in which their respective cases shall be laid before Him may hereafter be made the subject of a more formal agreement between the two Governments. I have the honor to be, with high consideration, Sir, Your obedient Servant, R. Pakenham.

LS in DNA, RG 59 (State Department), Notes from Foreign Legations, Great Britain, vol. 22 (M-50:22); PC in *Congressional Globe*, 29th Cong., 1st Sess., Appendix, p. 29; PC in Senate Document No. 1, 29th Cong., 1st Sess., pp. 161–162; PC in House Document No. 2, 29th Cong., 1st Sess., pp. 161–162; PC's in the Washington, D.C., *Daily Union*, vol. I, nos. 189 and 242 (December 9, 1845 and February 10, 1846), pp. [753] and 955; PC in the Washington, D.C., *Daily National Intelligencer*, December 13, 1845, p. 2; PC in the Richmond, Va., *Enquirer*, January 13, 1846, p. 4; PC in *Niles' National Register*, vol. LXIX, no. 17 (December 27, 1845), p. 265; PC in Crallé, ed., *Works*, 5:456–457.

From Z[ADOCK] PRATT, [Representative from N.Y.]

Committee Room of Public Buildings
and Grounds, January 15, 1845

Sir: The [House of Representatives] Committee on Public Buildings and Grounds are desirous to ascertain what new buildings, or what extension of the present buildings, may be necessary for the proper accommodation of the officers of your department, and for the preservation of the valuable archives and property belonging to it. You are, therefore, respectfully requested to direct the heads of the different branches of your department to communicate information in regard to the following points:

1. Whether the number of rooms at present disposable is sufficient for the transaction of business; and for the preservation of, and ready access to, the archives of the department.

2. What additional rooms (if any) would be required for those purposes.

3. Whether the safety of the archives of the department is secured by the present mode of keeping them.

The committee desire to know from you, on a review of the suggestions which may be thus made, what extensions or enlargement of the present building may be required, or what new buildings may be necessary, for the transaction of public business, and the preservation of the public property in the custody of your department.

On behalf of the committee, Z. Pratt, *Chairman.*

PC in House Report No. 185, 28th Cong., 2nd Sess., pp. 7–8; draft in DNA, RG 233 (U.S. House of Representatives), 28A-D23.1.

From GEORGE READ

U.S. Consulate
Malaga, 15 Jan[uar]y 1845
Sir, Enclosed I beg leave to hand Returns from this Consulate of American vessels arrived at and sailed from Malaga during the last six months of 1844; also of the Fees received during same period, and an approximate statement of the Exports of Malaga produce with specifications of the different articles & their total estimated values to the different ports of the United States.

The Commerce of the United States with this port has varied very little from what it was last year as to the Tonnage and number of vessels, but on the whole shewing a small increase of about 500 Tons in 1844. The Value of the Imports including Specie is greater in 1844 by $60,000 principally occasioned by an increased amount of Specie brought from the United States, being double of that received in 1843. No other articles than staves are imported at Malaga from the U.S. Catalonia receives Cotton from New Orleans through Havana; a Cotton Manufactory is to be established at this place also.

The Exports to the United States in regard to Tonnage are nearly equal in the two years; but the estimated Values shew an Excess in 44 of 40 per Cent, which is occasioned by an advance in the price of Raisins here, in Consequence of a more limited Crop than usual.

The Consumption of Malaga Raisins in the United States is nearly equal to that of all other Countries; any occurrence that should prevent this Consumption would cause infinite distress to the Cultivators of the vine in this district. Malaga wines are neglected very much in the United States, compared with former years—during 1844 however that was a Considerably increased Export over 1843. Latterly there has been a great falling off in the demand, and the Stock in the United States remains unsold. A Circumstance very Conclusive on this point is the fact, that all the wines exported hence to the U.S. go for acco[un]ts of the Shipper on this side, and not in consequence of a direct demand from the place of Consumption as was formerly the Case.

At this moment there is a considerable want of American tonnage to carry raisins to the United States and foreign flags are being employed for the purpose: the trade this vintage has been beneficial to those engaged in it, notwithstanding an encrease in price, here: a Corresponding advance has taken place at home probably from a rather more limited supply, or because our merchants at home had before them the high Cash duties in this article.

Spain is at present tranquil, the Government having adopted stronger measures to restrain the popular Commotions, by depriving the people of arms, and by the strict vigilance of a police established on a Military basis. The Cortes assembled in Oct[obe]r have been occupied in remodling the Constitution and as yet have not done any thing towards a Change in the Commercial regulations. There has been no change in the tariff of imports, and the System of Port Charges has not been varied, as was said to have been in Contemplation. The Charge of 7½ cents p[er] Ton is still collected under the head of "Cleaning the Port" though nothing of the kind has been done for more than twelve years. The Charge is therefore very heavy on the Am[erica]n Commerce for which it receives no equivalent, the funds so collected being Centralized with other imposts for general purposes.

The Quarantine regulations also have a very severe influence on the flag of the United States from their anomalous and vexatious inconsistencies. In august last I made a detailed exposition on this subject to [Washington Irving] our Minister at Madrid of many of these inconsistencies. He has written to me to say, that the subject has been laid before the Government of her Catholic Majesty [Isabella II].

Among other quarantine regulations are the following. Vessels from Norfolk or from the Chesapeak[e] north, sailing thence from 1 June to 31 October have eight days with purification and ventilation of the effects on board, clothes of the Crew and Cargo susceptible of Contagion. As the Cargoes are composed always of staves, these to avoid delay are towed in lighters ashore and are thrown overboard by the crew from the vessel at the beach, (the Crew not landing), & are then towed back again to the vessel in the empty lighter to be reloaded. A vessel under similar Circumstances arriving at Cadiz is placed in quarantine for eight days *before* she is *allowed* to *discharge*: If after being admitted she comes round here with the whole or a part of the staves, she is here again placed in quarantine, until they *are* landed in the usual way. At Gibraltar and at Madeira there is no quarantine from the above ports in the United States, but if a vessel come with her staves here, they must be landed before admission to pratique. If from Marseilles she is admitted immediately, because they say, she comes from a port where there is a regular lazaretto, & is presumed to have been admitted there in regular form. But in my humble opinion, it would never answer for Spain to put the ban of incommunication on a french port & in proof of this, Algiers & its dependencies are free from quarantine since France has them in her power, whereas the neighboring coast of Barbary, and the Spanish Military ports along the same, are still subject to four or eight days. Vessels from Trieste have eight days even now in winter, from Sicily four; from Naples none. Such are some of the inconsistencies of the quarantine regulations at this place, differing probably from those of any other port in the peninsula whilst none of them seem founded upon reason or Common sense.

Our countrymen continually were making complaints of the hardships of these sanatory regulations of which I felt aware, and laid the subject before our minister at Madrid as above stated. I sincerely trust he may be successful in obtaining some modification therein and indeed he gives me reason to hope that his intervention will be crowned with success before the next season comes round.

A question has often occurred to me, which the occurrences at Philadelphia between natives and naturalized Citizens has again brought to my attention. It is as to how far a Spanish subject returning from the United States with naturalization rights and residing in Spain, has a claim on the American Government and its agents.

The following case occurred here. A boy from Malaga was sent over to the United States for his education, and returned a naturalized citizen in 1840 as by documents exhibited to me, and as such I acknowledged him. He was included in the Conscription, incorrectly indeed, being beyond the age by Law to be enrolled; but he applied to me at the time to liberate him, as a citizen of the United States. Being unwilling to enter into the affair where his age was legally sufficient for his liberation, I advised him to put in that plea, which proved sufficient for the purpose. I considered it prudent not to raise a question, where not absolutely requisite to test an issue.

Spain does not acknowledge the principle of expatriation and claims power at all times over the born subjects of her soil wherever they may be, and more particularly within her own territories, whatever be their Character. The United States will protect her adopted Citizens in any part of the world. I certainly should be placed in a dilemma and on very weak ground, in a Case like the above, if I should have to contend with the authorities ["which" *altered to* "when"] these two rights come to issue. Which is the stronger *right?* the nation's on her own soil over her native subject, or the foreign shield of naturalization? One thing is certain; my claim would not be acceded to in Malaga, and I do not see that, by me, such a question could be definitively decided. I am therefore undecided in this complicated subject how far the spirit of the Laws of the United

States extend in a case like the above, in regard to her naturalized Citizens. I have the honor to be with Every Respect Sir Your mo[st] ob[edien]t Serv[an]t, George Read.

ALS (No. 50) with Ens in DNA, RG 59 (State Department), Consular Despatches, Malaga, vol. 4 (T-217:4), received 3/1.

From PEDRO DE REGIL Y ESTRADA

Consulate of the United States of America
Merida [Yucatan], 15th Jan[uar]y 1845

Sir, The address of the Department of State dated 25th October last, came to hand on the 2d inst., to which, as ordered, I have the honour to answer by this first opportunity, expressing my most sincere thanks for the confirmation by the United States Senate of my appointment for this consulate, on which occasion, it had been sent to the U.S. legation at Mexico [City], the commission to renew the application for an execuatur in my behalf, which no doubt shall be granted.

Enclosed you will find a copy of the only protest entered in this consulate by Mr. H[enry] A. Holmes Capt[ai]n of the Am[erica]n Brig ["]Henry Leeds"; but as from the disagreeable correspondence between Messr. C[harles] H. Todd & Co. & I the consignee of the cargo, I ["am" *interlined*] induce[d] to believe that this is not the protest to which you refer, I take the liberty to let know to the Department all what has occurred with the Henry Leeds and her cargo, which I hope will rectify any misunderstanding about it.

The Henry Leeds anchored at Sisal on 9th July last.

On the 10th, as soon as I knew what was her cargo, I informed Capt[ai]n H. Holmes that the corn, Corn meal, rice, biscuits, & shoes, he had on board, had always been prohibited by the laws of this country: that if the corn had been previously permitted in some circumstances, was by particular orders, expressing the time of its import and determining that in which it was to cease, but that then the prohibition was in all its force.

I also informed him that it was forbid[d]en by the laws, to any foreign vessels to land a part of her cargo retaining the balance on board, but that he could sail without paying Duties for the vessel or cargo, & if he had choice to discharged some part of her cargo, the vessel would have to pay the tunnage duties, and the admis[s]able goods also the Duties expressed in this Tariff; being in this case confiscated the prohibited goods; but not the vessel.

All was according to the laws to which Capt[ai]n Holmes knew it was necessary to be conformed; notwithstanding, desirous, as I was, to aid him as Consul & as consignee, I applied personally to the Government requesting for a particular permission in behalf of the Henry Leeds which by a mistake & not with the object of conculcating the laws, had fell in an involuntary error.

The Government been satisfied of the case, & wishing to show his good feelings in behalf of the Citizens and interest of the U.S., agreed and in consequence it was asked as p[er] Copy No. 1.

To let the Am[erica]n Brig Henry Leeds retain on board & to export where he thought best, the prohibited goods; to land those that were permit[t]ed, paying duties; and moreover a special grant for the vessel to go to the Coast to load with Logwood.

The Copy N. 2d shows the permission granted by this Government, without any charge or condition whatever which was not legal.

This permit being obtained, the Capt[ai]n did his business freely and spontaneously, exchanging the permitted goods with Logwood on the best terms, according to the circumstances of the market & to the quality of the goods, not suitable in general for the country.

The Government has not, as it is falsely supposed, nor any other influence obliged Capt[ai]n Holmes to make the bargain he did, and if the result was not as Messrs. C.H. Todd & Co. expected, it was on account of the bad judgement they formed from Baltimore and in the situation that Capt[ai]n Holmes placed himself with regard to the Logwood.

Messrs. C.H. Todd & Co. being wrongly informed of the causes which originated the bad results of which they complain, they begged Mr. Eneas McFaul [Jr.], Consul of the U. States for Laguna, to call to this city with the object of inquiring personally of what had occurred, & the copy of his letter to those gentlemen, Document No. 3, it shows to them not only that their complain[t]s are incorrect, but that what was done in those circumstances was the best could be made.

It was my duty, as Am[erica]n Consul and as consignee, to aid Capt[ai]n Holmes, and the postscript which appears in the said letter proves that he was satisfied of my services to him, as Mr. McFaul was.

The Enclosed letter of Capt[ai]n Holmes who arrived here to day, Document No. 4, proves that the only protest he has entered in this Consulate is the one I have already refer[r]ed to. With the highest esteem I am your most ob[edien]t S[ervan]t, Pedro de Regil y Estrada.

129

ALS (No. 7) with Ens in DNA, RG 59 (State Department), Consular Despatches, Merida, vol. 1 (M-287:1, frames 122–130), received 3/6.

[Thomas Scott, Chillicothe, Ohio,] to [James Wishart, St. Clairsville, Ohio, *ca.* 1/15?]. Scott gives his interpretation of the political fortunes of the Democratic party for the last thirty years and Calhoun's relations with that party. Looking forward to the next Presidential election, he asserts: "The integrity of the Union depends on the election of Mr. Calhoun in '48. My reasons for this opinion are drawn from the lights furnished by the history of the human race in every stage of its progress." Although this letter is incomplete, unsigned, and undated, Scott's authorship is established by the handwriting. James Wishart added the dateline "St. Clairsville, Jan[uar]y 15th, 1845," marked the letter "Confidential," and probably forwarded the letter to Calhoun. ALU (incomplete) in ScCleA.

From T[HOMAS] WYNNS

Turks Islands, Jan[uar]y 15, 1845
Sir, The few observations [on St. Andrews Bay, Fla.] contained in the enclosed letter [of 10/1/1844] which I have taken the liberty of of [*sic*] addressing to Your Excellency, were penned just previous to my embarking from New York in Oct[obe]r last, and which I now beg leave Most Respectfully, to submit for your Excellency's consideration.

Should they be deemed worthy of comment, I shall feel honored and obliged by Your Excellency's view of the Subject at your convenience—Via New York [City], to the Care of Messrs. G. & J. Laurie. Very Respectfully, I have the honor to remain, Your Exc[ellenc]y's most ob[edien]t H[um]ble Serv[an]t, T. Wynns.

ALS with En in DNA, RG 59 (State Department), Miscellaneous Letters (M-179:107, frames 266–270). NOTE: An AEI by Calhoun reads "Submitted for the consideration of the Secretary of the Navy." An AEI by John Y. Mason reads "Referred to Lt. [Matthew F.] Maury for opinion."

JANUARY 16–31, 1845

ⅠⅡ

On January 25 the House of Representatives passed a straight-forward resolution for the annexation of Texas, which had been introduced at the beginning of the session early last December. The vote was 120–98. In the minority were 70 of the 78 Whigs in the chamber and 28 Northern Democrats. In the Senate a struggle was ongoing, with Robert J. Walker of Mississippi, the annexation leader and a close associate of President-elect Polk, struggling to overcome the complicating amendments offered by Thomas H. Benton. There the matter stood for the time being.

The Secretary of State labored under the calls of Congress, claimants, and office-seekers, while trying to keep up with the management of the far-flung diplomatic and consular establishments of the Union. Prosecution of African slave traders, settling the accounts of the China mission, the Northeastern boundary survey, the ever-present question of claims against Mexico, were only a few of the matters brought to Calhoun's attention.

Calhoun kept in close touch with the American Minister in Texas, Andrew Jackson Donelson, or as close as was possible. Among numerous matters outstanding between the United States and Texas was the controversy ignited in Galveston by Duff Green's recent visit there. A despatch of January 16 by the American Minister in the City of Mexico reported on upheavals in that republic.

On January 20 Calhoun wrote instructions to the American representative in the Hawaiian Islands on matters that had arisen in regard to the legal rights of U.S. citizens. On the same day, also, he wrote to the representative in Brazil about trade with that country and about the unfortunate unending war between Argentina and Uruguay. The next day he reported to the British Minister that the President had declined to enter into an arbitration of the Oregon issue. There that major question would rest for the remainder of Calhoun's term.

On January 27 Calhoun instructed the new U.S. Chargé in Belgium, who happened to be his son-in-law. The next day he despatched another of his papers to the U.S. Minister in London against

131

the British position on extradition of slave fugitives. On January 29, the American Minister in Paris, William R. King, wrote describing at length the effect Calhoun's campaign against British antislavery was having in Europe.

Probably the toll of labor had something to do with the illness that struck late in the damp and wintry month, characteristically effecting Calhoun's weak spot, the lungs. The Washington Constitution *reported on January 31: "Mr. C[alhoun] has, for some days, been suffering under an attack of pneumonia, but we are happy in being able to state that he is decidedly better, and is rapidly regaining health and strength."*

◊

To Alexander G. Abell, "appointed" U.S. Consul, Hawaii, [Sandwich Islands], 1/16. Calhoun notifies Abell of his appointment and sends him instructions and documents relating to the performance of his duties. FC in DNA, RG 59 (State Department), Consular Instructions, 11:325–326.

To [William S. Archer], 1/16. "The Secretary of State has the honor to transmit to the Chairman of the [Senate] Committee on Foreign Relations, a statement of appropriations for Outfits, made at stated periods." Calhoun appended a list of diplomatic posts for which outfits for Ministers and Chargés d'Affaires were appropriated during the years 1825–1826, 1829–1830, 1833–1834, 1837–1838, and 1841–1842. FC with En in DNA, RG 59 (State Department), Accounting Records: Miscellaneous Letters Sent, vol. for 10/3/1844–5/-29/1845, p. 169.

To Benj[amin] W. Barlow, Washington, 1/16. Calhoun acknowledges receipt of Barlow's letter of 1/14 addressed to the President and in reply to it states that Congress has made no appropriation for the payment of a "corresponding agent of this Government in the Territory of Oregon to report upon the State of the Colony, the resources of the country[,] and all matters of interest to the United States." For that reason Barlow cannot be appointed to such a post. However, Calhoun and the President would be grateful to receive "any information you may obtain, relative to the actual State, or general prospects of that interesting portion of the Continent." FC in DNA, RG 59 (State Department), Domestic Letters, 35:75 (M-40:33).

To Peter A. Brinsmade, former U.S. Consul, Hawaii, [Sandwich Islands], 1/16. President John Tyler having appointed Alexander G. Abell to succeed Brinsmade, he is requested to deliver the archives and records of the post into Abell's hands. FC in DNA, RG 59 (State Department), Consular Instructions, 11:326.

From W[illia]m Crump, "Private"

Kingston Jamaica, Jan[uar]y 16th 1845

You will do[u]btless be somewhat surprised to be informed that Mr. [John A.] Bryan the Chargé d'affair[e]s to Peru and [the Chargé d'Affaires to Chile,] my self, are here at this date. We arrived here on the 19th of Dec[embe]r last, four days after the British Mail packet had left this port for Chagres. There has been no mail from this to Chagres since that date. Owing to some new arrangements entered into at that time by the mail agent here, the Liffey a new vessel will take her departure with the mail this fore noon for Chagres, goin[g] by Carthagena & St. Martha. Mr. B[ryan] and myself have taken passage in her. Two days after our arrival here we received a polite note of invitation from [James Bruce,] Lord Elgin the Gov[erno]r of the Island to spend three days with him at Spanish Town at the Queen[']s House, twelve miles from Kingston. We accepted his invitation and spent our time whilst there most agre[e]ably. His Lordship is a plain and agreeable gentleman, and seams [*sic*] to take great pleasure in conversing on agricultural subjects. He has established several agricultural Soci[e]tys, as he informed me, in the Island since he came out to take charge of the government.

The condition of this once productive Isle, has undergone many sad & disasterous changes, within the last few years. The fine fertile Sugar and Coffee estates that once produced there [*sic*] proprietors Lordly annual incomes, have become unproductive, and in some instances are abandoned to the Wild Bore and the reptiles of the Island. In my excertions into the mountains I have seen large quantitys of cain & extensive coffee fields nearly abandoned and the rich products actually rot[t]ing on the ground for the want of labour to gather them. Thousands of the Negro[e]s can not be prevailed on to labour, but for very short periods, at any price, and then but for a few days at a time. I have seen one of the Duke of Buckingham's estates, that contains twelve Miles Square, that was said to be the most productive estates in this vicinity, the superintendent of which informed me, that it formally [*sic*] produced a net income of forty Thousand dollars a year to its proprietor, that at this time it did not pay expences, and he was making arrangements to convert it into a stock farm.

I have been informed by all of the more intel[l]igent gentlemen here with whom I have conversed on the subject, that the present prostrated condition of this rich & productive Isle, is owing entirely to the emancipation of Slavery. The street[s] and public highways are constantly fil[le]d with fine looking men & women, ragged and half starved with a bit of sugar cain in their hand as food, perhaps the only kind they have eatten for days past. I wish old Mr. [John Quincy] Adams, [Joshua R.] Giddin[g]s & there associates could but see the miserable condition of these once happy, but now miserable people. Be pleased sir to accept assurances of high respect from your Obedient & Humble Servant, Wm. Crump.

P.S. May I trouble Mr. C[alhoun] so far as to ask of him, to give the letters herewith enclosed the proper destination, with his frank, if there is no impropriety in my making the request.

ALS in ScCleA; PC in Boucher and Brooks, eds., *Correspondence*, pp. 278–279.

From Ben E. Green, Washington, 1/16/"1844" [*sic*; 1845]. He asks that Calhoun furnish a certificate attesting to Green's service as Acting Chargé d'Affaires in Mexico from March 9 through September 1, 1844, to support a memorial before the House Committee on Foreign Relations asking compensation for those services. ALS in DNA, RG 59 (State Department), Diplomatic Despatches, Mexico, vol. 12 (M-97:13); draft in NcU, Duff Green Papers (published microfilm, roll 5, frames 883–884).

To [Charles J. Ingersoll], 1/16. "The Secretary of State has the honor to transmit to the Chairman of the [House] Committee of Foreign Affairs, a statement of appropriations for Outfits, made at stated periods." Calhoun appended a list of diplomatic posts for which outfits for Ministers and Chargés d'Affaires were appropriated during the years 1825–1826, 1829–1830, 1833–1834, 1837–1838, and 1841–1842. FC with En in DNA, RG 59 (State Department), Accounting Records: Miscellaneous Letters Sent, vol. for 10/3/1844–5/29/1845, p. 169.

To [James I. McKay], 1/16. "The Secretary of State has the honor to transmit, to the Chairman of the [House] Committee of Ways and Means, a statement of appropriations for Outfits, made at stated periods." Calhoun appended a list of diplomatic posts for which outfits for Ministers and Chargés d'Affaires were appropriated during the years 1825–1826, 1829–1830, 1833–1834, 1837–1838, and 1841–1842. FC with En in DNA, RG 59 (State Department), Accounting Records: Miscellaneous Letters Sent, vol. for 10/3/1844–5/29/1845, p. 169; CC with En in DNA, RG 233 (U.S. House of Representatives), 28A-D30.6.

From Ja[me]s B. Murray, National Hotel, Washington, 1/16. "I have received your letter of this date [*not found*] with the accompanying documents. The matters therein referred to will engage my early attention as I shall return to New York tomorrow, and I will take care to keep you fully advised of my proceedings." ALS in DNA, RG 59 (State Department), Miscellaneous Letters (M-179:107, frame 62).

To [Gustaf] de Nordin, [Swedish Chargé d'Affaires in the U.S., New York City?,] 1/16. "The Undersigned has the honour to inform the Chevalier de Nordin, in answer to his note of the 9th instant, that a nomination to the Senate of Mr. Jorgen Flood, as Consul of the United States, for the port of Porsgrund, has been laid before the President. Should it be confirmed by the Senate, the commission of Mr. Flood will extend his consular jurisdiction to such other ports as shall be nearer to Porsgrund than to any other Consulate of the U.S. within the same allegiance, and thereby include the ports of Skien, Brenig [*sic*; Brevig] and Langesund, within his Consular District." FC in DNA, RG 59 (State Department), Notes to Foreign Legations, Sweden and Norway, 6:11 (M-99:91).

From WILSON SHANNON

Legation of the U.S. of A.
Mexico, January the 16th 1845

Sir, A[t] the date of my communication of the 9th Inst. the result of the attack on the city of Puebla by the forces under the command of Santa Anna, was doubtful. I am now able to inform you that he entirely failed to make himself master of that place, and on the night of

135

the 10th Inst. left under an escort of five hundred cavalry with the view of reaching the coast and embarking for Havannah where he had sent his wife a short time since. His ultimate place of destination is said to be Bogota in Columbia [*sic*] where he intends residing, if he can get out of this country. In his flight to the coast however he has been stopped by the Government troops about fifteen miles this side of Jalapa, where he was at the date of the last advices, surrounded but not taken. He has written to the Government for a passport but I think it doubtful whether his request will be granted. All the troops under his command, except his escort, have sent in their adhesion to the Government. The revolution may therefore be said to be at an end. The loss in the attack on Puebla was not so great as I was led to believe from information received, at the date of my last dispatch. The truth is the loss in killed and wounded on both sides was inconsiderable.

It may now be taken for granted that the party in power will hold possession of the Government for some time to come. The elements, however, are not wanting to bring about a new revolution in due time, but in the nature of things it must be some considerable time before such a result can be brought about. I have purposely refraincd from expressing any opinion as to the disposition of the new administration towards the U.S. until I could form one, that I could advance with some confidence. It is unsafe at this time to express any positive opinion on this subject. For the last two months this Government has paid no attention to foreign relation[s]. The Ministers have been so busily engaged in the revolution that they have not been able to think of any other subject. I am induced however to believe that the new administration will be much better disposed towards the U.S. than the late one. The tone of the Government paper in which nothing is permitted to appear except with the approbation of the ministers, is greatly changed for the better. While under the control of the late ministers every number was filled with the most abusive articles against the U.S.; since the new ministers have come into power I have noticed nothing of an offensive character in their official organ. They have published an article from an American Journal animadverting in spirited terms on Mr. [Manuel C.] Rejon's two offensive notes [of 10/31 and 11/6] without any comments disapproving of the same, from which it may be infer[r]ed, they do not approve of the offensive language used by that minister. There are other reasons however that induce me to believe we may expect a more liberal, just and amicable policy from the new Government. The principal men engaged in the revolution have been compelled to make large advancements in money, to sustain the army and carry out the revolution successfully. They knew if they obtained possession of the Government, and could hold it, they would be able to reimburse themselves. They have succeeded in their views on the Government, beyond their expectations and their first object will be to secure themselves the money they have advanced. In order to do this they will be compelled to reduce the army and adopt a more liberal revenue tariff. The present military establishment, if continued would alone absorbe much more than the present entire revenues of the Government; leaving the civil list and the public creditors unprovided for. The army must be paid—there is no making terms with it. A reduction of the present army, would be received by all as a virtual abandonment of Texas forever; and the ministers on reducing the army, would have nothing to loose [*sic*] by avowing such to be their policy, and taking the ground that it was the best to adjust that question in an amicable way and on the best terms possible for the nation. I am strongly impressed with the belief, this is the ground they will take if a favourable door should be opened. The annexation of Texas to the U.S. would at once furnish the ministers the appology [*sic*] and create the necessity for entering into negociations with our Government in relation to boundary etc. in which they would hope to settle the Texas question on satisfactory terms. So far from annexation at this time being offensive to the present ministers it is more than probable they would look upon it as a fortunate turn whatever might be their outward professions. It would force things to a crisis and compell a speedy settlement of the question which is probably what they desire. Such are the views at least of many intelligent gentlemen with whom I have conversed. Instead of increasing the public contributions and taxes with the view of supplying the national treasury the Government will be compelled to reduce them or submit to a new revolution. The people are already borne down with taxes and cannot sustain their present burdens. It is therefore the political as well as the pecuniary interest of those now in power to cultivate amicable relations with all nations and especially with the U.S. and to adjust the Texas question in some peaceable mode and in such a way, as to relieve them from pecuniary difficulties. Should annexation therefore be consum[m]ated at the present session of congress I think there is good reason to believe that all questions growing out of that measure can be amicably adjusted with the present administration on terms satisfactory to both Governments, and with the final adjustment of the difficulties growing out of the Texas question, it is easy to see that almost every other matter of irritation between the two governments could be favourably disposed of without much difficulty. But so long as the Texas question remains open and unsettled there will be insuperable difficulties in the road of accomplishing any thing by negociation with this government, in relation to other matters.

While I am writing news is received that Santa Anna has made his escape and has most probably before this time embarked for Havannah. Yours with great respect, Wilson Shannon.

LS (No. 8) in DNA, RG 59 (State Department), Diplomatic Despatches, Mexico, vol. 12 (M-97:13), received 2/24; FC in DNA, RG 84 (Foreign Posts), Mexico, Despatches.

To Albert Smith, Commissioner, Portland, [Maine,] 1/16. "In reply to that part of your letter of the 13th instant, in which you inquire, whether, in paying the account of Lieu[tenan]t [William H.] Emory, you are to be guided by the rule laid down by this Department of having an account of the sum actually expended; or, that of the War Department, of a certain rate per mile; I have to inform you, that, inasmuch as Lt. Emory was in the military service of the United States, and was detailed to the Northeastern Boundary survey by the Department of War, the account for his traveling expenses should be paid according to the rule of that Department." Letterpress copy in DNA, RG 59 (State Department), Accounting Records: Miscellaneous Letters Sent, vol. for 10/3/1844–5/29/1845, p. 172.

From R[OBERT] WALLACE

Senate Chamber, Richmond, 16 Janu[ar]y [18]45
Dear Sir, I beg leave to inclose to you a report, I have had the honor to make to this body, on the Distribution of the Land fund, and trust it may be acceptable to you.

It was my intention to call on ["you" *interlined*] in Washington during the late recess of the Senate, but my time was so occupied that I could not. We are all anxious in regard to the new Cabinet, and, I say, without hesitation, that at home, between that place and this, and here, I have met with but one man who has not expressed his expectation, and earnest desire for your retention in the Department of State. I took the liberty to write a letter to Gen: [Andrew] Jackson on that subject, and at the same time expressing the opinion that Mr. [Andrew] Stevenson ought to be placed at the head of the Treasury.

I trust the reflections laid before Gen: J[ackson] may have a good effect.

My opinion is, that Colo[nel James K.] Polk will not be able to give us the requisite support from his administration, unless his Cabinet be composed of men of both ability and high reputation. He is so little known that we can derive no aid from him, and, as public confidence is indispensible to the success of his administration, it must be supplied through his Cabinet; in no other way can we have the benefit of the moral influence so necessary for the success of our principles and party.

Rumor, a few days since placed Mr. Stevenson in the State and Mr. B[enjamin] F. Butler in the Treasury Department. The latter would be an unfortunate appointment—he is the author of that part of Gen: Jackson's Protest which asserted such monstrous propositions. We have no confidence in the above rumor.

It is essential to the future success of our party, that Colo[nel] Polk's administration should be Southern and its leading members be of the South. Mr. [Martin] Van Buren is the only northern man whom I have known who has looked to our system in what he did; all others have been men of expedients—of shifts and contrivances for the time merely.

I earnestly hope you may be invited to remain in your present position and that you will not decline it. Much depends upon it. I am, dear Sir, very truly, R. Wallace.

ALS with En in ScCleA. NOTE: Wallace sent to Calhoun a printed copy of his "Report of the Select Committee of the Senate, on the Resolution of the House of Delegates, authorising the Treasurer of Virginia to receive of the Treasurer of the United States, a portion of the proceeds of the sales of the Public Lands," dated 12/7/1844. Wallace's report asserted that the Distribution Act was unconstitutional and called upon the Va. Senate to reject the House resolution and, thereby, the funds. An AEU by Calhoun reads "G[e]n[era]l Wallace."

From CH[ARLES] H. WINDER

Department of State
Washington, Jan[uar]y 16th 1845
Sir, A communication, from Hon. Z[adock] Pratt Ch[airman of the] Com[mittee] of Pub[lic] Buildings, dated 15th inst., to the Hon. the Sec[retar]y of State, has been referred to me for reply. The only portion of it that relates to my office, is embraced in the following enquiries:

1st. "Whether the number of rooms at present disposable, is sufficient for the transaction of business, *and preservation, and ready access to the Archives of their branch of the Department*?["]

2d. "What additional rooms would be required for these purposes?"

In reply to which, I have the honor to state—that I occupy one room, in every available spot of which, cases are placed from the floor to the ceiling, for the reception of Copyright Books, maps, Charts, Music, Prints &c &c.

These copy-rights are daily accumulating, and already I am at a loss to dispose of them. Every nook & corner of the room is occupied by them. Besides these, I have Charge of all Domestic Records and files, which are voluminous, and most of them important. For these I have no place whatever. They are not only without order for "ready access," but they are without the most ordinary means of preservation.

I felt it to be my duty to make these facts known to the Chief Clerk [Richard K. Crallé], which I accordingly did a few days ago.

The Seal of the Department is also in my charge—it is kept in a case of some size. I have not a spot in the room in which I can conveniently place it.

The Copy right and Home office requires at least two rooms for the "transaction of business, and preservation, and ready access to the archives of that branch of the Department." Respectfully Submitted, Ch. H. Winder.

ALS in ScCleA.

From Geo[rge] M. Bibb, Treas[ur]y Department, 1/17. "I have the honor to transmit herewith a report from the Register of the Treasury [Thomas L. Smith] accompanied by Tabular statements affording the information relating to the Trade between this Country and the Barbary and other African States, requested in your letter of the 28th December last." FC in DNA, RG 56 (Secretary of the Treasury), Letters to Cabinet and Bureau Officers, Series B, 5:6.

From Jo[sep]h A. Binda, [U.S. Consul], Leghorn, 1/17. Binda asks that James Ombrosi, acting U.S. Consul at Florence, be requested to surrender his seals of office. Ombrosi was appointed Consul there in 1830 but was never recognized by the Tuscan government. In spite of that, Ombrosi has acted in that capacity since 1830 and continues to do so. Binda protests that this is not only illegal but also it takes away the "emoluments & fees" of the Leghorn consulate.

Binda wishes to learn the opinion of the State Department in this case. A previous U.S. Consul at Leghorn had also complained of Ombrosi's actions. (A Clerk's EU indicates that this despatch was referred to the Secretary of the Treasury to be perused and returned.) LS in DNA, RG 59 (State Department), Consular Despatches, Leghorn, vol. 3 (T-214:3), received 2/22.

From MARY B. BLACKFORD

Mount Airy [Caroline County, Va.] Jan[uar]y 17th 1845

Dear Sir, Hearing with much disappointment of the arrival of the Oregon without my husband [William M. Blackford, U.S. Chargé d'Affaires to New Granada], and that the Capt. had said, he had waited for him as long as his orders admitted,

I hasten in exculpation of the former, from needlessly detaining the vessel, to copy a few passages from a letter received from him yesterday dated from the 1st to 6th of Dec[embe]r. I am perhaps encouraged thus to write to you, from a grateful recollection of your gentleness and kindness when I met yourself and Mrs. [Floride Colhoun] Calhoun at Bedford Springs [Pa.], years ago as Mary Minor, then a timid young girl alive to every touch of kindness.

"He says, "This is the forty fourth day since Mr. [Edward] Dixon left Carthegena, and he has not arrived. Nor have I any intelligence of, or from him, except a vague report that he had passed Momposa, which is within two days of the Barranca where he embarked. I am utterly at a loss to account for his delay except on the supposition that he has been ill somewhere on the river.

"There is a great fresh on the Magdelena which would retard his progress up very much, but it scarcely accounts for so long a detention. I cannot tell you how vexed and impatient I am under this unexpected delay. I have made all my arrangements for leaving here within two or three days after I get the Despatches, at least all arrangements which can be made before a day is fixed for departure.

"The Capt. of the Oregon [Lt. Arthur Sinclair] wrote me a letter reporting his vessel ["under" *canceled and* "at" *interlined*] my disposition under the orders of the Sec[retar]y of the Navy [John Y. Mason], and hoping I would reach Carthegena as soon as possible. I answered him that no urging was necessary as my anxiety would lead me to lose the least possible time in joining him, but he must on no account to return without me.

141

"The worst of it is I cannot make up my mind as to the length of time I should wait for Dixon, or whether in fact I ought to go at all without the *receipt* of my leave."

I hope you will excuse ["my" *interlined*] trespassing so much on your valuable time when you remember my anxiety to excuse my husband from all undeserved blame.

My letters can still be forwarded to Fredericksburg though I date from the Country where I am attending a sick child. With sentiments of respect I remain your friend, Mary B. Blackford.

ALS in ScCleA.

From D[ANIEL] S. DICKINSON, [Senator from N.Y.]

Washington, Jan[uar]y 17 1845

Sir, I am favored with letters from highly valued friends in New York acquainting me with Dr. Benjamin W. Barlow and speaking of him in terms of flattering commendation.

From these and a brief acquaintance which has followed I regard him as a gentleman worthy of confidence and warmly second his wishes touching his western mission. Y[ou]r ob[edien]t Serv[a]nt, D.S. Dickinson.

ALS in DNA, RG 59 (State Department), Letters of Introduction to the Secretary of State, 1820–1849. NOTE: An AEU by Calhoun reads "Mr. Dickinson recom[men]d[in]g Dr. Barlow."

From EDWARD EVERETT

London, 17th January, 1845

Sir, I enclose herewith a copy of a note addressed by me to Lord Aberdeen at the instance of Mr. E. Sheppard, requesting that certain paintings of Indian Chiefs belonging to him may be imported free of duty for the purpose of exhibition.

I did not feel myself quite at liberty to refuse a compliance with Mr. Sheppard's request, although there are considerable objections to the growing practice of seeking the assistance of the Minister of the

United States in the transaction of private business, capable of being performed without his intervention. It adds considerably to the burden of official duty, which is quite enough to employ all the time which can be given to it with due regard to health; and the greater the number of applications made by a Minister on occasions not more important than this, the less attention is likely to be paid to his interference in matters of gravity.

I do not allude to the evil as one that admits of any specific remedy. I have ever made it a rule, whenever it can be done without impropriety, to yield to our Countrymen every assistance in my power in their private concerns, without enquiring whether the matter-in-hand is within the line of official duty. Yet as I am sometimes obliged to decline making applications to the Government and the Court, at the instance of Americans in London, and this may occasionally be reported to you, I have thought it right that you should understand that it is always for some distinct reason of usage, delicacy or expediency, and never to save myself trouble. I am, Sir, with great respect, Your obedient Servant, Edward Everett.

Transmitted with despatch Nro. 243.
Mr. Everett to the Earl of Aberdeen, 17th January, 1845.

LS (No. 243) with En in DNA, RG 59 (State Department), Diplomatic Despatches, Great Britain, vol. 54 (M-30:50), received 2/22; FC in DNA, RG 84 (Foreign Posts), Despatches, 9:129–131; FC in MHi, Edward Everett Papers, 51:108–109 (published microfilm, reel 23, frame 608).

From Henry S. Eytinge, New York [City], 1/17. Eytinge, master of the American barque *Ganges*, states that he was recently at Leghorn preparing for a voyage to New York. He was obliged to wait at Leghorn two extra days because of the absence of the U.S. Consul [Joseph A. Binda] and his deputy from their posts. Respectable residents of Leghorn have informed Eytinge that the Consul had been absent for nearly two and one-half years during which time a Tuscan merchant who spoke little English had been acting as deputy Consul. That deputy had subjected vessels to "most vexatious delays & in many instances to onerous & illegal charges for fees." Eytinge calls upon the State Department to appoint a reliable Consul to Leghorn. ALS in DNA, RG 59 (State Department), Consular Despatches, Leghorn, vol. 3 (T-214:3).

From GABRIEL G. FLEUROT

St. Pierre[,] Martinique, 17 January 1845

Sir, I have the honor of offering you a Case of 12 Bottles of the choicest Variety & quality of Martinique Cordials universally Celebrated for its qualifications, deriving from the richness of the Fruit so peculiar to the Tropical Climes; and in this View I have Embraced an opportunity Via Norfolk, to Commit to the Care of Messrs. Robertson & Branda, my friends in that place, this small token, which I most respectfully present to your Kind regard & Consideration, hoping that it will meet your due approbation. I have the honor to be, Honorable Sir, With great respect, Your very ob[edien]t Servant, Gabriel G. Fleurot, U.S. Consul.

LS in ScCleA.

From SAM[UE]L L. GOUVERNEUR, "Private"

Washington, ["16" *altered to* "17"] Jan[uar]y 1845

My Dear Sir, You will see from the enclosed that the matter of Gen[era]l [Andrew] Jackson's letters is disposed of. They are (copies of them) with Mr. [Francis P.] Blair. What course he may adopt respecting them is left to himself. With G[rea]t respect &c Y[ou]rs, Saml. L. Gouverneur.

[Enclosure]

Andrew Jackson to [Samuel L.] Gouverneur, "Son in law
    to Ex President Monroe deceased, (Copy)"

Hermitage, Jan[uar]y 4, 1845

Sir, A friend of mine in Nashville, T[enn.] has placed in my hands the [Washington, D.C., Daily] National Intelligencer of the 24th of Dec[embe]r last, containing a publication over the letter *G.*

In speaking of the Treaty of 1819 with Spain it contains the following[:] "Its provisions were the subject of friendly consultation with [Thomas] Jefferson and [James] Madison, names identified with no concession unworthy of their country, and the policy dictated especially as to Boundary has the written approbation of [Andrew] Jackson &c &c &c."

I have no doubt but that you are the Author, and therefore I address you and request that you will give to my friend B[enjamin] F.

Butler Esq[ui]r[e] who will hand you this, for my use a full copy of my letter from which you have made the above extract together with a copy of the letter of Mr. [James] Monroe to which it was an answer. I trust you will see the propriety of complying with this request when it is made known to you that when my house got burnt, several of Mr. Monroe's private letters to me and my answers were lost. I regret that in your publication you did not give the date of my letter to Mr. Monroe, from which you made the statement of my approbation to the Boundary. From this omission you will discover the propriety of my request for copies. Let Mr. Butler compare the copies sent me with the originals & endorse true copies. I am very respectfully &c Y[ou]r m[ost] o[bedient] S[ervant], Andrew Jackson.

[Second Enclosure]

Sam[ue]l L. Gouverneur to Gen[era]l Andrew Jackson, "Ex President of the U. States"

Washington, Jan[uar]y 16, 1845

Sir, I have the honor to acknowledge the receipt of your letter of the 4th ult., enclosed to Mr. Benjamin F. Butler of New York, & by him transmitted to me, through Major W[illia]m B. Lewis of this place.

Referring to a publication in the Intelligencer of the 24th of De-c[embe]r last over the signature of *G*, of which you state, that you have no doubt I am the author, I respectfully reply that you are correct.

On the 2d ult., particularly alluding to that publication & the motives in which it originated, and after a friendly interview with Major Lewis on the subject, I addressed a letter to him, in which I respectfully tendered to you copies of any letters from yourself to Mr. Monroe, which you might be pleased to designate. Having been informed by him that he transmitted my letter to you on the 4th I ask permission to reiterate to you personally a respectful expression of every sentiment therein contained.

You will perceive that you are in error in supposing that I have made any extract whatever from any letter of yours in the publication referred to. Your approbation of the Boundary line in the Treaty with Spain, was stated on none other than a general authority in writing, which will account for the omission of date respecting which you express your regret.

In the spirit of my communication to Maj[o]r Lewis, & respectful Compliance with the request contained in your letter, I have now the honor to transmit to you copies of your letters to Mr. Monroe, most of them in reply to others from him, of date June 20, 1820, Jan[uar]y 1,

1821, Jan[uar]y 12, 1821, & Feb[ruar]y 11th 1821. In the absence of Mr. B.F. Butler I have caused their authenticity to be certified by Major Lewis equally acceptable, as I have supposed.

I deem it proper to state that I have not found among the papers of Mr. Monroe any other letter from yourself alluding to the Treaty of 1819 & to add that should any such hereafter be discovered, availing myself of your present request, I shall loose [*sic*] no time in transmitting it to you.

In delivering to me your letter of the 4th Major Lewis stated his intention, at your request to place copies of the letters referred to, & herewith transmitted in the hands of Mr. Blair. He has at the same time authorized me to communicate them to such individuals as I may think proper. I am with great respect &c Y[ou]r mo[st] ob[edient] S[ervan]t, Saml. L. Gouverneur.

ALS with Ens in ScCleA. NOTE: An AEU by Calhoun reads "Mr. Gouverneur[,] relates to the correspondence between Mr. Monroe & Gen[era]l Jackson in reference to the Florida treaty." Gouverneur's article defended Monroe and his administration from critics who, in 1844, suggested that the Florida Treaty had been too accommodating to Spain.

To Benjamin E. Green, [Washington], 1/17. "I have to acknowledge the receipt of your letter of yesterday, and to enclose the certificate which it requests." LS in NjMD, Presidential Autographs Collection.

From J[ohn] Y. Mason, [Secretary of the Navy], 1/17. "I have the honor to inform you, that Commander [John B.] Montgomery has been instructed to afford a passage in the U.S. Ship Portsmouth, to Delazon Smith Esq[ui]r[e] and to land him at such port in the Pacific as may be most convenient for him to reach his destination." LS in DNA, RG 59 (State Department), Miscellaneous Letters (M-179: 107, frame 66); FC in DNA, RG 45 (Naval Records), Letters Sent by the Secretary of the Navy to the President and Executive Agencies, 5:89 (M-472:3, frame 86).

From Edw[ar]d Stubbs

Department of State
Washington 17 Jan[uar]y 1845

The Undersigned [Disbursing] Agent of the Department has the honor to state to the Secretary, in answer to certain inquiries made by the Ch[airma]n [Zadock Pratt] of the [House of Representatives] Committee on Public buildings and grounds;

1st That he is, from the nature of his duties, liable to frequent interruptions; often when looking over and arranging papers, and vouchers of importance, and when making up accounts; and that it would tend much to his convenience, as well as security to have a second room where such papers, accounts &c. could be used without danger of loss or disarrangement.

2d That one additional room would be fully sufficient for the safe performance of his duties.

3d That the archives relating to his department are securely kept; having a a [*sic*] small fireproof vault for the purpose. Respectfully submitted, Edwd. Stubbs, Agent.

ALS in ScCleA.

To Mrs. MARY B. BLACKFORD, [Caroline County, Va.]

State Dept., 18th Jan[uar]y 1845
Dear Madam, I regret exceedingly, that the delay of Mr. [Edward] Dixon on the journey from Carthegena to Bogota has prevented the return of Mr. [William M.] Blackford in the Oregon & caused the keen disappointment, which you must have felt in consequence.

He was instructed to proceed on his journey with the least possible delay; and I am utterly at a loss to account for the long time he had been on his way without terminating his journey. The only information I have received has been through the Navy Dept. and your letter. From that derived from the former, I fear that he may have dieed [*sic*] on the way. With great respect I am & &, J.C. Calhoun.

ALS in NjMoN, Lloyd W. Smith Collection (Morristown National Historical Park published microfilm, Reel 8).

From Henry Y. Cranston, [Representative from R.I.], 1/18. "Pardon me for the liberty I take in requesting, that you would cause me to be furnished with such information as it may be in the power of the [State] Dept. to furnish, in relation to the matter referred to in the letter herewith enclosed." (The En has not been found but apparently concerned trade prospects in the Dominican Republic.)

ALS in DNA, RG 59 (State Department), Miscellaneous Letters (M-179:107, frame 71).

From C.G. Dill and others, Philadelphia, 1/18. Dill, "Master of Barque Venezuela & Late Master of Caracas & Rowena," and two other shipmasters, J.J. Wheeler and William Rugan, recommend W[illia]m T. Mann, acting U.S. Consul at Puerto Cabello, to fill that Consulship. LS in DNA, RG 59 (State Department), Applications and Recommendations, 1837–1845, Mann (M-687:22, frames 113–114).

From S. A. DRAKE

Sturbridge [Mass.,] Jan. 18, 1845

Sir, Permit me to intrude upon you at this time, to ascertain a fact and as I suppose to expose a fraud.

About the 1st inst., an individual, came into this Village, of respectable appearance and good address, representing himself as a *Mute*—and wishing to obtain a Writing School and in order to accomplish his purpose, he presented a letter of Introduction from you, of which the following is a true Copy.

Washington, Oct. 1844

Gentlemen—Permit me to introduce to your favourable notice Mr. Gustavus Wise—Nephew of the Hon. H[enry] A. Wise [U.S. Minister to Brazil]. John C. Calhoun.

P.S. Mr. Wise is a gentleman of high Standing, in society, any thing, which you may do for him to forward his wishes, will greatly oblidge J.C.C.

The above introduction, together with the fact that he was Deaf & Dumb, elicited Sympathy in his favour, and individuals, aided ["him" *interlined*] by their influence to procure a School—he obtained a large school, and, secured the tuition fee—and on the night that he closed his term he decamped without paying his bills—and took a valuable watch from one of the boarders.

Men went out in pursuit of him, and on the 16th overtook him ["in" *interlined*] Schenectady N.Y. and he is no[w] safely lodged in Jail to await his trial. Between this Sturbridge & Schenectady, he Call'd his name, Wise alias Sommerfield, ["alias" *interlined*] Manas-

148

seur[?] alias Wallace—and at every place he stop[p]ed went away without paying his bills.

Will you have the goodness to inform me by return of mail, Whether you know the man Wise—and whether the Certificat[e] is genuin[e] or a forgery and greatly Oblidge—I am very respectful[l]y Yours, S.A. Drake.

ALS in ScCleA. NOTE: An AEU by Calhoun reads "Wants an answer by return mail to a[s]certain whether a letter of introducing [*sic*] purporting to be signed[?] by me in favour of a Mr. Wise be false or not."

To J[abez] W. Huntington, [Senator from Conn.], Chairman of the Committee on Commerce, 1/18. "I have the honour herewith to transmit the papers requested in your letter [*not found*] of the 16th inst., relative to the qualifications of Jorgen Flood, and Jefferson Adams, nominated to the Senate as Consuls." FC in DNA, RG 59 (State Department), Reports of the Secretary of State to the President and Congress, 6:126.

From WASHINGTON IRVING

Legation of the United States
Madrid, 18th January 1845

Sir, I have received Dispatch No. 39 containing the commission of J.B. Lacey as Consul for Nueviatas and have applied for his Exequatur. I have received no answer as yet to my note to the Minister of State protesting against the exaction of fees for Consular Exequaturs. Indeed in speaking subsequently to Mr. [Francisco] Martinez de la Rosa on the subject he appeared to know nothing about it, so that he ["either" *interlined*] had not read my letter or its contents had escaped his memory. He made a memorandum however of the matter and promised to attend to it. It was the same with the remonstrances addressed in writing by this Legation against the eight days Quarantine imposed on United States' vessels although coming from northern ports. He knew nothing about the matter, made a memorandum and promised to attend to it. In fact he is quite inattentive and inefficient in official matters; his whole efficiency as a Minister lies in speaking in the Cortes; while he remains in the Ministry, therefore, all minor questions like the foregoing will be very liable to neglect.

The question of the duties on foreign and spanish flours introduced into Cuba which I adverted to in my last dispatch continued for some time to be discussed with animation and warmth in the public journals, but has latterly died away. I have endeavoured to learn from Ministers their intentions with respect to it, but they have avoided committing themselves. I am inclined to believe they are unwilling to meddle with it seeing it brings the interests of Cuba and the Peninsula into such angry collision. It may not therefore be brought before the Cortes at present. The project of a law relative to the ["abolition of the" *interlined*] slave trade has awakened suspicions of British intervention and influence which have been quickened by articles in the public papers charging the British Cabinet with a covert policy in this matter. A few days since Mr. Isturitz [*sic*; Xavier Isturiz] took occasion in the Chamber of Deputies to enquire of Ministers whether the proposed law was the result of any recent communications on the part of the British Cabinet, in which case he should wish to have all such documents laid before the Chamber when the subject should be brought up.

The Minister of the Interior would not say or not whether the Government had had communications on the subject but he would say that whatever they might have been, they had not been the motives of this law which had always been intended in compliance with treaty stipulations and had recently been rendered expedient by information collected in in [*sic*] the Peninsula and in Cuba.

It is probable the law will be attacked by Mr. Isturitz when it comes before the Chamber of Deputies. The same distrust of british agency and influence in the production of this law was manifested when a committee reported in its favor in the Senate. Some members refused to vote for the Bill so long as the intrusive policy of the British Government was permitted in the Spanish Colonies and a British ship of war was suffered to remain in the harbor of Havanna as a negro receiving ship.

Mr. Martinez de la Rosa exerted his eloquence to quiet these suspicions and to demonstrate how much the honor of Spain was committed in the case by her Treaties with Great Britain. He added that the receiving ship which gives such offence had been anchored in the port of Havannah with the consent of the Spanish Government on condition of being withdrawn whenever Spain should request it.

The sensitiveness of the Senate, however, still continued and was shewn when the penal clauses of the Bill came to be discussed, for though there was no longer a question of trying offenders by a mixed commission, and though offences were to be judged by the resident authorities, still there was an apprehension that any investigation as to the property in slaves, whether these slaves were native born or imported from Africa and the date of their importation etc. might give rise to inquisitorial proceedings calculated to throw the whole island into confusion. A Senator, therefore, Senor Olavarrieta moved an additional clause providing against any such inquisition. It was opposed in an animated speech by Mr. Martinez de la Rosa and a motion made to reject it but the motion was lost by a vote of 55 to 19. A proviso was consequently added to the penal clauses stipulating that "in no case and at no time can proceedings be instituted to disquiet or molest the proprietors of slaves under pretext of their (the slaves) origin." (Pero en ningun caso ni tiempo podra procederse para inquietar ni molestar a los propietarios de esclavos con pretesto de su procedencia.) When it is considered that the law in question has been brought forward and anxiously supported by Ministers, and that the Senate on most other questions have been completely at the beck of the ["Ministers" *canceled*] Cabinet, it will be perceived by the vote thus given that the Spanish public is wide awake in everything connected with Cuba and the Slave Trade and cautious of giving through motives of humanity any opening for foreign intermeddling in the interior affairs of their Colonies. In fact the Treaties concerning the Slave Trade entered into with G. Britain in 1817 and 1835 are felt as shackles by the nation. Even those conscientiously opposed to negro slavery begin to perceive how the efforts to suppress it may be misapplied or mismanaged so as to produce great evil. They are aware that the plea of philanthropy may be set up by politic statesmen to sanction dangerous invasions of national rights as in the fanatical times of the Crusades, the cross at the hilt of the sword was made to sanctify the weapon, however mischievously it might be used. I have the honor to remain Sir most respectfully Your obedient servant, Washington Irving.

LS (No. 59) in DNA, RG 59 (State Department), Diplomatic Despatches, Spain, vol. 34 (M-31:34), received 3/21; FC in DNA, RG 84 (Foreign Posts), Spain, Despatches, 2:125–129; PC in Aderman et al., eds., *Complete Works of Washington Irving, Letters,* 3:866–868. NOTE: This letter was received in the State Department after Calhoun had left office, but is included because it is a response to matters initiated by Calhoun.

From J[ohn] Y. Mason, [Secretary of the Navy], 1/18. "I have the honor to inform you in reply to your reference, that the application of Mr. [Clement H.] Stevens for a pur[ser]ship will be respectfully considered, nor will his claims be in any manner prejudiced by his being employed as Com[modo]r[e William B.] Shubrick's Clerk."

151

FC in DNA, RG 45 (Naval Records), Miscellaneous Letters Sent by the Secretary of the Navy, 34:366 (M-209:13).

From JAMES OMBROSI

Consulate of the United States of America for the
City of Florence in the Grand Duchy of Tuscany
Florence, 18 January 1845

Sir, Not having received a reply to the letter which I had the honor to address to the Department under date of 6th June last, & fearing it may not have reached its destination, I beg leave to recapitulate its contents, trusting that the embarrassing situation in which I am placed will be deemed sufficient apology.

Letters having been forwarded to me from the Department of State "for E[dward] Gamage Esq[uir]e Consul at Florence" & learning that the Gentleman was still in the United States I addressed him on the subject. He says in reply "the Consulate appointment for Florence has been conferred upon me" &c, "but in consequence of the determination of the Grand Duke [Leopold II], not to recognize at his Court, from this Country, any other than a Diplomatic representative, I declined officially visiting Italy." He adds, "all letters addressed to me from the Department of State, you will as *Deputy Consul* open, & attend to the contents."

Receiving no ulterior official instructions I have continued to perform the duties of the Office. *Now* however, Mr. [Joseph A.] Binda Consul at Leghorn calls upon me, & claims that the Consulate at Florence is abolished, & that a Vice Consulate shall be substituted in subordination to the Consulate at Leghorn. He says that he is willing to share with me the emoluments of the Office, if I will consent henceforth to act as his Deputy.

Having received no intimation that such a change was contemplated by the Government; and knowing that the Grand Duke, although he had through Courtesy recognized a Consul for the United States at Florence, had expressly stated that he could not accredit a *Vice* Consul, I feared that I might, by a compliance with the requisition of Mr. Binda, prejudice the interests of those whom I had heretofore had the honor to represent. I consequently declined any action in the case until I could hear from the Department.

Under these circumstances, I shall feel obliged by specific instructions for my guidance, and whether or not, my future services may be required by the Government, I shall ever retain a grateful sense of its past favors. I am with much Respect, Sir, Your obed[ien]t hum-[ble] Servant, James Ombrosi, Deputy Consul of the U.S. of America at Florence.

ALS in DNA, RG 59 (State Department), Consular Despatches, Leghorn, vol. 3 (T-214:3), received 2/22; ALS (dated 2/20) in DNA, RG 59 (State Department), Consular Despatches, Leghorn, vol. 3 (T-214:3), received 3/22.

From C[HARLES] S. TODD

Legation U.S. America
St. Petersburg, 6/18 Jan[uar]y 1845

Sir, I have entertained a great solicitude to be able, in a suitable manner, to bring the subjects contained in your Despatches Nos. 17 & 18 [of 8/27/1844 and 9/12/1844] before the Department of Foreign Affairs while at the same time I have felt some delicacy in taking any step that would seem to imply that we were anxious to vindicate our Conduct and character when these were not impeached. I should gladly have availed myself of any remark by Count [Charles Robert von] Nesselrode requesting information on the subject but no incident has yet presented itself by which I could make the explanation. In the meantime the annual Message of the President just received examines the subject so fully before the whole world that any conference in relation to it with this Government appears to be unnecessary unless Count Nesselrode should intimate a desire to receive further information.

The war on the Caucasus is another Florida affair upon a large Scale and continues to engage the attention of the Imperial Government. With a view to its more efficient prosecution Aide [de] Camp General Count Woronzow Governor General of Lesser Russia & Besarabia has been appointed a Field Marshal of the Empire and Lieutenant of the Emperor [Nicholas I] with the powers of a Vice Roy to conduct the war in such way as his own judgment may suggest. He was a distinguished Officer in the war with Napoleon and yet preserves the energy and activity of middle life. The most favorable results to the Empire may be anticipated from his genius & experience.

Allow me to recommend it to the Department to transmit copies of Capt. [Charles] Wilkes's [expedition] report and that upon the Coast survey, for presentation to the proper Department in this capital. These attentions create a favorable impression and may be expected since the recent present of the Coast Survey to [Louis Philippe] the King of the French & Lloyd's in London.

I have conversed recently with the former Russian Governor of the North West Coast who repeated, what I had obtained from other sources, that the Russian establishments on the Coast of Calefornia had been abandoned and he expressed the opinion that at no distant period it would be to the interest of the U. States to obtain a footing in that remote district of Mexico. A few Copies of Mr. [Robert] Greenhow's revised edition of his Essay on the North West Coast could be used advantageously with the prominent Ministers in this Capital.

The French Government has recently sent an Agent here to purchase extensively of timber for Masts of Ships and during the War with Morrocco [*sic*] an order was issued by the Imperial Government to equip the entire fleet at Cronstadt for Sea. It is intimated that a Committee, of which Aide-Camp General Count Orloff is President, has been appointed to examine into the propriety of modifying or repealing the duties on Exports and to increase the duty on raw cotton and cotton twists, as well as to admit the Coarser qualities of sugars on more favorable terms. The earliest authentic information on these points shall be transmitted to your Department.

I have the honor to enclose the last No. of the St. Petersburg Journal which, it is understood, is published under the eye of the Department of Foreign Affairs and of Count Laval, Secretary General of the Empire. The comments on the President's Message indicate a very favorable state of feeling, the neat and appropriate reference in the Message to the Emperor and to the Empire being calculated to produce a kind impression, notwithstanding the introduction into the same paragraph of an equally felicitous remark as to the King of the French.

I have read the President's message with unusual interest because the last annual message of every President leads to solemn and affecting reflections of which that of Mr. [James] Madison presents an illustrious example. The President, to whom I beg you to tender my cordial respects, can, among other causes of Congratulation, review with great satisfaction two interesting events in his Administration, respecting which there is scarcely a difference of opinion, that of the improved Condition of the Treasury and the Currency and the Treaty of Washington which removing the immediate causes of War led to a very triumphant arrangement as to the Squadron on the Coast of Africa that adds another guaranty during the next half Century to the maintenance of the freedom of the Seas. His administration, like the late War, has afforded an illustration of the efficacy of our Institutions to provide for all the contingencies to which the public affairs may be exposed. His ascent from the Vice Presidency presented a new and untried scene and was the more difficult from his not enjoying that great moral influence which General [William Henry] Harrison's fame and character brought to the guidance of the National Administration. I trust your own high sensibilities will pardon me for offering a passing tribute to the memory of the patriot in whose Councils and unreserved friendship I had the proud satisfaction of participating in peace and in war. Time as it rolls on will serve only to deepen the current of national affection for his exalted virtues; while I hope my own veneration for his character will mingle, in my last moments, with my reverence for that Supreme Power whose sovereignty and mercy we had both acknowledged. I have the honor to be with high Consideration & esteem, your friend & Ser[van]t, C.S. Todd.

ALS (No. 51) in DNA, RG 59 (State Department), Diplomatic Despatches, Russia, vol. 14 (M-35:14), received 2/22; FC in DNA, RG 84 (Foreign Posts), Russia, Despatches, 4406:232–234.

From W[illia]m W. Wallace

Warrenton [Va.], Jan. 18th 1845

Dear Sir: I avail myself of a visit, which my relation and friend Dr. G[ustavus] R.B. Horner of the United States Navy, makes to the seat of government, to enable him to call and see you. Permit me then to introduce him to your acquaintance. Dr. Horner, who is the brother of Professor [William E.] Horner of Philadelphia, and at present a resident of that city, is a gentleman of very considerable scientific acquirements and distinction; and will be pleased at the opportunity of taking you by the hand. I cannot let this occasion pass without congratulating you and the country that your labors in the cause of annexation are likely to be crowned with success during the present session of Congress. Such a measure, so deeply interesting to the people and government of the Union, cannot fail to leave a deep and durable impression on the public mind. In my judgment, it will constitute a new and important era in our government, as respects both its foreign and domestic policy. Very truly yours &c, Wm. W. Wallace.

ALS in ViHi, Gustavus Richard Brown Horner Papers. NOTE: Wallace marked this letter to be hand-delivered by Horner to Calhoun.

From William A. Weaver, Department of State, 1/18. Weaver reports to Calhoun the results of his examination into the accuracy of the Sixth Census. This examination is a formal State Department reply to memorials from the American Statistical Association and others questioning the accuracy of data collection and computation of census figures relating to free blacks in the U.S. The memorialists assert that errors in the census have distorted the true status of free blacks. Weaver has examined "each specification of error" and concluded that the memorialists have themselves erred in their claims. While there doubtless have been minor errors there have been no glaring methodological mistakes as charged. (Weaver incorporated into his report verbatim several pages of narrative and numerical tables that he had prepared in his draft report of 12/14/1844, entitled "Continuation of Report on the memorials relative to the alleged errors of the 6th Census (Part II)." However, he did not utilize materials from that earlier draft relating to the history of Africa or of Great Britain. Weaver had been superintendent of the Sixth Census in 1840.) PC in House Document No. 116, 28th Cong., 2nd Sess., pp. 3–30.

From [ROBERT MONROE HARRISON]

Consulate of the United States
Kingston Jamaica, Jan[uar]y 19th 1845
Sir, In consequence of the master of the vessel which takes this, being on the eve of his departure, I can only do myself the honor to inform you, that the Brig Phoenix of Baltimore commanded by Mr. Edward Myers has lately been wrecked on Folly reef in the neighbourhood of Point Morant the eastern end of this Island.

And I regret to say, that after the master and persons sent from here to save the property had landed a large proportion of the same on the beach it was forcibly taken from them by a band of some two hundred and odd negroes armed with hatchets and other offensive weapons; and if murder was not committed on the occasion it was owing to their having met with no resistance.

I addressed the Secretary of His Excellency the Governor on the subject a few days past, though as yet I have received no answer; but as I have enclosed a letter to him from the master of the Phoenix to me, and one from the persons who were employed to save the property by which some at least of the robbers may be identified, and others subsequently detected; I trust an example will be made of them in order to deter others from committing similar offences.

It is lamentable to perceive, that after all the expense and trouble of the British Government and people to educate and afford religious instruction to the negroes, they are as great savages in this Colony as ever; the amount of crime committed now is four fold what it was in the time of slavery, as may be clearly seen by the Criminal Calendars of the different Courts in this Island; Yet there are persons who declare that the negroes are not only improving in their moral and religious habits, but are industrious also; and by their endeavours the British Government are kept in the dark as regards the real state of things in these Colonies: And although several honest men in the House of Assembly have from time to time endeavoured to get a Committee appointed to report faithfully to the British Government on the subject, they have not succeeded, and the Island has therefore fallen to ruin [and] will never rise again. With great respect I have the honor to be Sir Your very ob[edien]t and most humble serv[an]t.

LU (No. 310) in DNA, RG 59 (State Department), Consular Despatches, Kingston, Jamaica, vol. 9 (T-31:9), received 2/17.

To George Brown, [Honolulu]

Department of State
Washington, 20th January, 1845

Sir: Your despatches to No: 16, inclusive have been received. It is to be regretted that a case like that of Mr. John Wiley, to which the last principally relates, should have occurred so soon after the recognition of the Hawaiian government by that of the United States. Your course in regard to it is approved by the President [John Tyler], who concurs in the views which you express. Notwithstanding the United States have no treaty stipulation with the government of the Islands, they cannot, under the circumstances, consent that the privilege of being tried by a jury of foreigners shall be withheld from our citizens while it is accorded to the subjects of Great Britain and France. We have every reason to expect our citizens shall have, in the dominions of that government, the same privileges as the citizens or subjects of the most favored nation. You will accordingly communicate these views to the Minister for Foreign Affairs, and repeat in the name of the government of the United States, your firm protest against the proceedings of the Hawaiian authorities in regard to Mr. Wiley, assuring him, in the strongest terms, that the United States will not submit to discriminations so unjust in their nature and so unfriendly in spirit as respects their citizens, and that the government of the Islands will be held responsible for all damages which may have been sustained in this case or which may hereafter be sustained by citizens of the United States under similar circumstances.

The United States, if it be desired by the Hawaiian government, are willing to enter into treaty stipulations, on the basis of those now existing between it and Great Britain; and I herewith transmit to you full powers to conclude such a Convention. But it is to be understood that the treaty is not to bar the claim for damages in the case of Mr. Wiley, (if any have been sustained) nor of any citizen or citizens of the United States for injuries accruing prior to its adoption, should it be made. I have further to say that if Great Britain or France should hereafter consent, in cases involving the rights of their respective citizens, to a trial by Jury *de mediatate lingua*, the United States would be willing to make the same concession. But whether there be or be not treaty stipulations between us and the Islands, the United States can never consent that their citizens should be put on any other footing than those of the most favored nations. I have the honor to be, With high respect, Sir, Your obedient Servant, J.C. Calhoun.

LS (No. 4) in DNA, RG 84 (Foreign Posts), Hawaii, Instructions; FC in DNA, RG 59 (State Department), Diplomatic Instructions, Special Missions, 1:201–202 (M-77:152).

From VESPASIAN ELLIS

Legation of the U. States
Caracas, Jan[uar]y 20th 1845
Sir, In accordance with the views expressed in your despatch of 30th October, I have embraced what seemed to me, a very favorable occasion, to urge upon this government, a reduction of the duties charged on American productions, & I have good reason to believe, that a very considerable change will be made therein.

I herewith enclose you a copy of my communication to [Juan M. Manrique] the Minister of Foreign Affairs, under date of the 16th Instant, which I hope will meet your approbation.

The National Congress of Venezuela commences its annual session, today.

Previously to preparing my letter to the Minister of Foreign affairs, I had numerous and repeated conversations, with members of Congress, and *others*, in official Station, most of whom, are favorably inclined to a reduction of duties on our productions. Several of them suggested, that a strong communication from this Legation, would have much weight with Congress, and would add strength to the recommendations of the Executive, on the subject, if any such should be made. There are political parties here, as in our own Country, and violent partisans, here, as there, not unfrequently range themselves, in favor of, or against the recommendations of the Executive, without reference to the wisdom of the measure recommended: & hence I have deemed it advisable, *Officially* to urge a reduction of the Venezuelan tariff of duties, not doubting, that my course would be fully appreciated by you, & that you would regard the present occasion, a very proper one, under the circumstances, for adopting the suggestions in your despatch, above referred to.

There is an earnest desire manifested by all Venezuelans, with whom I have conversed, both in & out of office, to cultivate the most friendly relations with us, and I doubt not such desire will be evinced, in the proceedings of their Congress, in relation to the Tariff.

Herewith you will receive a *duplicate* of my last quarters account, for the contingent expenses of this legation. The *letter* paper furnished me at Washington for use of the legation, was of so coarse & rough a texture, it was impossible for me to use it, & I had to purchase a better kind.

I am daily expecting from this government, a proposition to adjust all the claims of our citizens, at once, by a Treaty. It has been suggested to me, that such a proposition would be made ere long.

At present every thing is quiet, throughout the Country. I have the honor to be, with great respect, your obedient Servant, Vespasian Ellis.

ALS (No. 9) with En in DNA, RG 59 (State Department), Diplomatic Despatches, Venezuela, vol. 2 (M-79:3), received 3/9.

Duff Green, Washington, [Republic of] Texas, to James K. Polk, Washington, 1/20. Green has heard from a gentleman from Miss. who has talked with Col. [Gideon J.] Pillow, Polk's confidential friend, that Polk's "chief difficulty was how to get rid of Mr. Calhoun." This indicates to Green that the [Thomas H.] Benton and [Silas] Wright faction of the party is attempting to influence Polk against Calhoun through his personal friends. Since "Mr. Calhoun's self respect will prevent his doing any thing to counteract their machinations," Green fears that they may succeed. Green suggests that Benton and Wright are making coalition with leading Whigs to force Polk to do their bidding. Calhoun was confirmed by the Senate as Secretary of State in order to handle the Texas and Oregon negotiations. He is now engaged in "original and decided measures in relation thereto involving the destiny of the South." Green feels it to be his duty to advise Polk against conciliating Benton and Wright at the expense of Calhoun and his friends. If Polk does so, he will be going against the measures for which he was elected, will do the public interest and his own fame no good, will array the South against himself, and will be subject to the charge of violating obligations and of using his power to gratify the malevolence and personal ends of other men. Green asks Polk not to take offense at his frank advice, but he is no "court sycophant" and knows that he has no special claim on Polk's confidence. He writes as one who has devoted years to the cause of the South, as a citizen of Texas wishing to be annexed, as one involved in Polk's election, and with the realization that it is difficult for honest and truthful opinions to reach one in Polk's exalted position. He must warn that such a concession to Northern prejudice as removing Calhoun will be fatal to the success of the administration. His letter is written in a spirit of friendship, and, if Polk has already made up his mind to the contrary, it can do no harm. ALS in DLC, James K. Polk Papers (Presidential Papers Microfilm, Polk Papers, roll 32).

From Tho[mas] M. Hope, "Private"

Alton [Ill.,] Jan. 20 1845

Sir, It is due to you as well as your friends in Illinois that you should be informed of the position of certain men in this State, whose names will be sent to the Senate for confirmation to office in Illinois during the present session. These men were selected in *delegation* Caucus to take the place of *better* men and *better* democrats. The President [John Tyler] acted on the recommendation of this Caucus, and, *I know*, has expressed his regret, that he did not look *further* ("beyond the delegation") for information in regard to the appointments in Illinois. The individual [Abel C. Pepper] who was selected to succeed me, as marshal of this State, was selected on account of his *known* devotion to the Claims of [Thomas H.] Benton, [Silas] Wright & Co. for the succession in '48. The Receiver at, at Shawnee-town, the Register and Receiver at Dixon, the dist. Attorney and the Register in the Wabash dist. were also chosen to promote the views of Wright & Benton for the succession, and these men with the exception of the dist. Attorney were put in the places of your friends. In every instance except those mentioned above, *your known* friends were removed to make way for the men who were known to be hostile to every thing and every man *southern.* I was privy to the appointment of nearly all who the *Caucus* condemned to the gu[i]llotine. I dared the delegation to remove your friends and put Wright & Benton men in their places. I told them that I asked no favours, and that, if I was removed from the position I then occupied I would place myself in a *stronger one.* I consulted Mr. Kralle [*sic*; Richard K. Crallé] in this matter and he agreed with me in the opinion that your friends should maintain their honorable position, and not *beg* for mercy at the hands of a set of poli[ti]cal demagogues who had but *one term* more to serve. We were gu[i]llotined to a man. I returned home and established the "Alton Dem[ocratic] Union," out of my own private fortune, and assumed its editorial management, and with the help of God and the Calhoun party in this region, will sustain it. Since my connection with the paper, all sorts of overtures have been made to me from those who were most active in the execution of your *friends* here, which I have uniformly, moderately but firmly declined negotiation upon. We have rallied around the President to a man since the appearance of his message. We are entirely satisfied with the doctrines proclaimed in that most able state paper. On the Tariff he is right. As to Oregon we will not quarrel, even if the question should be settled on the parrallell of 49°. Texas is safe. Where is Benton[,] Wright & Co. as to these measures? As to the Tariff, I opine they are mum. Ad valorem don['] t suit *them,* because it *suits you.* As to Texas and Oregon, they are *nowhere.* I am afraid that you have blundered on the Oregon question. Time which cures all wounds will shew. In this, however, they occupy no better position than yourself. A word as to our delegation. [Robert] Smith & [Stephen A.] Douglass [Representatives from Ill.] I am inclined to the opinion will support you. The latter will however support [Lewis] Cass, if he deems him the most *available* man. He is a *great* man to ride on the popular wave. Judge [James] Shields is for Calhoun *first, next and always*; and he has more substantial influence in Illi[noi]s than any five of the delegation in Congress (Com[missioner] of Gen[eral] Land Office). You must *act* through your leading friends in the various States [or] your claims will be defer[r]ed until Time lays you on the shelf. We hold a State Convention *next month.* I am a delegate and will take that occasion to see all your friends from the various quarters of the State. My action shall be dictated with that caution and prudence without which, we cannot hope for success. I shall do all in my power to *rally the whole free trade southern* ["party" interlined] *in this State by uniting the friends of all southern men whose names will probably come up for the succession in '48.* If I succeed in this it is not difficult to determine, *even now,* whose party among these will be the strongest. Any suggestions you may deem proper to make I shall esteem confidential, and will conclude by saying that I was one of that Spartan Band in Virginia in '31, led on by the lamented Jones, my uncle, which would have *stood* by you and South Caroliana, or *fell* with you. I have the honor to be &c, Tho. M. Hope.

ALS in ScCleA.

From D[ANIEL] JENIFER

Legation of the United States
Vienna, January 20th 1845

Sir, Since my last despatch nothing has occurred here worthy of remark in regard to the United States. The Message of the President [John Tyler] to Congress has been read with much interest, and our relations with Mexico and Texas occasionally referred to, but with no invidious remarks as are common both in the English and French journals. I have as yet had no conversation with Prince Metternich upon the subject, since the reception of the President's Message. His health for some time has been delicate. It is my intention, the first favourable opportunity, without directly seeking it, to ascertain his views and opinions in relation to the position of the United States with regard to Mexico and Texas. My own opinion is, that in no event, will the Austrian Government interfere in this matter or countenance any hostile measure of the British Government towards us. Its policy and practice are conservative with regard to other nations and the best feelings exist towards the United States. In my next Despatch, however, I hope to be enabled to speak from authority and to advise the Government accordingly.

During my recent tour through the Italian States on my return from Palermo, I availed myself of all the means in my power to ascertain the disposition of those States. I do not hesitate to say that, as regards Great Britain and the United States, the feelings are almost universally in favor of the latter. At Rome I had an audience with His Holiness the Pope [Gregory XVI]. His Holiness was unreserved in the expression of the most cordial sentiments towards us which he repeated on my taking leave. From the interview I was led to believe that it would be desirable that more intimate diplomatic relations should exist between the United States and the Court of Rome. His Holiness spoke of the kind and liberal reception which was invariably given to the Roman Catholics who emigrated from Europe: of the growing prosperity of the Country and his gratification in giving audiences to Americans. Not so with subjects of Great Britain against whom at Rome and throughout the whole of the Italian States the deepest prejudices exist. The greater number of English who frequent Italy, and other States of the Continent leave behind them but few favorable impressions *except their money*. This feeling is general and attributed to their arrogance and general denunciation of any thing not English.

The British Government has no diplomatic representative at Rome and now would be a favorable period for the United States to profit by more intimate relations with that Court. It would no doubt have a good effect upon other Roman Catholic States of the Continent and be agreeable to a large portion of our own citizens at home. The Apostolic Nuncio at Vienna, who is an exceedingly intelligent and accomplished man—lately made Cardinal—has more than once assured me that it would be very gratifying to have instituted such relations. I merely make the suggestion growing out of the present state of things.

The Hungarian Diet has at last been adjourned after a prolonged and stormy Session of eighteen months. But few modifications in their political system have been made. Those of most importance are—allowing citizens not noble to hold real property from which they had heretofore been excluded, and some amelioration of inter-marriages between persons of different religious persuasions.

The Austrian Government is making rapid progress in their works of internal improvement. The rail-road from Vienna to Trieste is opened for passengers and freight as far as Gratz, the capital of Styria, with the exception of about eighteen miles over the Semmering Mountain, which it is contemplated to surmount by inclined planes and a Tunnel. The distance from Vienna to Gratz is 140 English miles and operatives are at work on 100 more. The rail road when completed to Trieste, a distance of 340 miles is looked to as the great mail route from England and all Germany to the East in connexion with the line of Steamers from Trieste, now in active intercourse with the Mediterranean, Levant and Black Sea. The harbor of Trieste is about to be made more safe for a greater number of ships at all seasons of the year; a consequent improvement in that City has already commenced and its commerce given a spur to.

My late sea voyage and tour in Italy have entirely restored me and I have returned to Vienna with greatly improved health. I have the honor to be, Sir, Your obedient Servant, D. Jenifer.

LS (No. 26) in DNA, RG 59 (State Department), Diplomatic Despatches, Austria, vol. 1 (T-157:1, frames 301–302), received 2/22; CC in DLC, Seth Barton and Daniel Jenifer Papers.

From Geo[rge] Latimer, Acting Consul, "St. John's, P[uerto] Rico," 1/20. Latimer acknowledges receipt of Calhoun's communications of 4/1, 6/14, and 11/14/[1844]. "Had the last [relating to sugarcane culture] arrived a few days sooner I could have sent some sugar cane to the agents of Mr. [Edward G.W.] Butler in New Orleans by a Spanish Brig bound to that port. I will do so by the next opp[ortuni]ty." ALS (No. 3) in DNA, RG 59 (State Department), Consular Despatches, San Juan, vol. 3 (M-76:4), received 2/25.

From R[ICHARD] PAKENHAM

Washington, 20 January 1845

Sir, I beg leave to enclose for your consideration an extract from a letter which I have lately received from Colonel [James B.B.] Estcourt, Her Majesty's Commissioner of Boundary, containing suggestions for the more rapid execution of the duties of the [Northeastern] Joint Boundary Commission during the approaching season; which suggestions appear to me to be worthy of the attention of the Government of the United States. I have the honor to be, with high consideration, Sir, Your very obedient Servant, R. Pakenham.

LS with En in DNA, RG 59 (State Department), Notes from Foreign Legations, Great Britain, vol. 22 (M-50:22). NOTE: In the En, dated 12/16/1844, Estcourt reported that during the previous work season the American Commissioners had completed only a small portion of their allotted section of the line, due to a failure of appropriations in Congress. The British Commissioners had completed their section and done much of the American portion with the understanding that the

American Commissioners would reciprocate the labor in the coming work season. Estcourt suggests that the American Commissioners be directed to begin their work on 5/1 and work through the summer.

To Charles S. Sibley, Tallahassee, Fla. [Territory], 1/20. "The President having, by and with the advice & consent of the Senate, appointed you Attorney of the United States for the Middle District of Florida, I herewith enclose your Commission. You will be pleased to inform this Department of the receipt of it." FC in DNA, RG 59 (State Department), Domestic Letters, 35:81 (M-40:33).

From C[HARLES] A. W[ICKLIFFE, Postmaster General]

[Washington, January 20, 1845]
I have exhausted all efforts to ascertain the cause of the delay of the Despatch Bag of the Depts. referred to in your communication, some days since [*not found*] and they have proved unsuccessful. Allow me to make a suggestion respectfully to you, upon this subject: and that is that you appoint the P[ost] M[aster]s of New York [City] & Boston your Agents—the amount allowed will enable them to hire each an additional Clerk and they will attend to this business and your instructions, particularly—and, if any delay, the Dept. will know whom to hold accountable. It is a fact that sometimes at Boston, in consequence of the absence of the despatch agent [Alanson Tucker, Jr.], you[r] bag is detained until he gets to the city and the regular mail is sent without it. C.A.W.

FC in DNA, RG 28 (Post Office Department), Letters Sent by the Postmaster General, N.2:411; draft in DNA, RG 28 (Post Office Department), Drafts of Outgoing Correspondence.

From W[ILLIA]M WILKINS

War Department, January 20th 1845
Sir, I respectfully transmit herewith, copies of the several reports, which have been received by this Department, in relation to the two white boys referred to in your communication of the 14: of August

last. Very respectfully Your Ob[edien]t Serv[an]t, Wm. Wilkins, Secretary of War.

LS with Ens in DNA, RG 59 (State Department), Miscellaneous Letters (M-179:107, frames 74–82); FC in DNA, RG 107 (Secretary of War), Letters Sent Relating to Military Affairs, 1800–1861, 25:453 (M-6:25). NOTE: Wilkins enclosed copies of six letters written during August, October, November, and December 1844 relating to the kidnapping of two Texas boys by Indians. According to one of the Ens, R[oger] Jones to Gen. M[athew] Arbuckle, dated 8/16, the boys had been captured after their parents had been murdered and they were among the Wichita Indians in the Choctaw Nation [in the U.S. Indian Territory]. Another letter, from Arbuckle to Jones, of 11/9, reported that the boys were held by the Commanches.

To HENRY A. WISE, [Rio de Janeiro]

Department of State
Washington, 20th January, 1845

Sir: I have the honor to acknowledge the receipt of your despatches numbered from 1 to 8, inclusive.

The subjects adverted to in your note to Mr. [Ernesto F.] França of the 8th of November, last, have an important bearing on the trade between the two countries; and I regret that the pressure of public business during the session of Congress, will not allow me sufficient leisure to examine them as fully as I could wish. The termination of the treaty with Great Britain presents a favorable occasion to secure advantages for our commerce which it has not heretofore enjoyed, and the system of reciprocal average duties which you suggest, seems to me ["as" *interlined*] well calculated to promote the object as any other. But as the subject is one of importance and requires both study and deliberation, and as a new administration is so soon to succeed the present, it is deemed advisable to postpone for the present any special instructions in regard to it. This is considered the more proper inasmuch as no definitive arrangement could be made before the 4th of March, next, when a new administration will come into power, unembarrassed by any preliminary steps on the part of the present.

The same considerations make it proper to defer, for the present, any special instructions in reference to the existing difficulties between the governments of Buenos Ayres and Monte Video. It is clear that the rights of neutrals, the general interests of commerce, and the common feelings of humanity require that the unhappy contest should be terminated; and to effect it, the suggestions of Mr. França would be taken immediately into consideration but for the reasons to which I have adverted.

As to the operation of the new Brazilian tariff, the Department concurs with you in the views you have taken of the subject, and approves the course you have adopted. It would be an act of gross injustice on the part of the Brazilian government to exact any other or higher duties on goods actually imported into the country prior to 11th November, than they would have been subject to under the treaty. To admit a different construction would be to give an *ex post facto* effect to the Decree, and to acknowledge a right equally indefinite in character and mischievous in operation. Goods imported prior to the expiration of the Treaty are entitled to a full discharge upon the payment of 15 per cent; an exemption which cannot be rightfully affected by subsequent legislation.

But you have so fully and ably considered the question, in your note to Mr. França, that it is deemed unnecessary to add any thing further to the argument.

The manner in which you have presented the claim of Mr. [Joseph] Ray cannot fail to have its effect on the Brazilian authorities, and while the steps you have taken meet with the entire approval of the President, it is earnestly hoped that your exertions will not fail to secure a final adjustment of all the claims of our citizens, now long outstanding, upon fair and liberal terms. I have the honor to be, with high consideration, Sir, Your obedient servant, J.C. Calhoun.

FC (No. 10) in DNA, RG 59 (State Department), Diplomatic Instructions, Brazil, 15:113–115 (M-77:23); CC in DNA, RG 84 (Foreign Posts), Brazil, Despatches, vol. 11; CC in DNA, RG 84 (Foreign Posts), Brazil, Instructions, vol. 2.

To George M. Bibb, Secret[ar]y of the Treasury

Department of State, January 21st 1845

Sir: I have the [honor] to transmit herewith the translation of a note [of 1/15] received from [Alphonse Pageot] the French Minister, in relation to a claim of Mr. [François] Durand to be refunded an alledged excess of duties paid on wines imported at New York. A translation of the Paper setting forth the grounds of Mr. Durand's claim is also enclosed. I have the honor to be, with high respect, Sir Your ob[edien]t Servant, J.C. Calhoun.

LS with Ens in DNA, RG 56 (Secretary of the Treasury), Letters Received from Executive Officers, Series AB, 1845, no. 13.

To [Henry Y.] Cranston, [Representative from R.I.], 1/21. "In reply to your note of the 18th inst. enclosing a communication addressed to you by Henry Holden, I have the honor to state that there is a gentleman (Dr. Caminers [*sic*; José M. Caminero]) in this City from the Islands of St. Domingo, who may be one of the persons referred to by Mr. Holden. I am not particularly informed as to the City of his residence, nor can I say how long he may remain here or in the Country. Neither am I able to state any thing as respects his powers to 'treat with individuals respecting trade.' The object of his visit to the Country so far as it may be of a public nature, and connected with the Government, could not, of course be communicated except in an official manner by the President." FC in DNA, RG 59 (State Department), Domestic Letters, 35:85 (M-40:33).

From Duff Green

Washington (Texas), 21st Jan[uar]y 1845

I wrote to you from Galveston that I had appointed Col. [Elisha A.] Rhodes the former Consul at Galveston as Vice Consul at that place. He is well qualified, is polite, attentive and conciliating in the discharge of his duty. There is a universal preference, as far as I could learn for him, over any one else, with all who know him, and I therefore take the liberty to urge his appointment as Consul. I have resolved to remove to Corpus Christi, and could not if I would discharge the duties.

I write thus because the difficulty with the President of Texas [Anson Jones], was to day, so far as he is concerned, arranged by a letter to Major Donaldson [*sic*; Andrew J. Donelson] withdrawing the imputations relative to the conversations which he made the pretence of revoking my Exequ[a]tur and it becomes necessary for to[?] make an appointment if it has already been done [*sic*].

Major Donaldson has promised me to write to you in Col. Rhodes' behalf. Yours truly, Duff Green.

ALS in DNA, RG 59 (State Department), Consular Despatches, Galveston, vol. 2 (T-151:2), received 2/10.

From GEORGE W. LAY, "Private"

Stockholm, January 21st 1845

My Dear Sir, I feel that the kind regard which you have ever manifested toward me personally has not been withdrawn in consequence of my abscence. From information which I have recently received, I am satisfied that I have been much indebted to your kindness & friendly protection.

The late New York papers brought to me a report stating that I was to be immediately superseded as the Representative of the United States at this Court.

This unexpected intelligence gave me much pain, and created no little surprise. There is nothing so well calculated to lessen the influence of a minister abroad, as the circulation of reports of this character.

It necessarily & unavoidably creates an impression, which nothing but a previous reputation well established can counteract. In the present instance, as soon as these reports reached Stockholm, they instantly called forth a manifestation of an interest & feeling in my behalf, and my personal welfare, as well as that of our Country, which could not but afford to me the most sincere & heartfelt satisfaction.

As soon as the King [Oscar I] heard of the report, he sent for the Minister of Foreign Affairs, and expressed to him much regret—directed him to say to me that it gave him great pain & that he should desire, that the Executive of the United States [John Tyler], through his Chargé d'Affaires, be apprised of the extreme regret he should feel should this take place. He also directed the Minister of Foreign Affairs also to assure me of the high regard & sincere estimation which he entertained towards me personally as well as Officially, and the sorrow he should feel at any change in the Official relations now subsisting between the two Countries.

The same warm interest & friendly feeling has been expressed by every member of the Administration, and all persons of influence & distinction with whom I have been acquainted in this City.

Altho the report which gave rise to this was to me exceedingly painful, it has nevertheless afforded to me the most ample & satisfactory evidence that I have acquitted myself, in the discharge of the high & important trusts committed to my charge, not only with credit to myself but honor to my Country. That my conduct during my whole residence at this Court has inspired the confidence & commands the respect of the Gover[n]ment to which I have been accredited.

Not having as yet had any intimation from the Gover[n]ment of an intention to supersede me, I feel myself constrained to consider these reports as without any proper foundation; or if there had been at any time such an intention, that your kind hand was extended to arrest it.

Agreeing with the Administration in every respect in all the great questions which have been agitated and decided by the recent election, it could not have been for any political considerations that I was to have been recalled. My sentiments in favour of the annexation of Texas, to the United States & in regard to the other questions were well known in the United States & to all my correspondents abroad. So far as it regards the Bank of the United States, it is I presume within your recollection, that at the session of Congress 1833 & 1834 [as a Representative from N.Y.], I was the only Whig in Congress from the northern States who took a decided stand against rechartering the Bank of the United States, & on Mr. [James K.] Polk[']s resolution against the rechartering the Bank I voted with Mr. Polk: & at the next election was opposed on this ground; but re-elected by an increased majority.

In regard to my standing & influence here, it is perhaps not necessary for me to say more than this, that I have the most unequivocal proofs, that no person could be more acceptable to the Gover[n]ment & the people, or who could at the present time be so useful to the United States.

I have taken much pains to make myself master of the Swedish language, as well as the customs, habits & history—past & present of the Country. In its present agitated state, about to adopt measures for a new organization, and an entire change of her Constitution, I am persuaded that no person can exert a more favourable influence than myself in behalf of the United States.

The principal object which I had in view in accepting the mission to Sweden, I have not yet been able to accomplish.

My time has been thus far mostly occupied in learning the language & in other respects preparing myself to be useful to my Country. It would be exceedingly gratifying to me to be permitted to remain here another year. This would not in any respect materially affect any plans the new Administration may have in view. In the present state of affairs I think you will readily see that it would be for the interest & most beneficial to the United States.

To me personally & as a favour, I feel that I can appeal to you, &

safely ask it, without any impropriety. For the past, no one can be more grateful than I am to you; and for the future I feel that I shall be able to afford to ["you" *interlined*] evidence, stronger than words can express, of my sincere & ardent devotion to the success & prosperity of yourself personally, and those great & leading principles with which you have so long been identified.

Your friendship to me during the past, and my knowledge of the truthfulness & sincerity of your character induces me to write you & leave this matter entirely in your hands. I have no correspondence with, or party connexions with any Senator or person at Washington & therefore communicate with you only.

It would be exceedingly gratifying to me to hear from you & if you allow me to do so, to write you more fully. With sincere regard, Your Friend, George W. Lay.

ALS in ScCleA. NOTE: In 4/1845 the James K. Polk administration appointed Henry W. Ellsworth to succeed Lay.

To Richard Pakenham

Department of State
Washington, Jan[uar]y 21st, 1845

Sir: I have laid before the President [John Tyler] your communication of the 15th instant, offering, on the part of Her Majesty's Government, to submit the settlement of the question between the two countries, in reference to the Oregon Territory, to arbitration.

The President instructs me to inform you that, while he unites with Her Majesty's Government in the desire to see the question settled as early as may be practicable, he cannot accede to the offer.

Waiving all other reasons for declining it, it is sufficient to state, that he continues to entertain the hope, that the question may be settled by the negotiation now pending between the two countries; and that he is of the opinion, it would be unadvisable to entertain a proposal to resort to any other mode, so long as there is hope of arriving at a satisfactory settlement by negotiation; and especially to one which might rather retard than expedite its final settlement.

I avail myself of this occasion to renew to you the assurances of my distinguished consideration. J.C. Calhoun.

FC in DNA, RG 59 (State Department), Notes to Foreign Legations, Great Britain, 7:60–61 (M-99:36); PC in *Congressional Globe,* 29th Cong., 1st Sess.,

Appendix, p. 29; PC in Senate Document No. 1, 29th Cong., 1st Sess., p. 162; PC in House Document No. 2, 29th Cong., 1st Sess., p. 162; PC's in the Washington, D.C., *Daily Union*, vol. I, nos. 189 and 242 (December 9, 1845 and February 10, 1846), pp. [753] and 955; PC in the Washington, D.C., *Daily National Intelligencer*, December 13, 1845, p. 2; PC in *Niles' National Register*, vol. LXIX, no. 17 (December 27, 1845), p. 265; PC in the Richmond, Va., *Enquirer*, January 13, 1846, p. 4; PC in the Lexington, Ky., *Observer and Reporter*, February 25, 1846; PC in Crallé, ed., *Works*, 5:457.

From R[ICHARD] PAKENHAM

Washington, 21 January 1845

Sir, In answer to your enquiry respecting "the disputed Territory fund," I have the honor to acquaint you that this subject has for some time past engaged the attention of Her Majesty's Government, with a view to the fulfilment, at the earliest possible period, of the provisions of the 5th Article of the Treaty of Washington.

The account at first presented by the Government of New Brunswick of the receipt and payments on the fund not having been found satisfactory, the matter became the subject of a correspondence, between Her Majesty's Government, the provincial Government of New Brunswick, and this Mission, and an amended account has been prepared which I hope to be able in a short time to lay before you, and at the same time to state that arrangements have been made for the payment of the amount which in pursuance of the 5[t]h Article of the Treaty will have to be made over to the Government of the United States, for the use of the States of Maine and Massachussets [*sic*]. I have the honor to be, with high consideration, Sir, Your very obedient Servant, R. Pakenham.

LS in DNA, RG 59 (State Department), Notes from Foreign Legations, Great Britain, vol. 22 (M-50:22); PC in House Document No. 110, 29th Cong., 1st Sess., pp. 55–56.

From Pedro de Regil y Estrada, [U.S. Consul], Merida, [Mexico], 1/21. "On account of certain claims made to this Government by the Spanish Consul at Campeachy, he was suspended in his functions, and also the American Consul of that City" as well as other diplomatic agents. Although he was not suspended at that time, soon afterwards, Regil y Estrada received from the Yucatan government a letter suspending him as U.S. Consul at Merida. "I have been personally assured that my suspension has had no other object than to equalize all the representatives of foreign powers." ALS (No. 10) with En in DNA, RG 59 (State Department), Consular Despatches, Merida, vol. 1 (M-287:1, frames 143–144), received 2/19.

From HENRY WHEATON

Berlin, 21 Jan., 1845

Sir, I have the honor to enclose herewith a Convention, this day concluded with the Bavarian Minister at this court, between the United States & the Kingdom of Bavaria, for the mutual abolition of the Droit d'Aubaine & taxes on emigration between the two countries.

As the Stipulations of this Convention are Substantially, & almost literally the same with the Conventions on the same subject with Wurtemberg & Hesse Darmstadt, which have received the sanction of the Senate, it appears to require no particular observations except as to the Sixth Article. This Article was proposed by the Bavarian negotiator, & as the same reservation is found in the last clause of the 14th Article of our Treaty of 1828 with Prussia, I saw no sufficient reason to object to its insertion.

Your several Despatches, nos. 58, 59, & 60, have been duly received, & their contents will receive due attention. I have the honor to be, with the highest consideration, Sir, Y[ou]r Ob[e]d[ien]t Serv[an]t, Henry Wheaton.

LS (No. 257) in DNA, RG 59 (State Department), Diplomatic Despatches, Germany, vol. 3 (M-44:4), received 2/22[?]; FC in DNA, RG 84 (Foreign Posts), Germany, Despatches, 4:168.

E[zra] W[illiams, Clerk of the Michigan House of Representatives, Detroit], to S[amuel] Y. Atlee, 1/21. Williams reports that a resolution favoring the "reannexation" of Texas has just passed the Michigan House of Representatives and that "every particle of abolitionism" was voted down. He encloses a copy of the resolution clipped from an unidentified newspaper. (This document is found among Calhoun's papers.) ALI with En in ScCleA.

To Shepard Cary, [Representative from Maine], 1/22. "With reference to your letter of the 29th Ultimo, relating to the 'Disputed Territory Fund,' I have the honor to Communicate to you, herewith for your information the copy of a letter addressed to this Department on the 21st instant, by her Britannic Majesty's Minister at Washington, the Right Honorable Richard Pakenham . . . ." FC in DNA, RG 59 (State Department), Domestic Letters, 35:86 (M-40:33).

From EDWARD EVERETT

London, 22d January, 1845

Sir, I duly received your despatch Nro. 115 with the papers relative to the outrage committed upon the American vessel the "Cyrus," P.C. Dumas Master, by Captain [W.] Bosanquet of the British Brig of war "Alert" off Cabinda [Africa] on the 2d of June last. I have drawn up a concise statement of the case in a note to Lord Aberdeen of the 20th instant a copy of which is herewith transmitted. I have thought it best to leave the description of the violent proceedings of the 2d of June in the words of Captain Dumas himself, and for that purpose I sent with my note to Lord Aberdeen an extract from his Protest made before the American Consul at Rio Janeiro [George William Gordon], commencing with the allusion to that occurrence, and continued to the end of the Protest.

As the British cruising officers are now required by their instructions to report every case of vessels detained and searched as soon as it happens, I presume we may expect an answer to my note without much delay. I am, Sir, with great respect, Your obedient Servant, Edward Everett.

Transmitted with despatch Nro. 245;
Mr. Everett to the Earl of Aberdeen, 20th January, 1845.

LS (No. 245) with En in DNA, RG 59 (State Department), Diplomatic Despatches, Great Britain, vol. 54 (M-30:50), received 2/22; FC in DNA, RG 84 (Foreign Posts), Great Britain, Despatches, 9:133–134; FC in MHi, Edward Everett Papers, 51:129–130 (published microfilm, reel 23, frames 618–619); CC with En in DNA, RG 46 (Records of the U.S. Senate), 29A-E3; PC with En in Senate Document No. 300, 29th Cong., 1st Sess., pp. 42–44.

From EDWARD EVERETT

London, 22d January, 1845

Sir, I received some time since a communication from Messrs. Brown, Shipley and Company a distinguished house at Liverpool, transmitting a correspondence with the Board of Trade, copies of which are herewith enclosed relative to the intercourse between this Country and Hong Kong, in American vessels. I thought it might be in my power to obtain a satisfactory explanation on the subject by personal conference; and for this reason I had an informal conversation with Mr. Mac Gregor [*sic*; John MacGregor], the Secretary of the Board of Trade, and a short time after with Lord Aberdeen.

Although the letter from the Board of Trade sent to me by Messrs. Brown and Shipley bears the signature of Mr. Mac Gregor, I gathered from what passed between us, that it had been signed by him in the routine of Office, and that the question had not particularly engaged his attention. The same was the case with Lord Aberdeen, at whose suggestion I made a written representation on the subject in a note of the 8th instant, of which a copy is herewith enclosed.

I did not feel warranted, in the absence of directions from the Department, in stating the case with much urgency, especially as it does not yet appear whether the restriction if persisted in, is to apply to the direct intercourse between the United States and Hong Kong or to the indirect only. The answer to my note will unfold the policy which is proposed in this respect by the British Government, and enable the President to give such instructions as may then appear requisite.

I am inclined to think that the result will be that the port of Hong Kong will be freely opened to foreign, vessels as their exclusion would be very apt to lead other European powers to obtain territorial possessions in the Chinese sea. I am, Sir, with great respect, Your obedient Servant, Edward Everett.

Transmitted with despatch Nro. 247;

1. Messrs. Brown, Shipley and Company to Mr. Everett, 15 October, 1844, enclosing a correspondence with the Board of Trade.

2. Mr. Everett to the Earl of Aberdeen, 8th January, 1845.

LS (No. 247) with Ens in DNA, RG 59 (State Department), Diplomatic Despatches, Great Britain, vol. 54 (M-30:50), received 2/22; FC in DNA, RG 84 (Foreign Posts), Great Britain, Despatches, 9:135–137; FC in MHi, Edward Everett Papers, 51:131–133 (published microfilm, reel 23, frames 619–620).

From ROB[ER]T MONROE HARRISON

Consulate of the United States
Kingston Jamaica, Jan[uar]y 22nd 1845

Sir, Herewith I have the honor to enclose you the copy of a letter which I addressed to His Excellency the Right Hon[ora]ble James

Earl of Elgin and Kincardine, Governor and Captain General of this Colony, on the 14th inst., in which I complained to him of the shameful and violent plundering of the Brig Phoenix of Baltimore (Edward Myers master) wrecked on Folly reef near Point Morant in this Island, by an armed band of negroes.

By His Excellency's reply which I also enclose, you will perceive, that, "immediate steps are being taken to punish the persons engaged in the plundering of the Brig Phoenix"; but as this is not the first time that American, Spanish and English vessels also, which have been cast away on this coast have been plundered by the negroes, who have always escaped punishment; I am much afraid that such will be the case in the present instance.

In stating to [*sic*] my letter of the 14th, that I was uncertain whether His Excellency, under such circumstances, would be able to punish them and afford any assistance to the Master of the Brig Phoenix, I had not only reference to these cases, but to the apathy, and disposition to palliate the faults of the negroes, on the part of many persons in authority here, for political reasons. With profound respect I have the honor to be Sir Your very obedient and most humble serv[an]t, Robt. Monroe Harrison.

LS (No. 311) with Ens in DNA, RG 59 (State Department), Consular Despatches, Kingston, Jamaica, vol. 9 (T-31:9), received 2/17.

To I[saac] E. Holmes, [Representative from S.C.], 1/22. "I have the honor to inform you that the Consulate at Matamoros, for which Mr. T[homas] D. Hailes applies in his letter of the 27th Ult[im]o—referred by you to this Department was filled on the 18th Ult[im]o by the appointment of J[ohn] P. Schatzell Esquire of that place." FC in DNA, RG 59 (State Department), Domestic Letters, 35:86 (M-40:33).

From J[AMES] I. MᶜKAY

Committee Room, Ways & Means, Jan[uar]y 22nd 1845
Sir, The Committee wish to be informed, by what authority, the arms taken from the Texian Troops under the command of Col[one]l [Jacob] Snively were sold, the amount of sale & how much thereof ha[s] been paid into the Treasury. Very respectfully, J.I. McKay.

P.S. Are the outfits that are asked for [*one or two words altered to* "Charges"(?)] Texas, Chile & Venezuela wanted for persons already appointed or appointments that are contemplated. J.I. McKay.

ALS in DNA, RG 59 (State Department), Miscellaneous Letters (M-179:107, frames 91–92).

From Isaac T. Preston

New Orleans, Jan[ua]ry 22nd 1845

Dear Sir, Allow me to introduce to you Judge Felix Bosworth of this State. He is a gentleman of much worth and has exercised great influence for many years in promoting the Cause of Democracy in this State. He deserves well of the party and his views and opinions in relation to public men and measures in Louisiana may be relied upon with great confidence. I am with great respect Your obed[ien]t serv[an]t, Isaac T. Preston.

ALS in DNA, RG 59 (State Department), Applications and Recommendations, 1845–1853, Bosworth (M-873:8, frames 943–944). Note: Lacking a postmark, this letter was probably hand-delivered to Calhoun.

To C[harles] H. Raymond

Department of State
Washington, 22nd January, 1845

With reference to the note of the 10th of August, last, addressed to this Department by Mr. [Isaac] Van Zandt upon the subject of two Texan white boys supposed to be among the Wichitaw Indians within the United States, the Undersigned has the honor to inform Mr. Raymond, Chargé d'Affaires ad interim of the Republic of Texas, that orders were given by the Department of War to the proper officers on the frontier, and that in consequence thereof, a detachment of dragoons proceeded to the village inhabited by that tribe, but after careful examination, the officer in command of the detachment and the Indian agent who accompanied it were satisfied that the boys were not in possession of the Wichitaws. It is stated that there was a mere rumor that they were held as captives by Kickapoos or Comanches, but whether by such of those Indians as inhabit the territory of the United States, does not appear.

The Undersigned avails himself of this occasion to offer Mr. Raymond renewed assurances of his respectful consideration. J.C. Calhoun.

FC in DNA, RG 59 (State Department), Notes to Foreign Legations, Texas, 6:80 (M-99:95); FC in Tx, Records of the Texas Republic Department of State, Copybooks of Letters Received from Texan and Foreign Representatives, vol. 2-1/103, p. 55; CC in Tx, Records of the Texas Republic Department of State, U.S. Diplomatic Correspondence; PC in Senate Document No. 14, 32nd Cong., 2nd Sess., pp. 130–131.

To C[HARLES] H. RAYMOND

Department of State
Washington, Jan[uar]y 22nd 1845
Sir: I have the honor to enclose herewith a copy of a Resolution of the House of Representatives of the 14th Inst.; and respectfully request to be furnished with such information as you may possess in reference to the subjects mentioned, not heretofore communicated by you to the Department, as may enable me to answer the call, at as early a day as possible. I have the honor to be, with high consideration, Sir, Your obedient Servant, J.C. Calhoun.

[Enclosure]
"Copy, 28th Congress, 2nd Session"
Congress of the United States
In the House of Representatives, Jan[uar]y 14, 1845
Resolved that the Secretary of State be directed to communicate to this House such information as he may possess or may be able to procure, of the whole amount of the debt of Texas, the amount for which bond or scrip have been issued, and the present market value of such scrip or bonds in Texas, in the United States and in Europe, the amount in value of the exports from, and the imports into Texas for the years 1843 and 1844, with the amount of revenue accruing and collected for the same years, with the expenditures for the same time; also, the present population of Texas, distinguishing the number between free and slaves; also, the quantity of acres of land which it is supposed is covered by valid grants, from the present and former Governments of that country, and the estimated quantity in acres of good and arable land, suitable for cultivation, which remains ungranted within the undisputed and acknowledged limits of Texas, as the same existed prior to the year 1834. Attest, B.B. French, Chief Assist. Clerk.

LS in Tx, Andrew Jackson Houston Papers; FC in DNA, RG 59 (State Department), Notes to Foreign Legations, Texas, 6:80 (M-99:95); FC in DNA, RG 59 (State Department), Domestic Letters, 35:86–87 (M-40:33); FC with En in Tx, Records of the Texas Republic Department of State, Copybooks of Letters Received from Texan and Foreign Representatives, vol. 2-1/103, p. 50; CC in Tx, Records of the Texas Republic Department of State, U.S. Diplomatic Correspondence; PC of En in *House Journal*, 28th Cong., 2nd Sess., p. 209.

From E[LISHA] A. RHODES

Galveston, January 22nd 1845

Sir, I respectfully submit to you the following extract of a letter I rec[eive]d a few days ago from the Hon[ora]ble A[ndrew] J. Donelson dated—

"Washington Texas, Jan[uar]y 16th 1845 Sir, The rovocation of Gen[era]l [Duff] Green[']s exequatur makes his Office Vacant, you will please attend to the duties as Consul until you hear from the Department, from whom I shall be pleased to hear also of your reception of the Appointment."

As Major Donelson has had every Opportunity of informing himself as to my Character and Capability, for discharging the duties of the Office, it affords me great Satisfaction to be able to transmit to you this testimonial of his Confidence, And I would respectfully solicit the appointment, if Consistant with the Views of the President. It may not be Amiss to State, that I have never become a Citizen of Texas. Never Voted, never Speculated in bonds, lands, or anything else; that I have never interfered in any way with the Politics of the Country, except in relation to annexation, which I have Warmly and Ardently advocated, looking upon it as a Measure fraught with the deepest interest to the United States and one that Cannot be too Soon Effected.

I wish it distinctly understood however that if Gen[era]l Green, desire to retain the Office, I am not an Applicant for it. I have the honor to be Your Obedient Servant, E.A. Rhodes.

ALS (No. 3) in DNA, RG 59 (State Department), Consular Despatches, Galveston, vol. 2 (T-151:2), received 2/9.

From DAVID SEARS

Boston, 22d January 1845

Sir, I take the liberty of enclosing a very singular case of injustice, connected with one of the Cantons of the Swiss Confederation. It is such, as seems to require of the General Government, on behalf of an American Citizen, a reasonable aid in the recovery of property, illegally and willfully withheld, and without whose mediation it must be lost.

The Property is acknowledged to belong to an American Citizen, but the interested persons, who now have it in possession, contrive, either from ignorance or knavery, to prevent a suit being brought before the Tribunals of the Country, under the plea that there is not sufficient evidence of the fact. The Swiss Consul here, will not move until instructed by the Council of State of the Canton de Vaud, and the Council of State will not give instructions, and thus the case cannot be presented. Every other means have been tried in vain, and an application is now respectfully made to Government for such instructions to their diplomatic Agent in Europe, as will establish the rights of Citizenship, and restore to an American Citizen property unjustly detained in a foreign Country.

The case is that of my daughter Mrs. Ellen Sears d'Hauteville, and the particulars are presented in her petition enclosed. In a few days my friend Mr. William H. Gardiner of this City, who has been Councel in the affair, will wait upon you at your convenience, and give you a statement of the remarkable facts, which demand and require the intervention of Government for obtaining a judgement, in what is apparently a plain and simple case of Justice. With great respect I have the honor to be your Obedient Humble Servant, David Sears.

ALS with En in DNA, RG 76 (Records of Boundary and Claims Commissions and Arbitrations), Miscellaneous Claims Records: France, Miscellaneous. NOTE: Sears enclosed a memorial from his daughter, dated 1/20, in which she set forth her claims against the Swiss government. At the time of her marriage to a Swiss citizen, Ellen Sears d'Hauteville's father had given her a marriage settlement of $20,000, legally secured to her use. When the marriage ended in divorce, she sought to recover the marriage settlement but collusion between her former husband and Swiss authorities has frustrated its recovery. Unable to obtain justice through her own efforts, the memorialist requests the U.S. to intercede with the Swiss government in her behalf.

To Morgan L. Smith, 1/22. Smith's letter of 9/27/1844 to President John Tyler has been received. Smith's reasons for not having traveled to his post [as U.S. Consul at Velasco, Texas Republic] have been deemed valid. However, it is expected that he will soon assume his post and undertake his duties. FC in DNA, RG 59 (State Department), Consular Instructions, 11:328.

From R[OBERT] J. WALKER, [Senator from Miss.]

Washington City, Jan[uar]y 22, 1845
Dear Sir, This letter will be handed to you by Gen[era]l Lewis Eaton who is one of our leading & most influential friends in the State of New York. Gen. E[aton] is the active & decided advocate of the immediate annexation of Texas & is with the genuine democratic party on all the great questions of the day both as to men & measures. Your[s] very truly, R.J. Walker.

ALS in ScU-SC, John C. Calhoun Papers.

To John W. Jones, Speaker of the House of Representatives, 1/23. In reply to a House resolution of 1/6 asking that he " 'communicate all such information in possession of the Department as may tend to show the cause of the increased expenditure for the relief and protection of American Seamen in Foreign Countries, with tabular statements of the amounts expended at the various consulates for a series of years; the number of seamen relieved at each of the Consulates; the amount accounted for by each of the Consuls as received by them on account of seamen discharged in Foreign Countries; together with all such other information as he may possess, and such suggestions as he may offer for the amendment of the system now in operation,' " Calhoun submits a lengthy report concerning the increase of American commerce, especially in whaling, and various ways in which the law requiring the payment of three months' wages to seamen discharged in foreign ports is circumvented. To guard the fund for the relief of these seamen from continued fraud, Calhoun recommends the following measures: "*First*—The individuals claiming its benefits should be citizens of the United States. *Second*—They should be regularly enlisted and registered. *Thirdly*—The masters or owners of vessels should be required to give bond and security before clearances are granted that they shall be returned to the United States, unless they shall have been regularly discharged by some Consul of the U.S. *Fourth*—No such discharge to be granted except in cases of sickness or insubordination, in which last case they shall not be entitled to relief. *Fifth*—Three months['] extra wages should in all cases be paid, to be charged by the Consul against the seamen for support and expenses while he remains at the public charge. *Sixth.* No relief to be granted except where proofs of a regular discharge are produced to the Consul. *Seventh.* Some further provision to secure a spe[e]dier passage to the United States; and to this end the national vessels should be required to call at distant Ports, and enquire for such as may have been left destitute, and to take them off." LS in DNA, RG 233 (U.S. House of Representatives), 28A-F1; FC in DNA, RG 59 (State Department), Reports of the Secretary of State to the President and Congress, 6:133–138; PC with Ens in House Document No. 95, 28th Cong., 2nd Sess., pp. 1–20. [The resolution to which this report is a response can be found in DNA, RG 59 (State Department), Miscellaneous Letters (M-179:107, frame 22) and *House Journal*, 28th Cong., 2nd Sess., p. 173.]

From Geo[rge] Latimer

Consulate of U. States
St. John's P[uerto] Rico, Jan[uar]y 23rd 1845

Sir, I transmit herewith a "Balanza Mercantil" and a "Cuadro Analitico" of this Island for the year 1843, they show in detail the receipts and expenditures and give every particular regarding the agriculture & commerce. I would respectfully request your attention to the great amount of the trade with the U.S. more than one fourth of the whole importations and exportations being in American vessels & mostly to or from the U.S. 311 ["American" *interlined*] vessels measuring 44,-192 tons entered the ports of the Island in 1843 while but 358 meas[urin]g 42,979 tons of all other foreign nations entered in the same time. They however paid but 68 3/4¢ p[er] ton tonnage money no matter from whence they came while the Americans paid one dollar p[er] ton—making a difference against the Americans of $14,222.50/-100 which they paid more, than any or all the other foreign nations ["had" *altered to* "did"] or would pay for same amount of tonnage and I beg to say that from the liberal policy & enlightened views of the present Capt. Gen[era]l the "Count of Mirasol" I think it would be a favorable time for the Gov[ern]m[en]t of the U.S. to move in the matter of getting this differential tonnage duty taken off. In conversations I have had with him on the subject he has expressed himself as ["favorable" *altered to* "favorably"] inclined towards that measure.

I have the Honor to be Sir very Respectfully y[ou]r Ob[edien]t S[er]-v[an]t &c, Geo. Latimer, acting Consul.

ALS (No. 4) with Ens in DNA, RG 59 (State Department), Consular Despatches, San Juan, vol. 3 (M-76:4), received 2/25.

To JAMES I. McKAY, Chairman, Committee [of] Ways & Means, House of Representatives

Department of State
Washington, 23 Jan[uar]y 1845

Sir, I deem it my duty to call your attention to certain reductions from the estimates of this Department, as well as omissions in the appropriation bill, now before the House of Representatives. Under the head of contingent expenses of the Department of State the item for extra clerk hire and copying is omitted.

You are aware, that, notwithstanding the vast increase in the business of this Department consequent upon the growth of the country, and the extension of its diplomatic and commercial relations; there has been, since the year 1827, but one clerk added to its regular force: and that a law was passed in 1842, prohibiting the employment of extra clerks, except during the sessions of Congress, or when necessary in consequence of calls of either house of Congress to be answered at its next ["ensuing" *interlined*] session.

In the bill making appropriations for the fiscal year ending 30 June 1844 the Contingent expenses of this Department were divided into specific heads, one being for extra Clerk hire and copying, $2000. A similar appropriation was made for the current year, but as the bill now stands there is none for that ending on the 30th of June 1846.

By the act of the 16th August 1842, it is made the duty of the Secretary of State to lay before Congress annually, at the commencement of its session, all such changes and modifications in the Commercial systems of other nations, whether by treaties, duties on imports and exports, or other regulations, as shall have come to the knowledge of the Department. The compilation and arrangement of the information called for by this act has to be performed by extra Clerks.

An appropriation was estimated for, of $481.90, being a balance, paid into the Treasury, of duties refunded by the Danish Government as having been erroneously collected from American vessels. Applications have recently been made by persons entitled to parts of this balance, and it is desirable that the Department should be enabled to pay them.

An estimate was made for the Contingent expenses of all the missions abroad of $20,000. It is reduced by the bill before the House to $15,000.

There are at present 23 foreign missions. The contingent expenses of 22 are restricted by a rule of the Department, to $18,500.

Loss by exchange on remittances and the drafts
of diplomatic agents &c may be estimated, at least, at   1,500

making as estimated $20,000.

Since that estimate was made it has occurred to me that some provision ought to be made for the infts of Ministers and Chargé d'affaires who may return to the United States during the ensuing year. According to long established usage, if five of each grade should return home, there would be required for the payment of Ministers the sum of $11,250

and for Chargé d'affaires   5,625

making an additional sum of $16,875

payable out of the appropriation for the Contingent expenses of the missions abroad, which added to the former estimate

will make $36,875

instead of $20,000.

You will see by a statement furnished to Congress (House Reps. Doct. No. 10—of the present session) that the amount of disbursements on this account, at this Department, and of accounts settled by the Fifth Auditor within the year ending 30 June last, was $37,680.

That amount was not for expenditures which had accrued within the year, as some of the accounts embraced longer periods. The same may be expected to occur during the ensuing year, on the final Settlements with such agents as shall return home.

The usual allowances upon the return of Ministers and Chargé d'affaires, have generally been paid out of the appropriations for Contingent Expenses of all the missions abroad. There are however instances where they have been specially provided for by appropriations. In the years 1819 and 1820, Laws U.S. Vol. 6[,] pages 396 and 478–9—

In those years there were but seven missions and the appropriations for their contingent expenses (exclusive of the return allowances) were $10,000

for each year.

The appropriations for the Contingent Expenses of the missions abroad from 1832 to 1842 inclusive, with the exception of

1836, were	$30,000
per annum making for eleven years	$300,000.

This did not include the Contingent expenses of the mission to Turkey from 1832 to 1840, inclusive for which appropriations were

made amounting to	57,000
making the total amount appropriated for Contingent Expenses of missions in Eleven years	$357,000
averaging per annum	$32,454.

A large balance from the appropriations having accumulated the usual estimate for the Contingent expenses of the mission to Turkey was discontinued in 1841, and that for Contingent expenses of all the missions, including Turkey, was for the Years ending on the 30th days of June 1843 and 1844 reduced to $20,000 for each.

That amount was appropriated for the former and but $15,000 for the latter year. In consequence of these reductions the existing appropriations will most probably be exhausted previous to the close of the current fiscal year and the amount latterly appropriated will not be sufficient to pay the ordinary Contingent expenses, exclusive of return allowances.

This must be apparent when it is recollected that in 1819 and 1820 the appropriations for seven missions were $10,000 per annum. In the two years which will end on the 30th June 1845 the appropriations amount to but $17,500 per annum for twenty three missions. I have the honor to be with high respect, Sir, Your obed[ien]t Serv[an]t, J.C. Calhoun.

FC in DNA, RG 59 (State Department), Reports of the Secretary of State to the President and Congress, 6:139–141.

From J[ohn] Y. Mason, [Secretary of the Navy], 1/23. "I have the honor to inform you, that the Commander of the U.S. Schooner Flirt has been instructed to afford a passage to Chagres to A[lexander] G. Abell Esq[ui]r[e] U.S. Consul at Hawaii, and to his lady; and I transmit herewith an order to the Commander of any U.S. vessel of war in the Pacific to afford them a passage to the Sandwich Islands." LS in DNA, RG 59 (State Department), Miscellaneous Letters (M-179:107, frame 94); FC in DNA, RG 45 (Naval Records), Letters Sent by the Secretary of the Navy to the President and Executive Agencies, 5:92–93 (M-472:3, frame 88).

To Publishers of Four Washington Newspapers

Department of State
Washington, 23 Jan[uar]y 1845

The newspaper now published by you has been selected for publishing the orders, resolutions and laws, except such as are of a private nature, passed during the 2nd Session of the 28th Congress; all public treaties entered into and ratified by the United States, except Indian treaties; and amendments to the Constitution of the United States.

Should you accept the appointment, you will, immediately on the receipt of this, be pleased to notify the Department of such acceptance, and name the person or persons who, as publisher or publishers, will be entitled to the Compensation for the publication herein authorized. To him or them, or to his or their order only, payment will be made. Should a transfer, into other hands, of the paper take place, a notification thereof from the person or persons so named, will be necessary.

It is expected that you will, on no account, divide any one act, unless from its great length it should exceed the limits of three pages of your print. And you will not fail, in publishing the orders, resolutions, laws, &c, to observe all the requisites prescribed by the Act of Congress of the 20th of April, 1818, "to provide for the publication of the laws of the United States, and for other purposes," so far as the same have not been repealed by the amendatory acts of the 11th of May, 1820, and of the 26th of August, 1842.

During the publication of the laws, you will forward your newspaper regularly to the Department of State. It has been usual for the publishers of the acts of Congress, to furnish the Department with their respective papers for the entire year, and it is expected you will conform to the custom, without, however, additional charge on that account.

A copy of the pamphlet, containing the orders, resolutions, laws, &c, published at the end of the Session, will be sent to you through the post office, as soon as it shall have been received from the press. You are requested, upon its reaching you, carefully to compare its contents with the publications in your newspaper, and should there be any omission in the latter, within the limits of these instructions, to supply the deficiency without loss of time.

Your compensation will be at the rate of one dollar for such printed page of the above named pamphlet laws, &c, published by you according to these instructions.

Together with the pamphlet, there will be transmitted a form of account and receipt, to be signed by you (or in case of a transfer of the paper, by the new publisher or publishers whose name or names shall have been communicated as above directed,) and sent to this Department for payment. I am Sir, &c, J.C. Calhoun.

FC (to [John B. Jones] publisher of the *Madisonian*) in DNA, RG 59 (State Department), Domestic Letters, 35:89–90 (M-40:33); PC in Jameson, ed., *Correspondence*, pp. 639–640. NOTE: A Clerk's EU reads "Same sent to Publishers of 'The N[ational] Intelligencer,['] and of The German National Gazette, & on the 29th same month, to the Publishers of 'The Constitution.'"

To [John B. Jones], Publisher of the *Madisonian*, Washington, 1/23. "In addition to the orders, resolutions[,] laws, &c mentioned in my letter of appointment to you of this date, you are requested to publish the private acts passed during the present Session of Congress and Indian Treaties, with copies of which you will be furnished by this Department." FC in DNA, RG 59 (State Department), Domestic Letters, 35:88 (M-40:33).

From CHA[RLE]S H. RAYMOND

Legation of Texas
Washington, January 23rd 1845

Sir, In reply to your note of the 22nd inst., I have the honor to submit the following statistical information.

It appears by President [Samuel] Houston's last annual message, dated the 4th ultimo, to the Congress of Texas, that the expenditures of the Government for all purposes, during his administration up to the 1st of November, last, excluding 50,873 82/100 dollars incurred during the administration of his predecessor and paid by this, amounted to $460,209.18. The receipts during the same period $466,158.09—leaving a balance, after carrying on the Government for the last three years, of $5,948.91.

It appears by a report of the Secretary of the Treasury of Texas, dated the 4th of December 1843, that the importations reported at the Custom Houses from the 1st of August 1842 to the 31st of July 1843 amounted to $417,205.32
The exports during the same period . . . . $415,768.75.
I have not been able to obtain an accurate statement of the duties

collected during the quarter ending the 1st of November 1842, but I believe they may be fairly estimated at $30,000. From that time to the 31st of July 1843—a period of nine months—the duties collected amounted to $102,450.60. The amount of direct taxes assessed in 1843 was $49,897.93, but how much of the same has been collected I am not informed.

According to the tax returns of 1843 the slave population, at that time, was 22,410. The increase since then I have, at present, no means of ascertaining.

From the 1st of August 1842 to the 31st of July 1843 there entered the ports of Texas 273 vessels, and there cleared during the same period 288.

By the last report of the Secretary of the Treasury of Texas, dated the 1st ultimo, it appears that the importations reported at the Custom Houses for the year ending July 31st 1844 amounted to $686,503.03. The exports during the same time to $615,119.34. The amount of duties collected on importations was $201,413.30. The expense of collecting was $23,551.45—leaving a nett revenue of $177,861.85. The amount of direct taxes assessed during the year 1844 was $50,-790.52. The tax Collectors have not yet made their returns of the amount collected.

I avail myself of this occasion to offer you renewed assurances of my distinguished consideration. Chas. H. Raymond.

ALS in DNA, RG 59 (State Department), Notes from Foreign Legations, Texas, vol. 1 (T-809:1); FC in Tx, Records of the Texas Republic Department of State, Letters and Dispatches Sent by the Texas Legation in Washington, 2:27–28; FC in Tx, Records of the Texas Republic Department of State, Copybooks of Letters Received from Texan and Foreign Representatives, vol. 2-1/103, p. 51; CC in Tx, Records of the Texas Republic Department of State, U.S. Diplomatic Correspondence; CC in DNA, RG 233 (U.S. House of Representatives), 28A-F1; PC in House Document No. 101, 28th Cong., 2nd Sess., p. 2; PC in the Washington, D.C., *Daily National Intelligencer*, February 6, 1845, p. 2; PC in *Niles' National Register*, vol. LXVIII, no. 1 (March 8, 1845), p. 4.

To HENRY WHEATON, [Berlin]

Department of State
Washington, 23rd January, 1845

Sir: You are aware that the period limited by the 6th Article of the Convention for the mutual abolition of the droit d'aubaine, and taxes on emigration, between the United States and the Grand Duchy of

Hesse, had expired, some twenty days before the exchange of ratifications, could take place; an informality, which the Plenipotentiary of Hesse [Baron de Schaeffer Bernstein] thought proper to waive after his attention had been particularly called to it by Mr. [Theodore S.] Fay. The question was submitted to the Senate, which formally resolved on the 13th instant, that the Senate advise and consent to the exchange of the ratifications of the Convention, at any time prior to the 4th July next, whenever the same shall be offered by the Grand Duchy of Hesse; and the said ratifications shall be deemed and taken to have been regularly exchanged, the limitation contained in said Convention to the contrary notwithstanding. A copy of the Resolution accompanies this despatch.

You will, therefore, on the receipt of these instructions, lose no time in taking proper steps to secure the formal sanction of the Government of Hesse to the act of the exchange of the ratifications of the Convention aforesaid, which took place on the 16th October last; which, when obtained, you will transmit hither without delay, to enable the President to proclaim the Convention at an early period. The difficulty is one of mere form, and the mode of executing these instructions is left to your good judgment and experience in diplomatic matters. It is not even deemed necessary to give you any new power beyond the authority which this despatch conveys.

It is not doubted that the Plenipotentiary of Hesse was satisfied in his own mind that his Government would approve of what he had done; and it is not improbable that this may already have taken place, upon the communication by him, to his Government, of the facts of the case. If this conjecture prove to be well-founded, it is conceived that an official announcement of any such action, would be sanction sufficient to satisfy the Senate, and enable the Executive to proclaim the Convention; and to supersede the necessity of exchanging formal certificates. The mode of effecting the object in view, as I have already said, will be left entirely to your discretion. I am, Sir, respectfully, Your obedient Servant, J.C. Calhoun.

LS (No. 64) in DNA, RG 84 (Foreign Posts), Germany, Instructions, 1:393–397, received 2/24; FC in DNA, RG 59 (State Department), Diplomatic Instructions, Germany, 14:88–89 (M-77:65).

To WILLIAM WILKINS, Secretary of War

Department of State
January 23rd 1845
Sir: I have just received a note from the Chairman of the Committee of Ways and Means of the House of Representatives, of which the following is an extract:

"The Committee wish to be informed by what authority the arms taken from the Texan Troops under the command of Col. [Jacob] Snively were sold, the amount of sale, and how much thereof has been paid into the Treasury."

I am not aware that the arms referred to have been sold; and respectfully request to be furnished with such information in regard to the fact, and the inquiries contained in the note from the Chairman of the Committee, as will enable me to return an answer to day. I have the honor to be, with high respect, Sir, Your obedient Servant, J.C. Calhoun.

LS in DNA, RG 107 (Secretary of War), Letters Received, Registered Series, 1801–1860, S-25 (M-221:135); FC in DNA, RG 59 (State Department), Domestic Letters, 35:87–88 (M-40:33).

From W[ILLIA]M WILKINS

War Department, January 23d 1845
Sir, In answer to your letter of this morning I have respectfully to refer to my official communications to the Department of State of the 13 of July and the 22d of August last, which ["contains" *altered to* "contain"] all the information possessed by this Department in relation to the arms &c taken by the order of Captain [Philip St. George] Cooke of the Dragoons, from Colonel [Jacob] Snively. The arms were deposited in the Ordnance store at Fort Leavenworth, where it appears by the enclosed report from the Adjutant General's Office, they still remain.

Should those papers have been mislaid duplicate copies will be furnished on further application. Very respectfully Your Obed[ient] Serv[an]t, Wm. Wilkins, Secretary of War.

LS with En in DNA, RG 59 (State Department), Miscellaneous Letters (M-179:107, frames 95–96); FC in DNA, RG 107 (Secretary of War), Letters Sent Relating to Military Affairs, 1800–1861, 25:456–457 (M-6:25); FC of En in DNA, RG 94 (Adjutant General's Office), Letters Sent (Main Series), 1800–

1890, 21:22 (M-565:14, frame 39). NOTE: Wilkins enclosed an LS from Assistant Adjutant General L[orenzo] Thomas to Wilkins, dated 1/23, stating that the arms confiscated from Snively were still at Fort Leavenworth and had been inventoried on 8/5/1844.

To J[AMES] I. McKAY, Chairman, Committee of Ways & Means, House of Representatives

Department of State
Washington, January 23rd 1845

Sir, I have the honor to acknowledge the receipt of your note of yesterday, and in reply to that part of it referring to the arms taken from the Texan troops under ["the" *interlined*] Command of Col: [Jacob] Snively, to transmit herewith, a copy of a Report from the Adjutant General's office to the Secretary of War, by which it appears that the arms have not been sold, as the Committee seems to have supposed.

As regards the outfits asked for Chargés d'affaires to Texas[,] *Peru* (not *Chile* as you suppose) and Venezuela, I have the honor to state that the appropriations are required for appointments made during the recess of Congress and that the Department has submitted no estimates for any prospective appointments of Chargés d'affaires. I have the honor to be, with high respect, Sir, Your Obedient Servant, J.C. Calhoun.

FC in DNA, RG 59 (State Department), Reports of the Secretary of State to the President and Congress, 6:132.

From Jesse W. Griffiths, Harrisburg, Pa., 1/24. Griffiths encloses to Calhoun a letter of 1/24 addressed to Calhoun from W[illia]m P. Wilcox, Speaker of the Pennsylvania Senate. In that letter, Wilcox recommends Griffiths for appointment to be U.S. Consul at Matanzas or another post. ALS with En in DNA, RG 59 (State Department), Applications and Recommendations, 1845–1853, Griffiths (M-873:35, frames 294–296).

From W[illia]m B. Hodgson

Savannah, Jan[uar]y 24, 1845

Sir, I beg to offer you for acceptance, a small volume of "Notes on Northern Africa," which I lately published.

This work is mostly ethnographic; but the first page will present to your mind, so eminently analytic, the conditions of that contest, which now exists in Barbary, betwixt civilization and semi-barbarism.

In the natural history of Man, I shall continue to assert the existence of an Organic law, by which the white and black races, when in contact, must ever stand in the relation of supremacy and subjection. If from any cause, this relation should cease, I should then maintain, that this organic law would require the removal of one race, from the presence of the other.

I am largely interested in this question, as one of property. And I have much anxiety for the fate of the great national measure now pending [the annexation of Texas], which I believe, will give greater security to that property, as well as larger guaranties for this Union.

I will only add, Sir, the expression of my hope, that you will remain in the National Councils, to give success to measures which you have initiated, and to protect the South, from those which may menace its prosperity. I have the honor to be Sir, with great respect Y[ou]r O[bedien]t Serv[an]t, Wm. B. Hodgson.

ALS in ScCleA. NOTE: Hodgson's *Notes on Northern Africa* was published in New York City in 1844. He had been U.S. Consul in Tunis.

From J[ohn] B. Jones, Madisonian Office, Washington, 1/24. "I have the honor to acknowledge the reception of your letter, appointing the Madisonian to print the laws of the 2d Session of the 28th Congress in its columns; and I take this occasion to inform you of my acceptance of the appointment." ALS in DNA, RG 59 (State Department), Miscellaneous Letters Received Regarding Publishers of the Laws.

From Farnham L. Tucker

New York [City], January 24 1845

The undersigned begs leave to Solicit from the President of the United States, the appointment of a Consul Ship to the Port of Truxillo Bay of Hondurus—he would also state, that at present there is no Consul or Commercial agent of the United States residing at that port. Respectfully, Farnham L. Tucker.

ALS in DNA, RG 59 (State Department), Applications and Recommendations, 1845–1853, Tucker (M-873:87, frames 522–525). NOTE: Tucker appended to this letter an undated affidavit signed by 15 New York City merchants stating that appointment of a U.S. Consul at Truxillo would be to the "interest of the Commercial Community" and recommending Tucker for the post. An AES by C[ornelius] P. Van Ness [Collector of Customs at New York City] reads "I concur in the foregoing request." Another AES, by J[ohn] Tyler and dated 1/31, reads "Mr. [Richard K.] Cralle will send up a nomination for the person within nam[e]d, unless there exists reasons known at the State Dept. ag[ain]st the establishment of a consulate."

From W[ILLIAM] P. WILCOX

Senate Chamber[,] Harrisburg, Jan[uar]y 24, 1845

Sir, Permit me to recommend Jesse W. Griffiths, M.D. of Philadelphia as a gentleman every way qualified for the appointment of Consul to Matanzas or some equally important station.

I have been well acquainted with Doct[o]r Griffiths for many years and know him to be a gentleman of education, intelligent, temperate, talented, and of irreproachable integrity of character, an active and uncompromising Democrat, well known to the Democracy of this State.

I can only say, that I have entire confidence in his ability to discharge the duties of any office, and I should be very much pleased to see that Doctor Jesse W. Griffiths should receive an appointment.

I have no doubt his appointment would be acceptable. I am very respect[full]y Your Ob[edien]t Ser[van]t, W.P. Wilcox, Sp[eake]r, Senate [of] Penn[sylvani]a.

ALS in DNA, RG 59 (State Department), Applications and Recommendations, 1845–1853, Griffiths (M-873:35, frames 295–296).

From J[OSÉ] M. CAMINERO

Washington, Jan[uar]y 25, 1845

Sir, As an addition to my note of the 8th inst., and in order that the Government may well understand, that the union of the Spanish portion to the Republic of Hayti in 1822, was not a spontaneous and

193

voluntary act, but was forcibly produced by circumstances, I have thought it necessary here more particularly to shew, the manner in which it was effected.

The Spanish portion of the Island of Santo Domingo, remained under the Government of Spain until the 30th of November 1821, on the night of which, the cry of independance was raised in the Capital City Santo Domingo, by Dr. Don José Nuñez de Caseres, then Lieutenant Governor and Auditor of War, to whom the officers in charge, gave free entrance into the Fortress, the arsenal, and the other forts in the vicinity, with the people of his party; and on the following morning, after the Governor and Captain General had been arrested, he published an act of Independance, assuming the title of President of the New State to which was given the name of Spanish Hayti, and hoisting the Colombian flag.

A few days afterwards, Brigadier General Don Pascual Real, the Governor and Captain General, together with the other head officers and garrison of the deposed Government embarked for Spain[,] Puerto Rico and Cuba.

The appellation of Spanish Hayti, coinciding with that of Republic of Hayti, which had been adopted by the negroes, and mulattoes occupying the French portion of the island, was a material error contributing to restrain the enthusiasm and prevent the cooperation of a part of the inhabitants. On the other hand the political change had not ["been" *interlined*] previously communicated to that part of the population of each place, which was required to make up the public opinion and to sustain it from the moment of the declaration of independance; from which omission, it had not been unanimously received by the people, and in a few days a difference of views and opposition manifested itself in two or three places on the north side, which was fomented by some European Spaniards, inimical to American Liberty, hoisting the flag of the Republic of Hayti, at Monte Cristi, and Santiago de los Caballeros, and entering into relations with the chiefs of that Republic.

The new President Nuñez de Caseres, had in the month of December, officially communicated the Declaration of Independence to [Haitian] President [Jean Pierre] Boyer, and made overtures to him for a treaty of alliance offensive and defensive, and the appointment of Commissioners to settle the proper stipulations to that effect: but Boyer being informed of the opposition declared by those places on the north side, which had raised the Haytian flag, and which already offered an opportunity for the breaking out of civil war among the Spaniards themselves, instead of acceding to the negotiation and recognizing Nuñez as President, replied in January 1822, styling him simply Political chief of the Spanish portion of the Republic of Hayti, inviting him to hoist the Haytian flag, with threats in case of his refusal, and manifesting all his views and plans for the immediate union of the two countries, and the dangers of an opposite determination.

This unexpected answer, demonstrated to Sr. Nuñez, how far his ideas and hopes had been disappointed, and caused the utmost consternation in the public mind; particularly among that great mass of peaceable inhabitants, the heads of families, who took no part in the political change, and who foresaw the great and immediate peril, to which their lives and properties were exposed, as well from the preludes to a civil war, on account of difference of opinions as from the approaching and inevitable invasion by the Haytian negroes; the new Government under Nuñez being entirely without funds and arms necessary to resist it.

In this deplorable state of things, all the civil and military authorities were convened in Council, at the Capital Santo Domingo, and having taken into consideration the threatening note of President Boyer, and reflected thereon, regarding it, as the only means of saving the people from the horrors of civil war, and from invasion on the part of the Haytian Republic, it was determined to submit to the unpropitious union thus forced upon them. The Haytian flag was accordingly raised and President Boyer made his entrance into the city of Santo Domingo, on the 12th of February 1822, at the head of more than ten thousand men: on the following day, he caused his constitution to be proclaimed, which had existed since 1816, for the French part only; he abolished slavery, and on his departure left Haytian Laws, and institutions, entirely different in character and customs from those of the Spaniards; for which reason, the two nations could never be united, as shewn by posterior acts, and by the general spirit with which all classes have fought, for the expulsion of the Haytians forever, from the Dominican territory.

I avail myself of this opportunity to observe, that the portion of the people of colour, that is mulattoes and samboes, free by birth are all natives of the same Spanish Dominican soil, and not of the French part; that these have always been in contact with the whites, and in the observance of the principles of religion and morality, to which they are accustomed from their infancy, according to the old laws of Spain; and that in the course of the operations to throw off the yoke of the Haytians and in the actions and combats, they have always taken the same resolution and displayed the same spirit and interest to repel them. All the Republics of the South contain members of

195

this class. I have the honour to be Sir Your Most Obed[ient] Ser-[van]t, Dr. J.M. Caminero.

State Department translation of ALS (in Spanish) in DNA, RG 59 (State Department), Notes from Foreign Legations, Dominican Republic, vol. 1 (T-801:1); PC in Senate Executive Document No. 17, 41st Cong., 3rd Sess., pp. 32–33; variant PC in the New York, N.Y., *Herald*, December 29, 1845, p. 2.

From JAMES H. CAUSTEN

Washington, January 25, 1845

Sir, Being the agent and representative of more than a majority of all the pending claims to indemnity against the Mexican Government, and more particularly, of that class which, under the Convention with Mexico of 1839, was submitted to and not decided by the Umpire [Friedrich Ludwig, Baron von Roenne]; I find myself called upon by existing circumstances to take some prompt action in that matter.

In all the proceedings heretofore had, I have regarded the movements of our Government, through the Executive, as not only the proper channel towards redress, but that it was the duty of the claimants to accord with its measures, and sustain its efforts by their concurrence—and upon that principle I have uniformly regulated my conduct, and desire still so to do.

It appears that quite recently the two Houses of Congress have volunteered aid to the claimants, and that Bills are now pending in each, through which a beneficial result is intended. It is very probable that these movements are designed to affect and sustain the proposed annexation of Texas to the United States, and may conduce thereto; to all which there can exist no motive for objection on the part of the claimants. I find that said Bills, however, are very imperfectly drawn, and do not cover the whole of the pending claims; but, although that fact is evident, still, I cannot attempt to amend them, without subjecting myself to the imputation of making an appeal from the Executive to Congress—to which I am utterly opposed.

Supposing it possible, nevertheless, that such Bills have received countenance or encouragement from you; and if so, that you would prefer such a modification of them as would cover the whole object and subject; I have ventured to submit to your better judgment a draft of a Bill, herewith enclosed, which, it is believed, will be satisfactory to all the persons interested in said claims.

If, as I hope, it may be your pleasure either to adopt said draft, or to modify it into a more suitable form, and cause it to be presented to Congress in such time and manner as you may prefer, I should be gratified in thus effecting what I consider my duty to those I represent.

And on the other hand, if you should decline that course, then, I would respectfully request the benefit of your judgment whether I may adopt it, of myself, without conflicting with the action or contemplated action of the Department of State. I have the honor to be With much respect Your Most ob[edient] Ser[van]t, James H. Causten.

ALS with En in DNA, RG 59 (State Department), Miscellaneous Letters (M-179:107, frames 102–106); ALS and draft in DLC, Causten-Pickett Papers. NOTE: Causten enclosed a draft of a bill "to provide for the ascertainment of claims to indemnity of American citizens, for injuries and losses inflicted on them by the Government and authorities of the Mexican Republic prior to the 1st day of January 1845."

From C[ALEB] CUSHING

Washington, 25 January 1845

Sir: I beg leave to render to you, in a connected form, and in explanation of the occasional details which appear in the course of my correspondence, a brief account of the personal organisation of the special Mission with which I have been charged by the Government.

Mr. Fletcher Webster, as Secretary of the Mission, was of great & important service, as well in the performance of the ordinary duties of his appointment, as of various special duties, which the peculiar nature of the negociations made necessary.

My instructions authorised me to introduce into the Mission interpreters, a draftsman, a physician, and a number of *attachés*, in order to give to it a certain degree of *éclat*, as well as to cooperate in its labors & duties: it being further prescribed to me that adequate compensation was to be made to the interpreters & draftsman, and payment if thought proper to a physician; but that the *attachés* were not to be a subject of charge to the Government.

In the selection of the gentlemen thus employed, I consulted (so far as I had opportunity & as circumstances admitted) the wishes of the Department; although much, of necessity, had to be arranged in China, without any means of previous reference to the Department.

The gentlemen thus attached to the Legation without pay were

197

Dr. Elisha Kane of Pennsylvania, & Messrs. John H. O'Donnell of Maryland, Robert L. MacIntosh of Virginia, & John R. Peters Jr. of New York.

Mr. George R. West of this District was employed as draftsman.

Dr. Kane officiated, for a time, as physician of the Legation.

But the most indispensable branch of assistance in the Mission, and that involving most expense, was for translation & interpre[ta]-tion, chiefly in Chinese & Tartar for intercourse with the Chinese Government, and in Portuguese for intercourse with the authorities of Macao. These duties were performed chiefly by Drs. E.C. Bridg-man and Peter Parker, American Missionaries in China, and by Mr. Stanislas Herniss.

To all the gentlemen mentioned, in their respective spheres of duty, great commendation is due for the services they have rendered the Government.

On Messrs. Bridgman, Parker, and Herniss, especially, there de-volved a great amount of writing, as well as of intellectual labor.

Drs. Bridgman & Parker are of that most praiseworthy & meritori-ous class of men, who devote themselves to the propagation of the Gospel in pagan lands, and deservedly stand among the highest in estimation of the American Missionaries in the East. They were pre-eminently useful to the Legation, not only as interpreters & trans-lators, but also as *advisers*, by reason of their long & exact knowledge of China.

Drs. Bridgman & Parker also officiated as chaplains to the Le-gation, in the performance of religious services at the residence of the Legation on the Lord's Day. I am Very respectfully Your ob[e-dien]t ser[van]t, C. Cushing.

ALS (No. 101) in DNA, RG 59 (State Department), Diplomatic Despatches, China, vol. 2 (M-92:3).

From A[NDREW] J. DONELSON

Houston Texas, Jan[uar]y 25[t]h 1845

Sir, I reached this place last evening, having, since my communica-tion to you of the 9th inst., been unable to transact business of any kind, until the 20[t]h inst., when the correspondence with this Gov-ernment was resumed relative to the objectionable conduct imputed to Gen[era]l [Duff] Green.

You will see from this correspondence, herewith enclosed, that

Gen[era]l Green's disclaimer of any intention to wound the feelings of the President [Anson Jones], or interfere in any manner with the independent discharge of his official duties, has been accepted by the President: and that thus this unpleasant affair has passed away, producing no injury to the friendly relations existing between the two countries, and leaving no sting behind on the private character of the Gen[era]l.

It was not deemed material or proper to ask for the reinstatement of Gen[era]l Green in his position as Consul, in as much as from the ground taken by him when he came to the seat of Government of Texas, he gave up substantially this character: and hence I treated the difficulty as public, only to the extent of the nominal responsibility imposed by an *Exequatur* still existing.

The papers relating to this subject, accompanying this despatch are No. 1—my letter of the 20[t]h to the Hon[ora]ble Mr. [Ebenezer] Allen—No. 2, Gen[era]l Green[']s letter to me of the 20[t]h. No. 3, a joint letter to Gen[era]l Green dated 1st Jan[uar]y from Messrs. [Robert H.] Williams, [A.S.] Thruston, & [J.C.] Meggenson. No. 4, the Hon[ora]ble Mr. Allen[']s answer to me dated Jan[uar]y 21st. I have the honor to be very respectfully Y[ou]r Ob[edien]t Ser[van]t, A.J. Donelson.

[P.S.] I send also, herewith, the No. of the Telegraph containing the letter of Gen[era]l Green referred to in the note of the Hon[ora]ble Mr. Allen. A.J.D.

[Enclosure]
Duff Green to A[ndrew] J. Donelson

Washington [Texas], Jan[uar]y 20[t]h 1845
D[ea]r Sir, I have read the copy of the letter from the Secretary of State giving the reasons for the revocation by the President of Texas of the *Exequatur* under which I acted as consul.

Nothing was further from my intention than to offer the slightest disrespect to him, or to resort to any improper means to obtain his sanction to the measures to which he refers: and I trust that as an act of justice to us both you will for me disclaim all intention to offer the slightest disrespect, or to interfere in any manner with the conscientious and independent discharge of his public duty.

I need not say to you that the measures referred to, as presented by me, were believed to be proper and expedient. My purpose is not to discuss them, but to enable you to make the most unequivocal disclaimer, and to put my intentions properly before the President. I do this as an act of justice to myself, leaving him to act as he may think proper.

My letter of the 2d Jan[uar]y published in the Telegraph was written under an impression that the President had intentionally sought a quarrel without a cause, and that although an effort was then making to bring about a reconciliation it could not be accomplished. It was but natural that under such circumstances, I should yield to the suggestion that he was in fact opposed to annexation, and was acting under the advice of the British Minister. Yet you will see by reading that letter, that I did not make the charge, but reserve my opinion subject to his future action.

That letter was placed in the hands of the Telegraph not to be published unless it became necessary for my vindication. When I learned that in an interview with you the President indicated a will-ingness to do me justice I would have written to Houston to prevent its publication, but found upon inquiry that it was too late for an ex-press to reach there in time. I regret its publication, as from the as-surances made through you, I am satisfied that injustice has been done the President. I have the honor to be &, (Signed) Duff Green.

[Enclosure]

A[ndrew] J. Donelson to [Ebenezer Allen]

Washington Texas, Jan[uar]y 20[t]h 1845

The undersigned, chargé d'Affaires of the United States, has the honor to submit herewith to the consideration of the Hon[ora]ble Mr. Allen, Att[orne]y Gen[era]l of the Republic of Texas and charged *ad interim* with the direction of the Department of State, a letter from Duff Green Esq[ui]r[e] in relation to the objectionable conduct imputed to him, and which was the subject of the communi-cation made to the undersigned on the 4[t]h inst. by the Hon[or-a]ble Mr. Allen.

Accompanying this letter is also one addressed to Mr. Green by three Gentlemen of this place. The object of both letters is to show that Mr. Green, however understood by the President, did not intend to misrepresent him or influence improperly his public conduct.

This voluntary disclaimer on the part of Mr. Green of all intention to wound the feelings of the President or interfere in any manner with the conscientious discharge of his official duties, it is hoped, by the undersigned, will justify a withdrawal of the personal imputations on his character, and produce a restoration of the friendly relations which would otherwise have continued to exist between them.

The undersigned regrets deeply that his confinement to the bed of sickness, from which he is yet hardly able to rise, has so long post-poned this explanation: but he is happy to say that he has received in the interval evidences of the most satisfactory nature that the disclaimer offered by Mr. Green is not only sincere, but is consistent with the exposition, which a closer examination has afforded, of the measures proposed to be accomplished by him through the agency of this Government, and in the interviews respecting which originated the misunderstanding between himself and the President.

Of the opinion entertained by the undersigned of those measures, he does not deem it necessary on this occasion to add more than was suggested in his note of the 6[t]h inst. on the subject. His object here is simply to be the medium of explanation for Mr. Green, being satisfied that the President will take great pleasure in withdrawing personal imputations on his character, when he is satisfied that they are not deserved.

The Undersigned renews to Mr. Allen the considerations of high regard and esteem with which he continues to be his most ob[edien]t Ser[van]t, (Signed) A.J. Donelson.
[Enclosure]
Eben[ezer] Allen to A[ndrew] J. Donelson
Department of State
Washington [Texas], 21st Jan. 1845

The undersigned Attorney General of the Republic of Texas, charged, *ad interim*, with the direction of the Department of State, has the honor to acknowledge the receipt of the note addressed to him on yesterday by the Hon. A.J. Donelson, chargé d'Affaires of the United States, relating to the "objectionable conduct" recently imputed to Duff Green, Esq[ui]r[e], originating in his interviews with the President; enclosing Mr. Green[']s letter to Hon. Mr. Donelson, under date of the 20th inst., and the copy of a communication from three Gentlemen of this place to Mr. Green—the two latter having relation to the same subject, containing a disclaimer on his part to offer "the slightest disrespect" to the Executive, or to interfere in any manner with the conscientious and independent discharge of his public duty; and manifesting the desire, that the Hon. Mr. Donelson should so present the matter to the President, as to place before him in a proper point of view the intentions of Mr. Green. Towards that gentleman, Mr. Donelson cannot but be perfectly aware, that the course persued by His Excellency, resulted alone from a sense of official obligations incident to his station; in adopting which, he neither entertained nor was in any degree influenced by motives of private pique or personal unkindness; and the undersigned having submitted the note of the Hon. Mr. D[onelson], and its accompanying communications, to His Excellency, has the satisfaction of announcing in reply, that His Excellency accepts the disclaimer of Mr. Green, coming as it does, with the explanations which the Hon. Mr. Donelson has presented.

A necessity for giving color to suspicions prejudicial to any individual, or wounding his feelings, or in any degree interrupting his private relations in society, be the justification ever so apparent or the duty ever so imperative, always presents an alternative to be regretted by the ingenuous and honorable. Alive to such feelings, His Excellency is happy to avail himself of the occasion to obviate so far as the tenor of the correspondence referred to will warrant, the injurious effects of any imputations resting upon the private character of Mr. Green, resulting from a possible misunderstanding of the motives which actuated him in his interviews with the Executive; who, as the undersigned is instructed to inform Mr. D[onelson], is willing to believe that he may have misapprehended the intentions of Mr. Green, and that his designs were in fact as expressed in the langu[a]ge of his disclaimer.

The President duly appreciates the honorable motives which induced Mr. Donelson to become the medium of explanation as stated in his note, for Mr. Green, but in announcing this acceptance of the explanations thus offered, and the propositions suggested by the Hon. Mr. D[onelson] in the matter under consideration; the undersigned must be permitted to remark, that he is happy to perceive from the letter of Mr. Green, that he regrets the publication of his communication addressed to the Editor of the Telegraph, under date of the 2d instant, and that acknowledged injustice has thereby been done to the President. The apparent charge conveyed by the language of that article, that the Executive was opposed to annexation and was acting under the advice of the British Minister, requires no no [*sic*] remark from the undersigned, as he conceives, to obviate any unfavorable impressions which such a charge would be calculated to make upon the mind of Mr. D[onelson] or to convince him of its fallacy and injustice. The state of the negotiations pending, between this government and that of the United States, the evidences of which are in Mr. D[onelson]'s possession, would furnish, a sufficient refutation.

Mr. Green, however, in his letter communicated with the note of Mr. D[onelson] to the undersigned, denies making such a charge, which would in fact have been wholly at variance with his own repeated declarations, as stated in the letter of the three gentlemen before alluded to, bearing date only one day before that of his communication to the Telegraph, a copy of which is relied upon as part of the explanation submitted in his behalf.

The recovery of Mr. Donelson from recent severe il[l]ness, affords to his Excellency an occasion of sincere joy and gratulation, in which the undersigned most cordially participating, renews to Mr. D[onelson] the assurances of the high regard with which he has the honor to remain His most Ob[edien]t S[ervan]t, Eben. Allen.

ALS (No. 10) with Ens in DNA, RG 59 (State Department), Diplomatic Despatches, Texas, vol. 2 (T-728:2, frames 472–478), received 2/11. NOTE: The enclosed letter of 1/1 from Williams, Thruston, and Meggenson to Green simply declared that Green expressed a belief that President [Anson Jones] would support any reasonable proposal for Texan annexation to the U.S. The issue of the *Telegraph* mentioned is not enclosed.

From Maj. J[AMES] D. GRAHAM

Washington, January 25th 1845
Sir, By direction of the Department of State my attention has been given to the communication addressed to it by the Right Hon[ora]ble Mr. [Richard] Packenham [*sic*], Minister from Great Britain dated the 20th inst., and to the abstract from the letter of Colonel [James B.B.] Estcourt, the British Boundary Commissioner, to Mr. Packenham, dated Quebec December 16th 1844.

So far as these communications bear upon the operations of the American Scientific corps, engaged in the joint Survey and demarcation of the Boundary under the Treaty of Washington, I have the honor to state to you, that as long as its organization remained as it was originally constituted by a special understanding between the two Governments, its efficiency was all that could have been desired, and its progress was quite equal to that of the British Scientific Corps.

The operations were, during that period, conducted in that conjoint manner which was no doubt contemplated by the Treaty. But the organization of the Scientific Corps upon our part has been twice interrupted, thereby diminishing its efficiency, whilst that upon the British side has been constantly preserved in full strength and in accordance with its original organization. Notwithstanding the energy and industry which have, I beg to assure you, been constantly displayed by our own officers and Engineers in the performance of all the duties devolving upon them, it was quite impossible that we should not, under circumstances so disadvantageous to us, fall behind our British colleagues in the progress of our work during the time that our force was reduced by our own Government. I have however the satisfaction to say that at the close of the field operations the past season, the British Corps was not in advance of our own so far as the Scientific operations, necessary to the accurate demarcation, were concerned. Immediately thereupon however our own Corps was again reduced by being deprived of the artillery detachment which had constituted a great aid to it, and this again places us in arrear with our office work.

The only plan which I can suggest, to prevent our continuing in arrear, is, that this detachment should be restored, provided it can be done without detriment to other branches of the public service. If there be any impediment to this course I would suggest the employment of an additional number of Civil Engineers as the only means of placing us on a par with our British Colleagues, and of ensuring the completion of the task before us in the rapid manner proposed by the British Commissioner. The work before us is an extensive one, and will require yet a great deal of labor to be performed, and if it be desired to complete it in so short a time as is proposed, it can only be done by a proportionate increase of force, and of pecuniary means to keep that force in active operation.

The detachment of Artillery is required to perform duties similar to those performed on the part of the British Commission by a detachment from the Corps of Sappers and Miners belonging to the British Army, with which the British Commissioner has been constantly aided, and will no doubt continue to be throughout the operations, it being a part of the System that was formally understood between the two Governments from the beginning.

In reply to your enquiry respecting the progress of the drawings, I have to state that we are much in want of the necessary office accommodations. Colonel [John J.] Abert has with no little inconvenience to his own immediate Department allowed one of the parties to occupy a room temporarily in his Bureau [of Topographical Engineers, War Department], but we cannot retain it long without encroaching upon that branch of the Service. In the mean time all our other parties are without any accommodation for drawing.

I have not, upon enquiry, been able to find any spare room in any of the Public [*one word canceled*] buildings. I would therefore recommend the hire of a building of moderate rent with a sufficient number of rooms to accommodate all our parties, to be retained until the termination of this service.

In accordance with your instructions I herewith submit an estimate contained in the paper marked A, for the transportation of the Artillery Detachment should it be restored to us, and for the rent of an office and the purchase of the necessary fuel. I have the honor to be very respectfully, Sir, Your Obed[ien]t Serv[an]t, J.D. Graham, Maj. Top[ographical] Engineers [and] Head of Scientific Corps on the part of the U. States.

ALS with En in DNA, RG 76 (Records of Boundary and Claims Commissions and Arbitrations), Letters Received by the Department of State concerning the Northeast Boundary Line, 1843–1850 and 1866; FC in DNA, RG 76, Letters Sent by James D. Graham, 1840–1844:106–109. NOTE: Graham's En estimated the amount needed for office space, fuel, and transportation to be $2,258.

From BEN E. GREEN

Washington, Jan. 25th 1845

Sir, In reply to your call for further information relative to the Instalments of the Mexican Indemnity, I have the honor to inform you, that Gen[era]l Waddy Thompson [Jr.] finding it impossible for him to attend personally to the receipt of the money and its transmission to the U.S., the high repute of the House of L[ewis] S. Hargous & Co., the fact of its being the most substantial and prominent house engaged [in] the U.S. trade, and the personal influence of its members with the Mexican Govt. pointed them out as the best persons for the agency. That House was accordingly selected by Gen[era]l Thompson for the purpose, and it has been principally owing to the exertions and management of the partner resident in the City of Mexico, to his acquaintance with the financial operations of the country, and the aid, which he has been able to afford the Mexican Govt., that the former instalments have been paid. In confirmation of this, I refer you to a letter from Gen[era]l Thompson, of the 25th March, 1844.

In relation to the alledged payment of the April and July instalments, and as a commentary thereupon, I refer you to my despatch of the 30th May, 1844, and to several notes addressed to the Mexican Govt., by date 4th & 8th of May and 24th July, and the replies of that Govt., dated 6th and 23d May and 27 July.

I have already explained to you the character of the payment mentioned in the note of Mr. [Manuel C.] Rejon, of the 2d Sept.; namely, that it was by orders on an empty treasury. Mr. [Wilson] Shannon, in his despatch to you [of 9/21/1844], announced the payment on the strength of Mr. Rejon's note, and because he felt confident that the orders would be paid out of the first funds coming into the Treasury, and although, up to the time I left Mexico, the urgent necessities of the Mexican Govt. had absorbed the revenues faster than they accrued, he continued to urge and was still in hopes, from day to day, that the orders would be cashed. The forbearance exercised towards the Mexican Govt., in thus waiting upon their necessities, was in accordance with the liberality invariably exercised by our legation and Govt. towards the Govt. of Mexico. It has been observed in all the later payments, none of which were made at the appointed day. In the case of the Instalment, which fell due on the 30 Jan. 1844, the greater part of the money was not paid until March, when a large sum was advanced by Messrs. L.S. Hargous & Co., our agents, to complete the payment. I have the honor to be Very Respectfully Your ob[edien]t serv[an]t, Ben E. Green, Secretary of the Legation at Mexico.

ALS in DNA, RG 59 (State Department), Diplomatic Despatches, Mexico, vol. 12 (M-97:13); PC in Senate Document No. 81, 28th Cong., 2nd Sess., pp. 20–21; PC in House Document No. 144, 28th Cong., 2nd Sess., pp. 20–21; PEx in Senate Document No. 85, 29th Cong., 1st Sess., p. 18.

From H[ENRY?] KING

St. Louis Mo., Jan[uar]y 25, 1845

Hon. Sir, The accompanying two German papers contain several articles of so much importance in relation to the affairs of Texas that I have taken the liberty of forwarding them to you. The letters from that country I recommend to your special attention. The company for the promotion of Emigration referred to has I understand, on good authority, never had its organization published before either ["in" *altered to* "on"] this Continent or in Europe. The character of its Officers and Board of Direction preclude the idea of its being a Company of speculators. It doubtless has had its origin in part in important state considerations at home, but there is also very strong reasons to suspect, that it was intended as an instrument to aid in securing no less important objects in Texas, to parties who, among the intelligent Germans of this City ["it is beleived" *interlined*] are secretly urging it forward. The operations of the Company extend I beleive over all Germany, and such I am informed, is the number of persons applying for emigration, that many are obliged to be rejected. The location of the Colony has been made as far as possible from the present settled portion of Texas, and a road is in course of construction from thence to a port on the Gulf but little frequented by other persons. These & other facts seem to indicate strong anxiety to isolate the Colony as much as possible from the American settlers, with the view it is suspected of securing the power & influence of the Company, to which some danger might be very properly apprehended by a too free intercourse with the Americans.

I have heard but one opinion expressed by the several intelligent German gentlemen of this City with which I have conversed on this subject, that is that if the question of annexation of Texas be deferred a few years its determination will be in the hands of this Company. What that determination may be, particularly, if the Company be, as suspected here & I understand also in Germany to be under the influence of Great Britain, there can be but little doubt.

Before closing it is perhaps proper for me to state that I know Mr. [Ferdinand] Lindheimer of Texas, and am intimately acquainted with the gentleman (Dr. George Engelman of this City) to whom the letters were sent and in whose hands I saw the originals. They are both gentlemen of the strictest veracity and in whom the utmost reliance may be placed. I have the honor to be Sir very respectfully Your O[bedien]t S[ervan]t, H. King.

ALS in DNA, RG 59 (State Department), Miscellaneous Letters (M-179:107, frames 100–102). NOTE: Dr. Ferdinand Lindheimer was an early German settler of Texas and a leading citizen of New Braunfels.

From Ja[me]s B. Murray, "Confidential"

New York [City,] January 25, 1845
Sir, In fulfilment of the object of your letter of the 16th Inst[an]t I placed myself in communication with Police Justice G.W. Matsell & with Mr. W[illiam] B. Taylor of the Post Office in this City for the purpose of adopting the preliminary measures requisite to discover the truth of the suspicions excited in the ["minds" *altered to* "mind"] of the Spanish Minister [Angel Calderon de la Barca].

Justice Matsell at once expressed his belief in the existence of associations among that particular class of persons, which if not already, might easily be converted into engines for producing the nefarious consequences suggested in the letter from the Spanish Consul at Vera Cruz.

He with great promptitude entered upon the duty of making himself better acquainted with the facts, & after further interviews with him wherein he made more full communications on the subject we decided that it would be requisite to employ at least two confidential

207

agents independent of and unknown to each other, but as they will have reason to apprehend much personal risk, they will probably expect a liberal contingent compensation.

As I did not construe the authority given to draw on your department as intended for such use, I preferred waiting to hear further from you, before committing myself by taking so decisive a step, which appears however to be unavoidable in arriving at the truth in relation to this extraordinary affair. I could enlarge were it not safer to await a personal interview and expecting your instructions in the present stage of the business [I] have the honor to be with great respect Sir Your mo[st] ob[edien]t S[ervan]t, Jas. B. Murray.

ALS in ViU, Crallé-Campbell Papers.

From J[OSEPH] T. WHITEFIELD

Anderson [S.C.], 25th Jan[uar]y 1845

Dear Sir, Your friends here are all extremely anxious to know whether you will continue in Mr. [James K.] Polk[']s Cabinet, take a foreign mission, or go again into the United States Senate. I believe your friends generally would prefer your remaining in the station you now occupy, or return to the United States Senate. I see the whigs are getting all the master Spirits in the Senate. [Daniel] Webster, [John M.] Clayton, and I have very little doubt [Henry] Clay can be prevailed on to return to the Senate—Moorhead or Crittendon [*sic*; James T. Morehead and John J. Crittenden] either would resign to give him the place. We have all come to the conclusion, that we have nothing to expect either from Congress, or the incoming Administration, and that the Southern States will have to take care of themselves. The course of the [Martin] Vanburen faction, on the 25th Rule, Tarriff, and the annexation of Texas—is so extraordinary—that we believe that we will have to take action and set up for ourselves. If so, would you not be of more service to us in the Senate, than any other place you could possibly occupy. I find that I am unable to educate my son [John C. Whitefield], as I could wish and I have an idea of getting him into a printing office in Washington, provided you continue there—so that you could have a Guardian care over him. It is certainly one of the best schools for improvement; I should like to have your advice as to this mode of Education for my son, & whether you would recommend it to me. I shall have either to do this, or to let his powerful natural capacity for the want [of] cultivation, like a di[a]mond in the quarry ne[v]er be polished—or have to resort to borrowing of funds and Mortga[g]ing all I have to enable me to educate him. The latter I should not like to do if I can avoid it—and if I was so disposed, in this section it would be very difficult [to] do—as those who have money, prefer purchasing property at forc'd sales, or if the loan, the least possible per cent it can be had at, is ten percent, & even at that to be paid, both principle & Interest in one year. At the north, especially in Newyork, it could be procured at much less interest, and for a length of time, by annually paying interest on the whole sum loaned, even this I could not do, without a friend being an entire stranger—not having a single acquaintance there except James Edward Bois[s]eau—and that a very limited one. I should like extremely to have a letter from you as early as your multifarious duties will admit—and your advice on this to me most interesting subject. I should (confidentially) like to know who will compose Polk[']s Cabinet—what pros[p]ect of the Annexation of Texas, what prospect of a reduction of the Tarriff—and especially what course you think Vanburen, [Silas] Wright, [Thomas H.] Benton cum multis alias, will take on all these interesting subjects—at the same time, not forgetting abolitionism. Wright's message [as Governor of N.Y.] is rather ominous I fear—so that I fear that his clique will desert the South on all the prominent issues made in the presidential canvass. I must confess my fears are great even as to the policy of Mr. Polk himself as regards the Tarriff. I should take it as a favour if you will file the enclosed affidavit & papers establishing the heirship of the widow & children of Glenn May who died in the United States service as a regul[ar] soldier, & let me know if their is any chance of their getting either land or money for them.

Tender my kind respects to Mrs. [Floride Colhoun] Calhoun, and accept for yourself, my esteem, my devoted friendship and my ardent aspirations for your individual prosperity, and that of my country. J.T. Whitefield.

ALS in ScCleA. Note: An AEU by Calhoun reads "J. Whitefield desires to have an affidavit filed in the case of ["he" *canceled*] a U. States Soldier." Joseph T. Whitefield was a lawyer and magistrate and was a member of the South Carolina House of Representatives occasionally between 1822 and 1851.

From A[NDREW] J. DONELSON

Galvezton, Jan[uar]y 26[t]h 1845

Sir, I transmit herewith the copy of a letter I have just addressed to the State Department of Texas requesting for Mr. [Elisha A.] Rhodes the usual privileges as a Consul until an appointment is made by the President. He is the Gentleman appointed by ["Gen(era)l" *interlined*; Duff] Green, Vice Consul: and I think would be a suitable appointment for the office of Consul.

He is highly spoken of by the citizens generally, has been long acquainted with the place, and has a large and interesting family dependent on his labor for support. I am very respectfully y[ou]r ob[edien]t ser[van]t, A.J. Donelson.

ALS (No. 11) with En in DNA, RG 59 (State Department), Diplomatic Despatches, Texas, vol. 2 (T-728:2, frames 478–479), received 2/11.

From WADDY THOMPSON, JR.

Greenville [S.C.,] Jan[uar]y 26, ["1844" *altered to* "1845"]

Sir, Some time during the spring of 1843 the Revenue cutter Woodbury was sent by Mr. [Daniel] Webster to Vera Cruz with a letter to me requesting my interposition in behalf of George B. Crittenden one of the ["Santa fe" *canceled*] Mier prisoners. I obtained his liberation from Gen[era]l [Antonio Lopez de] Santa Anna and as he was then as I was informed at Matamoros I directed the Captain of the Woodbury to touch at that Port and convey Mr. C[rittenden] to the United States. Before the arrival of the Woodbury at Matamoros Mr. C[rittenden] had been sent to Mexico [City]. The vessel having been sent to Vera Cruz for no other purpose I felt authorized to take this step. Very Respectfully Y[ou]r ob[edient] ser[van]t, Waddy Thompson Jr.

ALS in DNA, RG 59 (State Department), Accounting Records: Miscellaneous Letters Received. NOTE: Clerks' EU's indicate that this letter was received on 2/13 and that it related to a claim of Thomas C. Rudolph.

To Thomas G. Clemson, Brussels

Department of State
Washington, 27th January, 1845

Sir: Instructions given to your predecessors, so far as they may not have been executed, will, of course, be considered as forming a part of your own instructions.

The principal object of the present despatch, is to call your attention to the subject of the Belgian indemnification, for losses sustained by our commerce in the destruction of the Entrepôt at Antwerp; with which, it is presumed, you have now made yourself well acquainted. Mr. [Henry W.] Hilliard was informed that the new delays which had been interposed by circumstances to retard the payment of this indemnity, were a source of profound regret to the Government of the United States; and he was directed to take an occasion, before his departure from Brussels, to say so to the Minister of Foreign Relations [Albert Joseph Goblet] and to urge upon him the importance of inciting the Commission of Liquidation to prompt action, so as to afford to this Government some assurance that these long-pending claims of our citizens would be settled within a reasonable period.

You will, as early as possible, inform your Government of the present condition of these claims, and of the probability of their prompt liquidation; and take such measures as may be calculated to hasten the action of the Belgian Government in respect to them. I am, Sir, respectfully, Your obedient Servant, J.C. Calhoun.

FC (No. 4) in DNA, RG 59 (State Department), Diplomatic Instructions, Belgium, 1:56–57 (M-77:19); CC (in Anna Maria Calhoun Clemson's hand) in DNA, RG 84 (Foreign Posts), Belgium, Despatches, vol. 4; PEx in Holmes and Sherrill, *Thomas Green Clemson: His Life and Work* (Richmond: Garrett and Massie, Inc., 1937), pp. 74–75.

From A[ndrew] J. Donelson, "Private & Unofficial"

Galvezton, Jan[uar]y 27[t]h 1845

My D[ea]r Sir, I met at Houston your very acceptable letter of the 9[t]h inst., at which place I had arrived on the 24[t]h by slow stages from Washington [Texas], for the purpose of escaping the miasma of the latter place. I was attacked on the 4[t]h of Jan[uar]y with the prevailing epidemic and am among the very few cases of recovery from it.

When I reached Washington on the 4[t]h Jan[uar]y, Gen[era]l [Duff] Green's *Exequatur* had been revoked, and the worst possible feeling existed between him & the President [Anson Jones]. The Sec[retar]y of State, Mr. [Ebenezer] Allen, had prepared a statement of the case to be transmitted to their agent at Washington city. I immediately sought an interview with the President, and suggested to him the course which was adopted of stating the circumstances to me, and of permitting the explanations to pass through me to you. My first object was to remove the impression that Gen[era]l Green was authorised to commit his Government in any manner; and then to relieve him of the charge that he had sought to corrupt and menace the President, for you will perceive the statement of Mr. Allen makes this charge distinctly, and thus created a personal issue which under the circumstances could not have failed to injure the character of the Gen[era]l.

I considered the Gen[era]l, although out of his sphere, and not defensible as a consul, as not obnoxious to the severe imputations cast upon him. He was full of zeal in the cause of annexation, and mistaking the sense in which the members of Congress heard his project for the defence of the Western frontier and the invasion of Mexico, approached the President too familiarly, but without a doubt of his disposition, if not to concur in his views, at least to consider them in a spirit of kindness. Whereas in truth his movements were watched with suspicion from the beginning, and before he was aware of it, he was involved in the responsibility of measures, contemplating a serious change in the policy of the Republic, employing the Indians of the U. States & Texas in the invasion of ["Texas" *canceled and* "Mexico" *interlined*], and revolutionizing the country from the Rio Grande to the Pacific under the flag of Texas.

You will see that in my note to Mr. Allen of the 6[t]h inst., whilst I expressed my disapprobation of such projects, I treated the affair as not involving the United States, and reaching to no higher importance than what was due to private character and opinion. In this point of view it has been settled, and after a full disclaimer on the part of Gen[era]l Green of all intention to approach the President in the manner charged, the personal imputations on his character have been withdrawn ["in a manner" *canceled and* "to an extent" *interlined*] that ought to be satisfactory to him.

It gives me pleasure to say to you that the best feeling continues to prevail with the Congress of Texas on the subject of annexation.

Resolutions of various mass meetings on the subject have been referred to the committee of Foreign relations in the Senate, and have been the subject of a report from Mr. [David S.] Kaufman, the chairman, which he informed me would be unanimously adopted, recommending annexation as the true measure of safety for the Republic. The President also in my last interview with him, told me, that he would do his duty, and hold himself in readiness to call Congress together to take whatever steps might be deemed best to submit the action of our congress to the people of Texas for their confirmation and approval. Their Congress will probably adjourn tomorrow, having governed their legislation by the principle that, in view of annexation, the least that could be done, consistently with the administration and preservation of the Government, was the best.

The President called to see me repeatedly during my confinement, and after I became convalescent, stated to me, that he was assailed from some quarters as maintaining a position unfriendly to annexation: and that he was somewhat in doubt as to the course he ought to pursue to put himself right in the estimation of his own citizens. I suggested to him that I was satisfied with the course he had pursued in his intercourse with me: and that if he thought his position sufficiently well defined in the letter he had addressed to me on the 13[t]h inst., [sic; 12/13/1844] that there would be no impropriety in complying with a call from Congress for that correspondence—a course frequently adopted in other Governments for similar purposes. He seemed gratified at the suggestion, and there was a call accordingly made the next day, as I understood, for those papers. I had not considered that there might be something in my letter which would make its publication improper in the United States: if so, I shall exceedingly regret my imprudence, and must beg you to ascribe the weakness to the state of mind under which I was left by my sickness.

Determined to leave, during my absence, no influence inoperative in confirming the attachment of the people here to the measure of annexation, I left with a leading member of the House a letter of which the following is an extract and which he will publish.

"It gives me pleasure to say also in answer to your allusion to the active interest always manifested by Gen[era]l [Andrew] Jackson in behalf of Texas, that I had a letter from him a short time since in which he still expresses the same interest. He still looks upon the re-annexation of Texas to the United States as a measure of vital importance to the security and happiness of both Republics, and one that the people ought not to allow to be defeated. He considers that the inhabitants of Texas are entitled to the benefits guaranteed to Louisiana by the Treaty with France of 1803, and that reannexation is but a restoration of former rights, and a fulfilment of obligations which the Treaty of 1819 with Spain ought never to have disturbed.

"But independent of, and above, these considerations, he regards the will of Texas, made free and national, by the valor and prowess of her own citizens, and declared in favor of annexation, as constituting an appeal to the United States which cannot be resisted. This position of Texas remedies the errors of the Treaty of 1819, reopens the door for the consummation of the pledges contained in the Treaty of 1803, and restores to the valley of the Mississippi its unity in surface, in population, in Government, in defence, and in future security against foreign influence.

"With these views the Gen[era]l is still sanguine of the success of the measure of reannexation, and awaits with confidence the fulfilment of the popular wish in the United States by those charged with the administration of the Government."

I shall write you again from New Orleans, where I hope to meet my wife [Elizabeth Randolph Donelson], and will avail myself of the leave of absence the President has been kind enough to grant me.

There is one point of public interest, however, of which I will say a word in this letter, before concluding, and that is in relation to the unsettled question growing out of the order of President [Samuel] Houston to the collector at the mouth of the Sabine. The Secretary of State has not answered my communication on the subject, but replied verbally that instructions had been issued to the Collector which he was sure would prevent any future difficulty—that the subject being a delicate and difficult one, and requiring an examination of documents to which he had not now access, he hoped I would not press an answer immediately. I told him that all that was desired by me was the prevention of trouble, and an assertion of the rights of the U. States, and if his instructions to the collector had the effect attributed to them, that the delay he desired was not material. I am very respectfully y[ou]r ob[edien]t s[er]v[an]t, A.J. Donelson.

ALS in ScCleA; PC in Jameson, ed., *Correspondence*, pp. 1019–1022.

From Nath[anie]l Greene, Boston, 1/27. Greene recommends William T. Mann for appointment to be U.S. Consul at Puerto Cabello, Venezuela, in place of Dr. Franklin Litchfield, deceased. Mann is a Bostonian but has resided "some time" at Puerto Cabello "and his appointment appears to be desired by those of our Merchants doing business there." ALS in DNA, RG 59 (State Department),

Applications and Recommendations, 1837–1845, Mann (M-687:22, frame 115).

From GARRET D. WALL,
   [former Senator from N.J.]

Burlington [N.J.], Jan[uar]y 27, 1845
D[ea]r Sir, I take the liberty of enclosing to you, the Recommendations of the whole Sup[reme] Court of the State of New Jersey—the convention which recently formed the Constitution of N. Jersey, the whole Legislature of N.J. & the most respectable, and influential part of the Bar of N.J. presenting the name of Peter D. Vroom Esq. of Trenton for the office of Judge of the Supreme Court of the United States vacated by the death of Judge [Henry] Baldwin. These Recommendations are without distinction of Party and manifest the entire unanimity on this subject in N. Jersey. In fact, there is but one sentiment & one feeling, in relation to that appointment among the members of the highest courts in N.J. the Bar & the Legislature, & if it had been thought necessary to go among the Citizens, the same unanimity would have manifested itself. Gov. Vroom[']s qualifications as a ["Jurist" *canceled*] Jurist do not depend solely upon his reputation, at the Bar, where he now stands among the first, but have been displayed as Chancellor of N.J., & the Reports of Saxton & Green have given the materials for forming a Judgement of his character as a Judge. His friends with some confidence ask that he may be tested in that way.

Pennsylvania has given Judge [James] Wilson to the Bench of the National Judiciary & N. Jersey Judge [William] Paterson. When in the new arrangement of the Circuits Pennsylvania & New Jersey were thrown into one circuit there was no judge then on the Bench from either State and Judge [Bushrod] Washington was assigned to the Third Circuit, as it was denominated, & filled the station to the acceptance of both States. On his death, the first vacancy in that circuit occurred, and the claims of each State to fill the vacancy were equal, & both presented candidates. Judge Baldwin was appointed & New Jersey acquiesced without a murmur because ["like" *altered to* "the"] claims of each State, being equal at that time, neither had a superiority, on the score of the past. Now when Judge Baldwin[']s death, has again produced a vacancy, the situation of the States composing the Circuit is different. Pennsylvania has had one Judge, of that circuit, New Jersey none, & it is submitted to the wisdom of the appointing power that if N.J. presents a Candidate equal in all the qualifications for the office with any presented by Pen[nsylvani]a, that the Candidate of N.J. ["from that circumstance" *canceled*] ought to have the benefit arising from that fact. The Candidate presented by N. Jersey is the candidate of the Bench, the Bar, & the constituted authorities of the whole State with entire unanimity and it is doubtful whether any such unanimity can be produced, in favor of any Candidate from Pen[nsylvani]a. Another circumstance it is presumed is not unworthy of the Consideration of the Appointing Power. A Judge of the Sup[reme] Court of U.S. appointed in the 3d circuit, ought to be a learned & practical Equity Lawyer, which Governor Vroom undoubt[ed]ly is, and has given very decided & satisfactory evidence that he is so, while he presided as Chancellor of N.J. for many years. In all other of the qualifications necessary for the satisfactory discharge of the duties of that office, the friends of the N.J. Candidate will not shrink from a comparison with any Candidate presented by Pen[nsylvani]a.

As States New Jersey & Pen[nsylvani]a are on an equality as to rights and claims, and New Jersey ought not to have her claims, in the supplying the members of the Judiciary, pretermitted by the superior size and importance of Pen[nsylvani]a. That had its due weight assigned it on the former occasion.

Will you have the goodness to submit the Recommendations enclosed herewith & this Letter, to [John Tyler] the appointing Power, and to cause them to be placed on file for the action of a future Executive if no appointment should be made by the present executive. I have the honor to be Sir with great respect Y[ou]r ob[edient] Ser[van]t, Garret D. Wall.

ALS in DNA, RG 59 (State Department), Applications and Recommendations, 1845–1853, Vroom (M-873:89, frames 467–470).

From James W. Breedlove, "at Coleman's Hotel," Washington, 1/28. "I have the honor to hand herewith, a letter [of 11/20/1844] from Victor Roumage Esq[ui]r[e] of New Orleans appointing me his agent, and asking Information in relation to his claim against the Republic of New Greneda & Venezuella, which has been some years in charge of this Government. I should be pleased to be informed of the prospects of the recovery of this claim at your earliest convenience." ALS with En in DNA, RG 76 (Records of Boundary and Claims Commissions and Arbitrations), Miscellaneous Claims Records: Colombia, 1818–1825.

To EDWARD EVERETT, [London]

Department of State
Washington, Jan[uar]y 28th, 1845

Sir: The last steamer brought your despatch No. 216 [of 11/23/1844], giving an account of the conference between you and Lord Aberdeen in reference to the subject of my despatch No. 99 [of 8/7/1844].

I regret to say that the result is very unsatisfactory. The object of my despatch would seem to have been misunderstood. By reference to it, you will perceive that its leading object is to ascertain whether, according to the construction given by the British Government to the 10th article of the treaty of Washington, the *act* charged as a crime, must be such, in order to bring it within the provisions of the article, as would constitute the crime charged by the laws of the place where the fugitive criminal is found, as well as of that where it was committed.

The ground taken by the Nassau authorities in declining to surrender the slaves charged with murder and robbery in Florida, in the case to which my despatch refers, leaves no doubt that such is their opinion. It would be idle after an avowal of such an opinion on their part to take any further step in the case, until it is ascertained whether the Home Government will sustain the Colonial in it or not. To ascertain that, is the object of my former despatch.

Your account of the conference with Lord Aberdeen gives us nothing satisfactory on this important point. He, indeed, disavows the opinion of the Nassau Judges, except the portion which holds that an indictment is not sufficient in itself under the act of Parliament to carry the treaty into effect; and declares that the argument in illustration of the Court was not adopted by him; and, consequently as far as the Government was concerned, no inference like that on which my despatch dwelt, could be drawn from it. This, taken by itself, might be fairly considered as negativing the grounds taken by the Court—that the act charged as a crime must be such as the laws of the place where the fugitive criminal is found, as well as of that where it was perpetrated; and would be satisfactory were it not for the remarks which followed. I allude to those in which he says that "he did not, however, mean to say that in no case whatever which might arise hereafter, would the result of an application for the surrender of a fugitive charged with murder, depend in any degree upon the question whether he was a slave endeavoring to escape from his master. By the laws of all countries the same act of killing did or did not constitute the crime of murder, according to the circum-

217

stances of the case, which were often matters of very nice discrimination; and he could very well conceive that in cases which might arise, the fact of a person's being a slave might materially affect the question of his guilt on a charge of having committed murder. Her Majesty's Government must reserve to itself the liberty of dealing with cases of this kind when they present themselves and of being governed by circumstances which cannot be foreseen nor provided for, in any general regulations. He was, however, free to say that he did not share the opinion of those who hold that slaves as such cannot commit a crime. He regarded them as moral agents, and of course to be regarded in that light on a demand for extradition, leaving the consideration due to their condition as such to be decided by the circumstances of each individual case." The amount of these remarks as applied to this case is that the same act which may constitute the crime of murder in the United States may not constitute it in England; that the fact of the person charged with the commission of the crime being a slave, might materially affect the question of his guilt, according to the circumstances of the case, and that they were matters of nice discrimination, and that the home Government must, in consequence, assume to itself the liberty of deciding on cases of the kind.

It is admitted that an act which may constitute the crime of murder, in either of the two countries, may not constitute it in the other; not, however, because there is any difference between them in the definition of murder. It results from a different cause, which would seem to require from the remarks of Lord Aberdeen some explanation in order to a clear understanding of the subject.

In all such cases the cause may be traced, it is believed, to the fact that there are acts which are prohibited and made illegal in the two countries respectively that are not in the other. Whether a case of homicide in consequence of such act is murder, or not, in either, depends in such cases on the fact whether the act be prohibited and illegal or not in the country where it was committed. If it be illegal, it would; but if illegal [*sic*], it would not. Thus in England the killing of game, unless by certain privileged persons, is prohibited under severe penalties, and made illegal; while in the United States, there are no such laws. On the other hand, in many portions of this Union, including the Territory of Florida, domestic servitude is authorized by law, and it is made penal for a slave to resist the authority of his master, while in England it is abolished and prohibited by law. It results from this diversity between the laws of the two countries, in those cases, that it would be murder in England if an unauthorized person should kill an individual for attempting to arrest him save on his own premises; while in a similar case in the United States, where any man may lawfully kill game on his own premises, it would be regarded as justifiable homicide. The reverse would be the fact in the case of domestic servitude. In the portion of the Union where it exists, the act of killing ["which" *canceled*] would be murder in the slave attempting to escape from the authority of his master. It would not be so in England, because the relation which is legal in the former is prohibited in the latter. Other instances might be cited.

Nor is the difference confined to the case of murder. It extends to other crimes enumerated in the treaty. Take for example the case of forgery. Its definition is the same in both countries; but in both the acts constituting forgery depend upon particular municipal regulations, and are limited to special cases. Thus in England it is made forgery by particular acts of Parliament to forge a note of the Bank of England or the public securities of the country, or the stamps on which duties are collected—none of which constitute the crime of forgery by our laws. Examples of this kind might be cited on our side, and to which might be added many more, extending throughout the whole range of criminal legislation in both countries. Similar observations might with truth be doubtless made, in reference to nearly all other crimes enumerated in the treaty.

The remarks made by Lord Aberdeen in this connection, in regard to the difficulties which accrued in drawing up the Extradition Treaty between England and France, respecting the term murder in English, and *meurtre* in French, it seems to me are not relevant. There the difficulty grew out of the definition of the two words, which instead of being the same, (as the word murder is in the United States and England,) were of different signification—the latter comprehending several descriptions of crime which the former did not; and which therefore rendered additions to it necessary in order that the treaty might be made reciprocal in its operation between the two countries.

It is obvious from the preceding remarks that the question whether the criminality of the act is to be judged of by the laws of the country where the offence was committed or that where the fugitive may be found, is one of wide extent, and of the first magnitude in the construction of the treaty. We contend that it must be by the laws of the place where the crime was charged to have been committed, and not that where the fugitive is found; and hold that such construction is in strict conformity with the wording and true intent of the treaty; and that any other involves a palpable absurdity.

219

If our construction should be adopted by the Government of Her Majesty, ["though" *canceled*] all those nice discriminations and difficulties alluded to by Lord Aberdeen, and which would make it necessary to reserve the decision for the home Government, would vanish in this and the numerous other cases, as has been pointed out, on both sides, and which on any other construction would make the extradition portion of the treaty in a great measure nugatory. At all events, it is indispensably necessary that we should know what construction Her Majesty's Government intends to put on the article in question. It would make it indeed a one-sided contract if our Government should continue to place on it the construction we have, while that of Her Majesty adopts the one laid down by the Nassau Judges.

You are accordingly instructed to call again the attention of Her Majesty's Government to the subject, and to urge a speedy decision, in strong and earnest language.

In limiting my former despatch to the object to which it was confined, it was by no means intended to acquiesce in the construction given by the British Authorities to the statute for carrying the extradition article of the treaty into effect, that an indictment was not, of itself, sufficient evidence to warrant the arrest of the fugitive criminal; or that, if it did, the statute was consistent with the provisions of the article. On the contrary, the opposite opinion, it seems to me, is the sound one on both points. I limited it as I did, because I believed that the decision on the point it presented would certainly settle that in reference to the indictment; and that a decision could be more readily made on the former than on the latter. But as they are intimately united, and as we have been disappointed in getting a speedy and satisfactory answer, on the former, you are instructed to call the attention of Her Majesty's Government to, and obtain its decision on both. Indeed a decision that an indictment is sufficient evidence to warrant the commitment and delivery of the fugitive criminal would in a great measure decide both points and supersede the necessity of the other as the presentment of the Grand jury must always be founded on the criminality of the act according to the laws of the place where the crime was committed. I am, Sir, respectfully, Your obedient Servant, J.C. Calhoun.

LS (No. 120) in DNA, RG 84 (Foreign Posts), Great Britain, Instructions, 8:620–629, received 2/14; FC in DNA, RG 59 (State Department), Diplomatic Instructions, Great Britain, 15:241–247 (M-77:74); CC in DNA, RG 233 (U.S. House of Representatives), 28A-E1; PC in House Document No. 114, 28th Cong., 2nd Sess., pp. 9–12.

From S[amuel] C. Sample, [Representative from Ind.], 1/28. Peter Von Schmidt has petitioned the House of Representatives for compensation for a model of his "Pneumatic dry dock" that he furnished to the China mission at the instance of the State Department. As a member of the House Committee on Foreign Affairs, Sample has been requested to manage this petition. He asks Calhoun if Von Schmidt's request for $261.91 compensation is reasonable. ALS in DNA, RG 59 (State Department), Accounting Records: Miscellaneous Letters Received.

From CHARLES S. SIBLEY

Office U.S. Dist. Att[orne]y Mid[dle] Dist. of Florida
Tallahassee, January 28th 1845

Sir, I have the honor to acknowledge the receipt of your communication of the 20th instant, covering the Commission of his Excellency President [John] Tyler, to me, for the Office of Att[orne]y of the U.S. for the Middle District of Florida, for four years from the 15th instant—by and with the advice and consent of the Senate of the U.S. I have this day taken and subscribed the oaths of office before the Judge of this District, which have been filed in the clerk's Office of the Superior Court of this District in this City, and also endorsed on said Commission.

The course pursued by those who preferred accusations against me last summer has induced me to change the determination I had made to decline a continuance in this office. I was first appointed to it by President [Andrew] Jackson, re-appointed by President [Martin] Van Buren and being continued by Presidents [William H.] Harrison and Tyler, I was entirely willing if no unjust charges had been made against me, to have seen the Democratic principle of rotation in Office applied to me when my last commission expired. But the accusations preferred to your Department against my official conduct by Ex-Governor [Richard K.] Call and Mr. G.K. Walker demanded of me to pursue a different course. I feel that it is due to myself, to my friends, and also to public justice to accept this commission. No officer, conscious of rectitude, should be driven from the fulfilment of his duty to his Country by the calumnies of the wicked.

If I should after the next spring terms when I hope to have disposed of most of the important public prosecutions and civil suits now entrusted to my management surrender this Commission, it will be with the confidence that I shall have done nothing to encourage the enemies of public justice here, or the malevolent, to make charges against a successor for doing his duty fearlessly and impartially.

I trust however before then, the Office as a Territorial Office, may be abrogated by the recognition of Florida as a sovereign and independant member of the National Confederacy.

Be pleased Sir to convey to President Tyler my sincere declarations of respect for him personally, and gratitude for his public services, and accept for yourself like assurances. I am Sir Your Ob[edien]t Servant, Charles S. Sibley, U.S. Att[orne]y.

ALS in DNA, RG 59 (State Department), Acceptances and Orders for Commissions, 1845–1852.

From JOHN G. TOD

Washington-on-the-Brazos, Jan: 28th 1845

Sir, We had a message and accompanying documents today in the [Texas] Senate from the President [Anson Jones] upon the subject of annexation. I was present only to hear a portion of the same read. A motion was made to refer it to the Committee on Foreign Relations, by one of the Senators, who is known to entertain pretty much the opinions of the President. Another member made a motion to have it printed, as the Committee could throw no new light upon the subject, and the People were fully able to judge for themselves. This was objected to by another member on account of the expense, but amended the motion, that the Committee on printing make an arrangement to have the same printed in the [Washington, Texas, National] Register. This motion carried. I doubt whether they will be published this week, and as I expect to leave ["here" *interlined*] in a few days, I requested permission of one of the Senators to let me have the liberty of reading the accompanying documents; which was granted.

I was disappointed in not finding any thing of a late date, for I really expected from my conversations with different individuals here, who pretend to know much of our affairs, that some effective means were at work to offer us Independence.

I have taken a few extracts from Mr. [Ashbel] Smith's despatches (late Chargé to England and France) I am not sure but you have been furnished with copies of these documents by our Govt: I have been afraid to enquire, but if you have, you must only consider it as so much lost time in reading this.

In the despatch from

"London[,] 2nd June [18]44
In the course of the conversation, Lord Aberdeen said that Annexation would justify a War against the U.S. He also intimated clearly that in his opinion a decided representation to Mexico coming from the British Government as talked of, would not be unheeded nor unsuccessful. . . .

His remarks at this time have induc[e]d me to think that were the British and French Governments *assured* Texas would decline Annexation on condition of prompt and solid peace with Mexico, these Govts: would use *decisive* language to Mexico, even at the risk of themselves incurring a War."

From the same place under date of

"24th June [18]44
French & British Governments settle the whole matter by a *Diplomatic Act.* This Diplomatic act in which Texas would of course participate, would ensure peace and settle bounderies between Texas and Mexico, guarantee the seperate Independence of Texas &c. &c. . . .

A serious desire exists on the part of his Government to foster our interest provided we remain independent: and that Lord Aberdeen is prepared to adopt any proper course, all proper steps to bring about a peace with Mexico, if he felt assured that our Annexation to the American Union would in that event be prevented" . . . .

In a despatch shortly afterwards from Paris, he speaks of an interview he had with Louis Philip[p]e at Neuilly, "Of the lively interest the King of the French entertains for our having a *peace.*" The Chargé thinks "Commercial concessions could be made for our products with England & France, the latter power obtain for us, thro: her great influence with Spain, a recognition of our Independence, and great commercial facilities." All these things are to be done if Texas promises to give up the measure of annexation and remains independent. "The English & French Governments decidedly opposed to our annexation, and will act in the greatest harmony and union to procure us peace and Independence, and to prevent the union of Texas." &c. &c.

Now our Congress is to adjourn on next Monday: and I have no doubt this is the commencement of our Executive to open the war for "Independence and Commercial Relations with Europe."

It will all avail him nothing. If you can hold out a prospect, and offer this People annexation, any time this year or next, they will jump at it, unless they are out voted by Emigrants from Europe: of which I have no fear. Very Respectfully Your ob[edient] Servant, Jno: G. Tod.

ALS in ScCleA.

From A[NDREW] J. DONELSON, "Private"

New Orleans, Jan[uar]y 29, 1845

My D[ea]r Sir, The anticipated removal of the present incumbent of the office of Marshal in this District of La., by both parties, has produced, as is natural, many candidates for the vacancy. But it is said that the incumbent, Mr. [Algernon S.] Robinson, with the view of defeating the expression of public opinion on the subject will send in his resignation to you, with the expectation that an appointment will be made in his place, without a knowledge on the part of the President [John Tyler] of the wishes of the great mass of the people. If this should be attempted I trust you will advise the President of the propriety of his not acting hastily in the matter, or rather without knowing the state of public feeling here.

I make the suggestion in confidence to you at the instance of one of your friends in this city. I am very respectfully y[ou]r ob[edien]t ser[van]t, A.J. Donelson.

ALS in ScCleA.

From WILLIAM R. KING

Paris, January 29th 1845

My Dear Sir, I was much gratified by your very friendly letter of the 13th Dec[embe]r and I sincerely hope your anticipations may be reallised [*sic*], and this Congress may not adjourn without passing Mr. McDuffys [*sic*; George McDuffie's] resolutions for the annexation of Texas. I deeply regret the course pursued by Col. [Thomas H.] Benton, while I am at a loss to comprehend the motives which influence it. His position it seems to me is every way extraordinary, for while he professes to be desireous to promote the annexation of Texas, he cannot fail with his sagacity to see, that even should his Bill pass, it will in all human probability defeat the measure. All that England requires to perfect her plan of opperations, and to opperate successfully on Texas herself, is delay on our part to act deffinitively on the question. I am fully convinced of this from the change of op[inion; *ms. torn; one or two words missing*] produced on Ashbel Smith, [Texan Chargé d']Affair[e]s for France & England; He was the warm and decided advocate of annexation; but after making a visit to England and having an interview with Lord Abberdeen [*sic*], he avowed himself decidedly hostile to the measure. I entertain little doubt that he returns to Texas authorised to make proposals, or to use his influence to induce his Government to accept propositions which will be well calculated to produce their effect in Texas. Smith is a cautious man; yet in the conversations I have held with him he has thrown out remarks which convinced me that he will in this matter be a willing instrument in the hands of England. On more than one occasion he spoke of the time & *circumstances* being propitious for Texas to obtain the acknowledgement of her independence by Mexico. To procure the payment of her debt by granting certain commercial facilities to England; while at the same time the arrangement could be rendered greatly beneficial to Texas by a stipulation for the admission of her Cotton into British Ports free of duty. He did not say that these suggestions came from Lord Abberdeen, yet from the whole tenor of his conversations, he left that impression on my mind. Smith is the bosom Friend of the President elect, [Anson] Jones, and it is said will be his Secretary of State. I have thought it was but proper that you should understand his feelings and probable course. Would to God, our Congress could but understand the importance of prompt action to put an end to European intrigue, and the ultimate loss of that fine country, ["without" *canceled and* "unless" *interlined*] we resort to force to obtain it. The act done, we should hear no more of opposition on this side of the Atlantic. I shall use prudently the power you have given me to expend for [a] certain object $500. It is probable that nothing like that sum will be required, particularly if the contribution you mentioned should be made by the southern States. You do not direct on whom I shall draw—either do so, or transmit me a Bill for the amount. Tender my best respects to Mrs. [Floride Colhoun] Calhoun. Truly & faithfully I am your Ob[edien]t Ser[van]t, William R. King.

ALS in ScCleA; PC in Jameson, ed., *Correspondence*, pp. 1022–1023.

From WILLIAM R. KING

Legation of the United States
Paris, 29th January 1845

Sir, The publication of your instructions and despatches to me, produced quite a sensation here, as well as in England. On the other side of the channel the effect was disappointment and anger. The British papers not only accused this government of neglecting the interests of France in the Texas question; they did not hesitate to charge it with duplicity and treachery towards England. The public impression here was that of satisfaction, mingled with some regret on the part of the opposition that the ministry had not been guilty of the unwise and impolitic course of which it had been suspected and accused. I have deemed it the part both of policy and dignity to presume that the declarations of the government are entirely to be relied upon, unless retracted or modified in an authentic quarter. Of course I have not permitted myself to interrogate the ministry so long as it remained silent; but I have narrowly watched the course of its acknowledged organs. These have published your despatches without a word of contradiction or even of comment. The King [Louis Philippe] and his minister [F.P.G. Guizot] have both had opportunities of conversing with me upon the subject, but as they did not take advantage of them, I maintained a proper and prudent reserve. Public opinion would have strongly condemned any action of this government, unfriendly to the United States in their difficulties or disagreements with Mexico and England, and, as I have just observed, the Opposition was very sorry to be deprived of so popular a ground of attack. Indeed, I have supposed, that in the present critical conjuncture of affairs, the ministry was happy to be relieved of an imputation, which if just, would have rivetted the leading reproach against it, of excessive, if not humiliating deference to England. Whatever then, may be the personal dispositions of the Cabinet, or rather of its leader, irresistible popular opinion would forbid offensive or active interference against the annexation of Texas, even were ["not" *canceled*] the ministry not restrained by embarrassments which almost threaten its existence.

The election of presiding officers at the opening of the Session of the Chamber of Deputies, and still more the discussion of the address in reply to the Royal speech, revealed a serious defection in the ranks of the habitual supporters of the ministry. Its majorities have been small and fluctuating, and its fate is certainly somewhat problematical. There is wavering in the ranks, and, as in all such cases, timorous or suspicious friends may suddenly become open enemies. I will not venture to predict the result of what is generally admitted to be a ministerial crisis. The ministry may sustain itself but its march will be less steady and assured. Divided as the Chamber is, into so many shades and fractions, it is impossible to foretell the issue with such shifting and diversified elements of calculation. It is not prudent to predict when it is impossible for the ["str" *canceled*] shrewdest to tell what a day may bring forth. The paragraph of the address approving the conduct of the ministry in the Tahiti affair, was adopted but by eight votes, including ministers, a result which was admitted to be almost equivalent to a defeat. Yet the cabinet, strong in the cordial support of the King, has announced its intention to remain.

It is fortunate for us at this conjuncture, that nearly all the charges against the cabinet resolve themselves into that of subserviency to England; so that neither the present nor a future ministry can cooperate efficiently with Great Britain against the policy of the United States. Under this aspect the present posture of affairs here is of no small interest to our country.

The "right of search" treaties have accomplished little besides wounding the pride of the French people, and rendering odious the "entente cordiale," cordial understanding, which has been proclaimed with such ["prudent" *canceled*] imprudent ostentation by this government. During the debate upon the address in the Chamber of Peers, an amendment was moved to the effect that the *French Navy should be speedily replaced under the* ["surveillance" *canceled*] *exclusive surveillance of the national flag.* The ministry found it necessary to declare its adhesion to this important amendment, which was unanimously carried. The amended paragraph was adopted with like unanimity in the lower House, where, during the di[s]cussion, the refusal of the United States to submit to this odious right or rather wrong, was referred to in the most flattering and effective manner. Upon this subject, public opinion in France is almost, if not quite, united. Mr. Guizot announced the fact that England had consented to a revision of these obnoxious Treaties, provided something equally effectual can be found to repress the slave trade, for which purpose a commission is to be appointed. It is understood that the two commissioners will be the Duc de Broglie on the part of France, and Dr. [Stephen] Lushington on that of England, names which do not inspire much confidence, as both these gentlemen, however respectable, are known to be ardent abolitionists. I do not know that much will be accomplished by the expedient, but it is a satisfactory symptom of the force of public opinion against the politico-fanatical policy of

England, to which, it is to be feared, this government was too much inclined, or constrained, to lend itself. In connection with this subject, it may not be amiss to mention a circumstance which is not without interest. Upon inquiring a few days since, of the Chargé d'Affaires of Spain, the probable fate in the Cortes of the new bill for the suppression of the slave trade, he stated that it had passed the upper House, and would probably succeed in the lower, where a report in its favor had been made by the committee, but that hopes had been held out, if not assurances given by England, that the "pontons" would be removed. By pontons, ["tho" *canceled*] I understand those floating depots of liberated Africans which have excited so much offence and alarm in Cuba.

To revert to the ministerial crisis here, I must not omit to state my opinion that a change in the cabinet will not interrupt the friendly relations between France and England. All the leaders of the Opposition disclaimed the charge of hostility to England, while they maintained that the policy of France should be more independent of British influence or dictation. This is all we can require or desire.

Should the present ministry fall, Count [Louis-Mathieu] Molé will probably be at the head of the new cabinet, and it is understood that Mr. [Louis-Adolphe] Thiers has promised him the support of his friends. Mr. Thiers has, in conversation, ["t" *canceled*] expressed his unqualified disapproval of the surmised cooperation of France with England upon the Texas question, and his sentiments upon this subject have been strongly reflected by his acknowledged organ of the press. Count Molé has been generally considered the representative of the Russian *alliance* as contradistinguished from the English alliance; but this is a circumstance of little significance at this moment, as he ["had" *canceled*] has declared himself favorable to the maintenance of friendly relations with England, while he has condemned ["that" *canceled and* "the" *interlined*] exaggeration of this policy which he characterized as "la politique à outrance," a principle strained to a dangerous extreme.

In accordance with your instructions I have delivered to the authorized representative of the Spanish government at this Court, coupons corresponding to the amount of sixty thousand dollars, and his receipt for the same is herewith transmitted.

I have the honor to transmit also, an extract, communicated to me by the Minister of Foreign Affairs, from a report addressed to the Minister of Marine, containing information of the loss of the ship Elizabeth of New Orleans, a part of the crew of which was rescued by a French Ship on her voyage to Mexico. I have the honor to be very respectfully your obedient servant, William R. King.

LS (No. 10) with Ens in DNA, RG 59 (State Department), Diplomatic Despatches, France, vol. 30 (M-34:33), received 2/22.

From J.G. Klenck, Publisher of the National Zeitung, Washington, 1/29. "In answer to your note of the 23d inst. transmitting the authority for publishing the laws of the U. States in the 'National Zeitung,' I would reply that the appointment is accepted, and beg leave to state that payment for publishing the laws is to be made to me or my order." (A Clerk's EU reads "German National Gazette accepts.") ALS in DNA, RG 59 (State Department), Miscellaneous Letters Received Regarding Publishers of the Laws.

From ROBERT WALSH

Consulate of the United States of America, Paris
Paris, Jan[uar]y 29 1845

My Dear Sir, As the printed scraps heretofore sent to you have proved not unacceptable, I transmit a packet herewith, containing various editorial notices of the last day's debate on the Address, in the Chamber of Deputies, & the condition of the Cabinet down to this day. The English matter possesses some interest & may have escaped the notice of your purveyors in London. I would call your attention to the review (from the [London] Morning Chronicle) of the Oregon question. It is from a Source of authority official or personal. Encouraged by your letter of the 29th ult[im]o I may venture to indite a political epistle to you, on the 1st Feb[ruar]y, for the Steamer of the 4th, so that you may have the most recent facts & notions. The newspapers announce that the Senate have been pleased to confirm my nomination; but as I remain uncertain with regard to the dispositions of Mr. [James K.] Polk, I cannot yet (to use the vulgar phrase) "lay myself out" for the execution of the plans of office & public service which seem to me desirable. I am, Dear Sir, with the highest respect, your very ob[edien]t Serv[an]t, Robert Walsh.

ALS in ScCleA.

From HENRY WHEATON

Berlin, 29 Jan. 1845

Sir, In pursuance of the Instructions contained in your Despatch, No. 59 [of 8/23/1844], I have this day concluded & signed the Convention herewith enclosed, between the United States & Prussia, with certain other German States, for the mutual extradition of fugitives from justice in certain cases.

The terms of the Convention require no other explanation than what will be found in Mr. Secretary [Daniel] Webster's despatch, No. 39, with its enclosures, containing the original projet of the Convention, as agreed upon between him & Mr. [Friedrich Ludwig] von Roenne, Minister of Prussia to the United States; in my despatch No. 238, with its enclosures, containing the alterations proposed by the Prussian cabinet in the projet, with my observations thereon; and in your despatch, No. 59, authorizing me to assent to those alterations.

Your despatches, Nos. 61, 62, & 63, have been received, & due attention will be paid to their contents. I have the honor to be, with the highest consideration, Sir, y[ou]r ob[e]d[ien]t Serv[an]t, Henry Wheaton.

P.S. I beg leave to add that, as the Convention is subject to the ratification of each of the sovereigns & States of Germany therein enumerated, it will be necessary to transmit as many different Ratifications, on our part, as there are parties to the Convention on their part. H.W.

LS (No. 258) in DNA, RG 46 (U.S. Senate), 30B-B8, received 3/21; FC with En in DNA, RG 84 (Foreign Posts), Germany, Despatches, 4:169–176; CC in DNA, RG 59 (State Department), Diplomatic Despatches, Germany, vol. 3 (M-44:4).

From H[ENRY] WHEATON, "Private"

Berlin, 29 Jan. 1845

My dear Sir, Many thanks for your kind & confidential Letter of the 26 December.

I am very sorry to perceive by it that our divided & distracted councils render it doubtful whether you will continue in the Administration after the 4 March. The public interests must continue to suffer, as they have suffered for several years, by this want of *con-*

tinuity in the conduct of our foreign affairs which prevents any steady & intelligible line of policy being pursued in respect to our political & commercial relations with other Nations. I shall however cherish the hope, to the last moment, that the dissentions in the democratic party may be healed, so that you may find it consistent with your own feelings & views to remain in office.

As respects my own concerns, I mentioned to you in a Letter from Paris that I had ["wr" *canceled*] addressed the President [John Tyler] on the subject of my transfer, & am sure that you will support it with your opinion should *he advert to the subject*, or should an occasion occur in which you can, *with propriety*, break it to him. I am anxious to be useful to the public in a sphere of greater activity now that all the special objects of my mission here have been accomplished.

Baron [Heinrich] de Bulow has received despatches from Mr. Gerold [*sic*; Friedrich von Gerolt] coinciding with the information you give me as to the Zollverein treaty being again before the Senate. I continue still to be of the opinion that the most advantageous mode of revising the Tariff is by obtaining from foreign Powers equivalent concessions ["for" *canceled*] on our agricultural staples for the reductions we make on their manufactures, by which means the tariff question may be *finally* settled to the satisfaction of the planting States, without any material injury to the interests of the manufacturing classes, & to the great advantage of the navigation & commerce of the middle & northern States.

We send you today the treaty of extradition, which I hope will arrive in time to be laid before the Senate & ratified at the present Session. I beg leave to suggest the expediency of communicating to that Body the several papers enumerated in my Despatch, although I do not anticipate any objection to the ratification, as the arrangement is substantially the same with that contained in our recent Treaties with France & G. Britain.

I have desired a Copy of my Work upon the history of the Law of Nations recently published to be sent to you, which I have to request you will accept as a small token of my respect & esteem.

I had the pleasure on my way thro' Brussels to see Mr. [Thomas G.] Clemson & your daughter [Anna Maria Calhoun Clemson] who were in good health & spirits. I requested Mr. Clemson to write me whenever any thing should occur in respect to which he might wish to have another opinion, & he very cordially responded to this proposal. I am, my dear Sir, ever truly & faithfully your obliged friend, H. Wheaton.

ALS in ScCleA.

To JA[ME]S W. BREEDLOVE, Washington

Department of State
Washington, 30 Jan[uar]y 1845

Sir, I have to acknowledge the receipt of your two letters of the 28th instant and to inform you in reply that the representatives of the United States accredited to the Governments of New Granada, Venezuela and Ecuador are instructed upon the subject of the claim in the case of the Sarah Wilson, but this Department cannot form an opinion when it will be adjusted.

It is a rule of this Government to interfere by its good offices only for the recovery of claims of citizens of the U.S. on foreign governments originating in contracts. The claim of Mr. Victor Roumage founded upon his tobacco contract with authorities of the late Republic of Colombia will be prosecuted accordingly it being understood that the United States are not to enforce payment of the claim in the event of its being refused by the parties from whom it is due. I am &c, J.C. Calhoun.

FC in DNA, RG 59 (State Department), Domestic Letters, 35:94–95 (M-40:33).

From A[NDREW] J. DONELSON, "Private"

New Orleans, Jan[uar]y 30[t]h 1845

D[ea]r Sir, I reached this place last night and deposited with the postmaster, my letters to the Department relating to my public business. They will be a day in advance of this letter.

The British & French ministers at Galvezton are very active in their exertions against annexation, but have been deterred by the great fatality among the inhabitants at the seat of Government, from visiting that place. They report that no measure consummating annexation can get more than Twenty votes in our Senate: and that their information is from *high & responsible sources.* I hope they will be disappointed, even if the measure be limitted [*sic*] to the mere extension to Texas of the provisions contained in the 3d article of the Treaty in regard to La. The main point is to get the country, leaving for the future as they will be presented by Texas in her constitution, the difficulties, respecting slavery, the number of States & &.

I endeavored to sound Elliott [*sic*; Charles Elliot, British Chargé d'Affaires to Texas] in regard to his views about California and the

232

occupation of the country between the Nuesoes [*sic*] and the Rio Grande. My object was to get a clue to the mortgage, said by Gen[era]l [Duff] Green, to be held by Great Britain on a large portion of that country to secure the debts of British subjects. If there be any reality in that mortgage, as understood by Gen[era]l Green, Elliott knew how to keep it to himself.

My belief is that Elliott is sick of his position, and feels that interference with the annexation question was a false move for his Govt. He is saying boldly that the country is overrated, but affects great concern about the extension of slavery, insinuating that it will dissolve our Union, and, if Texas is annexed, bring upon her our troubles. He is a shrewd and cunning man, and of course is to be understood more by his actions than his words.

Not finding my wife [Elizabeth Randolph Donelson] here as I expected I shall proceed directly from this place to Nashville. I can go up and back again in about three weeks, and be ready to execute your instructions, should there ["be" *interlined*] any for me on my return. In addition to a necessity for attention to my private business, I wish to see Gen[era]l [Andrew] Jackson whose life hangs on a thread. I desire to converse with him particularly on the subject of his personal relations ["to you" *interlined*], which were brought to my notice by Governor [John] Branch [of Fla. Territory], and which I hope can be placed on such a footing as to take from them all impeachment of the character or motives of either of you. I am very respectfully y[ou]r ob[edien]t ser[van]t, A.J. Donelson.

ALS in ScCleA; PC in Jameson, ed., *Correspondence,* pp. 1023–1024.

To J O H N W. J O N E S , Speaker of the House of Representatives

Department of State
Washington, Jan[uar]y 30 1845

Sir, In compliance with the Resolution of the House of Representatives of the 14th instant, directing the Secretary of State "to communicate to this House such information as he may possess, of the whole amount of the debt of Texas—the amount for which land or Scrip have been issued, and the present market value of such scrip or bonds in Texas, in the United States and in Europe—the amount in value of the exports from, and the imports into Texas, for the Years

1843 and 1844, with the amount of revenue accruing and collected for the same Years, with the expenditure for the same time; also the present population of Texas, distinguishing in number between free and Slaves; also the quantity in acres of land which it is supposed is covered by valid grants from the present and former Government of that Country, and the estimated quantity in acres of good and arable land, suitable for cultivation which remains ungranted within the undisputed limits of Texas, as the same existed prior to the year 1834." I have the honor to transmit herewith a copy of a communication received from Charles H. Raymond Esq. Chargé d'Affaires of the Republic of Texas of date the 23d instant, which, with the Documents already communicated, accompanying the President[']s messages of the 10th of June 1844 and of the 3rd of December 1844 contain all the information in the possession of this Department in reference to the subjects of inquiry proposed by the Resolution of the House. I have the honor to be very Respectfully Your Ob[edien]t Servant, J.C. Calhoun.

LS in DNA, RG 233 (U.S. House of Representatives), 28A-F1; FC in DNA, RG 59 (State Department), Reports of the Secretary of State to the President and Congress, 6:142; PC with En in House Document No. 101, 28th Cong., 2nd Sess., pp. 1–2; PC with En in the Washington, D.C., *Daily National Intelligencer,* February 6, 1845, p. 2; PC with En in *Niles' National Register,* vol. LXVIII, no. 1 (March 8, 1845), p. 4. NOTE: The resolution to which this is a response can be found in DNA, RG 59 (State Department), Miscellaneous Letters (M-179:107, frame 48) and in *House Journal,* 28th Cong., 2nd Sess., p. 209.

To [J.G. Klenck], Publisher of the German National Gazette, Washington, 1/30. "As to furnish each paper, selected to publish the laws, resolutions, &c., mentioned in the letter of appointment to you of the 23rd instant, with copies of them, would put the Department to much inconvenience, they will be sent to the publisher of the 'Madisonian' only, from which paper you will be pleased to have them copied into your own." FC in DNA, RG 59 (State Department), Domestic Letters, 35:94 (M-40:33).

To S[amuel] C. Sample, [Representative from Ind.], 1/30. In reply to Sample's letter of 1/28, Calhoun states that the funds appropriated for the expenses of the Chinese mission were placed in the hands of [Caleb Cushing] the Commissioner and [Fletcher Webster] Secretary of that mission. Peter Von Schmidt's request for compensation for his "Pneumatic dry dock" should have been made to those officers and paid by them. Letterpress copy in DNA, RG 59 (State

Department), Accounting Records: Miscellaneous Letters Sent, vol. for 10/3/1844–5/29/1845, p. 211.

From John L. Stephens, 55 Wall St., New York [City], 1/30. On behalf of William H. Brown, Aaron Fuller, and John Bontey[?], owners of the steamboat *Planter*, Stephens claims compensation of $133,000 for various losses occasioned by the impressment of that vessel and crew into military service by Mexican authorities at Tabasco. Stephens hopes that Calhoun "will consider it within the province of your department to enforce the payment" of the claim. When requested to do so, Stephens will furnish proof of the claims. ALS in DNA, RG 76 (Records of Boundary and Claims Commissions and Arbitrations), Records of U.S. and Mexican Claims Commissions.

To President [JOHN TYLER]

Department of State
Washington, January 30th 1845

To the President of the United States.

The Secretary of State, to whom has been referred the Resolution of the Senate of the 2nd inst. requesting the President "to communicate to the Senate a copy of the letter [of 9/21/1844] of Mr. [Wilson] Shannon to the Department of State communicating the note of the Mexican Secretary of State [Manuel C. Rejon] in relation to the payment of the April and July instalments of the Mexican indemnity to the agent appointed by the United States to receive the indemnities under the Convention of 1843.

Also, to communicate to the Senate the name of the agent appointed to receive said indemnities, and the security if any, which may have been taken for the faithful performance of his duty, and the terms and condition of his appointment.

Also whether said agent has communicated any information to the authorities of the United States in relation to the non-payment of the instalments of the said indemnities due in April and July last.

Also to communicate to the Senate a statement of the indemnities actually paid to the United States agent, with the date of such payment to him, the date of the receipt of the money so paid at the Treasury of the United States, and a statement of the costs and charges made and allowed against such instalments before paid to the claimants"—Has the honor to transmit herewith copies of sundry documents on the files of this Department, numbered from 1 to — inclusive; and which contain all the information in its possession, having reference to the subjects of inquiry proposed by the Senate.

It may be proposed to observe that no communication has been received from Mr. Shannon in relation to the non-payment of the indemnities due in April and July last, since the date of his despatch of the 21st of September last. The note of Mr. [Ben E.] Green, the Secretary of the United States Legation at Mexico, who is now in this City, dated the 25th instant, (a copy of which is herewith communicated) explains the reasons which may probably have induced Mr. Shannon to defer any further communication in reference to the subject until he should have been fully satisfied that the assurances given in Mr. Rejon's note of the 2nd of September last would not be complied with. Respectfully submitted. J.C. Calhoun.

FC in DNA, RG 59 (State Department), Reports of the Secretary of State to the President and Congress, 6:143; PC with Ens in Senate Document No. 81, 28th Cong., 2nd Sess., pp. 1–21. NOTE: Tyler transmitted this to the Senate on 2/3. The resolution to which this is a response can be found in DNA, RG 59 (State Department), Miscellaneous Letters (M-179:107, frames 6–7) and in *Senate Journal*, 28th Cong., 2nd Sess., p. 64.

To President [JOHN TYLER]

Department of State
Washington, 30th January 1845

The Secretary of State to whom has been referred a resolution of the House of Representatives, of the 23d instant, has the honor to report to the President, that this Department has not any information to shew that any of the Officers of the United States connected with it, have been guilty of embezzlement of publick money since the 19th of August 1841. J.C. Calhoun.

LS in DNA, RG 233 (U.S. House of Representatives), 28A-E1; PC in House Document No. 96, 28th Cong., 2nd Sess. NOTE: Tyler transmitted this letter to the House of Representatives on 2/3. The resolution to which this is a response can be found in DNA, RG 59 (State Department), Miscellaneous Letters (M-179:107, frame 93) and in *House Journal*, 28th Cong., 2nd Sess., p. 249.

To HENRY M. WATTS, U.S. Dist[rict] Att[orne]y, [Philadelphia]

Department of State
Washington, January 30th 1845

Sir, A despatch was received yesterday from George W[illia]m Gordon Esq[ui]r[e] U.S. Consul at Rio de Janeiro, enclosing depositions against Capt. Hiram Gray & W[illia]m M. Ruhl late of the Brig "Agnes" & one R.S. Gough, implicating them in aiding & abetting, in a most positive manner, the Slave Trade—that they may be arrested, under the Laws of the United States for the suppression of that trade—& also enclosing a copy of a communication addressed to you, requesting the immediate arrest of the said parties, if found in your District. The object of this letter is, in case that communication has not reached you, to call your attention to the enclosed copy of it & to request that the promptest & strictest measures may be taken by you to secure the arrest of the persons therein named—of the result of which you will please advise the Department. I am, Sir, Very Respectfully Your obedient Servant, J.C. Calhoun.

P.S. A similar letter to this has been written to the District Attornies of the U. States, at N. York, New Castle [Del.], Princeton & Baltimore. From information received it is believed that William M. Ruhl, is now in Philadelphia.

LS in PHi, Gratz Collection; FC in DNA, RG 59 (State Department), Consular Instructions, 11:331–332.

From EDWARD EVERETT

London, 31 January, 1845

Sir, I transmit herewith Lord Aberdeen's reply received last evening to my note of the 8th instant, which accompanies my despatch Nro. 247, relative to the intercourse with Hong Kong in United States' vessels. It appears that while, somewhat contrary to my expectations, it is the present purpose of this Government to apply the Navigation Law to that island, the direct voyage from the United States is unquestionably legal.

It is scarcely necessary to say, that in presenting this subject to Lord Aberdeen's consideration, in consequence of the letter of Messrs. Brown and Shipley of the 24th of October, I had no thought of inviting a discussion of the general policy of the Navigation Law. The erection of Hong Kong into a free port was itself an exceptional measure, and it was of course a natural subject of enquiry how far the relaxation would extend. It was generally understood in this city and at Liverpool, that no restrictions whatever would be imposed on the Commercial intercourse with Hong Kong.

It is, however, a matter in itself of but little consequence. You will, however doub[t]less regard Lord Aberdeen's note as one of great significance. It seems to be an overture toward a reconsideration of the entire system of the Navigation Laws as between the two Countries. The only reason which would lead one to doubt whether so much can be intended is the unimportant nature of the occasion of making the suggestion.

Lord Aberdeen is, at present, at Windsor and it is doubtful whether I shall be able to have a conference with him before the departure of the steamer. But I shall lose no time in ascertaining the design, with which the suggestion alluded to has been made, and if possible the extent to which they are willing to go in modifying the Navigation Law and the Colonial System, which have hitherto been regarded as essential parts of the public policy of the British Empire. I am, Sir, with great respect, Your obedient Servant, Edward Everett.

Transmitted with despatch Nro. 251;
The Earl of Aberdeen to Mr. Everett, 27 January, 1845.

LS (No. 251) with En in DNA, RG 59 (State Department), Diplomatic Despatches, Great Britain, vol. 54 (M-30:50), received 2/22; FC in DNA, RG 84 (Foreign Posts), Great Britain, Despatches, 9:145–147; FC in MHi, Edward Everett Papers, 51:179–181 (published microfilm, reel 23, frames 643–644).

From GEO[RGE] S. HOUSTON, [Representative from Ala.]

Ho[use] of Rep[resentative]s, 31 Jan[uar]y [18]45
Sir, During the last session of Congress at my instance this House made a call upon the President [John Tyler] for the correspondence between the U.S. & Mexico growing out of the convention of 1839 (I think is the date) & the claims of our citizens against that government. The call has not been responded to. You will remember that I called to see you in person in relation to that correspondence at which time I was informed that the copy had been lost but was then found and I might look for it to be sent in to the House in a few days.

I have waited for near two months & it has not come in. I would be pleased for you to give it your earliest convenient attention. I have the honor to be D[ea]r Sir Y[ou]r fr[ien]d & ob[edien]t Serv[an]t, Geo. S. Houston.

ALS in ScCleA.

From C[HRISTOPHER] HUGHES, "Private"

The Hague: 31 Jan. 1845

My dear Mr. Calhoun, Here is a Ship from the Chesapeake at Rotterdam with a Box of "*Chawing*" tobacco—from Y[ou]r Excellency—to [Thomas G.] Clemson; & the "Backy" can't be *got hold* of—out of the *hold* of "the Katherine Jackson"—without *my* Instrumentality! Now—I'll lend my aid—in no such *Vices!* How can you encourage such doings? Here is [Sir James] Hudson (Fox's Secretary) as good a fellow as ever lived: & Baron Vincent Treyll[?]—who has married *one* of My Nieces (not 2 of them; so goes the *idiom*; "*one* of my &") a Grand Daughter of Gen. [Samuel] Smith—Miss Charlotte Mansfield—who came here to see my Daughter & found a Husband (Baron Treyll has also been in U.S.[)] & [William S.] Campbell—a clever capable fellow—& doing his Consul's duties well at Rotterdam; & I recommend him to your notice & protection—as a true American—& *very competent* in his office; [Charles] Nichols—at Amsterdam—is a *Regular Ass*—& really such "*a Spoon*"—that it is pitiful; burn this; or—as old [Richard B.?] Sheridan says—"it is *true*; but if you *repeat* it—I'll *deny* it"! Here are *all* these, & Clemson to boot—all more or less *Yankees*; "*chawing*"; and deluging *Holland* (this *Water*loo Land naturally) & disgracing America! &—unless a very unwarrantable use—is made of y[ou]r name—*You* are encouraging them. Sir, it is a shame! Now—if the Boys—would take Snuff (*as I do*—& in Lots) why—*that* would be all—allowable & perfectly legitimate & Gentlemenlike "I *reckon.*"

I suppose—I shall have to get the "*Bakky*" out of Limbo—& enable Campbell to send it on—to comfort Clemson! But seriously—I dont think he ought to *chew*; it certainly can do his Chest no good—tall & thin as he is. By the way he is a very clever fellow; getting on well—& has made a *most successful* impression upon Court—Government—Society & Colleagues at Brussels. King Leopold *told me so—both at Paris—& in his own Palace*; & I am happy to so assure you. Mrs.

[Anna Maria Calhoun] Clemson is exceedingly liked & admired & she has *promised me*—to apply herself to French; for everybody regrets that she dont speak it; & she *must* learn it. I saw y[ou]r Grand Children [John Calhoun Clemson and Floride Elizabeth Clemson] & nice little creatures they are! Your Daughter is certainly y[ou]r Daughter: I never "saw the *like*" of that *Likeness*. I enclose you a Letter just received from Colonel [William H.] Daingerfield—Texan Chargé d'affaires at this—Hague—Court; & a very clever & most respectable young man; amazingly improved since in Europe! a Marylander & cousin to my nephew & nieces—the children of Col. Geo[rge] Armistead! Let me say—that King Leopold spoke to me—most highly of your famous Despatch to Mr. King—which has "Kicked up a great Row" in Europe. Who cares? We dont I *guess*. Y[ou]rs truly, C. Hughes.

[Enclosure]

W[illia]m Henry Daingerfield to [Christopher] Hughes

Hotel de Russie, Berlin, Jan[uar]y 26th 1845

My very dear and most kind Friend, Your most acceptable and truly amusing letter of the 19th & 20th Inst. reached me yesterday morning; Last evening I went to Baron [Friedrich Ludwig von] Roenne and did every thing which you requested me to do except deliver him the letter which I did not find enclosed. I did not fail to ask Mad[emoise]lle Adelaide what a clock it was much to the amusement of Baron & Barroness, Pere et Mere; Among other persons there, were Mr. [Theodore S.] Fay & Mr. Johnson (son of Reverdy of Baltimore) so that you were quite amongst y[ou]r friends, and we did nothing for a good half hour, ["than" *interlined*] talk of nobody else but you & Miss Margaret [Hughes], who would be quite overcome if she were to hear repeated all the kind and admiring remarks made about her. My humble voice joined most *sinc[e]rely* in the general chorus ["to" *altered to* "of"] y[ou]r praises. Mr. [Henry] Wheaton I saw this morning and delivered your messages to him; The Duc Dalmatic I have not seen & shall not see as I leave here for Vienna tomorrow, where I am called by some business with the German-Texan Emigration Society; Baron Roenne & Mr. Wheaton, are both of the opinion, that in the present state of the Texan question with the United States a presentation to Baron [Heinrich von] Bulow, Min[ister of] Aff[ai]r[es] Etrangeres or any other *official visit* would be useless on my part; Prince Frederick of Prussia sent for me the other day & had a long conversation with me; Baron Roenne, Mr. Wheaton & Mr. Fay all send their kindest remembrances to you. Barroness R[oenne] requests & so does Mr. Fay that you would send each of them a copy of

Miss Hughes['s] letter. I am charged by the Baroness & Mad[emoi-se]lle Adelaide, to present through you to Miss Margaret, their kind-est and most affectionate remembrances to which, may I beg leave to add my own most respectfull salutations & to assure her of the very sincere pleasure it afforded me to hear her praises from persons so competent to judge of female excellence; Laudari a Laudatis, (the latin is for you not for Miss Margaret, and as a set off to y[ou]r *cudat*[?]) is always most agreeable. Baron R[oenne] & Mr. Wheaton have promised me to keep the question of recognition in case Texas shall not be annexed before the Prussian Gover[n]ment, untill the "Ides of March" shall have determined the fate of that Republic. Should Texas be annexed, by this Congress I shall only return to the Hague on my way home, which may be some time next summer. Under my circumstances my present determination is to return to the U.S. in the course of the ensuing Autumn; I am sure you will not fail to write to me at Vienna where I expect to remain all the month of February. You who are so scrupulously neat in all that concerns letters & letter writing must have been horrified with the appearance of a document so suspicious as that which you received for me at Paris, and had the goodness to forward to me here. It ["was" *can-celed and* "is" *interlined*] a copy of the Articles of Agreem[en]t as to the division between my Brother & myself of our Lands & negroes in Md. and ["was" *altered to* "is"] the work of a Maryland Lawyer. My negroes have all been sent to Louisianna and my Md. Land all sold at a good price; I am sure you will not feel so angrily towards that homely paper when I assure you it contained most satisfactory intel-ligence of my private affairs. From the Gover[n]ment of Texas I have heard officially nothing since my leave of absence which I shewed you & which you considered merely *facultative*; I shall con-tinue to consider it in that light untill I hear further from them.

I am quite gratified that you consider the opinions I formed of men & things at Hamburgh correct; I brought my matters there to the only practicable termination, viz a ratification of the treaty by Bre-men, and a written promise from the Minister, at the former place to ratify it ["in" *interlined*] case annexation did not take place ["before" *canceled*] during the present session of Congress; I could do no more. I am charmed to hear that you amused y[ou]rself so much, at Paris[,] London, & Dublin; Hudson writes me that you have returned quite renovated in spirits & health. Allow me to put my answer to his letter under this cover. Ask him to write to me at Vienna—And let me beg of you to do the same; You would really take the trouble of writing to me often if you only knew how much pleasure y[ou]r letters give me. Excuse the annoyance, the forwarding my letters may cause you. I am sure you will not be inflicted with any similar to that Doc[u-men]t so severely criticised, by you & so justly too. My best respects to those who have not *forgotten me* & my *love* to Hudson. He is all that you say of him. For yourself my dear & most respected friend accept the sincerest expressions of my respectfull love & esteem & believe me me [*sic*] ever faithfully yours, Wm. Henry Daingerfield.

ALS with En in ScCleA.

From Littleton Kirkpatrick, [Representative from N.J.], 1/31. Kirkpatrick seeks information from the State Department concerning the 1829 claim of Henry Dolliver against the Mexican government. This claim relates to the cargo of the American schooner *Lady of the Lake* and amounts, with interest, to $26,840. ALS in DNA, RG 59 (State Department), Miscellaneous Letters (M-179:107, frame 139).

To Farnham L. Tucker, New York [City], 1/31. Calhoun has received Tucker's letter of 1/24 seeking appointment to be U.S. Consul at Truxillo [*sic*; Trujillo, Honduras]. He reports that A. Follin is currently Consul at Omoa and Trujillo and it is not deemed necessary to establish a separate Consulate at Trujillo. However, if warranted, Follin will be authorized to establish a commercial agency at that place and to appoint Tucker to that post. Tucker is requested to notify the State Department if this arrangement is acceptable. FC in DNA, RG 59 (State Department), Consular Instructions, 11: 332–333.

To President [JOHN TYLER]

Department of State
January 31st 1845

To the President of the United States.

The Secretary of State to whom has been referred the Resolution of the House of Representatives of the 16th instant requesting the President to "communicate to this House any information possessed by this Government of the metes and bounds, or latitude and longitude of the Territory of the Republic of Texas, within which the authority and jurisdiction of the said Republic is recognized by the inhabitants dwelling within the said latitude and longitude: and also copies of all existing Treaties of the Republic of Texas with Powers other than the United States," has the honor, in reply thereto, to transmit herewith, printed copies of two Treaties now subsisting between the Republic of Texas, and the Government of Great Britain and France respectively; and a map of the territory of Texas compiled in the Bureau of the Corps of Topographical Engineers by Lieut. W[illiam] H. Emery [*sic*; Emory] under the direction of Col. J[ohn] J. Abert, exhibiting the boundaries of said Territory according to the best sources of information in the possession of the Department. Respectfully submitted, J.C. Calhoun.

LS in DNA, RG 233 (U.S. House of Representatives), 28A-E1; FC in DNA, RG 59 (State Department), Reports of the Secretary of State to the President and Congress, 6:144; PC with Ens in House Document No. 98, 28th Cong., 2nd Sess., pp. 1–11. NOTE: This was transmitted by Tyler to the House of Representatives on 2/3. The resolution to which the report is a reply can be found in DNA, RG 59 (State Department), Miscellaneous Letters (M-179:107, frame 63) and in *House Journal*, 28th Cong., 2nd Sess., p. 220.

From H[enry] M. Watts, [U.S. District Attorney], Philadelphia, 1/31. Watts has received a letter, dated 12/2/1844, from George W. Gordon, U.S. Consul at Rio de Janeiro, stating that sufficient evidence had been sent to the State Department to warrant the arrest of Capt. Hiram Gray, W[illiam] M. Ruhl, and others "for a violation of the laws of the U. States for the suppression of the Slave trade." Gordon also informs Watts that these individuals have returned to the U.S. aboard the *R.H. Douglas* bound for Baltimore. Watts has ordered an investigation which reveals that Gray and Ruhl are presently at Wilmington, Del. ALS in DNA, RG 59 (State Department), Consular Despatches, Rio de Janeiro, vol. 8 (T-172:9).

FEBRUARY 1–15, 1845

‖

The Senate continued to struggle to find a form in which Texas annexation could be approved. The Secretary of State, recovering from a quite serious bout of pneumonia, was confined to his rooms in the U.S. Hotel, but managed to get quite a bit of work done. Among much else, preparations were made to send an agent to view firsthand the situation in the new Dominican Republic; the doubtless long-anticipated protest of the Argentine Minister over the actions of the U.S. Navy against the fleet of that country last year arrived; and on February 8 Calhoun defended the facts used in his previous review of the depressed state of the free black people of the Northern States.

An Ohio Democrat wrote Calhoun on February 14 that the recent election was a vindication of Calhoun and his principles: "The result of the election has been to establish for the present, your opinions of the nature and policy of the general government . . . . He who is competent to interpret great events, must see in Mr. Polk's election the decided ascendancy of": and here the correspondent quoted Calhoun's Presidential campaign platform of the previous year: free trade, low duties, retrenchment, reform, and a strict construction of the Constitution.

If it was true that Calhoun's principles had decided the election, there had been no acknowledgement from the winner of that election, the President-elect, who had not consulted Calhoun in any way. On February 14 Calhoun wrote from his sickroom to a political intimate: "Nothing yet is known as to Mr. Polk's Cabinet arrangement. I think the probability is that he will form one of entirely new members."

‖

To [JAMES I. McKAY], Chairman of the Committee of Ways & Means, House of Representatives

Department of State
Washington, Feb. [*blank space*] 1845

Sir, The following table exhibits the number of foreign missions & Consulates, and the number of regular Clerks in the Department of State, together with their Compensation at different periods.

Years	Missions	Consulates	Total	Clerks	Compensation
1818	7	67	74	10	$13,400
1827	16	115	131	13	17,000
1845	24	177	201	14	19,250

From this it appears that from the year 1818 to 1845, a period of 27 years there has been an addition of only 4 to the regular number of Clerks in the Department of State, of which number only *one* has been appointed in the last eighteen years.

In the period embraced in the table, the number of Missions & Consulates ["have" *altered to* "has"] been nearly trebled, and the duties of the Department have, probably, been quadrupled. Many of these additional duties have been performed by extra Clerks employed under various acts & Resolutions of Congress. Of these there has been as many, at times, as eleven, exclusive of those employed on the Census. At present there are eight. Nor has there been less than this number at any time (except for short periods) during the last four years.

By the law of August 1842 it is enacted, "that no extra Clerks shall be employed, in any Department Bureau or office at the Seat of Government, *except during the session of Congress*, or when indispensably necessary to answer some call made by either House of Congress at one session to be answered at another." However beneficial such an enactment may be in its general operation, it is obvious that it must at times prove very embarrassing in a Department, in which there has been an addition of but one to the number of regular Clerks, in the long period of 18 years, during which the population and resources of the Country have been greatly increased, and the duties of the Department increased in probably an equal proportion.

The Act of August 16th 1842, makes it the duty of the Secretary of State, to lay before Congress, at the commencement of each session, "an account of such changes and modifications, in the commercial systems of Foreign nations, by treaties, duties & imposts, and other regulations, as may have come to the knowledge of the Department." Under this act, and under the various calls made by the Senate & House of Representatives, for information respecting our Commercial ["reg" *canceled*] relations with foreign nations, an irregular commercial & statistical Bureau, has grown up in the Department, composed exclusively of extra Clerks.

It is very desirable that there should be a permanent Bureau of this kind connected with the Consular Bureau; and as the Clerks in this Bureau must, for the proper performance of their duties, have a knowledge of the various foreign languages, and a minute acquaintance with foreign moneys, weights, and measures, together with much other general information, they ought to be suitably compensated for their labors.

Both, the British & French Governments have such Bureaux, which make very copious reports, on whatever is supposed to be of interest, in the commercial relations of other countries. The knowledge which they seem to appreciate so highly, cannot be of less importance to us than it is to them.

Under these circumstances I submit to your Committee, & through you to the House of Representatives the propriety of taking such measures, as will (without increasing the expenses of the Government) make it practicable to effect, a better arrangement of the Department, in respect to the Clerks employed than exists at present. I would especially suggest the propriety of passing an act, to authorize the appointment of a Clerk with a salary of $1450 p[e]r annum to take Charge of a statistical & miscellaneous Bureau, & also of making the usual annual appropriation, in the general appropriation Bill of $2000 for extra Clerk hire & Copying.

The accompanying table exhibits the amount paid for extra clerk hire, and Copying from January 1st 1841 to December 31st 1844 inclusive of what has been paid under resolutions calling for information, and other resolutions and acts of a specific nature. I am &c, J.C. Calhoun.

Years	From Con-tingent fund of Dept.	Fund for Expenses for Resolutions	For Indices Papers of Wash-[i]n[g]t[o]n	Total
1841	6178.14	"	"	6178.14
1842	5686.39	"	"	5686.39
½ of 1843	3491.64	"	475.00	3966.64
Fiscal year 1843–4	6322.	2184.00	1183.00	9689.
to 31 Dec. 1844	333.71	4463.60	572.	5369.31
	$22,011.88	6647.60	2230	30889.48

Average pr. annum   7722.37

The above is exclusive of payments for a proofreader and distributor of Laws, and documents, and for Compiling an Index to the laws amounting to $1150

and for compiling and attending to the printing of the Biennial Register which at $500 Bienially would be pr. ann.   250

making a total amt. pr. ann. $9122.37.

FC in DNA, RG 59 (State Department), Reports of the Secretary of State to the President and Congress, 6:148–150; PC in Jameson, ed., *Correspondence*, pp. 640–642.

James Ombrosi, Deputy Consul of the U.S. at Florence, to Edward Gamage, Charleston, S.C., 2/——. Ombrosi informs Gamage of attempts by Joseph A. Binda, U.S. Consul at Leghorn, to subjugate the Consulate at Florence to the authority of that at Leghorn. This action would be a great inconvenience to those trading at Florence, but Binda has announced publicly that "he expects to succeed in his efforts thro' the protection of his intimate friend John C. Calhoun of South Carolina, the Secretary of the Department of State." Ombrosi has written to the State Department on this matter but has received no reply. He asks whether Gamage has any knowledge of the views of the State Department. ALS in DNA, RG 59 (State Department), Consular Despatches, Leghorn, vol. 3 (T-214:3).

Floride [Colhoun] Calhoun to James E[dward Ca]lhoun, University of Virginia

Washington, 1[s]t February 1845

My Dear Son, Your letter of the 27th I have read with much pleasure, and from the tone in which it is written, I infer you have commenced your studies, with redoubled vigour, and have proffited some what by my good advice. As you now begin to see the importance of apply-ing yourself closely to study, and try and make up for lost time, I hope it will be the means of laying the foundation for usefulness, as well as literary acquirements in future life. I scarcely ever read a better letter. I read it to your father, who was equally pleased with it. He has been very sick for several days, but is now better. He would have rode out this morning, but thought it rather too cold. I see by the papers that he is thought very ill, and in fact they say past recovery, and that the Physicians have pronounced his lungs dif-fective. On the contrary, they say his lungs are remarkably sound, and that he is now free from disease of any kind. All he now requires is strength, and appetite, which rididing [*sic*] will soon restore. His complaint was the prevailing epidemic, that is a violent cold which stirred up the bile. His cough has nearly left him, and he sleeps well at night. You misunderstood me with respect to your father[']s not remaining here after the 4th of march. I do not know any thing about his remaining in the department after the 4th, that, is to be determined after Mr. [James K.] Polk, comes. I said we were to leave here for home, that is to spend the summer there; Even if we are to return and live here, we must go home first. I do not wish you to say any thing about it, as your father, does not wish any thing said about it yet, as soon as I know certainly, if we are to return here, I will let you know. If any one asks you about it say, you do not know your father[']s determination. I think it more than probable we will return. Be sure to burn this letter as soon as you read it, as I do not wish what I have written to be seen by any one.

I have heard from home often, all are well. [Martha] Cornelia [Calhoun] received a long letter from Cudy [Martha Maria Col-houn,] all are well. Your Uncle James [Edward Colhoun], came on to attend to some business, he has not yet returned from New York. Patrick [Calhoun] is well, and constantly employed among the Ladies. Quite as attentive to Miss Kate Wilkins as ever. She is a charming girl. He still persists, he has no idea of marrying. Eugenia [Calhoun] is still enjoying herself very much. She says, she dreads re- turning home again. Washington has turned her brains completely. Your Uncle James has just returned from Boston, he has been very sick but is better again, he has a bad cough. I do not think he will remain until the 4th. Your father looks quite well again, attended to business yesterday, and expects to be in the Office again next week. He is very thin, but will pick up again, as soon as he rides out. Per- sons, are anxiously looking out for Mr. Polk, I suppose he will be here the last of next week, or at last the first, of the week after. Cousin [James] Edward Boisseau, has requested me to have my likeness taken full length for him, and to have one taken for myself, and he will pay for both. He has sent your father a pair of suspenders, the handsomest I ever saw. I doubt if he will ever wear them. You ought to try and get them from your father, when you come. All are well, and join me in much love to you. your devoted mother, Floride Calhoun.

P.S. I forgot to mention having received letters from Brussells, all are well again. Also from John [C. Calhoun, Jr.,] he is not so well, has become very thin, and has had several attacks of virtico. Write often, at least once a fortnight to some of us.

ALS in ScU-SC, John C. Calhoun Papers. NOTE: An EU on the first page of this letter indicates that it was received on 2/9.

From EDWARD EVERETT

London, 1 February, 1845
Sir, I forward herewith a note from Lord Aberdeen in reply to mine on the subject of the "Cyrus," of which a copy accompanies my despatch Nro. 245. The Protest of Captain [P.C.] Dumas and the Affidavits attached to it, as furnished by Mr. [Henry A.] Wise to the British Minister at Rio de Janeiro [Hamilton Hamilton], having been transmitted to the Government here and an investigation of the case having been ordered, the further communication alluded to by Lord Aberdeen may, I suppose, be expected without much delay. I am, Sir, with great respect, Your obedient Servant, Edward Everett.
Transmitted with despatch Nro. 253;
The Earl of Aberdeen to Mr. Everett, 30th January, 1845.

LS (No. 253) with En in DNA, RG 59 (State Department), Diplomatic Despatches, Great Britain, vol. 54 (M-30:50), received 2/22; FC in DNA, RG 84 (Foreign Posts), Great Britain, Despatches, 9:148–149; FC in MHi, Edward Everett Papers, 51:188–189 (published microfilm, reel 23, frame 648); CC with En in DNA, RG 46 (U.S. Senate), 29A-E3; PC with En in Senate Document No. 300, 29th Cong., 1st Sess., pp. 44–45.

LEWIS E. HARVIE to Richard K. Crallé

[Richmond] Feb. 1th 1845

My dear Sir, I found on my arrival here that Mr. [Thomas] Ritchie had been informed that you were the author of "Silas," which I deeply regretted. He was much excited. It seems that, Cave Johnson [Representative from Tenn.] demanded the name of the Author & thus, it reached Mr. R[itchie]'s ears. I fell in with Mr. R[itchie] and took the liberty to say to him that I was entirely assured, that "Silas" was written without the instigation or knowledge of Mr. Calhoun, & he replied that he was satisfied of it. I did not say how I became satisfied of this, nor that I had any conversation with you. Nor did I say that Mr. C[alhoun; *one word canceled*] thought it too harsh a stricture on Mr. R[itchie]. I am sure you will understand & appreciate my course in this matter. I have thought it proper to make this communication, in order to apprise you that Ritchie was in possession of these facts, & that I had taken this course. Mr. Calhoun should not be brought into unnecessary collision with Mr. R[itchie]. We think that we have gained much upon the Whigs, by the proceedings in the House of Delegates on yesterday. I write in company & in great hurry. Very truly y[ou]r friend, Lewis E. Harvie.

ALS in ScCleA. NOTE: In the Washington, D.C., *Madisonian*, January 22, 1845, p. 2, "Silas" criticized the Richmond *Enquirer* for attacks on the Tyler administration and suggested that a "clique" in Richmond had made a share of the spoils of office a requirement for support of the incoming Polk administration. On January 31 the *Enquirer*, under the title "To the Friends of the Union," hinted that Calhoun had used the office of Secretary of State for self-aggrandizement for the 1848 Presidential nomination. To this article, "Civis" replied in the *Madisonian* of February 3, p. 3. On February 6, p. 4, the *Enquirer* published an editorial under the title "Mr. Calhoun," arguing that the *Enquirer* had been unjustly attacked by "ardent, devoted, but indiscreet friends" of Calhoun such as "Silas" and "Civis."

From R[OBERT] WALSH, "Private"

Paris, 1st Feb[ruar]y 1845
My Dear Sir, Yesterday, I committed to a gentleman going all haste
to London, a packet for you, with Some matter enclosed which I supposed would be acceptable. It will be forwarded to the Steamer.
This day, I offer a few more, & an autograph of Mr. [Louis Adolphe]
Thiers pressing the Service of an important member of the opposition,
for the Struggle in the Chamber of Deputies. The Member handed
it to me—under injunction of secrecy in regard to his name. It may
be curious in your private album. Some danger has been experienced by the cabinet, here, owing to the antipathies, of not a few of
the Conservatives to England & her power. The majority desire to
retain the cabinet; they detest, however, the *entente cordiale* carried
to the [F.P.G.] Guizot or Louis Philippe extent. This renders the
Situation of the cabinet more or less precarious at all times, as the
opposition operate upon the public feeling with it, and the Conservative Deputies fear their electoral Colleges. The cabinet would have
given you precious little satisfaction about Texas, if King & ministers
and the whole legislative majority had not perceived that the nation
would not endure a warlike league with England against the United
States. [George W.] Featherstonehaugh [*sic*], so Significantly appointed British Consul at Havre, has been introduced in all form at
Court, & most graciously received. He owes the double distinction
to his *Excursion through the Slave States*, replete with invention &
exaggeration. On the evening of the day after I received your Communication of the 27 Dec[embe]r, I went to the stated soirée of Mr.
Guizot, in order to observe the aspect of things in relation to the
Cabinet perils. Crowd, men, tone, prediction were all auspicious—
indicated confidence in the King's declared protection. Mr. Guizot
asked me—what American news: I told him that I could say, on your
authority, that the Texas bill might pass both House[s] of Congress,
this Session. His countenance at once indicated vexation: he made
no remark. I have held of late much conversation with principal
members of the two Chambers, chiefly Conservatives, & the others
of the Left Centre and the Gauche. All seemed to wonder at the
resistance made in Congress to the acquisition of such a region as
Texas, with the concurrence of its inhabitants; and none could believe that the adversaries were Serious on the topics of Mexican right
and Mexican war. Some mentioned spontaneously that no one of
the European governments—no division of any party in any of those

251

governments, would have hesitated a moment under like circumstances. The creation of the mixed commission respecting the Conventions between France & Great Britain about the Slave trade is regarded on all hands as a studied respite for the French cabinet, & an expedient for a better concert for the abolition of Slavery itself pursuant to the British plans. A Dr. [Stephen] Lushington, or a Lord [Henry Peter] Brougham, & a Duke de Broglie are the very pledged, determined, capable zealots for the purpose. The intelligence, arrived this morning, of Mr. [William E.] Gladstone's withdrawal from the British cabinet, produces a Sensation. He was the ablest member, except Sir Robert [Peel]. Mark the following language of the London Globe (Whig organ) of the 30th Jan[uar]y "How could Mr. Gladstone take the prominent part in *reversing* which he took in *advocating* the policy hitherto *affected* in favor of the Colonial & Free-labor interests, as regards the admission of tropical products?" It is constant matter of regret with me that your Southern delegation have not provided Some fund for a proper, frequent exposition of the question of American negro-slavery according to realities—to truth, justice and fair international judgment & dealing. For many years, you have been assailed by the British press and Societies countenanced or Stimulated by Statesmen [of] all parties, & the object has been, on the continent, to render the slavery so hideous & the communities of masters so generally odious, that open war on you, destructive of [*ms. torn; one or two words missing*] Southern & Northern prosperity, would not, in the end, p[*ms. torn; one word missing*] unwelcome or suspicious to the continental nations. [*Ms. torn; one word missing*] have scarcely been defended or excused at all. At Paris, at London, at Madrid, in the middle parts of Europe, the chief stations—in Germany—say Berlin, you have not of late been so represented as that any systematic earnest manifestations in your behalf could be expected. Nationality is called a *Sentiment* more powerful than a principle: it is not a mere official sense, or a general impression of the injustice of foreign denunciations, that you needed, so much as a direct, positive sympathy—a native community of feeling & concern. Your letter ["to Mr. (William R.) King" *interlined*] is widely efficacious; the impulse, however, must be repeated diffusively. I have wished to put forth what I have prepared with daily diligence & Sound materials—a view, in English & French, of the whole case & of American Statistics & Prospects; the expense would not be considerable, yet I am arrested by it—for the Consulship Scarcely defrays its own cost. Enough of this point.

A Deputy, a close friend & confidant of Count [Louis-Mathieu de] Mole, has just imparted to me this anecdote. He asked the Count why he, & his chief associates of the opposition, in the Coalition, proclaimed a cordial assent to the British alliance, & only lamented that ["the" *interlined*] *entente* was too devoted & obsequious on the side of Mr. Guizot. "Because," said the Count, "we must keep ourselves *possible* for the ministry: the King will accept—admit, tolerate, no Council with other policy or professions." You must understand that it would be a sorry game for these politicians to drive Guizot out without being able to get or *keep* in, themselves. If we deduct the Some forty or fifty Legitimists & Republicans (of the Deputies) who aim at the destruction of the government or Dynasty there remains a strong constitutional majority with the cabinet. Most resp[ectfull]y, R. Walsh.

ALS with En in ScCleA; PEx in Boucher and Brooks, eds., *Correspondence*, pp. 279–281. NOTE: Walsh enclosed to Calhoun an ALS in French from [Louis] A[dolphe] Thiers, dated 1/2/1845, summoning its recipient to a meeting for an unstated purpose. Thiers, a historian and politician, was President of France from 1871 to 1873.

From GEO[RGE] M. BIBB

Department of the Treasury
Washington, Feb[ruar]y 3d 1845

The note [of 1/15] of the Hon[ora]ble A[lphonse] Pageot the Minister of his Majesty the King of France, accompanied by the letter of Mr. [François] Durand of Perpignan, which you did me the honor to refer to me, have been duly considered.

Messrs. Aymar & Co., the factors or consignees of Mr. Durand, received at New York some Wines of Roussillon in France, imitative of, and assimilated to, the Oporto or Wines of Portugal.

Messrs. Aymar & Co., under the Act of 1842 for imposing duties on imports, were charged by the Collector of the Customs at New York, a duty of fifteen cents per gallon on those French Wines of Roussillon, which they paid.

The Secretary of the Treasury decided that under the treaty of 1840 between the United States and Portugal the Wines of Portugal could *not* be subjected to a higher rate of duty "than such as are or shall be payable on the like article being of the growth[,] produce or manufacture of any other foreign Country," therefore that as the red wines not enumerated of Austria & Prussia and in casks paid only six cents per gallon, that the red wines of Portugal could not be charged a higher rate of duty in the ports of the United States under the Act of 1842.

Mr. Durand farther states that he imported other wines of Roussillon into the United States paying only a duty thereon of Six cents per gallon.

That when application was made at the Custom House to have refunded the excess above Six cents per gallon paid on the French Wines of Roussillon assimilated to the port wines of Portugal, the Custom House Officer refused to refund such excess: which refusal Mr. Durand thinks strange, considering the decision of the Secretary of the Treasury as to the wines of Portugal and considering that he had, after the decision of the Secretary paid but six cents per gallon for duty on other wines of Roussillon so assimilated to the Port Wines of Portugal.

Upon the case of Mr. Durand I have to remark, that if the Collector committed an error in admitting other wines from Roussillon in France at a rate of duty of six cents, instead of fifteen cents per gallon, it by no means follows that the Collector should commit another error by refunding the duty correctly levied upon the former importation.

Secondly it is to be noted that where in those wines so assimilated to port Wines now imported from France there was no subsisting treaty between the United States and France to interdict the United States from imposing any rate of duty on the Wines of France which the Government might deem fit and proper: no treaty with France put the United States under any obligation to levy no higher duty on the Wines of France than such as were or shall be payable on the Wines of Portugal or of any other foreign nation:

Thirdly it is to be noted that the treaty with Portugal, whilst it ruled and governed the duty on the wines of Portugal and interdicted a higher duty than such as should be levied on any other foreign nation, Yet that treaty did not rule and govern the rate of duty to be levied on French Wines:

Fourthly it is to be observed that the Roussillon Wines on which the duty of fifteen cents per gallon was levied, were French Wines: that they were port wines by assimilation and imitation of Oporto Wines.

Fifthly it is to be noted that notwithstanding the assimilation, imitation or simulation, those Roussillon Wines remained in truth and fact, Wines of France that the imitation or simulation had not demolished the fact, had not transmuted those Roussillon Wines into veritable Oporto Wines into real wines of the product and manufacture of the Kingdom of Portugal.

Sixthly it is to be noted, that the Act of 1842 Section 8 paragraph 5th (p. 192) expressly provides, "That all imitations of any of the said wines & all wines imported by any name whatsoever shall be subject to the duty provided for the genuine article, & to the highest rate of duty applicable to the article of the same name."

That Act of 1842, imposed a duty "on Port & Burgundy Wines in Casks fifteen cents per gallon." From the premises the conclusion follows that when Messrs. Aymar & Co. paid upon these Roussillon Wines of France so assimilated to and in imitation of Port Wines, or the Oporto wines of Portugal, no excess of duty was paid: and that subsequently when a duty of six cents only was charged by the Collector on the other Roussillon wines of France, assimilated to the real Oporto Wines of Portugal and in imitation of Port Wines, such duty was less than that which should have been rightfully demanded.

The repugnance of the law of 1842 in some of its parts to subsisting treaties, does not abrogate its enactments in all its parts; So far as those enactments are not bridled and controlled by superior obligations of treaties, they must have force and effect.

The complaints of Mr. Durand and of Messrs. Aymar & Co. are without just cause. The refusal of the Collector of the Customs to comply with the demand made by them for the return of the supposed excess of duties levied upon those wines was proper and is approved of by the Secretary of the Treasury.

If for want of exact definition, or by lack of perspicuity to common understandings, complaints have arisen in the execution of the law of 1842, they are to be regretted, But from the imperfection ["of language" *interlined*] and of human comprehension, misunderstandings cannot in all things be avoided. With very high respect I have the honor to be Yours &c, (signed) Geo: M. Bibb, Secretary of the Treas[ur]y.

CC in DNA, RG 59 (State Department), Miscellaneous Letters (M-179:107, frames 147–151); FC in DNA, RG 56 (Secretary of the Treasury), Letters to Cabinet and Bureau Officers, Series B, 5:22–24; CC in DNA, RG 46 (U.S. Senate), 29A-D5.

To WILLIAM BOULWARE, Naples

Department of State
Washington, 3rd February, 1845

Sir: I am directed by the President to inform you, that he has yielded to your renewed solicitations to be permitted to quit your residence near the Government of Naples, and to return home. It is his wish that you should remain at your post [as Chargé d'Affaires to the Two Sicilies] until the arrival of your successor, that he may enjoy the advantages of entering upon the duties of the mission under your advice and experience. The President, however, does not entertain the idea that, under present circumstances, either policy or the public service will render your remaining at Naples, for this purpose, indispensably necessary; and if your private interests should make it important for you to return to the United States, you will be at liberty to embark as soon after the receipt of this despatch, as you may find it convenient; taking care to leave the archives and property of the Legation in the hands of Mr. [Alexander] Hammett, the Consul, or, of some other trustworthy citizen of the United States, to be carefully preserved till further orders. You are requested to transmit a correct inventory of them to this Department.

In accepting your resignation the President directs me to convey to you his entire approbation of the manner in which you have discharged the public duties with which you have been entrusted; and I transmit, enclosed, a letter addressed to the Minister of Foreign Relations of the Two Sicilies, with an office copy of the same, informing him of your recall, which you will present in the usual form, and accompany by assurances to His Excellency of the sentiments of friendship entertained by this Government towards that of the Two Sicilies.

Of the exact date of your taking leave, you will inform this Department and the Bankers of the United States; who will be desired to settle your accounts accordingly.

Your despatches Nos. 21, 23 and 24, (and one dated the 13th September last, not numbered), have been received. I have to direct your attention to despatch No. 11 from this Department, desiring you to transmit a copy of Mr. [Enos T.] Throop's No. 9—which has not yet been received. I am, Sir, respectfully, Your obedient Servant, J.C. Calhoun.

FC (No. 17) in DNA, RG 59 (State Department), Diplomatic Instructions, Two Sicilies, 14:22–23 (M-77:170).

From HENRY COLMAN, "Private"

London, 3 Feb[ruar]y 1845, 56 Charing Cross
Dear Sir, The kindness with which I have been honoured by you
induces me to write you on a subject in which as an American citizen
I feel the strongest interest, and to which I am prompted *entirely by
my own spontaneity without any suggestion of any person living*. I
know under such circumstances you will not deem it impertinent; and
as I never have been & never expect to be a candidate for any political favor whatever, ["I know" *canceled*] you will not distrust my
motives.

I know the influence which you will exert in the administration of
the Government of the U. States after the approaching change as well
as what you now possess; and I never hesitate to say that I do not believe there lives a man less under the influence of private & personal
motives or actuated by a higher regard to what you deem the good of
your country than yourself. Under these circumstances allow me to
say, that in my opinion nothing can be gained & much may be lost by
any change in the diplomatic representation of the United States at
this Court, & to express my earnest hope that such change will not be
hastily made.

I do not know what Mr. [Edward] Everett's wishes or expectations were or those of his family; but I do know that the situation is
not one of pecuniary emolument, as his allowance does little more
than half meet his necessary expenses. My only design is to speak of
the estimation in which he is universally held here. I have had constant & frequent intercourse here with many of the first individuals
in the country in rank, intelligence & political influence, and they are
unanimous & most emphatical in their expressions of personal respect
and confidence ["towards him" *interlined*]. Indeed I do not believe
that any man ever has done or could do more than he has done to
conciliate & secure a mutual good understanding between the two
countries without in any way compromitting the honor and interests
of his own. This circumstance gives him an influence which no
stranger could suddenly acquire, to say nothing of the advantages of
his experience in the office and his necessary and consequent familiarity with the relations of the two countries & the prominent subjects
of negotiation. I am no political partizan and beg you to understand
this letter as entirely private & personal. Feeling however the deepest interest in the welfare of my own country I beg leave to add, that
if in any way I can render any service to the Government while here

I beg you to command me. I shall remain here some months longer & go to the continent for a few months & then return here again. Or if, my dear Sir, while abroad I can do any thing *for you,* I assure you nothing would give me more pleasure than to serve you. I have the honor to be, With the highest consideration Your friend & ser[van]t, Henry Colman.

[P.S.] My address is London care of Baring, Brothers & Co.

ALS in ScCleA. NOTE: Colman, a native of Boston, was a Unitarian minister and agricultural writer.

From [J. C.] DE FIGANIE͂RE E MORA͂O

Her Most Faithful [Portuguese] Majesty's Legation
Georgetown D.C., February 3d 1845

Sir, On the 10th July 1843, and subsequently on the 23rd November following, I had the honor to lay before your Department, two claims made by subjects of Portugal, residents of the Province of the Cape de Verd Islands, for the abduction of two slaves, the property of said subjects; in the first instance, of the negro "Pedro," by John Holdridge, master of the whaling Bark called the "Romulus," of Mistic in Connecticut, and, secondly, of the negro "Marcelino," by Daniel Borden, master of the whaling Bark "Pantheon," of Fall-River Massachusetts.

These claims, with accompanying documents, were communicated by the President of the United States to the Senate, on the 14th March 1844, and referred to the Committee on Foreign Relations while your predecessor, Mr. [Abel P.] Upshur, assured me that instructions should be given to the respective United States' Attorneys, to prosecute the parties, if within the province of existing laws.

Since then, I have been deprived of communications from your Department in reference to this business, nor, am I informed, that the Committee alluded to has made any Report, or recommended any measure to prevent, in future, the commission of similar felonious acts, on the part of masters or crews of American vessels, and to redress those already committed: meanwhile, I have been directed by Her Majesty's Government to call your attention to those claims, and to inform you of a third and similar claim presented by John Baptist Livramento, a merchant of Villa da Praya of the the [*sic*] Island of

Santiago, as per enclosed documents, for the abduction, on the 28th of November 1844, of his slave "Alexander," a carpenter by trade, by James K. Turner, master of the whaling ship "Janus" of New Bedford, owned by W.C. Nye & Co. of Fair-Haven, the said Livramento incurring thereby the loss of Six hundred & fifty mil reis, which he claims.

I avail myself of this opportunity to renew to you, Sir, the assurance of my distinguished consideration. De Figaniere e Morão.

ALS with Ens in DNA, RG 59 (State Department), Notes from Foreign Legations, Portugal, vol. 3 (M-57:3, frames 528–551). NOTE: De Figaniere e Morão's numerous Ens are in Portuguese and are filed with State Department translations. All relate to the claim of John Baptist Livramento.

From Ja[me]s S. Green, [U.S.] District Attorney's Office, Princeton, N.J., 2/3. Green acknowledges receipt of Calhoun's letter of 1/30 enclosing one from Geo[rge] W[illia]m Gordon, U.S. Consul at Rio de Janeiro. He has recently received a similar letter from Gordon himself. "I have communicated with the collectors of our ports and with the Marshall and should the persons accused be found in the district of New Jersey the promptest and strictest measures will be taken to secure their arrest: the result of which I will communicate to your Department." LS in DNA, RG 59 (State Department), Consular Despatches, Rio de Janeiro, vol. 8 (T-172:9).

From O[GDEN] HOFFMAN

U.S. Attorney[']s Office
New York [City], 3d February 1845
Sir, I have the honor to acknowledge your letter of the 30th ult[im]o, in relation to charges against Capt. Hiram Gray & others, late of the Brig "Agnes," for being engaged in the Slave trade. On the 29th ult[im]o I received Mr. [George William] Gordon[']s letter, (a copy of which was enclosed in your communication to me) and immediately adopted the necessary measures to secure the arrest of the persons therein named, upon their arrival in this District. I am, Sir, Very Respectfully Your obed[ien]t Serv[an]t, O. Hoffman U.S. Attorney [signed] by W[illia]m C. Barrett.

ALS in DNA, RG 59 (State Department), Consular Despatches, Rio de Janeiro, vol. 8 (T-172:9).

To Littleton Kirkpatrick, [Representative from N.J.], 2/3. "I have the honor to acknowledge the receipt of your letter of the 28th ult., and to state in reply, that the latest information in the possession of this Department upon the subject of the claims of Citizens of the United States against the Mexican Government, is contained in the despatch of Mr. [Wilson] Shannon of the 12th of November, last a copy of which was communicated with the President[']s Message to Congress of the 18th of December last." FC in DNA, RG 59 (State Department), Domestic Letters, 35:98 (M-40:33).

From Z. Collins Lee, Office of U.S. Att[orne]y, Balt[im]o[re], 2/3. Lee acknowledges receipt of Calhoun's letter of 1/30 enclosing one from Geo[rge] W[illiam] Gordon, U.S. Consul at Rio de Janeiro. Lee has made inquiries and learned that the *R.H. Douglas* arrived at Baltimore three weeks ago. "It is presumed therefore that the persons named as implicated [in the African slave trade], who embarked in her, are still here—and the strictest search is now being made for them. It will be necessary to have the depositions referred to in the Consul's letter in the event of their arrest and I should be glad to recieve them by an early mail." ALS in DNA, RG 59 (State Department), Consular Despatches, Rio de Janeiro, vol. 8 (T-172:9).

From Francis R. Rives, London, 2/3. "I have the honor herewith to transmit you a letter resigning the office of Secretary of the United States' Legation at this court, with the request that you will be pleased to lay it before the President. Being anxious to return to America by the steamer of the 19th of April, I trust the Department will find it convenient to provide for the discharge of my duties after that time." ALS with En in DNA, RG 59 (State Department), Diplomatic Despatches, Great Britain, vol. 54 (M-30:50), received 3/13.

To J[ohn] L. Stephens, New York [City], 2/3. Calhoun acknowledges receipt of Stephens's letter of 1/30 with its claims against the Mexican government. "There is a convention pending between the United States and that government which is intended to provide for the adjustment of all claims of our citizens in Mexico. Its fate when known will be duly made public, and until then it would not under existing circumstances, be expedient to undertake a special negotiation with reference to the [steamboat *Planter*] claims which you represent." FC in DNA, RG 59 (State Department), Domestic Letters, 35:98 (M-40:33).

To President [JOHN TYLER]

Department of State
Washington, 3d February, 1845

To the President of the United States.

The Secretary of State, to whom was referred the Resolution of the Senate of the 10th of December, last, requesting the President "to communicate to the Senate, if not inconsistent with the public interest to do so, any further correspondence which may have taken place between the Minister of the United States to Mexico [Wilson Shannon] and the Government of that Republic, as well as any communications which may have been received from that Minister of later date than those transmitted with the Message of the 3d instant"—has the honor to lay before the President a copy of all the papers called for by the Resolution, with the exception of the despatch of Mr. Shannon of the 12th of November, a copy of which was communicated to Congress with the President's Message of the 18th of December. Respectfully submitted, J.C. Calhoun.

LS with Ens in DNA, RG 46 (U.S. Senate), 28A-F1; FC in DNA, RG 59 (State Department), Reports of the Secretary of State to the President and Congress, 6:144. NOTE: Enclosed herewith were two letters from Shannon to Calhoun, dated 11/30/1844 and 12/9/1844. Tyler transmitted this to the Senate on 2/5. The resolution to which it responds can be found in DNA, RG 59 (State Department), Miscellaneous Letters (M-179:106, frame 151) and *Senate Journal*, 28th Cong., 2nd Sess., p. 25.

From H[enry] M. Watts, Office of Att[orne]y of U.S., Phila[delphia], 2/3. "Having recieved your letter of the 30th ult., let me suggest the necessity of having the depositions, sent to your Department by George W[illiam] Gordon Esq[ui]r[e], as the basis of a warrant for the arrest of Capt. Hiram Gray and others, implicated in the violation of the law for suppressing the Slave trade. There is no one here to make an oath against them, even if they be found in this District."

ALS in DNA, RG 59 (State Department), Consular Despatches, Rio de Janeiro, vol. 8 (T-172:9).

From W[illia]m Woodbridge, [Senator from Mich.], 2/3. Woodbridge requests the return to him of recommendations and other papers he submitted last year in behalf of Robert Andrews, then an applicant for a Clerkship in the State Department. Having been unsuccessful at that time, Andrews wishes to receive the evidences of his qualifications then submitted. (A Clerk's EU indicates that the papers were sent to Woodbridge on 2/4.) ALS in DNA, RG 59 (State Department), Applications and Recommendations, 1845–1853, Andrews (M-873:2, frames 831–832).

From William H. Rogers, [U.S. District Attorney], Dover, [Del.], 2/4. Shortly before he received Calhoun's letter of 1/30, Rogers had received a circular from [George William Gordon], U.S. Consul at Rio de Janeiro seeking the arrest of Hiram Gray and others for violation of U.S. laws against the slave trade. Rogers visited Wilmington, the supposed residence of Gray, but learned nothing of his whereabouts. Rogers continues his search and states that if any of the suspects are within his district he will require copies of depositions against them in order to arrest them. ALS in DNA, RG 59 (State Department), Consular Despatches, Rio de Janeiro, vol. 8 (T-172:9).

To President [JOHN TYLER]

Department of State
Washington, 5th Feb[ruar]y 1845
To the President of the United States.

The Secretary of State, to whom has been referred the resolution of the House of Representatives of the 31st ultimo, requesting the President to communicate to that body, if not incompatible with the public interests, "any further communications which may have passed between the Government of Great Britain and our own, respecting the surrender of fugitive criminals from Florida, under the treaty of Washington, not heretofore furnished to that House," has the honor to submit to the President the accompanying copies of papers. J.C. Calhoun.

LS with Ens in DNA, RG 233 (U.S. House of Representatives), 28A-E1; FC in DNA, RG 59 (State Department), Reports of the Secretary of State to the President and Congress, 6:150–151; PC with Ens in House Document No. 114, 28th Cong., 2nd Sess., pp. 1–12. NOTE: Enclosed with this report were copies of Calhoun's letters of 8/7/1844 and 1/28/1845 to Edward Everett and Everett's letter of 11/23/1844 to Calhoun. Tyler transmitted this to the House of Representatives on 2/5. The resolution to which it is a response can be found in DNA, RG 59 (State Department), Miscellaneous Letters (M-179:107, frames 138–139) and in *House Journal*, 28th Cong., 2nd Sess., p. 304.

From C[ORNELIUS] P. VAN NESS

District of New York
Collector's Office
February 5th, 1845

Sir, I have the honor to transmit herewith a Statement prepared from the Books of this Office, in compliance with the request contained in your letter of the 24th December last. This Statement exhibits the quantity & value of the different articles imported into this District during the year commencing on the 1st October 1842, classified under three distinct heads, to wit, Articles free of duty, Articles paying duties advalorem, & Articles paying specific duties, with the rate of duty affixed to each article; & the specific duties reduced to *ad valorem* rates on the foreign cost. This reduction is based, as will appear from the statement, on the *aggregate* importations for the year of each description of merchandise liable to specific duty. The result in each instance is therefore the *average* advalorem rate. The range would be much higher in particular cases.

The period of the importations considered commences one month later than that fixed in the Resolution of Congress, greater facility being thereby afforded in preparing the statement from the *quarterly* accounts of this office, whilst the results cannot be materially varied. I am, Very respectfully Your obed[ien]t Ser[van]t, C.P. Van Ness.

LS in DNA, RG 233 (U.S. House of Representatives), 28A-F1; PC with En in House Document No. 73, 28th Cong., 2nd Sess., pp. 269–278.

To [Robert J. Walker, Senator from Miss.], 2/5. "Mr. Calhoun's compliments to Mr. Walker, and would be obliged if he would call at his lodgings to day, either as he goes to or returns from the Senate Chamber. Mr. W[alker] is requested to *send up his name* when he calls." LU in CSt, Harwood Family Papers.

To Z. Collins Lee, U.S. Dist[rict] Att[orne]y, Baltimore, 2/6. As Lee requested in his letter to Calhoun of 2/3, Calhoun sends him copies of depositions received from [George William Gordon,] the U.S. Consul at Rio de Janeiro, relating to the case of Capt. Hiram Gray, master of the *Agnes*, and others accused of engaging in the African slave trade. FC in DNA, RG 59 (State Department), Consular Instructions, 11:335.

To ALPHONSE PAGEOT

Department of State
Washington, 6th Feb[ruar]y 1845

Sir: Your letter of the 15th ultimo, preferring the claim of Mr. [François] Durand of Perpignan, for the repayment of an excess of duty supposed to have been improperly levied on certain French wines by the Collector of the Customs at New York, has been duly received at this Department. A translation of your communication and of the paper which accompanied it, were forthwith transmitted to [George M. Bibb] the Secretary of the Treasury, for his consideration, and I have now the honor to enclose to you a copy of his decision [dated 2/3] on the subject.

I avail myself of this occasion to renew to you the assurance of my distinguished consideration. J.C. Calhoun.

FC in DNA, RG 59 (State Department), Notes to Foreign Legations, France, 6:88 (M-99:21); CC in DNA, RG 46 (U.S. Senate), 29A-D5.

From CHA[RLE]S H. RAYMOND

Legation of Texas
Washington, February 6th 1845

The Undersigned, Chargé d'Affaires *ad interim* of the Republic of Texas, has the honor to acknowledge the receipt of the note of Mr. Calhoun, Secretary of State of the United States, of the 22nd ultimo, informing him of the measures taken by the Government of the United States for the recovery of two Texian white boys who were supposed to be in captivity among the Wichitaw Indians within the United States, and of the fact, that, after a careful examination through the village inhabited by that tribe, the persons making the search became satisfied the boys were not in possession of the Wichitaws.

The Government of the Undersigned will be gratified to learn of the earnest efforts so promptly and willingly made by the Government of the United States for the recovery and restoration of the two boys to their kindred and country; and although those efforts have, as yet, failed in effecting their humane purpose, they nevertheless furnish renewed evidence of the friendly disposition of the Government of the United States, towards the Government and people of Texas, and of its determination to fulfill, in good faith, its treaty stipulations with that country.

As there is a rumor, perhaps well founded, that the boys are held as captives by Kickapoos or Comanches, Indian tribes inhabiting the territory of the United States, the Undersigned entertains the hope that the Government of the United States will not relax its efforts until the place of their captivity be discovered and they be safely delivered into the hands of their friends.

The Undersigned avails himself of this occasion to offer Mr. Calhoun renewed assurances of his high consideration. Chas. H. Raymond.

ALS in DNA, RG 59 (State Department), Notes from Foreign Legations, Texas, vol. 1 (T-809:1); FC in Tx, Records of the Texas Republic Department of State, Letters and Dispatches Sent by the Texas Legation in Washington, 2:29–30; FC in Tx, Records of the Texas Republic Department of State, Copybooks of Letters Received from Texan and Foreign Representatives, vol. 2-1/103, p. 56; CC in Tx, Records of the Texas Republic Department of State, U.S. Diplomatic Correspondence.

To President [JOHN TYLER]

Department of State
Washington, 6th February, 1845
To the President of the United States.

The Secretary of State, to whom has been referred the Resolution of the Senate of the 4th inst: requesting the President "to communicate to the Senate, if in his opinion not inconsistent with the public interest, whether Mr. Duff Green does now hold or has lately held any diplomatic or official station near the government of Texas, and if so, what? when appointed? at what salary? and with what instructions"? has the honor to state, in reply thereto, that Mr. Duff Green was appointed Consul of the United States at the Port of Galvezton in Texas on the 12th day of September, 1844, and received from this Department his ordinary printed instructions as such, and none other; that no salary attaches to the appointment and that he neither holds nor has held any diplomatic or other official station near the government of Texas. Respectfully submitted, J.C. Calhoun.

LS in DNA, RG 46 (U.S. Senate), 28A-E3; FC in DNA, RG 59 (State Department), Reports of the Secretary of State to the President and Congress, 6:145; PC in Senate Document No. 83, 28th Cong., 2nd Sess.; PC (dated 2/10) in Jameson, ed., *Correspondence*, p. 643. NOTE: Tyler transmitted this to the Senate on 2/7. The resolution to which it responds can be found in DNA, RG 59 (State Department), Miscellaneous Letters (M-179:107, frame 146) and in *Senate Journal*, 28th Cong., 2nd Sess., p. 131.

To H[enry] M. Watts, U.S. Dist[rict] Att[orne]y, Philadelphia, 2/6. In reply to Watts' request of 2/3, Calhoun sends to him copies of depositions received from [George William Gordon], U.S. Consul at Rio de Janeiro, relating to the case of Capt. Hiram Gray, master of the *Agnes*, and others accused of engaging in the African slave trade. FC in DNA, RG 59 (State Department), Consular Instructions, 11: 334–335.

From CARLOS [MARIA] DE ALVEAR, [Argentine Minister to the U.S.]

Argentine Legation
New York [City], February 7, 1845
Sir, In the conference which I had the honour to hold with you, on the subject of the violence, (*atentado*) committed by Captain [Philip F.] Voorhees, of the American frigate Congress, on the Argentine vessels

of war, blockading the port of Montevideo, I had the satisfaction to hear you say—that the Government of the United States had deeply regretted that event, which could not be justified in any way: and, that so soon as the President should have received the official communication, of the American Commodore [Daniel Turner], who had sailed from Rio de Janeiro, for the Rio de la Plata, with the express object of inquiring into that matter, the Government of the United States would act in such a manner, as should be completely satisfactory to the Argentine confederacy. You at the same time had the kindness to offer to send me a copy of the communication from the Commodore on that subject, and to let me know the resolution which, the Government of the United States might take, in satisfaction for the insult committed against the Argentine flag. It is therefore with this object, that I have the honour to address you, considering it probable, that the Government of the United States will have received the communication from the Commodore, and will have resolved or be about to resolve what duty and honour may dictate, in reparation of an act, which has most particularly fixed the attention of the Argentine Government, as the Hon. Secretary of State may well have imagined. Flattering myself that the measure adopted by the Government of the United States, or which may be adopted by it, with regard to an occurrence so unexpected, will be directed not only to prevent that act of violence, (*atentado*) from remaining unreproved, but also to prevent such acts from being repeated as might be feared if the present one should go unpunished—which is certainly not to be anticipated, from the justice and honour of the United States' Government.

With this object, the Secretary of State will allow me to observe to him, that whatever be the measure adopted by the Government of the United States, with regard to Captain Voorhees, as it cannot in any way free that Captain from being tried for his act of violence, (*atentado*) according to the laws of the United States, and in reparation of an insult of an offence against a friendly nation, it is to be desired, that until this takes place, Captain Voorhees should be recalled, and removed as soon as possible from the Station in the Rio de la Plata where his presence after such an act, cannot but be regarded with the utmost dissatisfaction. This the more, inasmuch as his act of violence, (*atentado*) besides being committed without any provocation or appearance of common sense, does not inspire even that sympathy occasioned by deeds which from their difficulty and the risk attending them, have the character of audacity and intrepidity.

General Alvear avails himself of this occasion to renew to the Hon. Mr. Calhoun the assurances of his high consideration and respect. Carlos de Alvear.

State Department translation of ALS (in Spanish) in DNA, RG 59 (State Department), Notes from Foreign Legations, Argentina, vol. 1 (M-47:2). NOTE: Robert Greenhow, translator of the above document, inserted a note in his translation to explain that Alvear's use of the word "atentado" to describe Voorhees's action signified "an act very criminal and worthy of extreme reprobation and abhorrence."

From [WILLIAM H. GARDINER]

[Washington] Friday, Feb. 7, 1845
Mr. Gardiner, of Boston, presents his most respectful compliments to Mr. Calhoun, and encloses a letter [of 1/22] from Mr. [David] Sears, which he has withheld to the present time in consequence of learning that Mr. Calhoun[']s state of health was such as not to permit his attention to business.

Having today the satisfaction to learn that Mr. Calhoun's health is sufficiently reestablished for the purpose Mr. Gardiner will have the honor of calling upon him tomorrow.

A brief memorial to the State Department, containing a very general statement of the case, accompanied Mr. Sears' letter. This paper was handed to the Chief Clerk of the Department [Richard K. Crallé]. It refers for farther explanation to a much longer document in the files of the Department.

But a very short conversation will enable Mr. Gardiner to put Mr. Calhoun in full possession of the leading points and grounds for action on the part of the Government [on the petition of Ellen Sears d'Hauteville in regard to the Swiss government].

ALU with Ens in DNA, RG 76 (Records of Boundary and Claims Commissions and Arbitrations), Miscellaneous Claims Records: France, Miscellaneous.

From Fr[iedrich] v[on] Gerolt, [Prussian Minister to the U.S.], 2/7. Gerolt transmits to Calhoun a statement of the commerce between the U.S. and the German States of the Zollverein, itemizing imports and exports from 1840. The statement concludes with a lengthy memorandum on U.S.-Zollverein relations and a refutation of arguments used in the U.S. Senate to defeat ratification of the commercial convention between the U.S. and the Zollverein. ALS (in

French) with En (in English) in DNA, RG 59 (State Department), Notes from Foreign Legations, Prussia, vol. 1 (M-58:1).

JOHN HOGAN to "Mr. Clale?," [*sic*; Richard K. Crallé?]

Feb. 7th/[18]45

My Dear Sir, You will pardon me in troubling you so often in relation to those papers, but knowing your kindness I take liberties that I dare not take with other Gent[lemen]. I assure you I am exceeding anxious that they may be placed in the hands of Mr. Calhoun early tomorrow that he may look them over, which will enable me to leave [for the Dominican Republic] on Monday. With great respect I am Sir your ob[edien]t Serv[an]t, John Hogan.

ALS in ScCleA.

From Z[ADOCK] PRATT, [Representative from N.Y.]

House of Representatives
Washington, Feb. 7, 1845

Sir, It is my design to move additions to the Appropriation Bill, providing for the extension of our diplomatic intercourse: But before consummating that design, I am desirous of obtaining your views on the subject of ["a" *canceled*] missions for opening commercial intercourse with the empire of Japan and with the Kingdom of Corea.

The population and condition of those countries, in my Judgment, render them well worthy of attention from our Government; and, after the gratifying results of the mission to China, we may well feel encouraged to extend the offers of commercial intercourse with other nations equally advanced in civilization, though less numerous in population. The opening of commercial intercourse with those countries would indeed be important triumphs for American Diplomacy. Respectfully Yours, Z. Pratt.

LS in DNA, RG 59 (State Department), Miscellaneous Letters (M-179:107, frame 157).

From Ja[me]s T. Brady

New York [City,] Feb[ruar]y 8th 1845

D[ea]r Sir, Mr. Jno. T. Wymbs of this city wishes to be appointed our U.S. Consul at Paris. He has resided many years in the latter city, and acquired in his extensive mercantile experience an acquaintance with the Commercial interests of France and this Country which eminently qualifies him for the situation he desires. I beg leave to solicit in his behalf such aid as it may be in your power to bestow. Very truly Yours, Jas. T. Brady.

ALS in DNA, RG 59 (State Department), Applications and Recommendations, 1845–1853, Wymbs (M-873:97, frames 544–545). NOTE: Lacking a postmark, this letter was probably hand-delivered by Wymbs to Calhoun.

From F[e]r[dinand] Gardner, U.S. Consul, "St. Jago," Cape Verde Islands, 2/8. Gardner reports on a number of matters of routine Consular business and requests a short leave of absence. He wishes to be sent the published official documents by Calhoun on the Texas question. He is translating Calhoun's letter [of 8/12/1844] to William R. King into Portuguese "that I may be able to add my mite, to the *right* understanding of *British Philanthropy*." ALS (No. 73) in DNA, RG 59 (State Department), Consular Despatches, Santiago, Cape Verde Islands (T-434:3).

To J[ohn] W. Jones, Speaker of the House of Representatives

Department of State
Washington, Feb[ruar]y 8, 1845

Sir: In compliance with the Resolution of the House of Representatives of the 28th ult[im]o, directing the Secretary of State "to inform this House if any, and what steps have been taken to ascertain whether the errors imputed to the last Census by the memorials of Edward Jarvis, William Bingham and J. Wingate Thornton, and of Thomas Earle and others, presented to this House at its last session, praying that an inquiry should be made as to the accuracy of the last Census, and which memorials were referred to and reported upon by the Select Committee on Statistics, be correct, or not; and whether the result of the inquiry necessary for that purpose, has been such as to impeach, or not, the general correctness of the same," I have the honor to state, that I deemed it to be my duty, as the correctness of the late Census had been questioned during the last Session of Congress, and the errors imputed to it had received, to a certain extent, the sanction of one of the Committees of the House, to adopt such measures as the Department could, with propriety, in order to ascertain whether the errors imputed to that important statistical document, on which the distribution of power among the States of this Union and the legislation of Congress, for the time, must so much depend, were well founded or not. For this purpose I employed William A. Weaver Esquire, as a person in every way well qualified to perform the task of making a thorough investigation of the subject. He was originally appointed by Mr. [John] Forsyth, and continued by Mr. [Daniel] Webster, to superintend the taking of the late Census, including the correction of the returns of the Marshals and of the proofs of the printed documents. The memorials addressed to Congress impeaching its correctness with the report of the Committee in reference to them, were placed in his hands, with the direction to give the subject a thorough and impartial investigation, and to report the result to the Department.

A Copy of his Report is herewith enclosed, which will furnish the information called for by the Resolution of the House.

It would seem from its statements that great and unusual care was taken in order to ensure accuracy in the late census; and that many items charged as errors in it by the Memorialists are, in fact, errors on their part, while, as to the greater part of the residue, it is a matter of doubt whether they be errors or not. Many items, for instance, charged as errors under the head of education, involve mere questions of classification; and whether they be errors or not depends on the fact, whether the classification adopted by the Marshals or the Memorialists be that intended by the act providing for the taking of the Census.

But as the great object of the Memorialists in imputing gross and glaring errors to the late Census seems to be to destroy its credit, because it exhibits the condition of the free negroes of the non-slave-holding-States to be so much worse than that of the slaves of the other States in reference to the far greater prevalence of insanity, blindness, deafness, and dumbness, comparatively among the former than the latter, the Report has given this part of the subject a more full and thorough examination.

The result would seem fully to sustain the correctness of the Census on this highly important point. After examining and pointing out, in detail, the erroneous statements and Conclusions of the Memorialists, it proceeds to sustain the correctness of the Census in this respect, by evidence drawn from the preceding Census in 1830. That provided for taking the number afflicted by the same diseases, omitting that of insanity. Table marked A, (included in the Report) formed from the returns of the two, omitting cases of insanity in the latter, exhibits their comparative results, as to the number of deaf, dumb, and blind. It will be found, on reference to it, that the Census of 1830 strikingly confirms, throughout, the late census, as to the far greater prevalence of these diseases among the free blacks of the non-slave-holding-States, compared with the slaves of the other States. But as conclusive as this collateral evidence may be regarded, it is not more so than that drawn from a different source. It is well known that there is an intimate connexion between extreme physical wretchedness and crime. The same causes which produce the one, will the other. In order to bring this test to bear, a correspondence was opened with the proper State authorities with a view to obtain authentic statements as to the number of white and colored convicts, including both sexes, in their respective State prisons, for the year 1840 and the subsequent years. Table marked B gives the results as far as Statements have been furnished for 1840, the year the Census was taken. Like Table A, it strongly confirms the correctness of the late Census, by showing that the prevalence of crime, among the negroes of the non-slave-holding-States compared with the Slaves of the slave-holding States is not less striking than the greater prevalence of disease, as exhibited by the same document.

On a review of the whole, two conclusions, it is believed, will be found to follow inevitably. The one is, that the correctness of the late Census, in exhibiting a far greater prevalence of the diseases of insanity, blindness, deafness, and dumbness, stands unimpeachable. That it may contain errors, more or less, is hardly to be doubted. It would be a miracle if such a document, with so many figures and entries, did not. But that they have, if they exist, materially effected the correctness of the general result, would seem hardly possible. Nothing, but that the truth is so, would seem capable of explaining the fact that, in all the non-slave-holding-States without exception the Census exhibits, uniformly, a far greater comparative prevalence of these diseases among the free blacks, than among the Slaves of the other States. They are, indeed, vastly more so among the most favorable of the former, than in the least favorable of the latter. If to this be added the corroborative evidence furnished by the Census of

1830, and the returns furnished by the States showing a like greater prevalence of crime, as has been shown, the conclusion would seem to be altogether irresistible.

Why the fact should be so is a question of deep import. Without undertaking to investigate it, it may be asserted, that the cause, be it what it may, must be deep and durable. None other can account for the uniformity of its operation through so many States respectively, of such wide extent, and placed in such different conditions.

The other conclusion, not less irresistible, is, that so far from bettering the condition of the negro or African race, by changing the relation between it and the European, as it now exists in the Slave-holding-States, it would render it far worse. It would be, indeed, to them, a curse instead of a blessing. I have the honor to be, very respectfully, Sir, Your obedient Servant, J.C. Calhoun.

LS in DNA, RG 233 (U.S. House of Representatives), 28A-F1; variant FC's in DNA, RG 59 (State Department), Reports of the Secretary of State to the President and Congress, 6:145–148 and 151–153; PC with En in House Document No. 116, 28th Cong., 2nd Sess., pp. 1–30; PC in the Richmond, Va., *Enquirer*, March 14, 1845, p. 2; PC in the Charleston, S.C., *Mercury*, April 1, 1845, p. 2; PC in the Greenville, S.C., *Mountaineer*, April 11, 1845, p. 1; PC in *Niles' National Register*, vol. LXVIII, no. 14 (June 7, 1845), pp. 218–219; PC in Crallé, ed., *Works*, 5:458–461. NOTE: Calhoun enclosed a copy of William A. Weaver's report, dated 1/18, on his investigations of "errors imputed to the last Census . . . ." That document is abstracted under its own date. Calhoun's above statement was received by the House of Representatives on 2/12. The resolution to which it is a response can be found in DNA, RG 59 (State Department), Miscellaneous Letters (M-179:107, frame 116), and in *House Journal*, 28th Cong., 2nd Sess., p. 291.

From A[lphonse] Pageot, Washington, 2/8. Pageot acknowledges receipt of Calhoun's note of 2/6 enclosing the decision of the Secretary of the Treasury regarding the claim of [François] Durand for reimbursement for excess duties paid at New York City. Because the decision was unfavorable Pageot submits his and Durand's interpretation of the tariff law of 1842 and of the Secretary of the Treasury's circular of 7/1844 concerning the relationship of the tariff law to pre-existing treaties. According to Pageot and Durand, the duty on Portuguese wines is fixed by a pre-1842 treaty with the U.S. at 6 cents per gallon. Also, according to section 8, paragraph 5 of the 1842 tariff law, wines similar to or imitative of original varieties of wine, are to have the same tariff rates as the originals. Using this line of reasoning the rate of 15 cents per gallon charged against Durand's wine was excessive and incorrect. Pageot requests the Secretary of the Treasury to reconsider his decision because the higher duty constitutes a prohibitive tariff upon French wines. LS (in French) and two English translations in DNA, RG 59 (State Department), Notes from Foreign Legations, France, vol. 12 (M-53:8, frames 736–750); CC (State Department translation) in DNA, RG 46 (U.S. Senate), 29A-D5.

From S[TEPHEN] PLEASONTON

> Treasury Department
> Fifth Aud[itor's] Office
> 8th Feb[ruar]y 1845

Sir, Mr. Flectcher [*sic*] Webster, having presented to me his Account for Compensation and Contingent expenses, as Secretary under the Special Act of Congress of the 3d of March 1843, "providing the means of future intercourse between the United States and the Government of China," I have the honor to submit the same to you, together with vouchers in part, for the Contingencies, and to enquire what compensation, per annum, is to be credited to him, and if the dates stated for its commencement and termination, (23d April 1843, and 4th February 1845,) are correct? also, if he is to be allowed the items of Contingent expenses that are not supported by vouchers. I have the honor to be, With great resp[ec]t Sir, Y[ou]r Ob[edien]t Ser[van]t, S. Pleasonton.

LS in DNA, RG 59 (State Department), Letters Received from the Fifth Auditor and Comptroller, 1829–1862; FC in DNA, RG 217 (General Accounting Office), Fifth Auditor: Letters Sent, 5:203.

From H[enry] M. Watts, Office of Att[orne]y of U.S., Philadelphia, 2/8. "I have the honor to acknowledge the receipt of your note of the 6th inst. with the accompanying documents and to inform you, that on the strength of the affidavits Judge [Archibald] Randall, of the Dist. Court of the U. States, has issued warrants for the arrest of Capt. Hiram Gray, [William M.] Ruhl and [R.S.] Gough for violation of the provisions of the act of 20 April 1818 relative to the Slave trade. The Marshal will endeavor to apprehend the persons accused." ALS in DNA, RG 59 (State Department), Consular Despatches, Rio de Janeiro, vol. 8 (T-172:9).

From F[RANKLIN] H. ELMORE

Charleston, Feb[ruar]y 9, 1845
My Dear Sir, Mr. [Solomon] Cohen of Savannah, who has ever been a true Carolinian (a native of Georgetown & Graduate of our College) wishes to retire from his profession & reside in Europe for a time. He would like some Consular appointment of a rank & emolument suited to his real worth & standing. He has I know been observed by you as an intelligent & influential member both of our own & the Georgia Legislature—and also as one of your political friends. To me he has been known from our College days as a warm[,] sincere & energetic friend of every man & cause to which he has made profession. His qualifications for this or a Diplomatic appointment are certainly equal & if it should so fall out that you can aid his views, I am sure you will have no cause to regret it. Yours truly, F.H. Elmore.

ALS in DNA, RG 59 (State Department), Applications and Recommendations, 1845–1853, Cohen (M-873:16, frames 815–817). NOTE: This letter was hand-delivered by Cohen to Calhoun. An AEU by Calhoun reads "Mr. Cohen."

From G[regory] A. Perdicaris, Trenton, N.J., 2/9. "I have the honour to inform you that my affaires will not allow me to return to the Consulate of Athens; and though my leave of absence has not as yet expired I deem it my duty to send you my resignation, and beg that you would be so good as to lay it before the President." ALS in DNA, RG 59 (State Department), Consular Despatches, Athens, vol. 1 (T-362:1).

From G[REGORY] A. PERDICARIS

Trenton N.J., 9th Feb[ruar]y 1845
My Dear Sir, My affaires have, at length, imposed upon me the necessity of resigning my office, and the only duty that remains for me, is to thank you for your past kindness; and to commend to your care—not any particular individual as my successor—but our Consulate at Athens.

When I last saw you, I took occasion to lay before you, the condition of our Consulate, & to acquaint you with the humiliations to which it subjected me in consequence of being denied that pecuniary support which gives dignity and effect to office; in other words—in consequence of being left without a salary. You were pleased to request some memoranda of our interview, and I should have furnished it, had I not been unwilling to press a matter in which I was personally interested. As that consideration no longer exists you will allow me to call your attention to a subject in which our honor and interests are alike concerned. Our Consulate in Greece is either important to our interest and it ought to be properly supported, or unimportant and should be discontinued. Having held that office for the last eight years, I have had an opportunity of forming an estimate of its importance to our interest, and I do not hesitate in saying that it is necessary to our interests. Tho' our commerce with Greece amounts almost to nothing her Imports for 1840 were $1195,073.17, and her exportation to $3,862,000.59, and there is no doubt but that a profitable commercial intercourse may be fostered in that quarter. Nor is the political [con]dition of Greece, as unimportant as to be a matter of indifference to us. Greece is great in her position, and in the mental energies of her people she is the advance post of civilization in the east, and the strong hold of constitutional principles. It is my belief that an American Consul in Athens may do much to foster our commercial relations with the country, and his presence may give some support to those principles to which we are so much ["interested" *canceled and* "indebted" *interlined*]; but it is also my conviction that in order to attain these objects it is not enough to create the office and then leave it to share the fate of outcasts—no—the salary must follow the office, otherwise there is neither profit nor honor in the whole matter. It is better to have no Consul than to have one, and deny him the means necessary to his usefulness and dignity. I am My Dear Sir Your Ob[edien]t Serv[an]t, G.A. Perdicaris.

ALS in DNA, RG 59 (State Department), Consular Despatches, Athens, vol. 1 (T-362:1).

From Jacob Barker, New Orleans, 2/10. Barker introduces Madison Caruthers who will visit Washington "at the momentous change which is soon to take place in our political rulers" and has hopes of being appointed to a public office. (A Clerk's EU indicates that Caruthers was an applicant for appointment to be Collector of Customs at New Orleans.) ALS in DNA, RG 56 (Secretary of the Treasury), Applications for Appointment as Customs Service Officers, 1833–1910.

From SHEPARD CARY, [Representative from Maine]

House of Representatives
Washington, Feb. 10, 1845

Sir, I have received your note of the 22d ultimo, communicating a copy of a letter addressed to your Department on the 21st ultimo by her Brittannic Majesty's Minister at Washington [Richard Pakenham], in reference to certain monies and bonds constituting the "Disputed Territory Fund," and which, by the Treaty of Washington, ought long since to have [been] paid over to the U.S. Government, for the use of citizens of Maine and Massachusetts.

I should have addressed you earlier upon the subject, if you had not been disabled by a recent illness from attending to the affairs of your Department. I now beg leave to call your attention to the letters which I have heretofore addressed to you upon this subject, and also to the conversations which I have had with you.

I see no reason why the "*bonds*" belonging to the "Territory Fund" should not be immediately delivered over by the authorities of New Brunswick. If any difficulties exist as to the "*monies*" which by the Treaty of Washington ought also to be paid over, there can be none as to the "*bonds.*" At any rate, I see none, and it is my duty to press this point particularly upon your attention. Many citizens of Maine are largely involved in those bonds, as principals and sureties, and I should deeply regret being obliged to leave Washington, before the provisions of the Treaty in respect to them have been complied with.

Many of our citizens who are on these bonds as principals, obtained the names of citizens of New Brunswick as sureties, by depositing money with them as security. They cannot obtain a return of this money, until the bonds are given up and cancelled.

I would suggest that your Department should appoint an agent to receive these bonds, and that you request Mr. Packenham [*sic*] to urge upon the government of New Brunswick, to pay over to such agent without delay, the bonds referred to in the Treaty of Washington. I suggest this course, if it is not inconsistent with the relations of your Department. Shepard Cary.

ALS in DNA, RG 76 (Records of Boundary and Claims Commissions and Arbitrations), Letters and Miscellaneous Documents relating to the Maine-New Brunswick Boundary Dispute, 1824–1850.

From JOHN MCKEON

New York [City,] Feb[ruar]y 10, 1845
My Dear Sir, Having long & favourably known John T. Wymbs
Esq[ui]r[e] the bearer who is an applicant for a Consulate in France,
I take great pleasure in recommending him to your kind attentions
in the matter. He is a gentleman of great mercantile experience, has
long resided in France, is fully competent to discharge the duties of
the station he desires. There is no person whom I would more
earnestly recommend for such an appointment than Mr. W[ymbs].
His moral qualities & mercantile character are a guaranty[?] for a
proper discharge of the duties of the office. Yours Resp[ectfull]y,
John McKeon.

ALS in DNA, RG 59 (State Department), Applications and Recommendations,
1845–1853, Wymbs (M-873:97, frames 548–550).

From CHA[RLE]S H. RAYMOND

Legation of Texas
Washington, February 10th 1845
The Undersigned, Chargé d'Affaires *ad interim* of the Republic of
Texas, by direction of his Government, has the honor to transmit,
herewith, to Mr. Calhoun, Secretary of State of the United States, the
depositions of James Bourland, Collector of Customs for the Red
River District in Texas, and George W. Wright, a citizen of Lamar
county and Senator in the Texian Congress, in relation to the seizure,
in March 1843, by said Collector, of certain goods introduced into
that Republic, in violation of her revenue laws, by citizens of the
United States—the subsequent forcible rescue of those goods by the
importers, and their abusive treatment, at the same time, of the person of the collector—all of which has heretofore been the subject of
correspondence between the two Governments.

The depositions are properly authenticated before the Hon. M[il-
ford] P. Norton, Judge of the District Court of the 6th Judicial District of Texas, and establish most clearly the facts of the illegal introduction of the goods—their forcible seizure and taking away by
citizens of the United States, and, as near as possible under the circumstances, the amount of damage suffered in consequence.

The evidence being full and explicit, covering all the points sug-

278

gested in Mr. Calhoun's note of the 2nd of December, last, to the Undersigned on this subject, and the whole case having been fully examined and discussed, the Undersigned can, at present, see no obstacle to its speedy, final, and satisfactory adjustment—an event which he hopes soon to have the pleasure of communicating to his Government.

The Undersigned avails himself of this occasion to offer Mr. Calhoun renewed assurances of his distinguished consideration. Chas. H. Raymond.

ALS with Ens in DNA, RG 59 (State Department), Notes from Foreign Legations, Texas, vol. 1 (T-809:1); FC in Tx, Records of the Texas Republic Department of State, Letters and Dispatches Sent by the Texas Legation in Washington, 2:31–32; FC in Tx, Records of the Texas Republic Department of State, Copybooks of Letters Received from Texan and Foreign Representatives, vol. 2-1/103, p. 60; CC with Ens in DNA, RG 46 (U.S. Senate), 29A-D5; PC with En in Senate Document No. 38, 29th Cong., 1st Sess., pp. 1–5.

To William H. Rogers, U.S. Dist. Att[orne]y, "Newcastle," Del., 2/10. In reply to Rogers' letter of 2/4, Calhoun sends him copies of depositions received from [George William Gordon,] U.S. Consul at Rio de Janeiro, relating to the case of Capt. Hiram Gray, master of the *Agnes*, and others accused of engaging in the African slave trade. FC in DNA, RG 59 (State Department), Consular Instructions, 11: 336.

From ROBERT SMITH, [Representative from Ill.]

House of Rep[resentatives,] Washington, Feb. 10th 1845 Sir, I introduced a bill into the House of Rep. a few days since, to revive the "Act" requiring the Secretary of State to cause the laws, resolutions &c of Congress to be published in certain newspapers in the several States and Territories of the the [*sic*] United States. Which "act" was repealed in 1842; I am desierous of knowing the Cost of publishing the laws &c, in newspapers prior to 1842 for a series of years (say two or three): And what the cost has been since, and whether or not additional copies of the laws have been published ["in pamphlet form" *interlined*] and distributed, in consequence of the discontinuance of publishing the laws, as formerly, in certain Newspapers in each of the States & territories.

I would respectfully ask an answer to the foregoing enquiries at your earliest convenience. I have the honor to be very respectfully Your Ob[edien]t Serv[an]t, Robert Smith.

ALS in DNA, RG 59 (State Department), Accounting Records, Miscellaneous Letters Received.

From NEDHAM H. WASHINGTON

Washington, February 10th 1845

D[ea]r Sir, If you can with entire convenience, place your hands on a letter, from some of the citizens of King George [County,] Va., vouching for my qualification for office, sent as I am informed under cover to you for the President, it will be thankfully received, as should it meet my expectations, I intend to take it to him, at least as a letter of introduction, not having the pleasure of his acquaintance. I am in the hotel & will await the return of the servant. With wishes for your return to perfect health, I am with the utmost respect Yours, Nedham H. Washington.

ALS in DNA, RG 59 (State Department), Applications and Recommendations, 1845–1853, Washington (M-873:91, frames 471–473). NOTE: An AEI by Calhoun reads "All my letters received before I was taken unwell are at the office, and among them I suppose the one to which you allude, unless it was transmitted to the President." This letter was addressed to Calhoun at the United States Hotel and not postmarked.

To EDWARD EVERETT, [London]

Department of State
Washington, 11th February, 1845

Sir: The President [John Tyler] has learned with satisfaction, from your despatch No. 235, that in the conversation therein reported to have taken place with Lord Aberdeen, Her Britannic Majesty's Principal Secretary of State for Foreign Affairs, relative to the claim of the Government of the United States for the remission of the duties on Rough Rice, collected in contravention of the treaty existing between the two countries, His Lordship expressed himself in favor of your suggestions for bringing the question to a settlement by some fair mode of adjustment, and intimated that he would endeavor to overcome the repugnance of the Treasury to the method you have proposed for deciding the points in dispute. The President cannot but hope that this matter, long pending between the two Governments, will be speedily closed. Should it, however, not be settled at the time of receiving this despatch, you are directed to bring the matter again before the British Government, in such a manner as you may deem expedient, under the new state of circumstances which has arisen since the enforcement of the new law levying discriminating duties on Sugar. The order issued by the Lords of Her Majesty's Treasury, admitting Sugar from the United States under the lower duty, altho' produced by slave labor, entirely takes away all pretext for any longer withholding the duties collected on Rough Rice. The ground for the discrimination in the case of Rough Rice and Sugar is precisely the same; and the construction of the treaty by Her Majesty's Government, with respect to Sugar, must remove all doubt or dispute as to the Rough Rice duties.

You were right in bringing to the attention of Her Majesty's Government the fact that the United States require from Great Britain no other construction of the treaty of 1815, than we had conceded to other nations. Not only has a large amount of duties collected by the tariff law of 1841 [*sic*] been remitted on the wines of Portugal by virtue of a treaty similar in its provisions to that with Great Britain, but the same course has been pursued towards Holland, with respect to coffee imported from Java. Nor has the United States' Government, in refunding the duties referred to, inquired whether they were due to citizens of the United States, or to subjects of Portugal or Holland. It was enough that the duties were collected in contravention of our treaty stipulations. The truth is, both countries have, in their practical administration, put the same construction on the treaty of 1815; and your clear and unanswerable positions ought long since to have closed this matter.

The President relies on your efforts to bring this business to a speedy termination. I am, Sir, with great respect, Your obedient servant, J.C. Calhoun.

LS (No. 123) in DNA, RG 84 (Foreign Posts), Great Britain, Instructions, 8:648–652, received 3/18; FC in DNA, RG 59 (State Department), Diplomatic Instructions, Great Britain, 15:249–250 (M-77:74); PC in House Document No. 38, 30th Cong., 1st Sess., pp. 8–9.

From CHA[RLE]S H. RAYMOND

Legation of Texas
Washington, February 11th 1845

The Undersigned, Chargé d'Affaires *ad interim* of the Republic of Texas, has the honor to inform Mr. Calhoun, Secretary of State of the United States, that Major Tho[ma]s G. Western, Superintendent of Indian Affairs of Texas has received under date of the 6th ultimo, a letter from Messrs. L[eonard] H. Williams and B. Sloat, Indian Agents in the service of that Republic, from which it appears that the two children of Mrs. Simpson, a widow lady—the one a son named William about twelve, and the other a daughter named Jane about fourteen years of age who were stolen from their mother's residence at Austin on the Colorado river in Texas, early in the month of *November, last,* are now in the possession of the *Waco* and *Toweash* or *Wichita* Indians encamped in the *Wichita* mountains about 550 miles northerly from the city of Washington, Texas, and within the territory of the United States. The tribe of Indians with which the Wacos are encamped in the mountains is known indifferently as the *Toweash* or *Wichita.*

Messrs. Williams and Sloat were sent out, immediately after the news of the capture reached the ears of the President for the purpose of seeking and recovering these children from their Indian captors; but having reached a point some two hundred miles above the said city of Washington they found it impossible to proceed; the pra[i]ries for hundreds of miles across which they must travel being at that season destitute of grass, and furnishing no food for their horses. They however ascertained the facts stated in their letter to Major Western from the Camanches and other friendly Indians whom they met in their travels and at ["the" *canceled*] Torrey's trading house, as well as from their personal observation and knowledge of the course and character of ["of" *canceled*] the Indians committing the outrage. These Agents will recommence their journey so soon as the grass shall spring up, and will reach Fort Towson [in the U.S. Indian Territory] early in the spring.

In view of the foregoing facts the Undersigned is directed by his Government, formally, but most respectfully, to request of the Government of the United States the aid of its authorities to effect the release of these prisoners and their safe conveyance to Fort Towson or some other point, where they can be delivered to the Texian Agents and thus be restored to their home and friends, as provided in the 33rd Article of the Treaty of 1831.

The hope is confidently indulged that the efforts of the Texian Agents, seconded by the powerful assistance which the President of Texas [Anson Jones] doubts not will be cheerfully accorded by the Government of the United States, will lead to the speedy release of these youthful captives from their savage masters; and while engaged in accomplishing this humane object, it is not improbable that the *two boys* mentioned in Mr. [Isaac] Van Zandt's note of the 10th of August last, who were captured by the Indians on the Trinity river in the early part of last year, but whose place of captivity, the Agents of the United States have hitherto been unable to discover, may also be found and restored to their country.

The Undersigned avails himself of this occasion to offer Mr. Calhoun renewed assurances of his distinguished consideration. Chas. H. Raymond.

ALS in DNA, RG 59 (State Department), Notes from Foreign Legations, Texas, vol. 1 (T-809:1); FC in Tx, Records of the Texas Republic Department of State, Letters and Dispatches Sent by the Texas Legation in Washington, 2:32–34; FC in Tx, Records of the Texas Republic Department of State, Copybooks of Letters Received from Texan and Foreign Representatives, vol. 2-1/103, p. 61; CC in TxU, Alexander Dienst Papers.

From Farnham L. Tucker, New York [City], 2/11. Tucker acknowledges Calhoun's letter of 1/31 informing him that A. Follin is U.S. Consul at Omoa and Trujillo. Because Omoa and Trujillo are more than 100 miles apart, Tucker feels that Follin should appoint a Consular Agent at Trujillo. Tucker plans to sail for Omoa in 10 or 12 days "and will accept with pleasure the appointment from Mr. Follin should he think proper." He offers to carry communications from the State Department to Follin. LS in DNA, RG 59 (State Department), Consular Despatches, Omoa, Trujillo, and Ruatan, vol. 2 (T-477:2).

From J[AMES] HAMILTON, [JR.], *"Confidential"*

Galveston, Feb[ruar]y 12th 1844 [*sic*; 1845]

My Dear Sir, On my arrival here to day from my Plantation on the Brasos I found ["y" *canceled*] a few U.S. Papers which had been sent me from N. Orleans. It was with infinite concern that I perceived, some very unfavorable reports in relation to your health. I cannot but hope that from your natural stamana of constitution you will be able to surmount without any serious affection of your Lungs your reported indisposition and that before this can even reach you ["that" *canceled*] you will have been relieved from [*a few words canceled*] every thing like apprehended disease.

I am just about to embark for New Orleans & on the eve of my departure write this Letter to be deposited in the Post office on the moment of my arrival; to say that if your health was suffering or is suffering it has occurred to me ["th" *canceled*] that an excursion across the water ["may" *canceled and* "might" *interlined*] be of immense service to you. I therefore hope in this event you will think seriously of accepting the mission to England in case the state of your health should not allow you in case it has been offered to take the Department of State. That the former is at your option I cannot doubt. Should ["the former" *canceled and* "it therefore" *interlined*] be deemed expedient or desirable I beg ["you" *interlined*] My Dear Sir ["not to permit" *interlined*] for one instant the kind intimations which you made in reference to ["myself" *canceled and* "this" *interlined*] appointment for ["myself to interfere with your wishes" *interlined*]. I assure you if it was even at my disposal I would surrender it most cheerfully in your behalf not only *for such an object,* but under the conviction of your own superior qualifications for such a trust. Do not therefore regard for one moment the offer you made me to bring my name to the view of Mr. [James K.] Polk in case you were Sec[retar]y of State for this mission. As desirable as it may be to myself I should infinitely prefer seeing you in the occupation of this Post.

Should you however prefer remaining at home and the fact turn out that you have "a voice potential" in Mr. Polk's Cabinet a strong belief that in six months I can with Lord Aberdeen & Lord Ripon negociate a reciprocity Treaty and thus nullify the Tariff of 1842— would induce me to take the office personally inconvenient as it may be, more especially as I think without hazard to our friendly relations with G[reat] B[ritain]. I could under your advice & instructions place the slave Question before Her B[ritannic] M[ajesty's] Ministers in such a shape as to convince them, that it was not to the interest of the people of the United Kingdom to push this crusade of public opinion against the people of the South ["are" *canceled and* "who" *interlined*] are ["in point of fact" *interlined*] there best ["friends" *interlined*] & most natural allies. Your Letter to Mr. [William R.] King has doubtless produced some soreness in England, but your presence or the agency of one representing your feelings & views &

["representing" *canceled and* "having" *interlined*] your interests at heart, would soon take this ["impression" *interlined*] off.

Whilst I would wa[i]ve any claim even if I had ["it" *canceled and* "one" *interlined*] (which I have not) to the appointment in your favor, I must confess if my name was brought in competition with that of any other man I would not. I would make the same concession *to no other man in the Union, for be it vanity or presumption* I believe since you have told me [*ms. torn; one or two words missing*] that no ["other" *canceled*] individual in the ["Union be" *canceled and* "country" *interlined*] is better qualified for the office than myself, or who in the late struggle, has done more in consummating the great Revolution ["than myself" *canceled*]. If therefore my name for this ["mission" *canceled and* "appointment" *interlined*] should be brought up in competition with any other name but *yours* for the mission to St. James before the President & you should be in his Cabinet, I do not wish it to be withdrawn. Whilst I am willing that Mr. Polk should consult his own preferences more especially, as I cannot help such an exercise of discretion, yet I could not consent to concede my claims in preference to any man in the U.S. except ["your own" *changed to* "yours"].

As the die will have been cast before this reaches you as to the President's Cabinet write me immediately directed to the Oswichee P.O. [Ala.]—of the whole result of ["President Polk's" *canceled and* "the" *interlined*] organization in reference to his *Premier Pas* on which so much depends. On my arrival in New orleans I will write you in ["reference" *canceled and* "regard" *interlined*] to the impression the passage of the Resolutions for annexation in the House of Representatives has made in Texas at least at this place. The manner in which Congress propose to take the whole Revenues of their Custom House & at the same time throw their Creditors on their ["un" *canceled*] now unasailable[?; "public" *interlined*] Lands for payment has excited no small sensation. If Congress should adjourn ["without annexation" *interlined*] I think G.B. will submit proposals to Texas involving no injurious concessions on her part which will secure her independance & defeat annexation for ever. I am satisfied of this. I have barely space my Dear Sir to assure you of the esteem with which I am ever faithful[l]y & re[s]p[ectfull]y[?] yours, J. Hamilton.

ALS in ScCleA.

To J[AMES] I. MCKAY, Chairman of the [House] Committee of Ways and Means

Department of State
Washington, 12 February 1845

Sir: I have the honor to transmit herewith a copy of a note [of 2/10?] addressed to this Department by C[harles] H. Raymond Esquire, Chargé d'Affaires of the Republic of Texas, with the accompanying Papers, which I respectfully submit to the consideration of the Committee of Ways and Means, in order that an appropriation may be made to meet the claim to which they refer. I have the honor &c, John C. Calhoun.

FC in DNA, RG 59 (State Department), Reports of the Secretary of State to the President and Congress, 6:154.

From Neal & Co., John H. Silsbee, and others, Salem, Mass., 2/12. Twenty-six Salem merchants recommend William P. Peirce "as a suitable person to be appointed Consul at Macao, in China, where he now resides, and for a considerable time has acted as Vice Consul for that port." LS in DNA, RG 59 (State Department), Applications and Recommendations, 1845–1853, Peirce (M-873:67, frame 113).

From John Slidell, Alceé LaBranche, and John B. Dawson, [Representatives from La.], 2/12. The three men report that Samuel Haight of La. has been removed from his post as U.S. Consul at Antwerp "*solely* because the Executive wished to bestow his office on another person." The three seek Haight's reappointment to the Antwerp post or "Should the President not be disposed to reconsider his action upon this appointment, he will be an applicant for the Consulate at Hamburg." (Calhoun's AEU reads: "The Louisiana delegation recommends the reinstating of Mr. Haight as Consul at Antwerp.") LS and copy in DNA, RG 59 (State Department), Applications and Recommendations, 1845–1853, Haight (M-873:36, frames 99–102 and 113–114); CC in DLC, James K. Polk Papers (Presidential Papers Microfilm, Polk Papers, reel 33).

To ROBERT SMITH, [Representative from Ill.]

Department of State
Washington, 12 Feb[ruar]y 1845

Sir, In reply to your letter of the 10th inst[an]t relating to the publication of the laws, I have the honor to state, that, the act to provide for the publication of the laws, approved the 20th of April 1818, directed the publication to be made in not more than one newspaper in the District of Columbia, and in not more than three in each of the several States and Territories. It also directed that eleven thousand copies of the laws &c. of each session should be published in pamphlet form. The compensation for the publication in newspapers was fixed at the rate of one dollar for each printed page of the pamphlet form.

The act of the 26th of August, 1842, repealed so much of the former as required the publication to be made in the different States and territories, and in lieu thereof directed the publication in not less than two, nor more than four, of the principal newspapers published in the City of Washington, for country subscribers, the compensation fixed as before at one dollar per page of the pamphlet copy.

The cost of publishing, in newspapers, the laws of the 25th, 26th and a part of the 27th Congress was as follows:

For the 25th Congress.

1st Session (extra) In 28 States and territories, and the District of Colombia [*sic*], 82 newspapers	$1192.50
2nd Session. In 29 States and territories, and the District of Columbia, 85 papers	11,520.50
3d Session, In the same, 86 papers	7068.
Cost for the 25th Congress	$19,781.00

26th Congress

1st Session. In the same States and Territories and the District of Columbia, 87 papers	$5779.50
2d do do do 87 "	3489.
Cost for 26th Congress	$9268.50

27th Congress

1st Sess. (extra), In ["the same" *canceled and* "29" *interlined*] States &c. &c.	84 papers	$3454.75
2nd " In 27 States & Territories & the D. of C. 70 "		10595.
Making for those two sessions		$14,049.75
3d Session. In 4 papers in Washington City		618.
Cost for the 27th Congress		$14,667.75

28th Congress
1st Session. In 3 papers in Washington City $468

It will be seen by the foregoing that the annual average cost of publication in newspapers during five years prior to the repealing law, was $8,619.85 and, that that of the publication in the city of Washington subsequent thereto, has been 543.

No addition has been made to the number of copies published, in consequence of the discontinuation of the publication in the States and Territories, as no provision for that object has been made by law.

It may not be improper to state that Mr. [John] Forsyth, in 1840, in answer to a communication from Hon. John H. Prentiss of the Select Committee on Printing made a suggestion for stereotyping and printing an increased number of copies of the laws &c. in lieu of the newspaper publication. He stated that the amount paid for the latter would procure, in addition to the eleven thousand copies prescribed by law, 129,000 copies of the public laws and foreign treaties; or, 78,000 copies of the laws, public and private, and of treaties, foreign and Indian. I have the honor to be, Sir, Very respectfully, Your obedient Servant, J.C.C.

FC in DNA, RG 59 (State Department), Accounting Records, Miscellaneous Letters Sent, vol. for 10/3/1844–5/29/1845, pp. 223–[226]; CC in DNA, RG 59 (State Department), Accounting Records, Miscellaneous Letters Received.

To Joel W. White, U.S. Consul, Liverpool, 2/12. Calhoun reports that White's nomination to be U.S. Consul at Liverpool has been rejected by the Senate. FC in DNA, RG 59 (State Department), Consular Instructions, 12:112.

To W[illia]m Wilkins, Sec[retar]y of War, 2/12. "I have the honor to transmit herewith a copy of a communication addressed to this Department by C[harles] H. Raymond Esq[ui]re Chargé d'Affaires *ad interim* of the Republic of Texas, dated 11th inst. to which I respectfully solicit your attention. The circumstances stated by Mr. Raymond would seem to leave little doubt, but that the two unfortunate children are held in captivity by the Indians within the borders of the United States, and I need make, I am sure, no appeal to the Department of War, to ensure its hearty cooperation with the authorities of Texas to procure their liberation and safe return to their mother." FC in DNA, RG 59 (State Department), Domestic Letters, 35:105 (M-40:33).

BOND by J. C. Calhoun and And[re]w P. Calhoun

State of South Carolina
Pickens District [February 13, 1845]
Know all men by these presence that we, J.C. Calhoun of the State
and district aforesaid, and A.P. Calhoun of the State of Alabama and
Marengo County are held and firmly bound unto Placidia [Mayrant]
Adams, Administratrix of the estate of Jasper Adams deceased of the
district and State aforesaid, in the just and full sum of ten thousand
dollars, to be paid to the said Placidia Adams, her certain Attorneys,
Executors, Administrators or assigns: To which payment well and
truly to be made and done, they bind themselves and each and every
of their Heirs, Executors and Administrators jointly and severally,
firmly by these Presents sealed with seal of the said J.C. Calhoun for
himself and as Attorney for the said A.P. Calhoun and dated the
twentieth of March in the year of our Lord one thousand eight hundred and forty four, and in the sixty eighth year of the sovereignty
and independence of the United States of America.

The condition of the above obligation is such, that, if the above
bound J.C. Calhoun and A.P. Calhoun, their Heirs[,] Executors or
Administrators shall and Do well and truly pay or cause to be paid
unto the above named Placidia Adams, her certain Attorneys[,]
Executors[,] Administrators or Assigns, the full and just sum of five
thousand dollars whenever the said Placidia Adams, her certain Attorneys[,] Executors[,] Administrators or Assigns shall require the
same to be paid giving six months notice thereof in writing to the
said J.C. and A.P. Calhoun, their Heirs, Executors or Administrators
and shall till so required, well and truly pay legal interest thereon
each year semiannually, counting from the first of March Instant provided always that the said J.C. and A.P. Calhoun, their Heirs[,] Executors or Administrators shall at all times have the right to pay the
said sum of five thousand dollars and the interest which may be due
on the sum by giving six months notice thereof to the said Placidia
Adams, her certain Attorneys[,] Executors, Administrators or Assigns.
Then the above obligation to be void and of none effect, or else to
remain in full force and virtue.

Sealed and delivered by John C. Calhoun, in presence of A[rmi-
stead] Burt 13 Feb[ruar]y 1845 & by A.P. Calhoun in presence of J.C.
Calhoun Jr. [Signed by] J.C. Calhoun [and] And[re]w P. Calhoun.

DS in ScU-SC, John C. Calhoun Papers. NOTE: The two signatures and witnesses' statements have been cancelled.

From Everett & Battelle, New York [City], 2/13. The under-signed have learned that [William M.] Blackford U.S. Chargé d'Af-faires to New Granada has negotiated a commercial treaty between the U.S. and that country. Having been engaged in commerce with New Granada for some years, they state that the proposed treaty would be greatly advantageous to U.S. commerce and manufactures. They hope that the treaty may be ratified by the U.S. Senate. (An AES by Joseph Foulke & Son reads "We fully concur with Messrs. Everitt & Battelle in the views expressed as above.") LS in DNA, RG 59 (State Department), Miscellaneous Letters (M-179:107, frames 196–197).

From Fr[iedrich] [von] Gerolt

Prussian Legation at Washington, February 13, 1845
The Undersigned, Minister Resident of His Majesty the King of Prussia, has the honour to call the attention of the Hon. J.C. Calhoun Secretary of State, to a note from His predecessor Baron de Roenne, to the Department of State, dated August 31, 1842, claiming, in virtue of the 5th article of the treaty of commerce, and navigation between Prussia and the United States, a reduction of the duty on Prussian wines which has been by the last American tariff fixed at twenty cents per gallon in bottles, to fifteen cents per gallon the duty fixed on Sicilian wines.

This question having been decided subsequently by the Govern-ment of the United States, to the satisfaction of all the other Gov-ernments situated like Prussia, the Undersigned requests the Hon. J.C. Calhoun, to have orders given to the Collectors of the customs, not to collect more than fifteen cents per gallon, as duty on Prussian wines, and also to restore to the importers of those wines the differ-ence of five cents, which they have paid in excess on each gallon, since the tariff of 1842 has been in force.

On this occasion the Undersigned renews to the Hon. J.C. Cal-houn the assurances of his highest consideration. Fr. [von] Gerolt.

State Department translation of ALS (in French) in DNA, RG 59 (State Depart-ment), Notes from Foreign Legations, Prussia, vol. 1 (M-58:1).

From WILLIAM H. ROGERS

NewCastle [Del.], February 13th 1845
Sir, Under the circumstances connected with the case of Captain Hiram Gray, who is charged with certain acts in violation of the Laws of the U.S. for the suppression of the Slave Trade, I have deemed it advisable to communicate again with your Department before procuring his arrest.

He is now believed to be in Wilmington where he has a wife, and owns some real estate, which, it is said, he is offering for sale. The probability is that he will remain there for some time longer.

Upon examining the depositions transmitted certain doubts have been suggested which induce me to ask for further instructions. The papers transmitted are *copies* of the *copies* forwarded by the Consul at Rio, and I consider it very questionable whether in point of form they are sufficient to authorise the commitment of Gray. It appears to me that they are not such papers as are contemplated by the Act of Congress which makes certified Copies evidence. They are not papers "remaining in your office" but are sent home for the action of the Judiciary.

But further, as the Court of this District sits in the month of March unless the witnesses were then forthcoming the Party would necessarily be discharged. I am not advised sufficiently of the matter to know whether I may calculate certainly upon their attendance. In addition to these ["difficulty" *altered to* "difficulties"] I feel bound further to state, after examining the depositions, that I very much doubt the probability of procuring a conviction. The circumstances offer strong grounds of suspicion, but there are no facts which connect Gray directly with the transaction.

In this state of things I rather doubt the expediency of an arrest at the present time. It would put the government to an expense which might be fruitless; and I need scarcely suggest that the effect of an unsuccessful prosecution would be worse than doing nothing in the case.

Finding, upon an interview with the District Judge [Willard Hall] yesterday, that he feels the same doubts and difficulty, I have thought it my duty to apprise you of them. In the mean time—while waiting your further instructions—I shall have Gray's movements watched. I am very resp[ectfull]y Y[ou]r ob[edien]t Serv[an]t, William H. Rogers.

ALS in DNA, RG 59 (State Department), Consular Despatches, Rio de Janeiro, vol. 8 (T-172:9). NOTE: A Clerk's EU reads "Write to suspend operations for the present. The witnesses will arrive soon." An AES by John Nelson, Attorney General, dated 2/20, reads "I concur in the suggestions of the District Attorney."

From W[ILLIAM] M. CORRY

Cincinnati, 14 Feb. 1845

Dear Sir; The result of the election has been to establish for the present, your opinions of the nature and policy of the general government. Before that election, "the government had been divorced from the banks" and even the Whigs abandoned any re-union. He who is competent to interpret great events, must see in Mr. [James K.] Polk's election, the decided ascendancy of "Free trade, low duties, retrenchment, reform, & a strict construction of the Constitution."

Another, and a weightier question comes up. Prepared by previous events, the Texas contest involves the continuance of slavery. That pretext alone was wanting to set the North, especially N. England, northern New York, Penn[sylvani]a, and Ohio against any longer Union with the South, & its peculiar institution. As soon as annexation takes place, we will have the right of the majority of the people of the U. States asserted to dissolve the national compact, if indeed that act shall not be held a virtual dissolution. Our city is a stronghold of the anti-slavery feeling, and a daily Press and gifted *young* leaders make the abolitionists very formidable. Their legal gentlemen think that a majority of the R. Island adults had the perfect right to overthrow the existing constitution of that State; and of course apply their doctrine to every other State; & to the Union of the States. Equally remarkable are their notions of slavery. In a case of *hab*[*eas*] *corpus* for enquiring into the detention by his master of a fugitive slave from Arkansas who escaped into this State, now actually before Judge Read [*sic*; Nathaniel C. Reed] of our Supreme Court in this city, the most startling enquiries are pursued.

I. Arkansas was no State at the adoption of the F[ederal] Constitution; & therefore slavery cannot exist therein.

II. A fugitive slave can not be recaptured in Ohio, because the ordinance of 1787, forbade slavery throughout the N.W. Territory.

These, and like questions will be presented often, & when decided against the Petitioner, will be incessantly re-iterated by the agitators for the purpose of sapping slavery in all the slave holding States.

Space, will not allow me to enlarge on the certainty of an imminent struggle between South and North upon constitutional slavery itself. And when it does come, you may rely upon it, the battle must be fought by the West. Her position & responsibilities in the coming contest are of the very highest. It should therefore be the motto of the Administration *to fortify the West.* If the President at all comprehends the crisis, this will be his inclination; & it is the true policy of the whole south western section of the Union from which he comes. As yet that section is very little known in the Gen[era]l Government. She has indeed the political power in the House of Representatives, but her resources, moral, intellectual, physical and especially her present position demand a much larger share of of [*sic*] the weight in the national affairs. In the lap of the great West lie the keys of the Republic, and in her vast realms of power, and her attachment to the Union, are to be found its chief defence. It is but wisdom however, instantly to re-inforce this section for the coming attack on our System, which will be more formidable than any which has yet threatened its existence. Nothing but the firm democracy here with every advantage, can withstand the shock. That democracy should be strengthened, & its voice made irresistible, by the selection of ardent, able & *orthodox young* men of the party for office under the gen[eral] government. And nothing will require more judgment than the exclusion of the unworthy members of the party who either have no opinions, or who are incapable of upholding the true theory of our institutions. But the work must be done. From usurping Virginia, and grasping Massachusetts much of their ancient power is gone never to return, yet they, and vacillating N. York absorb the Federal patronage: henceforth let a portion of that fertilizing stream flow with kindest tides down the valley of the Mississippi.

A parity of reasoning which requires that you should waive the older portions of the country, also compels the waiver of the senior politicians. Both should be postponed alike at such a perilous moment to the sections and the men where the danger will be met, and by whom it must be encountered.

Retaining the first place under the new administration, you have the responsibility of the time upon you; and with far higher powers than belong to its head, you must avert the danger.

A new government organ should defend the measures and propagate the opinions of the administration. The [Washington] Globe is weak and heterodox. Mr. [Francis P.] Blair is beneath the emergency, & is in sympathy with the dull men whose magnet is Mr. [Thomas H.] Benton. None of them can do you justice for actual want of ability and probable want of the disposition.

It is the only object of this letter to recommend a person for that high station of leading Editor ["of the party—" *interlined*] Ellwood Fisher of Cincinnati, who is a State rights man, & goes for free trade, hard money, & the Constitution ["as it is" *interlined*]. You will soon see him at Washington on his return from Philadelphia where he goes on private business. As you can appreciate him, he needs no eulogium from me. I dare say, he will not consent to be employed as an editor even of the government paper. Indeed, he has frequently repelled the suggestion upon its being made to him by his friends. His fortunes now however, are unpropitious, and he might be induced to take a position which he would otherwise reject. He knows pretty well that he requires nothing but wealth to aspire to the highest; and it is probable he will still pursue that phantom for the present instead of politics. I have always advised him to the latter.

If not in the press of the country, I sincerely wish he could be employed otherwise by the administration so as to strengthen it, & advance his own reputation. An acquaintance with him from boyhood, enables me to predict for him at some day, a brilliant career of public service; and when I consider to what perfection he has brought himself out of obscurity, as a writer, debater, and orator by his own unaided exertions, no words can express my anxiety that he should by honorable means now enter upon it. This I do know that any post assigned him by the administration as long as he survives, will be impregnable to the utmost prowess of its enemies.

Mr. Fisher's pretensions cannot so properly be presented to any one as to you, for whose genius & patriotism he has been the very foremost advocate in this part of the Union. He left the city entirely ignorant that I would write to you in his behalf; & this letter is sent without consultation with any person. I cannot close it, till I have repeated the burthen of my last communication [of 6/19/1843?] so far as it was personal to yourself. Every consideration demands that you should not longer delay your promised visit to the Western country. You must, you will come. The cause will receive a fresh impulse among us; and your friends experience not gratification alone of the highest character; but a powerful accession of strength, and confidence. With true respect and admiration Yours, W.M. Corry.

ALS in ScCleA; PEx in Boucher and Brooks, eds., *Correspondence*, pp. 281–282.

To R[OBERT] M. T. HUNTER, [Essex County, Va.]

Washington, 14th Feb. 1845

My dear Sir, I have just received yours of the 11th Inst. [*not found*], and when I inform you, that I am not yet so far recovered as to be able to leave my chamber, I am sure you will excuse me for not writing before and the brevity of the present letter.

There is no foundation, as far as I know, for the rumour, that the Commissioner of Patents [Henry L. Ellsworth] is to be removed. I feel confident that he will not be removed before the present administration goes out, and I suppose that there is no certainty as to Mr. [James K.] Polk[']s views in reference to him.

There is at present no dispatch to be sent to Texas. The rule I have adopted is to send all dispatches by mail, except in extraordinary cases. Should there be one of a character as to require special Messenger[,] I will with pleasure present the name of Mr. Parker to the President [John Tyler] for the place but I do not think it probable, that there will be.

The fate of the Texian question is still doubtful in the Senate. Were it not for [Thomas H.] Benton's humbug move its success would [be] almost certain. Nothing as yet is known as to Mr. Polk's Cabinet arrangement. I think the probability is that he will form one of entirely new members. Yours truly, J.C. Calhoun.

ALS in Vi, Robert M.T. Hunter Papers; variant PC in Charles H. Ambler, ed., *Correspondence of Robert M.T. Hunter*, p. 75.

From J. Phillips Phoenix, [Representative from N.Y.], 2/14. Phoenix informs Calhoun that several of his constituents have claims against the Belgian government. They wish "to be informed of the cause of the delay in the adjustment and payment of their claims." If not inconsistent with State Department practices, Phoenix asks that he be "enabled to give some assurance to these gentlemen, that the U.S. government is determined to urge and [*sic*] immediate and final adjustment of these claims." ALS in DNA, RG 59 (State Department), Miscellaneous Letters (M-179:107, frame 202).

To President [JOHN TYLER]

Department of State
Washington, 14th February, 1845

To the President of the United States.

The Secretary of State, to whom was referred the Resolution of the House of Representatives of the 31st of December, last, requesting the President to communicate to that House "if in his opinion not inconsistent with the public interest, a copy of the despatch from Mr. [Wilson] Shannon to the Department of State, covering the communication from Mr. [Manuel C.] Rejon to Mr. Shannon of the 2nd of September, 1844, informing him of the payments of the instalments therein mentioned under the Convention of 1839—and such other communications as have been received from Mr. Shannon on the same subject; and to inform the House who is the agent of the United States to receive said payments, under what authority he exercises the power of agent, and whether any and what information has been received from said agent on the subject; whether any receipt was given to the government of Mexico for said sums of money, and copies of any orders on the Treasury of Mexico for said payments, what was done with them and where the same now are and whether any and what remonstrances or complaints have been made to the government of Mexico on the subject of the non-payments of said orders on the Treasury," has the honor to transmit, herewith, printed copies of sundry documents on the files of this department, which contain all the information in its possession having reference to the subject of inquiry proposed by the House of Representatives.

It may be proper to observe that no communication has been received from Mr. Shannon in relation to the non-payment of the indemnities due in April and July, last. The note of Mr. [Ben E.] Green, the Secretary of the United States Legation at Mexico who is now in this city, dated the 25th ult. (a copy of which is herewith communicated) explains the reasons which may probably have induced Mr. Shannon to defer any communication in reference to the subject until he should have been fully satisfied that the assurances given in Mr. Rejon's note of the 2nd of September, last, would not be complied with. Respectfully submitted, J.C. Calhoun.

LS in DNA, RG 233 (U.S. House of Representatives), 28A-E1; variant FC in DNA, RG 59 (State Department), Reports of the Secretary of State to the President and Congress, 6:154–155; PC with Ens in House Document No. 144, 28th Cong., 2nd Sess., pp. 1–21. NOTE: Enclosed with the last-cited source were approximately 30 letters and documents of 1842–1845 concerning the payment of the first instalment by Mexico and the non-payment of the last two. Tyler transmitted this report to the House of Representatives on 2/17. The resolution to which it responds can be found in DNA, RG 59 (State Department), Miscellaneous Letters (M-179:106, frames 480–481) and *House Journal,* 28th Cong., 2nd Sess., p. 77.

From ROBERT WALSH, "Private"

Paris, 14 [Feb. 1845]

Dear Sir, I send you Several interesting pamphlets, with a number of extracts from French and English papers. American interests are touched in the discussions of the Deputies, & in the press, of the schemes in relation to the transportation of American tobacco and cotton in French bottoms. As you receive London papers, I may advise attention to those parts of Lord Monteagle's speech (Feb[ruar]y 10th) in the House of Lords, which treat of the Custom House reports, the Sugar duties, and the reduction of the imposts on tea & *cotton.* The Paris official Moniteur contains an exposé of the character and purport of the Customs' law proposed by the Minister of Commerce, & of which the ready adoption by both Chambers is assured. The bill from the Committee of Commerce altering materially the Tariff regime of the French colonies, has passed the Deputies readily: Some of its provisions affect American trade. It is extant in the Moniteur. If the London Morning Herald is received at Washington, it may attract ["the attract" *canceled*] the attention of your Navy Department, for the various articles concerning British Naval architecture, experimental Squadrons & So forth. Three pamphlets have just fallen under my notice, that [*ms. torn*]e admission into the library of that department—[*ms. torn*]er to "An Apology for English Ship-builders" ["and" *canceled; ms. torn*]ts & Observations relative to the state of British [*ms. torn*]l Architecture," and "Reflections on British [Nav]al Construction." The great system of Coast Defence, harbors of *refuge* and *national security* with an additional steam-fleet, which the organs & oracles of all parties in Great Britain earnestly commend, cannot escape special heed in your meridian. Distrust of the pacific relations with France is the immediate and most operative motive. The French statesmen, of all denominations, are too conscious of their present naval inferiority to provoke seriously a rupture which the British are anxious to avoid. With steady, extensive preparation for war on both Sides, the extremity will yet be deferred as long as possible. The Soult-Guizot cabinet have manfully and finally thrown down the gauntlet to the combined opposition.

The question of granting the demand of Secret Service money, is the occasion, to be improved next week, on which the five or six coalesced divisions of malecontents will exert all their energies. It is anticipated that the Cabinet will prevail by a majority of thirty or more, & with this, deem the retention of power warrantable in every point of view.

The Minister of Marine means to push his bill for remoulding the administration of affairs (modifying Negro-slavery) in the French Colonies. It is regarded by the Colonial delegates as involving the question of Abolition. I enclose a note from Baron C[harles] Dupin [*not found*] to myself, by which you will see his uncertainty about the result. Mr. [Adolphe] Jollivet indefatigably, & with the materials which I ass[isted?] in collecting & digesting, sends forth a Small pa[*ms. torn*] every week, of more or less efficiency. You must [*ms. torn*] a permanent committee of the American Slave-[*ms. torn*] interest, to hold constant communication with sources of information in London, Paris, Madrid. Much may be obtained from London, but Paris is the place for action in reference to the whole continent. Mr. M[ichel] Chevalier is the chief writer of the Journal des Debats—the absolute authority—on American subjects. I wrote to him my compliments on his election to the Chamber, & my acknowledgments for a friendly article in the Debats about Texas annexation. I join his answer to Baron Dupin's note: his verbal assurances are more precise and emphatic. No one doubts that the Commission in London—ostensibly about the right of visit—is a sort of conspiracy against Negro-slavery in your hemisphere. The Duke de Broglie and Dr. [Stephen] Lushington are Abolition heroes—apostles—you will have seen the glorification of them, under that aspect, in ministerial speeches in both Houses of Parliament. I follow the debates in the Spanish Cortes—as they are reported at length in the Madrid papers—on the government bill for the suppression of the Slave-trade. The utmost jealousy of British influences & objects on the Slavery subject in general prevails in both bodies of the Cortes. Some of the speeches are able and comprehensive reviews and arguments. You will remark in my budget Lord Aberdeen's despatch to Mr. [Henry] Bulwer—*dictatorial* enough: it is a French version of a Spanish one. I have not ob[serv]ed the original in any London paper. This [Consu]late needs all the documents laid before [*ms. torn;* Congress?] this Session, & a good map of the U.S. w[hic]h is [not] to be procured here. With the highest respect [*ms. torn*] faithful Serv[an]t, Robert Walsh.

ALS in ScCleA.

From Cha[rle]s Henry Hall

Newyork [City], February 15th, 1845

Dear Sir, I had the honour to receive (through the intervention of R.R. [*sic*; Richard K.] Crallé Esq[ui]re) a reply to my respects to you relative to the Trade between this Country and China; and at the same time, a polite intimation, that further Correspondence upon this subject, would be acceptable. I need not perhaps say, that I feel highly honoured by this testimony of your approval of my communication, which will stimulate to a further collation of facts, and condensation of my views, and experience, to be submitted at my earliest convenience. In the meantime, permit me to remark that, I have not changed my views relative to the late Embassy to China since the return of Mr. [Caleb] Cushing, neither has his Report satisfied me, or his doings in that Country, although emblazoned by the Public Prints, as well as by his own blandishments. It was my hope, that this Gentleman might have *gone* to *Pekin*, and there made a Treaty, out of the *shadow* of *British* influence, and this he ought to have been instructed to do, or in the lack of instructions, he ought to have gone there of his own accord, not only for his own honour, but that of his Country. There could have been no objection to this measure on the part of the Emperor [Tao Kuang], as Ambassadors have always been admitted to him, saving in the last *negotiations* of the two nations at war, and concluded, by Commissioners on both sides. In Pekin I doubt not a Treaty might have been obtained of a highly satisfactory character and Based upon the reciprocal wants of the Two Countries and under mutual guarantees: as it is, we have a *faulty British* Treaty, *amended by* American negotiation. After all how do we know but England has *secret articles* quite unknown to Mr. Cushing? This certainly is her practice in most of her negotiations with foreign countries. I now notice our intention of sending out an Ambassador to China; if this be so, of course all the pomp and circumstance must go with him, usual in Embass[i]es; and probably sent out in a "Ship of the Line," in order to *ape England*, and other aristocratic rules, and to show the Emperor of China how potent a Nation we are.

Excuse me Sir, if this be ridicule—perhaps the occasion of it, warrants my familiarity. This branching out in unnecessary expenditure, and trouble in establishing an intercourse with China is quite unnecessary, as the Government of that Country is well informed as regards our own; and a plain "Commissioner," would be much more honoured than an "Ambassador clothed in purple and Gold, with a gold laced Cocked Hat, and Spurs at his heels." Witness the reception of Mr. [Edmund] Roberts at *Siam*, as our *Agent* for forming a Commercial Treaty—a plain unpretending man, received by the *King* [Rama III] and Court with more respect and Circumstance than any Ambassador previously, from any *other* Country. The *Court even* dispensed with the ceremony of *kneeling* which up to that time had always been observed at it, as well as at Pekin—and what was more remarkable, the Brother of the King, ["and" *canceled*] the Heir apparent, saluted Mr. Roberts in the English language, and much to his surprize, which led him to ask where he had acquired it? The reply was, "at *Ban[g]kok*["] through the aid of an "American missionary"! Here is proof that those Nations knew something of our People and *our Government*, and enough to render it quite unnecessary to send out other than an Agent, or a "Commissioner" bearing the *Eagle* upon his Button. This last distinction *is requisite*, as the Chinese hold all *Traders*, in the most perfect contempt. The Emperor of China no doubt instantly despatched Keying his *Commissioner* on having a request from Mr. Cushing for a meeting, an alacrity of movement on his part unusual, and probably never before known, which shows the desire he had to become on amicable terms with a People who had successfully resisted the invasions of his late barbarous Enemy, and able to cope with him even in his own Borders, and thus serve to check any further movement on the part of an insatiable foe, desirous of conquest and despotic rule. A British Treaty permit me to remark ought not to have been a guide for our Ambassador as the reciprocal wants of this Country and China are variant from those of England and the latter Country. China needs our *Raw* and manufactured *Cotton—Lead*—manufactures of *wool—Ginseng*— and many other articles of Commerce, in which supplies might be furnished upon lower terms than from England, or any other Country: and our Country as a return from thence needs the *Teas, Raw* and manufactured *Silks—Cassia*, matting—Grass Cloth and a great variety of other articles, and the interchange should be reciprocally *free* of Duties in both Countries. On this Basis a Treaty should have been made, and should it ever be gained, I would bid defiance to England in this Trade, even backed by her monopoly in *Opium* and *Furs* and products of her Asiatic Colonies. In this way we might not only supply ourselves, but, Germany and France more cheaply with Chinese Commodities than they could do it for themselves. Our great staples would circumvent all competition, and the balance of Trade, would be so much in our favour as to drain the Coffers of England of specie. I beg pardon for thus spinning out unintentionally at this time these remarks upon the China Trade, & shall reserve other matter for future communications, should you deem them worth having. Permit me here to briefly remark that our friends in this State are much relieved and gratified to learn your convalescence from your late illness, and trust your valuable life may be spared a long time for the benefit and honour of our common country; and I as one of them hope you may remain in Mr. Polk[']s cabinet, until you may have carried out the great measures you have so firmly, boldly and judiciously brought almost to a termination: then retire and await the call of your Country—and that the call will come, all parties here think, (although they all do not yet speak out), and with more unity than is publically expressed. All now approve *loudly* the call upon France, and the success, has gratified the vanity of the [*one word canceled and "*incorrigible*" interlined*] Whigs; as also the negotiations with Mexico, now, S[*an*]*ta Anna* is down.

Upon the subject of the Consular Laws, I shall have something to say at a future time, as I think they require immediate revision; and as regards the appointment of Party men, instead of those suitable for stations abroad it is much to the injury of Commerce, as well as the dignity, and honour of our Country. I hope the new ministry, will firmly and promptly set aside the example of the Two last Administrations in this matter of appointments, and select those men who may be suitable, rather than those professing political Opinions. With the most profound respect, I have the honour to be, Dear Sir, Your obedient Servant, Chas. Henry Hall.

ALS in ScCleA. NOTE: Hall was one of the leading American merchants in the China trade.

To CHARLES J. INGERSOLL, Chairman of the Committee of Foreign Affairs, H[ouse of] R[epresentatives]

Department of State
Washington, 15th February 1845

Sir: In answer to your inquiry as to what provision it is in my opinion desireable to adopt for a permanent Mission in China, I beg leave to suggest the expediency of making an appropriation for a Minister Resident with a Salary of six thousand dollars per annum, and an outfit of the same amount, to which the[re] should, it seems to me, be added, a Secretary and Chinese Interpreter with a Salary of two thousand and five hundred dollars per annum. This provision is much less than is made by other governments having similar relations with China; and the rate of compensation is but moderate, having in consideration as well the expenses of living in that country, as the importance of the duties to be performed by the Minister. I am &c, John C. Calhoun.

FC in DNA, RG 59 (State Department), Reports of the Secretary of State to the President and Congress, 6:155; PC in Jameson, ed., *Correspondence*, p. 643.

To [LEVI] WOODBURY and [GEORGE] McDUFFIE, [U.S. Senate]

[Washington, *ca.* February 15, 1845?]
I understand from [William Wilkins], the Secretary of War, that there are some objections on the part of the [Senate] Committee of Finance to the Contract with Gen[era]l [Alexander O.] Anderson & others for the removal of the Choctaw Indians. He informs me, that he has made a full report on the subject, which has proved satisfactory ["in reference" *canceled*] to the Committee of Ways & means of the House. The subject was brought by Mr. Wilkins before the Cabinet, and he acted under its decision after full consultation. It was believed to be the best arrangement which could be made under all the circumstances of the case. If the contract should now be arrested, it would cause great difficulty and bring much distress on the emigrating Indians. I have said ["so" *canceled and* "thus" *interlined*] much in order to attract your special attention to the subject. Truly, J.C. Calhoun.

ALS in ScU-SC, John C. Calhoun Papers. NOTE: In 9/1844, Alexander O. Anderson, [former Senator from Tenn.], John B. Forester, Samuel Cobb, and James Pickens, the latter two being Choctaw chiefs, contracted with the War Department to transport Choctaws from Miss. and Ala. to the Indian Territory. In response to a Senate resolution of 1/29/1845, Wilkins submitted a report on 2/6 detailing the contract negotiations. Wilkins's report is printed as Senate Document No. 86, 28th Cong., 2nd Sess. These circumstances have led to the assignment of a tentative date to this undated document.

FEBRUARY 16–MARCH 10
1845

〇

At the end of February the Congress passed the long-awaited joint resolution that would make Texas one of the sisters of the republican Union of the States. Most of the Northern Democrats swung back into line behind the administration their party had elected. The actual admission would not be accomplished until the following December, but on the last day of the Congressional session, March 3, the strength of the South was enhanced by the admission of Florida to the Union.

On that same day, March 3, Calhoun wrote detailed instructions to the American Minister to Texas on how to carry out the consummation of the long desired end. And on March 8 he received the expected protest of the Mexican Minister in Washington.

Though still recovering from a serious illness and in the last weeks of office, the conscientious Secretary of State continued to work hard till the end on a multitude of matters, large and small, not neglecting the relatively unimportant interests of obscure private citizens.

On March 3 the Tyler administration and the 28th Congress expired. Calhoun remained on duty until his successor, James Buchanan, was ready to take office on March 10. Public opinion seemed to feel that Calhoun was a part of the winning coalition, an important part, and would be asked to remain on hand and lend strength to the new administration. In an interview on February 27, Polk informed Calhoun that he intended to form an entirely new Cabinet. He expressed his high regard for Calhoun and offered him appointment as U.S. Minister to Great Britain. He probably was not in the least surprised when Calhoun declined.

The next day Calhoun submitted his resignation. Polk's "determination," he wrote, "has caused, on my part, no dissatisfaction, nor abatement of the kind feelings, personal or political, which I have heretofore entertained for you. According to my opinion, it is the right of every President to select his Constitutional advisers, without giving any just cause of offense to any one."

Calhoun added his "sincere hope, that your administration may confer lasting honor on yourself, & contribute to establish more firmly the liberty & prosperity of the country, by carr[y]ing out in practice the great measures put in issue in the late election . . . ."

⫿

To J[AMES] ED[WARD] COLHOUN, [Abbeville District, S.C.]

Washington, 16th Feb. 1845

My dear James, I opened the enclosed accidentally supposing it was directed to me.

My recovery has been very slow. I have not yet fairly left my chamber. I ride out in a hack every good day, and ventured so far to day, as to call on Mr. [James K.] Polk & the President [John Tyler]. I trust I shall be so far recovered before the end of the week as to be entirely off the sick list.

Nothing is yet known as to Mr. Polk's Cabinet. He is very silent, which I regard as very prudent.

Your Sister [Floride Colhoun Calhoun] and the other members of the Mess are well.

I hope your health is entirely restored & that you had a pleasant journey home. Yours truly & affectionately, J.C. Calhoun.

ALS in ScCleA.

From W[illiam] S. Archer, [Senator from Va.], 2/17. "I am instructed by the Committee on Foreign Relations, to enquire of you at what time the Commission issued to Mr. John A. Bryan as Chargé to [Peru] and at what time he left the United States. It would be desirable for me, to have the answer to these enquiries at the earliest moment." ALS in ScCleA.

From GEO[RGE] M. BIBB

Department of the Treasury
February 17th 1845

The note of the 8th of this month from the Hon. A[lphonse] Pageot, the minister of his majesty the King of France, to you which you did me the honor to refer has been duly considered.

The Act of Congress approved 30th August 1842, imposes specific duties of various rates on the different wines enumerated as well as on the imitations of wines. It is enacted amongst other things that duties be imposed "On Port & Burgundy Wines in Casks, fifteen cents per gallon. That all imitations of any of said Wines and all wines imported by any name whatever, shall be subject to the duty provided for the genuine article, & to the highest rate of duty applicable to the article of the same name."

Such are the positive enactments of the law passed by the Congress and approved by the President of the United States.

In this Section the intention is manifest to impose a duty of fifteen cents per gallon on all port wines, on all Burgundy wines and on all imitations of either of those wines imported into the United States, in casks, no matter by what names such such [*sic*] Port wines, such Burgundy wines, or such imitations of Port & Burgundy Wines may be called.

Port wine is a general name not applicable exclusively to the Wines of Oporto in Portugal, but but [*sic*] includes other such like red wines the product of other nations.

In the 8th Section of the act of 1842, a proviso is introduced "That nothing herein contained shall be construed or permitted to operate so as to interfere with subsisting Treaties with foreign nations."

By the treaty between the United States and Portugal, it is amongst other stipulations, declared "that no other or higher duties shall be imposed on the importation into the United States of America, of any article the growth, produce or manufacture of the Kingdom & possessions of Portugal, than such as are or shall be payable on the like article being the growth, produce, or manufacture of any other foreign Country."

Because the act has placed port wines and Burgundy wines in Casks under the same rate of duty; and because the Treaty with Portugal operating upon the provisions of the Act of 1842, has, by the decision of the Secretary, forbidden the levy of a higher rate of duty on the wines of Oporto than six cents per gallon, and because of the proviso so reducing the rates of duty, as not to interfere with subsisting treaties, it is agreed that the equality of duty between the Port wines of France & of Portugal, & the imitations of the Oporto wines so assimilated in France should be preserved.

To all this the Answers are, that the positive ["ena" *canceled*] enactments of the Statute are that a specific duty of fifteen cents per gallon on all port wines in casks, & on all the imitations of Port Wines, no matter in what country such wines are produced, shall be paid. The Statute imposes an equality of duty only, but does not confound all distinctions between the wines produced in one Country & the other, nor the distinctions between the effect of the Statute and the effect of a Treaty with a foreign nation which overrides and qualifies the Statute.

These distinctions in fact and law still exist. The Statute has not converted French wines into Portuguese wines: nor has the treaty between the United States and Portugal had the effect to put french wines upon an equality with Portuguese wines. The treaty operates as to the wines of Portugal, not as to the wines of France, French Wines are to pay duties according to the Statute not hindered, qualified, or deflected by any treaty. The Wines of Portugal are to pay duties under the Statutes as modified by the Superior obligations of the Treaty between the United States & Portugal.

An Act of Congress to impose duties on imports into the United States does not not [*sic*] desolve the obligation created by a subsisting treaty between the United States and a foreign nation. The tie of a treaty between two nations is fastened by the concurring Wills and mutual assent of the two contracting nations. The tie of a municipal law arrises out of the enactment of a single nation. The latter may be repealed[,] altered & modified at the will of the nation which enacted the law. But the former tie is to be dissolved by the concurring wills of the two nations who made the treaty, or may expire, or become null by consequence of the limitation, or provisions of the Treaty; The maxim "obligatio unumquodque dissolvitum eo ligamine quo ligatur" being as applicable to obligations of treaties as it is to Civil jurisprudence.

The introduction of the proviso into the law of 1842 against its interference with subsisting treaties with foreign nations, manifests the respect of the Legislature for the obligations of treaties, and of an intent that they be observed & fulfilled but that proviso has practically & in fact effected no other construction of the law than that which would have resulted from a Subsisting Treaty if the proviso had been omitted. It is tacitly implied and to be operative in other sections of the same act to which it was not expressly appended.

The several articles of the same treaty are not to be accounted as so many distinct and independent engagements, but as having a common relation: the contracting powers are understood to have agreed to each article in consideration of the others and by way of compensation.

The stipulation of the Treaty with Portugal before quoted in relation to the restriction of duties on imports into the United States, is compensated to the United States by correlative stipulations on the part of Portugal in the same article, and in other articles of that treaty.

Between the United States and France no such treaty for restrictive duty on imports is subsisting. France has no right to draw to her advantage the restrictive stipulations on the treaty between the United States and Portugal.

If the treaty between the United States and Portugal shall expire in pursuance of the limitations and conditions contained in the fourteenth article, or shall be otherwise abrogated, then and in such case the eighth section of the law of 1842 aforementioned would be operative to charge the duty of fifteen cents per gallon on Port wines of Portugal in Casks[;] the letter of the Statute is to impose such duty of fifteen cents per gallon on such wines in Casks: the letter of the Statute, the positive enactment of the law is qualified by subsisting treaties which are in conflict with the Statute, so far as necessary to fulfil the obligation of each subsisting treaty, but not farther, nor for a longer period than during the existence of the treaty. Where no subsisting treaty opposes the law must have its full vigour.

The proviso introduced into the 8th Section, in relation to subsisting treaties, can have no operation to impair the force of the letter of the Statute except so far as each particular treaty may require a deflection from the Statute to satisfy the spirit of the treaty.

No treaty with France, obstructs the effect of the Statute in imposing the duty of fifteen cents per gallon on such French wines. The proviso in the eighth section as to subsisting treaties does in no degree enure to protect the Wines of France called Port wines, or in imitation of Port wines from the duty of fifteen cents as enacted by the law of 1842.

It would be cause of congratulation to the undersigned, if he could, consistently with his sense of duty and obedience to the law of 1842 aforementioned, give the interpretation to that law favorably to the interests of France, the ancient and faithful ally of the United States; which two nations have so many considerations of mutual amity and reciprocal interests to cause them to cultivate a commercial intercourse upon terms of the most friendly character and equal reciprocity.

But I can not perceive any just cause for changing the Opinion expressed in the communication of the third of this month. With very high respect I have the honor to be yours &c, (signed) Geo. M. Bibb Sec[retar]y of the Treasury.

CC in DNA, RG 59 (State Department), Miscellaneous Letters (M-179:107, frames 210–216); CC in DNA, RG 46 (U.S. Senate), 29A-D5; FC in DNA, RG 56 (Secretary of the Treasury), Letters to Cabinet and Bureau Officers, Series B, 5:14–17.

From R[obert] P. Dunlap, [Representative from Maine], 2/17. Dunlap has heard that the *Morris* and *By-Chance* claims of U.S. citizens against New Granada have been settled by [William M.] Blackford, U.S. Chargé d'Affaires to that nation. He asks whether the claim of the heirs of Francis Adams in the case of the brig *Adams* has also been settled. Dunlap also seeks to learn whether papers relating to that claim were deposited in the State Department by Daniel Webster. ALS in DNA, RG 59 (State Department), Miscellaneous Letters (M-179:107, frames 205–206).

To A. Follin, U.S. C[onsul], Omoa and Truxillo, [Honduras], 2/17. Farnham L. Tucker will soon depart New York City for Truxillo. He has been strongly recommended for a Consular post at that place. However, because the port does not merit a Consul, Calhoun suggests that Follin appoint Tucker a Commercial Agent. "The Agent selected will correspond with, and make his Returns thro' you to the Department." FC in DNA, RG 59 (State Department), Consular Instructions, 11:337.

Cha[rle]s Henry Hall, New York [City], to R[ichard] K. Crallé, Department of State, 2/17. Hall encloses his letter to Calhoun of 2/15, requesting Crallé to present it to Calhoun. He also encloses a letter from an American missionary in China relating to Chinese-American commercial and political relations, clipped from an American newspaper. Hall annotated the clipping with his opinions and requests Crallé to send it also to Calhoun. Hall states that Calhoun's reputation is growing in New York as a result of his conduct of negotiations with Texas, Mexico, and France. ALS with Ens in ScCleA.

From J[AMES] HAMILTON, [JR.]

New Orleans, Feb[ruar]y 17[t]h 1845
My Dear Sir, Permit me to introduce Mr. W[illia]m H. Robertson
who goes on to Washington with an object which may be vastly im-
portant to we [*sic*] Cotton Growers—To wit to get introduced into
Russia as well as other portions of the North of Europe the Cotton
Waddings as a substitute for Blankets.

From Mr. Robertson['s] very remarkable capacity for business he
is well qualified to elucidate and recommend any improvement he
may take under his agency and control. You will readily comprehend the material relations of this subject on which he has a great
deal of information.

Mr. Robertson thinks that his appointment as Consul for St.
Petersburg will give him an influential consideration in Russia which
I sincerely hope he may receive from Mr. Polk as he is exceedingly
well qualified for such an Office by both his worth & Talents. If you
can serve him you will oblige—Sincerely & respect[full]y Your friend,
J. Hamilton.

ALS in DNA, RG 59 (State Department), Applications and Recommendations,
1845–1853, Robertson (M-873:74, frames 337 and 344–345). NOTE: An AEU
by Calhoun reads "Gen[era]l Hamilton recommending Mr. Robertson for the
consulate at St. Petersburgh."

From Daniel P. King, [Representative from Mass.], 2/17. King
transmits a petition from merchants of Salem, Mass., favoring the
appointment of William P. Peirce to be U.S. Consul at Macao. "Permit me to add that I am satisfied that Mr. Pierce [*sic*] is well qualified
for this appointment and that he would make a most able and faithful
officer. He is so well known to the Hon[ora]ble Caleb Cushing, late
Commissioner to China, and who will communicate with you on this
subject, that it is unnecessary for me to enlarge." ALS with En in
DNA, RG 59 (State Department), Applications and Recommendations, 1845–1853, Peirce (M-873:67, frames 110–113).

To J. Phil[l]ips Ph[o]enix, Representative [from N.Y.], 2/17.
Calhoun informs Ph[o]enix, in reply to his letter of 2/14, that the settlement of U.S. claims against Belgium is proceeding slowly because
of the "real difficulty of examining and deciding upon such numerous
and complicated accounts." Calhoun assures Phoenix that [Thomas
G.] Clemson, U.S. Chargé d'Affaires at Brussels, will do everything

in his power to expedite settlement of those claims. FC in DNA, RG 59 (State Department), Domestic Letters, 35:107 (M-40:33).

From S[tephen] Pleasonton, "5th Auditor's Office," Treasury Department, 2/17. Pleasonton submits the "account and vouchers" presented by Caleb Cushing, former U.S. Commissioner to China, for his contingent expenses. The accounts total $8,150.37. Pleasonton seeks to learn the beginning and ending dates for Cushing's salary and whether he is to be allowed one year's salary for his outfit and six months' salary for return transportation. ALS in DNA, RG 59 (State Department), Letters and Accounts from Despatch Agents at New York and Boston, vol. for August 1840–November 1847.

From NEDHAM H. WASHINGTON

Washington, February 17th 1845
Sir, In a personal interview a few days since I had the honor of exhibiting several letters from Gentlemen of Virginia & elsewhere recommendatory of my application for a situation within the range of your Department, having special reference to views which I entertained of procuring a Consulate abroad. I understand it to be usual & necessary to designate the particular position to which my views & wishes extend & for that purpose beg leave to state my decided preference for the appointment of Consul at Nassau, in the Bahama Islands. Will you oblige me so far as to consider me an applicant for that position & my letters & other recommendatory papers, speaking generally of a Consulate abroad, as pointed at that particular object. These letters, now in my possession, can be returned & exhibited at any moment it may be necessary to view them in reference to the present application. I have the honor to remain Very Respectfully, Nedham H. Washington.

ALS in DNA, RG 59 (State Department), Applications and Recommendations, 1845–1853, Washington (M-873:91, frames 474–475). NOTE: Lacking a postmark, this letter was probably hand-delivered to Calhoun.

From RICHARD M. YOUNG

Springfield, Illinois, Feb[ruar]y 17, 1845
My Dear Sir, Permit me to introduce to your acquaintance my friend Samuel Holmes Esq. of Quincy in this State, who is about to visit

Washington, and expects to arrive in time to witness the inauguration of our New President [James K. Polk]. Mr. Holmes is a merchant by profession, is one of my old neighbors and acquaintances, and among our most intelligent and worthy Citizens. He is also a republican in principle and practice, and has greatly contributed in elevating our party to its present lofty position in Illinois, and is in every respect well worthy of your attention and respect.

Any civilities you may find it convenient to extend to him, during his short stay at the Metropolis will be properly appreciated by him, and lay me under additional obligations for past kindnesses. I am very respectfully Your friend, Richard M. Young.

ALS in DNA, RG 156 (Records of the Office of the Chief of Ordnance), Application File, Samuel Holmes. NOTE: Young was a former Senator from Ill. and at this time a Justice of the Ill. Supreme Court. He was later Commissioner of the U.S. General Land Office (by appointment of President Polk) and Clerk of the U.S. House of Representatives.

From JOHN ACOSTA

New York [City,] 18 Feb[ruar]y 1845

Sir, Mr. [Alexander J.] Bergen of this City is an applicant for the Consulate at the Havana, and goes to Washington endorsed by both branches of the Legislature of this State, and by Gentlemen in this City whose reputation for high moral and political worth has been acquired, not only by force of talent, but by extreme caution in lending their names to none others than worthy and capable candidates for office. Mr. Bergen then, presents himself as no ordinary aspirant for the Post he solicits; the act of the members of the Legislature has made him the choice of the State, and that of leading merchants of the City, the chosen representative of its vast commercial interests with the Havana.

If the appointment is conferred upon a Citizen of this State, the strong testimonials which he bears must render him its prominent candidate. And while the Cotton, Rice and Tobacco interests of the South, require that these should receive the watchful protection of the Southern man at Liverpool, the important commerce of this City with Cuba, presents equal claims for the North in the appointment of the Consul for the Havana.

To an intimate acquaintance with commerce in its various branches, Mr. Bergen would bring to his aid a mind fruitful in its resources, energy rarely equalled, zeal and untiring devotion in discharge of his duties. His vigorous manhood, ardent and enthusiastic temparent [*sic*], combined with a disposition remarkably sensative and grateful for favours conferred, constitute qualities which in my judgment ought not to be overlooked in the selection of candidates for stations whose possession entitles the occupant to more than ordinary consideration among those over whom it may be desirable, at some future day, that he should exercise influence in furtherance of the principles of which you have so long been the distinguished exponent and able advocate.

Apologizing for this intrusion upon your valuable time, I will add that with your friends in this City, I should deem myself highly favored in the appointment of Mr. Bergen. With great respect I have the honor to be Y[ou]r Ob[edien]t Servant, Jno. Acosta.

ALS in ScCleA.

From Shepard Cary, [Representative from Maine], 2/18. "I enclose herewith a communication [of 12/28/1844 to Calhoun] from Samuel Lowder of Bangor, Maine, and also a letter [of 12/28/1844 to me] from John C. Dexter, Esq. in relation thereto, to which the early attention of the State Department is respectfully requested." [The enclosed documents concerned a claim against Mexico in the case of the schooner *Topaz*.] LS with Ens in DNA, RG 59 (State Department), Miscellaneous Letters (M-179:107, frames 219–222).

To R[obert] P. Dunlap, [Representative from Maine], 2/18. "I have the honor to acknowledge the receipt of your letter of yesterday and to state in reply that the claim in the case of the Brig Adams is not one of those which have been adjusted by Mr. [William M.] Blackford [U.S. Chargé d'Affaires to New Granada] nor have any papers relating to a claim of that description been lodged in this Department." FC in DNA, RG 59 (State Department), Domestic Letters, 35:107 (M-40:33).

From J[AMES] HAMILTON, [JR.]

New Orleans, Feb[ruar]y 18[t]h 1845

My Dear Sir, I was greatly ["relieved" *canceled and* "rejoiced" *interlined*] on my arrival here to find from the Papers that your convalescence was so far established as to relieve your friends of all anxiety in relation to your speedy recovery.

In the mean time let me beg of you not to regard any thing that has passed between us as the value of a tobacco stopper in regard to the mission to England if ["what" *canceled*] it becomes half as desirable ["to you" *interlined*] that you should occupy this Post as it is ["to" *canceled*] important prehaps [*sic*] to the public interest that you should do so. But I am probably making generous concessions at a very small price, as I very much question even if you do not take the appointment whether [James K.] Polk would authorize its being tendered to me. It is an old saying in the Kennel, that the greedy Dogs are always served first and I have no doubt some mouth is ready to receive this *Dotation* (as the King of France says) more rapacious than my own and I am content. I leave the matter in your hands to be managed as you deem most conformable to my character and your own sense of delicacy.

If you do not take the appointment yourself I shall be ["content" *canceled and* "satisfied" *interlined*] whether I obtain it or not, if you will only say to Polk what you have said to me that ["I am" *canceled and* "you consider me" *interlined*] the ["best" *changed to* "better"; *sic*] qualified for the duties of this office than any other man you know South of the Potomac & that no other individual but one on the South Side of this *fearful line* should occupy it at this crisis of anxiety & peril.

I confess if I were to go it would be without the motive of a single personal gratification of pleasure[,] novelty or ["ostentatious" *interlined*] honor, but for the single purpose of accomplishing *a great object in the smallest possible time,* and when that object is accomplished to come home.

If Texas is annexed I shall be relieved of every embarrassment I have in the world and if I go to England on my return I hope to go into Congress *immediately* and be felt again before I die in the cause of the South. I trust in God I may yet contribute to placing ["you" *interlined*] where your Country can alone reap the full fruition of your virtues & Genius. With this view whether you elect to go abroad or stay at home, if your health permits do not withdraw from the public eye, for I cannot but think in the next four years a Crisis will arise which will demand your services in the highest Post known to the Constitution to save both it & the Country from destruction.

Every thing but your health must be sacrificed to this consideration. As you will have vast power in controlling the movement of the Govt. thro' the treaty making power[,] your present Post I think would be far more influential than any other you could ["occupy" *interlined*]. I shall be delighted if Polk has the sensibility to what is due to your character and an apprehensiveness ["as" *interlined*] to what is due to your ability & his own interests to invite you cordially into his Cabinet.

On my arrival here I met [Thomas H.] Benton[']s *projet* for annexation which I think if it is made *definitive* as far as ["fact of" *interlined*] annexation is concerned is far more likely to obtain the concurrence of the people of Texas than the joint Resolutions of the House. These Resolutions really treat Texas as a conquered Territory. They appropriate her revenues ["for Customs" *interlined*] altho these are *solemnly pledged* long since to a certain class of her Creditors & remit the whole of them of all classes to the (*at present*) utter unava[i]ling & unavailable resource of her public Lands. This is not only countenancing but profiting by a most disgraceful repudiation.

I am satisfied that the most influential men in Texas connected with the Govt. would use the unceremonious arrogance and manifest bad faith of these Resolutions to defeat annexation forever. ["For" *canceled and* "And let it be understood" *interlined*] if Congress adjourns without consummating this measure I have *strong reasons* for believing that the British Govt. will submit to the people of Texas propositions providing for a recognition of the Independance of Texas by Mexico & a Peace between the two Countries without requiring any concessions on the Slave Question or any discriminations in favor of her Commerce but simply on the condition of *non annexation* & that Texas shall reduce her Tariff ["for" *canceled and* "to" *interlined*] 10 P[er]-Cent *ad valorem*. If I did not believe from the immense number of European Emigrants coming into the Country under the Emp[r]esarios of the Prince [Charles, of Solms, Braunfels, Prussia,] St. Johns[,] [Henry F.] Fisher & [Henry] Castro that in 5 years Texas would abolish slavery by a popular vote I would come out at once against annexation under a belief that a free port at Galveston would be a powerful Engine for free Trade in the U.S. but as it is I go for a Union between the two Countries. Ever My Dear Sir Yours faithfully, J. Hamilton.

P.S. It has occurred to me that Benton[']s ["Bill" *interlined*] if it were modified & divided into two sections the first to affirm that Texas was *ipso facto* from the passing of the act a member of the Union and his conditions made matters of detail to be arranged afterwards by Commissioners appointed by both Governments it would be far preferable for both & be much more likely to obtain the assent of Texas than the Resolutions of the House. Could not a compromise so as to insure the passage of an Act of Union be passed this session[?]

I forgot to mention one matter which I have much at heart. The continuance of our friend [Robert B.] Campbell in his present office [as U.S. Consul] at the Havannah [*sic*]. If you should not continue in Polk[']s Cabinet I still hope you will lend your influence to take of him [*sic*]. His *social* sympathies for [Henry] Clay never for a moment alienated his heart or his principles from *ours*.

Direct to me at the Oswichee [Bend, Ala.] at your earliest convenience. I shall drop Mr. Polk a Letter tomorrow on the State of things at Texas more in detail than this communication.

ALS in ScCleA; PEx in Jameson, ed., *Correspondence*, pp. 1025–1027. NOTE: This letter was postmarked in New Orleans on 2/19 and was marked "Express Mail."

To Samuel F. Haviland, U.S. C[onsul], Coquimbo, [Chile], 2/18. Haviland is asked to explain why the State Department has received no communications from him since his appointment. FC in DNA, RG 59 (State Department), Consular Instructions, 11:338.

From SIMEON HUBBARD

Norwich, Conn., 18 Feb[ruar]y, [18]45

You have been sick, Mr. Calhoun; very sick—*dangerously* so, as appears by a paragraph just seen by me in a last week[']s paper. I heard sometime past that you *had* been so indisposed as to give up business for a few days, *but was better*. Was there in your case, a *relapse*? If so, you have ["been" *interlined*] in great peril: And but for your *Anne*, would probably have failed. Ah! the Wife, the *Wife*, at *your* age, is the *all-in-all*. For the *Mother*[']*s* solicitude (and well for them) is more, or less, *less felicitous*[?] from *age*. But the *Wife*—whose cares never sleep in such extreme cases; and are ["never" *interlined*] more than momentarily abated by "cat-naps" suffereth no one to administer medicine, or prepare possets, or any outward application, but *herself*. No nurse, no watcher, however esteem'd or valued can the wife trust at such momentous periods. Nor is it possible to induce her by the most earnest entreaty to take care of herself; for *her*-self is merged in a *dearer* self. O *Woman Woman*! is there a man on earth that fully appreciates the ever-abiding divinity there is in thy *all-sustaining bosom*? Alas! no. Nor, except through an *un*-

speakable sympathy, can a woman with woman commune on those emotions which irresistable lead to a *self*-sacrifice for a husband[']s preservation. Will *Lordly man* ever legislate for woman to the full extent of the obligations imposed upon him by the God of nature—the God from whom sexual *organization,* and *adaptedness* are derived?

Mr. Calhoun *I* have had *sweet* experience of *precious* woman[']s innate heavenlyness. And that immediately preceeding the most embittered regrets, & painfull reflections following the death of a Wife of the [age] of *32 years!*

At that, her age, *I* was seized with a fearful malady—of which many [die] within a few days from the attack. The prostration was immediate & extreme. Physicians were called—consultations held. Best of nurses were obtained, & best of neighbourly watchers proffered nightly service. Yet the *wife,* with neither Physician, nurse or watcher would entrust the beloved one—one, for the preservation of whose life she would have gladly laid down her own.

For a fortnight, *critical* medicine was ordered to be taken at stated intervals; varying (as the disease progressed) from 3 to 5, *10,* and *15* minutes; and with the *utmost precision*; and the patient not suffered to sleep one minute beyond the prescribed limits. Not even *once,* in the whole course, was the *Wife* absent! No entreaty, either of the nurse, watcher, or any of the hous[e]hold could persuade her—nor even the plaintive voice of the *sick* could prevail on her to take care of herself—no, not in the least, *tho Big!*

I, became *convalescent*—then *she* was too overjoyed to *think* of herself. Her excitement was as *intense,* as her previous depression was *profound.* She mingled tears of joy with every congratulating *caller-in,* 'till she fell into labour. The *first* part past *happily. Not so the second.* The *Placenta adhered—nor could it be detached. Death was sure.* She *knew* it; and, doubtless, was *pre*-prepared for the event. For her calmness in conversation bespoke it; and in expressing her ulterior wishes, in regard to her little daughters, and the disposition of her numerous *keepsakes* ["she" *interlined*] made it manifest.

Death, delayed the execution of his mission. And her strength and spirits seemed to give assurance that he had *returned his warrent. Hope,* against every preceedent, resumed its empire; and in *two weeks,* extended it to *certainty.* ["Such" *interlined*] as was the unanimous voice of her Physicians ["as" *interlined*] fully expressed on the last, and fatal day of their daily assembling for consultation—a consultation which ended with a remark that it was *almost a miracle*—

the taking a joyfull glass of wine, and charging the *nurse* to be *care-ful* and not give her "good things" *too freely*. An immediate and joy-ful rush of sym[p]athizing neighbours suc[c]eeded. Then, true to the *woman*, her first act was *devotional*. Nor *less true* was her sec-ond; for she immediately sent for assistance to make the *husband a gown* for his *greater comfort*. For myself, being overjoyed ["I" *interlined*] ventured out for the first time, and still very weak. I visited my vegetable garden (2nd August)—From whence I was re-called by a hasty messenger.

She; whose *eyes* beaming with joyous love from under a tasty coif[f]ure befitting her dress of equal taste, and adapted, both, to the season & occasion I had for the last time so recently seen. She, whom I had so recently left occupied in giving orders to her hous[e]-hold, was in a *Death-ague* and *insensible*. Within a few hours she breathed her last, as my head was bowed down upon the same pil-low!!! Then; thoughts of the recently past, rushing in upon the mind like an overwhelming-flood, and rendered more aggravating by the recollection of a *fate-frought* incident at the *conception*, sank me into sorrows *deepest depths*.

I *need* pity and compassion, even, at this distant day—a day *dis-tant in annals only* ["(Aug[us]t 1813)" *interlined*]. *I can* [do] *no more this evening than retire for reflections.*

Morning.

Mr. Calhoun; have you in the course of life (from any circumstance) known one (never seen with the *bodily* eye) whose *finer feelings* you imagined to chord with your own? If so, you have not ["been" *in-terlined*] *quite lost in wonder* in reading the above.

Theme changed.

Being *adverse* to "safe preceedents" *I* am not desirous that you should remain at the post you now so honorably fill. You spoke, as you should have spoken to [William R.] *King*. And you are right in your views of *annexation*. The legitimate course *is by treaty*. But, as that *failed*; let it be done by *joint-resolution*, or any other way, *so that there be not even the shadow of restriction*. I were not for an-nexation 'till I saw *Aberdeen's* letter. What, them d[am]n[e]d *Ish-maelites of the ocean*—that *Marauding nation*; with impunity, say to an *American minister*, "your countrymen shall not keep slaves." (For that is no more than is plainly indicated in that insulting letter). Have the continental powers, been prepared to join in an *exterminat-ing-war* (as far as *War-ships* & *naval depots* are concerned) upon that aggressive nation? Or are they in a *course of preparation*? I wish the *19th Louis* was *twenty years younger than he is*.

In regard to Home affairs. Saving the *legitimate* offsprings of demagoguism; you have but little in Washing[to]n from *this region.* I continue to say to our demagogues (both right & left) *that the policy of S. Carolina* (saving nullification) is the *true policy of this bundle of nations.* And further (this to you confidentially) I have so said to our *Elect.* And, moreover, I have dwelt pretty largely on other topics of prime concern, in my apprehension—particularly on the immediate necessity there is of taking measures to bring both *rulers* & ruled within the *federal pale.* But, as is *most* probable (from the continued assailments to which his position renders him liable) the *breaking of the seals only,* has constituted *all* of its (the letter of a *stranger*) reception. On my private accounts I care not *more than two figs,* whether they were read or not. But, as evinsive[?] that even in *Connecticut* there are just views entertained of federal government, I have *strong desire.* You doubtless are aware that the *Press,* here, is but the creature (and a miserable creature too) of *demagogues.* And if your thought took one step corollaritively, you readily perceived the *impossibility* of getting through it any thing adverse to their views. (There is no safety for us as things *are.* There *must be* an *independent press* established here.)

Should occasion offer—and that pertinently—And were you to *incidentally* speak of Connecticut as a State in which formerly, as known to yourself, there existed *some* right views of federal government, it might awaken curiosity to read with a view of discovering whether in a *rejected* there was something worthy of *regard* or not.

Whether *innate,* or from *habit only,* is immaterial (in this case)[.] But so it is, that through *associations,* I am apt to come to conclusions ["*irrestable*" changed to "*irresistable*"]. A *long time ago* (speaking as would an *Ephemeris*) Through an intrigue that I joined you in thinking it *base,* there was a *breakup,* and an *assundering,* between *two noteables*—which was seized upon by certain political aspirants, to advance themselves in the favour of the *one,* under whose *broadshield,* they imagined their sinuous course might be made in greater security.

From *critical* observation, I perceived that the *sundering* had not, in, and of itself, the *essentials* of *permanency.* Yet through the *spirit of rivalry* (that most reckless of assassins) an unremitting endeavour extended it from *point* to *point,* as their *necessities prompted.* After a *suspension,* induced from *lack of pretence,* a certain *nomination;* while you were in the line of "*safe preceedents*" started the *Hornets.* But, *then,* it was admitted, it would be dangerous to loosen even a *single*-spoke in the *democratic wheel.* But the *point ahead* was kept in view. The *revolving-wheel, fortunately, stopped at the right spot. Then,* attention—*undivided attention* was given to the *point* that was *too high* in altitude. It must be *brought low*—nay *submerged in the ever alternating billows of abolition & protection!*

I was, in a certain office (high in estimation) asked what *I* thought about *filling the cabinet!* I replied by saying, *that thought, was, by right, the President[']s alone.* "Well, it will never do to keep *Mr. Calhoun in his present post".* Why not? "O, a *northern*-man—a *non-slaveholder must fill that office".* I instantly recognised, in that answer, the *length, breadth* and *depth* of *combined-intrigue.* Within a few days after, and in that same office, I was asked if I had *seen a certain paper.* No. One was handed me. I saw that the *resolve,* was going the round of affiliation, that *Mr. Calhoun must* be put *Hors du combat!* I said, on laying down the paper, that if *we* did not *damn the party press* it would bring *us* to *damnation!* And so it will.

Had I not, think you, better *wa[i]ve,* for the present, my aversion to "safe preceedents"? I *have resolved thus to do.* But what will that avail? *Nothing.* God bless you, *my staunch Frede[.]* Yours &c, Simeon Hubbard.

Norwich, Conn., Feb[ruar]y 20th, [18]45

Association has been at work again.

If you are well enough so to do; *you will laugh presently.* Sometime ago I was in a printing office, and there came in, from an adjoining town, an *honest,* though *rabid* politician of thorough *Tammany* principles—And whom I generally, to his head *only,* call *Marat.* He had often ["been" interlined] a *representative*—and once a *State senator.* "Well my good friend" (accosting me) "it always does me good to see you—for, *you* it was that *converted me to Jacksonism".* "Yes gentlemen" turning to the standers by, "I owe my conversion to *Major Hubbard[.]"* Then turning again to me, He began thus, "Well, who do *you* want for our next President"? "I *hear* you are *not* for *Mr.* [*Martin*] *Van Buren[.]"* "Are you for [John] *Tyler*"? *No.* But I would have been if he had not condescended—or rather *descended* so low as *to court the refuse of our V[an] Burenites[.]* "Well who would you have; [*Lewis*] *Cass*"? No great objection to *General Cass,* But I *should prefer Mr. Calhoun.* What! That *Calhown*—who quar-[r]elled with *Gene[ra]l* [*Andrew*] *Jackson!* would you take him for *that*"? (this in a stentorian voice)[.] *No,* not *for* that. "What then" (with a still louder voice) "Because he is a nullifier"? *No.* "What then" (*in a downright scream*) "Because *that Calhown* gave a casting vote to reject *Martin Van Buren that General Jackson had sent to England*"? *No[.]* "For what then" (in a softened voice) would you have that *Calhoun* for president"? Because he is the only one of our aspirants who pays a *profound* homage to ["the" *canceled*] *federal principles*. "What" with a rising voice "*You* turned federalist"! "*You*, who converted me from federal*ism* to Jackson*ism*"! I did not *seek* to *turn you from federalism*, but *to true federalism*. "*True federalism*"! Yes, that from which you say I turned you, *was a petty aristocracy*; that was *unfortunately called federalism*. We live under a *federal Government*. And the absurdity—*dangerous absurdity* of holding up the terms *Federalist* & *Federalism* as terms of reproach to the people living under a federal govt.; I *must and will* speak against. The *good old soul*, in parting, *urged me to call and see him*. The scene, was ludicrous in the extreme—so much so that the bystanders rushed out to give vent to their *laughing propensities*. S.H.

[P.S.] You will perceive by the *orthography* how your name was pronounced. Yet, to give you a more perfect idea, I observe that the last syllable was uttered both *loud & long*. From run[n]ing over the laughable scene, I have become *quite* of a merry mood, S.H.

[P.S.] And I have another *association* ["at my tongue(')s end" *interlined*]. But I fancy you have already enough of *that thing*[']*s* product. S.H.

ALS in ScCleA.

From R[OBERT] M. T. HUNTER

L[l]oyds, Essex [County,] Va., Feb[ruar]y 18th 1845
My dear Sir, I was very much concerned to learn that you were recovering so slowly from your recent attack and regret that I should have troubled you at such a time. I will communicate to Mr. Parker what you say in relation to him. I suspect however that his business will soon take him to Texas.

My friends against my earnest entreaties and expectations have placed me in a position which I fear will force me to run as a candidate for Congress in this District. No event in my political life has troubled me more. I fear it will prove to be an almost *disastrous* step. In every way it is calculated to be injurious to myself. My defeat in the district is almost certain as the whig majority though small is *fixed*. But either defeat or success will endanger my ["success" *canceled*] chances for the U. States Senate. Should we carry the spring elections my prospect for that place was fair until this untoward movement of my friends in this District. If I succeed it will be an excuse for setting me aside as a Candidate for the Senate. If I fail (as it is almost certain that I shall do), the idea of my being [*"a"* canceled] broken down will probably be still more fatal. I owe the nomination which I received in the Legislative Caucus mainly to the active exertions of our peculiar friends in the State. A conversation which you had with [Thomas H.] Bayly [Representative from Va.] on this subject last spring and which he communicated to some one or two of your friends in this State did much to turn the attention of your friends towards me for that post.

I do not know what are Mr. [Thomas] Ritchie[']s private feelings towards my nomination for the Senate. I suspect however that he would prefer some other person and would avail himself of any excuse for that purpose unless our friends should evince anxiety on the subject. Your own wishes on that subject would have great weight with the Calhoun men in this State. And if they adhere to me as a candidate for the Senate [*"notwithstanding the"* canceled] whatever may be the result of the District canvass, some of its injurious effects may be averted. But it will be necessary for this [*"purpose"* canceled and *"end"* interlined] that our friends should adhere steadily to this purpose. Any open expression of your opinion of course might be injurious to yourself but a word or a hint to [*"any"* canceled] some confidential friend in Virginia might be sufficient. I should never have ventured upon these suggestions but for your kind suggestions to Bayly which I presume of course indicated your own feelings on the subject and which were of *great service* to me. What however was judicious then might not be so now and it is possible that Bayly himself may now have some aspirations of the sort. If so he might take any interference on your part as unkind. And should such be his views I would be the last man in the State to [*"which"* canceled] wish you to do it. I desire the place, but not by the use of any means which would shake a single friend of yours in the State. Your friends in this State are most earnestly bent upon preserving their union and strengthening your interest. So far their conduct has been entirely fraternal[,] self sacrificing and cordial. I should be sorry indeed to set the example of a more selfish course of conduct. What is best for the general interest of our principles and of all who are engaged in supporting them I wish to be done and I would not set my private interests in opposition to them. I may be too partial to myself in supposing that my election as Senator would be beneficial to these interests but if I had not supposed it I should not have written this letter. Upon your judgment I rely more than upon my own and I shall be content with any course you may pursue. I have seen you already weakened and worried by the selfish contests of your friends and I have condemned it too much in others to be willing to follow such Examples. I do not therefore desire you to answer this, nor shall I ever enquire what you may do in this regard for I do not wish to embarrass you in the least in pursuing your own judgment on this subject. This letter is of course strictly confidential and when you have read it I beg that you will destroy it.

I infer from your letter that you will not be in Mr. [James K.] Polk[']s Cabinet. For your own interest it is perhaps better that you should not. But Mr. Polk should offer the place to you and in Virginia we shall enquire if he has done so. If he should not do it, he will run great risk of giving deep offence to your friends in Virginia. Yours truly, R.M.T. Hunter.

ALS in ScCleA.

From GEO[RGE] R. IVES, "Private"

Brooklyn, February 18th 1845

Respected Sir, Mr. Alexander J. Bergen of this City solicits the appointment of Consul at *Havanna*. In addition to the numerous friends of the Democracy who certify to his qualifications and would feel gratified at the appointment; may I be allowed to express that it would particularly give pleasure to your Friends if by your interference he should prove successful in his application.

The large and increasing trade would seem to indicate that some one from this State should represent the Commercial interest at that Port. I cannot allow the present opportunity to pass without expressing a hope that a *Southern Man* may be appointed to represent the great Staple interest of our Country at Liverpool. I am Dear Sir, Respectfully Your Ob[e]d[ien]t Servant, Geo. R. Ives.

LS in ScCleA. NOTE: Bergen was appointed U.S. Consul at Bermuda during the interval between the 28th and 29th Congresses but resigned the post in 12/1845.

[MEMORANDUM by Francis Wharton]

[Washington, February 18 and 20, 1845]
On Tuesday, February 18, I called on Mr. Calhoun. He was at his lodgings, at the U.S. Hotel, in Washington and I found him in his bedroom, he having only partially recovered from an attack of congestive fever which had much endangered his life. As he rose to meet me, on my entering the room, I was much struck with the emaciation of his frame, and the feebleness of his gait. He was much thinner than before, his eye was glased [*sic*], his cheek hectic, and his voice broken by cough. He spoke, after a few moments['] conversation on other subjects, about the Oregon negotiation. I saw him again on the Thursday evening following, and on both times he enter[ed] very fully into our foreign as well as our domestic relations. He said that the Oregon correspondence was, he trusted, coming to a satisfactory conclusion, and he spoke with great pleasure of the courtesy with which it had been conducted. He was sure, however, come what might, that the South w[oul]d earnestly stand up against the dismemberment of the continent.

The South had always done so;—e.g. The war of 1812, and the N[orth] E[ast] boundary negotiation, in which he believed he had rendered much service. He mentioned that when Mr. [Thomas H.] Benton's bill was pressing, to fortify the disputed territory, he called on Mr. [Silas] Wright, with whom he had previously had no intercourse, and told him a war was inevitable, if the bill passed. He suggested the bill to authorize the President to raise 50,000 volunteers on an emergency. The bill passed unanimously. He wished that on the Texas question, a similar spirit had been manifested by the North. He believed Texas was essential to the interests of the South, and North also. What it might work on slavery, he c[oul]d not say, but he presumed that it would gradually wear slavery southwards.

He said the words "concurrent majorities" were the essence of the Constitution. He thought that the safety of the country depended on checks. He objected vehemently to Dorrism, as breaking down all constitutional checks.

He spoke very kindly of Mr. [John Quincy] Adams, saying, however, that adversity had had an influence on him by no means genial. Mr. A[dams] was always in earnest; and when in Mr. [James] Monroe's cabinet, had shown much energy, public spirit, and knowledge of expedients, though but little tact. He was too apt to be rash &c.

Mr. [George] McDuffie he mentioned with great respect;

He said that sh[oul]d he not remain in the cabinet, he w[oul]d return home, and that his mind was firmly concluded not to return to the Senate. His health was decaying, and he was desirous also to finish a work he was then engaged in on political economy.

PC in Jameson, ed., *Correspondence*, pp. 644–645. NOTE: Jameson entitled this document, which he found in private hands, "Conversations with Francis Wharton, February 18, 20, 1845." According to Jameson, Wharton himself endorsed the document "Conversation with Mr. Calhoun, Feb. 1845."

From W[ILLIA]M WILKINS

War Department, February 18, 1845

Sir, In answer to your letter of the 12th instant, enclosing a communication of [Charles H. Raymond] the Chargé d'affaires, *ad interim* of the Republic of Texas, I respectfully transmit, herewith, copies of the orders given by the [Assistant] Adjutant General [Lorenzo Thomas] and the Commissioner of Indian Affairs [T. Hartley Crawford] under the instructions of this Department. Very respectfully Your ob[edien]t Serv[an]t, Wm. Wilkins, Secretary of War.

LS with Ens in DNA, RG 59 (State Department), Miscellaneous Letters (M-179:107, frames 207–210); FC in DNA, RG 107 (Secretary of War), Letters Sent by the Secretary of War, 25:476 (M-6:25); CC with Ens in Tx, Records of the Texas Republic Department of State, U.S. Diplomatic Correspondence; PC with Ens in Senate Document No. 14, 32nd Cong., 2nd Sess., pp. 131–132. NOTE: The first En, dated 2/13, from Thomas to Brig. Gen. M[athew] Arbuckle, directs that officer to "adopt such measures as may be necessary" to secure the release of the young son and daughter of "Mrs. Simpson of Texas" from their Indian captors and their delivery to Fort Towson. The second En, dated 2/17, from Crawford to W[illia]m Armstrong, Superintendent of the Choctaw Agency, transmits information regarding the two captive children and requests him to instruct those Indian Agents within his jurisdiction to cooperate with the military to secure the children's release.

To "Commander" J. C. DE FIGANIEÑE E MORAÕ

Department of State
Washington, 19th February, 1845

Sir: I have the honor to acknowledge the receipt of your note of the 3rd instant, relating to the two claims, of Portuguese subjects, residing in the Cape de Verd Islands, for the abduction of certain slaves in the whaling vessels Romulus, of Connecticut, and Pantheon, of Massachusetts, preferred by you in July and November, 1843; which, with their accompanying documents, were communicated by the President of the United States to the Senate on the 14th March last; and to the District Attornies for the Districts from which said vessels sailed, with instructions to examine into the cases, and to prosecute the parties according to circumstances and the law.

I have to acknowledge, at the same time, a document which accompanied, and is referred to in your note of the 3rd instant, submitting a third and similar claim, presented by John Baptist Livramento, a merchant of Villa da Praya, of the Island of Santiago, for the abduction, on the 28th November, 1844, of his slave Alexander, a carpenter by trade, by James K. Turner, master of the whaling ship Janus, of New-Bedford, owned by W.C. Nye & Co., of Fair Haven; the said Livramento alleging that he has incurred, thereby, the loss of six hundred and fifty mil-reis, which he, accordingly, claims.

In reference to the first case of complaint, that of the Romulus, the District Attorney of the United States for Connecticut [Jonathan Stoddard], informed this Department, on the 26th December last, that, at that date, the vessel, though expected, had not returned, and that he had taken measures to be promptly informed of her arrival.

As it regards the case of the Pantheon, the Department has not yet received intelligence of her return, nor of any action in the case, on the part of the District Attorney of the United States at Boston [Franklin Dexter].

I am directed by the President to inform you that, copies of the documents in the case of the Janus, will be transmitted, as soon as possible, to the District Attorney of the United States, for Massachusetts, with proper instructions; and also laid before the Committee of Foreign Affairs of Congress, to which, the papers in the former cases have been referred by the President.

The frequent recurrence of such acts of outrage is a source of much chagrin and pain to the President, who would be well pleased to recommend, or to take, efficient measures to prevent their repetition. I am, Sir, with great consideration, Your very obedient Servant, J.C. Calhoun.

FC in DNA, RG 59 (State Department), Notes to Foreign Legations, Portugal, 6:75–77 (M-99:80).

From J[AMES] S. MAYFIELD

Wood Lawn, Febr[uar]y 19th 1845

My Dear Sir, Some weeks since, I promised Gen[era]l Duff Green in Texas to address him under cover to you at Washington City.

The subject related to his late difficulties with the President of that Republic [Anson Jones]; they as I am informed by Major Donaldson [*sic*; Andrew J. Donelson] who arrived here a few days since have been adjusted not whol[l]y however to Gen[era]l Green's satisfaction.

The basis of the misunderstanding between them arose from supposed menaces, and the indisposition of the President to favour annexation, and a strong inclination manifested to favour the line of British policy indicated of late by Capt. Elliott [*sic*; Charles Elliot]. Gen[era]l Green's position in the Country as a functionary of your Government placed him in a false attitude. As a citizen of Texas, he could have sustained all his charges & that without subjecting himself & his friends to the Charge of intermed[d]ling in the policy of our domestic affairs. Allow me to premise this much, that the fact exists, and the proof can be made that England seeks territory between the Nueces & the Rio Grande and claims for British subjects large Grants of land lying within the Boundaries of Texas. I shall leave in a few days for N[ew] O[rleans] where I expect to meet Gen[era]l Green, when if it is desired to prosecute the enquiry further upon this subject; I will submit a full statement of facts. Having been for many years seperated from my personal and political friends in the U.S. I feel great delicacy in renewing the slight acquaintance of former years; permit me to add that I have watched with the pride and enthusiasm at all times the proud and elevated stand you have assumed as an American patriot and statesman. Yours truly with sentiments of high consideration, J.S. Mayfield.

ALS in ScCleA; variant PC in Boucher and Brooks, eds., *Correspondence*, pp. 282–284. NOTE: An AEU by Calhoun reads, "Mr. Mayfield[,] relates to Gen[era]l Green." Mayfield was Secretary of State of Texas in 1841. The version of this letter printed in Boucher and Brooks erroneously includes a three-paragraph portion of a different letter. While Mayfield was a Texan, this letter appears to have been written from the U.S. "Wood Lawn" has not been identified, but may have been a plantation in Mayfield's native Tenn. or possibly a town in Miss.

To Sam[ue]l Nelson, [Cortland, N.Y.?], 2/19. "The President having by and with the advice & consent of the Senate, appointed you Associate Justice of the Supreme Court of the United States, I have the honor herewith to enclose your commission. You will be pleased to inform this Department of the receipt of it, and, should it be accepted of the name of the State or Country in which you were born." FC in DNA, RG 59 (State Department), Domestic Letters, 35:108 (M-40:33).

From ALBERT SMITH

Washington, Feb[ruar]y 19th 1844 [*sic*; 1845]

Sir: I have the honor to lay before you a statement of the progress of the Joint Commission, appointed to run and trace certain portions of the "Boundaries between the Territories of the United States, and the Possessions of her Britannic Majesty in North America," under the Treaty of Washington of August 9th 1842.

The appropriation for the prosecution of the work, having been delayed until the seventeenth of June last, it was impossible to commence operations in the field, until late in the month of July.

Immediately after the appropriation was made, Maj. James D. Graham the head of our scientific corps was instructed to put the corps in action.

Six parties were organized on the part of the American Commission each under the charge of an Engineer, and placed along the Line, from the intersection of the meridian with the St. John, to the Height of Land, so called upon the ridge of Highlands at the intersection of the Kennebec Road.

Major Graham first visited the Height of Land, and determined accurately the Latitude and Longitude of that important position on the Highlands, and issued instructions in detail to the Engineers charged with the highland survey. During that visit the instruments which it was necessary to transport for the above mentioned object afforded him a favourable opportunity, without causing any loss of time in reference to the Boundary duties, to determine with accuracy the positions of the places where his party rested at night, on the journey between Boston and the Highlands. No occasion to multiply these observations was lost, and the Latitudes and Longitudes of Portland, Augusta, Waterville, Solon, the bridge over the W[est] Branch of the Kennebec, a little above the Forks, & Moose River Custom House and Post Office were determined from Astronomical Observations by him, aided by his Assistant, Lieut. [Amiel W.] Whipple.

Major Graham then ascended the St. John with his party and supplies in batteaux and canoes to the South West Branch of that river, where he erected an observatory, and was engaged during the season in making astronomical observations, surveying the straight line from the parallel of 46°25′ N.L. to the North West Branch of the St. John, and superintending the general work of the survey.

In ascending the river St. John between the Grand Falls and Latitude 46°25′ on the South West Branch, Major Graham determined a number of points astronomically both in Latitude and Longitude, which will be a great aid to the construction of a general map, exhibiting with accuracy, the geographical character of the country, in connection with the boundary line.

Many difficulties were encountered by him and his party in ascending the St. John, and especially its upper branches, arising from the very low stage of the waters at the late season to which the surveys were unavoidably delayed by a want of timely appropriations by Congress. The duties of his party were continued in the field until the ninth of November, the snow being then fifteen inches deep. He then descended the St. John from the astronomical station on the South West Branch, and for two hundred miles of canoe and batteau navigation many difficulties were encountered, by the masses of floating ice that surrounded the canoes and batteaux, and from the difficult and often dangerous rapids which had to be passed. The instruments & other public property were all however brought down in perfect safety and stored, the latter part of November, at Woodstock, N[ew] B[runswick] for the winter. The obstruction to the navigation from the ice, rendered it impracticable to transport them farther until the next season.

Leiut. George Thom was directed to survey the straight line from the outlet of Lake Pohenagamook to the North West Branch; a work which he accomplished with ability and dispatch.

Leiut. J[ames] L. Donaldson made a survey of the Great and Little Black Rivers, from their intersection with the boundary to their junction with the river St. John—an arduous and difficult duty by reason of the difficult and dangerous rapids in the former, and of ["the" *interlined*] want of sufficient water in the latter to ascend it in boats with supplies &c. for his party.

Mr. A[lexander] W. Longfellow, a civil Engineer, in conjunction with an Engineer of the British Commission, after erecting a large cast iron Monument at the source of the St. Croix, and several smaller monuments upon the Line to the St. John, (in addition to those placed there in 1843) went upon the meridian to its intersection with the

St. John, and, at that point, erected another monument of the largest size.

They then placed monuments of cast iron upon all the Islands in that river, below the St. Francis, having an inscription upon them, to designate the nation to which each Island belongs. These, as well as all the monuments upon the Boundary Line, were painted white. Mr. Longfellow then ascended the St. John, and made a survey of the portion of that river above the mouth of the St. Francis, and of the South West Branch to the parallel of 46°25' N.L. which had not been surveyed by Capt. [Joseph E.] Johnston in 1843.

To Leiut. W[illiam] H. Emory of the Corps of Topographical Engineers, and Mr. F[olliott] T. Lally, Civil Engineer, was assigned the difficult and arduous duty, of exploring the Highlands ["which divide the waters" *canceled*] which divide the waters which flow into the St. Laurence, from those which fall into the Atlantic, and of ascertaining and tracing the line of Boundary along the crest. They commenced operations with their respective parties at the Height of Land on the Kennebec Road. Mr. Lally, assisted by Mr. J[ohn] F. Anderson, Civil Engineer, taking the line extending North East, to the Metjarmette Portage, and Leiut. Emory, assisted by Leiut. Reynolds [*sic;* William F. Raynolds] of the Topographical Engineers, working South West in the direction to Halls stream. There being no road, or pathway accessible at that season to the Line, all the supplies, instruments, tents and camp equipage required for their parties, were transported to, and upon those mountain ridges, upon the backs of men. By constant and unceasing labor and perseverance, Leiut. Emory ascertained, surveyed and traced the Boundary, from the Height of Land to the head of Dead River—a distance, which it was not supposed possible to be accomplished in the time and with the force at his disposal. Nothing short of the most untiring and active exertions, in storms as well as sunshine, enabled him to do it.

Mr. Lally with his force completed the survey of the Boundary along the Highlands from the Height of Land to the source of the South West Branch of the St. John in the Metjarmette Portage, and, although the season was then far advanced, and ice had began to make in that stream, he determined to survey it to the parallel of 46°25' N.L. before he left the field. This he accomplished by the fifth of November, after undergoing, with his party many hardships and constant labour and fatigue.

The last party in the field upon that portion of the Boundary, did not leave their work until the fifteenth of January, when there was nearly six feet of snow upon the ground.

It gives me pleasure to state, that every Officer, and, with hardly an exception, every labourer engaged upon the Boundary the past season, have manifested, throughout, a commendable and prais[e]-worthy zeal in the service. Duty more severe has rarely been performed by any body of men.

The utmost harmony has prevailed, not only among ourselves, but between the parties of the two nations; and every possible facility has been afforded by the British Commissioner [Lt. Col. James B.B. Estcourt] to enable me to prosecute the work.

I am informed by Major Graham, that the astronomical calculations of the scientific Corps have been quite satisfactory and at the important points have agreed, as far as they have been compared, with those of the British Astronomers.

All the Engineers are now diligently employed in making plats of their surveys, and computations of the Astronomical Observations.

The number of labourers employed during the season has been about three hundred, and the whole cost of the survey for the year 1844—including salaries and contingent expenses so far as I am at this time able to estimate it, has been about thirty seven thousand dollars.

This has been enhanced by the increased cost of transportation at the late season of the year, that we entered the feild.

An examination of my report of the operations of the joint Commission in 1843—and of this communication, will shew the extent of the Boundary which has, thus far, been surveyed and determined.

It will be perceived, that the line has been surveyed, cut out and cleared thirty feet wide, and established by the erection of cast iron monuments, from the source of the St. Croix, to the outlet of Lake Pohenagamook.

From that point, to the head of the South West Branch of the St. John at the Metjarmette Portage, it has been surveyed by both parties, cut out, and cleared, and is ready for the erection ["of the erection" *canceled*] of the monuments which are ["now" *interlined*] being transported to the line upon sleds, to be placed early in the spring.

From the Metjarmette Portage to the head of Dead river, a line has been surveyed by the Engineers of both parties and cut out, but has not been verified and established by the Commissioners. This will be done early in the spring, and, if found to be correct, of which I have no doubt, the monuments, which are now upon the line will be erected.

I learn also that an exploratory line has been cut out and surveyed by the British Commissioner from Dead River to the head of Halls Stream.

The survey, therefore, which yet remains to be accomplished, extends upon the Line from Dead River to the River St. Lawrence—a distance upon a straight line of about two hundred and fifty miles, requiring more than a thousand miles of survey.

It is believed, that this may be accomplished, so far as the field operations are concerned, during the next season, if it be deemed indispensable. But, to accomplish it in the manner required by the Treaty, it will require the labour of six or seven hundred men, and an expenditure of seventy five or eighty thousand dollars. I have the honor to be, Sir—very respectfully Your ob[e]d[ien]t Serv[an]t, Albert Smith, U.S. Boundary Commissioner.

LS in DNA, RG 76 (Records of Boundary and Claims Commissions and Arbitrations), Letters Received by the Department of State concerning the Northeast Boundary Line, 1843–1850 and 1866; three variant drafts (dated 2/15, 2/17, and undated) in DLC, Albert Smith Papers.

To President [JOHN TYLER]

Department of State
Washington, 19th February, 1845

To the President of the United States.

The Secretary of State, to whom has been referred a Resolution of the Senate of the 17th instant, which is in the following words: "Resolved, that the President of the United States be requested to inform the Senate of the reasons which have prevented him from communicating copies of the correspondence, evidence and papers on file in the State Department in the case of the [claim of] owners of the Brig Gen[era]l Armstrong [against Portugal], called for by their Resolution of the 18th [*sic*; 8th] ultimo," has the honor to inform the President that, the documents called for by the Resolution are so numerous and voluminous, that the Department, with all the force it could devote to this object, has not yet been able to prepare the whole of them for communication. Respectfully submitted, J.C. Calhoun.

LS in DNA, RG 46 (U.S. Senate), 28A-E3; variant FC in DNA, RG 59 (State Department), Reports of the Secretary of State to the President and Congress, 6:158–159. NOTE: Tyler transmitted this to the Senate on 2/20. The resolution to which it responds can be found in DNA, RG 59 (State Department), Miscellaneous Letters (M-179:107, frame 218) and in *Senate Journal*, 28th Cong., 2nd

Sess., p. 174. The earlier resolution of 1/8 is found in Miscellaneous Letters (M-179:107, frame 35) and in *Senate Journal*, 28th Cong., 2nd Sess., p. 77.

To "Brigadier General" CARLOS MARIA DE ALVEAR, [Argentine Minister to the U.S.]

Department of State
Washington, 20th February, 1845

Sir: I have the honor to acknowledge the receipt of your note of the 7th instant, referring to a conversation between us in relation to the capture of the Argentine blockading squadron off the Port of Monte Video by the United States frigate Congress, under the command of captain [Philip F.] Voorhees.

In the conference referred to you correctly understood me to say that the government of the United States deeply regretted the occurrence, and that as soon as an official report of the transaction should be received from Commodore [Daniel] Turner, it would be prepared to adopt such measures as the circumstances of the case and the honor of the two countries should require. I regret to say that this information has not, as yet, been received. As soon as it shall have reached the Department it will be laid before the Executive and the result of its deliberations immediately communicated to you.

It is proper I should avail myself of the occasion to say that you seem in your note to have misunderstood some expressions in a part of the conversation referred to, which I beg leave to correct. The opinion I ventured to express as to the conduct of Captain Voorhees was confined entirely to the state of the facts as they were known to the Department, which did not seem to justify the course he had thought proper to adopt. I did not design to be understood as expressing any definitive opinion on the merits of the case, until the official report of the officer in command of the station should have been received. The government of the United States feels every disposition to cultivate the most amicable relations with the Argentine Confederation; and its final decision on the merits of this unhappy occurrence will show its readiness to do whatever justice may demand. I have the honor to be, with high consideration, Sir, Your obedient servant, John C. Calhoun.

FC in DNA, RG 59 (State Department), Notes to Foreign Legations, Argentina, 6:14–15 (M-99:1).

To Shepard Cary, [Representative from Maine], 2/20. "I have the honor to acknowledge the receipt of your Communication of the 18th inst. relative to the claim against the Mexican Government in the case of the Schooner Topaz, and to inform you in reply that the subject will receive all necessary attention from this Department." FC in DNA, RG 59 (State Department), Domestic Letters, 35:111 (M-40:33).

From F[RANKLIN] H. ELMORE

Charleston [S.C.], Feb[ruar]y 20, 1845

My Dear Sir, I yesterday met our friend Whitemarsh B. Seabrook Esq. & had a conversation of much interest with him in regard to himself & I am induced by what occurred to write to you on the subject. His health has not been good for many years. He has been really greatly enfeebled. Upon inquiring of him if he contemplated any movement for reinvigorating his constitution, he said he could not indulge in what really promised most, a travel to Europe, as he could not afford it. At the same time he said he would like very much some excuse for going, and if he could obtain some commission or charge that would pay expenses, he would very gladly avail himself of it to go. In the further conversation I found he only cared for something to last for a mere trip & that a Bearer of Despatches, Messenger of Govt. was what he limited his views to. Could you not give him some thing that would pay his expenses & give him a position of respectability suited to his worth & wishes? He is you know one of our truest & purest men & has done the State service. If you can I know it will be highly gratifying to him & may contribute to resuscitate & prepare him for better service hereafter when we may need him & all such.

If he can be sent, the sooner the better as the Season of the year approaches when his constitution ["is" *canceled*] begins to feel the effect of the climate.

All here are anxiously looking for the adjustment of the new Administration & the development of its policy—and I scarcely meet a doubting mind even as to your course. All concur that if your work is not done & you have the offer, that you should remain if no conditions *are required of you* inconsistent with your honor. As to yourself, once in fairly & honorably, we all feel perfectly assured, your own inherent strength will make for you all conditions you may require. In great haste Y[ou]rs truly, F.H. Elmore.

ALS in ScCleA.

From Hardy & Baker, [Boston, *ca.* 2/20]. They inform Calhoun that the bark *Zulette,* of Boston, was fired upon on 12/24/1844 as it was passing the Spanish fort at Tarifa, near Gibraltar. Although the vessel had not hoisted her signal flag, it was dark at the time and the flag could not have been distinguished if it were flying. They enclose an extract from the *Zulette's* logbook of that date. LS with En in DNA, RG 59 (State Department), Miscellaneous Letters (M-179:107, frames 238–239); CC in DNA, RG 84 (Foreign Posts), Spain, Instructions, 1:563–564.

To Thomas N. Herndon, "app[oin]t[e]d" U.S. Consul, Galveston, 2/20. Calhoun informs Herndon of his appointment. He encloses instructions for the performance of his duties and a blank bond form to be completed and returned. His commission has been sent to the U.S. Legation in Texas to obtain an Exequatur and then will be sent to him. FC in DNA, RG 59 (State Department), Consular Instructions, 11:339–340.

To C[HARLES] H. RAYMOND

Department of State
Washington, 20th February, 1845

Sir: In reply to your note of the 11th instant upon the subject of the two children of Mrs. Simpson of Austin, in Texas, who are alleged to be in the possession of certain Indians within the United States, I have the honor to transmit, herewith, a copy of documents which have this day been received from the Department of War.

I avail myself of this occasion to offer you renewed assurances of my respectful consideration. J.C. Calhoun.

LS in TxGR, Samuel Moore Penland Autograph Book; FC in DNA, RG 59 (State Department), Notes to Foreign Legations, Texas, 6:81 (M-99:95); FC in Tx, Records of the Texas Republic Department of State, Copybooks of Letters Received from Texan and Foreign Representatives, vol. 2-1/103, p. 63; CC with Ens in Tx, Records of the Texas Republic Department of State, U.S. Diplomatic Correspondence; PC with Ens in Senate Document No. 14, 32nd Cong., 2nd Sess., pp. 131–132. NOTE: Enclosed with this were copies of W[illia]m Wilkins' letter of 2/18 to Calhoun and its enclosures.

To Elisha A. Rhodes, Galveston, 2/20. Duff Green having resigned his post as U.S. Consul at Galveston, President John Tyler has appointed Thomas N. Herndon to succeed him. Rhodes is instructed to surrender to Herndon the consular records. FC in DNA, RG 59 (State Department), Consular Instructions, 11:340.

From CHARLES H. TODD & Co.

New York [City], Feb. 20th 1845
Sir, With reference to our letters of the 8th Oct[obe]r & 7th Dec[embe]r last due acknowledgments of which we have had the honour to receive from your department, we beg leave now to inform you that having received further accounts from Merida de Yucatan relative to the case of the Cargo of the Brig Henry Leeds, we have resolved to withdraw our claim on the Mexican Government in that case, as being untenable. We find on minute investigation which was made by Mr. Eneas McFaul Jun[io]r Consul of the U.S. for Laguna, who visited Merida on his way to his Consulate, and in whose ability and integrity we have full confidence, that we laboured under erroneous impressions as to the facts of the case; impressions caused by representations which we have since discovered to have been false.

We wrote some time since to Mr. [Pedro] de Regil y Estrada our Consul at Merida, complaining of the injustice that had been done us, and have received a long explanatory letter from him in reply, the truth of which has been confirmed by Mr. McFaul convincing us that neither Mr. Regil nor the Yucatan authorities were at fault. We have in consequence written to them that we should with draw the claim we had lodged with you for presentation, which we hereby do; and remain Very respectfully Your obed[ien]t Serv[an]ts, Charles H. Todd & Co.

LS in DNA, RG 76 (Records of Boundary and Claims Commissions and Arbitrations), Records of U.S. and Mexican Claims Commissions.

To Doctor J[OSÉ] M. CAMINERO

Department of State
Washington, 21st February, 1845
Sir: The letter of the President of the Dominican Republic [Pedro Santana] to the President of the United States of which you were the

bearer, with a copy of your credentials and also of the Constitution of your government and your memoir embracing a historical sketch of the events which led to the declaration of independence of the Dominican Republic and the establishment of a separate government have all been laid before the President and have received from him that deliberate consideration which their importance demands.

I am instructed by him to inform you that he has read your memoir with much interest and that he trusts that the people of the Dominican Republic will be able to maintain the independence they have declared and the government they have adopted; but that it has been the usage of this government before it recognizes the independence of one newly established to appoint a Commissioner to proceed to the country and to investigate and report his opinion on all the facts and circumstances on which it is deemed necessary to be informed before a decision is made. In conformity thereto, John Hogan, Esq[ui]r[e] of New York has been appointed a Commissioner and instructed to proceed to the Dominican Republic and report with as little delay as practicable on all the points on which the government desires information to guide it in its decision in this case. On the receipt of his report a decision will be made which will be communicated to you.

Mr. Hogan has been instructed to ["take" *interlined*] charge of any despatch to your government or communication which you may think proper to place in his custody. I have the honor to be, Sir, with high consideration, your obedient servant, J.C. Calhoun.

FC in DNA, RG 59 (State Department), Diplomatic Instructions, Special Missions, 1:210 (M-77:152).

To William P. Chandler, "app[oin]t[e]d" U.S. Consul at Puerto Cabello, [Venezuela], Wilmington, Del., 2/21. Calhoun informs Chandler of his appointment and encloses instructions for the performance of his duties. FC in DNA, RG 59 (State Department), Consular Instructions, 11:341.

To John H. Litchfield, Puerto Cabello, 2/21. William P. Chandler has been appointed to succeed the late Franklin Litchfield as U.S. Consul at Puerto Cabello. John Litchfield is requested to surrender to Chandler the consular archives and records placed in his custody. FC in DNA, RG 59 (State Department), Consular Instructions, 11:342.

To Washington Reed, Milton, N.C., 2/21. Reed is informed of his appointment to be U.S. Consul at Sagua la Grande, Cuba, and sent copies of a blank bond and various other documents. Abs in DNA, RG 59 (State Department), Consular Instructions, 10:285.

To William H. Rogers, U.S. Dis[tric]t Att[orne]y, Wilmington, Del.

Department of State
Washington, Febr[uar]y 21, 1845

Sir, Your letter of the 13th Instant, respecting the case of Capt. Hiram Gray, late of the Brig "Agnes" charged with certain acts in violation of the Laws of the U. States for the suppression of the Slave trade, has been received.

Under the doubt expressed by you and the District Judge [Willard Hall] of the sufficiency of the papers with which you have been furnished, to authorise the commitment of Gray, I have to request that you will suspend further proceedings against him for the present. A letter was received on the 19th Instant from the U.S. Consul at Rio de Janeiro [George W. Gordon], in which he states that the Witnesses in this case will soon be sent to the U. States. You will be advised of their arrival as soon as the Department receives the information, and in the mean time, to secure the arrest of Gray, I have to request that you will have his movements carefully watched.

It may be proper to mention, that [Henry M. Watts] the U.S. District Attorney ["at Philadelphia," *interlined*] to whom papers similar to those enclosed to you, were forwarded, has informed the Department, that on the strength of them, Judge [Archibald] Randall of the District Court of the U. States, had issued warrants for the arrest of Gray, [William M.] Ruhl & [R.S.] Gough. I am Sir &c, J.C. Calhoun.

FC in DNA, RG 59 (State Department), Consular Instructions, 11:342–343.

From Reuben Saffold, Cahawba, Ala., 2/21. Saffold recommends Benjamin Harrison for appointment to be U.S. Marshal for the southern district of Ala. Harrison's term as Sheriff of Lowndes County will soon expire. ALS in DNA, RG 59 (State Department), Applications and Recommendations, 1845–1853, Harrison (M-873:38, frames 159–161).

To President [JOHN TYLER]

Department of State
Washington, 21st Feb[ruar]y, 1845

To the President of the United States.

The Secretary of State, to whom has been referred the resolution of the Senate of the 14th instant, requesting the President to communicate to that body, if not inconsistent with the public interest, "the instructions given to the late Commissioner to China [Caleb Cushing], and any communications made directly to that Government," has the honor of reporting to the President the accompanying papers, which embrace a copy of the documents called for by the resolution. Respectfully submitted, J.C. Calhoun.

LS in DNA, RG 46 (U.S. Senate), 28A-E3; FC in DNA, RG 59 (State Department), Reports of the Secretary of State to the President and Congress, 6:159; PC with Ens in Senate Document No. 138, 28th Cong., 2nd Sess., pp. 1–9. NOTE: Enclosed with the last-cited source were three letters of May and June, 1843 from Daniel Webster and H[ugh] S. Legaré to Cushing and two documents of July 12, 1843, from John Tyler to the Emperor of China, all concerning the establishment of friendship and good commercial relations between the U.S. and China. This report was transmitted by Tyler to the Senate on 2/21. The resolution to which it responds can be found in DNA, RG 59 (State Department), Miscellaneous Letters (M-179:107, frames 203–204) and in *Senate Journal*, 28th Cong., 2nd Sess., p. 158.

From JA[ME]S WHITCOMB, [Governor of Ind.]

Indianapolis, Ind[ian]a, Feb. 21st 1845

Doctor Charles Parry, formerly of Philadelphia, but for the last eight years a citizen of this place, is desirous of receiving an appointment as Consul either at La Guayra, Guayaquil, Callao, Valparaiso, Rio Janeiro, Buenos Ayres, or Montevideo.

Doctor P[arry] is a gentleman of the most reputable standing, agreeable manners, well informed, has a large circle of acquaintances, and is highly esteemed. I am fully satisfied of his competency for the situation he seeks, and should be much gratified to hear of his appointment.

Doctor P[arry] has been an uniform and firm supporter of the principles, measures and candidates of the Democratic Party. Jas. Whitcomb.

ALS in DNA, RG 59 (State Department), Applications and Recommendations, 1845–1853, Parry (M-873:65, frames 758–759).

From BARNABAS BATES

New York [City,] Feb[ruar]y 22, 1845

Dear Sir, It gives me pleasure to inform you that a very large & respectable meeting was held in the Park this after noon at 5 O'clock, & strong resolutions in favor of Texas were passed unanimously, with the exception of *one* solitary voice in the negative. Preserved Fish one of our oldest & most respectable democrats presided. The meeting was addressed by R[obert] H. Morris our late Mayor, & Mr. Bosworth & other gentlemen with great power, & the audience responded with enthusiasm to their remarks.

It will be gratifying to you to learn that this measure is supported by the great mass of the democratic party in this region, & is growing more & more popular every day. The influence of Messrs. [Martin] Van Buren, [Silas] Wright &c &c, has little or no weight with the people on this subject. Texas they say must be annexed, ["&" *canceled*] *now* or *never*.

In connexion with this permit me to unite with your friends in expressing the hope that you will be induced to remain in your present important station. The best interests of the country require it, & I know that ["that" *interlined*] is with you a paramount consideration. I have made no professions of friendship, but it has not be[en] any the less sincere and devoted to you for the last 20 years, & I ardently hope that you may not leave the councils of the nation at this important crisis. Your letter to Mr. [William R.] King has made the hypocritical British wince because you have laid bare in that masterly & powerful production their real motives in promoting abolition. Let them look at home upon their millions of *white* slaves & relieve them from starvation & want, from ignorance & depravity before they attempt to look to this country, & when they cease to subjugate & enthral the millions of human beings in the East, they may then have some apology to whine over American slavery. Excuse this digression, I was led imperceptibly into these observations.

I will close by expressing my sincere hope that you will for the good of the country, forego your own comfort, & consent to remain in your present position. I remain Sir very sincerely your friend, Barnabas Bates.

ALS in ScCleA; variant PC in Boucher and Brooks, eds., *Correspondence*, pp. 284–285.

From J[osé] M. Caminero

Washington, February 22, 1845

Sir, I had the honour to receive your note of the 21 inst. whereby among other things you inform me of the appointment made by the President of Mr. John Hogan of New York as Commissioner to proceed to the city of St. Domingo with the object of investigating and obtaining information on the points ["of" *altered to* "on"] which the Government desires to be informed in order to guide it in its decision with regard to the recognition of the independance of the Dominican Republic, and allow me to avail myself of this opportunity to recommend to you for the interest of the said Republic that so soon as Mr. Hogan shall have made his report the Government will deign to give its decision and to make it known to me as you state in your said note; because the least delay may occasion the greatest injury, on account of the arrest of the progress of international and domestic affairs, supposing them to remain *in statu quo* until that time.

Permit me likewise to recommend to you Sir, to submit to the consideration of the Government, that if the Dominican Republic has directed itself in preference to the United States, it is because it desires to contribute to draw more closely, the bonds ["of" *altered to* "and"] interests of all America, and because it knows that in every point of America, the influence and controul of European nations, should be kept off. This great and important question cannot have escaped ["the" *altered to* "your"] perspicacity; and it appears moreover that the Confederacy of the United States, of America, as the oldest ["and" *canceled and* "nation and the" *interlined*] most powerful ["nation" *canceled*] from the force of ["their" *canceled and* "its" *interlined*] institutions from ["their" *canceled and* "its" *interlined*] extensive means and resources, and even from the order of nature, appears to be called to be the support and safeguard of the West Indies.

Being persuaded that the Commissioner Mr. Hogan, will find the accounts of the Dominican Republic given by me to this Government exact, it is to be hoped that its independance will be promptly recognised; the more as its firm establishment, must redound to the benefit of the greater security of the islands and possessions in its vicinity, where slavery exists, as it has freed itself from the Haytian negroes, and has thus ["by diminishing" *altered to* "diminished"] the force of the bad example offered by those negroes, and restrained them from usurping the territory of others. I have the honour to be Sir Your Obed[ient] Serv[an]t, Dr. J.M. Caminero.

State Department translation of ALS (in Spanish) in DNA, RG 59 (State Department), Notes from Foreign Legations, Dominican Republic, vol. 1 (T-801:1); PC in Senate Executive Document No. 17, 41st Cong., 3rd Sess., pp. 26–27. NOTE: In this translation, Robert Greenhow, State Department translator, referred to Caminero as the "Political Agent of Spanish Hayti."

To CALEB CUSHING, "late Commissioner to China"

Department of State
Washington, 22d Feb[ruar]y 1845

Sir, Your account for Contingent expenses of the Mission to China having been submitted by the Fifth Auditor [Stephen Pleasonton] for my decision, I have the honor to request, that you will explain the necessity for the employment of four Interpreters, charged for therein. Also that you will state the rate of compensation allowed to Mr. [Stanislas] Herniss, and the time he was employed; and the nature of the service of A. DeMiranda, assistant, for which a charge of $150[?] appears: That charge, as well as those for payments of $234 96/100[?] and $103.00[?], the former to John Miller for postages and newspapers, the latter to sundry persons for books, stationery, staff[?] &c are unsupported by vouchers, which you are requested to present. I have the honor to be, Sir, very respectfully, Your ob[edient] S[ervan]t, J.C. Calhoun.

Letterpress copy in DNA, RG 59 (State Department), Accounting Records: Miscellaneous Letters Sent, 1832–1916, vol. for 10/3/1844–5/29/1845, p. 242.

From Tho[ma]s Lloyd Halsey, Washington, 2/22. Halsey complies with Calhoun's request, made in a recent interview, and sends to Calhoun a history of his claim against the Argentine government. Halsey first applied for settlement of his claim in 1820 during the administration of James Monroe. Having gone through numerous negotiations and delays, the claim was finally decided by a commission of two appointed, without Halsey's knowledge, by the Buenos Ayres government. The commissioners determined that a payment "of $79,439.3rs[?] of hard dollars" was due to Halsey. This payment was originally to be paid in specie but in 1828 Argentine authorities offered to pay that amount in six per cent stock with interest. But by then the value of Argentine paper currency had depreciated by 150 percent. Halsey refused this payment and has since then continued to seek a settlement of the claim according to the 1826 decision. Halsey asks Calhoun to instruct [William] Brent [Jr.], U.S. Chargé d'Affaires to Argentina, concerning his claim. He also requests copies of correspondence between the Argentine and U.S. governments relating to his case. Halsey states his willingness to submit the claim and the 1826 judgment to a new group of arbitrators. LS in ScCleA; CC in DNA, RG 84 (Foreign Posts), Argentina, Correspondence Relating to Claims; CC in DNA, RG 76 (Records of Boundary and Claims Commissions and Arbitrations), Miscellaneous Claims Records: Buenos Aires, 1816–1849, Miscellaneous.

To JOHN HOGAN

Department of State
Washington, 22nd February, 1845

Sir: That part of the Island of St: Domingo which was formerly under the dominion of Spain, but which was subdued by [Jean Pierre] Boyer in the year 1822, has recently shaken off the authority of his successors and established a government for itself under the title of the Dominican Republic. Dr. J[osé] M. Camiuero has presented himself to our Government as its Envoy, with letters of credence from its supreme authority, and addressed a note to this Department, setting forth the events which led to the formation of the new Government, together with sundry statistical statements in reference to the population, resources and actual condition of the country, with a view to procure the recognition of its independence by the government of the United States. You will herewith receive a copy of these papers, the originals of which have been laid before The President, who has examined their contents with a disposition favorable to the acknowledgement of the Republic.

Before deciding, however, on so important a step, it is deemed advisable to take the course heretofore adopted by the government in similar cases, by sending a Special Agent to examine into and make Report to the government of the power and resources of the Republic, and especially as to its ability to maintain its independence; and you have been selected by the President for the purpose.

The points to which you will more particularly direct your inquiries are:

First. The extent and limits of the territory over which the Dominican Government claims and exercises jurisdiction.

Second. The character and composition of its population, the degree of intelligence amongst the better portions of the people, and whether there is a general spirit of unanimity amongst all classes, and determination to maintain their independence.

Third. The number, discipline and equipment of the troops, and what irregular or militia force may be brought into the field in an emergency.

Fourth. The aggregate population of the country and the proportions of European, African and mixed races, their mutual dispositions towards the existing authorities, and the names and characters of the principal persons in the Executive, judicial and legislative departments of the Government.

Fifth. The financial system and resources of the Republic, together with its foreign, coastwise and internal trade, and its connections, if any, with foreign Powers. In a word, your attention will be directed to all the points touched on in Mr. Caminero's memoir, and to such other subjects as may be connected with the main object of your mission.

You will be expected to communicate from time to time the progress of your inquiries and to return as speedily as possible to the United States, when you will make your final report to this Department. In no event will you remain more than six months from the date of your departure from the United States, unless specially directed by the Department. In the mean time your compensation will be at the rate of eight dollars a day, exclusive of your necessary travelling expenses, of which you will keep a regular account, sustained by proper vouchers, in order that it may be submitted to the proper accounting officer of the Treasury. I am, Sir, your obedient servant, J.C. Calhoun.

FC in DNA, RG 59 (State Department), Diplomatic Instructions, Special Missions, 1:211–212 (M-77:152); CC in DNA, RG 59 (State Department), Diplomatic Despatches, Special Agents, vol. 13 (M-37:13, frames 186–188); PC in Senate Executive Document No. 17, 41st Cong., 3rd Sess., pp. 33–34.

To WASHINGTON IRVING, [Madrid]

Department of State
Washington, 22nd February, 1845

Sir: I transmit, herewith, the commission of Washington Reed, of North Carolina, who has been appointed by the President, by and with the advice and consent of the Senate, Consul of the United States for the Port of Sagua la Grand, in Cuba, in the place of Patrick J. Devine, of New York, who was rejected by the Senate; on the receipt of which you will apply to the Spanish Government for an Exequatur, to be transmitted, when obtained, with the commission, to Mr. Reed, at the place for which he has been appointed.

Enclosed, is a copy of a letter [of *ca.* 2/20] addressed to this Department by Messrs. Hardy & Baker, representing that the Barque Zulette, of Boston, was fired into by the Spanish fort at Tarifa, and slightly injured. This act requires immediate attention, and you are, hereby, instructed to lose no time in presenting the case to the Spanish Government, and in demanding an explanation, or the punishment of the officer who may have been guilty of what appears to be a wanton outrage.

Your letter from Paris, dated the 16th October last, and despatches from the Legation to No. 58, inclusive, have been received; the three last, from yourself, written since your return to Madrid. The accounts which accompanied No. 58, have been referred to the Treasury; and those items which relate to expenses incurred by you in following the Court, as far as they may be found in accordance with former usage, will be allowed. They must be reasonable, and sustained by proper vouchers, as is customary. I am, Sir, respectfully, Your obedient Servant, J.C. Calhoun.

LS (No. 40) with En in DNA, RG 84 (Foreign Posts), Spain, Instructions, 1: 559–564; FC in DNA, RG 59 (State Department), Diplomatic Instructions, Spain, 14:184–185 (M-77:142).

To A[LPHONSE] PAGEOT

Department of State
Washington, Feb[ruar]y 22, 1845

Sir: I have the honor to transmit herewith a copy of a communication addressed to this Department by the Secretary of the Treasury [on 2/17], in relation to the subject of your note of the 8th instant.

You will perceive that the Department of the Treasury adheres to the decision heretofore given in the case submitted to its consideration. Should it be your wish to have the subject brought to the notice of Congress, it will give me pleasure, on a receipt of a note from you to that effect, to communicate it immediately, with a favorable recommendation, to the proper Committee of that body. I have the honor to be, with high consideration, Sir, Your obedient servant, J.C. Calhoun.

FC in DNA, RG 59 (State Department), Notes to Foreign Legations, France, 6:88 (M-99:21); CC in DNA, RG 46 (U.S. Senate), 29A-D5.

From Tho[ma]s G. Clemson

Legation of United States, Brussels
February 23d 1845

Sir, I have the honour to acknowledge the receipt of your Despatch, No. 4, dated Washington January 27th 1845.

The subject of the Belgian indemnification for losses sustained by our commerce in the destruction of the Entrepot at Antwerp is one that has recieved [*sic*] my attention since my arrival in Brussels. The business has been and is progressing regularly and had any thing occur[r]ed of note either to the advantage, or disadvantage of our claims I should have immediately ap[p]rized you of the circumstance. The Baron [Goswin-Joseph de] Stassart is president of the commission nominated to examine and liquidate the claims. I have seen him often, and since the receipt of your last Despatch, I have had an interview with Count [Albert Joseph] Goblet the minister of foreign affairs. Those gentlemen concur in assuring me that the business is progressing as rapidly as possible and that the interests of our citizens advance pari passu with the rest of the claimants of other countries. I am informed that a portion of the claims have already been liquidated by which is meant that those whose claims have been examined and found valid, have recieved a document assuring to them 50 per cent of the sum they will eventual[l]y recieve after all the claims are examined and the entire amount (Somme Global) shall be ascertained. Thus the claimant is enabled to raise money immediately after the receipt of the document. A portion of the claimants (those of a certain category) being sufferers for the necessaries of life and having claims under the sum of three hundred francs (less than $60) have been paid in money. I put the following question to General Goblet "What is the maximum of time that will elapse, before the entire settlement of all the cla[i]ms." To which he answered, "Two years have elapsed in the examination and we have progressed about half way, so that it will require two years more before the affair is entirely finished." This is also the opinion of the Baron Stassart. The Gentleman who holds the powers of Attorney of our claimants is a resident of Brussels, and had the time been longer before the departure of the next steamer from Liverpool I would have ascertained the number of Americans whose claims have been liquidated as explained above.

When conversing with General Goblet He asked me if I knew what position France had recently assumed on the Texas question, towards the United States. To which I answered that I knew nothing beyond the statements of the papers which were open to the world, and that I judged her position to be defined in Mr. Calhoun[']s letter to our minister in Paris Mr. [William R.] King. He told me very confidentially that he was assured that France was against annexation and that Mr. [F.P.G.] Guizot had very recently made certain promises to England to that effect. He also told me that he had recieved his information from England. I asked him if he was certain[;] he assured me that he was or very nearly. The same evening I was seated by the side of Mr. [Jean-Baptiste] Nothomb the minister of the Interior at a dinner given by Mr. Viron the Governor of Brabant. He asked me if I was aware of the position that France was about to assume on the question of Texas? to which I answered that I had heard something on the subject but I could not ["give" *canceled*] believe that France could possibly take a hostile position against the United States, so old and so faithful an Ally: Besides which we had the answer of Louis Phillippe [*sic*] to Mr. King. He then gave me to understand that there might be some mistake as to what Louis Phillippe did say, or that it might be denied. Among other things he said that before fifteen days had elapsed it would be known and make a great noise. I expressed some doubts about Mr. Guizot[']s announcing such a fact to the chambers & the French people and that I was disposed to think such a statement would destroy the ministry. To which he replied that he would announce it nevertheless. I then said "Grant the premises what will be the result"? to which he replied France would stand by and let England act. Much more was said upon the subject not necessary to repeat. I have no doubt but that the Belgian Government has recieved official information to the effect stated in the above conversations. To what extent it may be true you will doubtless be informed from other sources. My own individual impression is that the question of slavery is the question of questions and one upon which the peace of the world will turn sooner or later, ["but" *canceled*] independent

of that question the position which the United States has assumed latterly is well calculated to reinstate her in that exalted position among
nations from which she had almost fallen by a neglect of our foreign
relations & the handle that has been made of some of our errors,
among others Repudiation, by the English periodicals whose abuse
is incessant of every thing in or of the United States.

My relations with this Government are of the most agre[e]able
character, and I let no opportunity pass without doing all in my power
to convince them that the feeling is reciprocated on the part of the
U. States.

Mons. [Adolphe] Dechamps Minister of public works kindly put
into my hands, a few days back the accompanying Document which
he drew up at the instance of Mr. Nothomb and which was incited
by the clause in the President[']s message recommending the establishment of a line of steam boats between the United States and
Europe. It will be an important document for the U. States to refer
to in case they should conclude upon establishing so important and
almost necessary a means of communication between the two conti-
nents. Our Despatches now come through the English foreign office,
and all other papers, and documents are forwarded as freight, and all
arrive with great delay particularly the latter which are sometimes
lost. The Document sets forth the advantages offered by Antwerp
as one of the points of communication in case such a line, or lines
should be established, and also ["m" *canceled*] makes known a fact
which had escaped my memory; that Belgium had sent in a previous
year an agent to the United States with a view to the establishment of
Postal arrangements between the two countries.

Mr. Nothomb asked me a few days back whether I had recieved
an answer to the questions contained in my Despatch No. 3 dated
October 28th/44[;] on my answering him in the negative, he asked
me if it was my impression that they would be answered affirmatively.
I told him that I was inclined to think not. He then said that was his
own ["impression" *changed to* "opinion"], but before giving me a
form of a treaty he thought it his duty to guard himself against the
chambers by an official note on that subject from the United States,
and then went on to say that he was far advanced in the form of a
treaty, which he would give me before a very long time. I need not
add that the Belgian Government look forward to the ratification of a
treaty with the United States with great anxiety, and had it not been
for the business of the chambers, where ministers have been busily
occupied the matter would have progressed more rapidly. There
was a very strenuous effort made by the deputies to change the

ministry which was not successful, tho for a moment it [was] upon the verge of dissolution. At this time they have the subject of a treaty with the United States under anxious, and very serious consideration, and on that account I should be particularly well pleased to have your views on so important a subject. The reduction of the duties on Cotton in England will insure to us the statu quo of the Belgian tariff upon that important article. The reduction of the duty on Tobacco will be difficult. I had a conversation with Mr. Nothomb upon that subject. He said that the duty on Tobacco, here, was comparitively low, and was retained because they had need for the money, which that duty brought into the treasury. I told him that I was sorry to hear it; that the President had considered it of sufficient importance to mention it in his last annual message, and that it was my impression it would be the subject of negotiation when the treaty was entered on.

There is one mode by which the United States could be favoured viz. if Belgium would consent to increase the duty on all other Tobacco letting that upon American tobacco remain as it stands, we should in this way have a monopoly of the Belgian market, but this I fear they would consent to do with difficulty if at all. If it should be the wish of the President that I should ascertain the views of the Belgian government upon that or any other question I will doubtless be instructed to do so.

With this Despatch I send you a number of Galignani's Messenger which is interesting on account of a disscussion [*sic*] in Parliament upon the British government opening letters & private correspondence.

That discussion has brought to my recollection a remark made some time back by General Goblet to myself. He General G[oblet] having learned that our Despatches between the United States & the continent were carried by the English mail bag and passed through the English foreign office remarked jocosely it is true "That they sent their letters by that route when they desired to make their contents known to England." The practice of opening letters in England is undoubted and tho not so common as in some other parts of the world, no communication passing through England can be considered secure. This is another argument for the Establishment of a direct line of Steamers between the United States and this continent and particular Postal arrangements for official correspondence.

I forgot to mention in its proper place that Mr. Nothomb is generally believed to be very intimate with Mr. Guizot which gives to the conversation I have mentioned more weight than it would otherwise deserve. I can not myself vouch for the truth of this intimacy of course. Very respectfully your obedient Serv[an]t, Thos. G. Clemson.

ALS with Ens in DNA, RG 59 (State Department), Diplomatic Despatches, Belgium, vol. 3 (M-193:4), received 3/21; FC (in Anna Maria Calhoun Clemson's hand) in DNA, RG 84 (Foreign Posts), Belgium, Despatches, vol. 4.

To Jorgen Flood, [2]/23. Flood is notified of his appointment to be U.S. Consul at Porsgrund, Norway. Abs in DNA, RG 59 (State Department), Consular Instructions, 10:285.

From R[ICHARD] PAKENHAM

Washington, 23 February 1845

Sir, Her Majesty's Chargé d'Affaires in the Republic of the Uruguay has reported to Her Majesty's Government the valuable assistance rendered by Captain [Philip F.] Vo[o]rhees of the United States Navy, as well as by the other Naval Commanders in the River Plate, to Captain [Charles] Hotham of Her Majesty's Steam Vessel "Gorgon" while employed in the arduous task of getting that Vessel off the Beach at Monte Video.

I am instructed to express to you, Sir, the thanks of Her Majesty's Government for the efficient and ready assistance given by Captain Vo[o]rhees on that occasion. I have the honor to be, with high consideration, Sir, Your obedient Servant, R. Pakenham.

LS in DNA, RG 59 (State Department), Notes from Foreign Legations, Great Britain, vol. 22 (M-50:22); CC in DNA, RG 45 (Naval Records), Letters from Federal Executive Agents, 1837–1886, 8:174 (M-517:3, frames 132–133).

From C[ALEB] CUSHING

Washington, 24 February 1845

Sir: I have the honor to acknowledge the receipt of your communication of the 22nd instant.

I am aware that the amount expended for interpretation may seem to you large; but the circumstances called for the whole of the service; and the rate of compensation was the least for which such service could be obtained.

On entering upon the duties of my appointment, I found that the difficulties in the way of communication with the Chinese, were among the most serious of all the obstacles to the success of the Mission.

I had before me the admonition that Lord Amherst's Mission had failed, if not exclusively, yet immediately, in consequence of misunderstandings created by the want of adequate interpretation between him & the Chinese. I found, also, that great complaint existed at Hong-kong, on account of alleged discrepancies, of the most grave nature, between the Chinese & the English counterparts of the British Supplementary Treaty. These considerations rendered me willing to incur the hazard of the rejection of a part of my account, rather than that of any deficiency of the means of communicating with the Chinese.

In point of fact, I had less assistants in number than Lord Amherst, while the duty to be performed was more onerous, & involved more of responsibility, namely, the negociation of a treaty—and less, also, I believe, than Sir Henry Pottinger.

During the whole period of my negociations, & especially the latter part of the time, the gentlemen employed in the American Legation were most incessantly & laboriously occupied, in consequence of my anxiety to close the business in season for the action of the present Congress, and in consequence of the Chinese having, with honorable reliance on us, desired that all their communications, as well as ours, should be made through the interpreters of our Legation. To have dispensed with any of the assistance employed would have involved the consumption of much more time in effecting the objects of the Legation, and of course ultimately the expenditure of much more money, for salary of Mr. [Fletcher] Webster & myself as well as of interpreters; besides the evil of thus retarding the final accomplishment of objects highly important to the United States.

Drs. [E.C.] Bridgman & [Peter] Parker were engaged for a compensation at the rate of $1500 each per annum, and the payment in addition of all their extra expenses; Mr. [Stanislas] Herniss at the same rate of salary, which barely defrayed his expenses.

In going over the account at the Auditor's office, I called attention to the deficiency of vouchers in the three small items to which you refer; supposing it desirable that the whole of my claim should appear, and that those items would of course be suspended for the presentation of satisfactory vouchers. I am With the highest respect, C. Cushing.

ALS (No. 103) in DNA, RG 59 (State Department), Accounting Records: Letters and Accounts from Despatch Agents at New York and Boston, 1840–1860, vol. for 8/1840–11/1847.

From J[AMES] HAMILTON, [JR.], *"Private not official"*

New Orleans, Feb[ruar]y 24[t]h 1845

My Dear Sir, I have received the enclosed Letter for yourself which ["was" *canceled and* "is" *interlined*] written by a very talented Carolinian by the name of James Simmons who has settled in Texas and is well qualified for office. Indeed his qualifications are greatly superior to any employment he is likely to receive in the Country. I wish in case Texas is annexed and you should have any thing to do with the Govt. you would bear him in mind, as well as our friend [Barnard E.] Bee.

I have been in this City now about 10 Days and altho intensely occupied with business I have mixed much with the Democracy and I am happy to believe that of all our ["people" *canceled and* "public men" *interlined*] you stand *first* in their esteem. Your Letter to Mr. [William R.] King & conduct of the Question of Annexation will I am sure give you the united support of the whole South & South West in the next contest for the Presidency in case you should be a Candidate.

[John F.H.] Claiborne the Editor of the [New Orleans] Jeffersonian Republican is decidedly your friend and will warmly sustain your interests. I have had long & frequent conferences with him on the subject. I enclose you an Editorial ["for him" *canceled*] which at his *earnest request* I prepared for his paper designed to meet the Crisis presented by the contingency ["presented by" *canceled and* "of" *interlined*] the failure of the measure of annexation before Congress. I beg you will regard the fact of *my authorship as confidentially communicated.* [*Partial word canceled.*] He published it, as I prepared it, with the single addition of the words "bought up by their money"[—]a charge rather too strong for my charity to make.

I wish you *however particularly* not to say one word about my having had any hand in the article as Col. Claiborne starts for Washington tomorrow and I wish him if there be any *eclat* in so small an affair to have *it all* with the friends of annexation & the new Govt.

I am yet in doubts about your health except as far as the last advices thro the correspondent of the [Charleston] Mercury which represents it as improving which I trust in God may be the case. **If** it is not think seriously of the mission to England & a ["consequent" *interlined*] sea voyage.

As to myself I say again do not regard a straw what has passed between us. For altho there would be something very soothing & consoling to me after all the wounds of fortune to have such a distinction conferred on me at such a Crisis, yet if my own heart does not play me false I am sure I would be much better pleased to see you in possession of a Post where in spite of your passages with the British Govt. I know you could render such distinguished Services to the Country. *You* ["ought" *canceled*] out of the way I do not know any man in the Country who has a better claim to the appointment than myself. I do not thank [*sic*; John] Tyler could go through the Senate & it would injure [James K.] Polk to smuggle him upon the Country during the recess. The appointment would be regarded moreover as if our Govt. was not in earnest in our negotiations with England & that the whole affair was a compromise with a hungry expectant & a weak tribute paid to a frivolous woman [that is, Julia Gardiner Tyler]. I say this without the smallest ill will to Tyler but because I know this version of the affair is the only interpretation which would be put on it.

Besides after the vulgar abuse of England in which his ["son" *canceled and then interlined*; that is, Robert Tyler] has indulged, ["towards it" *canceled*] his appointment in regard to the British Govt. would be in bad Taste to say the least of it & to say nothing at such a time of the impolicy of sending to such a scrutinizing Govt. a vain *old* man with a *young* wife. I would despise myself if I could make this remark from a single selfish feeling of envy or jealousy. Yet I should not be at all surprized if he was sent for our foreign appointments have generally been given to those least qualified for them.

In regard to myself My Dear Sir do with me as you deem best. You know that I have n[ever(?) soli]cited the appointment—That the [*ms. torn; one word missing*] has been one of your own suggestion. I have written not a line ["to" *canceled*] or said one word to a human being on the subject *but yourself* nor shall I. If the appointment comes it must be from Mr. Polk[']s voluntary and unsolicited impulse *at least as far as I am concerned*. I feel that I have the will which some times in consciousness reflects the power of consummating great public usefulness and that with my old circle of friends in Downing Street I could take up our negotiations under your instructions and strike an important blow. But I am content to remain in the Privacy which belongs to my home ["& my fortunes" *interlined*] in Alabama for which I leave in a day or two.

If anything so unexpected by myself as that my name should be sent in for the mission to England pray have me charged to old So. Carolina. I know she will stand the *debit*. With sincere esteem Ever My Dear Sir very sincerely & faithfully Yours, J. Hamilton.

[P.S.] If you should have any *say so* with the new administration pray take care of Col. [Robert B.] Campbell & P[ierce] M. Butler in their respective appointments. Polk if he desires to fly a high pitch will not disturb [Henry A.] Wise and [Balie?] Peyton. He would consult a profound policy as well as generous magnanimity by taking such a course.

ALS in ScCleA.

From R o b [e r] t R. H u n t e r, "(Confidential)"

New York [City], Feb[ruar]y 24, 1845

Dear Sir, The mass meeting at Tammany Hall in favor of the annexation of Texas was one of the largest I have witnessed and I have to say that by the management of Robt. H. Morris[,] one of the leaders of the [Martin] Van Buren clique of this City, who, by an understanding, and for the sake of unanimity we consented should for that Evening preside as chairman, I was prevented from offering some resolutions I had prepared. The resolutions did not suit Morris, as they were void of Van Buren panegyric—but ["were" *interlined*] simply confined ["themselves" *canceled*] to the great leading political questions ,Texas[,] Oregon & Cuba, shadowing forth your views, and which I knew would have been unanimously responded to by the meeting.

The object however of this letter is to communicate to you that while at the meeting on the 22 inst. I was told that you were on terms of intimacy and in correspondence with an individual in this city, named Emanuel B. Hart. I *am unacquainted* with the man, but he was pointed out to me at the meeting, and I was informed by those who do know him well, that his reputation is bad, very bad, that he is well known here as the associate of Gamblers, and still more notorious as the *Companion* of a brothel keeper. If the report of his intercourse with you be true your friends here are undoubtedly to blame in not having informed you as to his true character. What I now write is from the dictates of my friendly feelings, and I trust you will look upon it, for what it is designed, merely as instance of my friendship.

I am *marked* here, and at Albany as your friend and the opponent of Van Buren, and I have only to add that you may depend upon my Services upon every occasion wherein I shall imagine your honor and dignity as well as y[ou]r interest is concerned. In one of the Journals some time since, I noticed that the appointment at Albany, of John Van Buren as Att[orne]y Gen[era]l and the throwing overboard of Sam[ue]l Young, the Sec[retar]y of State, and [Thomas] Farrington, the State Treasurer[,] seemed to be a puzzle at Washington. *Here* it is pretty well understood, to be Van Buren's move—the appointment of his son John, was of more consequence to him than the sacrafice [*sic*] of Young & Far[r]ington. These latter gentlemen were opponents to the Erie Rail Road & Erie Canal projects, and it was said that if they remained in the State Council, they could not be carried—that a bargain was therefore hatched, and a new Sec[retar]y of State & a new State Treasurer was [*sic*] appointed *together* with John Van Buren. Respectfully yours, Robt. R. Hunter.

ALS in ScCleA.

To "F.W." [*sic*; Freeman H.] Morse, Representative [from Maine], 2/24. Morse's letter of 2/18 with its enclosure from Nathaniel Cross, both addressed to President [John Tyler], have been referred to the State Department. The Department has previously communicated with Cross concerning his former imprisonment at Matanzas, Cuba. As explained before, the U.S. government considers this a civil affair and can only commend it to the attention of the Spanish and Cuban authorities, which has been done. "I am not aware that any further action on this subject is within the power of this Dept." FC in DNA, RG 59 (State Department), Consular Instructions, 10:286.

From A[lphonse] Pageot, Washington, 2/24. Pageot acknowledges receipt of Calhoun's note of 2/22 enclosing the decision of the Secretary of the Treasury regarding the claim of [Francois] Durand of Perpignan. He regrets that the Secretary of the Treasury continues to exclude the claim based upon his interpretation of the tariff act of 1842. Pageot restates his opinion of the matter but does not expect any change in the Secretary's ruling. He requests Calhoun to place the matter before Congress, as Calhoun has offered to do. Many importers of French wines, having interpreted the tariff as being charged at the lower rate of 6 cents per gallon instead of 15 cents, have made large orders. If the unfavorable ruling is adhered to, those importers will suffer financial losses. *LS (in French) and State Department translation in DNA, RG 59 (State Department), Notes from Foreign Legations, France, vol. 12 (M-53:8, frames 750–756); CC (State Department translation) in DNA, RG 46 (U.S. Senate), 29A-D5.*

From ALBERT SMITH,
[U.S. Boundary Commissioner]

H[ouse] of Representatives, Feb[ruar]y 24th 1845
Sir, The chairman of the Committee of Ways & Means [James I. McKay] has this moment informed me, that no letter or other paper has been placed before that Committee, upon which to base an appropriation for the prosecution of the [Northeastern] Boundary survey. I have the honor to be Most respectfully Your Ob[edien]t Serv[an]t, Albert Smith.

ALS in ScCleA.

From H[ENRY] BAILEY

Charleston [S.C.], 25 Feb. 1845
My dear Sir, I have been so earnestly solicited to write to you, for the purpose of asking your good offices in behalf of two of my friends who are candidates for Government patronage, that reluctant as I feel to be guilty of the impertinence, I have been induced to promise that I would do so; and having made the promise, I suppose I must now redeem it. I trust you will excuse it on this occasion, & I shall certainly not allow myself to be drawn into a repetition of it.

The friends alluded to are Solomon Cohen Esq., formerly of Georgetown, in this State, and now of Savannah, where he occupies a distinguished stand at the bar, and his brother Mr. Jacob Cohen, formerly of Georgetown, & now of this City. The former has his eye upon a foreign Consulate, that at Liverpool I believe; the latter desires some office in the Custom House, & would be content with any thing above tide-waiter, or surveyors as they are now called. I can cheerfully speak of them as gentlemen of integrity, & great moral worth, possessing high respectability of character, and eminently qualified for the stations they respectively seek, or any other that they would undertake to occupy. I will add, that both of them are natives of South Carolina, and have all their lives been firm, and unwavering republicans. They were nullifiers in the glorious era of 1832, and were active, zealous, and true on every occasion. The one was a member of the Legislature which called the nullifying convention, & I believe of the Convention itself; and the other was one of the volunteers who were specially pledged to rally upon General [James] Hamilton [Jr.]. In short both proved themselves true & devoted sons of their native State.

Solomon Cohen Esq. removed some four or five years since to Georgia, where as I have stated he has occupied an eminent place at the bar. But he has also distinguished himself as a politician, and become a leader in the democratic party. He was particularly influential in the late Presidential contest. I believe he has the undivided support of the Georgia democracy in his present application.

It would afford me great pleasure to learn that either of these gentlemen had been successful in their respective applications, for the promoting of which they will both be in Washington, perhaps as soon as this letter—but I must add, doubtless unnecessarily, that I do not desire their success at the cost of removing any incumbent, without just, & independent cause, merely to make room for them. I can never consent to be particeps in the humblest manner, to a policy, which I regard as degrading, and as unwise as it is ungenerous. In this community such a policy would render almost any administration unpopular, with the great majority of every party.

Something of the kind I know is threatened, & feared, in relation to [William J. Grayson] the present Chief of our Custom House, one of the most excellent of men, & acceptable of officers; but I trust such fears are groundless.

We are on the qui vive for the developements of the incoming administration, concerning which conjecture is quite at fault. I augur most favorably from Mr. [James K.] Polk's very discreet silence on the subject, from which I infer that he will seek advice in the very best quarter. [Franklin H.] Elmore has communicated to you the views of your friends here in relation to yourself, & I take the opportunity to say I concur in them entirely. With the highest regard & respect &, H. Bailey.

ALS in ScCleA.

From Tho[ma]s G. Clemson

Brussels, Feb[ruar]y 25th 1845

My dear Sir, I have written you quite along [*sic*] Despatch which you will excuse, for really I do not know how I could have said less consonant with my duty; besides it was the accumulation of a month. Now that Congress is no longer in Session [*sic*], and we have done all in our power for the annexation of Texas, you will perhaps have more leisure and blame me less for disobeying your orders.

We were very much distressed to hear of your illness, and shall await news of your recovery with great anxiety. Anna [Maria Calhoun Clemson] has written you a long letter, and expressed to you our feelings on that subject, besides having given you the news of the family. The winter here has been very severe and trying, but thank heaven we are all well & once more quite robust. The weather is now milder than it has been, and we hope to be able to enjoy it out of doors before long, from which we have been so long debarred.

I have cut the accompanying extract from a news paper. It will give you some idea of what is doing in the Diplomatic Corps in Europe. I merely send it that you may see the importance that is attached to these things on this side of the Atlantic. While on that subject I will give you an extract from a letter recieved [*sic*] from my col[l]eague Mr. C[hristopher] Hughes [U.S. Chargé d'Affaires to the Netherlands] at the Hague, in order that you may be assured that it is not myself alone that is of the opinion, expressed to you in a former letter. The more I see the more I am convinced of the importance of the subject.

"No one[,]" says Mr. H[ughes,] "has more experience of the stupidity of this use, or system than I have! It is a brevet of mediocrity & humiliation to tack to a man such a title. It is the effectual[,] the certain way of depriving him of the first element of success i.e. of public Court & social consideration. The very menials of the Palace— of the departments of Government and of the high *Personages* of

Court & society *mark* him—the Chargé d'Affaires; & treat him as an inferior person: & his words—his acts & his person feel the influence of this low Consideration." You know Hughe[s]'s queer way.

We were exceeding happy to hear of John's [John C. Calhoun, Jr.'s] much better health. The dry atmosphere of the Cane Brake [in Ala.] may be very beneficial & I hope will reinstate him entirely.

The steamer leaves on the fourth, but the English courier (by which this is sent) leaves to day & on the first of March[;] the last will be too late which explains why our letters are not dated later.

In haste. Your affectionate son, Thos. G. Clemson.

N.B. Please put your Franc [*sic*] on some of the letters which I send[.] There is one quite heavy to Mr. [Francis W.] Pickens. T.G.C.

ALS in ScCleA, Thomas Green Clemson Papers.

To George Evans, Chairman of the Committee on Finance of the Senate, 2/25. "I have the honor to transmit to you a copy of a letter addressed to [James I. McKay] the Chairman of the Committee of Ways and Means, of the House of Representatives, on the 19th of December last, requesting the necessary appropriation for running and marking the Boundary between the United States and Great Britain." Letterpress copy in DNA, RG 59 (State Department), Accounting Records: Miscellaneous Letters Sent, 1832–1916, vol. for 10/3/1844–5/29/1845, p. 250.

To C[HARLES] J. INGERSOLL, Chairman of the Committee on Foreign Affairs, H[ouse of] Representatives

Department of State
Washington, 25th February 1845

Sir: I have the honor to transmit to you, herewith, the copy of a recent correspondence between this Department and the French Minister at Washington, relative to the import duty chargeable on certain French wines, in virtue of the premises of the tariff act of 1842.

Permit me to recommend this subject to your favorable consideration, and, if upon examination by the committee on Foreign Affairs, the claim preferred by Mr. [Alphonse] Pageot should, in its opinion, appear to be well grounded—to hope that proper legislative measures will be forthwith adopted to effect the releif [*sic*] of those interested, and settle the true construction to be given to the particular clauses of the law referred to in the correspondence. I am &c, J.C. Calhoun.

FC in DNA, RG 59 (State Department), Reports of the Secretary of State to the President and Congress, 6:160.

From R[ICHARD] PAKENHAM

Washington, 25 February 1845

Sir, I have the honor herewith to transmit to you a Packet addressed to the President of the United States [John Tyler], which reached me yesterday by the way of Mexico and the Havana, containing as I am informed, certain Communications from the Government of the Sandwich Islands to the President. I have the honor to be, with high consideration, Sir, Your obedient Servant, R. Pakenham.

LS in DNA, RG 59 (State Department), Notes from Foreign Legations, Great Britain, vol. 22 (M-50:22).

From H[AYM] M. SALOMON, "Private"

New York [City], 25 Feb. '45

Dear Sir, Hearing that you had under Providence so far recovered as to attend to business again and other matters I thought it best to address you again a few lines in addition, on the last mentioned subject of a former letter.

Mr. [Daniel] W[ebster] having returned to this city waiting for the re assembling of the senate I called on his Confidential Mr. [Hiram] K[etchum] to enquire if he had progressed in our object by a conference—he said that it appeared to him better to wait the action of the new President [James K. Polk] in respect to the position which you might be induced to take in the next administration—which a lapse of two or three weeks would obviate and that then having matters before us pretty clear on the map we could shape our plans accordingly. I acquiesced, supposing it better to be Slow and sure than to[o] precipatate and fatal.

However I thought it still better to converce with W[ebster] himself to discover if any change in inclinations had taken place. When

I saw him the same day, on Friday last, and informed him of the sentiments of Mr. K[etchum] he said he perfectly agreed with those views and that he would be occasionally here & at Washington for three weeks to come. So you find by this that no abatement of inclination in the head men in this way exists as to my proposed ulterior project. It will be, when finally fixed on, for W[ebster] & K[etchum] to bring over [James Watson] Webb [editor of the New York *Courier and Enquirer*] who has taken Charles King formerly of "The American" as a Joint editor with him. The Commercial and the Express I can manage.

Proceed if you like *in every matter connected with men and things* under the present engagements you have made *as though you had not at all this great Point in View* for your own great Fame and the country[']s good[.] With regard and esteeme Undiminished your faithful Friend & Ser[van]t, H.M. Salomon.

P.S. My astonishment increases daily at the surprising neglect of the President [John Tyler] respecting his repeated promises to me.

You may remember that I had for the Consulate at Havre the Recommendation of Every Alderman and magistrate of the City of New York, besides those Testimonials from each of the Judges and from every Mayor for three terms of both parties besides mercantile Letters of *the highest grade*. Now I ask you and if it will not conflict with any views of yours respecting its propriety, could *you let me know* whether *you would present my claims to the new President* provided I could procure in addition to those testimonials from distinguished men—Those of our Governor and all the members of our Legislature?

once more on the first Subject

It ought to be no discouragement to you, to recollect that so far as it regards the great movements suggested by me to you and followed up heretofore, In no instance have you had cause to regret their issue, for in all the cases, you and your friends have obtained the results I contemplated. And I humbly think that had your southern friends consulted with me as to the instrument, they ought to use in *this quarter* in last summer[']s operations not half the funds would have been expended and your nomination obtained and election as certain as that of Mr. P[olk].

ALS in ScCleA.

From John Southgate, Norfolk, 2/25. Southgate seeks to learn whether Frederick Vincent, a claimant in the case of the *Ranger*, has

received from the Republic of Ecuador the sum due him on 7/12/-
1844. ALS in DNA, RG 59 (State Department), Miscellaneous Letters (M-179:107, frames 246–247).

To HENRY WHEATON, [Berlin]

Department of State
Washington, 25th February, 1845
Sir: I have the honor to acknowledge the receipt of your letter of the
21st ultimo, enclosing a Convention concluded that day, with the
Bavarian Minister at Berlin, between the United States and the Kingdom of Bavaria, for the mutual abolition of the Droit d'aubaine and
taxes on emigration.

This Convention, with a copy of your despatch, was submitted
yesterday to the Senate by the President [John Tyler]. I am, Sir,
respectfully, Your obedient Servant, J.C. Calhoun.

LS (No. 65) in DNA, RG 84 (Foreign Posts), Germany, Instructions, 1:401–
402; FC in DNA, RG 59 (State Department), Diplomatic Instructions, Germany,
14:90 (M-77:65).

From C[HARLES] G. ATHERTON, [Senator from N.H.]

Washington City, Feb[ruar]y 26 1845
D[ea]r Sir, Col. William Boardman, a Townsman of mine, who
brought Despatches from Mexico for the State Department, called on
me before leaving Town this afternoon, & as he had not an opportunity of an interview with you to day, requested me to make a statement in his behalf.

He says that Mr. [Wilson] Shannon desired him to take the Despatches as the mails were uncertain, & that unless they had been
committed to his care, he should have sailed directly from Vera Cruz
to Boston, thereby saving much expence incurred by coming by the
way of Washington.

Col. B[oardman] therefore wishes to know whether it would not
be consistent with the practice of the Department to make him some
allowance on account of the increased expence to which he has been
subjected by reason of his bearing the despatches as requested by

Mr. Shannon. I am, Sir, with great respect your Obed[ien]t Servant, C.G. Atherton.

ALS in DNA, RG 59 (State Department), Accounting Records, Miscellaneous Letters Received.

To T[homas] G. Clemson

Washington, 26th Feb. 1845

My dear Sir, The last Steamer ["brought" *interlined*] yours of the 28th Jan[uar]y [*not found*] with letters from Anna [Maria Calhoun Clemson] to her mother [Floride Colhoun Calhoun], Patrick [Calhoun], & John [C. Calhoun, Jr.].

I am happy to inform you, that I am in a great measure recovered from the effects of my late illness. It was a case of an inflammatory fever, with a strong congestive tendency. My recovery has been very slow; occasioned in part, I doubt not, from being compelled to see company and to attend to business, as soon as I was able to leave my bed.

I have delayed writing to the last day by the Steamer, in the hope, that I should be able to give you information of the fate of the question of annexation of Texas & the formation of the Cabinet. Strange as it may appear, neither is yet known, although it is now but six days to the 4th of March. It is thought the vote on annexation will be exceed[ing]ly close; ["It is thought" *canceled and* "so much so that" *interlined*] a single vote will turn the scale either way. It will probably be taken tonight.

Of the formation of the Cabinet nothing certain is known. The impression is, that the present will all go out, and an entirely new one [be] formed, at the head of which will be Mr. [James] Buchanan. Whether it be true or not, a few days will determine. As to myself, I have personally no solicitude. I am & have been throughout perfectly passive, & have requested my friends to be so. Indeed, if invited, I should not remain, unless the organization of the Cabinet should be such as to be in the main satisfactory.

I will see Mr. [Robert?] Beale on the subject of the patents, and let you know the result by my next; but I must say, I do not see how your right can be secured in them without your name appearing, or being liable to appear, which, although there is nothing wrong in it, would, I think, expose you in your present position to unpleasant imputations.

I am much obliged to Mr. Tampier[?], for the present of wine he proposes to send me as a sample, but, if I should not remain in office, which is probable, I would regret his sending it, in that case; as I would not be able to render him the aid, that I would otherwise desire, to effect the object he has in view.

I have not had time to read your publick dispatch, by the last Steamer. Your suggestions in reference to the grade of chargé de Affair[e]s, appear to me to be well founded, and will be taken into consideration, if I should remain in office. I see many changes, which should be made in connection with the Department.

I am rejoiced to learn, that the health of [John] Calhoun [Clemson] is perfectly restored. I felt very uneasy about him. I hope the indisposition of the child [Floride Elizabeth Clemson] will prove light. We are all well. Say to Anna that I have no time, or I would write to her. I must conclude, as the time for closing the mail is just at hand.

All join their love to you & Anna. Tell Calhoun that Grandfather hopes he is a good boy; & kiss him & his sister for me. Your affectionate father, J.C. Calhoun.

ALS in ScCleA; PC in Jameson, ed., *Correspondence*, pp. 645–646.

From Dallett Brothers, Philadelphia, 2/26. This company has received from the State Department and forwarded by the brig *Rowena* bound for La Guayra a tin case containing a U.S. flag directed to V[espasian] Ellis, U.S. Chargé d'Affaires at Caracas. "The expences were too trifling to warrant us in making any charge & we must consider the honour of forwarding a National flag as sufficient compensation." LS in DNA, RG 59 (State Department), Accounting Records: Miscellaneous Letters Received.

From EDWARD EVERETT

London, 26th February, 1845

Dear Sir, I have translated a couple of Editorial articles on the subject of Texas, from the "*Journal des débats*" of the 4th and 17th instant respectively, and forward them with this letter. This Journal is, as you are aware, the well-known organ of the French Government, conducted by persons entirely in its confidence, deriving from it pecuniary support, and occasionally it is supposed even receiving the assistance of M. [F.P.G.] Guizot's pen.

It is these circumstances which give significance to the articles in question, which are not characterized by any remarkable ability or intimate acquaintance with facts. I have thought it best to translate them just as they stand in the original, notwithstanding some objectionable expressions and statements, in order to convey accurately the spirit and substance of the articles, which will I think on careful examination be found to have a deeper meaning than might be supposed on a cursory perusal.

It is difficult to say whether they throw light on the views taken by the French Government on the question of Texas, or are intended to wrap them in additional mystery. While the negociation of the Treaty was in progress last year M. [Alphonse] Pageot, it is understood, was furnished with a protest against it, which he was dissuaded by Mr. [Richard] Pakenham from presenting, on the ground, it is said, that foreign interference of that kind would tend rather to promote than obstruct the ratification of the Treaty. The manner in which both the King [Louis Philippe] and M. Guizot expressed themselves to our Minister [William R. King] was certainly different from what might have been anticipated from such a demonstration. When the documents accompanying the President's Message at the opening of the Session were published in Europe, your allusions to the purport of those communications were commented upon in the London press and especially the [London] "Times" in the most pointed manner. The Government of France was openly accused of double dealing; the plainest intimations were thrown out that a different language had been held to Great Britain and to us; and a peremptory demand was made for an explanation. Of these loud calls of the English Journals no notice at all has ever been taken, as far as I am aware, by the Government press in France, although the Editorial articles in the "Times" on French topics rarely fail to command its attention. Instead of defending the French Government against the charge of double dealing, the *"Journal des débats"* has twice expressed itself in the remarkable manner, which you see in the accompanying articles, which certainly authorise the inference that the French Government will offer no violent opposition to the annexation of Texas and that no such opposition is anticipated by France on the part of England.

But notwithstanding the appearance of these articles and the inferences which they warrant, it has been plainly intimated in more than one article in the "Times" evidently of a semi-official character, that explanations of a satisfactory nature on this point have passed between the two Governments and that they will act if not technically in conjunction, at least with the same spirit and policy, in opposition to annexation; and a correspondence to this effect is understood to have taken place. Of this there has appeared however no trace in the "*Journal des débats,*" and its article of the 18th of February must be considered as a strange commentary on such an understanding.

I am unwilling to accuse or to suspect the French Government of want of good faith in either direction. The King, I am sure, has given the strongest proofs of a kind feeling toward us which could possibly be afforded. He took personally upon himself the responsibility of carrying through the Chambers the appropriations for the payment of the indemnity stipulated by Mr. [William C.] Rives' Treaty, a measure of which the odium is still fresh in France, not much to the credit of public sentiment in that country. Nor do I know that we have any grounds for distrusting the favorable disposition of M. Guizot.

I am inclined in some measure to reconcile the apparent inconsistencies which have disclosed themselves on this subject in the following way:

It is possible that M. Guizot entertains something of the jealousy which to a far greater extent is felt in England of the territorial extension and growth of the United States. The grounds of such a jealousy on the part of France are certainly not obvious as they are in the case of England, and it is not felt by the body of the people; on the contrary they regard us not only as good commercial customers but as natural political allies. There is however perhaps on the part of all the old Governments of Europe some jealousy of American progress.

It is possible that M. Guizot in the co-operation which he has yielded or promised to England in reference to Texas has been actuated only by a desire on a subordinate point to gratify her, in order to strengthen the very difficult position toward England, which he occupies in reference to the Right of Search, the occupation of Tahiti, and other great questions. He feels that without the good will of the present British Government his own would sink; as the Ministry here, on the other hand, believing that the peace of Europe is safer in his hands than of [sic] those of any minister in France who should supersede him, submits to a course of policy from him with which they would have quarrelled on the part of Mr. [Louis A.] Thiers.

On one or the other of these grounds, or partly on both, M. Guizot has no doubt promised England to co-operate with her in opposing the annexation of Texas.

But then neither England nor France intends to push this opposition to the point of war. In reference to France this was no more than might have been expected. As far as England is concerned I am not sure there are not many persons, who would have been willing that the Government should have made the annexation of Texas a *casus belli*, on the ground that it involved the rupture of Treaty engagements with this Government. I have, however, no reason to think that the Government has ever come to this conclusion; and though the point is not one on which it could be expected that I should receive any official information, I have good grounds for saying, that the annexation of Texas would not cause a breach of the existing relations between the United States and Great Britain.

This being the case the friendly assurances of the King and M. Guizot to our Minister [William R. King] receive a natural explanation.

No hostile measures are intended by either country. As to the remark made by M. Guizot to Mr. King referred to in your letter to Mr. [Tilghman A.] Howard of the 10th September last, that "France had not agreed to unite with England in a protest against annexation," this must of course be true, for M. Guizot is incapable of a mis-statement. It is however not less certainly true that he had even at that time himself authorised M. Pageot to protest against the measure, and that since the publication of the President's Message, there has been a correspondence and an understanding between the two Governments. That they have agreed on a joint protest, I will not believe in opposition to M. Guizot's assurance; but that they have agreed upon some plan of opposition cannot well be doubted. As it is certain that violent interference is not contemplated, the precise nature of the opposition is of no great moment. It will no doubt be addressed to the Government of Texas, and may be expected to be soon disclosed in that quarter.

How far a participation even in such a policy is to be reconciled with the language of the Government press in Paris I will not undertake to say. It has been intimated that, though the most confidential relations exist between M. Guizot and the *"Journal des débats,"* that paper nevertheless sometimes assumes an independent position and holds a language not sanctioned by the Ministry. The preference manifested by the *Débats* for M. [André] Dupin for the Presidency of the Chamber of Deputies at the opening of the present session over M. [Jean-Pierre] Sauzet the candidate of the Minister is quoted as a case in point. There is however some reason for thinking that M. Dupin was really preferred by the King. I have no belief that, if M. Guizot disapproved the tone of articles like those which accompany this letter, he would find any difficulty in preventing their appearance in the "*Journal des débats.*" For this reason I have observed, that it is not so easy as it ought to be to say, whether they are calculated to throw light upon the views of the French Government in reference to this question, or to involve them in greater mystery. They are at any rate apt illustrations of the circumspection required in forming judgments on any points of European policy, in reference to which it is deemed expedient by the Governments to pra[c]tise any concealment. I am, dear Sir, with great respect, ever faithfully Yours, Edward Everett.

LS (Private) with Ens in DNA, RG 59 (State Department), Diplomatic Despatches, Great Britain, vol. 54 (M-30:50), received 3/21; FC in MHi, Edward Everett Papers, 51:248–256 (published microfilm, reel 23, frames 678–682). Note: The enclosed articles both refer to the annexation of Texas to the U.S. as inevitable and, in itself, of little importance. The second article adds, "The true interest of the Texian question consists therefore in its being merged in that of the re-establishment of the Slavery of the blacks and the subjection of the red skins throughout a territory ten times as large as France." It concludes that even in such a case the citizens of Texas and even Mexico would be as well governed as by the present government of Mexico.

To R[ichard] Pakenham

Department of State
Washington, 26th Feb[ruar]y, 1845

Sir: I have the honor to acknowledge the receipt of your note of the 23d instant, expressing the thanks of Her Majesty's Government for the efficient and ready assistance given by Captain [Philip F.] Voorhees, of the United States' Navy, to Captain [Charles] Hotham of Her Majesty's steam vessel "Gorgon," while employed in getting that vessel off the beach at Monte Video.

I will take much pleasure in transmitting to the Navy Department a copy of your note, in order that it may be communicated to Captain Voorhees.

Be pleased to accept the assurance of my high consideration. J.C. Calhoun.

FC in DNA, RG 59 (State Department), Notes to Foreign Legations, Great Britain, 7:62 (M-99:36).

To C[HARLES] G. ATHERTON, [Senator from N.H.]

Department of State
Washington, 27th Feb[ruar]y 1845

Sir, I have had the honor to receive your note of yesterday's date on behalf of Col. William Boardman, who brought despatches from Mexico.

It frequently occurs that the Ministers of the United States send their despatches by private individuals returning to the United States, without an intention of any expense being incurred thereby. When occasions arise making the employment of a bearer of despatches necessary, for which compensation is to be made, an understanding to that effect is had between the Minister and the person employed, and notice to that effect is given to this Department. Mr. [Wilson] Shannon has not made any communication on the subject, and there-fore, agreeably to to [*sic*] the usage in such cases, no allowance for expenses can be made. I have the honor to be, Sir, Your ob[edien]t Servant, J.C. Calhoun.

Letterpress copy in DNA, RG 59 (State Department), Accounting Records: Miscellaneous Letters Sent, 1832–1916, vol. for 10/3/1844–5/29/1845, p. 258.

From C[ALEB] CUSHING

Washington, 27 Febr[uary] 1845

Sir: In reply to your inquiry of this morning, I have the honor to state that I think the sum of eight thousand dollars sufficient to cover the balance requisite to complete the service contemplated by the act of Congress authorising the late special Mission to China. I am very respectfully Your ob[edien]t S[er]v[an]t, C. Cushing.

ALS in DNA, RG 59 (State Department), Accounting Records: Letters and Accounts from Despatch Agents at New York and Boston, 1840–1860, vol. for 8/1840–11/1847.

To W[ILLIAM] S. ARCHER, Chairman of the Comm[itt]ee on Foreign Relations, of the Senate

Department of State
Washington, 27th Febr[uar]y 1845

Sir, I have the honor to transmit to you a copy of a letter [of today] from Mr. Caleb Cushing, late Commissioner of the United States to China, by which you will perceive that a further appropriation of eight thousand dollars for the expenses of that mission will be necessary. I have the honor to be, Sir, Very respectfully, Your Obed[ien]t Servant, J.C. Calhoun.

Letterpress copy in DNA, RG 59 (State Department), Accounting Records: Miscellaneous Letters Sent, 1832–1916, vol. for 10/3/1844–5/29/1845, p. 255.

To George Evans, Ch[airma]n, Senate Committee on Finance, 2/27. "I have the honor to transmit to you, for the information of your Committee, a copy of a letter [of 2/27] from Mr. Caleb Cushing, late Commissioner of the United States to China, from which you will perceive that a further appropriation of eight thousand dollars for the expenses of that mission, is necessary." Letterpress copy in DNA, RG 59 (State Department), Accounting Records: Miscellaneous Letters Sent, 1832–1916, vol. for 10/3/1844–5/29/1845, p. 254.

From WILLIAM R. KING

Legation of the United States
Paris, 27th February 1845

Sir, The news of the passage, in the House of Representatives, of a bill for the annexation of Texas, created no little sensation here. The general impression was favorable, & the idea that the measure might lead to a war with England, is now universally abandoned. As I have always said, nothing is to be apprehended from the open hostility of any European power, but much is to be feared from adverse influences exerted upon the councils of Texas herself, & I regret that my opinion is confirmed that the efforts of France are united with those of England to induce the young Republic to maintain her separate existence. Gu[a]rantee of independence, commercial advantages, proffers of pecuniary assistance &c, have been or will be, probably, held out to tempt her to reject the advances of the United States. It is to be regretted that this government is so blinded by its devotion to the English alliance, as not to see that its true policy in this question is neutrality if not active sympathy with the United States. France is not & probably can never be a predominant naval power. Her arm at sea, must ever rest upon that of ["the Un" *canceled*] America, and it is only by cooperation with us that she can hope to withstand the formidable ["pow" *canceled*] maritime power of England. There are no points of political or territorial rivalry, between us, and what makes us strong, so far from rendering her weak, must bring her strength in the hour of trial which is destined, sooner or later, to come. Unfortunately the present administration of the government, with no inimical disposition towards the United States, have lost sight of these obvious considerations, in their anxiety to maintain a thoroughly cordial understanding, upon all points, with Great Britain. I have every reason to believe that before my arrival, this government had in a measure pledged itself to cooperate with England, on the Texas question, & that if it subsequently modified its resolution, it was only to the extent of abstaining from overt & offensive acts of opposition to the measure of annexation. I have even been informed from a creditable source, that a protest was actually sent to the French minister at Washington [Alphonse Pageot] but withheld by the advice of Mr. [Richard] Pakenham, lest it should have an effect the opposite to that intended. There can be no doubt that French influence both at Washington & in Texas, is ["cop" *canceled*] cooperating with that of England, actively, perseveringly, and it is to be feared, efficiently. ["Their" *canceled*] Secret opposition is more to be feared than ["their" *canceled*] open hostility which latter would certainly promote, while the former may defeat, the measure in question.

Mr. [George W.] Terrell the new Texian Chargé d'Affaires, has arrived in Paris, after spending some time in London. He is an avowed opponent of annexation, and thinks that his opinion is rapidly gaining ground in Texas. He had frequent interviews with Lord Aberdeen, with whom it is to be presumed he has a cordial understanding. My conversations with him confirm the opinions above expressed, and which I had previously entertained. I learned from him, incidentally, that the instructions of the French government to its representative in Texas [Alphonse de Saligny] had been communicated to Lord Aberdeen, a significant indication of the harmonious views & action of the two cabinets. All these circumstances prove the necessity of prompt, able, & vigilant counteraction of the combined policy of England and France in Texas. The unfortunate rejection of the treaty has naturally cooled the ardor of the people for annexation, and every moment of delay, weakens our hands, while it strengthens those of our persevering adversaries. The question is now to be decided, not in London or Paris, or even Washington, but in Texas.

Since my last despatch the ministerial crisis has passed, & the cabinet has survived, somewhat crippled it may be, but with sufficient strength, probably, to go through the session sustained as it is, by the predominant will of the King, and, and [*sic*] the ostensible patronage of England.

I have the honor to acknowledge the receipt of your despatch No. 13, together with the packets of official papers for Col. [Sylvanus] Thayer, which shall be transmitted as soon as an opportunity presents itself.

I have received also a copy of the Treaty with Wurtemberg, for the mutual abolition of the "*droit d'aubaine*" &c; but before a similar one can be negotiated with Switzerland, it is indispensable that I should be furnished with the proper instructions & authority.

In compliance with your directions I have forwarded the work of M. [Eugène] Duflot de Mofras, on California & Oregon, which was but lately completed by the publication of the last number. It is accompanied by a beautiful copy of the same work which Mr. de Mofras desires to be presented to the Library of Congress, as a testimonial of his gratitude for the attentions which he received from the officers of the American [South Seas] Exploring Squadron [commanded by Charles Wilkes]. I transmit herewith, his letter [of 1/6] of that purport, which I request may be delivered with the work to the Librarian of Congress. I have the honor to be very respectfully your obedient servant, William R. King.

LS (No. 11) with Ens in DNA, RG 59 (State Department), Diplomatic Despatches, France, vol. 30 (M-34:33), received 3/21.

To R[ICHARD] PAKENHAM

Department of State
Washington, 27th Feb[ruar]y, 1845
Sir: I have the honor to acknowledge the receipt of your note of the 20th ultimo, communicating, for consideration, an extract of a letter you had recently received from Her Britannic Majesty's Commissioner of Boundary, which contains suggestions for the more rapid

execution of the duties of the Joint Boundary Commission during the approaching summer, and recommending Colonel [James B.B.] Estcourt's suggestions to the attention of this Government.

I have duly submitted your communication to the President [John Tyler], who cheerfully recognises the soundness of the suggestions therein made.

The attention of Major [James D.] Graham the Head of the American Scientific Corps, has also been invited to the subject; and it will be perceived, from the accompanying extract [of 1/25] of a letter from that officer, explanatory of some of the causes which have superinduced the delays adverted to by Colonel Estcourt in the execution by the American Commission of the labor assigned to it, that those causes were beyond the control of this Department, and are not attributable to any want of energy or industry on the part of that Commission, but principally to changes in the original organization of the American Scientific Corps.

It is much to be regretted that circumstances should have arisen to retard in any way the progress of a work in the completion of which the Government of the United States and that of Her Britannic Majesty both feel a lively interest; and I beg you to be assured that no efforts shall be spared by this Department in endeavoring to meet, as far as practicable, the suggestions of Colonel Estcourt in the further prosecution of the Joint Survey and demarcation of the line of boundary, in pursuance of the provisions of the Treaty of Washington.

I avail myself of this occasion to renew to you the assurance of my distinguished consideration. J.C. Calhoun.

FC in DNA, RG 59 (State Department), Notes to Foreign Legations, Great Britain, 7:62–63 (M-99:36); PC in Jameson, ed., *Correspondence*, pp. 646–647.

From JAMES K. POLK, [President-Elect]

Thursday mor[n]ing, Feb[ruar]y 27th '45

My Dear Sir: I beg leave to introduce to you my nephew Col. [J. Knox] Walker, who will hand you this note. I desire to have an inter[v]iew with you, and request that you will inform Col. W[alker] at what time it will suit your convenience. I am with sincere Regard Your ob[edien]t Se[rvan]t, James K. Polk.

ALS in ScCleA. NOTE: An AEU by Calhoun indicates that this letter was from "Mr. Polk, Pres[iden]t[-]elect."

From LEVI WOODBURY, SIDNEY BREESE, and W[ALTER] T. COLQUITT

Senate Chamber, February 27th 1845

Sir, The undersigned a committee of the Senate to make the necessary arrangements for the reception and inauguration of the President elect [James K. Polk] on the 4th March, next, have the honor to enclose to you copies of the arrangement for the occasion.

You will perceive that places are assigned to the Diplomatic Corps: and the committee have the honor to request that you will make the same known to the members of that body, in such manner as you may see proper, with a view to their being present at the inauguration.

That sufficient accommodation may be provided for them, the committee would be glad to learn, on or before the 3d of March, the number that may be expected. We have the honor to be, Sir, Your Obedient Servants, Levi Woodbury, Sidney Breese, W.T. Colquitt.

LS in DNA, RG 59 (State Department), Miscellaneous Letters (M-179:107, frame 252). NOTE: Woodbury, Breese, and Colquitt were Senators from N.H., Ill., and Ga., respectively.

CIRCULAR [to Foreign Representatives in Washington]

Department of State
Washington, 28th February, 1845

Sir: I have the honor to transmit to you, herewith, for the information of the Diplomatic Corps, a printed copy of the arrangements for the Inauguration of the President elect [James K. Polk], on the 4th of March, next; and should be pleased if you would, at your earliest convenience, signify to this Department whether you will probably be present at the ceremony or not, in order that the necessary accommodations may be provided for you.

I avail myself of this occasion to renew to you the assurance of my distinguished consideration. J.C. Calhoun.

LS (addressed to [Charles H. Raymond]) in Tx, Andrew Jackson Houston Papers; FC (addressed to [Jean Corneille] Gevers) in DNA, RG 59 (State Department), Notes to Foreign Legations, the Netherlands, 6:37 (M-99:75); FC (addressed to A[ngel] Calderon de la Barca) in DNA, RG 59 (State Department), Notes to Foreign Legations, Spain, 6:119–120 (M-99:85). NOTE: Abstracts of this circular, found in DNA, RG 59 (State Department), Notes to

Foreign Legations, in various files, indicate that copies were sent to the Ministers or Chargés d'Affaires of (in addition to Texas, Netherlands, and Spain) Great Britain, France, Russia, Prussia, Austria, Portugal, Belgium, Denmark, Sardinia, and Sweden. No copies of the circular to the representatives of Argentina, Brazil, or Mexico have been found.

From J[uan] N. Almonte, [Mexican Minister to the U.S.], 2/28. He gratefully acknowledges Calhoun's circular of this day but will be unable to attend the inauguration of President-Elect [James K. Polk] because of family illness. LS (in Spanish) in DNA, RG 59 (State Department), Notes from Foreign Legations, Mexico, vol. 4 (M-54:2).

From J[OHN] S. BARBOUR

Wash[ingto]n, Feb[ruar]y 28th 1845
My Dear Sir, I called yesterday at the State Dept. the moment you were leaving it, that I might hand you the enclosed.

It is from Gen[era]l [Robert] Wallace of the Senate of Virg[ini]a[,] by far the ablest member of that body.

As its perusal may interest you, I now communicate it. In great haste Y[ou]rs Truly, J.S. Barbour.

[Enclosure]

R[obert] Wallace to John S. Barbour

Warrenton [Va.], 22d Feb: '45
My Dear Sir, I have just rec[e]ived your kind note addressed to me at Richmond, whence I had left before it reached there, as you may well see by my letter of yesterday, sent under cover to the Hon: Mr. [Samuel] Chilton. In that letter I expressed my profound sense of the importance of retaining Mr. Calhoun in the Cabinet, and my deep regret at the information communicated by you to my brother, of his intention to retire. Your letter of today fills me with joy, when you say, "Mr. Calhoun will be invited to remain," although "nothing is *known*." That there is hope even is comfortable—that there could be certainty would give me a confidence in the fate of the country, the South and the administration, which I can not have if he retire. The space of a letter is not enough for me to place before you all the great considerations, direct and incidental, present and remote, which hang for their consum[m]ation on his remaining where he is. In a letter, which I informed you from Richmond, I wrote to Gen: [An-

drew] Jackson I placed this matter in its true and strongest light before him, and I shall not esteem him the sagacious man I have thought him, if they have not struck him with their full force. The [Richmond] Enquirer before the last, that of the 18th, means Mr. Calhoun when it speaks of the "first mind"; an expression I had often used to him [Thomas Ritchie?] in speaking of Mr. C[alhoun] and the importance, nay absolute necessity in the present juncture, of Mr. Polk's summoning to his aid the first minds and most able and experienced statesmen of the whole country. We can not get along with an inferior cabinet; the country must be governed wisely, or the Union—the South[,] the administration will all be in danger. Nothing but the wisdom of Louis Philip[pe] prevents a crusade against America, under the guise of humanity; treaty obligations to Mexico, defence of her rights to Oregon, &c, &c, by England, and some other powers who can furnish contingents of men. We are rising more rapidly into consequence in the eyes of the potentates of Europe from the moral force of our institutions than our physical or maratime [*sic*] advancement; and this it is which they would check if they could. Our first protection is in the wisdom of the King of the French, and our next in the affections of the French people. Do not understand me as underrating our own power. That you must recollect will not be exerted in such a war. The purpose of England will paralize the greater part of the North and East, and the South being the theatre of the war must bear its burdens and feel all its dreadful horrors. She ["(the South)" *interlined*] is now, however, stronger than the next twenty years will find her, after which she will raise a magestic [*sic*] head, and Virginia especially, if Texas have her doors open to receive our surplus and useless slaves. In this regard I consider Texas as most important for Virginia.

There is no man so capable of comprehending and baffling the profound and imposing movements of England, in all respects, as Mr. Calhoun, and we shall, comparitivly [*sic*], be pigmies in her hands without him. If it depend on him, urge him by every consideration of love and duty to his country and the South and the principles of the Republican party, not to quit his post. He must [*one word altered to* "stand"] by us in this hour of the greatest danger to which the country has ever been exposed.

I hope to see you in Washington soon.

Drop me a line as you may think any thing worth noting. Most truly, dear Sir, R. Wallace.

[Marginal P.S.] I have allways thought that Providence would give us Texas; & trust your fears may not be realized.

ALS with En in ScCleA. Note: An AEU by Calhoun reads "Mr. Barbour enclosing a letter from G[e]n[era]l Wallace."

From Geo[rge] M. Bibb

Department of the Treasury
Washington, February 28th 1845

The letter to you of the 13th of February 1845, from [Friedrich von Gerolt] the minister of his Majesty the King of Prussia, which you did me the honour to refer, has received the earliest consideration permitted by other pressing duties of this department.

The 1st, 2d, 3d, 4th, 5th, 6th, 7th, & 8th articles of the treaty between the United States of America & his Majesty the King of Prussia, concluded at Washington, on the first day of May 1828, have established between the their [*sic*] respective States a commercial intercourse, upon a system of entire freedom of Navigation & perfect reciprocity, based upon principles of equity mutually beneficial to the people of the two Countries.

The national vessels of the two contracting parties in the ports of the respective nations are placed upon an equal reciprocity as to the duties of tonnage, lighthouses, pilotage, Salvage & port charges, as well as to fees and perquisites of public officers &c, levied in the name or for the profit of the Government by authority of the one government & the other, upon their own national vessels:

All kinds of merchandizes imported into the United States, either the produce of, the Soil, or the industry, of the Kingdom of Prussia or of any other country, which may be lawfully imported in Vessels of the United States, may be imported also in Prussian Vessels, without paying other or higher duties or charges than if the same produce or merchandize had been imported in Vessels of the United States of America, whether clearing directly from the ports of the country to which they respectively belong or from the ports of any other foreign Country:

No higher or other duties shall be imposed on the importation into the United States of any article the produce or manufacture of Prussia, than are or shall be payable on the like article being the produce or manufacture of any other foreign country:

No priority or preference shall be given directly or indirectly by either of the Contracting parties, in the purchase of any Article of Commerce lawfully imported, on account of, or in reference to, the character of the vessel, whether it be of the one party or the other, in which such article was imported:

If either party shall hereafter, grant to any other nation any particular favour in navigation, or commerce, it shall immediately become Common to the other party, freely, where it is freely granted to such other nation, or on yielding the same compensation, when the grant is conditional.

Such are the principles of reciprocity mutually agreed by the subsisting treaty between the United States & Prussia. In respect of which, the Secretary of the Treasury accords [*sic*; accedes] to the proposition advanced by Mr. Gerolt the minister of His Majesty the King of Prussia "that a reduction of the duty on Prussian Wines which has been fixed by the last American tariff at twenty cents per gallon in bottles, to fifteen cents per gallon the duty fixed on Sicilian wines" ought to be made in the ports of the United States.

In accordance with these views the Secretary of the Treasury will prom[p]tly cause to be issued to the several Collectors of the Customs in the United States, orders not to collect under the tariff of 1842 more than fifteen cents per gallon on Prussian wines when imported in bottles; And also to restore any such excess which may have been paid on Prussian wines under the Act of 1842 when levied & collected from the importer, agent or consignee, under protest. It is to be noted that the bottles in which the wines are imported, shall pay a separate duty.

Permit me through you to assure the minister of His Majesty the King of Prussia, that the Secretary of the Treasury will use all the powers & authorities invested in him by law, to cause to be observed & fulfilled, by all the officers subordinate to the head of the Treasury department, the stipulations, all & singular, on the part of the United States, in the treaties between the two nations ["as for mentioned" *canceled*] subsisting, to the end, that the most scrupulous good faith shall be preserved on the part of the United States, (as he dou[b]ts not will be likewise observed on the part of His Majesty the King of Prussia & his government & officers,) and that the relations of good understanding which have hitherto so happily subsisted between the United States and the Kingdom of Prussia, & the Commercial intercourse between them, may be maintained upon a stable & permanent footing. Accept for yourself the assurances of my high respect, Geo: M. Bibb, Secretary of the Treasury.

ALS in DNA, RG 59 (State Department), Miscellaneous Letters (M-179:107, frames 253–257); FC in DNA, RG 56 (Secretary of the Treasury), Letters to Cabinet and Bureau Officers, Series B, 5:36–38.

From Geo[rge] M. Bibb, Secretary of the Treasury, 2/28. "Upon perusing the letter [of 1/17] of Mr. [Joseph A.] Binda, the Consul of the U: States at Leghorn, & the extract of the letter of Mr. Appleton, to me referred, I have to remark that it seems to me expedient & proper that the appointment of Mr. [James] Ombrosi as Consul of the United States, at Florence, should be revoked, & that he should be informed that his Consular certificates can not be respected in any of the ports or places of the United States, he not having been Accredited by the Tuscan Government." ALS in DNA, RG 59 (State Department), Consular Despatches, Leghorn, vol. 3 (T-214:3); FC in DNA, RG 56 (Secretary of the Treasury), Letters to Cabinet and Bureau Officers, Series B, 5:35–36.

From C[ALEB] CUSHING

Washington, 28 Febr[uary] 1845

Sir: In referring to the correspondence annexed to my despatch of the 20th of August 1843 numbered eighty eight (88) it will be seen that one class, of the subjects which it fell to me to discuss in China, remains open for such instructions as the President may see fit to give, in that behalf, to any future representative of the United States. I allude to the claim of the United States for reparation on account of the killing of an American citizen of the name of Sherry, by Chinese soldiers, and personal injury or restraint inflicted on Mr. Morse [*sic*; W.H. Morss], Mr. [Alfred P.] Edwards, & other citizens of the United States, in the course of the late war between China & Great Britain.

Connected with this, also, is the counter-claim of the Chinese, for reparation on account of the alleged killing of a Chinese by an American during this last year.

These topics I was under the necessity of leaving undisposed of, in consequence of my not having in my possession any authentic knowledge of the precise footing on which our claims had been left by Commodore Kearney [*sic*; Lawrence Kearny], to whose intervention therein reference was made by the Imperial Commissioner. I beg permission to call the attention of the Department to this subject, the means of pursuing which satisfactorily can, I presume, be derived from the correspondence of Commodore Kearney with the Navy Department.

While upon this subject, I cannot forbear to express my sense of the value & importance of the service rendered by Commodore Kearney, & the force under his command, at the period in question. I had evidence of the intelligence & zeal he had displayed, while on the coast of China previous to my arrival, in the protection of our legitimate commerce, in procuring redress for the injuries done our citizens, & in otherwise maintaining the dignity & promoting the interests of the United States.

And on this, as on other occasions, I have seen the advantages to be obtained from the judicious disposition of a naval force, under wise & brave commanders, in aid of our relations with a certain class of foreign Powers; and I earnestly hope that such a force will continue to be employed in China. I am Very respectfully, C. Cushing.

ALS (No. 105) in DNA, RG 59 (State Department), Diplomatic Despatches, China, vol. 2 (M-92:3). NOTE: W.H. Morss was injured and a young man named Sherry from N.Y. killed in a Chinese attack on an American boat crew from the ship *Morrison* on 5/21/1841. Edwards was an American merchant imprisoned at Honan in 11/1841.

From EDWARD EVERETT

London, 28th February, 1845

Sir, You are aware of the fact that in the Autumn of 1843, the President [John Tyler] did me the honor to send me a full power to negotiate with this Government for the adjustment of the Oregon question. Although the negociation was transferred to Washington by the appointment of Mr. [Richard] Pakenham, expressly with a view to give a new impulse to it—a step which had been decided upon before my full powers were received—I was led to have several conversations with Lord Aberdeen on the subject, the purport of which is contained in my despatches numbered 69, 82, and 106.

Since the arrival of the steamer of the 1st instant bringing intelligence of the progress in the House of Representatives, of a bill for erecting a territorial Government in Oregon, I have again had several conversations with Lord Aberdeen on this subject, which, though not precisely of an official character, I have thought to be of sufficient gravity, to be reported to you.

I have felt of course restrained in conferring with him on the subject, not merely from the want of any present powers to treat, but because I am uninformed of the precise views entertained by my Government, any farther than as they may be inferred from my own instructions in 1843, and the accounts given me by Lord Aberdeen of the progress of the negociation at Washington.

Under these somewhat unfavorable circumstances, I have applied myself with the greatest care to ascertain the extent to which this Government is prepared to go, with a view to the amicable settlement of the question, and the manner in which it stands affected toward the proceedings which have been had in Congress. Lord Aberdeen has expressed himself with as little reserve as I could expect, but has made the very reasonable remark to me, that as I was not authorised to make or receive proposals, he could not deem it expedient to endeavor to gain the assent of his colleagues to any specific plan, without knowing how it was likely to be met in the United States. A portion therefore of what I state must be regarded as matter of inference; drawn however from every source of information within my reach.

Lord Aberdeen having informed me that Mr. Pakenham had proposed to you to submit the controversy to arbitration, and that you had declined this proposal, I told him there was not as in the North Eastern Boundary a specific question between two rival lines to refer, and that I did not precisely see what issue could be made up for the arbitrator. He said there was a twofold question which could be referred, *First* whether the United States had an exclusive right to the whole, or whether as England says it is open to both parties; and if this were decided in favor of England, *Secondly*, what would be a fair line of boundary, by way of compromise.

I beg leave to remark on this point, that such a submission would be in this respect favorable to the United States, that it would give us a double opportunity of an adjustment favorable to our claims. If a decision for the first point were given for us, it would settle the whole controversy in our favor; whereas if the first point were settled according to the English claim it would give them nothing but an equal chance with us for a favorable decision of the second point.

I intimated that another objection to an arbitration would be the difficulty of finding an impartial umpire; England having an influence with the friendly powers of Europe which must naturally outweigh ours. Lord Aberdeen doubted whether there was much in this, and said they would (he thought) be willing to abide the decision of a power vizt. France, that might be expected to be fully as favorable to us as to them.

Lord Aberdeen is evidently much in favor of arbitration, and, as I am persuaded, because it affords the readiest method of an honorable adjustment of the question. They have twice refused our offer of running the 49th degree of latitude to the sea. They find us firm in resisting any further concession. I have uniformly assured Lord Aberdeen, that the United States would never accept a boundary much less favorable. He entertains on behalf of the Government of which he is the organ an invincible repugnance to receding in their terms, and accepting now what they have repeatedly refused; and he acknowledges the existence of the same difficulty on our side. He feels that these circumstances create a difficult and critical position, from which arbitration affords a ready and creditable escape; inasmuch as it is always honorable to accept the award of an arbitrator, even when you may think it less favorable than you might have expected.

Entertaining myself a clear conviction that our title is a strong one to the valley of the Colombia; that it is a respectable one up to the Russian limit; and that the offer of the 49th degree by way of compromise, is eminently reasonable and founded on the best and most obvious principles for settling such a question, I should feel entire confidence that the decision of an arbitrator would be to that extent favorable to us; and it would of course afford a mode of finally disposing of the subject as convenient to us, as far as the *point d'honneur* is concerned, as to Great Britain.

I have anticipated in some degree another point, to which Lord Aberdeen has given great prominence in all our conversations vizt. the entire impossibility that England should accept terms which she has already refused. I do not think I can be mistaken in saying that, unless it comes in the form of an award, she will never agree to the naked proposition of the forty ninth degree. I have, however, a pretty confident belief that she would accept that line with the modification alluded to in my despatches above mentioned; vizt. the southern extremity of Quadra and Vancouver's island, though cut off by the forty ninth parallel, to be theirs. Lord Aberdeen has never told me they would agree to this; but I am still of the opinion expressed in my former despatches, and for the reasons therein stated that they would do so, and I am confident that this is the best boundary which we can get by negociation. The concession of the southern end of the island, while of little importance to us, would be a great boon to them as giving them a passage through the straits of Fuca; and on the ground of this advantage I am of opinion that they would consider themselves justified in acceding in other respects to the forty ninth degree; but if the expectation prevails, that they can be led by negociation to agree to a boundary which we should regard as more favorable than this, I am confident that expectation will prove delusive. At the same time, I have spared no pains to impress upon Lord Aberdeen's mind the persuasion, that the utmost which the United States can concede is the forty ninth parallel with the modification suggested, taking care always to add, that I had no authority for saying that even that modification would be agreed to. Lord Aberdeen is also aware that since the receipt of my full power of September 1843, I have no precise information of the views entertained on this subject by my Government.

The position of the controversy is therefore obviously a critical one, and since the arrival of the steamer of the 1st instant has been, I think, contemplated with much seriousness, by this Government. The provisions of the resolution before the House for erecting a territorial Government have been the subject of repeated conversation between Lord Aberdeen and myself. I have stated to him my impression, that as far as I have been able to gather their nature from the debates, they do not go much farther than the British Government has gone in extending the jurisdiction of the Courts of Upper Canada to the residents in the Oregon territory. While Lord Aberdeen admits that there is a greater foundation for this statement than might at first be inferred from the imposing form which the measure assumes, and that it might perhaps be possible to execute the provisions of the bill without collision with British subjects and British interests in the territory, yet he adds that the measure is exclusive in its tendency and character, that it is an assumption of Sov[e]reignty, and is shewn to be so, in the proposal to put an end to the convention of joint occupation.

In this view of the subject Lord Aberdeen has assured me, with every appearance of sincerity, and in such a manner as to convince me that it is painful to him to contemplate the possibility of such an event, that if the United States proceed to take exclusive possession of the Country, England will feel obliged to throw a force into it adequate to maintain her present position. It would be wrong in me not to say, that this suggestion was in no degree made in the way of menace; but simply as the annunciation of a course which this Government would feel obliged to pursue in a given contingency, which is presenting itself too distinctly not to require consideration. I asked Lord Aberdeen whether he wished me to convey this suggestion to my Government, and he said he did not desire it nor make it for that purpose, but that I was at liberty if I thought proper to do so; that he had spoken from the fullness of his heart; that I well knew he was as much attached as any man in Europe to the preservation of the general peace; that he was the constant object of reproach on that ground, but that he regarded it as the privilege of a strong Government to disregard such reproaches, and to be able, if need be, to make some sacrifices to the continuance of peace; but that there was a point beyond which no administration could go, even if it were disposed, in that direction; and if the United States proceeded, while an amicable negociation is in progress[,] to put an end to the Convention of joint occupation and to appropriate to themselves the territory in dispute, war was inevitable.

I have regarded these observations as far too important not to be communicated to you, and I may perhaps with propriety add that I find from casual conversations with my colleagues of the diplomatic Corps, that they have formed the impression that the relations of the two Countries are in a very critical state. It also came to my knowledge a day or two ago that M. [F.P.G.] Guizot remarked to an American dining with him at Paris on the 18th instant, that he feared a conflict was impending between the United States and Great Britain on the subject of Oregon. The idea has been thrown out, that the addition of 4000 seamen to the number authorised last year was resolved upon, in consequence of the threatening purport of the last intelligence from Washington. I believe however that I may safely say that this additional force was determined upon, a considerable time before the arrival of the news. But that no reference was had by the Ministry, in thus providing for an addition of ten or twelve ships of the line to their disposable naval force, to the state of the relations between the two Governments is more I think than could be safely asserted.

1st March, 1845. Since the foregoing was written I have noticed an article of considerable significance in the [London] "Times" of this day, to some portions of which I am inclined to ascribe a semi-official origin. It contains a very superficial and inaccurate statement of the merits of the case, intended merely to rally public opinion in favor of the British side of the question. It speaks however of a readiness to accept "an amicable and equitable adjustment of disputable rights to waste territories"; and intimates that "the best method of arriving at this result would be by referring the matter to the arbitration of a third state." These expressions are no doubt intended to modify a little the confidence of the public in the unquestioned validity of the British title to the whole region, which is asserted in other portions of the article.

But the most significant remark is one, which occurs towards its conclusion to the following effect, that "in the present temper of

American citizens, we suspect that a silent but resolute determination to put our positions there in a state of defence and to send a sufficient squadron to that coast, is the wisest answer to these measures of the House of Representatives." I am inclined to think that this remark foreshadows the course of policy which has been contemplated, in the event of the enactment into a law of the bill now before the Senate. That measure would be regarded, I believe, as of a hostile tendency, but not in itself as a declaration of war. It would, however, I imagine be the signal for sending out an effective naval expedition to that region and for taking up a strong central military position on the Columbia river with outposts at the most important points of the territory. After the spectacle exhibited two years since of seventy five vessels of war in the Yang-tse-Keang, (of which a considerable portion were steamers,) and of a successful campaign in mid-summer in the latitude and under the climate of Charleston, we cannot entertain much doubt of the ability of Great Britain to take this step. Once established in the valley of the Columbia, the recovery of it from them, on our part, might be a matter of difficulty. Of the general results of the struggle which would ensue, (deplorable as a war must necessarily be, between the two nations able to do most good and most evil to each other), no apprehensions need be entertained by us. After hard blows given and received, we should doubtless come out of the contest with the national character elevated. But whether, in reference to the particular subject of controversy vizt. the partition of this territory, we should stand as well as we do now may be doubted. Prevented as England now professes to be by the *point d'honneur* from agreeing to the forty ninth parallel, is it probable that the events of the contest will be such, in that quarter, as to induce her to give way? Is it not more likely that she will be able to take and retain the whole country, and consequently go into the negociations for peace to great advantage?

It occurs to me also as worth considering, what will be the effect of a struggle for Oregon, on the possession of the Sandwich Islands. It is true that England and France have agreed to respect their independence; but a war for Oregon, unless France should at the outset throw herself into our scale, would be very apt to have for one of its first consequences, an understanding between France and England for a partition of the Sandwich and Society Islands, the result of which, I should apprehend, would be the final and permanent occupation by England of some portion of the first named group. Indeed I suppose the occupation of this *point d'appui* would be the first step of a naval movement on Oregon.

I hazard these suggestions with less diffidence (though with no great confidence in my impressions on such a subject,) because if I recollect right, a view substantially the same in reference to the power of Great Britain in the event of a war, to anticipate us, in taking military possession of the Country, was advanced by yourself in debate in the Senate of the United States. I am, Sir, with great respect, Your obedient Servant, Edward Everett.

LS (No. 269, Confidential) in DNA, RG 59 (State Department), Diplomatic Despatches, Great Britain, vol. 54 (M-30:50), received 3/21; FC in DNA, RG 84 (Foreign Posts), Great Britain, Despatches, 9:174–187; FC in MHi, Edward Everett Papers, 51:276–291 (published microfilm, reel 23, frames 692–699); variant CC in DNA, RG 76 (Records of Boundary and Claims Commissions and Arbitrations), Records Relating to the U.S.-Canadian Border, Documents Relating to the U.S. Case, no. 269.

From [Jean Corneille] Gevers, Dutch Chargé d'Affaires to the U.S., 2/28. He replies to Calhoun's circular of today that he will attend the inauguration of President Elect [James K. Polk] on 3/4. ALS in DNA, RG 59 (State Department), Notes from Foreign Legations, the Netherlands, vol. 2 (M-56:2, frame 184).

From J[AMES] HAMILTON, [JR.], *"Private* not official"

New Orleans, Feb[ruar]y 28[t]h 1845

My Dear Sir, I have been detained here and in its vicinity examin[in]g the best & most economical sugar works with the view of erecting them on my own place [in Texas] on Oyster Creek near the Brasos.

With this view I shall go up to the late Gen[era]l [Wade] Hampton's Est[ate] at the Houma's [La.] tomorrow and cannot reach the [Oswichee] Bend [in Ala.] before the 9[t]h which must account for my not answering any Letters from you which you may have addressed to that place.

Before leaving the City with [John S.] Preston for his plantation I have deemed it of some importance to send you the enclosed which is a most significant token.

You will perceive that it is a proclamation of the President of Texas [Anson Jones], revoking ["the issue of" *canceled*] all Letters of Marque & Reprisal against Mexico. As there happen to be I really [*sic*] not a single Letter of marque in existence I apprehend that this is a move at the instigation of the British Govt. to propitiate Mexico & to give facility to the pending negociations between herself & that Country for an ultimate pacification. I have no doubt that it is in the Line of policy which Lord Aberdeen suggested to A[s]hbel Smith it would be expedient for Texas to adopt if not the result of a direct movement of Capt. Elliott [*sic*; Charles Elliot, British Chargé d'Affaires in Texas,] on the Texian Govt.

I enclosed Mr. [Robert J.] Walker [Senator from Miss.] yesterday a leader from the Register[,] the Govt. Paper at Washington[,] Texas. I have no doubt the President[,] his Cabinet & all those in possession of national offices have thus come out ["in" *canceled*] against annexation and in favor of the British Alliance. I have no fears about the people altho disgust at the paltry & wavering conduct of the Senate is encreasing daily and if Mr. [James K.] Polk does not move with great promptitude & energy that Country will be lost entirely to this. There are serious objections to the Resolutions of Annexation as they passed the H. of R. The barren & for years unproductive source out of which the public Creditors of Texas are to be paid, in the face of the pledge which she has made of her Revenues by Customs in all the Bonds I issued & negotiated whilst the United States steps in & appropriates all these Revenues to ["itself" *canceled and* "herself" *interlined*] by absorbing within the vortex of her infamous Tariff all the imposts of Texas constitute well founded objections to annexation & will form an admirable handle for the Officers to agitate the Country. But still I think the game is in Polk[']s hands if he will play it with boldness & energy.

With this view I trust your health and the cordial kindness & confidence with which he may & only *can* if he has either gratitude & good sense invite you into the Cabinet will induce you to retain your present Post, altho I would rather see you at the head of the Treasury. But I deem it as indispensable to the honor & salvation of the Country that you should be in the Govt.

Our relations with England are becoming *sensitively delicate.* To combine a lofty spirit with consummate discretion requires a high & matured capacity for public affairs which I know not where Polk can find these qualities without he seeks them in you. He is however surrounded by such a Tartar horde from the East & West that I fear his being able with all his innate honesty & love of justice to maintain his equilibrium with such an immense pressure from without and entirely encompassing him.

Among the Eastern Politicians who has gone on for Spoils if not honors I see the name of Geo[rge] Bancroft of Boston. I know this man thoroughly. Three of my sons were at the Round hill [Mass.] school of which he with my good friend [Joseph G.] Cogswell was a principal. A more heartless[,] treacherous individual does not live. He is the very living Presentment of that Class of Metaphysicians ["of" *canceled*] which [Edmund] Burke describes so admirably in his work on the French Revolution. He is dry[,] acidulous & faithless and as scycophantic [*sic*] as faithless. I see his object by the Paper is the Cabinet. He would be a tool of [Martin] Van Buren[']s & [Thomas H.] Benton[']s and sacrifice you & Polk just with as little concern as he would kill a kitten. His Conduct to his Coadjutor Mr. Cogswell was compounded of all that was odious in ["gratitude" *changed to* "ingratitude"] & ["good" *canceled and* "bad" *interlined*] faith whilst for the mere purposes of popularity, he has pushed the doctrines of Agra[ria]nism & Dor[r]ism to the most disgusting & licentious extent. Have a care. He has no practical Talents for business altho possessed of much genius & great liberary[?] attaintments [*sic*]. In one word he is all head & no heart.

If you should go to England pray allow me to send you a batch of Letters to some of the best & most distinguished people in that Country who were among the most valued friends I had there.

In case you do not go in regard to myself I have but one word to say—in addition to all I have said. That you are the sole depository of the secret that I would accept the mission. My wife [Elizabeth Heyward Hamilton] from whom I rarely conceal anything is ignorant of such a disposition of my own Will, which I know in my circumstances would stagger the belief of my best friends that I should under take any thing if involving such pecuniary expence. But I believe I ["am" *canceled*] can obtain distinction [and] serve the Country without any perilous loss. I believe moreover that I can put myself in a situation to do you more good than any other man in the U.S. can atchieve [*sic*] for you. But still I am content[,] an amiable wife & devoted Children make a home humble [*one word or partial word canceled*] is it is [*sic*] too balmly [*sic*] & delightful to permit me to repine altho others may be prefer[r]ed to me for honors the duties of which peradvature [*sic*] I may as well fulfill.

I believe if you are a Candidate for the Presidency ["at" *interlined; the*] next Election in spite of the Sugar duty you will sweep the field. The ["session" *canceled and* "Legislature" *interlined*] & Convention [of La.] being in Session my intercourse with the Leading men of the State has been most intimate and to us [F.P.G.]

Gu[i]zot's phrase in relation to yourself the *"cordial understanding"* is most perfect between us. I have therefore spent a fortnight here not without some profit.

By the way I see by the Papers England has probably assailed Guizot for his declaration to ["Mr." *interlined*; William R.] King [U.S. Minister to France]. And that an apology has been either asked or demanded from our Govt. for the strong Reproof of your admirable dispatch to that Gentleman. I do not believe John Bull capable of such absurdity, but if he is I hope Polk will inform her Majesty's Govt. that our apology hangs at the point of our Bayonets, it must be sought *there* or *nowhere*.

Direct to the Oswichee P.O. & believe me My Dear Sir With esteem sincerely & faithfully Your friend, J. Hamilton.

ALS in ScCleA; PEx in Boucher and Brooks, eds., *Correspondence*, pp. 285–286.

From O[GDEN] HOFFMAN

U.S. Attorney's Office
New York [City], Feb[ruar]y 28, 1845

Sir, In the month of September last, my attention was called and directed by the State Department, to two Mexican Steamers, then being in this Port, the officers of which, it was alleged, were violating the provisions of the Acts of Congress of 1818 and 1838.

The case of these Steamers was the subject of a long correspondence with the Department, and to it my attention and consideration were constantly and zealously directed for some weeks. Mr. R[ichard] S. Coxe was subsequently associated with me, with whom I had frequent consultations in relation to the proper course to be adopted. The writs which I had prepared and placed, as a matter of precaution, in the hands of the Marshal [Silas M. Stilwell], in order that he might be ready to act at a moment's warning, were subsequently, in pursuance of your instructions, withdrawn, and the vessels were permitted to sail. All the proceedings were therefore out of Court, and no legal costs of Court can be taxed.

My remuneration for these services, must, therefore rest entirely with the justice of the Department, as to the counsel fee, or compensation, if any, that you may think fair and reasonable, for the time devoted and the labor performed. I make no specific charge for whatever you determine, with that decision I will be content.

I am anxious, that the matter should be considered and decided by you, who were conversant with the whole proceedings, and from whom my instructions came. I called, some two weeks since, when in Washington, to pay my respects to you, and intended then to have submitted the subject to you, but the state of your health denied me the pleasure of seeing you.

I pray your early attention to this matter, and to believe me with great Respect Your Ob[edient] Ser[van]t, O. Hoffman.

LS in DNA, RG 59 (State Department), Accounting Records: Miscellaneous Letters Received.

From [Johann Georg von] Hülsemann, [Austrian Chargé d'Affaires in the U.S.], 2/28. In reply to the circular of 2/28, he states that he will attend the inauguration of President-Elect [James K. Polk] on 3/4. ALS (in French) in DNA, RG 59 (State Department), Notes from Foreign Legations, Austria, vol. 1 (M-48:1); draft (in French) in DLC, John G. Hülsemann Papers (Toner Collection).

To R[ICHARD] PAKENHAM

Department of State
Washington, 28th Feb[ruar]y, 1845

Sir: I have the honor to acknowledge the receipt of your note of the 25th instant, transmitting a packet addressed to the President of the United States [John Tyler], which, you are informed, contains certain communications from the Government of the Sandwich Islands to the President; and to be with high consideration, Sir, your obedient servant, J.C. Calhoun.

FC in DNA, RG 59 (State Department), Notes to Foreign Legations, Great Britain, 7:63–64 (M-99:36).

To JAMES K. POLK, "Pres[iden]t elect"

Washington, 27th [*sic*; 28th] Feb. 1845

My dear Sir, Having been informed in the interview to which you invited me yesterday, of your determination to form an entirely new Cabinet, I deem it proper to apprize you of the fact, that I have resigned the office of Secretary of State to take effect, as soon as a successor is appointed & ready to assume its duties.

I regard it as not irrevelant [*sic*] to the occasion to assure you, that the an[n]unciation of your determination has caused, on my part, no dissatisfaction, nor abatement of the kind feelings, personal or political, which I have heretofore entertained for you. According to my opinion, it is the right of every President to select his Constitutional advisers, without giving any just cause of offense to any one.

In conclusion, I avail myself of the opportunity of expressing my sincere hope, that your administration may confer lasting honor on yourself, & contribute to establish more firmly the liberty & prosperity of the country, by carr[y]ing out in practice the great measures put in issue at the late election, & on which its success depended; by thoroughly reforming the Government & restoring the Constitution to what its illustrious framers intended it should be; by preserving peace abroad, without sacraficing [*sic*] the honor or interest of the country, and by restoring ["& preserving" *interlined*] brotherly feelings & harmony among the members of this mighty Union, ["in" *interlined*] the only way it can be, by effectually discountenancing all attempts at interference with the institutions & internal concerns of each other, and equalizing, among the various sections, the burthens & the benefits of the Government, especially in its fiscal operations. With great respect Yours truly, J.C. Calhoun.

ALS in DLC, James K. Polk Papers (Presidential Papers Microfilm, Polk Papers, roll 33). NOTE: An endorsement in an unknown hand reads: "Hon. Jno. C. Calhoun S.C. Resignation as Sec. of State. Received March 1st 1845."

From Ch[arles] Serruys, [Belgian Chargé d'Affaires in the U.S.], 2/28. "I have the honor to acknowledge the receipt of your note in date of this day and to inform you that I intend being present at the ceremony of the inauguration with my Secretary of Legation." ALS in DNA, RG 59 (State Department), Notes from Foreign Legations, Belgium, vol. 1 (M-194:1).

To President [JOHN TYLER]

Department of State
Washington, 28th February 1845
To the President of the United States.

The Secretary of State to whom has been referred the resolution of the Senate of the 17th instant, requesting the President to inform that body, if not incompatible with the public interest, "what measures, if any, have been taken by the Government of the United States, to obtain redress from the British Government for the illegal capture of the fishing Schooner Argus, of Portland, and other American vessels engaged in the fisheries, under a pretended infraction of the Convention of 20th October, 1818," has the honor to report to the President the accompanying copies and extracts of correspondence from the files of the Department, embracing the information called for. Respectfully submitted, J.C. Calhoun.

List of accompanying papers.

Acting Secretary of State to				
Mr. [Henry S.] Fox,	dated 10th July, 1839—Copy			
Mr. [John] Forsyth to Mr. Fox	24	"	"	"
" Forsyth to Mr. [Andrew] Stevenson	20	Feb. 1841		"
" Stevenson to Mr. [Daniel] Webster	7	April	"	Ext.
" Same to same	18	May	"	"
" [Abel P.] Upshur to Mr. [Edward] Everett	30	June	"	Copy
" Everett to Mr. Upshur	15	Aug.	"	Ext.
" Same to Mr. Calhoun	26	May 1844		"
" Calhoun to Mr. Everett	5	July	"	"
" Same to Same	6	Septr.	"	Copy
" Everett to Mr. Calhoun	9	Oct.	"	Ext.
Same to Same	4	Novr.	"	Copy.

FC in DNA, RG 59 (State Department), Reports of the Secretary of State to the President and Congress, 6:160. NOTE: The resolution to which this is a response can be found in DNA, RG 59 (State Department), Miscellaneous Letters (M-179:107, frames 217–218) and in *Senate Journal*, 28th Cong., 2nd Sess., p. 178.

From Carlos [Maria] de Alvear, [Argentine Minister to the U.S.], 3/1. He acknowledges the circular of 2/28 inviting him to the inauguration of President-Elect [James K. Polk] and plans to attend with his Secretary of Legation, Emilio de Alvear. ALS (in Spanish) in DNA, RG 59 (State Department), Notes from Foreign Legations, Argentina, vol. 1 (M-47:2).

From Steen Bille, [Danish Chargé d'Affaires in the U.S.], 3/1. He replies to Calhoun's circular of 2/28 that he considers it "both an honor and a duty to" attend [James K. Polk's] inauguration on 3/4.

LS in DNA, RG 59 (State Department), Notes from Foreign Legations, Denmark, vol. 2 (M-52:2, frames 95–96).

From A[lexander] de Bodisco, [Russian Minister to the U.S.], Georgetown, [D.C.], 3/1. He informs Calhoun that he and his First Secretary of Legation will attend the inauguration of President-Elect [James K. Polk] on 3/4. LS (in French) in DNA, RG 59 (State Department), Notes from Foreign Legations, Russia, vol. 3 (M-39:2).

From A[ngel] Calderon de la Barca, [Spanish Minister to the U.S.], 3/1. He replies to Calhoun's circular of 2/28 that he and the other members of his legation will attend the inauguration of President-Elect [James K. Polk] on 3/4. LS (in Spanish) in DNA, RG 59 (State Department), Notes from Foreign Legations, Spain, vol. 11 (M-59:13, frame 1033).

From [J.C.] de Figanièŕe e Moräõ, [Portuguese Minister to the U.S.], 3/1. In response to Calhoun's circular of 2/28 he states that he will attend the inauguration of [James K. Polk] on 3/4, accompanied by the Attaché of the Legation. ALS in DNA, RG 59 (State Department), Notes from Foreign Legations, Portugal, vol. 3 (M-57:3, frame 551).

To [FRIEDRICH VON] GEROLT, Minister Resident, Prussia

Department of State
Washington, 1st March, 1845

Sir: The note you did me the honor to address to me on the 13th ultimo, on the subject of a reduction of duty on Prussian Wines, was duly received, and referred to the Secretary of the Treasury for his consideration; and I have great pleasure in transmitting to you a copy of a note from him to this Department, dated on the 28th ultimo, which contains the decision the Treasury Department has come to, upon the question.

I take this occasion to offer to you the assurances of my distinguished consideration. J.C. Calhoun.

FC in DNA, RG 59 (State Department), Notes to Foreign Legations, German States, 6:102–103 (M-99:27). NOTE: This letter was addressed to "Baron de Gerolt."

From F[riedrich] v[on] Gerolt, [Prussian Minister to the U.S.], 3/1. Answering Calhoun's circular of 2/28, von Gerolt states that he will attend the inauguration on 3/4. ALS (in French) in DNA, RG 59 (State Department), Notes from Foreign Legations, Prussia, vol. 1 (M-58:1).

From G[aspar José] de Lisboa, [Brazilian Minister to the U.S.], 3/1. He acknowledges Calhoun's circular of 2/28 and plans to attend the inaugural ceremony on 3/4. ALS (in French) in DNA, RG 59 (State Department), Notes from Foreign Legations, Brazil, vol. 2 (M-49:2).

From J[ohn] Y. Mason, [Secretary of the Navy], 3/1. "I have the honor to return the two letters of Mr. T[homas] Wynn[s], submitted by you to the Department a few days since. Having referred them to Lieut. [Matthew F.] Maury for examination, I enclose a copy of his report, dated 25th ult[im]o." (In his report Maury suggested that, given the proximity of Pensacola, it was unlikely that St. Andrew's Bay would become an important naval center. He used the opportunity afforded by the report to suggest that a comprehensive coastal survey be undertaken for the Atlantic shoreline of the Florida peninsula in order to locate an Atlantic harbor suitable for a naval base and shipyard.) LS with Ens in DNA, RG 59 (State Department), Miscellaneous Letters (M-179:107, frames 263–270); FC in DNA, RG 45 (Naval Records), Letters Sent by the Secretary of the Navy to the President and Executive Agencies, 5:109 (M-472:3, frame 96).

From Gust[af] de Nordin, [Swedish Chargé d'Affaires in the U.S.], 3/1. He has received Calhoun's circular of 2/28 and plans to attend the inauguration of [James K. Polk] on 3/4. LS (in French) in DNA, RG 59 (State Department), Notes from Foreign Legations, Sweden, vol. 3 (M-60:2).

From A[lphonse] Pageot, [French Minister to the U.S.], 3/1. In reply to Calhoun's circular of 2/28, he states that he will attend the inauguration of [James K. Polk] on 3/4. LS (in French) in DNA, RG 59 (State Department), Notes from Foreign Legations, France, vol. 12 (M-53:8, frames 757–758).

From R[ichard] Pakenham, [British Minister to the U.S.], 3/1. He acknowledges Calhoun's circular of yesterday and hopes to attend the inauguration of [James K. Polk] on 3/4. LS in DNA, RG 59 (State Department), Notes from Foreign Legations, Great Britain, vol. 22 (M-50:22).

To F[RANCIS] W. PICKENS, [Edgefield District, S.C.]

Washington, 1st March 1845

My dear Sir, I wrote you a short time since. I hope you have got my letter. Since then, (on thursday last [2/27]) I had an interview with Mr. [James K.] Polk at his request, when he informed me that he had determined to form an entirely new Cabinet. He then expressed the highest esteem for me, personal & political, which he followed up by tendering me the appoint[ment] of Minister to England, & which he pressed me much to accept. I declined in mild but decided terms, & reciprocated the expression of esteem, and assured him that his annunciation was the cause of not the least dissatisfaction to me; that I had left my retirement with great reluctance to take charge of the negotiations in reference to Texas & Oregon, and felt relieved, as his determination would permit me to return to it, freed of all responsibility. Much more passed between us in the same friendly sperit. We parted, I wishing him a prosperous administration & he professing the strongest regard for me. I have since sent in my resignation to take effect as soon as my successor is ready to assume the duties of the office, and notified him to day of the fact.

He stated no reason for his determination to form an entirely new Cabinet, nor did he say who was to be my successor, or of whom his Cabinet would be formed. Rumour says, that [James] Buchanan is to succeed me; & such I believe is the determination.

Myself & my friends have abstained from taking any part in the various movements, which have been made to control in the formation of the Cabinet; and I have advised all ["of them" *interlined*] with whom I have had an opportunity of conversing to observe a dignified silence, let who will be appointed ["be appointed" *canceled*], & to show no dissatisfaction ["that" *canceled*] because I have not been invited to remain. It would be undignified and impolitick.

I hope our papers will observe the same course, or at least, if they should express regret that I am not to [be] a member of his cabinet, that no censure be cast on him for not inviting me. As far as I am individually concerned, what has occurred is probably the best for me. I retire with good feelings on all sides ["for me" *canceled*], with the exception of rabid whigs & the [Thomas H.] Benton & [Silas] Wright faction. I shall probably leave about the 8th or 9th Inst. and hope to see you on our passage through Edgefield.

All join their love to you, Mrs. [Marion Dearing] Pickens & family. Yours truly, J.C. Calhoun.

ALS in NcD, John C. Calhoun Papers. NOTE: An AEU by Pickens on this letter reads: "Mr. Calhoun—Polk—calling & determined to turn him out as Secty: of State & put in Buchanan—March 1845."

From Cha[rle]s H. Raymond, [Acting Texan Chargé d'Affaires in the U.S.], 3/1. In reply to Calhoun's note of 2/28, Raymond states that he plans to be present at the inauguration of [James K. Polk] on 3/4. ALS in DNA, RG 59 (State Department), Notes from Foreign Legations, Texas, vol. 1 (T-809:1); FC in Tx, Records of the Texas Republic Department of State, Letters and Dispatches Sent by the Texas Legation in Washington, 2:39.

To [JOHN TYLER], The President

State Dept., 1st March 1845

I hereby resign the office of Secretary of State to take effect as soon as a successor is appointed & ready to assume its duties. With high respect I am & &, J.C. Calhoun.

ALS in DNA, RG 59 (State Department), Letters of Resignation and Declination. NOTE: An AES by Tyler, dated 3/1, reads "The Chief Clerk of the State Department will file this among the proper papers of the Department."

To Brig. Gen. CARLOS MARIA DE ALVEAR

Department of State
Washington, 3d March, 1845

Sir: I have the honor herewith to transmit to you a copy of a communication this day received from the Honorable John Y. Mason, Secretary of the Navy, covering a letter from Commodore Daniel Turner, the officer in command of the United States naval forces on the Brazilian coast to Commodore [José] Baltierre, and also a Report from the same officer in relation to the capture of the Argentine blockading squadron off the Port of Monte Video, by the United States frigate Congress, under the command of Captain [Philip F.] Voorhees; copies of which are also herewith enclosed.

The President has carefully considered the statements contained in the Report of Commodore Turner and entirely concurs ["in the views expressed by him" *interlined*] in regard to the conduct of Captain Voorhees, who has been ordered home. As soon as he arrives, he will be brought before a Court of Inquiry, with a view to such examinations as may enable the Executive to decide finally on the course which it ought to adopt in regard to him.

The President trusts that this course will be satisfactory to the Government of the Argentine Confederation, and confidently indulges the hope that this unfortunate occurrence will not be allowed to mar the good understanding subsisting between the two countries. I have the honor to be, with high consideration, Sir, Your obedient servant, J.C. Calhoun.

FC in DNA, RG 59 (State Department), Notes to Foreign Legations, Argentina, 6:15–16 (M-99:1).

To WILLIAM BRENT, JR., [Buenos Ayres]

Department of State
Washington, March 3rd, 1845

Sir: In my general instructions to you on the subject of the claims of citizens of the United States, upon the Government of Buenos Ayres, I omitted a particular notice of that of Mr. T[homas] L. Halsey, which has been a matter of constant solicitude to this Department, and to which I now, in an especial manner, call your attention. This claim has long since been acknowledged and liquidated; and yet, notwithstanding the repeated remonstrances and applications on the part of our Diplomatic Representatives and Agents, it still remains unpaid.

On the 8th March, 1842, instructions were sent to Commodore [Charles] Morris, commanding on the Brazil Station, to demand the payment of it, in conformity to the basis set forth in the instructions. A copy of these instructions is herewith annexed. Commodore Morris held several conferences with the proper authorities on the subject; and, on the 20th December, 1842, addressed a communication to the Buenos Ayrean Government; a copy of which is also, herewith, annexed. To this communication the Minister of Finance replied, in a note dated on the 17th February, 1843; which note, (or a copy), will, it is believed, be found among the papers in this case, left by Commodore Morris in the hands of the Ex-Consul, Amory Edwards. By referring to the note, you will observe that *the Minister of Finance proposed,* for the first time, *to pay* to Commodore Morris, (the note was written after the Commodore's departure), the nominal amount of $108.831 of 6 per. cent. stocks, and the interest in paper money, which, if received and converted into specie, would not produce more than *an eighteenth part of the amount* due at the time of the award, the 26th July, 1826, the period at which it ought to have been paid.

The Government of Buenos Ayres having, *for its own convenience,* so long withheld the payment of this debt, to the great detriment of Mr. Halsey, and in *opposition to the constant appeals from this Department, it would be* an act of signal *injustice* to *pay him a less sum than the intrinsic value of the stocks and interest* at the *date of the award.* And I can not forbear to remark here that, this Department has found nothing in the note of the Minister of Finance of the 17th February, 1843, to cause it to alter, in any respect, the opinion that had been formed of the merits of Mr. Halsey's claim. *You will, therefore, take the earliest opportunity to express to the Buenos Ayrean Government, the just and confident expectations of the President that, the payment of this debt, in conformity to the basis laid down in the instructions of the 8th March, 1842, (which are only a repetition of previous instructions), will be no longer withheld.*

If, however, the Buenos Ayrean Government *should neglect* or *refuse* to *accede* to the just and natural propositions hereby again offered, and decline *the payment of* the *money in question,* you are then *authorised and* directed to agree, and to insist upon an arbitration, to take place at this city, by persons to be mutually appointed by the Minister of Buenos Ayres residing here, and the Department of State—and that the *award* of the arbitrators shall be final and decisive, and be *followed by the payment* of the due amount, in proper and convenient instalments, as the only fair means of bringing this protracted affair to a conclusion.

To *this claim I, therefore, direct your prompt and earnest attention;* and you are instructed to say, to the Government near which you reside, *that, any further delay on its part, in facilitating and effecting its final settlement, will be regarded by the President as indicating but a slight disposition to do justice to a citizen of the United States, and to cultivate and promote the friendly relations which so happily subsist between the two Governments.* I am, Sir, respectfully, Your obedient Servant, J.C. Calhoun.

LS (No. 4 [*sic*; 6]) in DNA, RG 84 (Foreign Posts), Argentina, Correspondence Relating to Claims; FC in DNA, RG 59 (State Department), Diplomatic Instructions, Argentina, 15:14–16 (M-77:10).

To A[NDREW] J. DONELSON

Department of State
Washington, March 3d, 1845

Sir: I herewith transmit to you a copy of the Joint Resolutions adopted by Congress for the annexation of Texas to the United States.

You will perceive that they consist of two distinct parts: the one embraced in the first and second sections, being the original Resolution as it passed the House of Representatives; the other, included in the third and last, being the amendment made by the Senate and subsequently adopted by the House. The former contains certain specific propositions for the admission of Texas into our Union; the latter gives a discretionary power to the President, if he should deem it advisable, to enter into negotiations with the Republic, as prescribed in the section itself, instead of submitting to its acceptance or rejection the proposals contained in the former.

The President [John Tyler] has deliberately considered the subject, and is of opinion that it would not be advisable to enter into the negotiations authorized by the amendment of the Senate, and you are accordingly instructed to present to the government of Texas, as the basis of its admission, the proposals contained in the Resolution as it came from the House of Representatives.

It is not deemed necessary to state at large the grounds on which his decision rests. It will be sufficient to state briefly that the provisions of the Resolution as it came from the House, are more simple in their character; may be more readily and with less difficulty and expense, carried into effect, and that the great object contemplated by them is much less exposed to the hazard of ultimate defeat.

That they are more simple in their character a very few remarks will suffice to show. According to the Resolution as it came from the House, nothing more is necessary than that the Congress of Texas should be called together, its consent given to the provisions contained in it, and the adoption of a Constitution by the people in Convention to be submitted to the Congress of the United States for its approval in the same manner as when one of our own territories is admitted as a State. On the contrary, according to the provisions of the Senate's amendment, the Congress of Texas must, in like manner, be convened: it must then go through the slow and troublesome process of carving a State out of ["a" *interlined*] part of its territory; afterwards it must appoint agents or commissioners to meet similar agents or commissioners to be appointed on our part, to discuss and agree on the terms and conditions on which the State shall be admitted, and on the cession of the remaining territory to the United States; and after all this, and not before, the people of the said State must call a Convention, frame a Constitution and then present it to the Congress of the United States for its approval, but which cannot be acted on until the terms agreed upon by the negotiators, and which constitute the conditions on which the State is to be admitted, shall have been ratified.

That they may be more readily and with less difficulty and expense, carried into effect, is plain from the fact that the details are fewer and less complex. It is obvious that the numerous and complicated provisions contained in the amendment of the Senate must involve much time and difficulty in their execution; while, as to the expense, the appropriation of $100,000 provided for by it, is a clear additional cost over and above that attendant on the execution of the Resolution of the House.

But the decisive objection to the Amendment of the Senate is, that it would endanger the ultimate success of the measure. It proposes to fix, by negotiation between the Governments of the United States and Texas, the terms and conditions on which the State shall be admitted into our Union, and the cession of the remaining territory to the United States. Now, by whatever name the agents conducting the negotiation may be known, whether they be called commissioners, Ministers or by any other title, the compact agreed on by them in behalf of their respective governments would be a Treaty; whether so called or designated by some other name. The very meaning of a Treaty is a compact between independent States founded on negotiation. And if a treaty (as it clearly would be) it must be submitted to the Senate for its approval and run the hazard of receiving the votes of two thirds of the members present, which could hardly be expected, if we are to judge from recent experience. This, of itself, is considered by the President as a conclusive reason for proposing the Resolution of the House, instead of the amendment of the Senate, as the basis of annexation.

But it may be objected that the Resolution of the House prescribes no means of rendering its provisions acceptable to the government and people of Texas, in case they should prove unsatisfactory. The objection, however, is more apparent than real; for although none are expressly provided, it cannot be doubted that the Congress of Texas may propose whatever amendments it may think essential, and transmit them to the government of the United States for its consideration and agreement; and, if adopted, to be binding on both parties, a far more satisfactory mode, in all probability, of obtaining the mutual consent of both, than that of negotiating through commissioners or other agents; while it is exempt from the decisive objections to which this is liable.

But it is deemed by the President of great importance that the Resolution should be adopted by the Government of Texas without amendment; so as to avoid the hazards and contingencies incident to delay; and you are accordingly instructed to use your best exertions to effect this object. Should you fail in this, you will next endeavor to induce the Congress of Texas to substitute, in place of amendments, separate and distinct propositions, expressive of their views of what the provisions of the Resolution ought to be, accompanied by a strong address setting forth their reasons at length, and expressing their reliance on the justice of the government of the United States for their adoption. If both fail, it will then remain for the Congress of Texas to amend the Resolutions as above suggested.

The President also directs me to instruct you to proceed with as little delay as possible to the seat of the government of Texas and to urge speedy and prompt action on the subject. Time is important, and not a day ought to be lost. The last hope on the part of any foreign power which may feel disposed to defeat annexation, will be to act upon the Government of Texas, and it can scarcely be doubted from the feelings expressed on the part of one of the leading European Powers against the measure, that no effort will be spared to induce Texas to reject the proposals contained in the Resolution. Your presence, intelligence, activity and influence are confidently relied on to counteract the attempt. I have the honor to be, with high respect, Sir, Your obedient servant, J.C. Calhoun.

[Enclosure]

"Joint Resolution for Annexing Texas to the United States."

[March 1, 1845]

Resolved, by the Senate and House of Representatives of the United States of America in Congress assembled, That Congress doth consent that the territory properly included within, and rightfully belonging to, the republic of Texas, may be erected into a new State, to be called the State of Texas, with a republican form of government, to be adopted by the people of said republic, by deputies in convention assembled, with the consent of the existing government in order that the same may be admitted as one of the States of this Union.

2. *And be it further resolved,* That the foregoing consent of Congress is given upon the following conditions, and with the following guarantees, to wit: First, Said State to be formed, subject to the adjustment by this government of all questions of boundary that may arise with other governments; and the constitution thereof, with the proper evidence of its adoption by the people of said republic of Texas, shall be transmitted to the President of the United States, to be laid before Congress for its final action on or before the first day of January, one thousand eight hundred and forty-six. Second. Said State, when admitted into the Union, after ceding to the United States all public edifices, fortifications, barracks, ports and harbors, navy and navy-yards, docks, magazines, arms, armaments, and all other property and means pertaining to the public defence belonging to said republic of Texas, shall retain all the public funds, debts, taxes, and dues of every kind, which may belong to or be due and owing said republic; and shall also retain all the vacant and unappropriated lands lying within its limits, to be applied to the payment of the debts and liabilities of said republic of Texas, and the residue of said lands, after discharging said debts and liabilities, to be disposed of as said State may direct; but in no event are said debts and liabilities to become a charge upon the government of the United States. Third. New States of convenient size, not exceeding four in number, in addition to said State of Texas, and having sufficient population, may hereafter, by the consent of said State, be formed out of the territory thereof, which shall be entit[l]ed to admission under the provisions of the federal constitution. And such States as may be formed out of that portion of said territory lying south of thirty-six degrees thirty minutes north latitude, commonly known as the Missouri compromise line, shall be admitted into the Union, with or without slavery, as the people of each State asking admission may desire. And in such State or States as shall be formed out of said territory, north of said Missouri compromise line, slavery or involuntary servitude, (except for crime,) shall be prohibited.

3. *And be it further resolved,* That if the President of the United States shall, in his judgment and discretion, deem it most advisable, instead of proceeding to submit the foregoing resolution to the re-

public of Texas, as an overture on the part of the United States for admission, to negotiate with that republic—then, *Be it resolved,* That a State, to be formed out of the present republic of Texas, with suitable extent and boundaries, and with two representatives in Congress, until the next apportionment of representation, shall be admitted into the Union, by virtue of this act, on an equal footing with the existing States, as soon as the terms and conditions of such admission, and the cession of the remaining Texan territory to the United States, shall be agreed upon by the governments of Texas and the United States; and that the sum of one hundred thousand dollars be, and the same is hereby, appropriated to defray the expenses of missions and negotiations, to agree upon the terms of said admission and cession, either by treaty to be submitted to the Senate, or by articles to be submitted to the two houses of Congress, as the President may direct. J[ohn] W. Jones, *Speaker of the House of Representatives,* Willie P. Mangum, *President pro tempore of the Senate.* Approved, March 1, 1845. John Tyler.

FC (No. 4) in DNA, RG 59 (State Department), Diplomatic Instructions, Texas, 1:107–111 (M-77:161); PC with En in Senate Document No. 1, 29th Cong., 1st Sess., pp. 32–35; PC in House Document No. 2, 29th Cong., 1st Sess., pp. 125–127; PC in the Washington, D.C., *Daily Union,* vol. I, no. 198 (December 19, 1845), p. [789]; PC in *Niles' National Register,* vol. LXIX, no. 18 (January 3, 1846), pp. 281–282; PC with En in Crallé, ed., *Works,* 5:393–399. NOTE: The En transcribed herewith is taken from the second-cited source.

From EDWARD EVERETT

London, 3d March, 1845

Sir, I received by the last steamer your instructions Nro. 120 of the 28th January in explanation of Nro. 99 of the 7th of August, on the construction of the tenth article of the treaty of Washington relative to the extradition of fugitives.

You will have perceived from my note to Lord Aberdeen of the 30th of January, a copy of which was transmitted with my despatch Nro. 250 [of 1/31], that I have anticipated in part your directions in maintaining that an indictment is sufficient evidence of criminality to warrant the surrender of a fugitive. I had intimated to Lord Aberdeen, in the conference of the 20th November which forms the subject of my despatch Nro. 216, that such was the view of the Government of the United States, which I should take another opportunity of enforcing.

As it was the principal purpose of my note to him of the 30th of January to suggest the various amendments in the Statute of 6 and 7 Victoria C. 76, shown by experience to be required to bring it into conformity with the treaty, I took the opportunity to present the indictment question among them, believing that by being brought forward in this way, as a matter of purely legal construction, it would be more likely to be considered on its merits, than if urged as incidental to the Nassau case. Further reflection has confirmed me in the expediency of this course.

In your instructions Nro. 120 you direct me again to call the attention of Her Majesty's Government to the point, whether on a demand of extradition reference is to be had to the question whether the criminal acts alleged constitute the offence according to the laws of the country where it was committed or of that where the fugitive has taken refuge; and also to the sufficiency of an indictment; and you add, "Indeed a decision that an indictment is sufficient evidence to warrant the commitment and delivery of the fugitive criminal would, in a great measure, decide both points and supersede the necessity of the other; as the presentment of the grand jury must always be founded on the criminality of the act, according to the laws of the place where the crime was committed."

This is precisely the order, in which the two questions presented themselves to my mind, and which led me to adopt the course which I have thus far pursued, in executing your instructions Nro. 99. Those instructions proceeded principally on the very natural assumption, that the reasoning of the Court at Nassau was sanctioned by the Government. This reasoning however was disavowed by Lord Aberdeen, and the principle that a slave cannot by possibility commit a crime and consequently cannot in any case be a subject of extradition, (a principle which you regarded as lying at the basis of the judgment of the Court of Nassau), was specifically disclaimed by him. This disavowal seemed to reduce the opinion of the Court of Nassau to a simple rejection of an indictment as sufficient evidence of criminality and to present that question as the first for consideration.

In a conference on other business a few days since with Lord Aberdeen, I told him that I had received instructions from you again to call the attention of Her Majesty's Government to the construction of the tenth article of the treaty, and that I hoped he would save me the trouble of doing so, by an early and satisfactory answer to my note of the 30th of January, proposing sundry amendments to the Act of Parliament. He said those amendments had been referred to the Law Officers of the Crown, and that they were he believed thought favorably of, but that he had not yet got their report.

When this report is received, if it admits the principle that an indictment is sufficient evidence, the whole matter will be satisfactorily disposed of; and on the opposite supposition, the entire question on the construction of the convention will be presented in the most convenient form for discussion. I am, Sir, with great respect, your obedient Servant, Edward Everett.

LS (No. 271) in DNA, RG 59 (State Department), Diplomatic Despatches, Great Britain, vol. 54 (M-30:50), received 3/21; FC in DNA, RG 84 (Foreign Posts), Great Britain, Despatches, 9:188–192; FC in MHi, Edward Everett Papers, 51:296–300 (published microfilm, reel 23, frames 702–704).

From Henry C. Flagg, Washington, 3/3. Henry Bouluquet, a merchant of Bordeaux, France, wishes to be appointed U.S. Consul there. He is the son-in-law of Paul Lajus, "a wealthy and respectable merchant" of Philadelphia. Flagg makes this recommendation on behalf of a retired New York City merchant, John K. Townsend. ALS in DNA, RG 59 (State Department), Applications and Recommendations, 1845–1853, Bouluquet (M-873:9, frames 54–55).

To [JOHN W. JONES], Speaker of the House of Representatives

Department of State
March 3rd 1845

Sir, By a resolution of the House of March ["23rd" *changed to* "3rd"] 1843, the Secretary of State was required to procure through the Consular and Diplomatic Agents of this Government abroad, and such other means as to him may seem most suitable:

First. Full and accurate information as to the wholesale and retail prices in foreign markets, during the year commencing on the first day of September 1842, of all commodities upon which duties are levied under existing laws, as well as of such as are imported free of duty.

Secondly. The rates of insurance, freight and commissions usually charged at the places of export, upon said commodities when imported into this country.

Thirdly. The modes and terms of sale customary there.

Fourthly. The average rate of exchange during each month in said year, and the true par of exchange between this and each foreign country.

Fifthly. The duties of export and import, and, as far as practicable, the various internal taxes levied upon such commodities, in either a crude, partially manufactured, or complete state.

Sixthly. The rate of wages in the various branches and occupations of labor and of personal service in the business of commerce and trade.

Seventhly. Full and regular files of price current sheets for said year, at each of the most important foreign markets, and such other documents and publications as may exhibit truly the information called for in this resolution.

The Secretary of State was further required to compile and have printed for the use of the House, a document embodying all the information called for by this resolution, arranged in such a manner as to be most convenient for reference and comparison—exercising especial care to give, in all instances, said information in Federal currency, weights, and measures.

By another resolution bearing date Jan. 24th 1844, the Secretary of State was further required, in making this report, "to state the rate of duties imposed on such articles on being imported into the United States, and, where specific duties are imposed, to reduce them to *ad valorem* rates on the cost of such articles abroad."

In compliance with these resolutions I have the honor to submit to the House the following returns from Consular, Commercial, and Diplomatic agents of the United States in foreign countries, with the quantities reduced to Federal denominations, and the whole so arranged as to be most convenient for reference and comparison. And also a statement [of 2/5/1845] from the Collector of Customs at New York [Cornelius P. Van Ness] giving the rates of duties on such articles when imported into the United States, the same being, where specific duties are imposed, reduced to *ad valorem* rates on the cost of such articles abroad.

In further compliance with the resolution of March 23rd [*sic*] 1843, I send to the House a number of Price Current sheets, a list of which is hereunto appended. I have the honor to be, Very Respectfully, Y[ou]r Ob[e]d[ien]t Serv[an]t, J.C. Calhoun.

LS in DNA, RG 233 (U.S. House of Representatives), 28A-F1; PC with Ens in House Document No. 73, 28th Cong., 2nd Sess., pp. 1–278. NOTE: The resolutions of 3/3/1843 and 1/13/1844 to which this letter responds can be found in *House Journal*, 27th Cong., 3rd Sess., p. 539, and *House Journal*, 28th Cong., 1st Sess., p. 288, respectively.

To [John Y. Mason, Secretary of the Navy], 3/3. "The Secretary of State presents his compliments to the Hon. Secretary of the Navy, and begs leave to call his attention to the Report of Commodore [Daniel] Turner in relation to the capture of the A[r]gentine Squadron off the Port of Monte Video—and to request an early communication from him in regard to the subject." LU in DNA, RG 45 (Naval Records), Letters from Federal Executive Agencies, 8:203 (M-517:3, frame 148).

From J[OHN] Y. MASON, [Secretary of the Navy]

Navy Department, March 3, 1845

Sir, I have the honor to enclose to you a copy of the despatch of Commodore Daniel Turner, commanding the U.S. Naval forces on the Coast of Brazil, numbered 152; also a copy of a letter addressed by that officer to Comm[an]d[e]r [José] Baltierre, of the schooner Sancalla; and to inform you that the course pursued by Commodore Turner, in regard to the schooner, her officers and crew, and his views in regard to the capture of the Argentine squadron, have been approved by this Department.

The Congress frigate has been recalled home, and an enquiry will be ordered into the conduct of her commanding Officer [Philip F. Voorhees], on his arrival. I am Very resp[ectfull]y Your Obed[ien]t Serv[an]t, J.Y. Mason.

LS with Ens in DNA, RG 59 (State Department), Miscellaneous Letters (M-179:107, frames 284–288); FC in DNA, RG 45 (Naval Records), Letters Sent by the Secretary of the Navy to the President and Executive Agencies, 5:110 (M-472:3, frame 97). NOTE: In his despatch of 11/4/1844 to Mason, Turner described the manner of his investigation of Capt. Philip F. Voorhees' capture of the Argentine blockading fleet on 9/29/1844. Turner determined that Voorhees' capture of the *Sancalla* was justified but that he had made errors in judgment in making the capture. Turner condemned Voorhees' taking of American seamen from vessels of the Argentine fleet and his release of Monte Videan prisoners from the Argentine vessels. This last act was an intervention by the U.S. in the war between Buenos Ayres and Monte Video. In his letter of 11/20/1844 to Com[mande]r Baltierre, Turner stated that he "entirely approve[d] of the conduct of that officer [Voorhees], in reference to yourself, and the vessel you commanded." Turner has ordered Voorhees to release the *Sancalla* and its crew solely out of respect for the Argentine government.

To E ph[rai]m F. Miller, [Deputy Collector], Salem, Mass.

Department of State
Washington, 3d March 1845

Sir, In reply to your letter [*not found*] of the 29th of October, I have to inform you, that, it has been determined to pay the expenses incurred for recasting &c. cannon for the Imaum of Muscat. You are requested to inform Mr. [David] Pingree, that, upon his transmitting to this Department the bill paid by him therefor, receipted as paid by its Agent, the amount, $2437.00 will be remitted to him, or, he may draw upon the Department for it, at his option. You will also inform Mr. Pingree that he may add to the amount one hundred dollars, to be laid out in a present to the Groom of the Imaum who accompanied the horses to this Country. I am, Sir, very respectfully, Your obedient Servant, J.C. Calhoun.

Letterpress copy in DNA, RG 59 (State Department), Accounting Records: Miscellaneous Letters Sent, 1832–1916, vol. for 10/3/1844–5/29/1845, p. 261.

To President [John Tyler]

Department of State
Washington, March 3d 1845

To the President.

The Secretary of State, to whom was referred the Resolution of the Senate of Feb[ruar]y 23rd 1843, requesting the President "to cause to be laid before the Senate a complete catalogue of all books &c." has the honor to submit, herewith, a Catalogue of the Books, Newspapers &c. in the State Dept. in addition to the one heretofore presented; and, also, a Catalogue of the Books, Phamplets [*sic*] &c. belonging to the Patent Office.

LU in DNA, RG 46 (U.S. Senate), 28A-E3. Note: Tyler transmitted this to the Senate on 3/3.

To Floyd Waggaman, 3/3. Calhoun informs Waggaman that he has been appointed bearer of despatches to A[ndrew] J. Donelson, U.S. Chargé d'Affaires to Texas, who is presently near Nashville, Tenn. Waggaman is to carry despatches to Donelson there and if he is not at that place to follow him to his location. He is then to return to Washington as quickly as possible "to make report of your proceedings." Compensation will be at the rate of six dollars per day plus traveling expenses. FC in DNA, RG 59 (State Department), Diplomatic Instructions, Texas, 1:111–112 (M-77:161).

To Henry Wheaton, [Berlin]

Department of State
Washington, 3rd March, 1845

Sir: In pursuance of the assurances given by Baron [Heinrich von] Bülow, in his note to you of the 10th of April last, which accompanied your despatch No. 247, dated two days later, that the Minister Resident of Prussia would, on his arrival at Washington, read confidentially to the Secretary of State, and to the Mexican Minister [Juan N. Almonte], the reasons on which the decision of the Umpire, [in the U.S.-Mexican Claims Convention of 1839] in the case of Mr. Aaron Leggett, was based, I have had, this day, a conference with Baron [Friedrich] Von Gerolt, who came prepared to execute the instructions of his Government on this subject. Having given to this case my deliberate attention, and having arrived at conclusions very different from those under which my predecessor appears to have acted, I have frankly stated to the Baron my belief that the whole proceeding originated in error and misconception; and I have signified to him that, as this Government is entirely satisfied that Baron [Friedrich Ludwig] de Röenne acted in this case, as in all others, with that love of justice and integrity for which his character was eminently distinguished, it feels constrained by duty as well as by delicacy, to decline the offer made by the Prussian Government, to communicate, confidentially, the information which had been solicited by this Government, under impressions which, it is conceived, ought never to have had existence. The very supposition strikes at the root of all faith in the Convention itself, and would probably be attended by the evil consequences of making all the other claimants unduly dissatisfied with the decisions in their cases.

It is not deemed necessary to go further into this subject. Baron Von Gerolt will communicate with his Government upon it; and you are, hereby, instructed to take the earliest occasion to give proper explanations, by conference or note, as may be most acceptable to the

Prussian Government. I am, Sir, respectfully, Your obedient Servant, J.C. Calhoun.

LS (No. 66) in DNA, RG 84 (Foreign Posts), Germany, Instructions, 1:405–408; FC in DNA, RG 59 (State Department), Diplomatic Instructions, Germany, 14:90–92 (M-77:65); PC in House Executive Document No. 83, 30th Cong., 1st Sess., p. 60.

J. Fr[anci]s Hutton to Dixon H. Lewis, Washington

New York [City], March 4th 1845

Dear Sir, Previous to your arrival in Washington I addressed a letter to you in which I stated that if Fernando Wood should resign the office he held as "Dispatch Agent" for this city that I should like you to ask the office for me from Mr. Calhoun.

The probable appointment of Mr. Buchannan [*sic*; James Buchanan] of Penn: as Sec[retar]y of State opens an opportunity for placing this office in my hands, for I presume you are aware this office is entirely in the gift of the Secretary. A simple request from you to Mr. Buchannan could obtain it.

The amount of salary is small and the duties would not prevent my attending to my regular business. I have avoided saying a word to any of our friends here on this subject neither have I mentioned to any individual any where, & should you not be able to obtain it for me—it ends the matter. Of course if Mr. Buchanan requires any evidence of claims &C I would remit them. I have the honor to be Very respectfully—Your Ob[edien]t Serv[an]t, J. Frs. Hutton.

P.S. Before you leave Washington our friends & myself desire to communicate with you.

ALS in ScCleA. NOTE: This letter was probably given by Lewis to Calhoun.

To [James K. Polk], The President

[Washington, *ca.* March 4, 1845]

Dear Sir, This will be handed to you by Mr. [Robert S.] Chew one of the Clerks of the Dept. who has been selected to assist your private

Secretary in the duties of his office. You will find him intelligent & familiar with the duties you may assign him. Truly, J.C. Calhoun.

ALS in DLC, James K. Polk Papers (Presidential Papers Microfilm, Polk Papers, roll 35).

From W[illia]m H. Robertson

Washington, 4 March [18]45

Sir, Aware of the value of your time at this period and your constant occupation I forbear to call upon you, to deliver the Enclosed [of 2/17/1845], anxious as I am to see ["you" *interlined*] & anxious as both Gen[era]l [James] Hamilton [Jr.] & Mr. [David J.?] McCord were that I should see you at an early period after my arrival. I shall wait untill you can signify the moment that I can have that pleasure. Gen[era]l [Alexander] Mouton has addressed Mr. [James K.] Polk on the subject but was particularly anxious that my views should be laid before you. I am very Respectfully and with great consideration y[ou]r ob[edient] ser[vant,] Wm. H. Robertson.

ALS with En in DNA, RG 59 (State Department), Applications and Recommendations, 1845–1853, Robertson (M-873:74, frames 337–338 and 344–345).

From J[uan] N. Almonte

Mexican Legation
Washington, March 6th 1845

The Undersigned, Envoy Extraordinary and Minister Plenipotentiary of the Mexican Republic, has the honour to address the Honourable John C. Calhoun Secretary of State of the United States of America; with the object of making known to him, the profound regret, with which he has seen, that the General Congress of the Union has passed a law, giving its consent, and admitting [*marginal interpolation*: "prestando su consentimiento y admitiendo"] into the American Confederacy, the Mexican Province of Texas.

The Undersigned had flattered himself with the idea, that on this question, the good judgement and sound counsels of the citizens most distinguished and most intimately acquainted with the conduct of the publick affairs of this Republic, would have prevailed in the deliberations of the legislative body, and of the Executive of the Union. Unfortunately however it has been otherwise; and contrary to his hopes, and his most sincere prayers, he sees consummated on the part of the American Government, an act of aggression, the most unjust which can be found recorded in the annals of modern history, namely that of despoiling a friendly nation like Mexico, of a considerable portion of her territory.

For these reasons, the Undersigned, in compliance with his instructions, finds himself required to protest, as he does in fact protest, in the most solemn manner, in the name of his Government, against the law passed on the 28th of the last month, by the General Congress of the United States, and approved on the first of the present month, by the President of these States, whereby the Province of Texas, an integrant portion of the Mexican territory is agreed, and admitted [*marginal interpolation*: "se consiente y admite"] into the American Union. The Undersigned moreover protests in the name of his Government, that the said law can in no wise invalidate the rights on which Mexico relies, to recover the above mentioned province of Texas, of which she now sees herself unjustly despoiled; and, that she will maintain and uphold those rights, at all times, by every means which may be in her power.

The Undersigned will say in conclusion to the Honourable Secretary of State of the United States, in order that he may be pleased to communicate it to the President of these States; that in consequence of this law against which he has just protested, his mission near this Government has ceased from this day. Wherefore the Undersigned prays the Honourable Secretary of State, to be pleased to deliver to him his passports, as he has made arrangements to leave this city without delay for New York.

The Undersigned avails himself of this occasion, to repeat to the Honourable John C. Calhoun, Secretary of State, the assurances of his high consideration. J.N. Almonte.

State Department translation of ALS (in Spanish) in DNA, RG 59 (State Department), Notes from Foreign Legations, Mexico, vol. 4 (M-54:2); PC in Senate Document No. 1, 29th Cong., 1st Sess., pp. 38–39; PC in House Document No. 2, 29th Cong., 1st Sess., pp. 130–131; PC in *Congressional Globe*, 30th Cong., 1st Sess., Appendix, pp. 202–203; PC in the Washington, D.C., *Daily Union*, vol. I, no. 198 (December 19, 1845), p. [789]; PC (dated 3/8) in *Niles' National Register*, vol. LXVIII, no. 6 (April 12, 1845), p. 84.

From H[ENRY] GOURDIN

Charleston, March 6th 1845

Dear Sir, I have to enclose you herewith a letter [of 12/5/1844] from the National Anti-Corn Law League of Great Britain. The volume referred to in the letter came safely to hand yesterday by the Barque Chieftain from Liverpool, and I await your instructions respecting it. I feel much flattered, and equal pleasure, that the League should have selected me as the channel of so pleasing a compliment to yourself. I am very resp[ectfull]y Your Ob[edien]t S[e]r[van]t, H. Gourdin.

ALS with En in ScCleA. NOTE: The enclosed letter of 12/5/1844 from George Wilson, Chairman of the National Anti-Corn Law League, can be found in *The Papers of John C. Calhoun*, 20:485.

From JAMES K. POLK

President's Mansion, March 6th 1845

Dear Sir: Feeling anxious to ascertain what action my predecessor has taken in regard to the Resolution to admit Texas into the Union, I would thank you to transmit to me, by one of your Confidential Clerks, any despatches on the subject which may have been sent to Mr. [Andrew J.] Donelson. I will thank you to send also the Resolution itself or a copy of it. Yours Very Respectfully, James K. Polk.

ALS in DNA, RG 59 (State Department), Miscellaneous Letters (M-179:107, frames 346–347).

From W[ILLIA]M H. ROBERTSON

Washington, 6th March [18]45

Dear Sir, Since I had the pleasure to see you, some of my Southern friends feeling a deep interest in this appointment of Consul to St. Petersburg, have thought it important to ask if you would be kind enough to address Mr. [James K.] Polk a few lines on this subject. These friends think that Mr. [James] Buchanan is a Northern man, & will not feel that Interest that you would ["would" *canceled*].

I take the Liberty, however, of Enclosing you a letter from an old friend of Mr. Buchanan from one of our Prominent men in Louisiana which may have some influence with Mr. Buchanan & who would no doubt have addressed him particularly could he have known or anticipated the appointment.

The whole [La. Congressional] delegation have addressed a strong letter to the President.

I should also feel obliged, to Mr. Calhoun if he would bear in mind, in his remarks to Mr. Buchanan, that the summer there is very short, and leaves but little time to put up machinery in that Country, [which] should be in operation before October, and if it is determined to give me the appointment, then it should be done as early as convenient, that a season should not be lost.

Begging you will excuse me for the liberty I have taken, I am with great Respect & Consideration Y[ou]r Ob[edien]t Ser[van]t, Wm. H. Robertson.

ALS in DNA, RG 59 (State Department), Applications and Recommendations, 1845–1853, Robertson (M-873:74, frames 348–350). Note: This letter was hand-delivered to Calhoun at the U.S. Hotel.

To Charles H. Todd & Co., New York [City], 3/6. Calhoun transmits copies of documents received from Pedro de Regil y Estrada, U.S. Consul at Merida [in Yucatan], relating to the case of the brig *Henry Leeds,* "chartered and loaded" by Todd & Co. Instead of neglecting the interests of Todd & Co., as charged by Henry A. Holmes, former captain of that vessel, Regil y Estrada has done everything possible to protect them. FC in DNA, RG 59 (State Department), Consular Instructions, 11:348.

From W[illia]m H. Chase, Pens[aco]la, 3/7. Eben Dorr has requested Chase to recommend him for continuance in office as U.S. Marshal for the Western District of Fla. [Territory] under the new administration. Chase has stated to Dorr that officeholders who have performed their duties "honestly & conscientiously" will likely be retained. "I believe that this will be the policy of the new admi[ni]stration, ["in respect of all in place" *interlined*] and I shall be confirmed in the belief if we happily find that you remain one of its advisers." ALS in DNA, RG 59 (State Department), Applications and Recommendations, 1845–1853, Dorr (M-873:24, frames 55–56), received 3/18.

To [JAMES K. POLK], The President of the United States

Department of State
Washington, 7th March 1845

Dear Sir, Agreeably to the request contained in your note of yesterday, I herewith transmit to you a copy of the instructions [of 3/3] given to Mr. Donolson [*sic*; Andrew J. Donelson], our Chargé to Texas, in regard to the Joint resolution of Congress providing for the admission of that Republic into our Union, together with certified copies of the Resolution itself. I have the honor &c, J.C. Calhoun.

FC in DNA, RG 59 (State Department), Reports of the Secretary of State to the President and Congress, 6:161.

To Mrs. PLACIDIA [MAYRANT] ADAMS, [Pendleton?]

State Dept., 8th March 1845

My dear Madam, My long continued ill health and the great pressure of official duties since I have been sufficiently recovered to attend to business, have prevented me from writing to you earlier.

I received your letter enclosing the bond; and among my first acts, after I was well enough, was to sign it & transmit [it] to my son [Andrew Pickens Calhoun] in Alabama, with directions for him to sign, & transmit it to you.

I will write to Mr. [Isaac E.] Crary before I leave, in reference to the Michigan case. The last letter I had from him was received in the early part of the session of Congress. The business was progressing, &, I hope, may be brought to a close during the summer.

I enclose a check for $100 on the rail road Bank of Charleston, to be credited to the interest on the bond. I would send the whole had not my expense here been such, that it would ["be" *interlined*] inconvenient to spare the balance. I will pay it on my return, which I hope will be in a few days after you receive this. The wheat account may stand, as you request until the September payment. With great respect yours truly, J.C. Calhoun.

ALS owned in 1959 by Mr. Holbrook Campbell, Springfield, Mass.

To WILLIAM R. KING

Department of State
Washington, 8th March, 1845

Sir: I have the honor to transmit to you the copy of an application addressed to this Department on the 20th of January last, by Madame Ellen Sears Grand d'Hauteville, together with transcripts of certain papers communicated to me in explanation and substantiation of a claim on the Swiss Government for property improperly withheld from her by the local authorities of that confederation; and soliciting the intervention of this Department to obtain redress in the premises.

The particular merits of this claim are fully set forth in the documents herewith sent to you. I take leave to recommend it to your prompt and favorable attention; and to request that you will use your best exertions to obtain for Madame d'hauteville, through the diplomatic Representative of the Swiss Confederacy at Paris, the measure of justice to which she obviously seems to be entitled. I am, Sir, with great respect, Your obedient servant, J.C. Calhoun.

LS (No. 16) in DNA, RG 84 (Foreign Posts), France, Instructions; FC in DNA, RG 59 (State Department), Diplomatic Instructions, France, 15:30 (M-77:55).

From Charles H. Todd & Co., New York [City], 3/8. Todd and Co. acknowledge receipt of Calhoun's letter of 3/6 relating to the *Henry Leeds* case. "As in our letter to you of the 20th of Feb[ruar]y we withdrew the claim we had instituted in this case, no further remark appears necessary, unless that we were placed in the position we assumed by misrepresentations on the part of Capt[ai]n Henry A. Holmes, who had charge of the vessel & Cargo, and whose statements are now proved to have been at variance with the truth." LS in DNA, RG 59 (State Department), Consular Despatches, Merida, vol. 1 (M-287:1, frame 150).

To [JAMES EDWARD COLHOUN, Abbeville District, S.C.]

Washington, 9th March 1845

My dear Sir, I leave day after tomorrow for Fort Hill, and am so busery [*sic*; busy] in preparing for my journey, that I can add but a few lines to the acknowledgement of the receipt of your letters, with their enclosures, all of which were duely forwarded agreeably to your request.

The sum due to the estate of your father [John Ewing Colhoun], of which you enclosed a statement, ["is" *canceled and* "are" *interlined*] the same that I collected & paid your share ["to you" *interlined*], with the exception of a single additional item. I will attend to that before I leave, if I can find time.

I hope you will make us a visit shortly after ["your" *canceled and* "our" *interlined*] return to Fort Hill. In the mean time I have only to add that the commencement of the new administration [of James K. Polk] appears to be little satisfactory to any one, except those who compose it & their immediate friends. Had I been invited to remain, I could not have ["excepted" *changed to* "accepted"] under circumstances. Yours affectionately, J.C. Calhoun.

ALS in ScCleA.

To Mrs. E[LIZABETH] A. R. LINN [in Mo.]

Washington, 9th March 1845

My dear Cousin, I had hoped, when I answered your note, I would be able to give you the pleasing intelligence, that what you desired had been done.

Had there been a vacancy Mr. [John] Tyler would certainly have appointed you [as Postmistress at St. Louis]. He felt strongly disposed to make one, but encountered an opposition, which he could not well overcome.

I mentioned the subject to Mr. [James K.] Polk, and strongly urged your appointment. He seemed to be well inclined; and I do hope he will confer it on you. I am sure he could not do a more acceptable act to the great body of the Party.

I leave for Fort Hill day after tomorrow, and I wish you, my dear cousin, to be assured, that in whatever condition of life I may be placed, whether in private, or publick ["life" *canceled*], I shall never be indifferent to what may affect you. Affectionately, J.C. Calhoun.

ALS in MoSHi, Lewis F. Linn Papers.

"Hon. J.C. Calhoun's ACCOUNT FOR SALARY"

[Washington, *ca.* March 10, 1845]

Fourth quarter of 1844		$1500 "
69/90 of the 1st quarter of 1845, being		
from 1st Jan[uar]y to 10th March, incl.		1150 "
		2650 "

1844					
31 Oct.	Receipt for October,	No.	1	$500 "	
	Paid Colman's account		2	1 "	
	" Brownson's Qy. Review		3	3 "	
	" Democratic Review		4	10 "	
16 Nov.	Check		5	100 "	
5 Decr.	do.		6	100 "	
13 "	do.		7	150 "	
18 "	do.		8	117.16	
19 "	do.		9	100 "	
27 "	do.		10	50 "	
3 Jany. 1845	do.		11	171.31	
7 " "	do.		12	50 "	
17 " "	do.		13	50 "	
6 Feb. "	do.		14	50 "	
20 " "	do.		15	195 "	
22 " "	do.		16	50 "	
3 March	do.		17	123 "	
6 March	do.		18	50 "	
10 " "	Check for balance			779.53	$2650 "

ADU (by Edward Stubbs) in ScCleA.

To J[AMES] BUCHANAN, [Secretary of State]

[Washington, *ca.* March 10, 1845]

Dear Sir, My friend Mr. [William A.] Harris of the [Washington] Constitution is desires [*sic;* "to" *canceled and* "of" *interlined*] obtain[in]g one of the South American Chargés, or some other equally respectable place. I know him well; he is every way well worthy of ["it" *canceled*] such a place as he desires. His character and intelligence are of a high order. I take great interest in his success, and would regard it as a personal favour if his wishes should be met. I say nothing of his political principles or his service to the cause as

417

they are both well known to you & the President [James K. Polk]. With great respect yours truly, J.C. Calhoun.

ALS in DNA, RG 59 (State Department), Applications and Recommendations, 1845–1853, Harris (M-873:38, frames 124–126). NOTE: An AEU by Calhoun indicates this letter was to be hand-delivered to Buchanan. Filed with the above is a letter from Harris to Buchanan, dated 3/14. In it Harris stated: "I simply enclose you Mr. Calhoun's note, which it seems he left for me on his departure from Washington, but which was not handed to me till last night. It expresses my object and wishes. I can add nothing to it, except to say, that in his note to me he says, that he has left a memorandum with the President, by which he has made my appointment to some respectable position, a matter of personal favor to himself."

To [JAMES] BUCHANAN

[Washington, *ca.* March 10, 1845]
My dear Sir, I learn from my friend Sam[ue]l A. Townes Esq[ui]r[e] that he is an applicant for the Consulate at Bristol, or some other of like grade or pay; and that his application is strongly backed by the Alabama & Georgia delegations & Mr. [George] Mc-Duffie. I take pleasure in adding mine to their's. I have long known Mr. Townes. He is a gentleman of sound political principles, of intelligence, integrity & gen[era]l good character, and would doubtless satisfactorily discharge the duties of the office for which he applies. I would be much gratified with his success. With great respect yours truly, J.C. Calhoun.

ALS in DNA, RG 59 (State Department), Applications and Recommendations, 1845–1853, Townes (M-873:87, frames 152–155).

From Richard K. Crallé, 3/10. "I hereby resign the situation of Chief Clerk in this Department, which you did me the honor to confer on me . . . ." ALS in DNA, RG 59 (State Department), Letters of Resignation and Declination.

From FR[IEDRICH] V[ON] GEROLT, [Prussian Minister to the U.S.]

10th of March 1845
Dear Sir, Having called this evening at your hotel without being able to see you, I beg to address you a few lines to express my sincere

regret of your separation from Washington and from public affairs and my most cordial wishes for your's and your family's health and wellfare.

In presenting my respects to Mrs. Calhoun, I take the liberty to inclose a curiosity from Mexico, an aromatic wood (Lina[l]oë) which preserves cloths & & against moths as is generally believed in that country. I have the honor to remain, dear Sir, Your most ob[e]-d[ien]t and humble Servant, Fr. v[on] Gerolt.

ALS in ScU-SC, John C. Calhoun Papers.

To [PETER HAGNER, Third Auditor of the U.S. Treasury]

[Washington, March 10, 1845]

D[ea]r Sir, I am of the impression, that items in the within statement [*not found*], are the same, that were allowed & paid through your office last summer, with the exception of the last ["item" *canceled*]. You remitted the amount to me, & I paid over the shares of J[ames] Ed[ward] Colhoun & J[ohn] E[wing] Colhoun. ["It" *canceled and* "The sum" *interlined*] was due not from the old bank [of the U.S.], as the writer supposes, but [from] some old unfunded debt, if my memory serves me. I will thank you to examine & let me know; and also if an item was omitted, ["if" *canceled and* "whether" *interlined*] it can now be drawn without the ["taxable" *canceled and* "trouble" *interlined*] & expense of taking out letters of adm[inistratio]n. Truly, J.C. Calhoun.

ALS in NcU, Hagner Family Papers.

From P[ETER] HAGNER

[Washington, March 10, 1845]

Dear Sir, I received your note this morning enclosing a letter to you from J[ames] Edward Colhoun Esq[ui]r[e] which I return, having ascertained that the two first mentioned sums as you suggested were paid to you and the third is erroneously stated at 53 dollars instead of that num[b]er of Cents as 53/100 noted opposite to the Items by the Chief Clerk in the office of the Register of the Treasury. Most respectfully Yours, P. Hagner.

ALS in ScCleA.

To [President JAMES K. POLK]

10th March 1845

The following are the names of a few friends, in whose welfare I take much interest, and the gratification of whose wishes would confer a great favour on me.

W[illiam] A. Harris Editor of the [Washington] Constitution. He is a gentleman of education, talents & honor; a warm and efficient supporter of yours. He has spent much of his time & means in conducting a very efficient paper in the late canvass. He would be glad to be appointed to any of the ["beau" *canceled*] head of the subordinate divisions of the Departments; or if there should be a vacancy to the place of Charge de Affair[e]s at Venezuela. He is well qualified in every respect for either.

To his name, I add that of Mr. [William A.] Elmore of New Orleans, for the place of District Attorney, should there be a vacancy; of Mr. [Hilliard M.] Judge of Alabama for the place of Charge in Peru or any other place of equal respectability; of Mr. [Solomon] Cohen of Savan[n]ah ["Georgia" *interlined*], for the place of Charge at Begota [*sic*], & Mr. [Francis] Markoe for that of Denmark should Mr. [William W.] Irwin be transferred to Austria. He has been a long time in the State Dept. and is every way well qualified. All the other[s] have strong recommendations for the places for which they apply. They are all well qualified to discharge their duties. I hope it will be in your power to confer the offices on them. J.C. Calhoun.

ADS in DLC, James K. Polk Papers (Presidential Papers Microfilm, Polk Papers, roll 34). NOTE: An AEU by Calhoun reads: "A memorandum for the President left by Mr. Calhoun."

MARCH 11–APRIL 30
1845

〚〛

Had Calhoun been as driven by personal ambition as the shallower of his enemies and biographers contended, mid-March might have found him headed North rather than South toward the spring plowing and a long period as a private citizen. He had been invited to be a guest of honor at the St. Patrick's Day celebration in New York City on March 17, which would have been the day before his sixty-third birthday.

Instead, he left Washington on March 11, the day after his official duties ceased, on the railroad to Richmond. Mrs. Calhoun and their daughter, Martha Cornelia, were in Philadelphia consulting a physician whom it was hoped could help the crippled girl, and were to follow him later. In Richmond Calhoun dined with several friends at the Exchange Hotel and spent the night at the home of one. Doubtless there was a good deal of discussion of what was to be expected of the new administration. He continued on the railroad southward the next day. The Richmond Enquirer, *March 14, 1845, found "Mr. Calhoun in better health, with excellent spirits, and blessed with great equanimity of temper—and retiring with the most courteous feelings towards Mr. Polk and his administration."*

At Wilmington, North Carolina, he left the railroad and transferred to the Charleston packet, arriving in that city on March 15. It had already been arranged by a public meeting a few days before that he would be the guest of the city. A Committee of Fifty met him at the wharf and later in the day called at the Charleston Hotel to tender him a formal dinner in honor of his just-completed services as Secretary of State. Calhoun made a few unreported remarks of appreciation, but declined the dinner. He could not refuse several less formal invitations to dine and numerous visitors. (Washington Daily Madisonian, *March 18, 1845.)*

Leaving Charleston, probably by the train to Hamburg, on the Savannah River opposite Augusta, and then by stage to Pendleton, he was at Fort Hill on March 21. He immediately threw himself into the personal matters that he had doubtless been anxious to take

421

up. Soon after arriving home, he went to Edgefield District to in-spect the "Cane Brake" plantation, property of his son-in-law Clem-son who was absent representing the United States in Belgium.

Finances, as always, were pressing. Despite the high produc-tivity and self-sufficiency of Fort Hill and of that other "Cane Brake" plantation, operated by his son Andrew in Alabama, the long-continued low price of cotton left the family destitute of liquid assets. On April 9 Calhoun wrote to the Boston manufacturer and financier Abbott Lawrence. They had been friends when Lawrence had been a member of the House of Representatives, and had often discussed political economy. Lawrence undoubtedly had access to liquid capital in amounts unknown to the South. Calhoun offered a business proposition in exchange for funds to refinance the mortgage of the Alabama property. Lawrence's courteous and detailed reply of April 30 indicated, however, that an agreement could probably not be reached on terms.

If Calhoun considered himself a private citizen, it was clear that the public still thought of him as a public man. He received con-gratulations and an invitation from the Democrats of Mobile. Clark Mills wished to make his bust. His correspondence was heavy. It came from diverse quarters and encompassed diverse subjects. Most of it, however, reflected uncertainties and differing opinions among representatives of many groups within the Democratic party over what to expect from the new administration of President Polk.

◫

From J[OHN] S. BARBOUR

Catalpa [Va.,] March 11th 1845

My Dear Sir, What is it that has provoked so much of Mr. [John S.] Pendleton's hostility to you?

I wish that I could learn, for I am told he is doing you & the late President [John Tyler] gross injustice.

He is a very base man, but he has many kindred in this quarter & has influence.

In his late mission to Chili [*sic*] he must have done something culpable in itself; & *his* fault is probably, the cause of his displeasure. I have never heard him myself but others inform me of his bitterness & malignity.

It is probable his accounts or Conduct abroad, have not had the sanction of your approbation as he expected. Something has wounded him & incensed him. With Great Respect & Regard Y[ou]rs Truly, J.S. Barbour.

[P.S.] If Mr. Calhoun *is gone* Mr. [Richard K.] Crallé will please write me in reply. J.S.B.

ALS in ScCleA. NOTE: This letter was enclosed in an ALS of 3/11/1845 from Barbour to Geo[rge] McDuffie, Senator from S.C., that reads: "Will you send the enclosed to Mr. Calhoun as soon as it reaches you? and if he has gone please send it to Mr. Crallé with a request that he will open it & answer it."

To Mrs. A[NNA] M[ARIA CALHOUN] CLEMSON, [Brussels]

Washington, 11th March 1845

My dear Anna, I leave today for Fort Hill. Yesterday I terminated my official character as Secretary [of] State, & passed the office to Mr. [James] Buchanan. Mr. [James K.] Polk did not invite me to continue. In an interview, which he requested, he informed me, that he had concluded to form an entirely new Cabinet, when he proceeded to express his high respect & confidence in me, ["&" *canceled*] which he concluded by offering & urging me to accept the Mission to England. I declined accepting in ["a" *interlined*] mild, but decided manner; reciprocated his kind expressions; informed him that I had heard the an[n]unciation of his course without dissatisfaction; that I had accepted the office ["I held" *interlined*] with reluctance and on the condition, that I should retire when the negotiations, which brought me in were finished, and concluded by saying, as he had decided that my services could be dispensed with, it releived [*sic*] me from all responsibility & permitted ["me" *interlined*] to return to the repose of private life earlier than I had anticipated, but not than I desired. After some conversation on other subjects, we parted, he renewing his kind expressions, and I wishing him success in his administration. I immediately resigned my office to take effect as soon as my successor was ready to take possession, and informed him of the fact.

At the desire of Mr. Buchanan, I remained in until yesterday. I acted towards him as kindly & liberally, as if I had been invited to ["accept the pla" *canceled and* "continue" *interlined*] & had declined, giving him full information, with my advice on all points

423

how to proceed. Throughout I have put myself above the suspicion of dissatisfaction or chagrin, of which I felt not the least. In fact, the course pursued towards me in not inviting me to remain, has releived me from a good deal of embarrassment. Had I been invited, I should, with my veiws [*sic*] of the probable course of events, judging from the composition of the Cabinet & the language of the ina[u]gural on the subject of the Tariff, [have] been compelled to decline, which I could not ["do" *canceled*] have done with satisfaction, on the part of my friends, without assigning my reasons; ["which" *canceled and* "& that" *interlined*] I could not have done without coming at once to an open rupture with the administration under unfavourable circumstances. But, as it is, I retire freed from all responsibility, with the good will of all, including the administration, and the regret, I may say, of almost the whole country, ["and" *canceled and* "with" *interlined*] no small censure on the administration, for not inviting me to continue. I may say, I never stood higher or firmer in the opinion of the country. I have been thus full, because I suppose, that both you & Mr. [Thomas G.] Clemson would desire to know, under what circumstances I retired from office. I doubt not, in Mr. Buchanan he will have a good friend in office.

Your mother [Floride Colhoun Calhoun] left for Philadelphia a few days since, in order to consult Dr. Muttur [*sic*; Thomas D. Mutter] on Cornelia's [Martha Cornelia Calhoun's] case. She expected, when she left, to be back yesterday; but the Doctor spoke with such confidence ["as" *canceled*] of ["to" *canceled*] restoring her hearing, & benefitting her in relation to the curve of the spine, that she has been induced to remain some time longer. Patrick [Calhoun] will join her in Philadelphia, & accompany her home. James [Edward Calhoun] is with me, and is looking well. He promises me, that he will wright [*sic*] to you. I heard from Andrew [Pickens Calhoun] & John [C. Calhoun, Jr. in Ala.] not long since. The former & family were well, & John's health improved. Patrick has determined to change his condition. He is engaged to Miss [Kate] Wilkins. She is said universally to be a very fine sweet tempered girl. I am glad he is about to change his condition. The Army is a dangerous place for the habits of a Batchelor [*sic*]. I say no more, as I take it for granted, he has written to you, or will, all about it.

My health is entirely restored, and strength in a great measure.

Say to Mr. Clemson, that I left the two drawings & specifications for patents enclosed to me by ["he"(?) *canceled*] him, with Mr. [Robert] Beale, who will correspond with ["you" *canceled and* "him" *interlined*] on the subject. After full reflection, I kept his name disconnected entirely from the ["subject" *canceled and* "transaction" *interlined*] & said to Mr. Beale, he might have two thirds, if he took out the patents. Any connection of his name with it might might [*sic*] subject him to unpleasant imputations.

Say to him, also, that I will make it a point to visit the Canebrake [plantation in Edgefield District] and spend a day or two there.

I ["am" *interlined*] happy to hear that the children are recovered. Kiss them for their Grandfather, & tell [John] Calhoun [Clemson] that he is glad to hear that he is a good boy. Patrick & James join their love to you & Mr. Clemson.

I write under continued inter[r]uption and must close. Your affectionate father, J.C. Calhoun.

ALS in ScCleA; PEx in Jameson, ed., *Correspondence*, pp. 647–648.

From SAM[UE]L HAIGHT

Washington, 11th March 1845
Sir, Some time since I had the honor to leave at your residence, a letter [of 2/12/1845] ad[d]ressed to you in my behalf by the delegation of Louisiana. As this letter is of some importance to me, ["and" *changed to* "I"] have to request the favor of its being returned to me should it be at present in your pos[s]ession. Begging to apologise for thrspassing upon your kindness I remain Sir With great respect Your ob[e]d[ien]t Servant, Saml. Haight.

ALS in ScCleA.

From ALONZO A. F. HILL and Others

Phi Kappa Hall, [Athens, Ga.] March 11th 1845
Dear Sir, It is the custom at all Universities to have an address delivered before the Literary Societies, sometime during their Commencement Exercises. Accordingly you have been unanimously— even with acclamation elected by the Phi Kappa Society of Franklin College—as our next Public Commencement Orator. The address to be delivered on the Thursday after the first Wednesday in August next.

We do trust that you will accept the appointment so gladly and willingly tendered you. It is one which the most gifted spirits of the South have filled. Her Chandler's, [Henry L.] Pinckney's, [John M.] Berrien's[,] [Francis W.] Picken[s]'s, [Alexander B.] Meek and others have all come up and laid before us the offerings of their genius. And now your youthful fellow-citizens burning with desire to add their mite to the already mountainlike glory of the American Statesman and Hope of the South, ardently hope that the name of her *Calhoun* shall be added to the roll. You could not refuse if you but knew the enthusiasm felt upon your choice. As soon as we learned that you were a while freed from the cares of public life, like the needle that points to the pole, all eyes looked to thee. Our fellow-collegians partook of our enthusiasm and the walls of old Franklin echoed with the name of the leading star of America.

We remember thee as one, whose voice has ever been raised for his country's good, whose every pulsation warms a patriot's breast, and never no never while the post of Honor lays within our power shall we forget the name of our *Calhoun*. With sentiments of profound Respect and Honor We Remain, Alonzo A.F. Hill, Joseph T. Elston, Edward H. Pringle, J.M. Tilley, George T. Hurt[?], Committee on part of the Phi Kappa Society.

P.S. Please answer us *immediately*. Should you honor us by accepting the appointment, I shall be happy to furnish you with any necessary information as to time[,] place &c. For the purpose of certainty in your getting this immediately, I send you a copy ["to" *changed to* "at"] your home in South Carolina. Direct to Athens, Ga. Yours, Alonzo A.F. Hill.

LS in ScCleA. NOTE: An AEU by Calhoun reads: "From a Com[mit]tee of the Phi Kappa Society of Franklin College informing me that I had been selected to deliver the Commencement Oration." Calhoun's reply has not been found, but he did not accept the invitation.

To [President JAMES K. POLK]

Washington, 11th March 1845

I learn from Dr. James A. Cherry that he is an applicant for some respectable place under the Govt. I have long known him & his family, which is highly respectable, & I take pleasure in bearing my testimony in favour of his intelligence, integrity & gen[era]l good character, & would be gratified if his wishes should be met. J.C. Calhoun.

ALS in DNA, RG 59 (State Department), Applications and Recommendations, 1845–1853, Cherry (M-873:15, frame 192). NOTE: An Alabamian, Cherry was an applicant for a U.S. Consulship at Barbados or Matanzas, Cuba.

From CHARLES F. OSBORNE and Others

Richmond, March 12th 1845

Sir, Being apprized of your arrival in this city on your passage Home, many of your republican friends here indulge the hope that you may be induced to tarry at least a few days amongst us. Animated by this Hope and acting on their behalf, we beg leave, while tendering our most cordial greetings, to express the high gratification which your presence will impart and to request that an opportunity may be afforded of exhibiting by appropriate public testimonial the high appreciation cherished here of your private virtues, your intellectual endowments and eminent public services. We would therefore solicit the honor of your attendance at a public Dinner to be given by your friends and fellow Citizens of Richmond and its vicinity at the earliest period which may comport with your pleasure and convenience. With sentiments of the utmost respect & esteem Yours most truly, Charles F. Osborne, Robert G. Scott, Francis Wicker, James A. Seddon.

LS (in Seddon's handwriting) in ScCleA. NOTE: This letter was addressed to Calhoun at the "Exchange Hotel, Richmond." The Richmond, Va., *Enquirer*, March 14, 1845, p. 1, carried a report: "Mr. Calhoun. This distinguished gentleman reached Richmond in yesterday's cars. He dined with some of his friends at the Exchange Hotel, and spent the evening with one of his acquaintances. He leaves the city to-day in the mid-day cars for his home in South Carolina." Another report stated that Gen. [Mirabeau B.] Lamar, former President of the Texas Republic, sat next to Calhoun at dinner.

From R[OBERT] M. T. HUNTER

L[l]oyds[,] Essex C[ount]y Va., March 14, 1845

My dear Sir, I was never more disappointed in my life than on day before yesterday when I missed the cars at Milford by five minutes.

On Tuesday evening I received your letter and on Wednesday morning I started to meet you having been misinformed as to the time when the cars left Fred[erick]sburg. I did not go down on Thursday because I understood ["that" *canceled*] from your letter that you would leave Richmond on that day. I thus missed the chance of seeing you which I very much desired and lost the opportunity of ascertaining from yourself personally Mr. [James K.] Polk[']s position towards you.

I see from the [Washington] "Constitution" which reached me this evening that your parting meeting with the President was "cordial and gratifying." I see also a letter quoted from a Charleston paper stating that you were "dismissed" because N[ew] York would not aid annexation upon other terms. I really am at a loss to know how you are yourself satisfied with Mr. P[olk]'s conduct. My own impression from the constitution of the Cabinet and from his failure to *offer* you the State Dept. was that he designed to destroy your influence and overlook your friends. The Tariff portion of his Inaugural had also an ominous "squinting" towards protection. I had supposed that frightened by [Thomas H.] Benton & [Silas] Wright he was disposed to offer you up as a sacrifice to propitiate them. Are these things so? Or was it done to pass the annexation bill and did he deceive himself into the belief that in the appointment of that cabinet he was crushing the pretensions of Wright and yourself and paving the way for ["your" *canceled*] his renomination for a second term? There is however a rumor in the [Richmond] Enquirer too that he offered Cabinet appointments to Wright and [Benjamin F.] Butler. If so there can be little doubt of his secret inclinations. Now my dear Sir it will be a matter of great interest to me and others of your friends in Va. to know your impressions and your views as to the course to be pursued towards him. Shall he be taxed at once with ingratitude in the public prints or shall we wait for his measures[?] I incline to the latter. If his measures are right and up to the Baltimore resolutions we must of course support them and that war of policy itself will do more to promote you than his patronage. His cabinet is such that you and your friends are not responsible for its course, and ["unless" *canceled and* "if" *interlined*] his measures are ["not" *interlined*] satisfactory public opinion will sustain us in attacking them. He must not tamper with the rights and safety of the South. I know nothing of the undercurrents which were at work. But his course so far wears the appearance of having been impolitic as well as unjust. It was his interest to have appointed one at least of your friends to the Cabinet. I do not see however that ["it" *can-*

celed] we could make public complaint of his failure to do so. Our motives might be misunderstood. But as to measures we may hold him to ["a" *interlined*] strict account. I think too that public sentiment will condemn any neglect of you on Mr. P[olk]'s part, and the more decidedly, ["the" *canceled*] as we say less about it.

Should Mr. P[olk] throw himself ["in favor" *canceled and* "(on) the side" *interlined*] of protection, we shall have a career of peril and labor before us. The distribution of the surplus in the shape of internal Improvements will add a strength to the Tariff with which it will be difficult to cope. The opposition too, would have to play its part with great delicacy and skill or soon be utterly wrecked. The absence of yourself too would be severely felt. Indeed I should almost lose hope if it were not that the reactions of these artificial systems are often so severe as to work a cure when human opposition seems to be unavailing.

I trust however that we have secured Texas. Altho I am not without my fears on that subject. I hope she will promptly accept the offer transmitted by you after the passage of the bill. And even then there may be danger of new difficulties to be thrown in the way by Mr. Benton. But much has been already accomplished—much for the good of the South—much for your own fame and I shall hope for the best.

I hope you have kept a private Journal during your service in the State Department. It will be necessary at some future day as an addition to your biography. Would it not be well for you at your earliest leisure to make a memo of as much as you would be willing to impart to ["you"(?) *canceled*] whoever may complete your biography. This might be delayed as long as you live unless there may be a call for another edition of your biography in the course of a year or two. I hope you will pardon me for suggesting this matter whilst events are yet fresh in your recollection. Most truly your friend, R.M.T. Hunter.

ALS in ScCleA.

From H[ENRY] BAILEY

Charleston, 15th March, 1845

Sir, The Joint Committee appointed by the City Council, and the Citizens of Charleston, to receive and welcome you, upon your return home, as the Guest of the City, and to tender its hospitalities to you during your stay with us, having had the honor of waiting upon you this morning in the discharge of the grateful duty assigned them, and of expressing, in the name of their fellow citizens, their high and grateful sense, as well of your distinguished public services, in a most critical period of the fortunes of our country, as of the devoted and self-sacrificing patriotism with which those services have been rendered by you, have instructed me now to request, that you would afford to the Citizens of Charleston the opportunity of a more full and free intercourse with you prior to your departure for your residence, by meeting with them around the social board. I have the honor, therefore, on behalf of the Joint Committee, to invite you to partake of a public dinner with the Citizens of Charleston, on such day as will best suit your convenience. With sentiments of the highest personal regard & esteem Your Ob[e]d[ien]t Serv[an]t, H. Bailey, Chairman of Joint Committee.

ALS in ScCleA. NOTE: An AEU by Calhoun reads "Invitation by the Joint Com[mit]tee to accept a publick dinner tendered [by] citizens of Charleston." This letter was addressed to Calhoun "Present" in Charleston.

To H[ENRY] BAILEY

CHARLESTON, 15th MARCH, 1845

Dear Sir: I greatly regret that it is not in my power to prolong my stay sufficiently to accept the invitation so kindly tendered by you, as the Chairman of the Joint Committee, appointed by the City Council and the citizens of Charleston, to partake of a public dinner with the citizens of Charleston.

My arrangements will compel me to leave your hospitable city to-morrow, for my residence in Pendleton.

I avail myself of the occasion to return my heartfelt thanks to the City Council, and the citizens of Charleston generally, for this and the many other marks of respect which they have extended to me. I never shall cease to remember them with the profoundest gratitude, while a pulsation of my heart remains. Never had a public man such cause to be grateful to his constituents as I have to them and the citizens of the State generally. It is my pride and consolation to be able to say that after thirty-six years of public services in various stations, and in passing through many and trying scenes, their confidence has never forsaken me. If it has been my fortune to render any service worth remembering during that long period to the State or the Union, to them the credit is due, whose firm and unwavering support never for a moment deserted me—*on that* I ever relied with confidence, while I followed the lead of Truth, Justice and the Constitution; and it was *that reliance* which enabled me to pursue the course I have without hesitation or faltering steps. With the highest respect, I am, &c., J.C. CALHOUN.

PC in the Charleston, S.C., *Courier*, March 19, 1845, p. 2; PC in the Charleston, S.C., *Mercury*, March 19, 1845, p. 2; PC in the Washington, D.C., *Constitution*, March 22, 1845, p. 3; PC in the Mobile, Ala., *Register and Journal*, March 25, 1845, p. 2; PC in the Milledgeville, Ga., *Federal Union*, March 25, 1845, p. 3; PC in the Edgefield, S.C., *Advertiser*, March 26, 1845, p. 2; PC in the Pendleton, S.C., *Messenger*, March 28, 1845, p. 1; PC in *Niles' National Register*, vol. LXVIII, no. 9 (May 3, 1845), p. 130.

To ALEX[ANDER] BLACK, "Chairman of the Stewards[,] Hibernian Society"

CHARLESTON, MARCH 15, 1845
Dear Sir—I greatly regret that my arrangements, which will compel me to leave your city to-morrow, will not permit me to accept the invitation of the Hibernian Society to dine with them on their approaching anniversary [of St. Patrick on 3/17]. Permit me to request you to tender to them my sincere thanks for this mark of their respect, and to assure them that if circumstances had permitted I would have been happy to join them in celebrating an anniversary dear to the sons of Erin, wherever found. With great respect, I am, &c., JOHN C. CALHOUN.

PC in the Charleston, S.C., *Courier*, March 20, 1845, p. 2.

From W[ILLIA]M GREGG

Charleston, March 15th 1845
My Dear Sir, I take great pleasure in complying with your request in sending you one of my pamphlets on Domestic Industry. I regret now that I did not, before it went to the Press in ["Phamphlet" *altered to* "Pamphlet"] form, extract such matter from it as may be deemed offensive to our leading ["Politicians" *interlined*]. I sought

the councel [*sic*] of discrete [*sic*] and intel[l]igent friends, selecting from both Political parties, and was advised not to suppress any part of the matter which had appeared in the [Charleston Courier] Newspaper articles, but to preface the work, with such remarks, as in my judgement, would exculpate me from the charge of unfriendly feelings towards our Political leaders. I regret that I did not extend more courtesy to Gen. [George] McDuffie, who (notwithstanding the morbid spirit he manifests of late) I regard to be one of the purest statesmen of the Age. The errors of great men when exposed, sets truth in bold relief, & this is the only excuse under which I may expect to escape ["the" *interlined*] censure of this Gentleman. As for my Politics, from my knowledge of your political course up to 1822, I became an advocate of J.C. Calhoun for President of the U. States, and have never had reason to change my ground, and not withstanding the Whigs of Charleston claimed me as one of their ranks, I have never hesitated, to express my opposition to the Tariff, to a new U. States Bank, and to manifest my preference to yourself over Mr. [Henry] Clay and all other men for the Presidency of the U. States. I trust you will give my pamphlet a careful perusal, pass over that which you may deem offensive, and weigh well, the undeniable facts which it has been my object to lay before the people of this State. I am with great respect your very humble serv[an]t, Wm. Gregg.

ALS in ScCleA. NOTE: In his pamphlet, *Essays on Domestic Industry: or, An Enquiry into the Expediency of Establishing Cotton Manufactures in South-Carolina* (Charleston: Burges and James, 1845), p. 7, Gregg stated: "It would indeed be well for us, if we were not so refined in politics—if the talent, which has been, for years past, and is now engaged in embittering our indolent people against their industrious neighbors of the North, had been with the same zeal engaged in promoting domestic industry and the encouragement of the mechanical arts. If so, we should now see a far different state of things in South-Carolina." This letter was addressed to Calhoun at the "Charleston Hotel." Gregg (1800–1867) was the leading cotton manufacturer of S.C.

From B[ENJAMIN] G. WRIGHT

Belmont [County, Ohio] March 17th 1845

Dear Sir, I cannot refrain from addressing you a few lines at this juncture of time on a subject on which, we I suppose, differ. That you are right, in the main, I frankly concede, but at the same time permit me to say to you that I humbly conceive that the best interests of this Union, & of popular rights, require of you a compliance with the wishes of your friends to visit the North & West. Your position is a peculiar one—not, however, owing to any act of yours but to the wicked & illiberal course of the press of the West & the North in refusing to let your true character, as a Statesman, be known to the masses of our people here & in the North. This you must well know to be true to the letter. And I do assure [you] that the same course will be pursued in future unless you consent to comply with the wishes of your friends by paying a visit to our Sections of the Union & acquiring personally that popularity which the press will never conse[n]t to give you.

This letter, for some time determined on, has been hastened by the annunciation in the N[ew] York Herald that your friends in that city have invited or intend to invite you to a public dinner. Now, my Dear Sir, at *this time* I do not think that the reasoning of your letter [of 7/9/1843] to your Cincinnati friends is at all applicable. You are not now a candidate for office & can certainly have no serious objection to visit our sections of this Union merely because your enemies & the enemies of our principles may, from unworthy motives, say that you do so ["from" *canceled and* "for" *interlined*] sinister objects. If such an accusation would ["be" *interlined*] valid against you, then no man worthy of the appellation of a great & eminent Statesman can consistently visit the Several States of this Union because forsooth he might hereafter from eminent abilities & high moral worth be put in nomination for the Presidency.

I trust that you will appreciate my motives for thus addressing you though you may not be convinced that I am right in urging you to accept invitations to visit our Sections of the Union. You will, however, agree with me that the men, who have stood firm & unflinching as a band of Brothers in the cause of constitutional liberty & "State Rights," can never, knowingly, so far forget what is due to their own characters, as to urge any one of this *"little Band"*, much less their *file leader*, to an act at war with the best interests of these States or at variance with the strictest rules of or Morality [*sic*] or the high & exalted precepts of christianity. On such visits your defence & illustration of the great American doctrine exhibited in your letter [of 8/12/1844] to Mr. [William R.] King would give you a place in the affections of our people which ["you" *interlined*] can never attain from any cause[?] of the press, much less from its past, present or future course. No man can win more popular applause from the Masses of our people than yourself. Your plain, terse & common ["sense" *interlined*] mode of treating great question[s] of ["public" *interlined*] concern would carry conviction to their minds from its irresistability [*sic*]. The Masses you know do not view things in the same light as corrupt & selfish politicians. Truth is their object & it would in all cases triumph were it ["not" *interlined*] for the course of the political press which has too often been to mislead instead of to enlighten the Masses. This is especial[l]y the case here where politicks may in fact be viewed as a trade instead of a high-toned devotion to principle.

If you are ever to visit our portions of the Union this is the time; & I feel confident that, unless you do most positively refuse to comply with the wishes of your friends, you ["ensure your" *canceled and* "can" *interlined*] by so doing confer lasting benefits[?] on your beloved country which, from your peculiar position ["& the course of the press" *interlined*] can be effected in no other way. I will add no more, & at the same time rest assured ["that" *interlined*] the expectations of your friends will not be disappointed.

In my last I requested an answer from you but on reflection I became satisfied that your position ["in" *interlined*] the Cabinet required unusual caution on your part. In this respect, perhaps, our friend Dr. [James] Wishart did not duly appreciate your situation. We are ignorant here of any *facts* as to the feelings of President [James K.] Polk towards ["you" *interlined*] but I suspect that the old feelings of the "*Proclamationists*" are averse to you & to the true "*State Rights Creed.*" Be this as it may the inaugural is not genuine—it asserts the *sovereignty* of the F[ederal] *Government*. To this all State Rights ["men" *interlined*] must object as a heresy.

Not recollecting your address I send this enclosed to the P[ost] M[aster] at Pendleton S.C. with a request to hand over or forward to you as the case may require. And let me suggest to you the propriety of [*illegible word canceled*] some such arrangement for your correspondents as will not excite any suspicion of ["any particular" *canceled*] of [*sic*] extensive correspondence.

Let me hear from you soon as convenient to yourself. With great respect yours &c. &c., B.G. Wright.

ALS in ScCleA. NOTE: Wright's second paragraph probably refers to a statement in the New York *Herald*, March 9, 1845, p. 2: "Mr. Calhoun. We understand that a large number of persons in this city have united in an invitation to the Hon. John C. Calhoun to visit New York, and partake of a public dinner." The same newspaper reported on March 18, p. 2, the proceedings of a St. Patrick's Day dinner the previous day, presumably the same dinner referred to in the earlier account. At this dinner the chairman "stated that he had received letters of apology from the Hon. John C. Calhoun, and the Hon. James Buchanan . . . ."

Ch[arles] Aug[ustu]s Davis, New York [City,] to D[ixon] H. Lewis, [Senator from Ala.], 3/21. Davis discusses recent political and commercial news from England. He observes that although the news is good for cotton producers, the real profits are to be made by manufacturers of cotton goods because they, rather than cotton growers, have "controul of Capital & Credit." For that reason they can manipulate the market. Davis also comments on Calhoun's popularity in the Northeast and wishes that Calhoun could be induced to make a tour of the region for "his health and *other reasons* . . . . Many of our people in this quarter [*mutilation*] through the medium that his political [*mutilation*] show him in—and few would suppose [*mutilation*] he [*mutilation*] amiable courteous Gentleman he is. They think him sour—morose—dark—designing &. &. when perhaps we have no public man so entirely the reverse." Calhoun's doctrines are working to throw a "wet blanket on our northern fanatics." (This letter was forwarded to Calhoun. An AEU by Calhoun reads "C.A. Davis.") ALS (mutilated) in ScCleA.

From Sam[ue]l Treat, "(Private)"

Reporter Office
St. Louis, March 21, 1845

Dear Sir: I take the liberty of addressing a note to you, on the supposition that it will reach you before you leave Washington. I need not remind you of the course pursued by Col. [Thomas H.] Benton during the past year, but the manner in which his avowed organ here [the St. Louis *Missourian*], established by him for the promotion of his own selfish objects, has been conducted, may not be equally familiar to you and your friends. Suffice it to say, that organ ["has" *canceled*] assailed the nomination of Col. [James K.] Polk, denounced the Texas movement and its advocates throughout the Presidential contest, lauded during the last session of Congress the *quasi* Abolition operations of [John P.] Hale, [Representative] of N.H., [Jacob] Brinkerhoff, [Representative] of Ohio, Orville Robinson, [Representative] of New York, and their co-adjutors, and has never omitted an opportunity of vilifying every Democrat who has refused to yield implicitly to the arrogant dictation of Col. Benton. Yet in the face of these notorious facts, an order was received by the Postmaster here [Samuel B. Churchill?], on yesterday, from the new

Postmaster General [Cave Johnson], directing that the publication of letters should be hereafter made in the Missourian, instead of the Reporter. The trifling amount of patronage thus taken from a Democratic paper, and conferred on a Benton journal, is unworthy of comment, except so far as it has a moral force against the Annexation and Democratic cause, in Missouri, Illinois, Iowa and Wisconsin. You are aware that the tone of public opinion in, at least, two States and Territories is received from the papers published in St. Louis. During the last twelve-months the Reporter has been the only Democratic paper in this city that has upheld the Texas measure and Southern rights, and the Missourian as well as the other Benton, and all the Whig journals have assailed the South and Annexation with every weapon which could be brought to bear. The change, therefore, made by the new Postmaster General, will give the impression throughout the whole Northwest that Col. Polk's administration has fallen at the start into the embraces of Benton and his co-workers. This should not be. The gallant band that rallied around the Reporter, and struggled against the most fearful odds, should not be paralyzed, by such unjust treatment. *The Texas battle is not yet over.* At this point it is well known what are Col. Benton's intentions for the future. The struggle will be renewed at the commencement of the next session of Congress, and before many months have elapsed, the preparatory movements will be made in this State by Col. Benton ["himself" *interlined*]. Yet the whole weight of the new administration is, ["in" *interlined*] effect, cast against those who, from motives of patriotism, are prepared to maintain, as becomes Southern men, that policy which you so happily commenced in the State Department. I confess that I rejoiced that an American Secretary of State had at last been found, to strip from England the mask of philanthropy which she has worn for too long a period, and in the fullness of my joy dared to undertake an invidious task in this State—to assail Col. Benton and reply on the stump to his Anti-Texas speeches. It has been my good fortune to stand up, in the presence of assembled thousands in St. Louis, and vindicate what I considered the American policy, *par excellence*, as fully displayed in your letter to Mr. [William R.] King. Whether erroneously or not, I considered that the time had come when our Republic must either hide its head in shame, or take a determined stand against British Abolitionism. Many movements here, under the auspices of Col. Benton's confidential friends, led me to believe, that he was preparing the way for an attack upon slavery in Missouri. Fearing for the safety of the Republic, and being confident that Missouri is to be the first great battle field in the coming contest, I felt the greatest anxiety that the few who had determined to meet the gathering storm should be sustained, by at least the countenance of the Federal Administration. I know that the mass of the people are true to the country, and that they will not desert the South in the coming trial, unless our efforts are paralyzed at the very beginning. I have seen them tested fully within the last year; and if I may be permitted to refer to my own personal knowledge, without appearing to be too vain, I would say that not only in St. Louis, but in the different counties in which I have addressed the people from the hustings, a most enthusiastic approval of your diplomacy has been given by the masses, regardless of party distinctions. I have heard crowd after crowd rend the air with approving shouts, as the true character of the controversy between us and Great Britain has been laid before them, and your spirited defence of American honor and rights explained. In all this, I have acted from feelings which I believe to be those of patriotism. I confess, then, that my emotions at this hour are ["deeply" *canceled*] painful in the extreme, on learning that those on whom we had a right to rely, if not for moral aid, at least for no opposition, have been deceived, in the most unaccountable manner, into strengthening the arms of our enemies and the enemies of true principles. I have spoken in the first person merely to illustrate the effect that the Postmaster General's new movement, is to have upon the Administration. My feelings are shared by those of Mr. Polk's true friends in the Northwest. It will be in vain for us to attempt to resist the combined hosts arrayed against us, if the Federal Administration is to lead them, and cheer them on in the conflict. I ["st" *canceled*] write, perhaps, warmly on this subject, because I feel the magnitude of the questions at issue, and soon to agitate this Republic. It appears to me obvious that we are at the threshold of one of the most trying crises our country has ever had to meet, and I believe that the Postmaster General has been deceived by some unknown person into the adoption of a measure which will give strength to the enemies of the country—a moral power which will not only inspirit them, but unnerve the friends of the Administration. To be sustained, the Administration must be just to those who are ready to battle for it. Their confidence, high-wrought as it has been, must not be destroyed, or the worst must be anticipated.

I must beg to be excused for troubling you with this hasty letter, about what may appear a trivial matter. The amount of patronage in dollars and cents *is* trifling; but not so the moral effect. At the moment of a successful beginning, when the true Democrats here had succeeded in procuring *instructions* to Col. Benton, and when his friends had commenced deserting his treasonable operations by platoons, it is indeed strange that ["they" *canceled and* "we" *interlined*] should be called to endue [*sic*] a rebuke like that given by ["the" *interlined*] Postmaster General. The consequences of this new movement are important, and I hope that the necessity of an immediate restoration of affairs, as they stood, will take place. At all hazards, a devoted band in Missouri will not desert American honor and Southern rights, even if deserted by the Government. If you can, through any of your friends, represent this matter in its true light, I trust you will do so. Yours truly, Saml. Treat.

ALS in DNA, RG 56 (Secretary of the Treasury), Miscellaneous Letters Received, 1815–1914. NOTE: This letter was endorsed by Calhoun "Mr. Treat of the Reporters office," and endorsed in another hand, "Public Printing[,] Sam[ue]l Treat." Treat, a native of N.H., was later a State and federal judge in Missouri.

To T[HOMAS] G. CLEMSON, [Brussels]

Fort Hill, 23d March 1845

My dear Sir, I wrote Anna [Maria Calhoun Clemson] by the last Steamer, just before I took my departure from Washington; and informed her, that on my return, I would visit the Cane Brake [in Edgefield District] and write you, as to the State of your affairs there. I now write to fulfil my promise.

I spent one day there, & road [*sic*] over the whole place, with your neighbour Mr. Mawbly [*sic*; John Mobley], with whom I quarte[re]d at his request while there, in company with Mr. Bland your new overseer. It may be proper to premise, that his predecessor had left of his own accord without notice a short time before, & without insisting ["for" *canceled*] to ["being" *changed to* "be"] paid, for the two months he had staid [*sic*] in the second year; and that Mr. Mawbly after sending for Mr. [James] Vaughn ["& consulting him," *interlined*] in the absence of Col. [Francis W.] Pickens on a visit to Alabama, had employed Mr. Bland, at the rate of $200 a year. He is experienced in the business, having been engaged in it for 9 years, and has the reputation of being a good overseer. He is married, but has no children, and is to be found bread & meat.

I found the place, all things considered, in good order. The fences had all been new built, or repaired; the oats were up & looked well; the ploughing nearly finished preparatory to planting. It seemed to me to be well done. He intended to commence planting corn the day after I left. His crop will ["will" *interlined*] consist of 120 acres in cotton, 110 in corn & 70 in oats. The Horses ["& Mules" *interlined*] were in reasonable good ["plight" *interlined*]; the hogs I saw looked well, & had, I learned, increased fast, & the sheep appeared to me to be in fine order. There were 19 lambs. I did not see the cattle.

The negroes all continued to enjoy health; and appeared contented. The House had advanced slowly for the want of lumber. Mr. Mawbly has been, I have no doubt, ["very" *canceled*] very attentive. He informed me, that he ["had" *interlined*] written you, that he could not ["longer take" *canceled*] continue his supervision ["longer" *interlined*] than July next; but would cheerfully give any advice to Mr. Bland, whenever desired. He puts great confidence in him, both as to skill & attention to business; &, I think, the prospect is fair that he will do well.

I got home ["day before" *canceled*] yesterday, & found all well except William Lowndes [Calhoun], who had the measels. He was very sick when I arrived, & spent a very bad night; but seems quite convalescent to day. I went over my place to day, & find it in excellent order. It has been greatly improved since you saw it. I venture to say, that few places in the State, ["is" *canceled and* "are" *interlined*] in better order. I have not ["yet" *canceled*] seen the Devon Bull yet; but hear, that he is a fine animal, & is in good order.

I left Mrs. [Floride Colhoun] Calhoun & [Martha] Cornelia [Calhoun] behind. She had taken Cornelia to Philadelphia to consult Dr. [Thomas D.] Mutter about her case, and received such encouragement from him, that she resolved to remain 8 or 10 days to give him a fair opportunity to try his skill. She will be accompanied back, as far as Charleston by Patrick [Calhoun], & expects to be ["back" *canceled and* "home" *interlined*] early next month.

On my return home, I spent a day in Richmond, & had a most cordial reception from my friends. I saw & conversed ["all" *canceled*] with all the prominent men of the party, including Mr. [Thomas] Ritchie, who presided in a dinner party of about 20 plates, given by my intimate friends. He gave a toast complimentary of me, which was followed by three others, expressly naming me as the candidate for '48. The whole was unexcpected [*sic*] to me. My friends there are intelligent, ardent & united. They will open the campaign for the April election on high anti Tariff grounds. Mr. [James A.] Seddon, one of the most intelligent & ardent, was nominated by a large convention, the day I was there, as the candidate [for Representative from Va.], ag[ai]nst [John M.] Botts; & will turn the discussion on the Tariff. The inaugural is regarded as not satisfactory on the subject by our friends.

I also spent a day in Charleston; & was most cordially received, without distinction of party. The Hospitality of the city was voted me. A large party of Gentlemen, not less than 100 dine[d] at the Hotel with me, & a publick dinner was tendered, which I declined. I had requested to be received quietly. I found in Charleston, & as far as I have learned, that the Cabinet & the ["inag" *canceled*] inaugural are both unpopular ["in the State" *interlined*]; as I believe they are throughout the South, if not the Union. I say but little ["on the subjects," *canceled and* "in reference to either" *interlined*] especially ["on" *canceled*] the former. It would be both impolitick & improper. My course towards the President [James K. Polk] & his Cabinet has been marked with great liberality, & has been felt ["by them" *interlined*] to be so. Mr. [James] Buchanan has spoken every where in the highest terms of it, as far as he is concerned. He pronounced it to be above all praise.

William Lowndes joins his love to you & Anna. Kiss the dear children [John Calhoun Clemson and Floride Elizabeth Clemson] for their Grandfather. My health is quite restored. Your affectionate father, J.C. Calhoun.

ALS in ScCleA; PEx's in Jameson, ed., *Correspondence*, pp. 649–650. NOTE: Seddon defeated Botts in the election for Representative from Va.

To Col. JA[ME]S ED[WARD] COLHOUN, [Abbeville District]

Fort Hill, 23d March 1845

My dear James, I arrived here yesterday & found all well except William Lowndes [Calhoun], who has the measeals [*sic*]. He was very sick when I arrived & spent a bad night, but is quite convalescent to day.

I left your Sister [Floride Colhoun Calhoun] behind. She took [Martha] Cornelia [Calhoun] to Philadelphia to consult Dr. [Thomas D.] Mutter about her case, expecting to return to Washington before I left; but the Doctor gave such hope of restoring her hearing, that she resolved to stay some 8 or 10 days to give him a fair trial of his skill. I expect her early next month.

I enclose a note [of 3/10/1845] from Mr. [Peter] Hagner in answer to one from me, which will explain itself without any remark on my part.

I hope you will make it a point to pay us a visit at some early period. I have much to say to you, which can better be communicated in conversation than by letter. I was sorry that Francis [W. Pickens] was absent, on a visit to Alabama, as I had made my arrangement to spend a day or two with him, when I could have conversed fully with him about the state of things in Washington. I fear he will find himself mistaken, as to Mr. [James K.] Polk's course.

I spent a day at Mr. [Thomas G.] Clemson['s] place [in Edgefield District], and was glad to find things were going on well there. I have been over mine to day & find it in high order. I think there are few places in the State in better. Yours affectionately, J.C. Calhoun.

ALS in ScCleA.

To JAMES BUCHANAN, [Secretary of State]

Fort Hill, 24th March 1845

My dear Sir, I enclose several letters, which I hope you ["will" *interlined*] have forwarded to their destination.

May I express the hope, that Mr. [Henry A.] Wise may be continued at Brazil. I am sure one better qualified cannot be selected to take his place, and I know that it would be convenient & desirable for him to remain longer there. I am aware, that there was no kind personal relations between him & the President [James K. Polk], while they were both members of the House; but I know, that Mr. Wise took a decided interest in his election, and has ceased to have any unkind feelings on his part. The President can best judge, what course it would be proper for him to take, but it seems to me, that a decision on his part to retain him would be an act of magnanimity, which would do him credit. Yours truly, J.C. Calhoun.

ALS in PHi, James Buchanan Papers (published microfilm, reel 8, frames 640–641); PC in Jameson, ed., *Correspondence*, p. 651.

From A[NDREW] J. DONELSON, "Private"

New Orleans, March 24, 1845

My D[ea]r Sir, Your despatch by Mr. Waggeman [*sic*; Floyd Waggaman] although later than you may have wished, in reaching me, on account of the circuitous course by Nashville, was in time for the earliest conveyance to Galvezton since the passage of the bill. I was yesterday at Mobile to lay in supplies for my plantation, and am still waiting for the departure of the Marmora, a steam ship, that has been advertised to sail, for some days, but will not get off before morning. She furnishes the only opportunity for a conveyance until the return of the New York, which is the regular packet.

You may rely on my best exertions to effect annexation on the terms of the House part of the Resolution: and have but little doubt of success, unless the existing Government with[h]olds its agency in its reference to Congress or the people. Without a great change in the popular feeling since I left Texas, no personal influences can stand up against the measure as now offered by our Government.

It would have been gratifying to me to have seen this important measure closed before you left the Government, but I suppose it was not a matter to you of much moment, individually, after ascertaining that the new administration would endeavor to adjust it without altering the basis of the negotiation. The Union is under deep obligations to you for the prompt and enlightened ["measures" *canceled*] aid you have rendered in snatching from the grasp of Great Britain a Territory so essential to our peace and safety.

I would have written to you from Nashville, in reference to the cause of your misunderstanding with the Gen[era]l [Andrew Jackson], but that I did not feel authorised to do so. Although in the general his feelings were kind, yet, as he seemed to take an unchanged veiw [*sic*] of the circumstances in the Seminole war which led to the inter[r]uption of your personal intercourse, I did not see that any good would result from reopening the question. I have a great desire that ["you" *canceled*] the point of difference between you should be settled in such a manner that the friends of both may look at ["it" *interlined*] hereafter, without the pain it would occasion as it now stands.

I am aware of the delicacy of the question, and of the impropriety of my touching it with an expectation of presenting it in any new light. It is one of the cases that cannot be settled by argument. You are aware that it was at [Fla.] Gov[erno]r [John] B[ranch']s instance that I have moved as far as I have in the matter. If I have done wrong he must be responsible.

I tender you my thanks for the kindness I have received at your hands, and my best wishes for your health & happiness, and am very truly y[ou]r ob[edien]t ser[van]t, A.J. Donelson.

[P.S.] I am just informed that the boat is about to start, and that I will have no time to copy, or correct this scrawl. Pardon therefore the rudeness of making it necessary for you to decipher it. Y[ou]rs &, A.J.D.

ALS in ScCleA; variant draft (dated 3/20) in DLC, Andrew Jackson Donelson Papers; PEx in Boucher and Brooks, eds., *Correspondence*, pp. 286–287.

From DANIEL E. HUGER, [Senator from S.C.]

Charleston, March 24th 184[5]
My dear Sir, The Senate adjourned on Thursday the 20th and I reached this City yesterday the 23d.

Nothing occurred at Washington but what was in due course. The nominations of the President were confirmed generally. He refused to communicate to the Senate anything which had been done by Mr. [John] Tyler or himself, under the resolutions for admitting Texas. The Zoll-Verrein [*sic*] treaty was postponed until the next session of Cong[res]s. Mr. [Daniel] Webster appeared to understand perfectly the object of this Treaty & it's [*sic*] policy. Other gentlemen of his Party appeared to regard it as simply an attempt to reduce the Tariff—which they said ought not to be done but with the concurrence of the House of Representatives.

I was informed by [James Buchanan] the Secretary of State that the wish of the Presid[en]t was to send a minister to England from the Southern States & if possible from South Carolina. I have no doubt your indication of one would be attended to. Hopes are yet entertained that *you* might yet be induced to go. I said your friends had pressed you on this subject but that you appeared inflexible.

Mr. President and myself had some conversation as to Proscription in S. Ca[rolin]a. The result was a declaration on his part, that no removals should take place here except for *cause*.

The death of Senator [Isaac C.] Bates [of Mass.] afforded me an opportunity of taking ground which I was happy enough to perceive, was regarded as indicative of So[uth] Carolina feeling.

The course pursued by Gen[era]l [George] McDuffie & myself on the Oregon question excited at first, unpleasant feelings, but before we parted, I think, even the Gentlemen of our Party had ceased to indulge even disapprobation of our course.

Mr. Buch[ana]n spoke to me of the course ["of" *canceled*] the [Charleston] Mercury had pursued with respect to him. He declared to me he had done nothing & even had not a wish, to have you supplanted in the State Department. He said you had been generously kind to him and for which he felt grateful. He did not appear entirely satisfied with his position—a seat in the Senate he thought preferable. Should you ever concur in this opinion, I beg you will without hesitation signify the same to me. We want you in the Senate. The Whigs there are much stronger than we are & I mistake much if the contest between the two parties does not in a very short time shew the necessity of some change—particularly in the Cabinet. If the Secretary ["of the Treasury" *interlined*; Robert J. Walker] does not turn out much more than is expected of him & far superior to his brother Ministers a change in the Cabinet must take place. Mr. Buch[ana]n may fall on the Bench. No one has been nominated to fill Mr. Justice [Henry] Baldwin's place. The President said to me he was determined to have a *first rate man* there & that this was the cause of his delay. He moreover said that in his opinion sufficient attention had not been given to this subject even by General [Andrew] Jackson himself.

We have a rumour in circulation that Mr. [Levi] Woodbury is to go to England. I attach no consequence to it, for the reason above given.

Should you at any time feel disposed to communicate to me your wishes or views a letter addressed to me here will be attended to. Yours &ca, Daniel E. Huger.

ALS in ScCleA; PC in Jameson, ed., *Correspondence*, pp. 1027–1029. NOTE: An AEU by Calhoun reads "Judge Huger." In 11/1845 Huger resigned to make room for Calhoun in the Senate.

To GEORGE WILSON, [Manchester, England]

Fort Hill, 24th March 1845

Dear Sir, I accept with much pleasure the Copy of the 1st Vol. of the League, which you transmitted to me by the direction of the Council of the National Anti Corn Law League, for my acceptance. I feel greatly honored by this mark of their respect.

I regard free trade, as involving considerations far higher, than mere commercial advantages, as great as they are. It is, in my opinion, emphatically the cause of civilization & peace—of wide spread civilization & durable peace among the nations of the earth. It belongs to England and the United States to take the lead in this great cause, and I hope that ["day" *interlined*] is not distant, when they will set the noble example to the rest of Christendom of freeing Commerce of every shackle & imposition, excepting such duties as may be laid exclusively for revenue. With very great respect I am & & &, J.C. Calhoun.

ALS in ScU-SC, John C. Calhoun Papers; PC (from the London, England, *League* of 5/3/1845) in the Washington, D.C., *Daily Union*, June 7, 1845, p. 3; PC in the Washington, D.C., *Constitution*, June 9, 1845, p. 3; PC in the Raleigh, N.C., *North Carolina Standard*, June 11, 1845, p. 2; PC in the New Orleans, La., *Jeffersonian Republican*, June 16, 1845, p. 2; PC in the Milledgeville, Ga., *Federal Union*, June 17, 1845, p. 2; PC in the Columbus, Ga., *Times*, June 18, 1845, p. 2; PC in the Edgefield, S.C., *Advertiser*, June 18, 1845, p. 1; PC in the Natchez, Miss., *Mississippi Free Trader and Natchez Gazette*, June 24, 1845, p. 2; PC in the Pendleton, S.C., *Messenger*, June 27, 1845, p. 1; PC in the New York, N.Y., *National Anti-Slavery Standard*, July 31, 1845, p. 2; PC in *The Liberator*, vol. 15, no. 34 (August 22, 1845), p. 133.

To A[NDREW] P[ICKENS] CALHOUN, Faunsdale, Marengo County, Ala.

Fort Hill, 26th March 1845

My dear Andrew, I wrote you under the same date with this, and advised you to sell our cotton crop without further delay, & among other things to remit without delay the interest due Mrs. [Ann Mathewes] Ioor.

Since I sent my letter [*mutilation*; "to the"?] Post office, I have had a letter from her, by which I learn, that she had drawn on Mathew[e]s & Bonneau for the amount due & sold the draft to a merchant in Greenville, & that they had not paid it. At her request, I have given her a draft on them, to relieve her from her embarrassment, which was occasioned by her not having got my letter in time, informing her, that we would not be in funds before the end of March, & that you would remit her a draft as soon as our cotton was sold. I have written ["of" *canceled and* "under" *interlined*] this

445

date to John [Ewing] Bonneau, explaining the facts, why it was necessary for me to draw, before his firm was in funds, but that you would remit the amount to his firm without delay, to replace to my credit, the money advanced on the draft. I hope it will be done with as little delay as possible. Your affectionate father, J.C. Calhoun.

ALS in ScU-SC, John C. Calhoun Papers.

From DUFF GREEN

Washington, 26th March 1845

My dear Sir, I regret not seeing you before you left here. I had much to say of the future & of the past, and especial[l]y of Texas. [Anson] Jones & [Samuel] Houston are opposed to Annexation, but a very large majority of the people are for it.

The Resolutions of Congress propose that Texas shall surrender her public property & her customs, & retain her land & pay her debt, the federal Govt. having the right to determine her boundary. If [Thomas H.] Benton's line be assumed Texas will not have land to meet the head rights & bounty warrants now authorized & she will upon these terms have surrendered her customs & taken a debt which she cannot pay, but by her customs—this would be disgraceful to her & to the U. States. The federal Govt. assumed the debt of the old thirteen States, the debt of the Revolution[,] because the States surrendered the Customs & Texas will demand the same.

[Willie P.] Mangum [Senator from N.C.] tells me that the Whigs will now assume that the national faith is pledged & will vote for admission & the payment of the debt upon that ground. He says that they could have beaten [James K.] Polk with any other man than Mr. [Henry] Clay and that they intend to make a better choice of candidates the next time. Their ticket will, as I learn, be [John] McLean of Ohio & Mangum for Vice Pres[iden]t & I for one will go for McLean if I am compelled to choose between McLean & [Silas] Wright or any Democrat of that wing of the party.

I learn that there has been a warm discussion in the Cabinet which has resulted in selecting the [Washington] Globe as their organ, & [William A.] Harris of the Constitution told me that the President's private Secretary had asked him if he would consent to be associated with [Francis P.] Blair in the Globe and that he had assented if he could agree on the terms—one of which was that the succession should not be agitated for three years!! The Madisonian comes out and ["takes" *canceled*] says as by authority that any one who agitates the succession before three years will incur the President's displeasure.

This may be wise, but to me it ["is" *canceled*] appears that if you give Blair, Benton & Wright three years to organize and pack another convention that there will be an end of the matter. Whoever the Globe nominates will be the democratic candidate and that candidate will be defeated.

In my humble opinion the South should organize without delay. They should organize on the principle openly avowed that they would not only refuse to support any man who did not go for a repeal of the tariff and against a caucus but that they would not tolerate any man who did not. This is the crisis of the slave holding interest—to hesitate now is to be lost. You have a weighty responsibility on you. You cannot escape it. Silence on the part of your friends will be attributed to a desire to wait events and to take advantage of the chances to promote your own ambitious views. And rest assured that this is not the time for inaction. Bold, decided, uncompromising support of your measures and an unsparing war on your enemies is your true policy, whether you look to yourself or the country. For myself I do not believe there is either public or private virtue in the South to meet the crisis. Mr. [George] McDuffie betrayed the South when he quailed before Benton in the Senate. If the South makes an effort, however feeble it may be[,] I am with her, but I fear the slave holding race has become so degenerate that they have surrendered their birth right for less than a mess of pottage. Do not flatter yourself that you can retire and escape censure, unless your friends make a vigorous and uncompromising rally against the tariff & against the caucus. I will remain here some weeks & will be glad to hear from you. Your sincere friend, Duff Green.

ALS in ScCleA; PC in Boucher and Brooks, eds., *Correspondence*, pp. 287–289.

To R[OBERT] M. T. HUNTER, [Essex County, Va.]

Fort Hill, 26th March 1845

My dear Sir, I regret much, that I did not see you on my way home. I spent a day in Rhimond [*sic*; Richmond] and saw and conversed freely with all our friends, both in in [*sic*] reference to my position in relation to Mr. [James K.] Polk and his administration, & the course we ought to take in relation to the portion of the inaugural, in which he speaks of the Tariff.

Personally there is no hostile feelings towards him or his ["Cabinet" *canceled*] administration, on my part. It is no greivance [*sic*] to me, personally, that he did not invite me to remain, as one of its members. If he had, I would not have accepted, but on the condition of continuing until I had completed the Texian & Oregon ["questions" *canceled*] subjects, & that it should be announced, that I remained for that purpose, at his special request. Even then, I would have felt no little hesitation, with my impression in reference to the composition of the Cabinet and the ground taken in the inaugural on the subject of the Tariff. I hold the latter to be unsound, & the former unsafe, both in reference to the Tariff & the Oregon question. In the event of the failure of the negotiation, its influence will be thrown on the side of re[s]cinding the joint occupancy, the innevitable effects of which will be, the loss of the Territory and hostilities with England. She is desireous of settling the question, and does not want war with us; but would encounter its hazard, if we should, by re[s]cinding the Convention, make it a question of force, who should occupy it. If on the contrary, we hold on to the joint occupancy, & England should not re[s]cind it, the whole Territory must become ours by the natural progress of our population; & that in a far shorter space of time, than the most sanguine calculate. It is, indeed, the only way we can obtain the whole; and if the influence of the administration ["be" *canceled*] should be brought to bear efficiently & in the proper direction, publick sentiment might be controlled in the West, and the whole Territory secured, even if the negotiation should fail. Composed as it [the administration] is, I have no hope that it would. Thus thinking, I had no desire to remain, and felt rather relieved, than otherwise, that I was not invited to continue. In the interview, I had with ["him" *canceled and* "Mr. Polk" *interlined*] at his request, he treated me with ["the" *interlined*] greatest respect, which left nothing to disturb our personal relations. Thus much as to myself.

As to the publick, it is for ["them" *canceled and* "it" *interlined*] to decide, whether Mr. Polk's course, in reference to me, was right or wrong; & what indications it gives, as to the line of conduct he intends to pursue. To it, and my friends, I leave the decision.

It seems, indeed, strange, that one ["who had" *canceled*] who had been forced into the office in reference to two important negotiations, by the united voice of both parties, & who had brought one to a successful close, as far as it depended on him, and made satisfactory progress in the other, should without the slightest objections be superceded ["& that" *interlined*] without leaving ["time" *interlined*] to bring to a close, the duty which he had thus far successfully performed, & to the performance of which, he had been unanimously ["called" *interlined*], but a short time before. I must say, that I can see but one explanation, & that is, that I stood in the way of the restoration of the old [Andrew] Jackson Regime, both as to individuals & policy. The ground taken in the inaugural is nothing, but a repetition of Jackson's judicious Tariff, in different language. There is not a man in the Cabinet, who did not continue throughout a thorough Jackson man. If Virginia stands fast on the issue, on ["which" *canceled*] which Mr. Polk was elected ["especially in reference to the Tariff" *interlined*] the scheme will fail; otherwise it will terminate in the overthrow of the party, & the triumph of the whigs.

I explained fully to our friends in Richmond the ground we ought to occupy in reference to the portion of the inaugural, that relates to that important measure, in your pending Canvass. It will not do for us to endorse it, on the one hand, or to come, at this time, into conflict with the Administration in reference to it. Either course would be fatal. In order to avoid both, I suggested to our friends to admit frankly in the canvass, that [the] ground taken in the inaugural was not satisfactory; that to say the least it was ambegious [*sic*]; but to add, that there was no ambiguity as to their principles; that they were in favour of a revenue Tariff, with no discrimination, but on revenue principles, and with a maximum not exceeding 20 per cent; that is, in a word, in favour of the compromise. And to conclude by adding, if such was the meaning of the inaugural, they would give Mr. Polk a cordial support in car[ry]ing it out; but if not, they would be constrained to oppose his views, however reluctant; and that they would leave him to explain his ["intention" *canceled and* "meaning" *interlined*] by his acts at the next session.

I do hope, our friends have acted accordingly. On no other ground can we safely stand on this vital question. If we give away in reference to it, all will be lost. Texas, I regard as settled, unless there should be gross mismanagement, which will leave no other living question ["question" *canceled*] between the parties, but the Tariff, and those connected with it. Our friends by taking the ground firmly can control Virginia, & that will the administration. Otherwise, every thing will fall into confusion, & the whigs rise permanently into power. Our course may be ["a" *canceled*] difficult, but it is a clear one. Let what will come, ["let us" *canceled and* "we must" *interlined*] adhere to the issue on which we succeeded at the late election. Three fourths of the whole party are opposed to a protective Tariff, either inc[i]dental or direct. The movement of England towards free trade will greatly strengthen us, especially in the North West. To restore the old Jackson Van Buren party will be impossible.

I kept no journal, while in the Department of State; but will, if I shall find leisure, put down in writing the principal occurrences during the period.

I hope there is no doubt of your election. Yours truly & sincerely, J.C. Calhoun.

ALS in Vi, Robert M.T. Hunter Papers; variant PC in Charles H. Ambler, ed., *Correspondence of Robert M.T. Hunter*, pp. 75–77.

To [JAMES K. POLK], The President

Fort Hill, 26th March 1845

Dear Sir, I understand that Dr. W[illiam] A. Sparks of this State is an applicant for the place of Consul at Naples.

I am personally, but slightly acquainted with Dr. Sparks ["personally" *canceled*], but have no doubt, from the favourable opinion of Gentlemen of high respectability well acquainted with him, that his qualifications are ample for the place, & that he would fill it, should the appointment be confer[r]ed on him, in a manner, which would do credit to himself & the Government.

I have only to add, that should circumstances warrant ["justify" *interlined*] his appointment, I would be much gratified. With great respect I am & &, J.C. Calhoun.

ALS in DNA, RG 59 (State Department), Applications and Recommendations, 1845–1853, Sparks (M-873:82, frames 129–130).

From HENDRICK B. WRIGHT

Wilkes-Barré, March 26, 1845

My dear Sir, From recent developements at the Metropolis I am inclined to think, or at least fear, that my fate for the Collectorship [of Customs] of Phila. will share the fate of my friend General [Romulus M.] Saunders for the Post office department. I had intended to have asked you for a letter to the President [James K. Polk] before I left Washington, but did not like to do so for the reason that it might put you under some obligation to the appointing power, which you might not feel inclined to assume. I write you now, Sir, for a letter to the President; *but desire to be expressly understood* that if it conflicts in *any way* with with [*sic*] your course of policy not to do it. I would be exceedingly averse to throwing around you any incumberance [*sic*], when you might have a disposition to serve me in this matter even at some personal sacrafise [*sic*]. Should you be willing to write the President, (in view of what I have already said) I would regard it as a favor of much magnitude & would so remember it. I am told the ap[pointmen]t will be made in about two weeks. Very truly Yours, Hendrick B. Wright.

ALS in ScCleA. NOTE: This letter was addressed to Calhoun in Charleston and was forwarded from there to Pendleton.

From H [ENRY] GOURDIN

Charleston, March 27th 1845

My Dear Sir, You have, ere this, I trust safely reached your home, and your health and strength improving from rest, and the change to a better climate.

The news by the British Steamer is most important. Sir Robert Peel's bill of 1842 exercised a wonderful influence in our North Western States, and did more to strengthen the "free trade" party of America than any thing that could have been done at home. The present measure is decisive as to the tariff party. It will utterly destroy them, and our only danger now is, that a compromise may be forced upon us too soon, for our keen sighted brethren of New England, seeing the storm which is hanging over them, and in which their fate is involved, will endeavour to make the best bargain they can, and they know full well that the longer they delay now, the worse for them.

My object in writing to you is, to inquire the address of a Mr. Wiley, with whom you had a conversation relative to the shipment of Cotton to China. The Agricultural Society of St. John's Colleton, has placed funds in my hands to make trial of some of their Sea Island Cottons, in that m[ar]k[e]t, and I desire to obtain information as to the best mode of accomplishing it. If you can give me any information on the subject, or a letter to Mr. Wiley, if he can serve

451

us, in your opinion, I shall be obliged to you. I am Dear Sir, Very resp[ectfull]y Your Ob[edien]t S[er]v[an]t, H. Gourdin.

ALS in ScCleA.

From AUG[USTUS] A. NICHOLSON

Washington, March 28th [18]45

My dear Sir, I give you the rumour of tonight; I think it is to be relied on—[Robert J.] Walker takes the State [Department]—[James] Buchanan the vacant Bench in Penn[sylvani]a. [William L.] Marcy the Treasury. Can't Ellmore [*sic*; Franklin H. Elmore] take the War?

In great haste—the Mail closing. Respectfully & most truly Y[ou]r friend, Aug. A. Nicholson.

[P.S.] Oblige me with a letter. You know that you *can* write to me.

ALS in ScCleA. NOTE: An AEU by Calhoun reads "Maj[o]r Nicholson."

From MEMUCAN HUNT

Galveston [Texas,] 29th March 1845

My Dear Sir, I write to request your reference to our annexation resolutions which were adopted at this place on the reception of an assurance of the passage of the joint resolution, by the Congress of the United States, offering us a union—and to tender you my most hearty congratulations on the consum[m]ation, by your government, of the momentous question. We appreciate, at this place, your great agency in accomplishing this desirable end, and availed ourselves of the first op[p]ortunity, which offered, to manifest our estimate of the service you had rendered us, and to declare also our estimate of you as a private and public man.

Being desirous, at all times, to render you any service in my power, I have the honor to remain your personal & political friend, Memucan Hunt.

ALS in ScCleA.

From JOHN MARSHALL

Southern Reformer
Jackson, Mis[sissi]p[pi,] 29th March 1845

My dear sir, I assure you sir it is with more than ordinary interest that I have witnessed your course on the great question of annexation. The able manner in which you laid before congress, the details of the negotiations, & treaty, has been a source of pride and gratulation to your friends everywhere, but more especially in Mississippi. It is indeed ["to" *canceled*] the manly & independent position which you occupied before the nation that contributed to the success of the party in the presidential election; had you for a moment quailed before the quasi-advocates of anne[x]ation everything would have been lost. The next congress will be a most important assembly. The ultimate success of the great measure will depend upon its action. It cannot be lost. But is it not vitally essential that the South should be scrupulous in her election of members to that body? Should we not select men upon whose integrity we can rely in every emergency? Will not the last abolition & British struggle against us be made, and may it not be a fearful one? Vermont, Massachusetts, Ohio, and other federal States that have declared against it, cannot leave the field without making a bold and concerted attack. Another question of great magnitude presents itself. The tariff must be modified at the next session of congress. What it shall be when given to us, remains in a great measure to be decided by the South. On this question we can think of electing none but strictly revenue men. We want no discriminations for protection. We want no plea for raising money from the people for other purposes than revenue. We must meet this question as it becomes the interests of the south—the interests of the great consuming portion of the country.

I assure you, sir, that upon both these questions the democracy of Mississippi, repose the most implicit confidence in your opinion. It would afford them great satisfaction to see you again in the senate. No man we believe more capable to take the lead at the present juncture of affairs. I assure you we feel a deep & abiding interest towards you; one that will assure you of support in every emergency in which you may be placed; and I trust the time will come when we will be able to place you at the head of the affairs of the nation. In view of our approaching election, & the high favor in which you stand in our State, I trust you will not fail to lay before me the views you entertain of the importance of the questions to be decided at the next congress. I anticipate everything from their publication that can promote our success; and I hope for the good of the cause alone you will not fail to comply with my request.

With my best wishes for your health & happiness, allow me to remain your devoted friend, John Marshall.

ALS in ScCleA. NOTE: John Marshall (*ca.* 1812–1862) was a native of Va. but not closely related to Chief Justice John Marshall. He was at this time editor of the Jackson *Southern Reformer* and later of the Jackson *Mississippian.* About 1854 he moved to Texas and became editor of the Austin, Tex., *State Gazette.*

From ENOCH E. CAMP

New York [City], March 30, 1845
Most Respected Sir, The state of public opinion is now better prepared, than at any other period, for your friends to commence action in this State and the east. Were I intimate, or even partially acquainted with those who feel as I feel, I should address this letter to them and not to you, as it would be better fitting their ear than yours. All that is necessary to secure the confident support and prompt action of thousands of the honest, young democracy of this city and State, is the establishment of a daily press, about the size of the "New York Herald," through which their views and opinions can be inculcated and a complete organization effected for 1848. Mr. [James G.] Bennett is opposed to the selection of *my choice* for the Presidency, and as he leaves for Europe in a few weeks, this is the favorable period to commence the enterprize. My long experience and full practical knowledge of the business is such, that with capital sufficient to sustain it six months, I could, after that period, render it profitable and lucrative to those who had started the enterprize. Now is the time, before the new Common Council come into power—before the offices ["and printing" *interlined*] are distributed and while the Texas and oregon questions are yet unsettled.

As I am one of but few words, and feel the necessity of prompt action, either let this letter be placed in the hands of some one who can stir up the proper feeling and address me at once. Being a practical printer, I can issue the first number in a week's notice, and my almost ["universal" *canceled*] universal acquaintance is such that I can command all the able political talent of the city—except the *rankest* old Hunkers—[*two words canceled.*]

I will guarantee with the sum of $5,000 to place such a press on solid, permanent footing in less than six months from commencement. With respects to Mr. [Richard K.] Crallé, I remain, sir, Yours, Enoch E. Camp.

[P.S.] (Address at Herald office).

ALS in ScCleA. NOTE: This letter is addressed to Calhoun in Charleston with an AEU on the cover sheet that reads: "If Mr. C[alhoun] is not at Charleston, will P[ost] M[aster] please forward to his residence." Camp began publishing the long-lived *National Police Gazette* in 1845.

To [WILLIAM W.] CO[R]C[O]RAN & [GEORGE W. RIGGS], Bankers, Washington

Fort Hill, 30th March 1845

Sirs, Mrs. Calhoun, before I left Washington, went on to Philadelphia with our youngest daughter [Martha Cornelia Calhoun], to take the advice of [Dr. Thomas D. Mutter] an eminent Physician of that City in reference to her case, expecting to return in time to accompany me home. The case of our daughter required her to be detained much longer than we calculated, & it is still uncertain when the state of her health will permit her to return. In consequence, the sum that was supposed, to be ample to meet her expense, has proved to be insufficient, which compels me to ask the favour of you to accept & pay her draft on you for a sum not exceeding $300, should she find it necessary to draw on you. I will make arrangement to return, ["it" *canceled*] at an early day, whatever you may advance. With great respect I am & &, J.C. Calhoun.

ALS in DLC, Riggs Family Papers. NOTE: Calhoun addressed this letter to "Messrs. Cocran & Briggs."

From F[RANCIS] W. PICKENS

Edgewood [S.C.], 30 March 1845

My dear Sir, We arrived home [to Edgefield District] a few days ago and found all well. Mrs. [Marion Dearing] Pickens suffered very much from the traveling home & exposure, it being very cold with ice in Ala: & the stages rough.

I rec[eive]d your letters on my return and feel rejoiced that you are now free from all responsibility not by your act but by the acts of others who now have the power of the Gov[ernment] in their hands. It is better for you & will be better for your fame. Office can confer no power on you or your name. I take it for granted from the inaugural & the Cabinet that [James K.] Polk is preparing to break down the Tariff of 1842 by tactics & organization rather than by boldness or decission [*sic*]. I suppose his object will be to detach Pennsylvania from N[ew] York & the ["the" *canceled*] other tariff States & thus divide them, and that [Robert J.] Walker [Secretary of the Treasury] is appointed from the old [Andrew] Jackson party & from his connexions in Pennsylvania & position in Mississippi to head the Fiscal opperations [*sic*] of the Gov[ernment] so as to effect his gen[e]r[a]l purpose of dividing the Tariff party itself. With that view I suppose he will move to detach the iron interest by protecting it & bearing upon the other interests so as to relieve the cotton or exporting States by reducing taxes on most things except iron. I suppose [William L.] Marcy [Secretary of War] is taken to divide New York politics & thus balance that State by equal parties within her own borders. ["Marcy" *canceled*.] Marcy was conservative & went off from [Martin] V[an] B[uren] in 1837 with [Ephraim H.?] Foster[,] Beardsley &c.

The danger of all this is that it will fail and then the Adm[inist]r[ation] will sink into imbecility & contempt. As far as will & high purpose is concerned it is an ordinary Cabinet. Walker has more than any. It may be that the country is so corrupt that it is not able to bear any thing higher. If so nothing but a ["conf"(?) *canceled*] convulsion can save us. I never saw such indifference as prevails in Ala: & Geo[rgia]. The excitement of last Fall is followed by a perfect paralysis. Even the admission of Texas produced no sensation.

I understood from our friends in Montgomery [Ala.], who said they heard it from [James E.] Belser & [Dixon H.] Lewis, that you were perfectly satisfied with every thing and that all would come right. I trust in God it may be so, but things look to me like it was going to be a very ordinary Adm[inist]r[ation]. It may be that by their politic system they may succeed in their results, as the country is so far sunk as to be prepared to bear nothing more at present. But I fear they will sink in a year into perfect impotency. I dread this at least.

I have just rec[eive]d a letter from Columbia which states [Franklin H.] Elmore is to go to England.

I rec[eive]d two letters from Mr. [Thomas G.] Clemson on my return home. They were well & in one which he appears to intend for publication he seems to dread any thing like disunion as he sees what is the feeling ag[ain]st us in Europe &c.

I did not see Andrew [Pickens Calhoun] while in Ala: as I had no time and the roads were utterly impassible [*sic*]. I heard he was very well. Arthur Simkins just left here yesterday and is sued or about to be for what he owes in the purchase of lands from men who are themselves under executions &c. He made certain & unqualified promises by the 1st Jan[uar]y from what Mr. Clemson told him as to his payment from Andrew. He wrote to Andrew who told him he might calculate with certainty on it by the 10th Jan[uar]y but afterwards wrote he could not remit as cotton was too low. He has not heard since although he wrote to send it back by me. Arthur came and put the mortgage of Clemson's place in the hands of an Att[orne]y yesterday to foreclose it immediately as he was compel[l]ed to do so to save his own property & the property of those whom he owed. I interposed & got him to wait until Monday (Tomorrow) week Sale day. He says he will wait no longer & if so the place will be sold in three months. I write to let you know about it as Mr. Clemson put it somewhat under my charge until last December when he said you or John [C. Calhoun, Jr.] would then take charge of it. I do not know what to do. You know even if Andrew did not wish to sell he could take an advance on his cotton. Arthur went into Bank with my name so as to keep off things up to the present time, but the Bank debt becomes due in 20 days from this.

I am glad you went by the Canebreak. You see that the Overseer left it while I was gone to Ala: & another [Bland] was employed. The man Mr. Clemson got I told him I had no confidence in his integrity, but Mr. C[lemson] seemed to be perfectly delighted with him, & has writ[t]en back confiding every thing to his judgment & care. So much so that he left a book with him and particular memoranda of every little thing he would [have] done on the place, and his last letter is full of directions to me about building & manuring & stock, which if it were properly attended to strictly would prevent a crop almost. I will do what I can as a friend cheerfully, but I fear he is so particular that he will be greatly disappointed as I have no time to attend at all to details. I can scarcely see to my own business. There ought to be three more mules on the place to work it right. I should be very glad if John could take charge of it.

His being on the plantation would make a great difference. I have written Mr. Clemson about the matter, & shall write in a few days again. I understand Cousin Floride [Colhoun Calhoun] did not return with you. Very truly & sincerely, F.W. Pickens.

ALS in ScCleA.

From H[aym] M. Salomon

New york [City,] March 30, [18]45

Dear Sir, I did not receive any reply to my last letter of enquiry directed to your chief clerck [Richard K. Crallé] while yet in Washington. It must have been owing to his press of business.

This is now to say that the great progect for the good of the country and your future fame is *yet on the tapis* confidentially between me and the ["others" *altered to* "other"] Principal[.] After writing me only one letter expressing confidentially your own mature ["&" *interlined*] deliberate reflection on this subgect Then, you will see the propriety of procuring some highly honourable—influcntial—and persevering friend at the south to whom you will make known my progect and the fact of its actually being entertained as desirable and salutary for the nation by the old Head and Chief of the —— party to whom I had made the first proposition—as well as to his Confident—which gentleman to whom you communicate at the South must act for your Interests and be the correspondent with me.

Thus you will have me in the centre, The sole recipient of the plans and actions of both the parties to the greatest of political atchievments yet attempted in this country[.]

One of our papers says that you are writing a Book, "a History of your times" if you will take the advise of an old and disinterested friend. Publish *nothing* until our progect has its determination—I will of course give you notice. When you do print a Book, let *every* speach you have delivered from *the beginning* of your public life be inserted. There is not one (no flattery to you) but what may be compared with no disadvantage to yours, to the highest speciments of demosthenian oratory. With the greatest respect I am as ever your Faithful friend, H.M. Salomon.

P.S. I have never yet heard from the late President [John Tyler] about many autograph testimonials which I was to have had returned.

Is not my fate most Singular as a politician tho' the last appellation perhaps does not exactly apply to one so often regardless of policy as to effects on his own interests. With claims and testimonials unprecedented as to force and truth and the reading of which caused the last President to make me three *promises*—added to which your constant defender and supporter politically for nearly Thirty years—and am up to this day without ever having received one cent of government patronage[.] On looking the other day over some old scraps of former times I found that when you were Vice P[resident] you gave me a letter to Mr. [Samuel D.] Ingham who was of the then Cabinet but by the time I arrived at Washington (only a few days) he had been removed[.]

I have not the satisfaction of being personally known now to *any* of the S.C. delegation or to the President [James K. Polk] or one of his present Cabinet.

ALS in ScCleA.

From BEN E. GREEN

Washington, March 31st 1845

Dear Sir, I met Mr. [Charles A.] Wickliffe this evening at the cars, as he was about leaving for Kentucky, and he requested me to write to you & enquire whether the despatch to Mr. [Wilson] Shannon, which was read, corrected and approved of in Cabinet council, about a week or ten days previous to the inauguration was ever sent. No traces of it remain in the Department, and Mr. Wickliffe says he has learned that some difficulty will be made about it. He also requested me to ask you to write to Judge [John Y.] Mason about it.

There is nothing new here beyond what you see in the papers. Yours truly, Ben E. Green.

ALS in ScCleA. NOTE: Mason, who had been Secretary of the Navy under Tyler, continued in Polk's Cabinet as Attorney General.

By Dr. William L. Jenkins, [Pendleton], 4/1. Jenkins recorded in his daybook services rendered to the Calhoun household: "Hon. John C. Calhoun. To extracting Tooth [of a] Woman (Jane) [$]1.50." Entry in ScCM, Waring Historical Library, William L. Jenkins Daybook, 1840–1848, p. 43.

From HENRY NEILL

Philadelphia, April 1st 1845

Respected Sir, Although I have not the honor of ["your acquaintance" *canceled*] being personally known to you, yet my great admiration of your political opinions, and the very masterly manner in which you defended yourself from the joint attack of two of our most eminent statesmen ([Henry] Clay & [Daniel] Webster,) together with the ability with which you have made it manifest that a National Bank was a National Evil, and the improper extension & continuance of the protective system, ["an injustice not to be borne," *interlined*] induce me to hope you will forgive the liberty I have taken in addressing you. The publication of your speeches I consider a standard volume of best political opinions that have been presented to our country, and I have no doubt thier [*sic*] influence on the rising Generation will be such as to bring increasing respect to your memory long after you & I have been laid in our graves.

I was very much disappointed that Mr. [James K.] Poalk [*sic*] did not invite you (if he did not) to continue in the office of Secretary of State, taking into consideration the important services you have rendered to your Country. I owe you many apologies for writing thus to a perfect stranger, but ever since I read your speeches on the great points of political controversy, I have longed to become acquainted with you, and had at one time almost determined to make a visit to Washington for the sole purpose of making your acquaintance.

If you had been there as a private citizen, instead of an influential officer under Government the inducement would have been greater, as it would be difficult to do such an act without subjecting oneself to the suspicion of sinister motives. You are now in the retirement of private life, and no motive connected with office seeking can be suspected.

You are in the decline of life as well as myself, I was born on the 12th of March 1783, like you descended from Irish parentage, our Grand-Fathers being both born in Ireland.

It remains that I should tell you who I am. A Marylander who received his medical education at the University of Pennsylv[ani]a and after graduation married & settled in Philad[elphi]a where I have remained a practitioner of medicine to the present time.

Should you honor me with an answer to this letter I should be glad to know your opinion with respect to the Naturalization Laws, I have considered 5 years long enough if the law was faithfully executed. With the greatest admiration for your public character, I subscribe myself your's very respectfully, Henry Neill, M.D., 140 S. fourth St., Philad[elphi]a.

ALS in ScCleA.

To [FRANCIS W. PICKENS, Edgefield District, S.C.]

Fort Hill, 1st April 1845

My dear Sir, I do not think the object of Mr. [James K.] Polk in the formation of his Cabinet was such as you suppose. I am of the impression, that he does not contemplate the ["adjustment" *with* "ment" *interlined*] of the Tariff as a part of his system of policy; but on the contrary, ["it is" *interlined*] to take, under another name, Gen[era]l [Andrew] Jackson's position of a judicious Tariff, as a mid[d]le ground between the free trade party and the advocates of the protective system. He intends, ["indeed," *canceled*] his administration, as a continuation, if I may so say, of the Jackson dynasty; and has accordingly framed it altogether of individuals, who stuck to Gen[era]l Jackson to the last. It was formed in Tennessee before he left home; but considerably changed after his arrival at Washington. A highly respectable Senator told me he saw the list, in Gen[era]l Jackson's hand writing. It consisted of [James] Buchanan for the State Dept.[, Azariah C.] Flagg[,] one of the Albany Regency[,] for the Treasury, [Andrew] Stevenson of Virginia for the War, [George] Bancroft for the Navy, [Cave] Johnson for the Post Office & [Robert J.] Walker Attorney General. The changes were forced on him. His appointments clearly prove, that he intends to give the influence to the wing of the party, which was defeated at Baltimore.

There must be some mistake on the part of our Montgomery [Ala.] friends, in saying that I approved of the arrangement of the Cabinet, on the authority of [Dixon H.] Lewis [Senator from Ala.] & Belcher [*sic*; James E. Belser, former Representative from Ala.]. I said little on that subject, for reasons which are obvious; and what little I did say, was to intimate friends. Lewis knows I was not, nor is he, or scarcely any other Southern man. The error probably originated in their saying, that as far as I was concerned personally, I was satisfied. I was rather relieved, than otherwise, in not being invited to continue, as I could not have remained with what I conceived to be the object of Mr. Polk's policy, had I been invited. Had I been,

461

I could not have retired without incur[r]ing the displeasure of a large portion of my friends, without assig[n]ing my reasons, & I could not have done that, without deeply offending the administration. As it is, I retired without giving offence to any one or incur-[r]ing any responsibility.

I stopt a day in Richmond, where I saw al[l] our prominent friends, and had much conversation with them & Mr. [Thomas] Ritchie. I foun[d] things in a very statisfactory [*sic*] state there, especially on the free trade subject. You see their address to the people of Virginia, signed by Ritchie, takes sound ground on that vital question. That & the movements in Parliament, will give great prominence to the question at the next session. It is then the battle will have to be fought. I hope the whole South will back Virginia in her position.

But to drop politicks & return to private matters. I can not but be greatly surprised at what you write, as to the course which Arthur Simkins threatens to take, on the mortgage. Arthur wrote to me on the subject ["of the instalment during the winter" *interlined*] & I informed him, if my memory serves me[,] that Andrew [Pickens Calhoun] had been at Mobile & found cotton selling as low as 4½ cents, and that he found it impossible to obtain ["an" *interlined*] advance on his cotton, in consequence of the heavy advances, which the factors had made to the planters whose crops had not come down from the low state of the river or other causes. I wrote to him, not to sell, unless he could get six cents, until the ["market" *canceled and* "month of" *interlined*] March, as I felt satisfied there would be an advance in the price. I was confident that Great Britain would be compelled to repeal the duty on cotton & hoped, that the March Packet would ["bring" *interlined*] intelligence of the fact. I said in my letter to Arthur, that he must indulge us under such circumstances, until we could sell, which would be in March. I heard nothing from him & concluded, that he had acqui[e]sced in the arrangement. I would have sent for him the day I spent at the Cane Brake; but understood his wife [Mary Bonham Simkins] was at the point of death, to converse with him on the subject. Under such circumstances I cannot [*the remainder of this letter is missing.*]

ALU (fragment) in ScU-SC, John C. Calhoun Papers; variant PC in "Letters from John C. Calhoun to Francis W. Pickens," in *South Carolina Historical and Genealogical Magazine*, vol. VII, no. 1 (January, 1906), pp. 12–14. NOTE: At some later time Pickens added several marginal notations to this letter. The first was written in response to Calhoun's initial comments on Polk's tariff policy and reads "How little verified by the facts afterwards." A second notation referring to Polk's patronage and Cabinet appointments reads "How totally at variance with the facts—[William L.] Marcy Sec[re]t[ar]y of war—a bitter opponent of [Martin] Van Buren." A final notation adjacent to the mention in the third paragraph of the address to the people of Virginia reads "written by Mr. Calhoun." The "Address of the Democratic Central Committee, to the People of Virginia" was printed in the Richmond, Va., *Enquirer*, March 25, 1845, pp. 2–3, and was signed by Thomas Ritchie. Pickens's somewhat spiteful statement that Calhoun was the author of this document seems doubtful. The address, which fills five and a half newspaper columns, does not resemble Calhoun's style at all and the bulk of it is taken up with a detailed criticism of the behavior of members of the Whig party in Virginia in the legislature and on the hustings, in regard to the Texas question. However, it is certainly possible or even likely that Calhoun had some input into the beginning and the conclusion of the document. These state explicitly that the Whig party has always represented consolidationist principles and is now also tainted with abolitionism, and that Southern Whig leaders have allowed party discipline to force them into betrayal of Southern interests. Mary Bonham Simkins, wife of Arthur Simkins, died on March 21, 1845.

From JOHN BRODHEAD

Philadelphia, April 2, 1845

My dear Sir, If an apology is necessary for the frank expression of sentiments of the highest esteem and admiration then, Sir, I ask one for this letter.

Some two or three years ago, after a conversation with several young fellow members of the bar, I determined to address you, and make known to you how dearly your name was cherished by many of our fellow citizens in this Northern State, and how anxious thousands were that you should become the nominee of the Democratic Convention, but my humble situation, and the fear of transgressing deterred me. However, ever since that time I have been influenced by a desire to write to you. Shortly before your being chosen by Pres[iden]t [John] Tyler Secretary of State, I was about to address you, but then I feared my motives would be misconstrued and I determined to be silent. But now that you are once more, thro', in my view, a mistaken policy of Mr. [James K.] Polk's, a private citizen, with no offices to dispense and no favors to ask, I can at least have one admirable character with my letter—disinterestedness.

I am a Pennsylvanian—a native of the "banner" county Pike. Up to the age of 16, I read of you and thought of you as a sort of monster, a most hideous enemy to your country; such was the prejudiced and unjust character of the works that came before my eyes, and the speeches that fell upon my ears. But since I have become able to think for myself—to read and reflect upon all sides of a question, how different my opinion of you, and what delights me as much, how changed the ideas of the masses.

For the last two years I have made it a point of asking the opinion of every one with whom I conversed on political subjects, and the men of our nation, as to the merits of John C. Calhoun, and, it is great happiness for me to declare, that I met very few democrats with whom you were not a favorite, very many who spoke of you, as I always must, with the greatest enthusiasm—and no Whig but who expressed great respect for you.

In the State of New York I found "Calhoun men," with sentiments like my own. In the County of Orange especially did it seem to me you were very popular.

It is evident from this that a straight forward, high minded unbending course, altho' it may for a season thro' the influence of wire-working demagogues render one abused and unpopular, yet, as the old hero says "Truth is mighty and will prevail," and honesty of purpose is sure to triumph—it finally will receive its reward.

Your late course in regard to the Texas question, your letter to Mr. [William R.] King &c—altho' snarled at by some of our *democratic* papers is beginning to be properly appreciated.

And I trust and believe that should Heaven spare you long enough, that the American People will do Justice to her brightest son.

I pray you, Sir, excuse the incoherent and imperfect manner in which I have expressed myself, and believe me, that there is not one sentiment however coarsely uttered that does not find a place in my heart.

Of course, this letter is written for your eye alone—and I am sorry that it is not more worthy of your notice. But it is truthful altho' homely, and it comes from your friend and ob[edien]t ser[van]t, John Brodhead.

[P.S.] I am a young man, and before the present generation is 10 years older, a new set of men will be on the political carpet. My first vote went for James K. Polk—my next went [*sic*], if opportunity occurs will go for John C. Calhoun.

ALS in ScCleA. NOTE: This letter was addressed to Calhoun "Near Charleston," S.C., with a request to the Postmaster to forward it to Calhoun's residence.

To JOHN A[LFRED] CALHOUN, Eufaula, Barbour County, Ala.

Fort Hill, 2d April 1845

My dear John, Your letter received by yesterday[']s mail, gave me the first intelligence I had of the death [on 3/11] of your good mother [Sarah Caldwell Martin (Mrs. James) Calhoun]. It deeply affected me, notwithstanding the reflection, that it must be to her a happy deliverance from her long affliction. Few have been more afflicted, and none ever ["bore" *interlined*] such affliction with greater fortitude.

It is, indeed, melancholy to witness the departure of one after another of our early acquaintances. I am now the last survivor of the first generation after the emigrants on my father's side, except Alex[ande]r Calhoun, & old aunt Gellium [*sic*; Elizabeth Caldwell Gillam] the last on my mother's side. I saw ["her" *interlined*] on my way from Washington, at the residence of her son's Gen[era]l [James] Gellium [Gillam]. She is 87 years of age. Her memory is almost entirely gone. Our family on the father's side emigrated in 1733. The in[ter]val is a long period to be filled up, with 2 generations.

I felt not the slightest dissatisfaction because Mr. [James K.] Polk did not see proper to invite me to remain in his cabinet. On the contrary, it was rather a relief. Had he invited me, I could not, on principle, have remained in ["it" *interlined*] with my impression of what is to be the course of his policy, both as to the Tariff and the Oregon question, in the event of the failure of the negotiation, now pending to settle it. I fear, that if not settled by treaty, the policy of the administration will be to re[s]cind the joint occupancy. If so, it will not improbably lead to the loss of the Territory to be followed by hostilities with England, which may be avoided & the territory secured, if the opposite policy, of hold-on to the joint occupancy be adopted. Had I been invited to remain, I could not have retired, without offending a large portion of my friends without assigning my reasons; nor could I have assigned them, without offending the administration. As it is, I retire without offence to any one, or incurring any responsibility.

Publick employment is no way necessary to my happiness. I do not even miss it. My time is fully and agreeably employed. My old attachment to agricultural pursuits is not in the least abated.

It is too late for me to think of commencing the History, to which you allude. If I write any thing, it will be on the elementary princi-

465

ples of political science, preliminary to a discourse on the Constitution of the U. States.

My ["publick" *interlined*] course will require no vindication with posterity. *Time* will be my vindicator. The truths, which I have stood by, however obscure at present, will shine forth under its clear developement of that powerful ["advocate" *interlined*].

I hope you & your family continue to enjoy good health. Mine is completely restored. Give my love to Mrs. [Sarah Norwood] Calhoun & family. Your affectionate Uncle, J.C. Calhoun.

ALS in ScU-SC, John C. Calhoun Papers.

To "Col." JAMES ED[WARD] COLHOUN, [Abbeville District, S.C.]

Fort Hill, 5th April 1845

My dear Sir, The letters to, which you refer in your note of the 20th March [*not found*] were all received & forwarded as you desired, of which you were informed by a letter written before I left Washington, and which I hope you have since the date of your note received. I should regret its miscarriage, as it contained a good deal of private matter, not intended for the publick.

I wrote you since I returned home, in answer to yours, about the claim of the estate on the U. States, information of which you got from the editor of the Courier. I hope you have got my letter.

I expected your Sister [Floride Colhoun Calhoun] this week. She wrote me, that she would be at Aikein [*sic*] on the 1st April, and I accordingly sent down the Carriage to meet her, but the next day after it left, I got a letter from her, stating that Cornelia's [Martha Cornelia Calhoun's] spinal affection began to effect her general health, & to show symptoms of rather an alarming character, and that it was quite uncertain, when she would be able to leave.

William Lowndes [Calhoun] has got entirely over the Measels, & joins his love to you. Yours affectionately, J.C. Calhoun.

ALS in ScCleA.

From C[HARLES] J. INGERSOLL,
[Representative from Pa.]

Philad[elphia], April 5, [18]45

Dear Sir, Owing to the hackman disappointing me the morning I was to leave Washington, after I took leave of you the evening before, I did not get off as expected and therefore thought it best instead of carrying the letter you gave me for Mrs. [Floride Colhoun] Calhoun, to mail it to her address here. She told me when I called on her that it was attended by no inconvenience. I intended to write and explain to you why I happened not to be the bearer of the letter but Mrs. C[alhoun] made it unnecessary.

Last Evening your warm adherent and my worthy friend John Hastings of Ohio passed an hour with me on his way home from Washington where he thinks things are in an unsettled state. I have no correspondents there so that I know not much more than the Newspapers publish. I have no doubt that your policy as to Texas and our foreign relations generally particularly as regards England will be persevered in: as to Oregon I am not so sure as I think Mr. [James] Buchanan did hold a different opinion.

The next Session of Congress will disclose many curious and striking circumstances in the distribution of parties and course of Events. I consider it uncertain where the majority will be found in either house.

The interval from now to then is the first holiday I have had for several years from the wasting distractions of continual party contests, and I mean to turn my back on them while I employ my time much more profitably and pleasantly in finishing the first Volume already nearly done of a historical sketch of the war of 1812 whose philosophical influences duly explained on the legislation, jurisprudence[,] finances, economy and all other elements of republican government may be rendered as striking and more instructive than its military exploits and reverses[?].

However employed I shall always cherish a lively sense of the times of political association in which nearly always from the period of that conflict till the present I have always lived in harmony with you and remain with sincerity your friend, C.J. Ingersoll.

ALS in ScCleA. NOTE: Ingersoll published *Historical Sketch of the Second War between the United States of America, and Great Britain, Declared by Act of Congress, the 18th of June, 1812, and Concluded by Peace, the 15th of February, 1815* (2 vols. Philadelphia: Lea and Blanchard, 1845–1849).

To JAMES BUCHANAN, Sec[re]t[ar]y of State

Fort Hill, 6th April [1845]
Dear Sir, I omitted to mention to you, that I had authorised Our minister ["at Paris" *interlined*], Mr. [William R.] King, to spend out of the contingent fund a sum not exceeding $500 for the purpose of disseminating correct information in reference to our Government & its views & policy, in order to counteract, at that important center of European intelligence and diplomacy the gross misrepensations [*sic*] which daily go forth as all that relates to the Government & the country. I have suggested to him, that it would be the most advisable course for him to draw on the Department for whatever sum he might find necessary not exceeding that allowed. With great respect I am & &, J.C. Calhoun.

ALS in DNA, RG 59 (State Department), Accounting Records: Miscellaneous Letters Received.

From LEWIS S. CORYELL

Washington, 6th Apr[il] 1845
My dear Sir, It seems dreary here without you. I came at the especial instance of my friend [John P.] Heiss who I have for a long time been encouraging to establish an organ for the Govt. and [due] to his indomitable perseverence the desirable object will be effected. When the attempt failed to procure Donnoldson [*sic*; Andrew J. Donelson], the Globe was *almost* selected, but Heiss was indefatagable & I obligated to supply the means to either establish a new press or buy out the Madisonian [and] Constitution, which made him more firm, and [James K.] Polk at last selected old Tom [Thomas] Ri[t]chie, and Heiss paid him a Visit and after much pursuasion he came up here, had an interview with the Pres[ident] and agreed &C & the Pres[iden]t then sent for [Francis P.] Blair & told him that he had been elected upon issues that forbid that the Globe c[oul]d be the organ &C &C & after much talk, reflection & *feeling* Blair yesterday agreed to sell his types and fixtures at a price to be agreed upon by a man chosen by each party & they to fix on a third man in case of disagreement and on Tuesday they commence the Inventory so now you see, what I began long ago is about to be realized. We have gained a great Point in dismissing Blair & [John C.] Rives but I am far from being satisfied with Ri[t]chie, and the

Pres[iden]t holds open a place in the concern for Donnoldson. [William] Selden Tr[easure]r advances Ri[t]chie $13,000. I procure all Heiss needs. My opinion is that the Constitution will have to be purchased or they will divide the Congress printing.

Gen[era]l [Simon] Cameron our new Senator [from Pa.] is with *us* and he will influence [James] Buchanan instead of vice versa. The reason Cameron was elected was [George W.] Woodward had the caucus machinery in his favor, was a devoted Bentonian, and in convention proposed 21 years probation & never to hold office in Penn[sylvani]a by a foreigner, so you see he was heavy on their necks & they let the election of Cameron take place as the only way to get rid of Woodward. Cameron will be perfectly orthodox in all his votes, except the Tariff, nor will he be very obstinate on that point.

Polk has a timid Cabinet—& we have carried this project in the absence of Buck [James Buchanan] & [George] Bancroft who are away.

I mean to have a full talk with Polk and as I want no office I will speak the plain language to him.

I dined with Mrs. [Floride Colhoun] Calhoun yesterday. She goes home Tuesday, but I will send this by mail as she may be detained on the way.

You have vastly improved your estimation while Sec[retar]y of State, and lost nothing by your retiring. Indeed the impression abroad is, that you will have to be recalled to finnish up negociations already begun.

If you write me direct to me at New Hope[,] Penn[sylvani]a. Y[ou]r f[rien]d Sincerely, Lewis S. Coryell.

[P.S.] Cameron is y[ou]r devoted fr[ien]d. You remember the talk we had together with him & [Benjamin H.] Brewster.

ALS in ScCleA; variant PEx in Boucher and Brooks, eds., *Correspondence*, pp. 291–292.

From JAMES S. LANE

Saint Louis Mo., Ap[ri]l 6th [1845]

My dear Sir, After a severe political struggle we find it impossible in this part of the Union to ascertain whether any thing has been achieved for the benefit of *Sound* Democracy or not.

For a series of years a small portion of the party has had but little confidence in Col. [Thomas H.] Benton and for the last three bold and vigorous efforts have been made to place Missouri on the true ground. Although we were unable to prevent his re-election to the Senate in consequence of the timidity and treachery of a few of the Members of our Legislature, pledged to vote against him, yet we are by no means discouraged or irresolute.

The high ground assumed by yourself on the Texas and other questions, has enabled us to rally the Democracy with enthusiasm in favor of true American principles and in such a way as to diminish the confidence of the masses still more in Col. Benton[']s political integrity.

It is impossible in one letter to explain the exact position of affairs in this State or to analyse the elements at work to effect a complete political regeneration here. But I can assure you that Col. Benton[']s power is rapidly declining and nothing can save him from a total overthrow but the influence of the Federal administration.

Should President [James K.] Polk determine to use the power conferred on him by the Democracy of the Union to fasten upon the Country again the Benton and [Martin] Van Buren dynasty, the Democrats in Missouri who have heretofore fought gallantly against that cabal, will once more enter the field and under more favorable circumstances than before, to make Missouri in political matters what she should be—a Southern State.

To effect this important result we are anxious that as far as the Federal Government can effect this State its influence shall be neutralized, if it cannot be secured for right principles.

We have here a young gentleman who has been among the first and foremost in the contest against the Benton influence for the last three years. Col. Benton endeavored to procure his services at the commencement of the conflict and although the Col. was then in the height of his power—that young gentleman spurned the overtures made and repelled them personally by an insult which would not be brooked. The gentleman to whom I refer is Samuel Treat Esq[ui]r[e] of this City. As the associate Editor of the Missouri Reporter, he has written more and labored harder than any man west of the Allegheny Mountains to destroy the ascendency of Col. Benton. For months at a time and at the most critical moments he has had the Sole charge of that Paper. During the eventful period from Nov. 1843 until the Baltimore Convention had settled down against Mr. Van Buren and again during the late session of Congress, he was compelled (Mr. [Shadrach] Penn being absent) to strike out a course for the Reporter and to pursue it, without assistance or counsel from others. What that course was and what the ability displayed, you probably have the means of deciding.

His exertions as editor, were equalled by his boldness, enthusiasm & eloquence as a popular speaker.

On all important occasions when the strongest supporters of Col. Benton or the ablest Whigs ["were" *interlined*] brought forward, he was called upon to meet them on the Hustings. He canvassed several counties, speaking daily to large crowds and throughout the conflict here and elsewhere spared no pains either as Editor or popular speaker to maintain the right, against Bentonism and Whiggery. Such is the man for whom we wish to procure the appointment of Chargé at some European Court.

If we can succeed in this measure our cause will be greatly strengthened. We can then bring a moral power to bear in its behalf which we have heretofore been unable to exert. He will be strengthened for the new contest and additional weight given to his actions.

If it were necessary he could procure the signatures of nearly all educated men in this part of the Country to a petition for this purpose but he has too much pride & self respect to take such a step himself or to suffer others to take it for him.

At the same time his circumstances are such as to require that he should receive such an appointment—the only one he will accept, or withdraw from political life altogether. He has a family dependent upon him and for its sake he must devote himself for the future to some profitable employment unless his services to the country can be secured in the way indicated. He is now in the vigor of early manhood—was educated at Harvard University—read Law in New York and was for some time at the head of a Literary Institution in that State—and since he has been in Missouri has been employed in public affairs as an Editor.

His health is somewhat impaired although he labors as much as any man in Saint Louis.

The question for us to decide here is, shall we aid him and ourselves by securing for him an appointment worthy of his intellectual abilities and attainments and commensurate with his political services? To accomplish our purposes it is necessary that those with whom we have co-operated and with whom we intend to co-operate hereafter, should assist us in this enterprise. We may encounter the determined opposition of Col. Benton in it whenever he shall ascertain our designs, but if we can induce our friends elsewhere to unite with us, we can succeed.

It may be that you will feel some delicacy in requesting any appointment for a friend, but permit me to suggest that the times require that no honorable efforts for the country should be left untried. It is earnestly desired therefore that you should address Col. Polk in reference to this matter.

It has been the uniform policy of Col. Benton to prevent any Missourian from receiving a general appointment from the Federal Government. No one from this State has ever been honored by promotion to even as high an office as Chargé with one exception [Vespasian Ellis] and that was under the administration of President [John] Tyler. That gentleman has been recalled. Now Missouri has no one in a high station. It can therefore be asked with propriety that Mr. Treat should receive the appointment desired. The growing trade of the West seems to demand that a Chargé to some of the German Courts should be a western man say to the Hague [*sic*] but I would not confine my request to any one of them.

We wish to acquire the moral and political power which the elevation of Mr. Treat would give. We wish it for the sake of sound principles of the country. His firmness and ability have been tried. His qualifications for the post of Chargé are indisputable. He deserves all that it is in the power of the Anti-Van Buren Democracy to bestow—and if they do not cheerfully assist this movement then we have no inducement to labor hereafter. All that is expected or sought, is that friends should mutually aid and strengthen each other.

In Missouri we have more to contend against than in any other State in the Union and if we can succeed in this appointment we shall be ready for the onset.

I have written to you freely so that you might be in possession of the facts and views of those who co-operate here with your friends in other States.

The Office of Chargé is not local and consequently there can be no [*one word canceled*] objection to exertions out of Missouri in behalf of Mr. Treat. Your friend & Serv[an]t, James S. Lane.

ALS in ScCleA.

To Henry Wheaton, [Berlin]

Fort Hill, 6th April 1845

My dear Sir, Your letter of the 29th Jan[uar]y found me a private citizen, at my residence ["here" *interlined*]. Mr. [James K.] Polk did not see proper to invite me to remain, which permitted me to return, freed of all responsibility, to a retirement, which I had left with great reluctance, at the unanimous call of the country, to take charge of the Texian & Oregon negotiations. The one I have concluded, & the other I have left in a fair way.

I greatly regret, that no opportunity was afforded me of giving you more substantial proof of the high estimate I place on your talents & services, than the mere expression of my opinion.

At the session preceeding [*sic*] the last, Congress withheld all appropriations for outfits for ministers, except the three that were vacant; to Paris, to Rieo [*sic*; Rio de Janeiro] & Mexico, with an understanding, that all appointments which should be made without outfits, should be rejected, unless in case of a vacancy in the recess. During the last session ample appropriations were made, but not until just ["before" *interlined*] the close of the session, and with the understanding, that the appoin[t]ments should be made by the incoming administration.

All I could do, I did, to call your long & faithful services & great experience as a negotiator to the attention of my successor [James Buchanan], with a strong expression of my hope, that they would [be] duely appreciated by the President [James K. Polk]. What policy the administration will adopt, whether the wretched & corrupt ["principle" *canceled and* "one" *interlined*], that to the victor belongs the spoils, or the enlightened & patriotick one of bestowing its patronage, with the single eye to the good of the country, remains to be seen.

I regret exceedingly that the ZollVerein treaty still remains unacted on; which may be attributed, in part, to the all engrossing subject, Texas, occupying so much of the attention of Congress, and the belief, on the part of its friends, that it would be much more likely to be ratified at the next session. I cannot but think the prospect of its ratification then, is good. Should Texas come in, there will be 6 additional Senators; two from there, two from Florida, & two from Ioway [*sic*], all, as we have good reasons to believe, on the side of free trade. I do hope, with such a prospect, that the ZollVerein States will waive the formality, as to the time for ratification, until the close of another session. Yours truly & sincerely, J.C. Calhoun.

ALS in NNPM, Wheaton Papers.

To Hendrick B. Wright, [Wilkes-Barre, Pa.], "Private & Confidential"

Fort Hill, 6th April 1845

My dear Sir, I received by the mail of yesterday, yours of the 26th March, & would with much pleasure comply with your request, if I could under circumstances do it with propriety. I say under circumstances; because, before I left Washington, I left with the President [James K. Polk] a few names of personal friends, who had been uniformly his ardent supporters, & were strongly backed by the support of their States respectively; not one of whom has, as yet, received the least notice. While I am thus left in a state of uncertainty, as to the course the administration intend to take in reference to my friends, it seems to me that self respect forbids any farther application on my part in their favour, especially, as I have no certainty, whether it might not be of more disservice, than service. My own course has been marked throughout with the greatest kindness & liberality towards the President & his administration; and his language has been towards me kind & cordial; but as ["far as" *interlined*] facts go, it has thus far ended in that. But, be ["it" *canceled and* "his course" *interlined*] what it may, while it cannot influence my publick ["course" *canceled and* "conduct" *interlined*], towards either, yet it imposes on me certain rules of propriety, which I am bound to respect. Indeed, in your case, if the prominent and influential part you acted, in bring[ing] about the state of things, which ended in the election of Mr. Polk, should fail to secure ["to" *canceled*] you his favour, I feel, that it would be in vain for me to interpose in your behalf. I wish you to be assured, that if circumstances permitted, it would afford me great pleasure to serve you. You have strong claims on the party, which ought to be respected; & I would suppose, the head of the treasury Dept. [Robert J. Walker], who is so familiar with them, will not overlook them. Yours truly, J.C. Calhoun.

ALS in PWbWHi, Hendrick B. Wright Papers; microfilm of ALS in NjP, Hendrick B. Wright Papers.

From F[ranklin] H. Elmore

Charleston, Ap[ri]l 7, 1845

My Dear Sir, Mr. Clarke [*sic*; Clark] Mills of this city is the inventor of a new & improved process for takin[g] bust impressions. His success & talants [*sic*] have induced many of your friends here to insist on his taking yours & at his & their instance I submitted a request to you to that end when you were here on your first return from Washington after taking charge of the State Department. You then consented to sit for the operation at some future day. Mr. Mills is now anxious to procure your sitting & in this he is but the exponent of very many here who wish to have copies. He has called to see me today & tells me he intends writing to you on the subject, but is unwilling to do so without some introduction, and I have great pleasure in the opportunity he affords, to bear testimony to his merits & to the general desire felt by your friends here that you will accede to his request.

The operation will not exceed 15 minutes & is I am assured as little inconvenient as such a thing can be. I am My Dear Sir Very truly Y[ou]rs, F.H. Elmore.

ALS in ScCleA. NOTE: This letter was addressed to Calhoun at Pendleton as if it was to be delivered by Mills.

From ELLWOOD FISHER

Louisville, 4 M[onth *ca.* 7] 1845

Esteemed Friend, I have defer[r]ed writing since my return in order to be definite in describing the present and future political aspect of this section. But I cannot delay my congratulations on the intelligence we receive from Europe and from Texas, all so favourable to the United States, to peace, free trade, and to all the objects of the late Diplomatic labours. It is perhaps happy for thy own fame, and in its consequences I trust happy for the country, that thy retirement from the state Department occurred ["at" *canceled*] in time to be so promptly followed by events that ["must" *canceled*] confer so much éclat on thy recent public service. Such good fortune could hardly be expected to follow for a protracted period even the same desert.

I hope our friends of the Press will impress on the public mind the causes of these results. The paper printed here, is conducted by persons not wedded to the late regime of the party, but are I think disposed to better counsels. When here I write an occasional editorial for the paper, and I mean to morrow to devote a column to our late Diplomacy.

The Administration has so far followed the course which I thought to be indicated by its formation. The second assistant Post Master

Gen[era]l—the appointing office—has been given to [former Representative William] Medill—a decided Ohio [Martin] Van Buren man. I learned a fact yesterday however from [James Walker] a brother-in-law of the President [James K. Polk], passing here on his way to Tennessee that looks otherwise. It is that [Francis P.] Blair is to quit the [Washington] Globe, which is to be taken by [Thomas] Ritchie of the [Richmond] Enquirer and Maj[o]r Donaldson [*sic*; Andrew J. Donelson] our Chargé to Texas who returns for the purpose. The arrangement however is subject to the ratifacation [*sic*] of Gen[era]l [Andrew] Jackson—to whom it seems Blair insisted on refer[r]ing it—evidently with the hope the General would interpose to save him.

Donelson I saw on his return from the Balt[imore] Convention [of 1844]—of whose undercurrents he gave me some account. He said the Tennessee delegation voted at first for [Lewis] Cass—himself among them—he voting as well as two or three others, with the rest for Cass on an understanding that these should vote with him and his friends if another more available man should be designated by them. He told me that some time before leaving home he was impressed with the idea that Gen[era]l Jackson's course on Texas would displace Van Buren. Can it be that the General and he[?] had actually selected Polk[?] For he told me that although Polk was nominated in the Convention by [David] Hubbard it was after a consultation with himself and some others. Walker the President[']s brother-in-law spoke to me in terms quite disparaging of the present standing in Washington of the Van Buren clique. And I was informed in coming home by General [Sackfield] Maclin of Arkansas, formerly connected with Polk in the State government of Tennessee ["that" *canceled*] and evidently yet a confidential friend that [Thomas H.] Benton and Polk had no intercourse for Polk considered and even knew that Benton had been hostile to him.

I have conversed freely with many persons since my return home, on the course of the administration—and have found few very few much pleased with it. The West is discontented at her exclusion from the Cabinet. And the young men of talent do not recognize enough ability in the government to regard it with pride, and support it with zeal.

The Cincinnati Enquirer undertook two or three weeks ago ["to" *canceled*] when it understood the Calhoun men were not satisfied with the Cabinet and the Inaugural, to denounce them in quite violent terms. Although the print is a low and dull concern I thought it inexpedient to have the minds of its readers prejudiced in that manner, so I caused it to be intimated to the editor [Charles Brough] with whom I hold no intercourse, that the friends of Calhoun in the Senate might cause the rejection of his brother John Brough who is a candidate for an Auditorship—and I have heard no further abuse of that kind.

There is here a very respectable house—Thomas J. Read & Son con[nected] with another at New Orleans. Read is a decided friend of thine though a personal friend and intimate of Jackson and Polk. Read wrote a very strong letter published in the [Washington] Constitution with his proper signature not long before the Baltimore convention, urging thy nomination. I have proposed to Read to import into Texas from England prior to next session of Congress, a considerable quantity of merchandize to be reshipped to other ports ["into" *altered to* "in"] the United States after the annexation—and thus realize a profit of the difference between the present tariff of Texas and U.S. And out of the profit thus made to appropriate a fund sufficient to establish a few leading presses in Indiana and Ohio. He thinks very favourably of the plan—and I hope will act upon it. I intend to take measures to have the same thing done in the North as well as in the South. And if merchants do not open their eyes to the operation, the profits realized will suffice to secure through[?] the country what is so much needed—a due proportion of sound public [papers].

What shall be done with the Convention system[?] Shall it be tolerated, reformed, or destroyed? It is a question of difficulty to which I have designed bestowing some consideration—and should like to have thy views—as on every other matter of interest. Please address at Cincinnati. Thy friend, Ellwood Fisher.

ALS in ScCleA; PEx in Boucher and Brooks, eds., *Correspondence*, p. 289. NOTE: This letter was postmarked in Louisville on 4/8. Fisher (1808–1862) was a prolific journalist and an anti-abolitionist Quaker from Ohio. The newspaper referred to in the second paragraph has not been identified with certainty but may have been the Louisville *Democrat* or the Louisville *Courier*.

From H [AYM] M. SALOMON

New York [City,] April 7, 1845
Dear Sir, The result of the efforts of the [Martin] Van B[uren] Party continues daily to manifest itself in the operations at Washington[.] They are reaping the advantages of the promises and the

deceptions practiced on you and your friends at Baltimore for not only the Ninety ninth but also the one Hundredth time[.] *I* would never from what I have seen of them in this quarter believed in anything they proposed apparently for the interest of Others. I have told my friends often I rather take their intentions to be directly opposite what they propose.

You need not be reminded that however critical your position might have been considered at periods heretofore as connected with the history of your political Life—none yet have arisen like the one now presenting itself and through which you will have to progress within two years[.]

The Papers say they are progecting to send you as a Commissioner to a neighbouring province to br bring [*sic*] about that which you had ["pergected" *canceled*] perfected a year ago and the consummation of which was obstructed solely by the sinister movements of [Thomas H.] Benton and Van Beuren[.] Away with such a progect to be executed by John C. Calhoun! *he* whose arguments have shut up the mouths of the most adroit ministers of the principal European governments in a matter regarding the vital interests of his nation[.] Shall he be sent to patch up breaches willfully made by such a faction? No.

Should the proposal come I would simply say to such a Cabinet[,] "I decline the commission[.]" I am &c &c[.]

Then, let them discover your reasons if they can[;] they should have no more texts from letters of J.C. C[alhoun] on which to build injurious paragraphs.

It is also said that old Mr. [Thomas] Ritchie is to be brought to their aid at W[ashington]. I venture to predict that he also will fall into their net unless he is perfectly independant in his worldly affairs.

Among unexpected things to which the acting Governors or agents of the faction *might feel compelled* to submit and thus seal another leaf in the history book of their degradations would be the intreating recall of John C. Calhoun to Washington as a Hercules to their salvation. If providence thus wills it, Let him then *like another Aristides* accept it—but ["as" *interlined*] this call would suppose on its face that he was *the only or most* competent person in the nation to manage its affairs—Let the national undertaking on your part be with an unequivocal written understanding that The Ministers and Consular agencies abroad to carry out your views should only be those whom your position alone would ["call" *inter-*

lined] on *you to nominate.* With profound regard As Ever I am &c &c, H.M. Salomon.

ALS in ScCleA.

From St. Geo[rge] T. Campbell

94 So[uth] 4th Street, Philadelphia
April 8, 1845

My dear Sir, I learn with pleasure your improved health & sincerely trust that the temporary retirement you now enjoy from the excitement & labor of public service will speedily and permanently restore it.

No longer serving the nation each citezen may claim an interest in your experience and judgment: and for myself I feel anxious to have the result of your reflection ["upon" *canceled and* "as to the" *interlined*] effect of the proposed changes in the Tariff of Great Britain both upon American products and manufacturing interests.

As an English measure its object seems apparent—to undersell American labor at all hazzard, especially in China & the whole East. But is it not also prudent and most popular—for [Sir Robert Peel] the great minister of that nation, retains his tax upon the wealthy while he assists the poor and calms that excitable & alarming mass— the manufacturing population.

But the experiment is intended to be tested in some manner at *our cost* & great interests in every Section of the Country are staked upon its result.

What American legislation does it call for? What change in the principle of the compromise act does it require? What in the tariff of '42? & to what general System of duties and commercial regulations does it tend?

No statesman of our own has ["given" *canceled and* "expressed" *interlined*] to us his views—nor given a direction to public opinion upon the subject. Mingling as I do in no political contest yet feeling not the less interest in every measure affecting the stability & policy of our government, I trust you will at your convenience express to me your opinion of the proper american policy to meet this movement which seems to mark a new era in the British system for revenue. Very Sincerely Y[ou]rs, St. Geo: T. Campbell, April 8, 1845.

ALS in ScCleA. NOTE: St. George T. Campbell, a son of Alexander and Maria Dallas Campbell, was a prominent Philadelphia attorney.

To T[HOMAS] G. CLEMSON, [Brussels]

Fort Hill, 8th April 1845

My dear Sir, I wrote to Anna [Maria Calhoun Clemson] shortly after my arrival Home from Washington. I hope ["it" *canceled and* "my letter" *interlined*] arrived in Boston in time to go by the last Steamer, & that it has ere this reached its destination. I gave her an account of my visit to the Cane Brake [in Edgefield District] on my way up, & in what condition I found things there.

The spring continues very fine. The weather clear, rather dry & moderately warm. I am more than half done with planting corn; have nearly all my cotton ground sowed, but not yet covered, except a few acres in detached patches; and I expect in the course of 10 days to have my whole crop planted, except the old Mill ["pond" *interlined*] and the adjacent new ground. I am busy ditching the former, & do not expect to plant it before the first of May. My place is really in beautiful order. Mr. Fredericks has done full justice, as far as the plantation is concerned; but report in the neighbourhood speaks unfavourable of him in other respects.

I wrote Anna, that her Mother [Floride Colhoun Calhoun] had gone to Philadelphia, to consult Dr. [Thomas D.] Mutter about [Martha] Cornelia [Calhoun's] hearing & spinal affection; but that I expected her to be at home early this month. She was to have been at A[i]ken on the 1st Inst., & the carriage went down ["in time" *canceled*] to meet her there at the time. The day after it left, I received a letter from her dated on the 25th March, which informed ["me" *interlined*] she could not leave when she expected; that Cornelia's spine began to be troublesome, and that some of the symptoms were of an alarming character, & that it was quite uncertain when she could leave. Her letter made me quite uneasy about poor Cornelia; but I have since had a letter from Patrick [Calhoun], dated ["on" *canceled*] the 30th March, which gives a more favourable account & expresses the hope, that they would soon be able to leave for the South.

In this remote corner, I have but little political news. Judging from all I see & hear, I fear Mr. [James K.] Polk will not carry out the great issues, on which he was elected. It seems to me, judging at this distance, that the primary object with him is to restore the very ["party" *canceled and* "clique" *interlined*] which ["was" *interlined*] thrown over board at Baltimore in order to elect him. I hope, however, I ["may" *interlined*] be mistaken.

We have no local News. Every body is well, except those who have the measels. We have had two cases, but trust it will not spread on the place. Willy [William Lowndes Calhoun] got over his very easily. My health is quite restored. I hope you are all well. The children [John Calhoun Clemson and Floride Elizabeth Clemson], from what Anna writes, must be the picture of health, & be very interesting. I think Floride is becoming the favourite with her. Tell them, that their Grandfather thinks often of them, and would be glad to see them.

We expect Andrew [Pickens Calhoun] & family to be with us this summer. Margaret [Green Calhoun] & the children, under the escort of John [C. Calhoun, Jr.], will come some time in May, & Andrew as soon as the crop is laid by.

Willy joins his love to all of you. He has grown very much the last six months. Your affectionate father, J.C. Calhoun.

ALS in ScCleA.

From CLARK MILLS

Charleston, Ap[ri]l 8th 1845

Honored Sir, When in Charleston on your way to take charge of the State Department at Washington, you were kind enough to give your consent to have your bust taken by me, at some future day, as you could not make it convenient to delay your departure at that time. Having obtained a list of one hundred of our most respectable citizens who were desirous of having it taken, I had made arrangements to proceed to Washington for that purpose, when the news was received of your illness. In thus taking the liberty of addressing you, my object is, most respectfully to solicit that you would allow me the opportunity as early as your convenience may admit, to gratify the wishes of those of your fellow citizens who have honored me with their names.

I beg permission to state that the process I have adopted for taking busts is altogether different from the usual mode, & inflicts scarcely any inconvenience, and does not occupy more than fifteen minutes.

I have so arranged my business that I will be prepared to visit ["you" *interlined*] as soon as you may appoint for me to do so. The honor of an answer, and at your earliest convenience is most respectfully solicited. With great respect & consideration Y[ou]r Ob[edien]t Serv[an]t, Clark Mills.

ALS in ScCleA. NOTE: An AEU by Calhoun reads "Clark Mills."

From JAMES BUCHANAN, [Secretary of State]

Washington, 9 April 1845

My dear Sir, I have just returned to this City after a brief absence in Lancaster [Pa.].

The President [James K. Polk] does not intend to remove Mr. [Henry A.] Wise [U.S. Minister to Brazil] & he authorised me to say so to you. He yesterday offered the mission to England to Mr. [Franklin H.] Elmore. I hope that gentleman may accept it: though I still deeply regret that you did not consent to go to London yourself.

We have received no Despatches either from Mexico or Texas since you left. Messrs. [Thomas] Ritchie, [Andrew J.] Donelson & [John P.] Heiss will take the Globe & publish the official paper (as I suppose).

Please to remember me kindly & respectfully to Mrs. [Floride Colhoun] Calhoun & believe me, with the highest regard, to be Your friend, James Buchanan.

LS in ScCleA; PEx in Boucher and Brooks, eds., *Correspondence*, p. 292.

To A[BBOTT] LAWRENCE, [Boston]

Fort Hill, 9th April 1845

My dear Sir, This is a letter on business, and I hope you may find it not inconsistent with your interest to meet my wishes in writing to you.

My son Andrew [Pickens Calhoun] & myself purchased some years since, when cotton was at a fair, but then regarded a very moderate price, a very valuable cotton plantation in Alabama, Marengo County, consisting of upwards of 2000 acres of land, every acre of which is good; fertile, durable, and what, in that region is extraordinary on such lands, perfectly healthy. With a family of 140, white & black, we have not paid a dollar to a physician for the last three years. We have now upwards of 1200 acres cleared, and in a high state of cultivation, & completely stocked in every respect. Our crop this year, already planted, is 900 acres in cotton & 350 in corn. The former estimated on the average product of the place, ought to yeild [*sic*] upwards of 250,000 pounds of clean cotton. My son resides on the place, and is industrious, economical & skilful, as a planter.

When we purchased, we paid a part of the purchase money, & expected at the then price of cotton, to pay the whole with ease in a few years. Our calculation has all been realized except the price, at which we estimated the price of cotton. That fell the ["very" *canceled*] next year, and has ever since been runiously [*sic*] low, which has embarrassed us in meeting the purchase money, & which has caused this letter to be addressed to you.

We find, that we want more time, than our creditors can afford to give, and a lower rate of interest, than the legal, in this State & Alabama, where they reside. It is 7 per cent in this, & 8 in that. If that can be effected, we feel confident, we can discharge what is due at 6 cents the pound for cotton, with ease; and as you are one of the greatest manufacturer[s] of the article, of which we are the growers; and as money is plenty in your section, & scarce in ours, owing to ["the" *interlined*] fair price of the manufactured articles, & the very low of the raw material, I hope, it may be effected through you.

Our place is becoming more productive yearly. The expense of the first settlement of a place has all been incurred; our force increasing from the great health of the location, and the land more productive in cotton, with the reduction of the extreme fertility of new cleared land.

What I propose is, to raise a sum, say $30,000, to be repaid by a shipment annually of at least 100,000 pounds of clean ["cotton" *interlined*], or a sum, that shall equal that in value, at the selling price in Boston, to be delivered or remitted on or before the 1st ["of June or" *interlined*] July each year. If it should ["be" *interlined*] any inducement, we would take our supply, until the debt is paid, of sum[m]er & winter clothing for our people; say 200 in number. For security, we would give a mortgage on the ["land" *canceled and* "place" *interlined*], with our bond. The ["land" *canceled and* "the place even" *interlined*] at the present great depression, would sell for at least $40,000 and is entirely free of all incumbrance. We hold property, which would sell for three times, as much as we owe, at present prices.

What I desire to know ["is" *interlined*], first, whether the loan can be obtain[ed] on these terms, or what other, & what would be the lowest rate ["of interest" *interlined*] at which it could be obtained. An early answer is desirable. If it can be obtained on terms sufficiently favourable, my son will go on with full authority to close the transaction, and, if you should require it, with such evidence, as to the value of the place, and its freedom from all liabilities, & our entire solvency as you may desire. It is proper to add, that our place produces a cotton of excellent staple, strong & long, and of sufficient fine[ne]ss. With great respect I am &c &c, J.C. Calhoun.

ALS in MH. Note: An account of Calhoun's dealings with Abbott Lawrence appeared in *Historical Magazine*, 3rd series, vol. I, no. 2 (February 1872), p. 113. This account contains a number of substantial errors.

From A[sa] Whitney

New York [City,] 10 April 1845

D[ea]r Sir, I avail myself of the permission you kindly gave me, to explain the plan by which I propose to carry into effect my project for a railroad from Lake Michigan to the Pacific Ocean.

I have as you are aware asked of Congress to grant to me of the Public Domain 60 miles in width from the Lake to the Ocean, the proceeds & avails of which to be applied exclusively to the building & completing the said road, after which the surplus lands to belong to me as a reward for the work and in order fully to attain such object I would have commissioners appointed, same as our Judges now are, whose duty it should be to dispose of said lands with my consent they holding the avails thereof subject only to the building of said road, responsible & bound to report to each Congress, they not having power to dispose of the lands without my consent, nor I power to use the lands or their avails without their consent, thus being a check upon each other.

Having friends who have offered to me means which I think adequate to the commencement of the work & believing that its commencement, will draw to it so much enterprise, that it cannot fail of success, gives me full confidence.

From Lake Michigan where I propose to commence the work to the Missouri river, a distance of about 650 miles making about 25 millions of acres, through which I learn from good authority that a road can be built with great facility, I also learn that the land is all good & would be likely to sell & settle quite as fast as the road can be built, that the road will facilitate the sale & settlement cannot be doubted.

I estimate that the road will cost about $20,000 p[e]r mile for its complete construction, thus for 650 miles would cost $13 millions[;] the 25 millions of acres at $1¼ (the government price) would be $31 millions leaving a surplus of $18 millions, or equal to build 900 miles beyond the Missouri river.

From all accounts from those who have passed over the Country & particularly that from Ramsey Crooks Esq[ui]r[e], the lands from the Missouri to some distance beyond the mountains, are very poor, not producing enough to sustain their animals[,] generally covered with a wild sage & nothing else, therefore but little can be realized from them.

The whole length of road with its windings will probably be 2400 miles, the lands from the Lake to the Missouri providing for 1550 will leave 850 miles to provide for out of the poor lands from the Missouri to beyond the mountains & what good lands there may be between the mountains & the ocean. The estimated cost of the road is $50 millions, & not producing any returns till its full completion, would require $15 millions more to keep it in repair & operation.

I understand from Lieu[tenan]t [John C.] Fremont (whose report is to be published by order of Congress) that to build a road through the rocky Mountains to the Pacific is not only feasible, but offers a more favourable rout[e] than any we have known or read of on any part of the Globe, that the entire rout[e] from the Missouri to the Ocean can be built on a grade less than seven feet to the mile, so that it would seem nature has given it to us for this very purpose.

Considering the poor quality of the lands from the Missouri o[n]ward for a long distance & considering the magnitude of the enterprise, I do not feel that I have asked for too much. The value of the lands from the Lake to the Missouri & their undoubted increase in value from the building of the road through them, their avails *all* of which to be applied to the continuance of, I consider a sufficient guarantee to the government, that the road will be completed.

It is my intention to pass over, examine & partially survey 7 or 800 miles of the rout[e], the coming summer. The reasons for commencing the road from Lake Michigan are many & obvious. First as the road is to be built from the lands, it is necessary to commence at a point, where or near to where the lands are unappropriated, & where there is sufficient timber for its construction. Secondly the great necessity for a cheap & easy water communication from the important Atlantic cities to transport settlers, labourers & materials directly to the road. And last tho not least, the great importance of the commerce of England, with the vast coast of South America & Mexico, with China, Australia & a great part of India—England could make her depot at Montreal or some point in Upper Canada, use the Lakes then the rail road to the Pacific, & then her own Vessels again thus for a small toll, enjoy all the great advantages of the road. The great saving of time so all important to the merchant, of far greater consideration than any reasonable cost of freight, would force commerce through this channel, and this road would have the advantage of others in the cost of freight, having no interest or cost of construction to provide for. Merchandize may be transported upon it for less than half a cent p[e]r ton p[e]r mile, costing from Oregon to Lake Michigan less than $12 p[e]r ton weight & one ton weight being equal to 2 to 2¼ tons measurement of Teas or such like Merchandize, it would cost less than $6 for the transportation of one Ton measurement of Teas from the Pacific to the Lake. This road would make a saving of more than six months in time on all the business of both England & the United States with China &c[;] for instance a Vessel sailing from the United States or from England in from March to May (later will not do on account of the moonsoons in the Chinese Seas) arrive in China from June to September & must then wait till November or December for the Tea Crop, they return[,] arrive in England or the United States in March to may, about 10 to 12 months. The sales of American & English manufactured goods take place in China in September to January, their Tea Crop coming into market from November to January, so that Merchandize or other funds may be sent by this road to meet the market there, as also the Tea crop for a return & save full 6 months, often much more.

I have given my reasons for commencing from the Lake which I think you will fully understand & agree with me in its importance. You will also see that this road must force the opening & completing, all the veins of communication from all the Atlantic cities to it, when you will have a direct line of railroads[,] rivers & canals from each & all the Atlantic cities to the Pacific ocean, which can be traversed in 8 days, look at the picture & where is the man who can withhold his voice & hand, required, without effort, for this great work. I believe that the granting of the land which I ask for, & the commencing the work, will open such a field for industry & enterprise, as the world has never before known & that the wealth & enterprise of the world must be attracted & drawn to it by an irresistable force, & where is the man amongst us who may not expect benefit.

Here is a vast region of country, a wild, a waste, a delightful climate suited to the people of the north of Europe & of our own States, much of it a beautiful country, the soil rich & fertile. Open this road through it, it unites the two great oceans of the world, it becomes the great th[o]roughfare of nations, subject to a toll so small as to be almost free, it will be as a new found world, the one population of Europe must & will flock to it.

Let us consider, that our present population is 20 millions but in 22½ years more will be 40 millions & perhaps many of us may desire the benefits which this road ["& the world" *canceled*] will open to us & to the world.

It appears to me that we now have the power & means (means which costs nothing & will be exchanged for a valuable consideration, a productive[,] industrious population) of accomplishing a work greater than has been done by men or nations, the results of which must change the whole world. We are now at the extreme of the Globe, build this road & we are in the center, with Europe on the one side & Asia & Africa on the other. You Sir can see, you can read what must then be the destiny of our nation, we can then traverse the vast Globe in 30 days, we bring all the vast world together as one nation, one family. It will harmonize, it will civilize, it will christianize, it will do more, than all mankind before us have done, and where is the man who will not say let it be done, and it shall be done. I believe that this work will bring our vast country so directly together as one family, that all the sectional jealousies, interests & differences will harmonize, each State & section left to manage its own domestic affairs in its own way, as was intended when the compact was formed—the scale being so grand & interests so diversified, that no one can predominate, the Agricultural by its extended influence must harmonize all, while it can never require the subjection of any other interest to its own. My imagination may have been led astray in the grandness of this project, but I believe not, for to me it appears not only clear but plain & simple. It is my desire that you may fully understand the subject. If I am wrong I know you will see it & shall be greatly obliged for your opinion, if I am right, it is my strongest desire to have not only your friendship, but your powerful influence to aide it. Respectfully Your ob[edien]t Serv[an]t, A. Whitney.

ALS in ScCleA.

To John "Broadhead" [*sic*; Brodhead], [Philadelphia], 4/12. "I have . . . been gratified to learn, that there is so great a change in public opinion at the North in reference to my political course. In pursuing it, and acting on the principles of the Old State Rights Republican Party, I have been governed by a deep conviction of duty, regardless of the popularity of the movement, or any consideration personal to myself. I am firmly of the opinion that on no other principles can our free[,] popular and glorious system of government be preserved; and have no doubt but time and experience will prove the correctness of my opinion. They have been greatly departed from since the termination of the old race of Virginia Presidents, and to that, I attribute the increased corruption and glowing [*sic*; growing] disorders, which every patriot must lament to behold, and which, if not arrested, must lead to the loss of liberty and the downfall of our institutions. To avert so great a calamity to our country and the cause of free government over the globe, I look to the rising generation . . . ." PEx in *Autograph Letters, Manuscripts, Documents*, Catalogue 48 of Kenneth W. Rendell, Inc., (Somerville, Mass.: [1970]), p. 6.

To C[HARLES] J. INGERSOLL, [Philadelphia]

Fort Hill, 12th April 1845
My dear Sir, I agree with you in opinion, that the next session of Congress will disclose many divisions & striking circumstances in the distribution of parties and the course of events, and that it is quite uncertain, where the majority will be found in either House.

There is no telling what will be the result of the next four years. Things were never more uncertain than at present. I look on, from this distant point, silently & clamly [*sic*].

I am not at all surprised, that you should be tired of the wasting distractions of continual party contest. They have, of late, turn[ed] out as fruitless, as they have been exhausting. I have long believed, that our system has been working wrong, and cannot but fear, that it is reaching a crisis, which it will be difficult for it to pass.

I am very much gratified to learn, that you ["are" *interlined*] engaged in writing an historical sketch of the late war, and that you have already made such considerable progress in the work. I hope you will make it *more than a sketch* before you are done, especially in its political & philosophical aspect. In that, it is a rich subject, which, as yet, remains untouched. Its battles, are nothing comparatively. In your fuller understanding of the subject, in its more interesting aspect, you will have great advantages over all, who have yet attempted the history of that important event in our history.

It is to me, as to yourself, a source of much pleasure, in taking a retrospect of the passed [*sic*], to reflect, that our long acquaintance has never been mar[r]ed by a single incident, ["through" *canceled and* "in the" *interlined*] various scenes, through which we have passed together.

I, on my part, have commenced an enquiry into the elements of political science, preliminary to a treatise on the Constitution of the U. States; but know not whether I shall ever have time to finish it. Yours sincerely & truly, J.C. Calhoun.

ALS in PHi, Ingersoll Papers; PC in Jameson, ed., *Correspondence*, pp. 651–652.

To [DIXON H. LEWIS?, Washington]

Fort Hill, 14th April 1845
My dear Sir, I do not think, that there can be any serious intention of offering me the place of Commissioner to Texas. I doubt, whether there will be any necessity to send any one, unless, indeed, the instructions, which I gave Donolson [*sic*; Andrew J. Donelson], in reference to the House resolution have been altered. They provided for the possible contingency of Texas declining to agree to the terms proposed. But should it be offered, I certainly should not think of accepting, unless, indeed, a case was made out, showing that there was ["a" *canceled*] real necessity for the step, & satisfactory reasons assigned to show, that my services were necessary, & that there was reasonable prospect they would be successful. Of that, I have no expectation, and can scarcely imagine that such a case could be made out. I have just heard from [Lewis S.] Coryell, that the Globe is to be dismissed and a new organ established at the head of which Mr. [Thomas] Ritchie will be placed. The intelligence is important, and I hope it will prove correct. It will certainly be a great point to get clear of the Globe, & [Francis P.] Blair & [Thomas H.] Benton, even if we cannot escape wholly from the Albany Clique. If Ritchie could be made to go right, it would, indeed, be a great movement, and of that, we must not dispair. Our friends in Virginia have great influence over him, and they are united, firm & determined to oppose

him, if he should take a false track. I had much conversation with them & him, the day I spent at Richmond, on my return home. It was very satisfactory. The prospect every way was better, than I ever saw it in Virginia. You being on the spot, have it in your power to do much. I hope you will remain during the whole recess at Washington. It will enable you to do much good.

Hoping, that the dismissal of the Globe, indicates a favourable change in the course of the administration, I take the liberty of enclosing a letter [of 3/21] from one of the editors of the Missouri Reporter [Samuel Treat], on the subject of the transfer of the patronage of the Post office Department to the Missourian. The facts it states, in reference to the course of that paper, if known to Mr. [James K.] Polk, and if he assented to the transfer, would indicate, that he is resolved to bestow his countenance & patronage on the portion of the party, which did all they could to defeat the great question, which elevated ["him" *interlined*] to the presidency. I hope they were not known to him, & that the transfer was made without his knowledge. If there should be reason to believe that such is the case, it would be desirable, that he should be made acquainted with the facts.

I know not that you can do any thing in the ["matter" *interlined*]. My object in transmitting ["it" *canceled and* "the letter" *interlined*] is to put you in possession of the facts to be ["used" *canceled*] be [*sic*] brought to the knowledge of Mr. Polk, if a favourable opportunity should offer &, if there should be reason to believe, that the Post Master General [Cave Johnson] acted without his knowledge, or that he was ignorant of them. I have taken the step, on the supposition, that he has not yet definitely made up his mind to restore the old Hunkers with Benton as their leader to power. If in this I mistake, or you should think, that no use can be made of the facts, destroy the letter.

I see from the Madisonian, of which a copy was sent me by the last mail, that it has changed editors, and that Mr. [Theophilus] Fisk takes charge of it. I presume he sent me the copy to apprise me of the fact, and to obtain my subscription. I will thank you to request him to send me the weekly Madisonian, & put my name on his list of subscribers.

I am a subscriber to the Constitution; but have not received it since my return home, and will also thank you to request Mr. [William A.] Harris or Hart [*sic*; John Heart] to send it to me. I put you to this trouble in both cases to avoid the expence of Postage. I do hope, that in the new arrangement of the press at Washington, Harris ["could" *canceled and* "may" *interlined*] get some permanent & respectable position. He is able, & honest and would, with some ["more" *interlined*] practice & experience, make one of the best editors in the country. I would be glad to hear from you fully on all points, which you might think interesting.

With best respects to Mrs. [Susan Elmore] Lewis. Yours truly, J.C. Calhoun.

ALS with En in DNA, RG 56 (Secretary of the Treasury), Miscellaneous Letters Received, 1815–1914. NOTE: The address leaf of the letter is missing, and the only certain evidence as to whom it was addressed is the mention of "Mrs. Lewis" in the closing. It is known also, corroboratively, that Lewis remained in Washington for some time after the adjournment of Congress in March. The letter is found in the records of the Treasury Department presumably because Lewis gave it to Secretary of the Treasury Robert J. Walker or some other official along with Treat's letter enclosed.

To SAMUEL TREAT, St. Louis, "Private"

Fort Hill, 14th April 1845

Dear Sir, Your letter of the 21st March reached Washington after I left, and followed me to my residence here, where I received it a few days since.

The course of the Postmaster General [Cave Johnson] in bestowing the patronage of his Department on [the St. Louis *Missourian*] a paper which pursued ["the course" *interlined*] it did, on the great question, which elevated Mr. [James K.] Polk to the presidency & placed Mr. Johnson in the office, which he holds ["is indeed surprising" *interlined*]. I cannot think, that it was done with the knowledge & consent of Mr. Polk; for surely nothing could be more suicidal, than to turn his back on those, who nobly sustained the great issue, on which he was elected, & to give his countenance & support to those, who opposed, & did their best to defeat it. Nor would the policy be less suicidal to attempt to conciliate all, by placing those who sustained & supported, on the same level ["with those who opposed it" *interlined*]. It would be to confound friends & foes; the faithful & unfaithful. The honest & safe road lies directly before him; to carry out the great issue on which he was elected & bestow his confidence & patronage on those who triumphantly carried it through against the mighty opposition of the whigs; & to leave those, who faltered or opposed to pursue their own course. Any other course, on his part, must end in the prostration of his administration.

Any attempt to elevate the wing of the party, which was defeated at Baltimore, will prove utterly abortive. They can never regain their popularity, or the publick confidence, and may be regarded among things that are passed, and ["have become" *interlined*] obsolete. I know not, that any thing can be done, at present, to correct the false step, to which your letter refers; but I have taken the liberty of transmitting it to a friend [Dixon H. Lewis?] in Washington, and requested him to act in the case, if he saw any prospect of doing any thing. The [St. Louis] Reporter for its bold and independent course, richly deserves the support of the government, and party. With great respect I am & &, J.C. Calhoun.

ALS in MoSHi, Samuel Treat Papers.

From F[RANKLIN] H. ELMORE

Charleston, Ap[ri]l 16, 1845

My Dear Sir, The Board of Directors [of the Bank of the State of South Carolina] have directed me to discount your note for $4,000 until 1 Jan[uar]y next. I have not done so yet, because you sent no check for the money & no direction how to apply the proceeds. If they are to be paid away here you had best, send a check in blank to your agent [Mathewes & Bonneau], who is to apply the money. If you want the money elsewhere & we can forward for you, you must send the check payable to the Cash[ie]r Mr. Cha[rle]s M. Furman with instructions as to the application. I have not said what is the amount you may check for as it will vary slightly every day & I have not filled your note nor discounted until the proceeds can be applied by your orders that you may not pay more interest than is necessary.

I rec[eive]d a few days ago a *private* letter from Mr. [James K.] Polk tendering me the mission to England. The manner this has been done is highly gratifying to my feelings, but I have felt constrained to decline it, for many reasons. The time to prepare for sailing is indicated as in May—much too short for me. The position for 4 years would ruin me. *No special duty* or service was indicated & I therefore infer that no special service is to be intrusted to the Minister. If a commercial treaty is to be considered, I presume Mr. [James] Buchanan will either take it to himself or direct it according to the Pennsylvania views & these would not suit me. But apart & beside all these considerations, my affairs would not allow of an absence so early nor beyond a year & as I could not make terms nor suggest them even I have today explained my reasons & declined acceptance. I am My Dear Sir Yours truly, F.H. Elmore.

P.S. In case of my absence, which may occur, if you write on this Bank business, you had best direct to me and Mr. Furman.

ALS in ScCleA; PEx in Boucher and Brooks, eds., *Correspondence*, pp. 292–293.

From [Miss] M. H. McKni[ght]

Phila[delphi]a, April 16th 1845

My very kind friend, I regret to have occasion to trouble you on a subject of so painful a nature to myself, but your long and tried friendship suggests the propriety of so doing[.]

In the [Washington] Globe of Sat[urday] the ["14th" *altered to* "12th"] you will see that the President [James K. Polk] has dismissed my [step-]Brother Lt. W[illia]m Decatur Hurst from the Navy, in consequence of having waived his Rank, whilst first Lt[.] of the Brig Truxton on the Coast of Africa, to engage in a Duel with pass[e]d Mid[shipman] [J. Blakeley] Creighton of the same vessel. Brother in his letter to the Secretary of the Navy [George Bancroft] acknowledged that he had offended (in a moment of exasperated feelings) against the discipline of the Service, and most deeply regret[t]ed it, he did not attempt to palliate it, but to you, I may. Mr. Creighton was twice rebuked for improper conduct between 8 & 9 P.M. Next morning Mr. C[reighton] charged Brother with ["improper" *canceled and* "ungentlemanly" *interlined*] conduct in his manner of inforcing duty the night previous & stated to him, that if he could not obtain satisfaction in any other way, he would report him to higher authority. Brother replyed he would give him personal satisfaction if he wished it. The next morning they met. Brother did not fire at his antagonist, but received his. The Ball passed through the right leg five inches above the ancke [*sic*], through the left leg, shattered it completely, the Large bone was so sharp as to split the Ball[.] Half remained in[,] the other part passed out & fell on the Ground. He has almost recovered, walks without a Kane [*sic*], no shortening of the limb. I must observe that Brother requested the Surgeon Dr. [Silas?] Holmes to go to Creighton and settle it amicably if possible[.] Mr. Creighton declined. It is a very hard case that the Secretary should make an example of one, whose family, every male relative has been in the Navy, and he for Sixteen

493

years has been most exemplary. This is the first moment of sorrow he ever gave his sisters, left an Orphan at 4½, by my dear Mother bequeathed to me, as a dying Legacy, and ["has" *interlined*] been and is still the cherished object of my affections. Every Officer that he ever sailed with, gives him the highest testimonials. For this momentary error on the score of discipline, I fear unless he is speed[i]ly reinstated his high & noble Spirit will be crushed forever. I went to Washington with him, he called on Mr. Bancroft to give an explanation. He refused to see him, but that very afternoon, recommended the President to dismiss him, and without enquiry of any kind. Both Com[modor]e[s] [Lewis] Warrington & [William M.] Crane interceded for him, but the Secretary was resolute.

Will you not my dear Mr. Calhoun, for the sake of my ever to be lamented Uncle [Stephen Decatur] use your influence ["of" *altered to* "for"] his reinstatement ere it is too late. If you knew him, I am sure you would [see] he not only resembles Uncle in person but every respect, is one of the best of Brothers[;] ever since he has been a Lt. has allowed me Six hundred a year out of his pay. I will not say any more on this subject feeling assured that we have a firm friend in you.

Please say to Mrs. Calhoun, I was in Boston with my Brother & Sister [Mr. and Mrs. Francis B.] Stockton, when she was in Phila. or should have been with her. My kindest love to her. I often very often think of the happy times passed under your Roof. With my warmest regards I am Very Truly Yours, M.H. McKni[ght].

P.S. We are at Major [Levi] Twiggs, Marine Barracks[,] Phila-[delphi]a Navy Yard.

ALS in ViHi, Mason Family Papers.

From F[RANCIS] W. PICKENS

Charleston, 17 April 1845

My dear Sir, I was obliged to come down to take up my children and return to-morrow. I suppose Cousin Floride [Colhoun Calhoun] is with you now. I hope she got up safely. If it had not been for my having made the arrangements to meet me at Aiken I would have sent up my carriage with her home. As Arthur [Simkins] wrote you I thought it was unnecessary to say any more about the mortgage &c. I hope it will turn out all right.

[Franklin H.] Elmore shewed me [James K.] Polk's letter offering him the mission to England and his reply. He refuses it solely on account of his embarrassments and the time allowed him being too short to prepare for leaving. Polk urged an immediate departure at the urgent request of [Edward] Everett.

I see from Elmore's letter that he has expected it from the "correspondence of friends at Washington." I take it for granted that time will be allowed Elmore & that he will yet go. It will be an excellent appointment—the best that can be made considering the issues. I understand that there will be a change in the Cabinet & [James] Buchanan will go on the bench &c. [Robert J.] Walker is the ruling spirit. [Thomas] Ritchie will certainly go to Washington as "the organ." So Elmore informs me. It is said here that if Elmore does not accept that he has urged Gov[ernor James H.] Hammond to go in his place. It is thought he will go. I think next to Elmore he will be the ablest man for us. If Elmore goes, I do hope a sound[,] safe man will be put at the head of our Bank [of the State of South Carolina], for I do assure it is all *rotten* now. There must be a crush in it, so say all business men. I do hope you will not interfere at all as to the Pres[i]d[enc]y of the Bank even in suggestions. You have no idea of its ramifications. In haste but truly, F.W. Pickens.

P.S. As to your kind invitation to visit you I do not think I can leave home at all this Summer, but if I were of course there is no place on this earth I would rather be at than with Cousin F[loride] & yourself. F.W.P.

ALS in ScCleA; PEx in Jameson, ed., *Correspondence*, p. 1029.

From Ro[bert] Tyler, "Private"

Philadelphia, April 19th [1845]
My dear Sir, I have been intending to write to you for a fortnight past, but have been delaying the execution of my desighn, because I desired to watch the developments made at Washington, and to obtain from them, facts, to sustain my own decided conviction, as to the course of policy Mr. [James K.] Polk has determined to pursue.

From what I observe & learn the Albany Regency are in power, if not openly at least by way of Kitchen Cabinet, at Washington. We are to have a repetition of the old *game*, the *actors* being changed, that[']s all. [Martin] Van Buren played thro [Andrew] Jackson at your expense, the Albany Regency with [Silas] Wright at their head play, or attempt to play the same game with Mr. Polk (a most acces[s]ible man to their schemes) on precis[e]ly the same terms & conditions. I have many reasons to believe, & some to know, that this policy has been agreed on, after a world of deliberation & consul[t]ation had before Mr. Polk Came to Washington, thro convenient agents (Major [Auguste] D'Avezac being one), and that such policy is slowly, laboriously and cautiously, but they hope, *surely* being perfected. It is Certain that Mr. Polk *has been* & *is* in the most close & confidential relation with the N[ew] York politicians. Tho, I confess there is much of *mere suspicion* in my views I wil[l] relate certain facts to you.

John P. Heiss, may be regarded I presume (tho for the most part a very worthless person) a credible witness to a specific fact in ["connection with" *interlined*] which he proclaims himself as an actor. He incautiously made (for he is a great fool) a singular revelation to me some ten days ago here in Phila[delphia], & he related, I understand, the same circumstance to others. He informed me that when Van Buren's anti-Texas letter appeared, "Cave Johnson & the other politicians in Tenn[e]ssee insisted that the Nashville Union should endorse his letter & position;" The Editor [Alfred O.P. Nicholson] of the paper (Heiss not having the ability to write but being *proprietor*) wrote an article under the dictation of Johnson & others *endorsing* fully *Van Buren[']s letter,* and brought it [to] him to be inserted in the Union. He, being an ardent Texas-man, positively refused to lend his paper to so shameful a proceeding. "Those men then threatened to establish a rival paper at Nashville." But for his obstinacy, he declares, Tennessee would have thus, as far as the Politicians could do it, endorsed Van Buren's position. Mr. Polk was then [before the Democratic convention] a candidate for the Vice Presidency. He was, indeed the chosen man of the [Washington] Globe clique for that office before the Texas quarrel. Cave Johnson is now Postmaster General, & the man who was then editor of the Union [Nicholson] has been instantly provided for by being made recorder of the Land office. Johnson is Mr. Polk[']s Confidante. Mr. Polk before Van Buren's letter against Texas appeared, was an ardent Texas man, he then not having the remotest idea that Van Buren would oppose Jackson[']s views on the question—the Union was regarded as his organ—Johnson &c &c as his *particular friends.* This fact demonstrates that he was willing to give up Texas, anything, & everything, *to Party,* for he believed that Van [Buren] would be, in despite of all opposition, the nominee of the Convention. From the day of his nomination, nay from the day Van Buren[']s letter appeared, he has not opened his lips about Texas, untill [Robert J.]

Walker[']s intrigues & treachery with [Thomas H.] Benton & [Lewis] Cass lost the Treaty plan of annexation as the foundation of the Joint resolution, & the Joint Resolution with Benton's amendment (Polk concurring) passed the Senate. All this I say smells rankly of the Hunker school.

I will mention another fact. When the Country asked why it was that *you* to whom Mr. Polk was so much indebted, was not Cordially invited to remain in the State Dept., the answer was, "I wish to avoid all the cliques." But lo & behold it now appears that at this very moment Mr. Silas Wright had been offered his choice of places in the Cabinet, & that Mr. [Benjamin F.] Butler had been offerred [*sic*] the War Dept. The [New York] Morning News & Albany Atlass & other Wright papers assert this fact, it has no where been authoritatively contradicted, Mr. [Thomas] Ritchie in his paper of Ap[ri]l 1st gives a hint partly significant of its truth, & I have private information on which I confidently rely as to its truth. It is useless to dwell on the helpless inconsistency of this act with his professions of purity.

Another fact. Every appointment yet made for N[ew] York, Pen[n]s[yl]v[ani]a & M[a]ss[achusetts] is a complete restoration of Hunkerism.

The transfer of the Globe is a farce. You perceive that Mr. Ritchie has already attacked my father [John Tyler] for sending on the Joint Resolution to Texas. Rest assured that there is a perfect understanding among all these men of the old Regime. Benton[']s amendment cures all difference among them. [Francis P.] Blair & [John C.] Rives still retain half of the Globe it is said & believed, and I rather suspect that not a dollar has gone out of their hands. I look upon it all as a trick from beginning to the end. They have given too much ostentation to the movement, representing Blair as being in a bad humor, and they have gone so far as to say that *you* have furnished the funds for the organ. It is all intended to catch gulls.

One after another all my father's friends are being, or to be butchered, while all the time they profess kindness & great admiration for him. The Ear of the administration is turned from them, and the few who are encouraged to hope that they will be suffered to remain, are compel[l]ed by the course pursued to forswear their faith & honor. The idea in reference to yourself is quietly to *drop you*, and to buy off your friends as far as practicable. But this cannot & must not be done. We all now look to you. Will you permit me to advise that you Come back to the Senate[?] There is a vast deal of dissatisfaction prevailing everywhere in the Country at the

Course pursued, and these men must not be suffered to play their game out. They should be checked at the start, in the bud. It is easier to crush the egg of a serpent, than to kill a strong & slippery snake.

Mr. Polk is very cunning. He apparently throws a vast deal of responsibility & power upon his Cabinet, while in fact he holds the whole power tight in his own hands. For instance he votes as one in Cabinet sessions. But how is the Cabinet composed—Walker, [James] Buchanan, [John Y.] Mason vs. [George] Bancroft, Johnson, [William L.] Marcy—three & three. Mr. Polk has the casting vote.

Mr. Walker is playing for the Vice Presidency with Cass as his candidate for the Presidency with a hope for the succession. [Vice-President George M.] Dallass [*sic*] is content to be Sec[retary] of State of *that* administration, & *the family* then take *two* chances for the Presidency. Buchanan goes for the Presidency in his own right but will be destroyed at a moment[']s warning. Polk & his three Hunkers for themselves—Polk for reelection, & Wright or Benton to succeed. This *is* the state of the game, I care not how they attempt to disguise the moves. I prophesy that Benton is Sec[retary] of State before the administration ends. Buchanan & Walker are used mainly as tools for the time being. They are made to serve useful purposes, to countenance proscription &c &c &c but they get very few offices for their immediate partisans. Mr. Mason is a friend but he is timid & irresolute tho an excellent man.

Mr. Van Buren & Mr. Polk are in close & constant correspondence.

Now when you come to reflect that the Hunker school adopt a dishonest and intriguing course of policy in the attainment of an end *by choice* always, you will probably think there is some force in what I have said. Under all the circumstances of the case you must come back to the Senate. We want the aid of your voice, your position before the Public, *for we do not intend to submit to this state of things.* My Father, I will frankly say, might perhaps be made m[ore] *available* than yourself, but he has n[ot] the intrinsic popular strength that you have.

It is my firm impression that the [Democratic] party cannot stand together & that the next President will be chosen by the House of Representatives, if a whig be not elected. In fact the only way of preventing the choice of a whig will be to look to the House.

I have thus frankly written to you my views upon the politics of the day. I might say much more in confirmation of my views, but I will not fatigue you. My object is to express to you the wish of all your friends here, & my own ["wishes" *changed to* "wish"], to see you in the Senate again. We wish one man before the Country who has some fixed principles to stand by, & to whose good sense & patriotism we can rally. With great respect Y[ou]r fr[ie]nd & ob[edien]t S[ervan]t, Ro: Tyler.

ALS in ScCleA; variant PEx in Lyon G. Tyler, *Letters and Times of the Tylers,* 3:160–161. NOTE: The partial text printed by Tyler is based on a different ms. than the ALS cited above, a ms. which has not been located.

From FRANCIS WHARTON

Philadelphia, April 19, 1845

My dear Sir, It gave me the greatest pleasure to hear a few days since from your son [Patrick Calhoun?] of your thorough recovery since your arrival home. The country can ill dispense with your valuable services, and I trust that you will find strength, if not to return to public life, at least to complete those literary labours which, after all, will weigh more with posterity than efforts, either in the cabinet or the senate. The friends of constitutional law and of true political science, expect much from you now; and many an eye is turned to you at the present parenthesis in your life with eager and proud hopes. We want a full, thorough, and just, disquisition on the theory of our Constitution, and we want, in addition to it, what [Henry] Hallam has given to Great Britain, a sketch of ["our" *interlined*] constitutional history.

We met with a great loss some weeks ago in the defeat of Mr. [George W.] Woodward for the U.S. Senate. He was the regularly nominated caucus candidate and was beaten by a combination between whigs, natives, and bank-democrats, of the most disgraceful character. The great cry against Mr. Woodward by the seceders was that he was a "Calhoun man," & that he was vitally opposed to the tariff of 1842. The last is pretty much the fact, but it certainly shows a progress of light that such a man, suspected of the former error, & convicted of the latter, should receive the vote of a democratic caucus, & of three fourths of the democratic members of a Pennsylvania legislature. I trust that the tariff is weakening its hold on the bowels of our immediate fellow citizens, though it is hard to tell how far the increasing iron and coal speculations will add to its strength. I very deeply regret Mr. Woodward's non election, as you would have found in him an ardent friend, & the Senate an able member. He is decidedly the most powerful man in the party in Pennsylvania.

Mr. [James] Buchanan, it is said, is ill at ease with the president [James K. Polk]. Mr. Polk does not understand Mr. B[uchanan]'s acquiescence in Mr. [Simon] Cameron's election [as Senator from Pa.]. Be that as it may, there is a rupture which will soon take place, if it has not already done so, between the [George M.] Dallas & Buchanan wings of the party. The impression here, from the tenor of the appointments, is that Mr. Dallas, as far as presidential favour is concerned, is entirely floored. If so, I cannot help feeling that the result arises from the great error made by him & his friends in adhering to Mr. [Robert J.] Walker, as their candidate for the office of Secretary of State. If they had rallied around your standard, perhaps the republic might have been saved the blow it received through Mr. Buchanan's appointment.

It seems that your prophecy in regard to your letter to Mr. [William R.] King on slavery is fulfilled. England has bowed before it. Never did an event more thorough[ly] justify a movement of so important & bold a character as does the present conduct of the British press & ministry justify your letters on the Texas question. Even some of the most ultra [Martin] V[an] B[uren] presses of the North are now acquiescing in the correctness of the stand.

I trust that if I ever can be of any service to you here you will at once command me. That homage which at the beginning I felt towards your character, I can never forget. With great respect, I remain yours most truly, Francis Wharton.

ALS in ScCleA. NOTE: This letter was addressed to Calhoun at Fort Hill and was postmarked in Philadelphia on 4/21. At the bottom of the last page of the letter, Wharton wrote and then canceled the date "April 21, 1845."

From W[ILLIAM] GILMORE SIMMS

Woodland[s], [Barnwell District, S.C.] April 20, 1845

Dear Sir, I trust that the nature of this communication will excuse me for trespassing on your time and attention. I have been solicited by the Editor of the Democratic Review, to prepare a brief biography of Mr. [George] McDuffie to accompany an engraved portrait of that gentleman which is to appear in a forthcoming number of that work. Esteeming Mr. McD[uffie] as one of the greatest men that our country has produced, I am desirous of bestowing the utmost care upon the article, and to present no facts, and urge no opinions, without first securing for them, the sanction of those best informed in the one and best prepared to determine upon the other. To you, Sir, I turn, therefore, in order that I should be equally prepared in both respects. I should like to know what, in particular, are the chief characteristics of Mr. McD[uffie]'s mind, what have been his best achievements, what were the several steps in his mental and political career, what were his best passages of arms in debate, what is his manner—what his peculiarities, whether of taste, temper, thought, action ["and" *canceled and* "or" *interlined*] expression. Of course, I should be sorry to confess, that, on most of these points, I had not formed some general notions of my own; but I wish to have my own views fortified, or to be enabled, from good authorities to review and adjust them. All such matters, ["as" *interlined*] are suitable for such an article as that I propose to prepare—all matters which may be honorable to Mr. McD[uffie] are necessary to the subject—the training of his mind, its first *public* beginnings—its various successes, and a fair examination of his political ethics—all of which, I assume to be in your power to impart—I should be most happy to receive at your hands. In particular, as furnishing material least likely to be exceptionable and most likely to be attractive, I should be glad, if you could dwell upon his best forensic and public displays—suffic[i]ently indicate the opposing parties to give interest to the contest, and sum up the general merits of the issue. For a work like the one mentioned—the Democratic Review—I should, of course, avoid all matter likely to pr[o]voke disenssion [*sic*]. My purpose is simply to satisfy ["curios" *canceled*] a reasonable curiosity in regard to the *mind* of our subject, and to do him honor in making this attempt. With profound respect, Sir, I am, Very faithfully, Your ob[edien]t and obliged Servant, &c W. Gilmore Simms.

ALS in ScCleA; PC in Oliphant, Odell, and Eaves, eds., *The Letters of William Gilmore Simms*, 2:56–57. NOTE: The *Democratic Review* of May, 1845, contained an engraving but no sketch of McDuffie.

From PERCY WALKER and Others

Mobile, April 21st 1845
Dear Sir, At a Democratic meeting held in this city on the 14th Instant, the undersigned were appointed a committee "to express the cordial approbation of the meeting of your public conduct, their gratitude for your services, and to offer to you on the part of the

meeting, such other manifestations of their respect and esteem as we might think proper."

In carrying out the purpose of this resolution, we beg leave to assure you of the high sense felt by your Democratic fellow-citizens of this place of your distinguished public services, and especially of the wisdom, firmness and patriotism that marked your conduct as Secretary of State under the late administration.

Grateful as this duty is to us, we fear that we can but lamely express, the admiration felt for those talents, that have lifted you so high in the world's regard, and the devotion of which to the public interests, has tended so much to a right understanding of our peculiar form of Government, and reflected lasting glory upon the country. It is to your public efforts that your fellow-citizens are mainly indebted for a true exposition of the relative powers and duties of the State and Federal Governments. From you they have learned the great truth, that the harmony of all, can only be preserved by each one's confining it's actions within the allotted sphere, and that the rights of the people and the States can only be properly secured, by carefully guarding against the centralizing tendency of our Federative system.

["But, Sir" *canceled*] It was made especially our duty, to thank you, [for] the manner, in which as Secretary of State, you conducted the negotiation for the re-annexation of Texas. You were chiefly instrumental in effecting the settlement of that ["measure" *canceled*] great question, upon which national prosperity and the security of the South so much depend. In your official papers is to be found a noble vindication of the character and rights of the Southern people, and our gratitude is due to you for the rescue of that rich section of our Continent from fanatical influence, and European dominion.

And now ["while"(?) *canceled*] when every indication promises the addition of Texas to our family of States, thus affording security to the Southern Seaboard, and opening a wider field, for the march of republican institutions, permit us to assure you of our grateful sense of your agency in effecting this great result.

Many, very many of your fellow-citizens in this quarter of the Union, earnestly desire to see, & hear you and to *shake* you by the *hand*, and for them we would press you to gratify their wishes.

As an evidence of their approbation of your public and private life, we are instructed to tender you a Public Dinner, to be given in this place, at such time as you may designate.

We have understood that it is your intention, ere long to visit this State, and we trust that you will extend your journey to Mobile, and afford us an opportunity of manifesting the sincere regard in which you are held by Your Friends & fellow-citizens, Percy Walker, Thomas Holland, Thomas McGran, W[illiam] R. Hallett, J[ohn] A. Campbell.

LS (in Walker's hand) in ScCleA; PC in the Mobile, Ala., *Register and Journal,* May 27, 1845, p. 2; PC in the Charleston, S.C., *Courier,* June 3, 1845, p. 2; PC in the Richmond, Va., *Enquirer,* June 11, 1845, p. 4. NOTE: Calhoun's AEU reads "Invitation to partake of a publick dinner at Mobile."

From ISRAEL HOGE, "Private"

Post Office, Zanesville [Ohio]
Ap[ri]l 22, 1845

My dear Sir, Your friends in this neighborhood deem the enclosed due you for your past services & hope in the future that you may be still farther elevated in the counsels of the nation. Yours most respect[fully,] Israel Hoge[,] P[ost] M[aster].

[Enclosure]

Ap[ri]l 22nd 1845

Dear Sir, A number of States-rights republicans of Muskingum County Ohio, wishing to testify to you their high esteem for many eminent services you have rendered our common country in the different situations ["which" *interlined*] you have been ["placed" *altered to* "called"] to serve her, particularly the distinguished part you have taken in the various important questions which have agitated the public mind within the past year—embrace this mode of conveying to you an expression of their strong personal regard and their sincere thanks for the many sacrifices, which you have made in behalf of those principles we hold to be necessary to perpetuate our glorious Constitution—The doctrines of [17]98, which were maintained *then* by our republican Fathers, with [Thomas] Jefferson at their head and which we believe to be equally true *now* and equally essential to the welfare of our country. W[illia]m Pringle, Israel Hoge, Jno. Burwell, John Sockman, Stephen Burwell, Ja[me]s Taylor, J[unio]r, Daniel DeDejearmett[?], A. Wilkins, J[ohn] S. Parkinson, W[illia]m Galigher, Samuel Clark, Charles McDill, W[illia]m M. Wallace, B. Van Horne.

ALS with En in ScCleA. NOTE: An AEU by Calhoun reads "["States right" *canceled*] From several individuals of Zanesville Ohio, belonging to the States rights party." The En, in Hoge's handwriting, was signed by each man personally.

From A[NDREW] J. DONELSON, *"Private"*

Washington Texas, April 24, 1845

My D[ea]r Sir, It gives me pleasure to inform you that upon the basis of the first and second section of the Joint Resolution for the annexation of Texas, which you instructed me to present to this Government, there is now a probability amounting to almost *certainty* that the measure will be consummated before the next session of our Congress.

Upon my arrival here there was excitement in the public mind, growing out of an impression that the President of this Republic [Anson Jones] would not accept the proposals, or refer the subject to either Congress or the people. And there was unfortunately some ground for such an apprehension in the delay of the President to issue his Proclamation, yet he never for a moment in any interview with me intimated a wish to interpose an obstacle to the judgement of the people.

You will be surprised, however, when I inform you that Gen[era]l [Samuel] Houston brought all his influence to bear against our proposals, and in favor of resorting to the negotiation contemplated by the Senate amendment to the House bill. Upon the latter basis there is no doubt, aided by his influence, this Government expected to throw me back for new instructions; but my communication was prepared with a full knowledge of the temper of the cabinet, and I presented it the morning after my arrival as containing the *ultimatum* of President [James K.] Polk in which he had the concurrence also of President [John] Tyler.

Great hesitation and indecision were manifested throughout the corps of officeholders, and it was not until Gen[era]l Houston could be seen, and until there were returns from other points in the State, that the President announced the issue of his Proclamation to call Congress.

It is useless, however, to trouble you with the details of the various incidents which marked a settled purpose here to change the basis selected by my Governm[en]t, nor will it be interesting to you to know the particular steps taken by me to defeat such a purpose. It is proper for me, however, to say to you that in a long correspondence into which I have been drawn by Gen[era]l Houston I have been obliged to refer to certain statements from him representing the willingness of Texas to retain her public domain and pay her own debts. In a letter directed to you from New Orleans I urged upon you to let go that feature of the Treaty, stating to you that Houston thought Texas would be better off *retaining* than *ceding* her public lands. At the time he made this declaration our attention was confined to Mr. [George] McDuffie's bill, and it is obvious that when you took out of that bill the provisions concerning the public debt and lands of Texas, there was nothing left but the general provision admitting Texas as a Territory, and securing to her citizens a community of rights and privileges as citizens of the United States. In rebutting the objections made by Gen[era]l Houston to the House bill—objections drawn out with care and intended to influence President Jones—I have maintained that he was committed substantially to that bill, and could not oppose it without a change of the position occupied by him in December last, when I communicated to you *confidentially* [in a letter of 12/24/1844] the extent to which the provisions of the Treaty might be modified without danger to the measure, so far as it depended upon the approbation of Texas. As that letter may be important to me I wish you to preserve it.

Without further reference to the progress of the measure since my last arrival at this place, I may say to you that President Jones in convoking Congress has removed the only possible obstacle to its consummation, which was the necessity of obtaining *"the consent of the existing Governm[en]t,"* to the proposals contained in the House bill. Congress will give this consent most cheerfully, and authorise a convention of the people at an early day, when the new constitution and a Government adapted to the changes made necessary by the admission into our union, will follow in time for the next meeting of our Congress.

The people of Texas are holding public meetings throughout the Territory, and are expressing their approbation of the terms offered to them by the United States with a unanimity which no other debated question has ever received.

This great measure is therefore consummated unless the spirit of faction, appearing again in our Congress, may refuse to pass the law redeeming our pledge to Texas when she brings forward her Republican form of Governm[en]t.

I congratulate you on the possession of an additional guarantee for our safety from internal as well as external foes—a guarantee which you have sacrificed much to obtain, and for which the country can never thank you & President Tyler too much.

With my thanks for your personal kindness on all occasions to me;

and my great respect for your exalted public & private character, I have the honor to be very sincerely & truly, Y[ou]r ob[edien]t Ser-[van]t, A.J. Donelson.

P.S. Consider the reference I have made to Gen[era]l Houston as private & confidential. I still have a hope that he will withdraw his opposition. A.J.D.

[Marginal P.S.] See the enclosed paper said to be the organ of the Govt. After I see Gen[era]l Houston I will write again. Do not therefore on any account, let my name reach the public, as having indulged a doubt about his course.

ALS in ScCleA; PEx in Jameson, ed., *Correspondence*, pp. 1029–1032.

From ABBOTT LAWRENCE

Boston, April 24th 1845

My Dear Sir, I beg to acknowledge the receipt of your favor of the 9th [of April], which I have under consideration. You shall hear from me again in two or three days. I remain Dear Sir Very faithfully yours, Abbott Lawrence.

ALS in ScCleA.

To T[HOMAS] G. CLEMSON, [Brussels]

Fort Hill, 25th April 1845

My dear Sir, The last mail brought me yours by the Great Western of the 24th March, and one from Anna [Maria Calhoun Clemson] to her mother [Floride Colhoun Calhoun] by the same conveyance.

My letters subsequent to that of the 26th Feb., acknowledged by yours, will give you all of the political news up to the date of the last, transmitted, if I recollect aright by the Hibernia. Since then, the most important, is the dismissal of [Francis P.] Blair & the [Washington] Globe, and the adoption of [Thomas] Ritchie & a new paper [the *Union*] to be published by him, as the organ of the administration. I am not certain, that it indicates any change of policy; but it is a great point to get clear of Blair & his "filthy sheet." Ritchie will be at least decent and decorous; but I apprehend too little elevated for a Government paper, and too much devoted to the old clique & party taticks [*sic*] to produce any considerable change in the policy of Mr. [James K.] Polk & his cabinet. I hope, I may be deceived. I am sincerely anxious, that the administration should go right, and shall take no ground against it, unless I should be forced by its acts to believe, that they are resolved to restore to power the miserable clique, which was overthrown at Baltimore; and on the overthrow of which, Mr. Polk was raised to power.

You are right in your opinion, in reference to [Edward] Everett [U.S. Minister to Great Britain]. [Franklin H.] Elmore has had the mission he fills tendered to him. He has declined the place, but on grounds ["which" *interlined*] will lead ["probably" *interlined*] to the renewal of the tender, & his acceptance.

But to pass from politicks to private affairs. The price of cotton is, indeed, so low at present, that it yields but little profit. Our sales, between this & Alabama this year, amounted to 400 bales averaging nearly 500 pounds to the bale, which at 10 cents would have given a gross income of $20,000 and a net income of about $15,000, after deducting expenses of every discription [*sic*]; but instead of that, it has not netted $5,000. The Alabama crop sold at a price averaging less than 5 cents, and leaving a net profit of less than 3 cents the pound. Yet I would not advise you to sell your place & hands. The low price of cotton depresses the price of land and negroes, although they both keep up, especially the latter, much better than you would suppose; but I do not think you could sell without a loss at this time. Cotton must rise. The very low price must discourage its production, while it must greatly increase its consumption. When it rises, every thing will rise with it, and especially land & negroes, when, if you should feel disposed to sell, you might at a great profit. In the mean time, you may do something more than clear expenses, though not a great deal more, at the present price of cotton; but your gang will be rapidly increasing, not less certainly than 3 or 4 per cent, and your place be improving in value, by putting it [in] good condition. The great point is to get & keep a good overseer, [even] if you have to pay high wages. Your present one has a high character & I think will do well.

I am not a little surprised, that Col. [Francis W.] Pickens should write you about the instalment due Arthur [Simkins]. If he did it without his request, it was volunteering in what he had no concern; but, if at his request, he ought to have stated all the facts, which he has not.

The facts are these. Arthur wrote me before the instalment became due, and desired to know to whom he must look for payment.

I informed him to Andrew [Pickens Calhoun]. Shortly after, I received a letter from Andrew, who wrote me, that he had been to Mobile, & found cotton selling at but 4½ [cents] per pound. I felt confident it would rise some, and wrote him not to sell before March, unless he could get 6 cents, calculating that the duty on cotton in England would be repealed, and that it would raise the price to 6 cents. I wrote also ["to" *interlined*] Arthur, stating what I had written to Andrew, and informed him, that I could not think of sacraficing [*sic*] our crop at the then very low price; & that he must wait with us, 'till March, when I had directed our cotton to be sold, be the price what it may. I heard nothing from him, and concluded, that he had acquiesced in the arrangement and remained under that impression, until after my return home in March. In the meane time Andrew had gone to Mobile to sell about the mid[d]le of March. The steamer arrived late in the month, & the news of the repeal of the duty did not reach there until after he had sold, by which we lost nearly $2000 on the sale of our crop. The sales left a nett balance, but little more than sufficient to meet the instalment due on the Cuba purchase (the place purchased from Glover).

As soon, as I heard of the result, I took immediate measures to place John [Ewing] Bonneau in funds to meet the instalment due Arthur, and wrote to him to draw on him for the amount of the instalment with interest from the 1st January, & wrote, at the same time to Mr. Bonneau to credit us with the amount on your notes. The conduct of Arthur in the affair surprised me. The request for the short indulgence was reasonable. He ought not to have asked, or expected a sacrafice of our cotton crop, at the low price it was then selling, which would have involved a loss equal to ⅔ of the amount of the instalment, compared to what it was reasonable to expect the rise would be in a few month[s]. At all events, he ought to have informed ["me" *interlined*], that the arrangement I proposed did not suit him, & that he wanted the amount immediately.

The long continued low price of cotton falls with great weight on us. Our estate in Alabama is a noble one; and, if possible, must not be sacraficed. At present prices, but a little more can be done, beyond keeping down interest, & preventing the increase of debt. If that can be done, we must wait patiently for the rise of price. In the meane time, our force is increasing rapidly [and] our places, both here & there, improving. My improvement on this place during the last year has added more than $500 to its value.

The spring thus far has been very dry; more so, than I have ever known. We have had no rain, but one or two light sprinkles, for the last four weeks. Cotton, which has been planted for a for[t]night, is only very partially up. The prospect for rain is still bad.

The measles seem to be universally prevalent all over the country. There have ["been" *interlined*] two or three deaths in consequence of them, and among others, Mr. [Fair] Kirksey, the late partner of Mr. [John S.] Lorton. We have had three cases in the yard; but the quarter has as yet escaped. Cornelia's is the last of the three, & she is on the recovery.

All join their love to you & Anna & the children [John Calhoun Clemson and Floride Elizabeth Clemson]. Kiss them for their Grandfather. Your affectionate father, J.C. Calhoun.

ALS in ScCleA; PEx in Jameson, ed., *Correspondence*, pp. 652–653.

From E. J. Peterson

Dandridge Tenn., Ap[ri]l 25th 1845

Sir, A part of the students of Murray Academy have formed themselves into a body corporate, for the mutual benefit of its members in oratory, and for the promotion of Literature &c. It is to be termed "the Animicultus society of Murray Academy." Being desirous of obtaining Gentlemen of high literary attainments as honorary members, we respectfully solicit your name as one. Any books or money that you would feel disposed to give would be very thankfully rec[eive]d. Y[ou]rs very Respec[t]fully, E.J. Peterson, Cor[responding] Sec[retary] &c.

ALS in ScCleA. NOTE: An AEU by Calhoun reads: "Informing me of my appointment to an honorable membership of the Animicultus Society of Murray Academy Ten[ness]ee."

To J[OHN] Y. MASON, [Attorney General]

Fort Hill, 26th April 1845

My dear Sir, I am not sufficiently acquainted with the case of Lt. W[illiam] Decatur Hurst refer[r]ed to in the enclosed [letter to me from M.H. McKnight, dated 4/16], to form an opinion in relation to it; but it does seem to me, taking the facts of the case to be as stated therein, that it is a hard case. I am not the advocate of duelling, but

[as] it is not one of those offenses which demoralizes and destroys the efficiency of a navy, I doubt exceedingly the policy of punishing it, by inflicting the highest penalty on it known to the Naval code. There ["are" *interlined*] many offences very lightly punished, far more prenicious to the service than it.

But be this as it may, surely his near relationship to [Stephen Decatur] the most heroick commander that ever adorned our service, & the iden[t]ity of the family with the establishment & his own good conduct heretofore, ought not to pass for nothing.

I hope you will give your attention to the case. I write to you because of your recent connection with the [Navy] Department and the deep interest, which I know you take in the prosperity of the establishment, and because I am not intimately enough acquainted with Mr. [George] Bancroft [Secretary of the Navy] personally to write to him on such a subject. If on examination, you should think the case is a hard one and that the rules of the service may be relaxed in relation to it without injury, and that you can interfere in it without impropriety, your own good sense will best direct you what steps ought to be taken.

I take deep interest in whatever is related or connected with the name of Decatur. I was intimately acquainted with the Commodore, and was much attached to him, as he was to myself, which is my apology for interfering in any manner with the case. With great respect your's truly, J.C. Calhoun.

ALS in ViHi, Mason Family Papers.

From ROBERT G. SCOTT

Richmond, April 27th 1845

My Dear Sir, I have postponed writing to you as I promised until I could speak with certainty of the result of the Virginia elections. That result is now known & a glorious one it is. We shall have a majority on joint ballot ranging from 15 to 25 & it may go up to 30. I think this majority will be of the right stamp. But more than this—[Robert M.T.] Hunter & [James A.] Seddon are elected [Representatives from Va.]. The former by nearly 200 majority; & the latter by 262, in this ["heretofore" *interlined*] strong Whig population. Never have I seen such a triumph. Old Hanover [County] has come back to us by a majority of 32. Hunter[']s own county Essex, returns to the Democratic family. Bailey [*sic*; Thomas H. Bayly] is elected in the Accomac[k] District by at least 120 majority. [Archibald] Atkinson, [George C.] Dromgoole, Treadway [*sic*; William M. Tredway], Hubbard [*sic*; Edmund W. Hubard], [Shelton F.] Leake (from the Albemarle District), [Henry] Bedinger, [William] Taylor, [George W.] Hopkins or [John B.] George, [Augustus A.] Chapman, [Joseph] Johnson, [William G.] Brown & Taylor, are all elected, leaving the Loudo[u]n District alone to the Federalists, & that has elected a Texas Whig. Thus you will see my Dear Sir that our old State has been waked up, & that she may now be counted on to lead the South, in the coming struggle. Could we have done more[?] Your best & strongest friends go to Washington. They will with your own State delegation present an array of talent, firmness, sound judgment, fidelity to our principles & elevation of character, above vastly above their adversaries. But a new enquiry at once arises. Hunter[']s election, removes him from the list of those from whom a selection of Senator will be made. Our present Governor [James McDowell] goes out next winter & we have to elect another. Who are to fill these high stations[?] The West will expect to have one of these. For years our Governors have come from beyond the mountain. [William S.] Archer our Senator lives in Amelia. The West will then probably claim the Senator & the East the Governor. But who are they to be[?] Our present Governor will not do for the Senate. But he is young comparatively & talented. Many of the Western members will prefer him. But I have no idea he can be elected. Judge [Isaac S.] Penn[y]backer is the next ["choice" *interlined*] with that branch of the party. But he can hardly be elected, for reasons as strong if not stronger, than those applicable to our Governor. In looking about Dr. [Austin?] Brockenbrough, who is quasi a resident of the West has occurred to some of us. But is he sufficiently separated from the old leaven[?] If not he would be worse than either, for his control[l]ing influence over the new organ at Washington, would be fatal. Yet I have strong reasons for believing that the Doctor is at heart with us. Do *you* know anything on this subject? If you do, fail not at once, to let some friend here be informed of what you do know. If he will go with us, to place him in the Senate, would be a measure of inestimable value. Your own observation will at once picture out the great advantages. I have taken measures to procure information on this head, but it will be some weeks before I can procure it in a reliable form. The selection of our Governor, is hardly of less importance, than the Senator. A sound, able, practical man at the head of the State, would give a direction at home to our movements, ["of" *canceled*] such as would rapidly give power, efficiency & cohesion to our party. We shall have less difficulty as to this selection than the other. For in the East, we can present several names, upon which our friends can rally. William O. Goode, Richard Kidder Meade &c would give us all we could desire. Already are our friends quietly yet decidedly looking to these matters. The last evening brought me several letters. Dromgoole might have been in our way, but his intemperate habits, places him I think out of the chance of further elevation. Such is a brief outline of our position, as to men. But my Dear Sir, old Virginia is now sounder than for 20 years on the great principles which you hold dear. Texas & the Tariff have this spring done the work. Texas, because that is truly a question, connecting itself with the South & the Slavery of the South. The Tariff, because Virginia has firmly resolved, to abide not by the plundering bill of 1842, but resolutely at *all hazards*, to demand its modification. In this, the tide water country of Virginia are nearly unanimous. And especially, that long, populous & rich peninsula between the waters of the York & the Rappahannock, extending from New Point Comfort, to the foot of the blue Ridge, & embracing the counties of Matthews [*sic*; Mathews], Middlesex, Gloucester, King & Queen, King William, Essex, Hanover, Caroline, Spotsylvania, Orange, Madison, & Green[e], from which *not a single Whig* has been elected to our Legislature. Accomac[k] too, sends us both Democrats & Warwick & Elizabeth City elects a Democrat, & turns out a Whig. Indeed looked upon in every aspect, I do from my soul, most heartily congratulate you on this victory, as the pristige [*sic*; presage] of what is to follow. Our people look [*one word canceled*] *now* to your State, to give us in due season, the successor of the ["Pre" *canceled*] present President. In regard to Mr. [Thomas] Ritchie, & his taking charge of the Government organ at Washington, I can not undertake at this moment to for[e]shadow what may come [of] it. But I have but slight fears as to the consequences. We here stand *now* in a position to restrain any offensive action. We are too strong to be trifled with, much less deceived, even was there a disposition to do either, which I by no means suspect. But the possession of strenght [*sic*] & its wise use, is the position of safety. The former we have, & the latter I have no doubt will be practiced. I am deceived in our men, if this be not proved. Already the supporters of the [Richmond] Enquirer in Virginia, are appealing to us, to keep up its vigor, & to take measures for preserving its future influence & efficiency. As to Mr. Polk[']s dispensation of office, we look here but for little. Indeed in my judgment the less we get the better. None certainly ought to be sought or taken, by begging for it, as the mendicant seeks his daily bread. I have little question the office of Secretary of State is already too hot for the present incumbent [James Buchanan]. What with our Texan negotiations, Mexican troubles, Brazilian squabbles & the growling of John Bull, I rather suspect the Pen[n]sylvanian would be glad to be back in the Senate. Or has a longing eye to a quiet seat on the bench of the Supreme Court. And then among the on dits ["of the day" *interlined*] we hear Mr. [Andrew] Stevenson is to become premeir [*sic*], & [Attorney General John Y.] Mason to retire, or go abroad. About all this I know but little, & care less. If Mr. Polk & his Cabinet do right, I will approve; if wrong I will ["not" *interlined*] spare them the less, but on the contrary condemn them the more because I gave my aid to bring them into power. But I have wandered from the main purpose of this letter, which was to let you know how stood things in Virginia; that accomplished I designed to stop. With my best & sincerest wishes for your health & happiness, I am with high regard & respect yours truly, Robert G. Scott.

P.S. Say to your friends to command me in all things here. Where is [Franklin H.] Elmore[?] He wrote me 3 or 4 weeks since & said he would write[.] I [*two or three words canceled*] replied fully to his letter, & since then he has been as dumb as an oyster. I rejoice *he* did not agree to go to England. We want much more such men at *home* just now. R.G. Scott.

ALS in ScCleA; variant PEx in Jameson, ed., *Correspondence*, pp. 1032–1035.

From H[ENRY] W. CONNER

Charleston, April 28, 1845

Dear Sir, The late advices from England, Mexico & the Brazils represent our relations with those countries to be in an unsettled & precarious condition & the fact has created in our minds some uneasiness with regard to the future.

Occupying the position that the Bank of Charleston has occupied & must always occupy towards the public it is very important that we should prepare ourselves by anticipation for any possible contingency that might happen.

With the means of ["our" *canceled*] information in our possession at present we feel ourselves incompetent to arrive at any satisfactory conclusion but relying upon your uniform willingness to impart the benefits of your superior knowledge & experience in all matters pertaining to the public good we have taken the liberty of asking your opinion so far as you may feel it proper to give us with regard to the probable course of events for the next 12 months or two years.

Are the probabilities in favour of a war with England or Mexico or both?

Is it probable that whether the result be peace or war the public mind will be kept agitated & unsettled by the action of our next Congress to the disturbance & injury of the business of the country?

What would be the effects of a war upon the Banking System of the country & particularly upon the Banking & business of the South?

These are questions of great moment to us & it is their importance with the motives that prompts them that induces us to appeal to you for their answer.

Whatever you may please to say to us will be considered confidential. My ideas extended no further than to communicate its substance to not exceeding 3 of our most active directors—if more agreeable to you however the information shall remain [with] myself exclusively.

If an emergency arise you may expect again to be called for by the voice of the people. I percieve [*sic*] evidences I think already of the public mind turning in that direction. Very truly Y[ou]rs &C, H.W. Conner.

ALS in ScCleA.

From W[ILLIA]M HOGAN

Boston, April 28th 1845

When last I had the honor of seeing you, My dear Sir, I handed you a letter from my friend Judge [James M.] Wayne of Sav[a]n[na]h [Associate Justice of the U.S. Supreme Court] & the Hon. Isaac [E.] Holmes [Representative] of S.C. recommending me as a fit person to fill the Office of Consul at Trinidad ["Cuba" *canceled*] West Indies. I had then some fears & I believe I took the liberty of mentioning them to you—whether the South would benefit by the change of Administration which took place & have not since visited Washington; nor should I ever do so, had I any weight in the country, untill there was a [*ms. torn; one or two words missing*] drawn between

514

North & South, for [*ms. torn; one or two words missing*] seems to me that untill this is [*ms. torn; one or two words missing*] Southern men will permit themselves to be the dupes of Northern politicians; but as I have no political weight I will thank you for the letter which I left with you, or what would be still better, a line from you to Mr. [James] Buchanan, Secr[etar]y of State, recommending me for the Consulate of Trinidad, Barbadoes, or any of any other place in Spain, France, or Germany. Emolument is not my principle object, but I am in pursuit of health & information.

I have written a small volume recently, entitled "Popery as it was & as it is" which you will please accept from me. I shall follow up the subject. I send it to my friend Mr. Holmes of Charleston who will forward it to you together with this letter[.] I have the honor to Remain Sir Respectfully, Wm. Hogan.

ALS in ScCleA. NOTE: Hogan (1788–1848), an Irish-born former priest, was the author of (among many other works) A *Synopsis of Popery, as It Was and as It Is* (Boston: Saxton & Keir, 1845).

From ABBOTT LAWRENCE

Boston, April 30th 1845

My Dear Sir, I received in due course of Mail your favor of the 9th and in reply have to state, that I am not a money lender, nor are my particular friends, with whom I am associated in the manufacture of Cottons, or those engaged in Foreign Commerce. We however entertain and cherish feelings of kindness toward our brethren of the South, and notwithstanding the disturbing causes that have existed between us for sometime past, we do not forget that we are of the same blood and Country, living under the same Government, and subject to those alternations of prosperity and adversity, which have been often experienced throughout the length and breadth of our land. We cannot therefore be indifferent to the prosperity of the South, when we see and feel that our own is identified in a great measure with that of the *whole* Union.

I have a strong desire to accomplish the object of your wishes, and I beg here to remark that I entertain the highest respect and regard for your private character, and have full confidence in your honor and integrity. *I am* [*one word canceled*] not personally in condition at this time to extend the accommodation you wish, and have therefore taken the liberty to call on friends who approve the views I have presented, and are ready to join me in the sum of $6000 each.

We cannot of course know anything of the security you propose—this we leave, believing you will give us ample security for the loan under any and all circumstances. Our proposal then is to loan to you the sum of $30,000 with interest at six per cent payable annually in Boston, with $6000 of the principal in annual payments, the last payment to be made at the expiration of five years—and to be secured by Mortgage on property in the State of Alabama with the joint and several note or Bond of yourself and Son [Andrew Pickens Calhoun]. The papers to be made to Francis C. Lowell Esq[uir]e in trust for himself, Abbott Lawrence, Nathan Appleton, David Sears, ["&" *interlined*] John A. Lowell ["and" *canceled*].

The money shall be ready for you at any time after the first of June, or whenever it may be convenient for your son to visit us.

You are aware that we are Merchants, and that punctuality is an essential element in all transactions with us. *I know your habits of business*, and perhaps the remark is superfluous—yet I am quite sure you will excuse me for the hint, after the experience we have had in transactions of this kind, with numbers of men of elevated character and standing.

With respect to sending your Cotton here for sale, we have no wish to make a condition of that sort. You shall be left free to send it to that market where it will yield the most money. The clothing for your people you will also purchase where it may be most convenient. The only condition we impose for this loan is, *perfect security*, and the punctual payment of the interest annually—and $6000 of the principal ["annually" *interlined*] for the term of five years.

I rejoice to know you can produce cotton at 6 cents per pound, and make a fair business of it. The price is now very low, although somewhat better than three months since. It would be greatly to our interest, if it bore a higher price. We find the consumption of manufactures much larger, when Cotton bears a full price, than when it comes down to about the cost of production. The American market is becoming of more importance to us every ["day" *interlined*]—the quantity of Cotton to be spun in the United States, I think will be doubled in eight years—(the present consumption being at least 400,000 bales) I have little doubt that in 1856 with a steady course of legislation, the consumption in this Country, will reach One Million of bales—(New Orleans). You may be surprized at this statement, but the history of our Cotton spinning, with the prospects before us, brings conviction to my mind, that the above estimate is not exaggerated. We are now exporting coarse cotton cloths to every quarter of the Globe, where they are admitted—and I assure you our goods have the preference in every market to which they have been shipped.

When I look at the Colonial policy of Great Britain, and the efforts *made*, and *continued*—to produce Cotton in India, in which they have succeeded in improving the quality and increasing the quantity, and that the price of our Cotton has been reduced ["in" *canceled*] by this competition, and that we have forced the British Government to repeal the duty on Cotton, in consequence of the competition of our fabrics in Foreign markets—I am compelled to believe that one of the best securities for the Cotton planter may be found in raising up a powerful competitor to Great Britain in our own Country.

There are now under construction in the United States more than 300,000 spindles, many of which are designed for goods suited to foreign markets. The demand for Cotton goods is much greater than the supply, and I cannot see that there will be any diminution the present year—the prices however of all Cotton goods will be materially reduced, when the mills now constructing shall be in operation. It is the demand for foreign Countries that enables us to maintain the present prices. If I had not already written a long letter, I would give you some statistical facts upon the growth and manufacture of Cotton. I must however leave the subject for a future occasion—with this expression of opinion, that I have full confidence in the rapid increase of the culture ["& manufacture" *interlined*] of Cotton in this Country, and believe ["that(?)" *canceled*] if prosecuted with economy and vigour, the grower and manufacturer will find their interests the same, and reap an ample remuneration for the Capital employed.

I had anticipated the pleasure of a visit to South Carolina, the present season—but the spring is so far advanced that I must postpone it till another year.

I pray you, Dear Sir, to accept the assurances with which I remain Very faithfully yours, Abbott Lawrence.

ALS in ScCleA; retained copy in MH.

From B[ENJAMIN] G. WRIGHT

Belmont [County,] Ohio, April 30th [1845?]
Dear Sir, I received your favour, without date, Postmarked April 4th
a few days since. And though I am ["not" *interlined*] convinced
that your friends are wrong in their solicitations I must acknowl-
ed[g]e that you are right if the people were true to themselves.

Your letter breathes the true spirit of exalted & disinterested
patriotism; & my object in this is, not to ask your leave to publish
that letter but, to ask you to prohibit its publication if you deem such
a prohibition necessary. If not you will please let me know as soon
as convenient, & send me a date to be affixed thereto.

As you may not have retained a copy of your letter to me I send
the last sentence but one, which is all that I think you could have
any objection to being published. It is as follows; "If I could be so
corrupt, as to consent to be an instrument in their hands—if I would
withdraw my opposition to a protective Tariff & wasteful & extrave-
gant [*sic*] expenditures, & come out an advocate for the principle,
that [to] the victors belong the spoils, the road to the White House
would be a broad & open way to me."

In conclusion I trust that you will not prohibit the publication &
if so your friends will have reason to look for you to visit the West
& North in your own way & at your own time. Truly yours &c, B.G.
Wright.

ALS in ScCleA. NOTE: This letter has been assigned tentatively to the year 1845
because it seems to be a continuance of the correspondence represented by
Wright's letter to Calhoun of 3/17/1845. This is, however, not a certainty.

From JAMES BUCHANAN, [Secretary of State]

Department of State
Washington, April 1845
Sir: I transmit to you enclosed a letter addressed to this Department
by Gen[era]l [Duff] Green, presenting his account as Bearer of
Despatches to Mexico and Texas. As there is nothing on file here
to show what was the understanding between this gentleman and
yourself as to the allowance to be made to him in compensation for
this service, I will thank you to state your opinion to be used as a
voucher as to the correctness of Gen[era]l Green's account, which I

am disposed to settle according to your wishes. I am Sir, very respectfully, Your obedient servant, James Buchanan.

FC in DNA, RG 59 (State Department), Domestic Letters, 35:172 (M-40:33).

From W[illia]m Gregg

Charleston, April 1845

Dear Sir, Your esteemed favour of 27th ult[im]o came to hand in due course of mail. Your remarks about the protective system are correct, and I concur with you fully. But I cannot think for a moment, that the introduction of the kind of cotton manufactures which it will be our interest to adhere rigidly to, can by any possibility cause those engaging in such pursuits, to change in the sligh[t]est degree their politics. It will be decidedly our interest to stick to the coarser fabrics, in which the raw material gives us a great advantage. And while we can make cloth as I am now doing, at a cost for the labour of all employed (including the keeping our Machinery in order) of 3 c[en]ts per lb[.], a sum not equal to the cost of carrying the cotton from Aiken to Liverpool, what interest can we have to seduce us over to the protective system? Many of the coarse spinners at the North are opposed to it in all its forms, and I believe all would be, were it not that they live in an atmosphere peculiar to its growth, surrounded by so many persons, and interests which live by its bounty. They are not so short sighted as not to perceive that every increase of the Tariff, produces a rise in wages & brings new capital into the business without creating additional outlets, yet they are either silenced, or carried along with the crowds around them.

I cannot immagine [*sic*] any interest which may spring up among us with the change I propose, unless it be the manufacture of Iron, the proprietors of which might be induced to abandon their allegiance to Southern principles by joining in the clamour for protection. I will not say more on this subject but refer you to an article No[.] 1 which will appear in the Charleston ["Courier" *interlined*] in answer to [a] letter from W[illia]m F. Davie Esq. recently published.

I think you have fallen into error in two particulars, and as I feel well assured that you, like all other great men, follow the rule of gathering knowledge wherever you may meet it, however humble the source, I will therefore endeavour to put you right in these two particulars. In the first place, you state, that the old Atlantic States

519

engaged in the culture of Cotton[,] Rice & Tobac[c]o now manufacture all the coarse cotton fabrics necessary for their consum[p]-tion. This is an error, and it is possible my pamphlet may have led you into it. I should have been more explicit ["and have stated" *altered to* "in stating"] distinctly what I ["meaned" *altered to* "meant"]. I alluded to osnaburgs, which article constitutes but a small portion of the coarse fabrics which it would be our interest to make, the range of which covers all the brown goods sold in this market, as well as those from which all the bleached and printed cloths are made of a fineness not exceeding 55 threads to the inch. To give you ["some" *altered to* "an"] idea of the consumption of such goods in this State and Georgia, I will give the amount of sales of this species of goods in one year by a single House in Charleston, and leave you to draw conclusions as to the quantity which may be brought into those two States, through other merchants of this City, Augusta, Columbia, and other smaller Towns whose merchants trade directly with the Northern & Eastern Cities. The sales of the house alluded to amounted to 4035 ["Bales" *canceled and* "packages" *interlined*] making 3,379,727 yards of cloth which would give employment to double the ["number of" *interlined*] spindles or twice the capacity of all the Mills now in Georgia & South Carolina, ["see note 7th page" *interlined*] this added to the immense quantity of linseys which we will supply ourselves with so soon as our planters can supply Southern wool in sufficient quantities ["will require a large additional force & gives a new featur(e) to the case" *interlined*]. Taking this view of the subject you will perceive throws our present manufacturing establishments altogether in the shade. This house it is true is engaged largely in this particular trade but notwithstanding it furnishes but a limited portion of all the goods consumed.

The second error is in looking only at the persons directly employed in the operations of spinning without taking into the count the increased number of employments the Factory operative brings around him over that of an Agricultural labourer. To illustrate the matter, I will take the statement in my pamphlet, giving an account of a Mill in Lowell making osnaburgs. The capital of that Mill, that is the Lowell Company as shewn in the index is $600,000 but the company have three establishments[,] one making Carpets, an other linseys, the third Cotton Osnaburgs. The latter establishment employs a capital of $200,000. It appears that in this in this [*sic*] department they employ 175 hands, whose wages amount to $35,867 per an[n]um, which is about equal to $200 to each person. The Mill it seems produces a gross profit after paying this sum for wages, of

$180,196. From this take 9 per cent which is given in the index as the average dividends declared, and you have ["$172,196" *altered to* "$162,196"], which is of course expended in the various ramifications of conducting the business, and goes to compensate the various classes of persons which are drawn around such an establishment. This sum you will perceive gives employment at $200 per an[n]um, to upwards of 800 persons, or 4½ to each Factory operative. Taking another view of the subject, By the same statement you will perceive, that, after deducting 9 per cent interest for the capital employed by the owners in conducting the business, say $18,000, ["and" *canceled*] there will be left the sum of ["$198,072" *altered to* "$98,072(?)"] equal to ["$1188" *altered to* "$1131"] per hand produced by the aid of machinery. ["which" *canceled and* "This sum" *interlined*] leaves an excess after paying ample wages to feed and clothe the operative and pay interest on ["the" *interlined*] capital which may be engaged in the business of ["$988" *altered to* "$931"] to each hand employed, and this is why a Factory of 5000 spindles and which gives employment to 175 hands never fails to build up a Town around it, and give an impetus to a high state of Agriculture to a large circle of country in its vicinity. And how is it with the force employed in the growth of cotton? I will fall below your estimate of the number employed, and suppose the Crop to be 24,000 thousand [that is, 24 million] bales, allotting to each hand 2½ bales, will give 960,000 as the number employed. At present prices these bales will not average over $25 each, and this is a yield of but $62½. It is true he raises more provisions than he consumes but cotton is the only marketable article which he produces. Out of this you have to shoe & clothe him, and from the sum left take the interest of vallue of the labourer, the land which he cultivates, the horse & agricultural implements, the ballance will be the sum left to support other labourers, and idlers, which of necessity will be around him. I think it will be found that before much is expended in this way, a large portion of the interest which should have gone into the pockets of the owner will have been absorbed.

Reverting again to the number of hands necessary to spin and weave into coarse fabrics the crop of the U. States, when you come to take into count the the [*sic*] goods, other than osnaburgs, which I have alluded to in an other page, you will perceive that ["that they are so much finer than osnaburgs that" *interlined*] inste[a]d of 100,000 persons, it would take nearer 300,000 to manufacture 24,000 thousand ["bales" *interlined*]. It is needless to comment further on the innumerable sources of profitable employment a cotton manufacturing establishment necessarily creates around it, and when we shall have such establishments scat[t]ered throug[h]out our State, which I trust in God we will both live to see, how much good will be done by giving employment in the shape of clerkships & overseers, to the idle young men, now to be found in throngs, lounging about our Villages & Towns, with little else to do, than smoke segars & whittle with their knives. And although by adding to the vallue of our Staple by manufacturing it into yarn, we will increase the burthens of the protective system now, bearing so heavily upon us, when we come to take into the count the sum which we will add to our gross products, by availing ourselves of our immensely vallueable water power, and the great number of idle persons, who as things now exist, are a dead weight to us, the idea of additional burthens sink into insignificance.

From the earnest manner in which my pamphlet is writ[t]en, you cannot have failed to perceive my deep solicitude for this cause. I am not a politician, and regret now, having made allusion in the pamphlet to the protective system, for it ought to have no connection with the subject. The remarks relative to Gen. [George] McDuffie & Mr. [James F.] Simmons were penned in a moment of excitement, after reading Gen. McD[uffie]'s Richmond Speech, which I thought at the time to be full of absurdities. This together with being some what out of patience with what are termed the Bluf[f]ton boys, lead to all the remarks about the Tariff & State resistance.

I trust my Dear Sir, after turning this matter over in your mind you will think more favourably of introduceing manufactures in South Carolina. I do sincerely hope that you may see the subject in the light I do, and come to the conclusion, that it is not only our interest to manufacture our cotton, But that sound policy would dictate to us the propriety of turning the arms of our adversaries against themselves, by not only manufacturing for our own consumption, but by spinning up every pound of our cotton were it possible. The 40 Million of dollars worth of yarn which the various Markets of the world take from England, to say nothing of England herself as a market, will be ["a" *interlined and* "guaranteed" *altered to* "guarantee"] that the labour which we may bring into this business from the idlers around us, or by withdrawal from other pursuits to be employed in spinning, will be fully remunerated.

I fear that your patience has been ["already" *interlined*] exhausted, but I feel so much interest in the subject that I will at the expense of becoming tiresome extend my remarks a little further.

What do we intend by the change which ["is" *interlined*] proposed, in going to manufacturing? Some people seem to think that every planter should go to work and spin his own cotton into yarn, others that the present system of Agriculture will be at once overturned, and we become as it were by magic, a farming, and great manufacturing people. Any change for the better must be very gradual, or it will not be permanant [*sic*], in attempting to make changes no doubt many foolish things will be done, much capital will be wholly lost to its owners by injudicious investments in machinery. The idea of a planter manufacturing his own cotton into yarn, is impractical, and must not be attempted untill manufacturing knowledge is more general with us, unless it be by those who can go largely into it, availing themselves of all the advantages which manufacturers obtain, in employing men understanding the Science of manufacturing.

To proceed we will ask again how is the change to work? I would say, let the present labour and capital engaged in Agriculture remain very much as it is. Those engaged in these pursuits must be content to look for their advantages in the general prosperity which will be brought around them, in a home market for their agricultural products, increased vallue of real estate, & good roads for the transportation of produce to market. They must learn to keep out of debt, to raise their own horses, mules, and hogs, to raise more sheep, in short plant less cotton and become [*partial word canceled*] by degrees more agricultural. But the question about manufactures is yet to be answered. I would say we want in South Carolina about 40 new Factories similar to the Mills owned by the Massachusetts Co. in Lowell, say to contain about 7000 Spindles each. I would have them put in operation and owned by the capitalists now in the State, not engaged in Agriculture. They should work White, or Black labour, Spin yarn and weave it, or Spin it alone, just as their interest might prompt them. These Mills might be expected to work up about 2500 Beales [*sic*] each per An[n]um or 100,000 Bales takeing them collectively, into yarn ranging from No. 12 to 24. And we might estimate each Mill to require 225 workers and this you will perceive would give employment to 10,000 persons. They would be Whites or Blacks as inclination might lead the owners, the presum[p]tion is that a majority would be Whites, and these we have in abundance around us. So you will perceive, the force ["the" *canceled*] requisite to carry out this operation, would not materially breake [*sic*] into that now employed in agriculture. It may be asked where the capital is to come from to build these forty Mills, $8,000,000 of dollars would build them and furnish all the capital necessary to conduct their operation. Prove the business to be profitable and this sum would soon be forth coming. It would however be years before it could all be applied, a single Factory could not be put in operation in less than two years and with all the earnest we could bring to our aid, ten years & maybe fifteen would elapse before we could start forty Mills. And what would be the effect of establishing forty such cotton Factories in South Carolina? There is a field for the imagination which I will not venture to lead you into, but suffer you to be your own pilot. Suffice it to say, that they would be equal to the capacity of all ["now in" *interlined*] Massachusetts to spin. These Factories well managed could not fail to take a business from her, which has made her the richest and the proudest State in the Union. She has heretofore done the coarse spinning of the U. States, and the advantages she has had in the Raw material, has given her the supremacy over England in all the markets of the world, and we possessing almost, if not quite as much advantage over Massachusetts as she has had over England, what is to prevent us from strikeing for this immensely valuable trade? While our ["present" *interlined*] agricultural population would remain to be employed very much as they are now, planting cotton, though we think in a very improved condition, These forty Factories with their ten thousand operatives could not fail to do for us, what they have done for Massachusetts, Double our white population, clear up our swamps, and put the thousands of acres of our wilderness land into a high state of cultivation, elevate the condition of our San[d]hill population, and give, as it has done in Massachusetts, a new impetus to every thing around us. In all this change what is to be our position as to England ["and" *canceled*] and other foreign countries now our customers for cotton? just what it is now. England has long since given up the coarser numbers as you will perceive by her manufacturing and export statistics. The yankees are now treading on their toes in the finer numbers, and our competition will only be felt through them, when we shall have driven them all onto finer numbers. My impression is that the day ["when" *canceled*] will come when a great portion of the world will be looking to the cotton growing States for yarn to supply their hand, and even power looms. And is our Politics to be changed by the introduction of this branch of industry? Massachusetts was the last State to come into the protective system, and guarantee that our Southern cotton manufacturers will not be the first to call for protection from Government.

You occupy an enviable position in South Carolina, every eye is fixed on you, and much depends on your decession [*sic*] in this matter. We have $200,000 ready to go into cotton spinning in Charleston and only wait the the [*sic*] action of the Legislature to obtain a charter of incorporation such as has been granted in this State and such as other States are in the habit of granting. If our politicians set their faces agains[t] manufacturing by incorporated companies, such charters will not be granted, and much of our capital disposed to go into this species of investment will find its way to Georgia where they are going into the business with a determined spirit. Let us not permit that enterprising State to go ahead of us, but let us set about at once to encourage the bringing about this chang[e], let us endeavour by all means to take advantage of resources which nature has so bountifully bestowed upon [us], and we may be the richest and the hap[p]iest people on Earth. I am with profound esteem your very humble se[r]v[an]t, Wm. Gregg.

P.S. The Saluda & Vaucluse mills now running at a greatly increased speed, make together but about 650,000 yards per an[n]um, and this is more than double the quantity produced by all the other mills in South Carolina. W.G.

ALS in ScCleA; PEx in Boucher and Brooks, eds., *Correspondence*, pp. 290–291. NOTE: An AEU by Calhoun reads "Mr. Gregg." Gregg took his statistical information from the appendices to his pamphlet *Essays on Domestic Industry: Or, an Inquiry into the Expediency of Establishing Cotton Manufactures in South-Carolina* (Charleston: Burges and James, 1845), and his references to page numbers and "index" in the above letter also refer to the pamphlet.

MAY 1–JUNE 30
1845

⫿

"Mr. Calhoun is now at his residence near this place," reported the
Pendleton *Messenger, "busily engaged in agricultural pursuits. He*
seems to have entirely recovered from the attack of sickness which
he had at Washington. We understand that his correspondence is
large; and we think it nothing but right to remind those who write to
him on business of their own, that he no longer enjoys the franking
privilege, and that his postage bill must be a heavy one." (Quoted
in the Washington Daily National Intelligencer, *May 19, 1845.)*

Busy with his "agricultural pursuits," Calhoun received a disap-
pointment, neither the first nor the last that his sons would bring.
James Edward Calhoun, fourth of his five sons and ninth of his ten
children, had been expelled from the University of Virginia. The af-
fair was not entirely dishonorable, however, since James's main
offence was to refuse to give testimony against classmates who were
guilty of riot.

The heavy political correspondence indicated continuing dis-
satisfaction and uncertainty among many of the diverse groups that
made up the Democratic party, Calhoun's "friends" being by no
means the only group who were or felt themselves to be out of favor
with the administration. His relations with Polk and the adminis-
tration remained friendly, though certainly not intimate. He ex-
pressed freely, to those who asked, his doubts as to whether Polk
would prove himself up to the mark in regard to Oregon and the
tariff. Calhoun had refused the mission to Britain. It was offered
in succession to two of his closest South Carolina allies, Francis W.
Pickens and Franklin H. Elmore, both of whom declined. This
could be regarded as a gesture of friendship to Calhoun and South
Carolina—unless one believed that the offers were only made on the
certainty they would be refused.

Calhoun's only public statement was in a letter on May 15 to a
committee of Mobile Democrats who had invited him to their city.
In a statement he no doubt intended for wide circulation he reviewed

*what he felt were his successes in the State Department and gave
his opinion of the present state and needs of the Union.*

*On June 8, at The Hermitage, the indomitable Andrew Jackson
lost his last battle and was gathered to whatever realm harbors the
spirits of warrior chieftains. Calhoun's feelings at the news are not
recorded.*

*Just after the middle of June, Calhoun went down country to
Abbeville District and the scenes of his childhood and youth. He
visited numerous relatives and Senator George McDuffie, whose
critical health was due at least in part to the effects of duels he had
fought on Calhoun's behalf more than two decades before. In those
long gone days the chief enemy had been William H. Crawford, now
vanished from the earthly scene more than a decade.*

*Calhoun's main purpose in Abbeville was to see to the erection
of gravestones for his mother, father, and sister, and to the construction of a wall around the family burying ground at the Long Canes.*

◫

To [GEORGE] BANCROFT, [Secretary of the Navy]

Fort Hill, May 1845

Dear Sir, I understand John Johnson, the son of the late Dr. [Joseph]
Johnson of Charleston, has been recommended to your Department
for the place of Midshipman by some of the most respectable citizens
of the city. My object, in addressing ["you" *interlined*], is to add my
name to the list of those, who have recommend[ed] him.

I am not personally acquainted with the applicant, but understand, that he is [a] lad of about 16 years of age, & I infer from the
high standing & respectability of those, whose names are attached
to his recommendation, well qualified for the place. His family is
highly respectable. His father was a very respectable physician, &
the late Judge [William] Johnson of the [U.S.] Supreme Court, was
an uncle of the applicant.

Under the belief, that he is well qualified for the place, & my
great respect for his family & connection, with whom I am personally acquainted, I take pleasure in recommending him, & would
be gratified with his success, if it should be in your power to appoint
him; but fear it cannot be done, under the act of Congress, which
prohibits such appointments; until the number of Midshipmen shall

be reduced below that fixed for the Naval establishment. Yours truly, J.C. Calhoun.

ALS in MHi, Bancroft Papers. NOTE: Johnson did not receive an appointment as a midshipman. Many years later, as a Confederate military engineer, he was active in the defence of Charleston harbor.

To H[ENRY] W. CONNER, [Charleston]

Fort Hill, 2d May 1845

My dear Sir, In answer to your first enquiry, as to the probability of a war with England & Mexico, one or both, I am of the opinion, there is but little danger of one with the latter, unless she should be backed by the former; and that is not probable, unless England should conclude, that a rupture between us & her is probable from the Oregon question. I am of the impression, that all danger of hostility is from that question. Indeed, I was so strongly impressed with that opinion, that I deemed it my duty to give Mr. [James K.] Polk & Mr. [James] Buchanan, a full statement of the state of the negotiation; my impression of the mode in which the negotiation ought to be conducted, in order to avoid hostilities, and effect, at the same time, our object; and the great danger of being involved in hos[t]ilities with England & of losing the Territory, unless the question should be managed with great delicacy, combined with great firmness and address. I also stated my opinion, ["that" *interlined*] the quiet & successful termination of the Texian question depended much on the Oregon; that England had no ground on which she could stand to come[?] to a rupture with us, in reference to the former, and that if she intended to give us any trouble about it, she would make Oregon the pretext, unless it was so managed as to prevent it. I, in addition, emphatically stated, that the joint occupancy was the key of the Oregon question; that if we held on to it & conducted the question, as it ought to be, it was hardly possible we could fail; but, if we re[s]cinded, it would be very difficult to avoid hostilities & the loss of the territory. I acted on that belief throughout, and it was owing to my efforts & influence, that the resolution to re[s]cind did not pass at the last session.

My conversation with Mr. Polk ["took place" *interlined*] on my first interview with him, & long before his inaugural was prepared, as I supposed. It was intended to guard him. When I saw it, & saw how directly he had gone against my views, I said at once to some of his friends, that I much regretted it, & that the course he had taken, would give much trouble; endanger the peace of the country, &, not improbably, the loss of the Territory.

You will see from all this, that, I think, there is much danger. Mr. Polk, Mr. Buchanan, ["&" *imperfectly erased*] Mr. [Robert J.] Walker [Secretary of the Treasury] & Mr. [Cave] Johnson [Postmaster General] are openly committed to the policy of re[s]cinding the joint occupancy, & taking possession of the Territory. If that is done, hos[t]ilities are innevitable. I fear they will neither have the pat[r]iotism, nor manliness to change their ground; and, if that should be so, every thing will depend on the Senate & the South to arrest so mad a course. I call it mad, for it is something worse than folly. If they do their duty, peace may still be preserved. England does not desire war. On the contrary, she dreads its effects, & wishes for peace. I cannot but think, it will yet be avoided, but there is much danger.

The probability is, that there will be much agitation of the question of peace or war at the next session, unless the administration should retract & settle the ["Oregon" *interlined*] question, by fixing the boundary between the ["two" *interlined*] countries in the recess. The difficulty of doing that has been much increased by the grounds taken in the ina[u]gural & the late Debate in Parliament; but it may still be done, I think, if Mr. Buchanan should have the nerve to settle it. I believe him to be inclined to do so; but I doubt his firmness. As to the effects of the war, if it should occur, I cannot doubt, but it will be calamitious to both countries, and especially so to our banking institutions. It would be difficult for them to avoid suspension either South or North.

You now have my opinion. I do not intended [*sic*] it for the publick, but have no objections to its being made known to such friends, as you may think proper, & in whose discretion you can confide[.] Yours truly, J.C. Calhoun.

ALS in ScC, John C. Calhoun Collection; photostat of ALS in DLC, Henry Workman Conner Papers.

From DUFF GREEN

Washington, 2nd May 1845
My dear Sir, I enclose you a copy of a letter to Mr. [Francis W.] Pickens. It explains itself. I do not see how ["you" *canceled*] he can hesitate to adopt the course I recommend, and I hope that it will meet

your approbation. By going to England, on a special mission, charged with these important negociations you will, I verily believe be able to conclude a favorable treaty. [*One word canceled.*] You will find a powerful and influential party who believe that it is the interest of England that all her colonies should, as soon as they [are] capable of self government, become independent governments with friendly commercial treaties with England, and these will be glad to surrender Oregon, as part of a commercial arrangement with this country.

If you fail you will have discharged your duty, and identified your name with the honor, & interests of the United States so that you can do more than any other man to guide future events. A new crisis has arisen since the coming in of the new administration, and your acceptance of the office under these circumstances will give you new claims on the confidence of the country and be considered every where as an acknowledgement of your merits & superior qualifications.

If you refuse, it will be charged that you are soured & disappointed, and you will be held responsible for any failure in the negociations which may occur.

Some of your friends say that if you make a treaty it will be assailed, because it is made by you. I admit that the history of the Texas negoti[ati]on would seem to justify such an opinion, but I think it will be otherwise because, the new negociation will be sustained by Mr. [James K.] Polk. [Thomas] Ritchie will be here and will be committed in advance. [Thomas H.] Benton's power to do you injury no longer exists & all parties will fear to assail a good treaty if it makes an end of the controversy, & if you fail, you will have the American feeling to fall back on, which will be stronger as the pretensions ["& objects" *interlined*] of England will be exposed by you.

I hope that you will place what I have done to the proper motives. Believe me as ever your sincere friend, Duff Green.

[Enclosure]

Duff Green to F[rancis] W. Pickens, "(Copy)"

Washington, 2d May 1845

Dear Sir, When the late news from England arrived I called on the President [James K. Polk] and suggested that under the new aspect of our relations with that country I believed that Mr. Calhoun could be induced to accept the mission to England if he were charged with negotiating a commercial treaty and the adjustment of the

Oregon question. He replied that he regretted that it was not now in his power to tender him the appointment, as it had been tendered to another, and that he could do nothing unless the person, to whom it had been tendered, should decline to accept it. He did not say that you are the person, but I inferred so from what he said.

I see by the papers of today that there is a rumour that Mr. [Martin] Van Buren will be sent on a special mission and seeing this I no longer hesitate to write to you and suggest that you have it in your power to recommend to the President the appointment of Mr. Calhoun, and thus enable him to render a great service to the country and relieve himself from the imputation of having declined to perform his duty in a trying crisis, for the public will not properly appreciate the change, which has taken place, and will hold him responsible in case of war, and will give great credit to Mr. Van Buren in case he adjusts the Oregon question, as I believe he can do. He will be lauded for his magnanimity, while Mr. Calhoun will be censured for yeilding [*sic*] to his mortified vanity and refusing to obey the call of public duty. In making this suggestion it is proper that I should say that the President told me that, if he believed Mr. Calhoun could be induced to accept the appointment, but for the circumstance that he had tendered it to another, he would write to Mr. Calhoun, a letter, entreating him to accept and that he should be charged with the negotiation respecting ["the" *canceled*] Oregon with unlimited discretion. He told me further that he desires to make a commercial treaty.

I do this because you will see that if Mr. Calhoun is appointed he will be charged with negotiations of vital importance, and for which, it is no disparagement to you to say he is better qualified than any man in the country, and which, it is obvious, will not be entrusted to you in case of your appointment. I have the less hesitation in making the suggestion because your relations to Mr. Calhoun are such that I hope it will give you great pleasure to serve him, as I believe, you will do in this particular. By doing so, you will place yourself on much higher grounds than you would otherwise occupy, and should you desire the appointment, you will have but postponed the gratification of your wishes, because Mr. Polk will not expect Mr. Calhoun to remain abroad longer than it may be necessary to enable him to conclude the important treaties, with which he will be charged.

I hope, my dear Sir, that you will rightly appreciate the motives, which prompt me to write this letter. I am yours truly, (Signed) Duff Green.

ALS with En in ScCleA; another copy of En in ScU-SC, John C. Calhoun Papers; PC in Jameson, ed., *Correspondence*, pp. 1035–1036. NOTE: On the same date, Green wrote to Calhoun's son (and his own son-in-law) Andrew Pickens Calhoun, urging him to influence his father to accept the "appointment" discussed: ALS in ScU-SC, John C. Calhoun Papers. Then, on 5/15, Green wrote to Polk urging Calhoun's appointment to a mission to Great Britain. Green pointed to newspaper comments favorable to such an idea, stated that the commercial interests of New York City were in favor, and stated that Franklin H. Elmore had informed him that Calhoun could be induced to accept: ALS with En in DLC, James K. Polk Papers (Presidential Papers Microfilm, Polk Papers, roll 37).

From W[ILLIA]M B. ROGERS

[May 2?, 1845]

Dear Sir, It becomes my painful duty to communicate to you the above copy of the proceedings of the faculty in relation to your son. Regretting that he should have given such occasion for their action, I have the honor to remain, With very great respect Your Ob[edien]t Serv[an]t, Wm. B. Rogers, Ch[airman,] fac[ulty,] U[niversity of] V[irginia].

[Appended:]

University of Virginia, April 26th 1845

It appearing to the satisfaction of the Faculty, that Mr. James E[d-ward] Calhoun evaded the process of the Civil Authority whilst engaged in the investigation of the late riots at the University—

Resolved, that he be dismissed from the University.

Copied from the minutes, W[illia]m Wertenbaker, Secretary of the Faculty.

ALS with appended ADS in ScCleA. NOTE: An AEU by Calhoun reads "The order dismissing James from the University." Rogers's letter is undated but is postmarked May 2.

From F[RANCIS] W. PICKENS

Edgewood [Edgefield District, S.C.]
Sunday, 4 May 1845

My dear Sir, I hasten to let you know that I re[ceive]d yesterday from Charleston the amount of the note due from Mr. [Thomas G.] Clemson to Arthur [Simkins] ($3,070) from Mathew[e]s & Bonneau or rather through them. Arthur got me to write for it for him, & I will deliver the amount to him to day. Mr. [John] Mobley was here the other day and told me all were well at Mr. Clemson's except the overseer [—— Bland] who was taken sometime since with a paralitic affection but is better. I sent my overseer there yesterday & he will return this evening. As to finishing that house it will be difficult to do so with that carpenter. He is a very smart man but will not work and if he were pushed I am sure he would run off. There are a great many things that Mr. Clemson has written to be done, such as ditching, manuring, and building that will be difficult to be done if he expects a crop. He wishes the barns & stables moved off. Would it not be better to make the carpenter do that, and if any thing is to be left let it be the house, as they will not be back for years, & even if not entirely finished when they return it could be done to their own taste? If you could send down there your overseer or John [C. Calhoun, Jr.] with any directions at all—it would do good, as it would let the overseer & the negroes all know & feel that you had an eye towards them. You need not think of interfereing [*sic*] with me at all, as I merely act as a friend now. I promised *only to take charge* of it until the 1st Jan[uar]y last. His idea was that either you or John would take charge of it then. They have had rain there—but we have none here. I never saw such a parching drought at this season. Miss Elizabeth [Barksdale Pickens] re[ceive]d a letter the other day from Anna [Maria Calhoun Clemson]. They were all well & she says Mr. Clemson is now the most thorough American she ever saw, but of course you heard by the same steamer.

I rec[eive]d a letter from Mr. [James K.] Polk dated the 21st April and made the following answer:

Edgewood, 27 April 1845
My dear Sir, I re[ceive]d yours of the 21st instant on yesterday, and return you my thanks for the distinguished honor you are pleased to tender in offering me the appointment of "Envoy Extraordinary & Minister Plenipotentiary to Great Britain."

Highly important as I know the position to be in the present juncture of our affairs, and gratifying as it might be personally to me, yet under existing circumstances I most respectfully decline the appointment.

There are questions of grave import connected with the future policy of our government which I fondly hope and believe will be adjusted under your Administration so as to give *permanent justice*, equality, and protection (meaning the slave question) to all, but *until they are settled* I could not (unless in the contingencies of war) accept any office consistently with the *feelings* of *allegiance* I bear to my *own State*. With great personal regard[,] I have the honor to be very respectfully your obed[ien]t serv[an]t, F.W. Pickens.

The news from England looks a little uncertain, but I take it for granted there can be no war at present. I saw the letter of [Franklin H.] Elmore to the President, & I thought it very low in its tone.

Present us affectionately to Cousin F[loride Colhoun Calhoun] & [Martha] Cornelia [Calhoun]. Very truly & sincerely, F.W. Pickens.

ALS in ScCleA. NOTE: An AEU by Calhoun reads: "Col. Pickens acknowledges the receipt of $3000 due by Mr. Clemson to Arthur Simkins paid by J.C. & A.P. Calhoun ["by" *canceled*] from the proceeds of a note discounted the Bank of the State for $4000."

From J[AMES] HAMILTON, [JR.]

Wilmington Steamer
Harbour of Charleston
May 5[t]h 1845

My Dear Sir, I owe you a thousand apologies for not having written you before in reply to your kind favors written at the close of the session of Congress. But I have been almost ever since either travelling or engrossed by the most anxious & interesting occupations connected with my variously diversified engagements.

I was not however indisposed to wait (as I knew that I should have to go North) to see how [James K.] Polk[']s administration would work & how your exclusion from his Cabinet seemed to influence the public mind. I cannot think as yet it has elicited a very high degree of confidence whilst your not being in it is a source of profound Regret with every man who happens to be beyond the reach of Faction either on the one side or the other. The President committed a great mistake in this matter which he will find it difficult to remedy—more especially at a crisis which demands the first experience & Talent in the Country.

I had a long interview & a free one with him & with his Secretaries of the Treasury & State [Robert J. Walker and James Buchanan]. The President assures me that the whole power of the Executive will be exerted to modify the Tariff to *the Revenue Standard.* The question naturally arises what he regards a Revenue Standard as in adjusting such a Balance we may differ very essentially with him and his Cabinet. The latter however think they can hit on a Compromise which will be altogether satisfactory to the South. I trust it may in its measure of justice. The administration are acting in good faith & with the most earnest & effective Zeal to remove every objection to Annexation & consummate this great measure, whilst the Tone of the President is quite pacific on the Oregon question. I think he will propose to the British Govt. the Line on which ["it is supposed" *interlined*] you were willing to adjust this vexed point in dispute. The negotiations with Mr. Packenham [*sic*; Richard Pakenham] will be resumed next week.

When I wrote you from New Orleans that I was willing to go to England on a special mission to negotiate a reciprocity Treaty it was under the idea that I was to act *under your administration* of the State Dept. otherwise I never would have allowed you even in all your kindness & friendship to bring my name to the President[']s view for this mission.

My object was to repeal the tariff in effect thro a commercial Treaty. Buchanan of course would not permit me to consummate such a triumph & therefore when I went to Washington I informed the President that whilst I was exceedingly flattered by your most complimentary recommendation that circumstances would have compelled me to decline the appointment ["if it had been tendered" *interlined*] as Resident Minister to the Court of St. James. I assure you My Dear Sir I feel far more flattered by your testimonial of my fitness for this station, than I should have been for the appointment itself.

Three Days since on my return to Washington on my way South he told me that he had tendered the appointment to [Francis W.] Pickens after [Franklin H.] Elmore had declined it. He then went on to say that he should have tendered it to me after yourself (as he was pleased to say from my superior qualifications to both of the former Gentlemen) but from the fact of my having represented Texas at St. James that this incongruity of Citizenship might have created embarrassment. Without excepting to the validity of this objection, I told him for the reasons I had disclosed in our first interview I was quite gratified the matter had taken the course it had done. That on no mission could I be absent from my interests in this Country more than 4 months and hence an acceptance of appointment with its outfit under such circumstances would have been impossible. I am glad he has appointed our friend Pickens as its suits both his fortunes & his inclinations I presume. I shall write him tomorrow and put him up to the reciprocity Treaty & other matters of importance before he goes.

I shall propose now [Dixon H.] Lewis is here a meeting of a few of your confidential friends as to the best course we ought to take in regard *to your prospects ahead.* If with the Leaders of the different parties & factions in the Country you are weak you *never were as strong* with the people if you run as the AntiConvention Candidate, which is the only ground on which you can be brought out. ["I think your success highly probable" *interlined.*] This is the opinion of some of our friends in Virginia whom I saw at Richmond. Gen[era]l [Duff] Green thought Pickens ought to decline that you might go to England, and I promised him to write Pickens to this effect. But upon reflection I shall abstain as if this matter does not occur to ["Pickens" *canceled and* "himself" *interlined*] it ought not to be prescribed by a third person. Upon mature reflection I think your true position is Retirement. In the glare of public action you would only invite the malice & envy of the Leaders of the factions of the various parties[;] where you ["you"(?) *canceled and* "are you" *interlined*] excite the admiration & sympathy of the people as a man to whom injustice has been practiced & that it will beho[o]ve them to call you from that Retirement. This I believe firmly. I remain My Dear Sir Sincerely & faithfully Your friend, J. Hamilton.

[Marginal P.S.] I must apologize to you for paying the Postage on this Letter. All your correspondents should do this as really your postage otherwise would be an enormous Tax.

P.S. I shall remain in Charleston six or seven Days and after a full consultation I will write. I think I can sketch a ["the" *canceled*] campaign which must end in a glorious triumph of our principles in your person. Be so kind as to direct to Savannah where I shall be [*ms. torn;* next?] week.

ALS in ScCleA. NOTE: An EU on this letter reads: "cowardly."

From DIXON H. LEWIS, [Senator from Ala.]

Charleston, May 6th 1845
My Dear Sir, I am this far on my way home from Washington and after repeated conversations with your friends at the North, & with Gen[era]l [James] Hamilton [Jr.] who travelled with me from Washington, I have come to the conclusion once more to urge on you the

propriety of your visiting the North this summer. I know your almost insuper[able] objections, & to some extent believe there is force
in them; but I am convinced, there is still more force in the almost
unanimous wishes of your friends, founded on a belief that nothing
but personal intercourse can relieve you from the misconceptions
which so generally attach to ["you;" *interlined*] among the masses
of the North. They think you are proud & haughty—even aristocratic
in your manners & bearing, & austere to a degree which would make
you personally offensive to all but to your personal friends of a class
in Life far above the body of the People. Cha[rle]s A. Davis'[s]
letter [of 3/21/1845] which I sent you shows this, & I have it from
so many of your friends who have visited Washington since the adjournment that it can[no]t be doubted.

Your enemies keep up the idea of your social & sectional exclusive-
ness by saying that "John C. Calhoun goes to Washington & when the
session ["is over" *interlined*] returns back strai[gh]t to South Carolina, that he knows nor cares for ["any" *canceled and* "no" *interlined*]
thing, north of the Potomac." This imputation as unjust as it is, receives a semblance of plausibility from the fact, that it has been so
much your *destiny* of late, to defend the South from the sectional
Legislation & plunder of the North, that the world has ceased to contemplate your ["political" *interlined*] character in any thing like ["a"
canceled and "its" *interlined*] national aspects. The very fact of your
visiting the North would go far to correct this impression, while a
free & unreserved intercourse with your fellow citizens ["during your
journey" *interlined*] would remove it entirely. Hence although
others have made but little by such visits, when their object has been
to increase the veneration of the Public for admitted talents or great-
ness, the result promises greatly more success, in an attempt to *correct misconceptions as to character*, so gross as to be dispelled by the
slightest acquaintance.

But I know you are as unprepared in character as you are in
feeling, to play off the the [*sic*] Pageantry which has sometimes accompanied the visits of distinguished ["men" *interlined*] through the
Country—& that to you, the severest process of philosophical induction or mathematical reasoning, is not half so difficult, as one of those
unmeaning & heartless congratulatory addresses, which are so flip-
pantly passed off now a days, by light heads & hollow hearts of those
who seek notoriety in their journey, by flattering every locality which
honours them with a crowd. If I were in your place, I would leave
home with the avowed intention of passing myself as a *private citizen*,
& in *no event*, would I give colour to the charge that I was seeking

any political object—by making a political speech, or any object of personal advancement, by being drawn out in a public address, to avow any opinions, or to justify or defend any portion of my past history. I know this will be a departure from the common rule, & that it will be difficult, but you can take with you one or two younger friends who by being accessible to the People, will be consulted in advance on all such matters, & who by a course of resolute & determined resistance when any such thing is proposed, can protect you from all importunity in such matters. You once said to [Robert M.T.] Hunter & myself, that if you travelled north one or both of us must go with you. I regret that I can[no]t go with you this summer but Hunter is just elected & can—& I know will, if you require it. General Hamilton of all others would be just the man for you, & in consulting with me on the subject expressed his great willingness to do so & proposed to do so in the Fall in a trip through Alabama, Missis[s]ippi[,] Louisiania [*sic*], Texas, Arkansas, St. Louis, Cincin[n]ati & then through Kentucky & Tennessee back to Carolina—provided you should desire it. I told him that it was all important you should take a trip through the North this summer & asked him if he could then accompany ["you" *interlined*]. He said he was *compelled* to to go to England, but even if he goes—he could accompany you as far as Boston—which is the most material part of the journey & then with Hunter you could make the rest of the Tour.

I hope you will excuse me in these suggestions. I am convinced the Government never can be reformed without your aid & if you will now as a *private citizen*, while your relations are kind to [James K.] Polk, who is not looked to for another term & before the question of the succession is raised—if you will take this trip & your friends without naming you, will direct all their batteries against a National Convention—I have no doubt we can make you the next President. I *know* you were never as strong before, & stronger because you are in retirement *against* the will of the People. In that retirement, you can as another citizen visit the North without having a political Flag[?] to follow you—& I beg you to do so in July next.

My health is better than it has been for five years. Write me to Lowndesboro [Ala.] in reply to this & *particularly* as to your *own health*. Great anxiety is felt by your friends as to the effect of your late attack on your general health. [Franklin H.] Elmore is at Columbia but returns tomorrow when Gen[era]l Hamilton & a few of your friends will meet for consultation as to future movements. Y[ou]r friend, Dixon H. Lewis.

ALS in ScCleA.

To F[RANCIS] W. PICKENS, Edgefield, S.C.

Fort Hill, 6th May 1845

My dear Sir, I cannot disapprove of your declining the mission to England. I see many difficulties in any Southern man accepting it under existing circumstances, and yet, it is highly desireable that it should be filled, on many accounts, by a man true to the South & all its interests. In addition to the reason you have assigned, there are others connected with the Oregon question as it stands, which, I fear, would make the position of a minister in England who is true to the South embarrassing, should he be charged with any duties connected with it. I fear Mr. [James K.] Polk has taken a false view of that important question. The remarks of the inaugural in reference to it, have made it impossible to settle it by negotiation, unless he retracts, or explains away, what he has said, which would ["be" *interlined*] almost as embarrassing. But, what I regard as still more unfortunate; it will, I fear, make it impossible to take the only course, if it should fail, by which we ever had any chance of getting the whole Territory; ["that is" *interlined*] by standing still & letting time & emigration settle the question. Our true policy was to treat the subject amicably & quietly, and, if negotiation failed, hold on to the joint occupancy, & leave it to England to terminate it, if she should so decide. I doubt whether she would, had the proper course been pursued. In that case, it would have fallen quietly into our hands.

I saw the danger, and endeavoured to guard Mr. Polk, in my first interview, against it; but, as it seems, in vain. I, also, endeavoured to guard Mr. [James] Buchanan, but I know not whether with more success. A war with England about Oregon would be the most fatal step, that can be taken; & yet there is great danger it will come to that. In my opinion, if prevented, it must be by the Senate & the South. The question might have been successfully managed. I saw my way clearly through it, and left it in a good way.

We have been, and still are very dry. We had a light shower yesterday, which just laid the dust. To day there is no sign of rain.

I had not supposed you took my direction in conducting Mr. [Thomas G.] Clemson's affairs, ["other" *interlined*] than what you state; and I only abstained from advising because I supposed you knew the place so much better than I did, that my opinion ought not to have any weight against yours. Most certainly the crop ought not to be sacrificed or interfered with by the House, or any other job; and all his directions ought to be held subordinate to that view of the subject.

539

I cannot possibly attend to it, either by myself or overseer, at so great a distance, and it is entirely out of the question for John [C. Calhoun, Jr.] to do it. He has no experience, & the restoration of his health is paramount to all other considerations. All that can be done is to have a good overseer, as I believe the present [—— Bland] is, & trust to him. If his health should [be] restored & he should feel, that he was responsible for the management of the place I think he would do well.

All the family join their love to you, Mrs. [Marion Antoinette Dearing] Pickens & family. Yours truly, J.C. Calhoun.

[P.S.] Mrs. Calhoun requests me to say that she has received her spectacles & that she is much obliged to you.

ALS in ScU-SC, John C. Calhoun Papers; PEx in Jameson, ed., *Correspondence*, pp. 653–654.

F[RANCIS] W. PICKENS to Col. J[ames] Edward Colhoun, Calhoun's Mills, Abbeville District, S.C.

Edgewood [Edgefield District, S.C.,] 7 May 1845
My dear Sir, Arthur [Simkins] desires that land sold which belonged to Maria [Simkins Colhoun]. You know of course that it is now subject to division—as it was inherited by her. You are entitled to one third of it. He told me the other day that he would file a bill for sale & partition & I told him to drop you a line about it. I have no doubt it ought to be done. A few days after I arrived from Charleston I re[ceive]d from the President [James K. Polk] the offer of the mission to England; & the following is my reply in full—which I send you as I know you feel interest in my character &c.

"Edgewood, 27 April 1845
My dear Sir, I re[ceive]d yours dated 21st inst. on yesterday and return you my thanks for the distinguished honor you are pleased to tender in offering me the appointment of 'Envoy Extraordinary & minister Plenipotentiary to Great Britain.' Highly important as I know the position to be in the present juncture of our affairs, and gratifying as it might be ["to me" *canceled*] personally to me, yet under existing circumstances I most respectfully decline the appointment.

There are questions of grave import connected with the future

policy of our government which I fondly hope & believe will be adjusted under your administration so as to give *permanent* jus[ti]ce, equality & protection to all, but until th[ey; *marginal interpolation:* "meaning the institution of slavery from Foreign interference &c &c."] are settled I could not (unless in the contingencies of war) accept any office consistently with the feelings of allegiance I bear to my *own* *State*. With great personal regard I have the honor to be very respectfully your ob[e]d[ien]t Serv[an]t, F.W. Pickens.
To the President of the U. States.["]

I saw [Franklin H.] Elmore's letter in reply to Polk & I thought it was low in its tone. I thought if I accepted it might be supposed that it was a favour conferred & I scorn to accept favour from any man living. Besides I would not travel myself in the slightest degree until I could see something certain in the future destiny of So. Ca. in relation to the odious act of 1842. The State is now too much in the hands of weak, selfish, or prejudiced men; I rejoice that an opportunity was given to shew that there were in So. Ca. at least some few who disdained office.

I have re[ceive]d several *strange letters* since the offer was made, and to-day one from Gen[era]l [James] Hamilton [Jr.] & one from Duff Greene [*sic*]. I see from Hamilton's that Mr. Calhoun had written him when Sec[re]t[ar]y of State that if he was continued he (Mr. Calhoun) would appoint him to negotiate a reciprocity treaty with G. Britain &c &c. And I think also from his letter that he has been on to Washington expecting still the appointment. It was there he found out I was offered it. I do hope Mr. Calhoun never urged his appointment. Considering the history of the last few years since 1837 &c—it would be a fatal error to [*ms. torn;* recomm]end[?] or urge any such man. Duff Green has also been talking very foolishly to the President in rela[tion] to Mr. Calhoun, & has been speaking as if he were in the confidence of Mr. Calhoun. His letter to me [*ms. torn;* was?] extremely med[d]ling & weak, *such men as* these *would ruin any man in the world*.

I see no paper has known of the offer to myself—& I hope it will not get into the papers, & least of all ["the" *canceled*] that no friend of mine will make it public.

We have the most distressing drought I ever saw. Things seem ruined. There is rain about but none here.

Write me fully & often. When you see Dr. [Henry H.] Townes present me to him. Truly & affectionately, F.W. Pickens.

ALS in ScU-SC, Francis W. Pickens Papers.

From J A [M E] S S. J O H N S T O N and
B E N J A [M I N] F. S I M M O N S

Halifax County[,] No[rth] Ca[rolina,] May 9th 1845
Dear Sir: Please think this not intrusion. The object of this communication is to obtain your advice on subjects momentous to us.
You will at least Sir in consideration of the motives by which we are
actuated pardon us for this application, a compliance with which will
cause such infinite condescension on your part. You may have had
in your youth the same views & feelings which we have, and therefore know how to appreciate advice.

There are many other able and distinguished men in the United
States to whom we might have applied; but your course of life appears to us more exemplary than that of others. We have thought
you the most appropriate person from whom to obtain the desired
advice both from the character of your mind, and from the fact that
with us your views will be enforced by public and private worth.

We are both young men twenty two or three years of age, with
collegiate educations obtained in Virginia and in this State, and have
just taken up the legal profession as our business of life. The advice
desired then has respect to law. The course of human life is so short,
that but little can be performed at best; but much less if our efforts
are misdirected. As beings possessed of intelligence, reason and
responsibility we have a part to act in the world—a fortune and character to make—much to perform in the short time allot[t]ed us. We
are hence impressed with the importance of proper application.

We have employed our time since we commenced the study of
law as our own reason dictated, and we have thought for some time
past of taking a regular course of study at Cambridge [Mass.] or
some other Northern law school. Some of the points then on which
we are anxious to obtain your opinions are the following[:] 1st. With
regard to the propriety of taking a course at a Northern School[;]
2nd. If such a step be proper what institution of the kind you think
most eligible[;] 3rd. Your opinion of the law Department of Harvard
University at Cambridge. We should be glad Sir to obtain your
views on these heads, or we shall be equally obliged to you for a
sketch of your views as to the proper course generally for young men
in our situations.

We know the difficulty of giving advice for the peculiar cases of
individuals whose mutual habits are unknown to the adviser. But
notwithstanding this we believe that you may materially affect for

the better, and determine our future course. It may occur to you that we should have applied for information on some of the points which constitute the object of this letter to one who had spent much of his life in the forum; but in addition to what was said above as to the views which determined ["us" *interlined*] to make this application to you, we remark that we are anxious to become lawyers, but not *mere* lawyers. We do not look upon the legal profession as a mere money making machine but entitled to a much higher rank. Our idea of a lawyer is, that he ought to be a Statesman[,] scholar and a christian. Many have succeeded at law tolerably well without much acquaintance with its theory, this course appears to us objectionable. Law also ["appears" *interlined*] to be the stepstone to political preferment. Your views upon a political course of life will be very acceptable. This arena seems most enticing yet there may be other fields of action in which the young aspirant may gather wreaths of glory and renown.

On any or all of these topics your views will be received with the greatest pleasure. We can find no principles for our guida[nce in(?)] the biographies of most men. We see that one rises app[arently] by labor & industry—one by the concurrence of favorable circumstances—another by pecuniary fortune. Such diversity in the affairs of men would only lead us to the belief that life is a mingled yarn subject to no fixed laws.

Nothing but our unbounded confidence in your judgment of these matters and a thorough conviction that your advice will be more valuable than that of others, have induced us to trouble you with this communication. We are young and inexperienced individuals, and an answer to this letter can of course add nothing to your reputation. But we conceive that all true patriots of enlarged philanthropic principles like yourself feel an interest in the rising generation and will willingly contribute to its proper direction. For the several reasons enumerated we make the application, attention to which will put us under the greatest obligations to you.

With assurances of our highest regard & esteem we have the honor to be your friends truly, Jas. S. Johnston, Benja[min] F. Simmons.

[P.S.] We shall receive your letter if directed to Halifax N.C.

LS in ScCleA.

543

From D[IXON] H. LEWIS

Charleston, May 9th 1845

My D[ea]r Sir, I have kept your letter till this time to give you an account of the conference with your friends. R[obert] B[arnwell] Rhett, James [S.] Rhett, [Ker] Boyce, [Henry] Gourdin & [James] Hamilton [Jr.] met at [Franklin H.] Elmore[']s last night. We discussed the course proper to be pursued in reference to placing you in the best position for [18]48. It was thought your friends should pursue as long as possible a conciliatory course towards the administration, at the same time they should cause ground at once to be taken by all the presses in your interest, against any future National Convention as an organization which put the Party in the hands of the office holders & seekers—& to urge this in the abstract without any reference to your interest. All concurred in the opinion you should travel North this summer, & I think two of the Company would like to accompany you—& that you should go as a private Citizen, & make no developements by speeches or otherwise.

I think the opinion was that you were doing well in your present position & that it would not be well to abandon ["your present position" *canceled*] a position in which you commanded so much of the sympathy of the Party, while at the same time you were ["not only" *interlined*] exempt from the responsibility of any failure on the part of [James K.] Polk & his administration, but for every such failure the public would give you the credit of saying & believing that if you were in his Cabinet—it might by your prudence have been averted.

Still if [Francis W.] Pickens declines the mission to England, Polk may appeal to you in a way you can scarcely refuse the acceptance. He may offer you *plenary powers* & put it on the ground that you are called in reference to an Exigency in our foreign affairs; which you cannot decline. Again if the Whig Party should bear down our forces in the Senate by their superior ability—the public voice may *require* you to come to that Body. These are contingent results which may possibly *constrain* you to leave your retirement, but as long as you can well avoid it, I think your best position for the *present*, is to remain in private life. So far, instead of retirement withdrawing you from the public interest & sympathy—I am persuaded that it has increased it.

Excuse these suggestions as the conclusions of my own mind aided by the suggestions of your other friends. I give them to you, as I give all my suggestions on affairs concerning yourself—only for what you may think them worth—deferring always to your better judgement.

I hope however you will not decline the visit to the North this summer. In that I think I & all your other friends cannot be mistaken. Write me in reply to Lowndesboro Alabama. I am truly your friend, D.H. Lewis.

P.S. Elmore suggested that if Polk offers you ["plenary powers & in addition offers you the you were to" *canceled*] the mission with such Instructions as you may think proper & *then pledges* himself with *the whole weight of the Administration* to sustain a Treaty of the Oregon Question which you may make, & then gives you power to negotiate a Commercial Treaty, it will be exceedingly difficult for you to decline & to stand justified. In this opinion your other friends concurred—though for my part I had rather see the Cross pass by you—as I know the difficulties of the question.

ALS in ScCleA; variant PC in Boucher and Brooks, eds., *Correspondence*, pp. 293–294.

F[RANKLIN] H. ELMORE to [Duff Green]

Charleston, May 10 1845

My Dear Sir, Col. [Francis W.] Pickens declines the London Mission because the Tariff is not adjusted & South Carolina has the highest claim on his allegiance & & [*sic*] services until that is done. He does it in the most kind & respectful manner, but firmly. Will not this strengthen the Commercial Treaty scheme? Does it not give additional reason why the Tariff shall be settled by Treaty?

If Mr. Calhoun is again offered the mission, he will not take it except on terms that will enable him to do good—serve the Country & *not ruin himself*. What are they[?] First—If the Oregon negotiation is given him, to settle, he will want, *not powers* merely—but *instructions* covering the *very terms of the treaty*—rendering the Administration *responsible* in their own instructions & bound therefore to fight for what is done as *their own act*.

Second—Liberal *instructions* for a commercial treaty.

Third full powers to press the question for the rendition of fugitive slaves.

With all these the fullest pledge of support in what he should do. With these granted or offered, he might accept. I don't think he could refuse well, if the instructions as to Oregon were such as he approved. Without all these are arranged to his satisfaction in the offer, he will hardly accept. If they are it will afford him so ample a field for usefulness that I hardly think he can refuse.

Now I would suggest to you if you confer with the President [James K. Polk], impress these things on him. Let him deal in no stinted confidence or support—either all or none. He will secure the services of one most able to make them useful by it—and not without.

No Southern man can settle the Oregon without infinite hazard of sacrificing himself, if he concedes a foot south of 54 40′. It would only be safe with *instructions* to do so & the fullest committal of the Government to sustain it. In haste Yours truly, F.H. Elmore.

ALS in DLC, Duff Green Papers.

From ——

Warrenton Virginia, May 11th 1845
Sir, I would most respectfully yet most earnestly call your attention to the claims of the Honor[a]b[le] William Smith of this place, to Executive patronage—as the phrase is. Mr. Calhoun, I am so in-digna[n]t at the President's conduct on this subject, as are all Mr. S[mith]'s friends and they are the greater portion of this State, that I know not whether to write you or not lest I do some one injustice. Mr. [James K.] Polk is well acquainted with Mr. Smith's political life; he has been informed of the long, continued and ceaseless efforts of Mr. S[mith] in the Republican Cause; he is not ignorant of Mr. S[mith]'s many and heavy sacrifices for the benefit and success of our Faith; and yet in the face of all these facts he seems determined to overlook and pass unrewarded the claims of this gentleman and scholar and that too after many recom[m]endations in favor of Mr. S[mith] from some of the most prominent of the Democratic leaders in the State and repeated petitions very numerously signed by the Mass of the people. Such injustice is vile, ungrateful and, from his manifest contempt of the petitions, un-Democratic. Would a man like yourself have done so? No: my head on the contrary; and it is in this belief that I now address you, confident of your interference in the matter. We, the people, did believe that Mr. Polk would prove a just as well as wise man, but now we think somewhat that ["we" *interlined*] have been mistaken.

You are doubtless acquainted with Mr. S[mith]'s political life, but it may not be amiss to give a brief summary of it and state his present public position and private condition. I will be very brief. He commenced public life about the time of Gen[era]l [Andrew] Jackson's first attempt for the Presidency, and though he sometimes disagreed with him, battled in those contests under him. In Mr. [Martin] Van Buren's first campaign he was among the first of our leaders, and in his last, when all were depressed in spirits, he came to the rescue, took up the Word and went forth to the fight—and it is admitted generally, and by every unbiased man that his influence and exertions saved our Old Dominion from Federal thraldom. In the last election Mr. S[mith] was justly considered the master-spirit— the leader of his party in this State, and did more towards the Democrat triumph in it than any other man, and this can be said without disparagement to any one. He is beyond comparison the most popular man in the State with the people, and though his straightforwardness and consistent independance has caused him to come in contact and occasionally clash in opinion with some of the selfish and arrogant of the "Spartan Band" and particularly with the veritabl[e] "Leonidas" himself, yet these little concussions have invariably increased his influence with his peculiar friends the bulk of the people although they have proved detrimental to his immediate interests. Your intuitive insight and wonderful knowledge in such matters will readily inform you as to the estimation in which Mr. S[mith] is held and the position which he occupies.

Mr. Smith will be elected, without doubt, this winter to the U.S. Senate if he is not sent abroad, or should he prefer it the Gubernatorial Chair of our State will doubtless be at his command. Judging from present manifestations anything in the gift of the State he can get, but unfortunately he is too poor to receive—with justice to himself and family—anything that the State can give. He is very poor, his property is very small and what little he has, I fear, cannot retain much longer unless justice is rendered him by the General Government. He calculated I doubt not upon an appointment when he purchased his little farm, and if he is disappointed it must we think ruin him, paralyse his every effort and in fact drive him from the political arena of our State. Virginia can ill sustain the loss of such a man, nor would our cause generally throughout the Union suffer much less, for he is a growing ["and improving" *interlined*] man. For six and twenty years Mr. S[mith] has labored in the Democratic vineyard assiduously, and without ceasing; & it may truly be said of him that hitherto he [*ms. torn*; has(?) kn]own[?] "no variableness or

547

shadow of turning." And [*two or three words missing*] he has received not one substantial indication of gra[titu]de or commendation from the Government, notwithstanding the notorious fact that his devotion to party has proved the most fruitful source of his present pecuniary difficulties. The people think that Mr. S[mith] ought to have anything in the gift of the President. Do you not think so too? He would prefer the Mission to Spain. Mr. [Washington] Irvin[g] is sick if I mistake not and might be recalled with perfect consistency, I think. I have felt myself at liberty to address you on this subject knowing that you are aware that Mr. S[mith] has ever been one of your warmest friends and most earnest admirers, and being very anxious that Mr. S[mith] might by a mission be relieved of his pecuniary embarras[s]ments and be free and untram[m]eled to weild [*sic*] his good sword in the cause of the "Great South[r]on" in the fall of 1848. I beg you to exert your influence for Mr. Smith. *Haste is very requisite.* My name would add but little to the weight of this paper—being only one of the people, though *a zealous and earnest-minded Calhoun Man.*

ALU in ScCleA. Note: An AEU by Calhoun reads "Anonymous[,] Relating to Hon. W. Smith's application for appointment." Although datelined "Warrenton, Virginia," this letter was postmarked "Charleston, S.C., May 15."

From A[ndrew] J. Donelson

New Orleans, May 13[t]h 1845
D[ea]r Sir, I addressed a letter to you from Washington in Texas, in relation to the progress of the annexation question, but find since my arrival here, that the vessel to which it and my despatches were entrusted has not yet reached this port.

When that letter was written I was fearful that Gen[era]l [Samuel] Houston would throw impediments in the way; and being in a correspondence with him in which it became important for me to show that he had given his assent to the feature of the joint resolution which leaves with Texas her public lands, I referred to the statement of the fact in a confidential letter to you: and I took the liberty therefore of calling your attention to the subject, and requesting you to preserve that letter if it had been received.

Since then, however, Gen[era]l Houston has brought the correspondence referred to, to a close, and has declared that he will make no opposition to the proposals for the annexation of Texas. The great question then may be said to be settled, for without Gen[era]l Houston's aid the opposition to it becomes at once too small to command any respect or consideration.

The Congress of Texas will meet on the 16th of June, and will accept the proposals from the United States without a dissenting voice. In the convention to be afterwards assembled to form the new constitution there will be equal unanimity on this subject; but as in that convention there will be a representation of local interests which have ["been" *canceled*] heretofore been almost irreconcilable, it may be expected that some delay will mark the proceedings.

Of the result, however, no doubt can be entertained. The powerful voice of the people cannot be disregarded, and I predict that the convention will ratify our proposals without the cross of a t, or the dot of an i, in the way of change.

Congratulating you on the prospect, finishing so brilliantly a work of so much importance to our country, and to which you have contributed so much of your time and labor, I beg you to accept assurances of my great respect & esteem. Y[ou]r ob[edien]t S[e]r[van]t, A.J. Donelson.

ALS in ScCleA; PC in Boucher and Brooks, eds., *Correspondence*, pp. 294–295.

To Abbot[t] Lawrence, [Boston]

Fort Hill, 13th May 1845

My dear Sir, I received a few days since your letter of the 30th April, containing the conditions, on which you & your friends propose to accept the offer of myself & my son to borrow $30,000. On due reflection, I have concluded to decline accepting them.

In offering to pay annually 100,000 pounds of clean cotton of good quality, or its value at the time in the Boston market, on the loan of the proposed sum, my calculation was based on an estimate, that at 6 cents the pound, we could spare that amount after deducting all expenses. Believing that it might be safely estimated, that the article would not fall below that price, I felt safe in making the offer. But as our means depended on cotton, I regarded ["it as" *interlined*] proper to offer it as the basis on which our annual payment would depend, until the loan should be redeemed. The affair was intended to be a business transaction, and our engagements, accordingly, to be met with perfect punctuality, as well as the debt to be perfectly secured. Thus intended, I must decline ["decline" *canceled*] accepting your offer, because at 6 cents the pound (the present average) we would not be able to pay (as you propose) $6000 annually on the principal and interest in addition.

You must permit me to suggest another reason, which, if my impression is correct, would of itself compel me to decline. The impression your letter makes on my mind is, that your offer is made from a disposition to oblige me on the part of yourself & friends, & that not without inconvenience to yourself & them. If I am right, as greatly as I am indebted to you & them for your kind feelings, I could not accept, for reasons, which on reflection, I feel assured, you & they will duely appreciate. When I wrote you, I had supposed, a loan might be effected from the state of your money market, on terms mutually advantageous. It was only on that supposition, that I could make the offer, or accept the loan with propriety.

I am much gratified to learn, that the manufacturing interest is so prosperous, & its prospect so bright. I hope it may be fully realized. I am particularly so to hear, that you are so successful in commanding the foreign market. It is impossible for manufactures in their present advanced state to attain high prosperity, if exclusively dependent on the home market. The great point for that purpose, is to get possession of the foreign market; but high duties, instead of aiding, is a great impediment to that. The relation between imports & exports is so intimate, that the one depends on the other. This the manufacturers of England begin to understand; & hence the immense exertions, which they are making in favour of reducing duties & free trade. They have already succeeded in repealing the duty on cotton, in order that they may get the raw material as cheap as you do; & will not stop until they repeal them on food, when they shall be able to feed their operatives, as cheaply as you do yours. In repealing, they look to the foreign trade; and when it shall be fully effected, & low duties & free trade become the established policy, they will successfully compete with you in the general market of the world, with high duties & restricted commerce.

No one can be more desireous than I am that you should be comple[te]ly successful in commanding the foreign market. I would much rather see our cotton go abroad in the shape of yarn & cloth, than in the raw state; when the price, instead of being ruled by the foreign, would be controlled by the home ["market" *interlined*]. When that is accomplished, all competition, and conflict between the interests of the planter & manufacturer would cease; but until then, every measure, which restricts our foreign exchanges, acts as a burthen on the former, while it retards ["while it retards" *canceled*] the period, when their interests would be identified. This, among other reasons, constitute my objection to the restrictive system. I am no opponent to manufactures, or manufacturers, but the reverse. I rejoice at their in their [*sic*] prosperity & would do nothing intentionally to injure them. With great respect yours truly, J.C. Calhoun.

ALS in MH; autograph draft in ScCleA; variant PC in Jameson, ed., *Correspondence*, pp. 654–656.

From THO[MA]S G. CLEMSON

Brussels, May 14th 1845
Dear Sir, The bearer of this letter Mr. [Louis] Chitti is about visiting the United States, with a public mission from the Belgian Government to study our institutions with a view to increasing the commercial relations of the two countries. Mr. C[hitti] has been professor of social economy & director of one of the Banks of Belgium and is advantageously known as the author of several works on political economy. He is equally distinguished for his intel[l]igence and honourable character.

Mr. C[hitti] is proprietor of a large tract of land in Virginia and Kentucky, and will be occupied a portion of his time in attending to those interests.

I have seen a good deal of Mr. C[hitti] since my arrival and I take great pleasure in making you acquainted with a gentleman of his attainments &c. Your affectionate son, Thos. G. Clemson.

ALS in ScCleA. NOTE: An AEU by Calhoun reads: "Mr. Clemson, ["recommends" *canceled*] Introducing Mr. Chitti."

To PERCY WALKER and Others, [Mobile]

Fort Hill, 15th May, 1845
Gentlemen: From some delay in the mail, I did not receive, until a few days since, your letter of the 21st April, informing me, that at a democratic meeting held in the city of Mobile on the 14th of the same month, you were appointed a committee to express the cordial approbation of the meeting of my public conduct; their gratitude for

my services, and to offer on the part of the meeting, such other manifestations of their respect and esteem as you might think proper.

I will not attempt to express the deep gratitude I feel for the warm approbation of my public conduct and services expressed by the meeting in their resolutions, and the very acceptable manner in which you have performed the duty entrusted to you.

In performing it, you have alluded with particular approbation to my conduct and services in reference to State Rights, and during the period I filled, for a short time, the State Department under the late administration.

To no part of my public life do I look back with greater pleasure, than that devoted to expounding and maintaining the relations between the Federal and State Governments, on which the doctrine of State rights depend, and it is a great consolation for me to think it has not been in vain.

The Federal Government regarded in its federative character, in which States and not individuals, are its constituents, is the most remarkable ever formed; and promises, if carried out honestly and fairly as such, a higher degree of prosperity and happiness, than has ever fallen to the lot of any people. On the other hand, regarded as a national Government, in which individuals and not States are the constituents, it has nothing novel or remarkable about it. Instead of a great Federal Republic, as it is, it would be in that character a huge, unwieldy democracy, destined to be torn into fragments by hostile and conflicting interests, and to terminate in convulsions. Such being my conviction, I felt it to be my duty to maintain the Federal character of the Government against the national or consolidative, at any sacrifice and hazard, and shall continue to do so so long as it shall please the author of my being to spare my life.

The services I rendered during the period I filled the State Department, were performed under great difficulties and embarrassments. Nothing, indeed, but the magnitude of the questions involved in the negotiations in reference to Texas and Oregon, with the difficulties and embarrassments encircling them, and the unanimous call of the country to take charge of the negotiations, could have induced me to leave my retirement and return to public life. Besides those that were intrinsic, there were many that were of an extraneous character.

Among others, the administration was literally without a party in Congress and very feebly supported by the people; and the presidential question was pending, which experience had taught me overruled in a great measure all others.

The negotiation in reference to Texas first claimed my attention, because it was the most pressing and could not be delayed without hazard. In order to avoid the difficulties and embarrassments which I apprehended from the presidential election, I resolved to keep entirely aloof from the party politics of the day, and especially from questions relating to the election, and to use my effort to induce the candidates not to commit themselves against annexation. I had little apprehension that Mr. [Martin] Van Buren would, as a great majority of his friends with Gen. [Andrew] Jackson at their head, had declared for it. The position of Mr. [Henry] Clay was different. The masses of his friends in the north opposed it, which I feared would sway him. In order to prevent it if possible, I saw some of his most prominent friends, with whom I was on friendly terms, and used every argument I could with them, to exert their influence to prevent him from coming out against it.

It was all in vain. His letter in opposition soon after appeared, and Mr. Van Buren's followed shortly after, most unexpectedly to me.

Their effect was great. Mr. Clay's friends were rallied against it almost to a man, although the great body of them in the West and South, were strongly disposed to support it, and not a few of the prominent, openly committed in its favor.

It was different with Mr. Van Buren's. The great body of his supporters remained firm in its support; but an active, influential and not an inconsiderable number adhered to his course. Indeed, the stand taken by the selected candidates of the two great parties, with the influence of the presidential question and the feebleness of the administration in Congress and the country, seemed, for a time, to render the prospect of success almost hopeless.

To these causes of opposition there must be taken into consideration another, to realize the difficulties and embarrassments that stood in the way of the success of the measure. I allude to abolition. It may indeed, be truly regarded as the main spring which put the others in motion.

The abolition party in the North and West had taken an early and decided stand against it, and had gone so far as to adopt measures to influence the party in Great Britain, and through them the British Government to oppose it, as the most effectual means of abolishing slavery in the United States and throughout the continent. The scheme was to abolish slavery in Texas as the most certain means of doing so in the United States, and that of doing it throughout the continent. To consummate this grand and well laid scheme, it was indispensable that Texas should be prevented from being annexed to our Union; while the only possible way to defeat it and prevent the mighty consequences which would flow from it, was the annexation of Texas.

The course of the British Government at an early stage of the negotiation, made it manifest that it had warmly and fully embraced the scheme. The declaration made by its minister at Washington to our Government before it had fairly commenced (a copy of which was left at the Department of State after I had entered on its duties,) left not a doubt on that point. It indeed, as well as avowed it, by declaring that Great Britain desired to see slavery abolished in Texas and throughout the world, and that she was using constant efforts to effect it, and by inference, that she was using her influence and diplomacy with Mexico to agree to recognize the independence of Texas, on condition that she should abolish slavery.

I saw in this declaration, thus formally made to our government, a confirmation of what I believed to be her scheme of policy in connection with Texas, from other but less conclusive evidence in my possession. I also saw clearly, that whether it should succeed or not, depended on the fact whether Texas should or should not be annexed; and that if it succeeded, its inevitable consequences would be the final consummation of her great and deep design, to be followed by the desolation of the south, the prostration of the commerce and prosperity of the continent, with a monopoly on her part of the great tropical products of sugar, coffee, rice, tobacco and cotton, which are almost exclusively, as far as this continent is concerned, the result of slave labor.

Seeing all this, the question presented to me was, how shall the declaration of the British government be met? Shall it be silently passed over, leaving annexation to be urged on other and different grounds, or shall it be directly and boldly met and exposed?

It is not in my nature to hesitate between such alternatives. My conviction is deep, that truth, honesty and plain dealing is the true policy on all occasions in the management of public affairs, including diplomatic; and I resolved, without hesitation, to take them as my guides on this memorable occasion. The defeat of this deep laid scheme; the success of annexation, (as may now be almost certainly said,) the vindication of the great institution on which our safety depends, and the rescue of the commerce of the continent from the grasp of commercial monopoly, have been the result, and I may add, as far as I am individually concerned, your approbation, that of the meeting you represent, and if I may judge from indications, nearly of the whole country now of my course.

But at the time the approbation was not so unanimous. Denunciation *then*, loud and deep, fell on my head.

I was charged with introducing a new local subject of little importance into the Texan issue, with the base design of injuring the prospect of one of the presidential candidates, and of dissolving the Union! And many, who did not go so far, even southern men whose all was at stake, thought that I acted injudiciously in introducing the slave question and giving it such prominence; that it was calculated to have a bad party effect and to drive off some of the party who were not sound on the subject of abolition, or who desired to obtain the votes of abolitionists. But I pass them by without remark or comment now, when time and experience and the approbation of the country sanction the wisdom of the course I adopted.

The absorbing character of the negotiation in reference to Texas, did not so engross my attention as to neglect that of Oregon. As soon as the former was sufficiently dispatched and the business of the department brought up, I entered on that. I left it in an unfinished state; and as it is still pending, I am not at liberty to speak of the course I took in reference to it; but I trust, when it comes to be made public, it will not be less successful in meeting your approbation and that of the country generally. It is a subject not without great difficulties; and I feel assured I shall be pardoned for expressing a hope that it may be so conducted by those to whose hands it is entrusted to finish the negotiation, as to bring it to a successful and satisfactory termination, and thus avoid an appeal to arms. Neither country can possibly gain any thing by such an appeal, or can possibly desire it if it can be honorably avoided.

In conclusion, I assure you and through you those you represent, that it would afford me great pleasure to partake of the public dinner you have tendered me in their name, and of forming the personal acquaintance of my numerous friends in your city; but it is not now in my power. It is probable, however, that I shall visit my son who resides in your State some time next autumn; and in that event, I will make it a point to visit Mobile, when I shall be happy to meet you and all my friends. With great respect, yours truly, J.C. Calhoun.

PC in the Mobile, Ala., *Register and Journal,* May 27, 1845, p. 2; PC in the New Orleans, La., *Jeffersonian Republican,* May 31, 1845, p. 2; PC in the Charleston, S.C., *Mercury,* June 2, 1845, p. 2; PC in the Charleston, S.C., *Courier,* June 3, 1845, p. 2; PC in the Washington, D.C., *Constitution,* June 5, 1845, p. 2; PC in the Washington, D.C., *Daily Union,* June 5, 1845, p. 123; PC in the Milledgeville, Ga., *Federal Union,* June 10, 1845, p. 2; PC in the Camden, S.C., *Journal,* June 11, 1845, p. 2; PC in the Edgefield, S.C., *Advertiser,* June 11, 1845, pp.

2–3; PC in the Richmond, Va., *Enquirer*, June 11, 1845, p. 4; PC in the Green-ville, S.C., *Mountaineer*, June 13, 1845, p. 1; PC in *The Liberator*, vol. LI, no. 24 (June 13, 1845), p. 94; PC in the Pendleton, S.C., *Messenger*, June 13, 1845, p. 1; PC in *Niles' National Register*, vol. LXVIII, no. 15 (June 14, 1845), pp. 231–232; PC in the Jackson, Miss., *Mississippian*, June 18, 1845, p. 3; PC in the New York, N.Y., *National Anti-Slavery Standard*, June 26, 1845, p. 1; PC in the Jackson, Miss., *Southern Reformer*, June 28, 1845, p. 1. Note: Besides Walker, the addressees of this letter were Thomas Holland, Thomas McGran, W[illia]m R. Hallett, and J[ohn] A. Campbell.

To [Dixon H. Lewis]

Fort Hill, 16th May 1845

My Dear Sir, I entirely concur in the view taken by our friends, in their consultation in Charleston, as stated in your letter [of 5/9], with a single exception, that of travelling this summer. My impres-sion after a review of the whole ground is unchanged, on that point; especially that of travelling this summer. Admitting it to be expedi-ent, I am of the impression, it ought to be defer[r]ed untill next year. To be still and quiet for *the present* strikes me as the proper course.

I will visit my plantation in Alabama to see my son [Andrew Pickens Calhoun] and his family, some time this fall. In that case I shall extend my visit to Mobile[,] N[ew] Orleans and perhaps Vicks-burg and farther. Another year, if, my friends, shall think it advis-able I will yield to their opinion to visit the North and West.

The first point at present is to develope in a proper way our de-termination not to yield to the dictation of a Convention, and through [it] to office holders and office seekers, the right secured to the people of the U. States by the Constitution to elect the Chief Magistrate. For that purpose after full consultation by correspondence with our Virginia friends, a pamphlet ought to be ["put" *interlined and* "ought" *changed to* "out"], stating our grounds and the reasons for it in op-position to a Convention. It should appear in Virginia and be pre-pared by [Robert M.T.] Hunter, [James A.] Seddon, or some talented friend there.

A letter from you to [Robert G.] Scott, would put the thing in motion. On its appearance, the Southern papers should be put in motion to attract publick attention to the subject and in due time, the Southern Review[,] the Literary Messenger and Bro[w]nson[']s Review should contain articles, of which the pamphlet should be the subject. When the publick mind in the South is sufficiently [prepared] for it, then ["if" *canceled*] my friends if they should choose to present my name as the people[']s candidate in opposition to the Convention Candidate may do it with success, provided they determine to nail the Colours to the mast. If we are resolute and determined, the office holders and office seekers will succumb. They are a compromising race. With them a half loaf is better than none, and no prospect of success is better than no prospect. In no other way, be assured, my friend, can we succeed. The mercenary corps will never permit power to be put in my hands, if they can elect another. That is fixed, but [they] had rather see me elected than an opponent from whom they can have nothing to ["to" *canceled*] hope. That is the philosophy of the whole affair. We can only succeed by showing them, that I am the only man of the party who can be elected, which we can easily do if our Virginia ["friends" *interlined*] choose to take the stand, early and firmly. Without it, establishing news papers[,] travelling and every other thing is in vain. Indeed if I am to travel I would greatly prefer to do it openly as the Candidate of the people and the Constitution, and under invitation from them to meet them in that character. It would be far more respectable to do it in that than any other character.

Such are my views. If you concur, you can do much to execute them. Write at once to Scott, [Franklin H.] Elmore[,] [James] Hamilton [Jr.] and such other friends at other points, as you may think judicious.

Elmore should call a small meeting of our friends in Charleston and place the subject before them in extenso, and organize a systematic movement begin[n]ing it at a few important points, and address our friends in Richmond as the Organ of the meeting on the subject of preparing and issuing a pamphlet.

What is wanted is action, action, action; quiet and still but wide spread and efficient action. Among those you ought to write, I would add [William A.] Elmore of New Orleans and Redwood [*sic*; Ellwood] Fisher of Cincinatti [*sic*]. He was at Washington last Winter and is efficient and faithful. He may be fully trusted. He writes well and if you would put him in possession of the line of action, would, I have no doubt prepair [*sic*] an able pamphlet suited to the Western meridian.

You are at liberty in your correspondence if you ["should" *interlined*] think proper to us[e] my name and give such extracts from what I have written to you on the subject as you may think proper. I particularly concur in the opinion of the Charleston meeting, that retirement for me at present, is the proper position for me. I have no idea, that the mission [to Great Britain] will be offered to me on the terms you suggest it might. If it should it would be difficult to decline, although it would be ["difficult" *canceled*] very adverse to my inclination. There is but one possible reason which as far as I can see, should in any contingency force me into publick life at this time. The Oregon question might take a turn, that might make my presence in the Senate almost indispensable. War must not grow out of it. I know it need not, or rather I ought to say needed not. [James K.] Polk[']s inaugeral [*sic*] has greatly embarrassed the subject, as I apprehended at the time. I have no confidence in the administration in refference to the subject.

I did my best to put him in the right direction in relation to it before he delivered his inaugeral but as it turned out in vain. I fear if he is not overruled War will be [the] consequence, a ["conseq" *canceled*] war which must end in the loss of the territory and countless ["disasters" *canceled and* "disaster" *interlined*] to the Country.

The government itself will hardly survive it. I have for years kept my eyes on it and what I have said is the result of deep reflection. He can I fear be only overruled by the Senate and not by that unless the South is true to itself. If my efforts [are] necessary to prevent so great a calamity as such a war I must meet the responsibility as great as it may be. Yours truly, John C. Calhoun.

Contemporary ms. copy in Vi, Robert M.T. Hunter Papers; variant PC in Charles Henry Ambler, ed., *Correspondence of Robert M.T. Hunter*, pp. 77–79; variant PEx in Joseph G. Rayback, "The Presidential Ambitions of John C. Calhoun, 1844–1848," in *Journal of Southern History*, vol. XIV, no. 3 (August, 1948), p. 335.

From R[ICHARD] K. CRALLÉ

Lynchburg [Va.,] May 18th 1845

My dear Sir, I have just returned from an excursion through some of the western Counties of the State; and though I have learned but little which it would interest you to read, I still trouble you with a letter, as I desire to be informed as to your health and that of your family. When I met with [your son] James [Edward Calhoun], very unexpectedly, in the mountains, on his way from the University [of Virginia] to his brother's [Andrew Pickens Calhoun's] in Ala. he had neither heard from you nor his mother. I hope she has safely arrived at home, and that Miss [Martha] Cornelia [Calhoun] has improved;

tho' of this I am not sanguine, however full of promises the Doctors may be. I hope you will spare me a few moments, as soon as you receive this, and let me know whether you have entirely recovered your strength, and got rid of all the symptoms of your attack in Washington.

Besides this there are some other matters on which I wish to hear from you. The result of our elections shows an increased strength in the Democratic Party in almost every section of the State; and as yet I have met with but two or three individuals who are not decidedly friendly in their feelings towards you. Almost every influential man in the Party openly professes this; and your friends have better reasons to be satisfied with the present state of things than at any past period. Still the time must come for some action, and much depends on the *manner* and the *moment*. I have written to [Robert M.T.] Hunter, and requested him to consult with others upon the subject. In the west your friends are waiting the action of others. Taliaferro, Trigg, Latham, [David] McComas, [William H.?] French and others in the Abingdon District–[Augustus A.?] Chapman, Miller, [John B.?] Calwell and the two Thompsons–[Samuel L.?] Hays, Johnson, and most of the Democratic members of the Legislature from the West are decidedly favourable in their feelings. Many of these I have seen, and have no doubt of their fidelity. But the time *when*, and the *manner* how we should take the first step deserve full consideration. If we act too precipitately we shall furnish the corrupt Junta in Richmond with weapons against us; while, on the other hand, if we delay too long we shall allow them to mould public sentiment to their own purposes. [Thomas] Ritchie's position at Washington has not be[en] taken, I apprehend, without full advisement. His probable views and projects I have not been able to learn, as I have been so much in the mountains since we parted. Hunter, to whom I have written since my return, may probably furnish some clue to his future designs. In the meantime I have no idea they can be friendly. He attributes the failure of [Andrew] Stevenson to get a seat in the Cabinet to you or your friends in Virginia. I learned this from [Washington] Greenhow after we left [Robert G.] Scott's in Richmond. His plan, I expect, is to run [Silas] Wright with Stevenson as Vice President—or, if that fail, to take some other Northern man to subserve the same end. A fulsome eulogy on Stevenson which I casually met with in my travels serves to convince me of this; for after the events of the last winter he [Ritchie] cannot hope to get him [Stevenson] into the Senate or the Executive chair of the State. He is resolved, however, to get him in some place, and the one I suggest opens other and further prospects. At present he is insidiously silent as to the succession; and I have no doubt when he breaks ground it will be on the old topic of the Baltimore Convention, the Union of the Party &C &C. Ought we to consent to go into a Convention? If not, ought not the matter to be discussed, without reference to individuals, in the public prints? Is not this the proper time for it, before Parties have taken position? Would it not, at least, draw from our opponents, their purposes in the future? I should like to have your views on these points.

It is evident that every thing depends upon the position Virginia shall take; and I hazard nothing in saying that the hands of your friends would be greatly strengthened by a visit to the State. Indeed this is essential. You ought, in justice to them, to yourself, and to the cause, to visit the State during the summer. There is a stronger and more general interest felt by the *people* to see you than any other public man; and I venture to urge it on you as a public duty, that you visit the Springs as early in the season as possible. Your purpose to do so should be made public, as thousands would probably go to see you who might not otherwise be aware of it until too late. I could have the annunciation made here. Your health, I am sure, would be greatly improved by it, while it would subserve other good purposes. I act but as the organ of thousands when I say, I hope you will consent to come on early in July.

I have received a note from Judge [Daniel E.] Huger, enclosing one from J[ohn] S. Barbour addressed to you, or, in your absence, to me, desiring to know the causes of Mr. J[ohn] S. Pendleton's extreme hostility to you. I have not replied to it—as I am not aware of any, except such as necessarily must exist between an honest man and a scoundrel. His enmity is not worth notice. I have a letter too from [Theophilus] Fisk, who I understand, has promised the public my cooperation in his Paper. He acts without authority; for I am not so well satisfied as to the sincerity of his friendship. Rumor said, at first, that he would sustain the pretensions of [Lewis] Cass. I have not seen a number of his Paper, nor have I written to him in reply to his letter. Do you know anything of his views? How comes it that the [Washington] Constitution was not united with the [United States] Journal, if he was to be regarded as a friend of yours? He tells me he knows that [John] Heart is a *"traitor to you."* Can this be so? I fear there may be treachery on one side or the other, and shall not correspond with either until I learn more. But surely [William A.] Harris is above every thing that smacks of dishonesty. I cannot believe he would do anything unworthy of the gentleman—and Heart could not without his permission.

I see that the mission to England has been offered to Mr. [Francis W.] Pickens, but have not learned whether he would accept or not. I am not prepared to determine whether he ought or not. Of course he will consult you before he acts. [William M.?] Blackford, who has been here, says that there is a schism in the Cabinet between [Robert J.] Walker & [James] Buchanan, and that he would not be surprised if the Administration should desire you to return. Bettie [Elizabeth Morris Crallé], who has improved a good deal, desires her most affectionate regards to you, Mrs. Calhoun and Miss Cornelia; and joins me in the earnest wish and hope that we shall meet shortly at the Springs in the mountains. Mary also desires her best love to each. In haste yours truly, R.K. Crallé.

ALS in ViU, Richard Kenner Crallé Papers; PEx in Frederick W. Moore, "Calhoun as Seen by His Contemporaries," *Publications of the Southern History Association*, 7:422–423.

From J[AMES] HAMILTON, [JR.]

Savannah, Geo[rgia], May 18, 1845

My Dear Sir, I was so much occupied whilst in Charleston that I had not time to write you again but having a moment of leisure here I am induced to drop you a line altho I did not find ["here" *canceled and* "in this city" *interlined*] as I anticipated a reply to my Letter at this place.

Your friends at Col. [Franklin H.] Elmore[']s had a very gratifying meeting whilst I was in Charleston. I laid before them the result of my observations at the North—that you never were as strong with the people as at the present moment, and that free from all caucus & Convention nominations we must run you next time against the field & commence at once to organize for the Battle. I gave them distinctly to understand that there were two men at least at the South who would nail your colors to the mast[,] [John H.] Howard of Georgia & myself[,] and that there must be no *capitulation this time*. That we would not consent to their ["its" *canceled and* "being hauled down" *interlined*]. That hitherto you had been invariably sacrificed by the *timidity* of your friends to the *malice* of your Enemies. That if we failed we would stand justified before the world & posterity for declaring you at the proper time a Candidate by the fact universally acknowledged that you are better qualified than any man in the Country for the highest Office in the Gift of the people.

I moreover told them that I had made one President [Andrew Jackson] & contributed largely to making another [James K. Polk?] & that if God spared my life & Texas enabled me to pay my Debts in the next year, I should take a vehemently active part in your election by organizing & confederating with your friends from one end of the Union to the other, & endeavour to make a third.

It was deemed my Dear Sir vastly expedient that all fastidiousness aside ["that" *canceled*] you should travel North & West during the ensuing year & let the people see *who and what you are.* That the impression would be most decisive & and [*sic*] potential I have no doubt. It would be well that this trip should be made before you become *an announced Candidate,* and therefore your Journeyings [*one word canceled and* "ought" *interlined*] to cease by next Autumn twe[l]vemonth.

Mr. [Henry] Gourdin & myself would meet you in Charleston in July, if it suited you to go on ["again" *canceled*] this summer. I could be with you in New York during your stay there in July, and accompany you to Boston but there I should be constrained to leave you as on some very important private business, I shall have to take the steamer for England on the [*manuscript torn; one number illegible*]st Aug[u]st. If you postpone your Northern jaunt until the next summer, I should be able to ["to" *canceled*] go with you throughout your whole Excursion. As I deem it indispensable that the people should have some personal knowledge of you thro social ["sympathy" *canceled and* "contact" *interlined*]—I beg you to wa[i]ve all feelings of ["personal" *canceled*] delicacy & assent in this particular to the wishes of your friends.

I deem it likewise of much importance you should visit Louisiana next winter. Why can you not go down with me in Nov.[,] see your son [Andrew Pickens Calhoun,] be in New Orleans when the Legislature meets which is in Dec. and return home by ascending the River to Louisville[,] Kentucky[,] & travelling thro Kentucky & Tennessee & by this route reaching Fort Hill before planting time?

But whilst I am delineating an excursion to keep you at home you have probably decided to go abroad, for I have very good reason to believe that the President [James K. Polk] has pressed again upon you the mission to England consequent on [Francis W.] Picken[s]'s declining it, and that this offer has resulted from the far greater complication of our relations ["now" *interlined*] with England than at the period when you declined the appointment before. If the mission is made a special one and the administration will agree upon a line which you shall consider as a fair basis for the adjustment of the Oregon Question and will pledge themselves to sustain any treaty you may make, *at all & every hazard* and you think such a compromise will be accepted by England I would run the hazard of striking a great blow for your public reputation both at home & abroad—more especially if the President will authorize you to negotiate a reciprocity Treaty, which I have frequently said to you, I deem entirely feasible in the hands of a Southern & free Trade man. These present strong views in favor of your accepting the mission whilst it is not to be ["concealed" *canceled and* "doubted" *interlined*] if you fail in your mission, the result might be unpropitious to your political fortunes. Nor is the fact to be con [*sic*] concealed that your present retirement under the circumstances which attended ["is in" *canceled*] it is a source of strength, for there is not a man unprejudiced by party who does not feel that you ought now to be in the Dept. of State & it is unjust you should not.

If you should accept the mission I must time it in such a manner as to go out to England in the same vessel with you as I think from my knowledge of Downing Street & ["the" *interlined*] mode of living in London I could be of essential service to you.

Write me immediately what has been your decision in this matter directed to the Oswichee P[ost] O[ffice,] Russel[l] County[,] Ala. & believe me My Dear sir yours ever, J. Hamilton.

P.S. I have sent in an article to the [Charleston] Mercury on the subject of your postage & [Henry] Clay[']s which I hope will induce all your correspondents to do what I will do *prepay* ["your" *canceled and* "their" *interlined*] postage. Upon reflection I have determined to send the article to the [Washington] National *Intelligencer.*

P.S. Do not fail to write me by return mail & if you have accepted the English mission let me know when you will leave Fort Hill that I may meet you either in Charleston or at the North.

ALS in ScCleA. NOTE: This letter was postmarked in Savannah on 5/20 and was marked by Hamilton, *"post paid."*

Thomas Ritchie to John Y. Mason

[Washington] May 18, 1845
My Dear Sir, In writing to Mr. Calhoun, as you told me last night you intended to do, I will thank you to be explicit with him, as you can be, (as I begged you) ["but" *canceled and* "and" *interlined*] to say [to] him at once, not to listen to the idle gossip in the newspapers. I enclose you a specimen, which I cut out of [James G.] Bennett's [New York] Herald, just at hand this morning. His Editorial A. and an extract of his Washington correspondent B. are both dictated by spleen, in consequence of my contradicting their previous misrepresentation. I found it necessary to arrest their stories, 1st. that we may correct that incessant tendency of the letter-writers at Washington to misreport all public matters, and their prurient disposition to abuse the public ear—& 2ly. because in this particular case, the story about the *Special* mission was agitating the commercial community, with all sorts of hobgoblins about war. I am sure I need not tell Mr. Calhoun, that I am the last man to "proscribe" him—and as to Mr. [Francis W.] Pickens's *Italics*, there was no "malice" in it—but simply a desire to point out to the reader, that in *that* particular statement alone the N.Y. scribbler was correct. I had previously announced Mr. [Franklin H.] Elmore's declining—and not having noticed Pickens's I called the attention of the Reader specially to *that* by my unfortunate Italics.

If you could place these simple facts before Mr. Calhoun (along with what you may think it right to say about *"The Executive"* article, you would oblige Yours Truly, Thomas Ritchie.

ALS in ScCleA. NOTE: This letter was doubtless forwarded to Calhoun by Mason. The Washington, D.C., *Daily Union* of May 14, 1845, p. 3, disavows a recent article in the New York *Herald* stating that Calhoun would be offered a Special Mission to England to treat on the Oregon and tariff issues and that he would accept this mission. The same article mentions that the regular appointment to London had been refused by "both Messrs. Elmore and *Pickens*" as well as Calhoun. The article entitled "The Executive" appears in the *Daily Union* of May 7, 1845, p. 3, and comments favorably on the "efficiency, energy, and capacities" of the James K. Polk administration and its appointments thus far.

From ISRAEL HOGE

Post Office[,] Zanesville Ohio
May 19, 1845

My dear Sir, The enclosed address was mailed to you on the 22nd of last month but supposing that it was not properly addressed—I again enclose it to you.

You have many warm friends in Ohio many who would like to see you again in the counsels of the nation at this particular juncture of affairs & many also who would have been pleased to have you accepted [*sic*] the Mission to England—all of them hope some day to see you el[e]vated still higher in the public [*one word canceled and "counsels" interlined*] of this great & mighty nation. Your friend most sincerely, Israel Hoge, P[ost] M[aster].

ALS with En in ScCleA. NOTE: Hoge enclosed a copy of the same address to Calhoun from the "States-rights republicans of Muskingum County Ohio" which he had transmitted with his letter of 4/22 above. The second copy, however, included additional signatures of C. Moore, H. Reed, and George James.

From J[OHN] S. BARBOUR

Catalpa, [Culpeper County, Va.,] May 21st 1845

My Dear Sir, I was in Washington a few days past. I saw [John Y.] Mason, [William L.] Marcy, [James] Buchanan & [George] Bancroft. These people are the vilest of hypocrites if they are not your friends. I am old enough to distrust all politicians, for they are the pests of every community in which they are members. The loss of personal hopes & the consequent lapse of selfishness into patriotism, make them your friends (as far as they can be friends of any body) in spite of antient predilections. Several little anecdotes were told me to satisfy me of Bancroft's admiration of your ability in the despatches to the British Minister. And one of these occurring in Cabinet Council. Men like animals of every other class have their instinct, & you cannot mistake the instinct that is "north of the Tweed." Victory said Bonaparte is never [*one or two words canceled and "called to an" interlined*] account for her actions. And the "flesh pots of Egypt" are scented in the distant gale. These people doubtless think that having exhausted both their powers & their hopes in wrangles for other uses than those of the Country, they may now fall back in commendation of you, as the offering which "vice gives to virtue." The agent I believe is according to the masters in Ethics, vicious or virtuous according to his intention, but the act good or ill according to its tendency. Be this as it may these people are professedly at least to your friends very laudatory of you. And I may add that which was my chief purpose in picking up my pen to write you. The President (Colo[nel James K.] Polk) is so ["also"(?) *canceled*] likewise.

Mr. Polk is by nature a good man, plain in understanding, raised into aspiration by the advent of peculiar combinations of powers, parties, & persons; and successful to the highest limit in the altitude of aspiration. He may naturally & I believe ["patriotically" *with the* "c" *interlined*] wish first that he may be succeeded by the most worthy for his own gratification & secondly for the country[']s weal. I have the best reason to think that his present hopes & wishes lean to you. It was he who recounted to me Mr. Bancroft[']s eulogy on reading (or hearing) your letter to the British Ambassador. I know that [Thomas] Ritchie is decidedly your friend. And I know he is a friend to be valued. The young Ritchies [that is, Thomas Ritchie Jr. and William F. Ritchie] I know nothing of; but the old man is far more sincere & honest than we might expect from a hacknied politician.

The President asked me why it was that the South Carolina Statesmen declined the mission to England? I replied that it was a matter of which I was wholly uninformed. I thought his views correct. In this—1st That the mission ought to go to a slave State—2d. particularly to South Carolina. I was alone with Mr. Polk for near two hours & I am greatly deceived if he is not sincerely your friend. He spoke of [Silas] Wright as being powerless, and in a tone of the feud of [Vice-President George M.] Dallas & [James] Buchanan which left me with the belief that he regarded them both as feeble for ill or injury to others or profit to themselves. I may have been deceived in all that I heard, yet I do not think so. When kindness is felt & is sincere in its tendency & object, it cannot always be repulsed with justice or policy. Unsolicited support for political trust, by those towards whom we have acted in opposition, ["or who" *canceled*] & who are without personal regard to us, is perhaps high commendation[?] to the object of support, & moreover commendable[?] to the patriotism which offers its aid under such circumstances. To repulse it is I think neither wise nor dutiful. The substance of my thoughts is this: those people at Washington wish to be your friends—

whether the motive be good or bad is it wise to discard their favour? With great Respect & sincere Regard Y[ou]r friend, J.S. Barbour.

ALS in ScCleA; variant PC in Jameson, ed., *Correspondence*, pp. 1036–1038.

TO A[NNA] M[ARIA CALHOUN] CLEMSON, [Brussels]

Fort Hill, 22d May 1845
My dear Anna, The last Steamer brought me yours of the 13th April.

I have been very punctual in writing to you or Mr. [Thomas G.] Clemson excepting the interval of my sickness. If you have received fewer from me, it was because I was almost his sole correspondent in the family, while you had several besides myself. Latterly, however, since I left the [State] Department, I have written you & him alternately.

It was scarcely in the power of Mr. [James K.] Polk to treat me badly. I would consider it, at least, as much a favour to him for me to remain in office under his administration, as he could to me, to invite me to remain. Indeed, as his Cabinet was organized and the views expressed in his inaugural in reference to the Tariff & his imprudent declaration in the same in reference to the Oregon question, I could not have remained in, had he invited me. I did my best in a conversation I had with him, a week or ten days before he delivered his inaugural, to guard him against the course he took in reference to Oregon, but it seems in vain. I fear it will give the country much trouble to escape from its effects. It has greatly increased the difficulty of settling the question, and ["has" *interlined*] lost us the only chance we ever had to secure the whole, & may, in the end, lose the whole.

You will have seen, that after I declined the mission [to England], it was offered to [Franklin H.] Elmore, who declined it, & then to [Francis W.] Pickens, who did the same; & that it is now rumoured, that it will be offered to me, with full powers to adjust ["it" *canceled and* "the Oregon question" *interlined*] & to negotiate a commercial treaty. I have no idea it will, &, if it should be, I certainly will not accept, if I can possibly avoid it.

I was not aware until I took charge of the State Dept. of the immense influence, which may be exerted through it on foreign & domestick relations. I found its duties had been shamefully neglected. I had nothing to sustain me; the administration without a single advocate in Congress & very feeble in the country, with a most inefficient organ [the *Madisonian*], and both parties, or rather the acknowledged leaders of the one party & both leaders and followers of the other, opposed on its leading measure, that of the Annexation; and yet with all these disadvantages, I have succeed[ed], by a bold unhesitating course, to secure Annexation, & leave a strong impression ["behind" *interlined*], both at home & abroad, in the short space of less than 11 months. I say secured, for Maj[o]r [Andrew J.] Donelson, our Charge writes me by a letter received by the last mail, that he regards annexation as now certain. The publick voice of Texas is almost unanimous, & the Govt. has been compelled to secumb [*sic*]. While conducting the Texian question successfully by bold & decisive measures, I was conducting the Oregon with equal success, by a quiet, amicable, but firm course. I saw my way clearly through it, and would have terminated the negotiation last winter in time to be laid before Congress, had Mr. [Richard] Pakenham received instructions from his Government, as early as he expected, at [the] stage of the discussion at which I left it.

I am rejoiced to learn that your health & Mr. Clemson's is as good as it is, after so long & disagreeable a winter, & that the children[']s [John Calhoun Clemson's and Floride Elizabeth Clemson's] is so fine & they so rapidly improving. You must really ["have" *interlined*] been tired with a Belgian winter; and I am glad, that you think of travelling. It will after such long confinement be of service to your health & sperits. I am glad to learn both by yours & his letter, that he has concluded a project of a treaty, & hope that it ["will" *interlined*] be approved by the Administration. It will add to the reputation & influence he has already acquired. I have no doubt, a change should be made in our Diplomatick & consular arrangements, to give both increased efficiency & respectability, & intended to have taken the subject up, had I remained in the Department.

In our remote situation, we have little news of a domestick character, and still less, that is not old, of a publick. We are all well. The season has been very dray [*sic*]. We have had but one wetting rain since the last week in March. Much of the cotton has just come up, but that which had come up, & the corn & small grain look much better, than you would suppose. I understand Mr. Clemson has had rather more than the usual share of rain, which has fall[en] in that quarter of the State this season. I have favourable intelligence of our Alabama crop.

We expect John [C. Calhoun, Jr.] from Alabama daily, &, you will be surprise[d] to have it added ["and" *canceled*] James [Edward Calhoun] with him. He, with a larger [*sic*] portion of the students, left the Virginia University during the late row, rather than become witness ag[ai]nst his classmates; and, instead of coming home directly, he took the route by N[ew] Orleans & the Canebrake, where I understand he has arrived, & expects to return with John.

Poor [George] McDuffie I hear has just had paraliticke stroke, which has been followed by loss of speech & the use of his left side. His case must be hopeless. It makes me sad to think of it.

All join their love to you & Mr. Clemson & send their How Do & kisses to the children. Your affectionate father, J.C. Calhoun.

[P.S.] If an opportunity should offer, I will forward a half dozen copies of my speeches & &c to the State Dept. to be sent to Mr. Clemson. I have put another volume a part for Calhoun, with his name inscribed. I have recommenced in good earnest my prelimitary [*sic*] treatise on the elementary principles of political science, and made good progress towards finishing the rough draft. When finished I shall commence the treatise on the Federal Constitution, which I hope to finish in the course of the year, if I can remain at home. J.C.C.

ALS in ScCleA; PEx's in Jameson, ed., *Correspondence*, pp. 656–657.

To A[ndrew] J. Donelson, [New Orleans]

Fort Hill, 23d May 1845
My dear Sir, The last mail brought me your two letters of the 24th April & 13th Inst.; the latter containing the gratifying intelligence, that all the obstacles in the way of the annexation of Texas have been removed, & that there is no doubt now of the consummation of the great measure. It is, indeed, a great ["measure" *canceled*] measure, in whatever aspect it is regarded, and has been effected under great difficulties. For the very important part you have acted towards accomplishing it, the country is greatly indebted to you. I saw from the first the use, which it would be attempted to be made of Mr. [Robert J.] Walker's amendment to the House bill, & that, it endangered the success of annexation. Gen[era]l [Samuel] Houston & the Government of Texas could not have taken any other ground, so well calculated to defeat it, if such had been the design, as to

have the negotiation opened anew under the amendment. Had it succeeded, whatever may have been the terms agreed on by the Commissioners, the treaty (for such it would have been) would most assuredly been rejected by the Senate. There is a settled and fixed opposition to the measure in all and every form in that body, which can not be overcome. Seeing this, I could not doubt, that whoever was opposed at bottom to annexation in Texas would take their stand, not in direct opposition to annexation, but against the House bill, & in favour of the amendment; & that all the foreign influence—that of Great Britian [*sic*] & France would ["be" *interlined*] thrown in the same direction. Under this impression, I took a most decided stand against it from the moment that the amendment was first offered in the shape of an independent measure by Col. [Thomas H.] Benton, and it was with great difficulty, and after much exertions, that I defeated it in that shape; in which, had it passed, annexation would, from what has transpired, been clearly lost. The *Government* of Texas would have had the whole game in its own hand, and could have defeated it by delays & throwing in embarrassing propositions ["in its way" *interlined*]. I also used my best efforts to defeat it in the shape of an amendment from the same impression, but in vain. Failing in that, I lost no time in preparing and giving the instructions, based on the House resolutions, which I did, as the only possible means of preventing the loss of annexation, & which, most fortunately, you have so ably & successfully carried out. The presenting it, in the first instance, as an ultimatum, was a bold & masterly stroke. On that the success of your movement depended. The course taken by Dr. [Ashbel] Smith, Secretary of State [of Texas], in opposition to annexation surprised me. I had regarded him as a firm friend of annexation. I received two letters from him in 1843; one after I had left the Senate & retired to my residence here, giving me a full account of the intrigues of the abolitionists with the British Government, in reference to Texas, and the countenance, which they received from Lord Aberdeen. I enclosed the one I received here, to Mr. [Abel P.] Upshur [then U.S. Secretary of State], in a long letter addressed to him, & urging on him the necessity of adopting some decided measure to defeat a scheme, which, if it should succeed, must prove fatal to the South, & the Union. The information, which the Doctor's letter contained, & the views I presented, I doubt not had due influence in bringing about the negotiation, which followed, & which we may, I trust, now say with certainty, will end in annexation.

I received the information you give in reference to Gen[era]l

Houston's course, in strict confidence, as you desire; and wish you to consider what I write in the same way. I have not looked over my papers, but have no doubt, but that the letter to which you allude is among them, if it has been received, as I doubt not it has. With great respect yours truly, J.C. Calhoun.

ALS in DLC, Andrew Jackson Donelson Papers; retained copy in ScCleA; PC in Jameson, ed., *Correspondence*, pp. 658–659.

From F[RANCIS] W. PICKENS

Edgewood, 23 May 1845

My dear Sir, I am glad you wrote me in relation to Duff Green's letter; not that I supposed you had countenanced what he had done, but from his letter I infer[r]ed that he made Mr. [James K.] Polk believe he was acting for you by authority. According to his own letter to me his conversation with Mr. Polk was unmanly & mean. I do hope the President well knew that Greene [*sic*] did not act from any correspondence with you. I have not answered Green's letter & do not intend it as I could not trust myself with such a man. I see he has been the means of stuffing the N[ew] York letter writers with all sorts of nonsense. While on the subject, I fear Gen[e]r[a]l [James] Hamilton [Jr.] has talked imprudently recently in Washington. As soon as he found out the Presid[en]t had offered me the mission he wrote me, and mentioned the substance of a letter which he said you wrote him when you "supposed you might be continued as Sec[re]t[ar]y" of State. The letter was in refference [*sic*] to you desiring to appoint him on a special mission to England &c &c &c. Now the only point I fear is that he was urging his appointment from the President & that he mentioned your name in connection with it, for he says he spoke of his being able to negotiate a Reciprocity Treaty &c—but did not mention the "first part"—which I infer[r]ed to mean that he did not mention the fact of your having desired him to hold himself in readiness to accept a special mission &c. Now Hamilton is so utterly prostrated and pressed in his private affairs that he cannot act as he did when you used to know him.

His name is laughed at in Charleston by all the gentlement [*sic*] of standing.

He wrote me about my appointment when he took it for granted I would of course accept and immediately presented a name as

Sec[re]t[ar]y of Legation, & I know he did it at the instigation of [James] Buchanan, as [Dixon H.] Lewis had done the same in a very low-toned letter—shewing that he was ready to do any thing Buchanan desired. I felt it due to me that I should write Gen[era]l Hamilton & gave him my resasons [*sic*] for declining the appointment, & he immediately shewed my letter to Col: [Franklin H.] Elmore & others. Of course what I write you about these gent[lemen] is entirely confidential. The country is so utterly corrupt & prostituted that it is difficult to know to whom we can trust ourselves in public matters. You would be surprised to see the letters I have rec[eive]d urging my acceptance of this Mission *even in this State,* and then the congratulations from the North &c. But they all came too late as I did not hesitate a day to send back my answer.

Mr. [Thomas G.] Clemson's overseer [—— Bland] is permanently disabled from paralysis and I have to employ another overseer. I send there to-morrow to give possession to another man. I really do not know what to do about his business. I know it is neglected but I cannot attend to it properly. I wish some other arrangement could be made as to it.

I only returned yesterday from my River place where I had been with the whole family for 10 days past.

We had fine rains, and my crop is uncommonly fine there—my cotton particularly. It is all hoed over twice & to a stand—one stalk—& is about half leg high—of course in places higher—all squaring well. The drought has put my corn backward but not injured—except as to a stand in places. I have made ["a" *interlined*] contract to deliver 5,000 bushels—& am interested in it as a crop. I have in 975 acres from ankle high up to breast high—it is all growing now beautifully. My first stand of peas is also good. You know peas are an important crop with us. I think with good reason. I will be able to sell 10,000 bushels of corn sorted. If you want bagging & Rope you had better get it now. I got 2500 yds. of the best I ever saw one lb. ⅝ to the yd. at 12½ cts. & Rope at 3 Cents. Every thing of that kind is now low. The K[en]t[uck]ys[?] have glut[t]ed the market. Our love to all. Truly, F.W. Pickens.

ALS in ScCleA.

From Lewis S. Coryell

Washington, 27th May [18]45

D[ea]r Sir, You are always right. You saw signs early, that I only now begin to discover.

I have the riddle solved, and now lament my stupidity. I give you in confidence the secret. [James K.] Polk only aspired to be Vice[-President], and was content with [Martin] Van [Buren] for Pr[e]s[iden]t who he supposed w[oul]d get the national nomination and therefore courted the leading Vans by way of propitiating himself with them for Vice; hence the app[ointmen]t of Henry Horne [*sic*; Horn, former Representative] of Penn[sylvani]a, [Benjamin F.] Butler of N[ew] York[, George] Bancroft of Massa[chusetts] who had his letters to rise up worse than Banquo[']s ghost and instead of an independent man we have elected a Pres[iden]t bound hand & foot to the Van's! And unless we proffit [*sic*] by their abuse of power we are again in a bad way.

In New York all are of the magician stripe; in Phil[adelphi]a not one of [George M.] Dallas['s] men has been ap[poin]t[e]d & only 2 of [James] Buch[ana]n[']s[;] in fact nobody is pleased but the base incumbents.

I have been much in N.Y. & Phil[adelphi]a, & assure you, fermentation has begun.

I have learnt today from a reliable source that *Buck goes on the Bench* as soon as Congress assembles, but the Cabinet as a whole know nothing of it. Tis said that [John Y.] Mason [Attorney General] is beginning to think well of himself, and [Robert J.] Walker [Secretary of the Treasury] is Heir presum[p]tive but Polk means to oblige the wishes of the Poeple [*sic*] a second term or I am mistaken. I begin to think your retirement will bring you more certainly before the *poeple* than ever before, "So wrote it he." Sincerely Y[ou]rs, Lewis S. Coryell.

ALS in ScCleA; PEx in Boucher and Brooks, eds., *Correspondence*, p. 295. NOTE: This letter was written on stationery headed "Tyler & Birch's United States Hotel, Washington, D.C. Board, per day, $1.50."

To J[OHN] Y. MASON, [Attorney General]

Fort Hill, 30th May 1845

My dear Sir, I am much obliged to you for your attention to the subject of Miss [M.H.] McKnight's letter, which I enclosed to you.

I have not been without deep solicitude about Texas, & am much relieved by the intelligence you give through [former] Gov[erno]r [Archibald] Yell [of Ark.], that unconditional annexation is certain. I did not doubt, that many of the influential men of Texas were at heart opposed to the measure, & apprehended, that they would sieze on the amendment made in the Senate to open the negotiation anew, if possible, under pretex[t] of objections to the House resolutions, but in reality to defeat the measure. If that had been done, annexation would have been lost. It would have placed the question completely in the hands of the Texian Government. Even as certain as the success of the measure may now appear, I trust, the administration will not be so confident, as to relax its vigillance [*sic*]. England has her heart deeply fixed on defeating it; as I saw from the first, & will leave nothing undone to accomplish it; & unfortunately the Texian Government, whatever professions it may make, will zealously cooperate with her.

I am glad to learn, that a feeling exists in the administration in reference to the Oregon question, such as you believe, I would not object to. I have all along regarded, that, & not Texas, as the dangerous question; & have believed, & still do, that, if England intends to take a belligerent stand against us, Oregon will be made the pretex[t]. She has nothing to stand on, as far as Texas is concerned; & would have to submit quietly, when annexation shall have been accomplished, however deeply opposed to it, if no other question of controversy between us could be drawn in as a pretex[t]. Hence, while I conducted with decision & boldness the Texian question, I treated the Oregon with gentleness, but firmness at the same time. I have, in fact, on more general view thought, from the begin[n]ing that to be *quiet—to do nothing to excite attention, and leave time to operate*, was our *true* policy—the *only one*, indeed, by which we could secure the *whole* Territory; & that the opposite, not only involved the hazard of war, but the final *loss of the whole Territory*. My aim was ["so" *interlined*] to conduct the negotiation, that its failure should not involvue a rupture of the friendly relations between the two countries, & in that case, to use the influence of the press & the Government to curb in the West, so as to prevent the re[s]cinding of the joint occupancy & the taking of any step, that might be considered a a [*sic*] violation of the Convention; & leave it to time to decide the question. I regard the joint occupancy as our trump card, which secured the game, so long as we held it. I would not give Great Britain a farthing for her claims, if she would stipulate not to disturb it, on her part; my dread was, that she would re[s]cind; & have [*sic*; hence] the importance I attached to keeping quiet. Thus thinking, I could not but regret, that Mr. Polk mentioned the subject in his inaugural, &, especially in such a way as to give the British Government the opportunity of coming out as it has.

I see the English papers already talk of re[s]cinding on their part. I am of the impression, that we have lost the opportunity of secureing the whole territory; & that the only alternative left is to settle it by negotiation, or by the Sword. The last would be a sad appeal. I cannot doubt but it would end in the loss of the territory, or a disgraceful peace; one condition of which would be to take the offer of Great Britain. We might take Canada, but we would have to surrender it back, to get Oregon, or rather a part of it. My hope now is, that the aversion of both countries & both governments, I trust, to such an appeal, may lead to an adjustment on reasonable terms by negotiation. Such was the hope I entertained, when I left the [State] Department. I am the more encouraged now to hope, from the strong prospect, that the annexation question will succeed by the almost unanimous voice of the people of Texas, which will cut off all motives for hostilities on that score. I see nothing to change in the opinions I delivered three years since in the Senate on the subject of Oregon.

I am obliged to you for enclosing Mr. [Thomas] Ritchie's note, although it was not necessary for the object he had in writing it. I saw the articles from the Herald it enclosed, but they made not the least impression on me.

I know too well what credit is due to political letters to permit them to make any impression on me.

I take the occasion to say, that I was gratified, when I learned that Mr. Ritchie had become the Organ of the administration, & have no doubt, he will acquit himself with ability & honor in his highly responsible position. He has my best wishes for his success. Of his friendly feelings towards me, I do not doubt; though, candor compels me to say, that I think from some early unfavourable impressions he has, or rather, I hope I may say, had formed an erroneous opinion of my motives & course as a publick man, which has prevented him from doing me full justice.

As to the special Mission [to Great Britain], I am & have been of the opinion, it would be an injudicious step, & have frequently so expressed myself. The question can best be settled at Washington; & if I recollect aright, I so expressed myself to Mr. [James] Buchannan [*sic*] before I left the Department. I am sure, it is useless for me to say, that whatever movements may have been made in reference to it, were made without my knowledge, and against my judgement. All I wish is, that Mr. Polk and his administration may carry through successfully the Texian, the Oregon, & Tariff questions with all others, which may touch the peace, the liberty or prosperity of the country.

The dispatch, or rather the letter [of 12/20/1844] to Mr. [Wilson] Shannon, to which you allude, was not sent. If you will recollect, it was confined to expressing the views of the Government in reference to the course, which led to the suspension of diplomatick intercourse between him & the Mexican Government. It supported him in general, but expressed disapprobation of the part of his last communication, which looked like an appeal to the Mexican people against their Government. The letter was approved by the Cabinet, but it was thought advisable not to send it, until there should be further developments of the course events might take; as things were very uncertain at the time in Mexico.

Shortly after, intelligence was received of the br[e]aking out of the Revolution, which ended in the overthrow of [Gen. Antonio Lopez de] Santa Anna. Deeming it highly important, that we should be ably represented in Mexico, in the turn events had taken, & that Gov[erno]r Shannon's position & relation to the Mexican Government were such, as to forbid intercourse between them, & of course, to make his services of no avail at so critical a period, I saw the President, stated my views to him, & suggested the propriety of his addressing a private letter to the Gov[erno]r, as a friend, stating the circumstances, which might render diplomatick intercourse of great importance, & the difficulty of opening it with him, & suggesting for his consideration, the propriety of resigning under such circumstances. He agreed to adopt the course, & requested me to prepare the letter. The next day I was taken sick, & continued unable to attend to buisness for more than a month. After my recovery, I brought up the subject with the President at my first interview, & it was concluded to be too late & the administration too near its close, either to send the letter I had prepared for Governor Shannon, or to write the letter he intended to address him.

In conclusion, I reciprocate the expression of pleasurable feelings, which the recollection of our association, & that of the other members of the late Cabinet, always excite in my bosom.

Mrs. Calhoun joins me in kind remembrance to yourself & Mrs. [Mary Anne Fort] Mason. Yours truly, J.C. Calhoun.

Retained copy in ScCleA; PC in Jameson, ed., *Correspondence*, pp. 659–663. NOTE: The handwriting of this document is perhaps that of John C. Calhoun, Jr. Calhoun made a few corrections in his own handwriting and added the AEU, "Copy of my answer to Mr. Mason's letter."

From ELLWOOD FISHER

Cincinnati, 6 mo[nth] 1, 1845

Esteemed Friend, I received thy letter of April 24 and concur fully in its view of the momentous consequences of Texas Annexation, immediate and remote. Although the Territory itself is much less than Louisiana as acquired by [Thomas] Jefferson, even if not part of it, yet the geographical position of Texas considered in connexion with the character of existing governments on this continent, and in the other hemisphere renders its acquisition of importance scarcely less, perhaps greater politically and socially, than that of Louisiana itself.

The sectarian discord and disunion now progressing in reference to African slavery, as events concomitant with annexation, and connected with it, from the principles involved in their discussion illustrate and vindicate very fully the wisdom of that measure. It must materially influence if not controul the destiny of our own political and social institutions, and through them those of all other North American territory: whilst the great momentum it will impart to the action of American power moral and physical on Europe gives, to the total result an extent and sublimity beyond the faculties of mortal mind to comprehend.

The idea that our government or union is weakened by extending our territory—and the notion of the northern whigs that this is peculiarly the case when the extension is southward I presume are both precisely the reverse of true. I consider the late ecclesiastical division [of the Methodists and Baptists] also as an omen favourable rather than adverse to the durability of the Union. For if as we believe centralization of power is the great evil of our system[,] extent of territory particularly in the South will tend to counteract that

577

propensity. For the remote members whilst they enjoy equal benefits with the central from the legitimate action of government, suffer more and in the proportion of their distance from usurpation, and have accordingly a readier disposition as they possess a greater facility to resist it. If too a remote circumference can have no interest in centralization of power, that part of it which ranges along southern latitudes is peculiarly exempt from such an influence. For the South being essentially agricultural and therefore identified with the great mass of the republic which is agricultural also can scarcely propose any policy of a partial character in its own favour. At the same time the effect of extending territory in one direction is to change the geographical locality of the centre and thereby destroy the established and proscriptive abuses of centralism—and break up its combinations. It is for that reason I am in favour of changing the seat of government. I would locate it on the Ohio or Mississippi, and would make Philadelphia[,] New York, & Boston, with all their newspaper and money power and State influence, the enemies instead of the advocates of centralism. The day they become frontier towns, and can no longer go down via Rail Road after breakfast, and take the Government by the button and whisper in his ear, and invite his servants over to dine to be cajoled, threatened or bribed—that day they will reverse the policy heretofore pursued.

Ecclesiastical divisions will promote the same result. Anniversary week at New York will no longer be attended by representatives, as to a great ecclesiastical congress of the United States. Nor will the eyes of the devout be always directed to the East as those of Musselmen to Mecca. The course of pilgrimage will be changed. Conferences, Assemblies, and Conventions will be held at Charleston, Memphis, Louisville and Cincinnati—and opinion will be formed under their local influences rather than fabricated according to the mode at New York where the steamers are coming over every day from London and Paris with the latest fashions—the newest style of John Bull[']s hypocrisy or of French infidelity.

I perceive that the leading whig paper of New York (the Tribune) is advocating the removal of the property qualification of negro suffrage in that State in the convention soon to be held. The increased negro vote is computed at 10 to 20,000—enough with the abolition vote to hold the balance of power in that State. Waiving the effect of such a change in the social character of the State, its influence on the existing organization and usages of the Democratic party deserve to be considered. Suppose New York to be thus permanently withdrawn from the Democratic ranks—Ohio now perhaps the next largest State is in a very unpromising condition also. Yet these two States in a convention for nominating President would have the same vote, as if Democratic, both in selecting the man and declaring the principles which they could do nothing to aid. Both of them ["would" *canceled and* "might" *interlined*] also be of the most inferior grade of Democracy—that is a Democracy of expediency and of hypocrisy. For when a party is in a minority yet strong enough to contend with some hope of success, the temptation is very strong to temporize, to equivocate and to assimilate with the enemy. Such a disposition would be manifested in its avowals of principle and its choice of men. And such principles and such men would be embarrassing and detrimental to both the truth and the triumph of the party elsewhere and in the main contest. How is this to be averted? The Compromise of the Constitution by which in case the President is not elected by a majority of the electoral vote, he is chosen by a majority of the States, is somewhat observed by adopting the two thirds rule in the Convention—which requiring more than a majority of the delegates but less than such a majority as would always repres[ent a] majority of the States seems to take something like a medium between them—although it might sometimes happen that two thirds even of the delegates would not represent more than a mere majority of the ["people" *canceled and* "party" *interlined*]. Still however under the two thirds rule Ohio and New York would have one third of the power required to decide—whilst if the decision belonged to the States, they would not possess one sixth of the required ["four"(?) *canceled*] number of fourteen, the majority. The convention system relying on party organization not only dispenses with personal popularity and ability but ostracises them. And they are qualities which for obvious reasons abound much more in the Slaveholding than free States. The only solution of the difficulty which occurs to me, if the convention system is preserved, is to have Conventions composed like Congress of two houses—the States represented as in the Senate, and the concurrence of both bodies necessary to a nomination. Even this would give the States as such less power than they practically exercise under the Constitution without conventions. For there can seldom be an election by the people, and consequently it must be frequent by the States. But by the modification I ["propose" *canceled*] suggest, a majority of the States would have equal power with a majority of the people, or rather of the districts.

Whether Conventions under any form to nominate candidates are not incompatible with the elevation of great men; whether our institutions themselves are favourable to mediocrity, or whether meddling men be not the creatures of tranquil times, are all questions involved in the problem. Perhaps the experiment we are now making to determine the minimum of ability requisite for the government of the country may throw light on these questions. I am glad that annexation was not left to the results of this experiment—since I have seen its effects on the Oregon question. I hardly hope the administration will so far transcend its instincts as to offer thee extraordinary powers to England to treat for free trade as well as Oregon. A free trade treaty might possibly fail the Senate, but not in the country. I should rejoice at such a movement, because the negotiator and the treaty would go before the country together—and would triumph together. With very great regard thy friend, Ellwood Fisher.

ALS in ScCleA.

From DUFF GREEN

Washington, 1st June 1845

Dear Sir, I was surprised and remonstrated with Mr. [James] Buchanan, for sending my account to you. I explained to him that the understanding between us was that I would be absent longer than the usual time taken to go with Despatches to Mexico, and that I was not to charge for all the time absent, but was to charge & be allowed for the longest time allowed for such service. I did not ask or expect, greater or higher compensation than was allowed to bearers of despatches. It was the time & not the rate of compensation, and this I wished him to allow or rather to fix himself.

I have been to Albany. The Regency are at war. A portion of the party have united with the whigs in ["a" *canceled*] favor of a bill for calling a Convention to reform the Constitution for the avowed purpose of taking from the Executive the appointments which now constitute the political capital of the Regency. [Martin] Van Buren & the leaders fought hard but being defeated are now disposed to come in and if possible get a majority in Convention and thus retain power. [Governor Silas] Wright & [Comptroller Azariah C.] Flagg are very much dissatisfied with the administration here and threaten open opposition. [Francis P.] Blair is very much dissatisfied and has operated on [Andrew] Jackson so as to induce him to write letters very offensive to Mr. [James K.] Polk, copies of which have been circulated in Albany & New York [City]. As if to put an end to Van Buren's influence letters going as far back as far as [*sic*] 1824, between the leading partners to the old Albany Regency & including [Thomas] Ritchie[,] Van Buren, Jessee [*sic*] Hoyt, [Churchill C.] Cambreleng, [James Watson?] Webb, Benrette [*sic*; James Gordon Bennett?,] [William J.] Duane, [John] Coddington, [William L.] Marcy & many others showing their operations in stocks and betting on Elections and the combinations and intrigues for office and the manner of obtaining the control of Jackson & managing Elections, & the establishment of presses, have been discovered in the Custom House of New York and the originals were secured, & copies multiplied so as to prevent any arrangement for the suppression of the originals. Some of the copies have been exhibited to the President & he now understands, that he has every thing to fear and nothing to hope by identifying himself further with that clique.

I startled Ritchie by telling him the fact but refused to give him any of the particulars. He declared that he was your friend and that your friends in Virginia ["wer" *canceled*] knew it & had confidence in him as such. He said that neither he or Mr. Polk would know any difference in democrats. I told him that the profession was good but the practise bad—that so far almost all the appointments were given to partisans of Van Buren, & that not content with this anti Van Buren democrats were removed to make place for those who were of the true faith. That for one I held him & those who had Mr. Polk's ear responsible and that I intended to judge them & the administration by its acts, & not by its professions. He received it well, because I took care that while the declarations were decided the manner should be unexceptionable.

I know that your friends think that you should retire. There is a growing disposition in those about the President to involve the country in war with England. I differ with your other friends. If you do not go to England, I think you should come to the Senate. Parties will organise this winter, and if you are not here the tendency on the part of your friends will be [to] rally on Judge [John] McLean. I prefer him to any probable Candidate after yourself, & I have spoken to many of your friends who are of opinion that if he is to be a candidate it is better that he shall be brought out and elected by the Conservative portion of the democratic party, which is now strong enough to control the Elections & is therefore responsible for the future course of the Government. I give you facts to enable you to decide for yourself. If you do not decide soon your friends will move in the other direction. Yours truly, Duff Green.

ALS in ScCleA; variant PC in Boucher and Brooks, eds., *Correspondence*, pp. 295–297.

From N. E. Jenkins

Boston, June 2d 1845

Honored Sir, Altho' an humble individual and wholly unknown to you, I take the liberty of addressing a few lines touching the political aspect of affairs, in this section. I was an humble Inspector of Customs at this Port, appointed under Mr. [John] Tyler's Administration, and hoped to remain under the new regime. But no, Marcus Morton the abolitionist, could not tolerate the adhesion of any one who had thro' good & thro' evil report sustained the principles of the man whom I delight to honor. Nineteen individuals, including myself this day ceased to be officers of the Government, and solely on the ground that they were favorable to the election of Mr. *Calhoun* for the next Presidency. Some 2 or 3 Whigs were at the same time ejected, but more remained. I give you these hints that you may be enabled to judge between friends & enemies. With the highest Consideration and Respect I am Very Respectfully Y[ou]r Ob[edien]t Serv[an]t, N.E. Jenkins.

ALS in ScCleA. NOTE: This letter was addressed to Calhoun in Charleston and forwarded on 6/10 from there to Pendleton.

To [George] Bancroft, "Sec[re]t[ar]y of the Navy"

Fort Hill, 3d June 1845

Dear Sir, The writer of the enclosed [*not found*] is well known to me personally; and I have no doubt would execute with fidelity & perfect satisfaction either of the offices, for which he applies, should the Executive think proper to confer either on him. He is well educated, sober, attentive & capable; & has been in politicks a uniform & firm supporter of the Republican cause. With great respect yours truly, J.C. Calhoun.

ALS in IGK.

From S. C. Kell

Huddersfield Yorkshire, June 3d 1845

Sir, On the part of a society in England formed for the purpose of diffusing information on Commercial & Economical subjects (confessedly among the most important questions of the present day) I have taken the liberty of sending you by Steam[er] a copy of the London "Economist" & shall with your permission continue to forward the successive Nos. by each Steamer Gratis.

I trust that you clearly understand that our object is solely the diffusion of Knowledge & that I am totally unconnected with the paper, our only reason for choosing that paper being that we consider it one of the best written & most able works on Political Economy of the present day.

Feeling sure that you will be glad that such a publication has been thrown in your way and trusting you will excuse the liberty I have taken in addressing you I am Sir Yours respectfully, S.C. Kell.

ALS in ScCleA. NOTE: An AEU by Calhoun reads "Mr. Kell of Huddelsfed [*sic*] England." This letter was addressed to Calhoun in Charleston and was forwarded on 7/26 from there to Pendleton.

From LEWIS S. CORYELL

Washington, 4th June 1845

My dear Sir, I begin to think you know most; certainly your views I begin now to reallize. I will give you a few facts, for your information to shew you how matters are. There is no union in the Cabinet. [James] Buchanan goes on the Bench—but his fellow Sec[retar]ys don[']t know it. [John Y.] Mason goes to England & [Andrew] Stevenson comes into the Cabinet, but of this I am not positively certain. [Cornelius P.] Van Ness [Collector at New York City] goes out, [William C.] Bouck comes in, which is a matter that will please nobody, but this is yet unknown out doors, and the gang of applicants are becomeing a daring band; very good quiet clerks are daily giving way for roudies. Penn[sylvani]a goes against us next fall certain. New York must and the result upon the nation will be felt. The Old Hero [Andrew Jackson] won[']t die but is now reviving on Excitement and is as despotic and devilishly inclined as ever. The Albany regency mannage in their letters not only to excite him on Topics & matters in which they have purpose but elicit replies from him, which they use variously. He is outrageous yet about the [Washington] Globe, and insists on [Francis P.] Blair being restored &C &C & but all won[']t prevail. Interest holds it now where it is. [James K.] Polk is run down with the floating trash and knows nothing about the real feeling of the Poeple [*sic*]. God knows what will become of us. The Senate will certainly reject very many app[oint-men]ts next winter.

I write in much haste, but perhaps you have had all I tell you, but I get it from undoubted authority and from a friend at court. Y[ou]r friend truely, Lewis S. Coryell.

[P.S. Robert J.] Walker [Secretary of the Treasury] is the Bull of the Woods. Hoping to be Heir apparent[,] he is kind to all who he hopes to govern.

ALS in ScCleA.

From Lewis S. Coryell

Washington, 6th June 1845

D[ea]r Sir, Since I wrote you, a new order has prevailed. C[ornelius Van] W[yck] Lawrence & not [William C.] Bouck will be Collector [at New York City]; the latter was too objectionable to the [Martin] V[a]n B[ure]n party, and the former is neither one or the other and all are dissatisfied. Altho Vanness [*sic*; Cornelius P. Van Ness] committed a capital error in agreeing to resign yet as that was improperly urged & obtained his friends are determined that he shall not resign, but stand firm & be turned out. The cabinet are no unit, 4 of them are [Presidential] candidates, and [James K.] Polk[']s vigor is daily falling off. Suspicions fill every circle and the idea of the Hermitage having had potent power in the general arrangement of the adm[ini]s[tration] is becomeing unpleasant. In fact the Adm[ini]s[tration] is for Politicians & not for the country so far. Y[ou]r letter [of 5/15 to the Mobile Committee?] is spoken of in the highest terms. Would you believe it Gen[era]l [Andrew] Jackson thinks dear [Francis P.] Blair, should come back into the printing depart-[men]t[?] Gov[ernor] Van Ness is expected here this Evening and if he has not too far committed himself his friends will prevent his resigning, and then the fight will begin. The fact is to me very clear, that all things were arranged at the Hermitage before Polk came on here. [Vice-President George M.] Dallas has not been obliged in *one single appointment.* Penn[sylvani]a & New York in their next Legislatures will be against us—and there will be any thing but a smooth time here ["in the" *interlined*] next Congress. Polk begins to fret, and has become petulant.

I leave for New Hope [Pa.] tomorrow but may remain to ["fix" *canceled and* "look" *interlined*] over their movements a day longer.

[Postmaster General] Cave Johnson refused to dine with [Richard Pakenham] the Brittish [*sic*] Minister[,] saying that the poeple['s; *sic*] business required all his time! I have written this in a moment of haste for your own eye. Truly y[ou]r friend, Lewis S. Coryell.

ALS in ScCleA.

From [John R. Mathewes], "At Home (Accoa,)" [Clarkesville, Ga.?], 6/6. Mathewes comments on the long interval since he has heard from Calhoun and fears that his letters may have miscarried. "This may be the fate of mine in this age of Political Guillotinism. Mr. [James K.] Polk by this time may have issued the ukase 'Off with his head' in which my pains [letters] would be wasted to the desert air. I am anxious to write & will if there is any certainty of its reception." Mathewes's principal object in writing is to exchange information on gold mining. He wishes to meet Calhoun and to discuss his own and Calhoun's reported mining successes. Mathewes states that his mine is turning a "steadily handsome profit" and that, unlike cotton or rice, "gold when harvested is gold; like 96, turn it which way you will 'tis the same—not dependent upon the subtraction or addition of subsequent causes or effects," (by which he means tariff duties that influence the prices of cotton and rice). (Two of the four extant pages of this letter are badly mutilated and other pages may be missing entirely.) ALU (mutilated) in ScCleA.

From KER BOYCE

Charleston, June 7th 1845

Dear Sir, I have no doubt but you will have many applications made to you to give letters to the President [James K. Polk] or heads of Department to obtain office. I have no doubt but you have refused, to interfear and as faire [*sic*; far] as, I have heard you have allways declined, to apply to any administration, in behalf of any. I write you now to say to you, that It will be a wise course to preserve towards any office which may be applyed to from hear or to keep any one in office which his office may be applyed to for. At the present moment Col. M.I. Keath [*sic*; Matthew I. Keith?] is about to apply to the President to remove the present Post Master Mr. [Alfred] Huger who has held it some 15 ["or 18" *canceled*] years as he received It from Gen[era]l [Andrew] Jackson, as his pay for turning from a

Nullifyer to a Union man. He has ceartinly not been, a very strong friend of yours at no time. Now on the other hand Col. Keath has been a strong friend of yours thr[ou]gh all changes and has never faltered under any circumstance. Col. Keath feels now, that he [is able] to call on you for friendship but would not ask you, to stoop ["so low as" *canceled*] to interfear, as he thinks your station is different from all others in this State and you ought not to be drawn in to so unpleasant a business as to meddle with your acquaint[anc]es in office.

We feel hear that injustice is about to [be] done us the Democratick party, that all the offices should be heald by old fedrales and those that have allmost to a man been against the State and you, should hold office while those that stood up when the odds was against us [are forgotten]. Judge [Daniel E.] Huger, [Senator from S.C.,] is against proscription, because his friend is P[ost] Master (as the people think). Homs [*sic*; Isaac E. Holmes, Representative from S.C.] is against removial because he knows his Brother ought to be removed from a[n] office which he obtained for him in so disgraceful a way[—]as Representative of this City [he] made use of his office to obtain that he could not obtain unless he had been our Representative. But Sir we the Democraticks of Charleston do not intend to allow our day to lay [*sic*] still, and heave [*sic*] any Representative say to the administration, that So[uth] Carolina wants no office. Sir We feelt hear much for the course which thear self conceited dignity, they put on not go in Mass with Geo. & Ala. to the President and to have said to him the South wish you to remain as Secr[e]t[ar]y of State and that they felt that it was only their wright. But their dignity would not allow them to stup forward for you but they could as to retain in office and app[oint?] in office Whigs. Now we will not subject [ourselves] any longer, to such[,] as our members to Congress never was sent thear to speak for us in that particular[?]. I write you this as a priviate letter, to give you some of what is now grown to a[n] Excitement in our town. I thearefore wish this ["as" *canceled and* "to be" *interlined*] considered confidential. Y[ou]rs most Sinsarely, Ker Boyce.

ALS in ScCleA. NOTE: An AEU by Calhoun indicates that this was a "Confidential" letter and that it was answered on 6/30. Boyce's remarks about the brother of Isaac E. Holmes apparently refer to Arthur F. Holmes who had been appointed an appraiser of merchandise in the Charleston Customs House by President John Tyler.

To T[homas] G. Clemson

Fort Hill, 7th June 1845

My dear Sir, Your letter of the 29th April to me and Anna's [Anna Maria Calhoun Clemson's] of about the same ["date" *interlined*] came by the regular packet.

Your political reflections are just. Nothing is wanting to enable the South to have a decided control in the presidential election, but firmness, but the great difficulty has heretofore been with Virginia, under the guidance of Mr. [Thomas] Ritchie. His policy has been to act in concert with the party in Pennsylvania & N[ew] York, as the most certain way of succeeding in the election; & for that purpose to concede something of our principles to secure their cooperation. The effect has been to detach Virginia, in great measure, from the South, and to lower the standard of the principles, which first brought the party into power, and to divide & distract the South. But things have much improved of late in Virginia, as the last election shows. The Whigs have been signally defeated; but what is still of much more importance, defeated in a fair canvass & by State rights men on State rights principles. The State may now be said to be under the control of our friends; young men of talents, decision & integrity, who are on good terms with Mr. Ritchie, but not under his control. They are resolved to oppose him, if he should refuse to sustain our principles, and policy, which he will not do, should he find it would place him in a minority in the State, as it certainly would with their opposition. I hope for much from this state of things. If Virginia should go right, the whole South will rally around her, when victory would be certain, bring with it the restoration of the Constitution & the reformation of the Government. The prospect is certainly better than it has been for many years.

Far as I can learn, there is no hostile feelings towards me on the part of Mr. [James K.] Polk & the administration. I learn from a friend, who spent several days ["there" *canceled*] at Washington a short time since, & had free conversation with the President and most of the members of his Cabinet, that they spoke in the kindest & most respectful terms of me, and my conduct while in the State Department, especially of my communications to Mr. [Richard] Pakenham on the subject of Oregon. It seems, that they were read in Cabinet, & the highest eulogy pronounced on them, particularly by Mr. [George] Bancroft. Nor do I think, that Mr. Ritchie is hostile; on the contrary, I have many reasons for thinking, that his feelings have undergone much change of late in reference to myself, but it may be, not sufficient to give me a preferance [*sic*]. All things considered, I think, the opposition to me has abated greatly, while my positive strength has greatly increased within the last 12 months.

Mrs. [Floride Colhoun] Calhoun is writing to Anna by the conveyance, which takes ["this" *interlined*], and will give all the local & domestick news, which will make it unnecessary for me to repeat it. It is excessively dry. I have had but one good rain in upwards of 2 months, and that did ["not" *interlined*] wet the ground thoroughly. But my crop is better, than you could expect under such circumstances. I have my small grain in the big bottom, which this year hits exactly. My wheat is fair, say 10 or 12 bushels to the acre. I have just finished cutting it. I am cutting my rye. It is the best I ever saw, & think it [will] yield at least 15 bushels round to the acre, which is great for our climate. The oats is fine. The corn & cotton small, but a good stand. The pease well up.

John [C. Calhoun, Jr.] & James [Edward Calhoun] bring good accounts from Alabama. The season had been good, & the average h[e]ight of the cotton crop (900 acres) was two feet on the 20th May, when they left, & the corn shoulder high on horseback.

My place is in fine order. My ditches greatly extended & improved since you saw them; and I shall after another year begin to attend to manuring[?] & improving the soil.

I agree with you, that our breed of Horses require improvement, and from what you say of the Norman[?] ["cross" *canceled and* "horse" *interlined*], I do not doubt, that its cross with ours would greatly improve them. I will bring your offer before our agricultural society; and, if the pressure of the times do not prevent it, I think, they will authorise you to make a purchase for them. I think so, because the colts of the Candadian [*sic*; Canadian?] horse, which is of the same stock, have proved so fine. I have two remarkably fine; the best I think I ever had.

The Devon Bull is a fine animal & is in good order. He appears to be very thrifty. I intend housing him in a cool place, as a precaution against the distemper, next week. The weather now has become warm, after a long continuation of Cool weather.

I think, I mentioned ["in" *interlined*] my last, that Christian[?] has left the county, & that he gave an order to Mr. McDow on you for repairing the Dearborn before he went. I refused to pay before I could hear from you, if it was just, as I am of the impression you had paid him.

We are all well, & join in love to you & Anna, & the children. From what their mother writes, they must be making great progress,

& be very interesting. Kiss them for their grandfather. Your affectionate father, J.C. Calhoun.

ALS in ScCleA; PEx in Jameson, ed., *Correspondence*, pp. 663–664.

To A[NDREW] P[ICKENS] CALHOUN,
Faunsdale, Marengo County, Ala.

Fort Hill, 9th June 1845

My dear Andrew, I was glad to learn by your letter & John [C. Calhoun, Jr.] & James [Edward Calhoun] that you were well & the crop looks so well. I hope health & the good prospect continues. You must be careful of yours, especially by avoiding the extreme heat of the sun & getting wet. We are all well, but our prospect of a crop indifferent except the small grain. We have not had a rain to wet the ground a half inch in 10 weeks, but one & that although a good rain did not wet it more than 3 or 4 inches. Notwithstanding, I have a good stand of cotton & corn, although both are backward & small. My small grain, which fortunately happened to be in the big bottom is good. The rye the best I ever saw & the wheat & oats a full average.

I see in looking over the accounts of the sales of our cotton crop, that you have sold 341 ["bales" *interlined*], weighing in the aggregate 176,876 pounds & that the gross amount of the sales is $8408.21. John informs me that there remains to be sold about 35 bales, which at $20 the bale would raise the amount to $9108.21. Add the rent, which I think you informed me was $1200 or [$]1500 would make the income of the place upwards of $10,300. Deduct expense, say $3,800; would leave a clear income of $6500, which would be ample to keep down interest on our debt and leave something toward the principle, after deducting the expense of your family. I hope you have been able to do something towards keeping down, at least the interest on the debt due to Mr. [Ker] Boyce & Mr. [John Ewing] Bonneau. I feel uneasy about both. Mr. [Thomas G.] Clemson, I suppose, will not need his, so long as he continues in Europe, as he is resolved to live within his income; so that if those two could be paid, the rest of our debt might be considered as funded. I see by the papers, that corn is selling at Marion at $1 the bushel. John says, that you can sell 2000 bushels. I hope you will be able to realize something considerable from that ["source"(?) *canceled*] source. If you should be able to sell for 75 cents it would amount to $1500 & would raise our gross income to $11,800 say, & our nett to $8000, estimating the expense at what I have assumed. Such an income at a period of such great depression of our staple, show how great the capacity of the place is for production, & ought to prevent us from being discouraged. I hope, if you get a fair offer for your corn, you will not hold back too long, so as to lose the opportunity of selling.

I propose to go out in the fall. I hope your mother [Floride Colhoun Calhoun] will agree to go with me. I shall leave home as early as is safe.

All join in love to you & Margaret [Green Calhoun] & the children [Duff Green Calhoun and John Caldwell Calhoun]. John speaks very highly of them & the place. Patrick [Calhoun] seems delighted with it. I hope you will write often & fully. I get very few & very brief letters from you. I write two or three for one I receive. Your affectionate father, J.C. Calhoun.

ALS in ScU-SC, John C. Calhoun Papers. Note: This ms. is badly faded.

To James Ed[ward] Colhoun

Fort Hill, 9th June 1845

My dear James, I have fixed on the 18th Inst. to be at the old place [in Abbeville District] to put up a plain monument, which I have had prepared to the memory of my father [Patrick Calhoun], mother [Martha Caldwell Calhoun] & sister [Catherine Calhoun Waddel]. I propose to go down some days before hand to have time to make a short visit to you & other of my relations, who I have not seen for a long time. I expect to leave on the 12th (Thursday); & go directly to Millwood; thence [*one word or partial word canceled*] to Dr. [Henry H.] Townes, & thence to Mr. [Armistead] Burt, & Edward Calhoun, if I have time. You may expect me on the 13th. I write to let you know, so that you may be at home.

Tom got up safely yesterday. We are all well & all join in love to you. Yours affectionately, J.C. Calhoun.

[P.S.] If you should see Dr. Townes let him know my arrangement.

ALS in ScCleA. Note: Edward Calhoun (1809–1862) was an Abbeville planter and the son of John C. Calhoun's brother Patrick Calhoun.

From Sam[ue]l W. Dewey

Washington D.C., 9th June/[18]45

Honor'd Sir, In consequence of the loss of the Hebrew & other testimonials respecting my good friend Major [Mordecai M.] Noah, all of ["which" *interlined*] you saw & examined, I am confident you will pardon me for thus intruding upon the quiet of your retirement, ["&" *interlined*] requesting you to so far favor your old & well tried friend Major N[oah] as to acquaint President [James K.] Polk or Mr. Secretary [James] Buchanan at your earliest convenience, with the nature & purport of those testimonials. Against my intention they were left in the hands of President [John] Tyler, till too late an hour. For several days previous to his departure, I tried to get possession of them, but as they were packed away among other papers, he desired me to wait till he got home, when he promised to send them to me without delay.

He went home. I wrote him repeatedly, asking for the papers, & after the lapse of several weeks, was informed they were lost, together with other valuable papers of his own. Since then, I have used every possible exertion, to recover them, but as yet without success.

I have made the same request of President Tyler, that I now make of you, but fear he may not comply, as he is doubtlessly much troubled & annoyed at the unceremonious removal of his friends from office. The papers in question, presented the combined application of the *Trustees* & *Managers* of all the Synagogues, together with numerous individual applications from the principal Hebrews in this Country to President Tyler, praying him to appoint thier [*sic*] Hebrew brother Major Noah, as Minister to Constantinople.

Also, there was a very important letter from Sir Moses Montefeore [*sic*; Montefiore] of London to Major N[oah] evidently intended to be shewn to our Government. If I remember correctly, you observed after perusing those documents, "*The Major certainly had reason to consider himself the Head of his people.*" I beg you to enter thoroughly into the spirit of my request, & be assured it is made from a firm & sincere conviction, that if you will comply with it & address the parties above named, giving them your views as to the importance of those documents, thier contents & general bearing, & the true character of the talented & patriotic individual in whose behalf they were presented, you will do a *great good* to society at large. It is morally certain that a few lines from you, to either of those high Functionaries, would exercise a mighty influence over thier minds at this lowering crisis.

Those documents so unfortunately lost, set forth in the strongest possible terms, the united & heartfelt testimony of all the principal Hebrews of this country in behalf of the superior merit of thier brother Major N[oah]. One of them contained this important announcement[:] "The Hebrews, hold full *one hundred Millions* of dollars (*$100,000,000*) of the public stocks of this Country, & still they never have had as yet, one of thier co-religionists in the service of the United States as a foreign Minister." Circumstances entirely beyond the control of President ["Tyler," *interlined*] prevented him from making the desired appointment, consequently the Hebrews one & all, including Major N[oah] have become disheartened & dejected, & determined to never again make an effort to attract the attention of our Government, towards thier peculiarly imposing claims. They certainly have cause to feel aggrieved, but I hope with your timely & efficient assistance, to turn thier mourning, into rejoicing, by bringing the spirit & intent of thier applications to President Tyler, to bear with redoubled effect upon the present Administration.

It surely would be a master stroke of policy for President Polk to place our Government on the best possible terms of amity & friendship with the Great-Money-Power of the Old World. Money is justly said to be the sinews of war, & if we wish to cripple or completely paralyze those sinews on the other side of the Atlantic, we have but to send Major Noah as Minister to Constantinople, or as a special Agent to look after our interests in the East.

He would produce the most important effect on the minds of the Hebrew Bankers throughout Europe.

His Mission to that Country would utterly benumb & deaden the arm of European warfare, as he would prevail upon the Great money holders of the world, to withhold in future, thier money, when loans are wanted by the Heads of Europe, for war purposes. Besides this, no doubt it would hasten the coming of that sublime spectacle "The Restoration of the Jews to Palestine." Napoleon might have done much towards effecting that great object, although it would seem as if the times were hardly ripe for the consum[m]ation of that soul-stirring event in his day. I am however clearly of the opinion, that had he conciliated the Jews, instead of treating them as he did, his last breath would have been drawn elsewhere, than on "The lone Isle of St. Helena." Major Noah is a clear headed statesman, a ripe scholar, a fast friend, a warm & pure hearted patriot, & as you said "he has ever been right on the great subject that governs the destiny of the South."

No one can for a moment doubt his consum[m]ate tact, skill & ability as a diplomatist. The Hebrews of the Old World, are anxiously looking to this Country for another Governmental demonstration in thier behalf, when they will move en masse to the Land of thier Father Abraham.

Our Nation was the first to abrogate all political disabilities of the Jews, & on us, they depend for the final signal which shall cause thier glorious return to the Holy Land.

Thier most sanguine expectations will be realized, if you but aid in getting Major Noah appointed as above.

I trust you will pardon me for transcribing the following lines from my Memorandum Book, "Gen. McNeill wishes some friend of J.C.C. to enforce his obligation *to shew himself*. He owes it to his Country. No one should be permitted to doubt his allegiance. His friends would expect him, but, that he has so long deferred to his own judgement without reference to thier affectionate wishes." This Impromptu, was noted down at the close of a most interesting conversation between Gen. W[illia]m G[ibbs] McNeill, Samuel L. Gouverneur Esq. & your humble servant, on the importance of your visiting the North the present year, or as early as convenient. I fear there is too much truth in the saying of the day, that "the sceptre of influence is fast departing from the hands of superior Intelligence, & falling into those more democratic." Should this be the fact, it is not to be wondered at, when we reflect how young & inexperienced are a majority of our voters, & how purely selfish are grown, the mass of our politicians.

Beyond doubt, the major portion of the intelligence of our Country, for the last fifteen years, has been in favor of having you or Mr. [Henry] Clay as our chief Magistrate. But it is said by the "Unterrified Democracy, no man ought to be elected as President, who will not conform to party usages, & *Lay Pipe* &c. &c. according to circumstances."

Again requesting you to write Mr. Secretary Buchanan, or President Polk, relative to the documents in question, & to give them your views, respecting the *great good* that in the main must inevitably be conferred upon society at large, should our Government send Major Noah, as Minister to Constantinople, or as Special Agent to the Old World, to place our Country in the most favorable position before the Money Power of Europe, & to see if a favorable treaty can be effected with Egypt, &c. &c. &c.

With the tender of my best services at all times, & wishing yourself & family, health, prosperity & all other blessings & enjoyments, without measure, I remain your Ob[edien]t Servant, Saml. W. Dewey.

ALS in ScCleA.

From SOLOMON COHEN

Savannah, 11 June 1845

My dear Sir, As I desire a little political information, and know no one so able to give it to me, or on whose opinions I have so much confidence, I have taken the liberty to address you on the subject. The Governor's election in this State will be warmly contested, and as it is probable that my friend Mr. [Matthew H.] McAllister will be the democratic nominee for that office, I desire to be armed at all points. The subjects on which I seek information are the following—Why was the Tariff not modified at the last session of Congress and is it probable that a sufficient number of the Northern democracy will unite at the ensuing session to place the Tariff in a state agreeable to the South. I would also desire your opinion as to the causes which have led the British Government to relax their system of restrictions. In asking your opinion I have no intention to give any publicity to your reply; but am only seeking information that may be useful to the great cause in which you take so deep an interest, and may the better enable me to advocate that cause. Knowing how much you have to engage your time I will conclude, with the assurances of the sincere regard & respect of Y[ou]r ob[edien]t Ser[van]t, Solomon Cohen.

ALS in ScCleA.

From EDWARD NOBLE

June 14th 1845, Alabama

Dear Sir, My sister Floride [Noble Cunningham] has kindly informed me of some ungracious words reported to you as my expressions. They are so devoid of thruth—so vulgar & withall showing such wrong judgement & bad taste, that need I say, sir, I feel myself lessened in my own estimation that my capacity should be so low marked, and my taste so poorly appreciated. Permit me then to explain to you

594

why "I prefer Mr. [William C.] Preston to yourself" and "would as leave fish in a mud-puddle as read one of y[ou]r speeches," by a direct & unmistakeable contradiction of ever having used the vulgar language. I would hardly feel myself permitted to trouble you with a letter denying this slanderous report, were it not that I have also been informed of the remarks you made on hearing it—viz—"that you felt hurt; but remembered whose son I was"—"that you were so intimate with my Father & Mother [Patrick and Elizabeth Bonneau Pickens Noble] it hurt you to think one of their children were [*sic*] against you[.]" I hope you are satisfied that you have heard falsely of me. You will I trust read this letter in the spirit it was written. I wrote it not to push myself upon y[ou]r notice, or give myself consequence by supposing what I could say would be taken as aught against you, or that you would think so; but solely & simply, Sir, to disabuse y[ou]r mind of a report so little to my credit and so false as to fact. Believe me sir with due respect y[ou]r ob[edien]t Serv[an]t, Edward Noble.

ALS in ScU-SC, John C. Calhoun Papers. NOTE: This letter was postmarked in Selma, Ala., on 6/14.

From BABCOCK & CO.

Charleston, June 15, 1845

Honor'd Sir, Your esteem'd favor was rec[eive]d. We are much gratified to learn that you are pleased with the "His[torical] Col[lections] of Virginia" [by Henry Howe]. It is also very gratifying to hear that you approve of our design in producing a similiar work on our own State.

Will you be so kind when at leisure, to inform us, if you think much traditionary lore can be found in your section of the country—particularly that [kin]d which is connected with the ["very" *canceled*] first settlement of that part of the State. S. Carolina is very rich in that description of material which a work of this character requires. Still, it will demand much research and travelling to obtain it. Mr. Howe is we think, well calculated for this undertaking—as he is not only a young gentleman of education, but agreeable in his manners, and of excellent connexions—while he possesses a strong inclination for pedestrian excursions, having traversed all over the States of N[ew] York, N[ew] Jersey & Virginia in every direction & mostly on foot. With the utmost respect we remain yours truly, Babcock & Co.

LS in ScCleA. NOTE: William Rogers Babcock (1800–1859) came from New Haven, Conn., to Charleston in 1818. He was a publisher and bookseller.

To J[AMES] ED[WARD] COLHOUN, Terrysville, Ab[beville] Dist[rict, S.C.]

[Abbeville District, S.C.] 19th June 1845
My dear Sir, I sent word by Andrew, that we intended to enclose the grave yard and ["that we intended" *canceled*] to employ him, if you could spare him to do the mason work. Since then, there has been a meeting of the family; and the details arranged. It is proposed to make ["it" *canceled and* "the wall" *interlined*] 65 feet square, 18 inches thick[,] 5 feet 3 inches in h[e]ight from the bottom, of which 15 inches will be in the ground, below the surface.

I was requested to write to you to ascertain from Andrew how much lime it would require, & to let me know by letter at Pendleton, and whether you could spare Andrew to do the quarr[y]ing & build the wall. It is intended to commence after laying by the crop; and to guard ag[ai]nst sickness, the arrangement is for him to sleep at the summer establishment of Frank Calhoun, which has proved perfectly healthy. It is about 1½ mile from the quar[ry]ing.

I hope you have had good rains & that you will be sure to make us a visit, when Mr. Toomy [*sic;* Michael Tuomey] shall be in our vicinity; or if inconvenient then, some time during the season. Exercise will be of service to you & we shall all be very glad to see you.

When you write let me know whether you can spare Andrew at the time refer[r]ed to, say about the 20th July, & if not then, when, to do the Job. Yours affectionately, J.C. Calhoun.

ALS in ScCleA.

From A[LEXANDER] J. BERGEN

New York [City,] June 22, 1845
My Dear Sir, I made an application in March last to the President [James K. Polk] for the Havana consulate. I am now informed that

the cause of the nonremoval of the present incumbent [Robert B. Campbell], is at your request. If so, it is useless for me to continue the contest.

Will you please inform me, what are your feeling[s] on this subject. Circumstanced as you were on the incoming of the present administration I could not ask your aid when in Washington, and did not then suppose that you would take part in appointments.

I am regarded here as one of your friends and have the undivided strength of that portion of the party both in this and other States, therefore can ask nothing of Mr. [Martin] Van Buren and his friends so that if you are in favour of the retention of Mr. Campbell and opposed to me, I should know it, and I will withdraw from the field at once.

Your early reply will oblige, Your friend & Ob[edien]t S[er]-v[an]t, A.J. Bergen.

ALS in ScCleA.

To Tho[mas] G. Clemson, Brussels

Fort Hill, 23d June 1845

My dear Sir, I am in the receipt of yours of the 12th May brought by the last steamer, & am happy to hear, that you are all well.

You must, indeed, have had a very disagreeable winter & spring. Ours on the contrary have been more than usually pleasant, with the exception of dust from the severe drought. I have never known such an one so early in the year. I had but two rains to wet the ground more than half an inch since the 25th March. The last fell a few days since, & has done much to revive the crop. The corn will be very low, but with good seasons now, may ear well. The cotton, for the most part, is small & backward. About two thirds of mine looks well. I am now engaged in the oat harvest. I have harvested, & brought in all my wheat & rye. My small grain crop is good.

I do not think it would be safe with my bilious habit to visit your place during the summer season. Much of the intermediate country is bilious & sickly. If I should not go to Alabama, I will visit it in the fall, & do what I can to keep things right; but your reliance must be on your overseer. You ought to have a first rate man; and to obtain one, you must give good wages. I am of the impression, that you ought not for the present to aim at doing much in the way of manuring. Your first object should be to put the place in order, & to clear ["sufficient" *canceled and* "as much" *interlined*] lands as will be ample for your force. You cannot expect to do much in the way of manuring in your absence. Few overseers know much about it. In my own case, I pursued the course, I suggest for you. I do not expect to commence a regular system of manuring & fertilizing my fields until ["next" *canceled and* "the" *interlined*] year after the ensuing.

I do not recollect w[h]ether the calves, to which you refer were sent down or not; but should an opportunity offer, I will send down some of the best I have. They are, however, not at all promising. The breed proved inferior.

I fear with you, that [Henry A.] Wise [U.S. Minister to Brazil] is pursuing an injudicious course in reference to the slave trade. My instructions to him were full & pointed on the necessity of preserving the most friendly relations with Brazil in every respect. It would be greatly to be regretted, if he has taken any step, calculated to have a contrary effect.

We have had several occurrences of deep interest growing out of the movements of the abolitionists. The Baptist & Methodist Churches have both been divided into slave holding & non slave holding. The exposition of the cause leading to the separation of the latter has been put forth in pamphlet form. It was written by Dr. [Henry B.] Bascom; and is one of the fullest & most powerful vindication[s] of the South & its institutions, which has yet appeared. It will do great good. [Former] Gov[erno]r [James H.] Hammond has published two letters to Mr. [Thomas] Clarkson, which are attracting great attention. They are well written & must do good. It is gratifying to see the South taking higher & higher ground on this vital subject. If I had a spare copy, I would send you Dr. Bascom's pamphlet.

I made a visit to Abbeville last week to errect the monument to my father, mother & sister [Patrick Calhoun, Martha Caldwell Calhoun, and Catherine Calhoun Waddel]. I found Mr. [George] McDuffie much better than I expected. His speech is not effected, and he still retains the power of moving his leg. The nerves of sensation are not at all effected. He is cheerful & hopeful.

I saw nearly all of our relations, & found them all well. Crops, with few exceptions, looked badly.

We are all well & all join in love to you, Anna [Maria Calhoun Clemson] & the children [John Calhoun Clemson and Floride Elizabeth Clemson]. Kiss them for their Grandfather.

Mrs. Judge Wardlaw [that is, Sarah Allen (Mrs. David L.) Wardlaw] died a few days since. She had been recently confined. Your affectionate father, J.C. Calhoun.

ALS in ScCleA; PEx in Jameson, ed., *Correspondence*, p. 665. Note: Bascom's pamphlet was entitled *Methodism and Slavery; with Other Matter in Controversy between the North and the South; Being a Review of the Manifesto of the Majority in Reply to the Protest of the Minority of the Late General Conference of the Methodist Episcopal Church, in the Case of Bishop Andrew* (Frankfort, Ky.: 1845). Hammond's letters to Clarkson were published in the Charleston, S.C., *Mercury*, in June, 1845, and were also printed as pamphlets, one of which was entitled *Two Letters on Slavery in the United States, Addressed to Thomas Clarkson, Esq., by J.H. Hammond* (Columbia: Allen, McCarter & Co., 1845).

From LEWIS S. CORYELL

New Hope [Pa.,] 23d June 1845
My dear Sir, I have just returned from N[ew] York [City] and Albany. The course pursued by the Ex[ecutiv]e and his Cab[i]n[e]t in regard to [Cornelius P.] Vanness [*sic*] & his removal [as Collector of Customs at New York City] is any thing but dignified, and the [Martin] V[a]n B[ure]n men are more dissatisfied with [Cornelius Van Wyck] Lawrence than Van Ness but to crown the whole they are infuriate[d] with the Ap[pointmen]t of Louis McLane [as U.S. Minister to Great Britain]. In fact the Adm[ini]s[tration] is daily loosing [*sic*] strength, and unless there is a union of North & South the middle ground won[']t save it. Strange as [it] may appear there is a disposition of the V[a]n B[ure]n men *now* to unite with the South as there [*sic*] only hope to avoid [Robert J.] Walker or [Lewis] Cass who begin already to cheer the hope of [Presidential] succession. Would you believe it, a high Priest of the Tam[m]any Club[?] offered to toss up with me whether [Silas] Wright or Calhoun should ["be" *interlined*] our *next man!* To this I c[oul]d do no less than object, & told him, that they could reasonably have no hope except through Calhoun[,] that Wright was unavailable from associations, Political & sectional &Ct. and that the only man to secure success was Calhoun and [Levi] Woodbury Vice[-President], and that then they might come in with vigor under such an adm[ini]s[tration] which he seemed to think was reasonable &Ct.

[George M.] Dallas ["is" *canceled and* "has" *interlined*] not ["been" *interlined*] gratified in *one* single app[ointmen]t. Nobody is *obliged, & all dissatisfied.*

And you were right in all your prognostics, and now I sincerely

599

hope you will not come back to the Senate and let them feel the absince of strength. [James] Buchanan is lost in Penn[sylvani]a. His fr[ien]ds have been disappointed & fell off. Penn[sylvani]a and New York, will but have opposition Leg[islatu]r[e]s[?], and next winter will produce a panic over the Democracy of the nation, and prove that there is no Safety in weak men. Besides the Hero is gone ["who" *interlined*] was their countersign for all things designed. I am with great Respect y[ou]r fr[ien]d truly, Lewis S. Coryell.

ALS in ScCleA. NOTE: Coryell's comment that "the Hero is gone" refers to the death of Andrew Jackson on 6/8.

From W[illia]m P. Duval

St. Augustine, June 23rd 1845

My dear sir, I had the pleasure, previous to your leaving Washington last spring to receive your letter on your retiring from the office of Secretary of State. I confess it surprised me, that under the pending controversey between our government and great Brittain you were not retained. I do not believe their is a statesman as competent to manage the great questions, between the two nations in the united states as yourself and we the people of the united states may yet have too much cause to regret, the negociation, devolved on your successor[.] We have had much excitement, in our late election for Governor and Representative to congress—and no doubt you have learned the signal overthrow of the Whig party in Florida. I took the field and hope I rendered some aid, in securing the democratic victory. next to your noble State Florida is determined to sustain you, and we pray for the occasion, to prove our love, and energy, in maintain[in]g the policy, of the South. My friend Mr. [David] Levy [Yulee] will be one of our senators to congress where I hope you will once more take your stand in defence of southern rights and principles. I do not entertain a doubt, that I could have been also elected to the Senate, if I had sought the station in the manner, & way too often resorted to by politicians. I cannot electioneer for myself, although, I am, not backward in the service of men whos[e] conduct and principles are in accordance with the democratic doctrin[e]s of 1798. I am a candidate for no office, and in my public speech[e]s said so to the people, and am now convinced, my disinterested support had influence with the voters. Mr. Levy however is entitled to more thanks for the triumphant result of our election than any one individual in Florida[.] I have been strongly urged by my friends throughout the State to meet the General Assembly at Tallahassee and urge my pretentions to a seat in the senate. I have decidedly refused to do so or to visit Tallahassee while the Legislature is sitting. If that body believes that any other gentleman of our party will be more servic[e]able to our State—They should elect him. I will under no circumstances blow my own trumpet, and shall be content to act in the service of our cause, with all the energy and limited influence I may possess. I am so much gratified at the success of our principles in this State and con[s]cious that Florida will never desert you or your doctrines, that personally I care little for myself[.]

It would afford me much gratification to see, and converse a few days, with you, on the leading subjects that so deeply involve the honor, and prosperity of our country, and if any thing should call me in 100 miles of your residence—I should certainly pay you a visit. I hope you have a good crop, for in this State, the drought threatens us with famine[.]

Present me most respectfully to Mrs. [Floride Colhoun] Calhoun and believe me as ever your sincere and affectionate friend, Wm. P. Duval.

ALS in ScCleA. NOTE: Florida had been admitted to the Union on 3/3/1845.

From S A M [U E] L W. D E W E Y

Washington D.C., 25th June/45
Hon[ore]d Sir, Respectfully referring you to my former communication, I beg leave to renew the sentiments of esteem & the request therein contained. I most earnestly hope you may agree with ["me" *interlined*] as to the importance of your addressing a few lines to President [James K.] Polk or Hon. Ja[me]s Buchanan respecting the lost papers of your early & fast friend Judge [Mordecai M.] Noah, & the appointing him as Minister to Constantinople or as special Agent to Egypt.

At the present moment (as I have learned through a gentleman just from Egypt) England has her active agents in Egypt strenuously opposing the will of all the other European Powers as regards a Canal across the Isthmus of Suez. France, Russia, Austria &c, are strongly in favor of having a ship Canal communication from the Mediterranean to the Red Sea, sufficiently capacious to admit the passage of ships of the largest class—England opposes the Canal project on the ground that it would give France & the other European Powers a decided advantage over her. Russia has her ports on the Black Sea & in case a Canal is completed she will open a water communication with China & India, whereas she now only carries on trade with those countries by land. France, Austria, Italy &c have thier large commercial cities on the Mediterranean, & Rail Roads would transport to any part of their dominions the light goods of China, India &c.

England would be but a small gainer by such a Canal, as she would be compelled to carry by water all her goods from Alexandria down the Mediterranean to the Atlantic, thence to her own shores, therefore she is in favor of having nothing more than a RailRoad across the Isthmus. She has even gone so far as to place Rails on a portion of the route, & has used every possible exertion to get permission from the Viceroy to lay a RailRoad all the way across. At present, Englishmen are engaged in transporting coal from the Nile to the Red Sea on the backs of Camels for the supply of the British Steamers in the Red Sea. The camels carry about 500 pounds at a time. This fact alone, proves that England opposes the making of a canal, for no very small or trifling reasons. This Canal & Rail Road dispute may ultimately produce a general disturbing of the peace of Europe.

We as a great Commercial people certainly should have a voice in that great commercial enterprise. It has been truly said that "Commerce wields an incomprehensible power over the destiny of the human race. With it unshackled, we can exist as a great & enlightened nation, without it, we can no longer boast of freedom or liberty, we should be slaves."

We have none but an Englishman (Mr. Todd [*sic*; Alexander Tod]) to represent our Government in Egypt at this time. If our Government wishes to send important Dispatches to Europe, thence to India, China &c, we are obliged to put them on board of English steamers, have them sent through English Post Offices & finally handed over to our Consul in Egypt (a full blooded John Bull) for him to forward at his pleasure via other English conveyances.

Now as one of the sovereign people of these United States I do most solemnly protest against these proceedings. England is a nation who has no feeling in common with us. Was it in her power, she would immediately arm the slaves of the South & aid them to murder their masters. England is philanthropic & humane to her own interest & self aggrandizement. The manner in which she used to furnish the Indians on our frontiers with tomahawks & scalping knives, & then pay them in British gold for each murder & scalp, shews up in a proper light English humanity & philanth[r]opy. It seems to me that we are insulting the memory of those who achieved our independence by thus doing all we can to promote the welfare of England while we neglect our own commercial interests. England gives her money freely where she can get back two dollars for one. She has established her steam packets all over the world, & now it is impossible that private individuals should be able to compete with her. If we want steam ships of our own to carry our mails back & forth, Government must do a little something towards bringing about this great object. I think we are bound to shake off the present bondage which we are under to British Steamers. The surveil[l]ance exercised by England over the correspondence of this Country, is contrary to the spirit & intent of our institutions, if it is not directly unconstitutional. As well might we permit England to send her agents over to this country & allow them to establish communications from Maine to Georgia—build RailRoads & carry mails from East to West, & North to South.

I trust the day is not far distant when we the people, in our might will rise, & with the aid of our Government (which is ourselves) break down this odious monopoly of the ocean, by England. Judging from all the documents I have lately met with from your pen, I conceive you are in favor of perpetual peace, & of a rigid exercise of national economy. I am sure no movement that can be devised by human wisdom or ingenuity, would go farther towards ensuring a perpetual peace, than would the speedy Restoration of the Hebrews to Palestine, & surely nothing would sooner cause the rapid accumulation of a large surplus in our national treasury, than would the complete removal of all fears of war. You may rely upon it, if public feeling is once fairly excited & roused on the subject of Restoration, all ideas of a war, or of wars, will be banished from the minds of the great mass of mankind. If Judge Noah is sent by our Government to Constantinople or Egypt via England, France &c, besides doing all he can to bring about the speedy Restoration of his people to the Land of thier Fathers, & securing for us a lasting interest with the Hebrew Bankers of the Old World, his great aim will be to get them to become interested in a Line of Steamers intended to run between this country & Constantinople, via the Western Islands, Gibraltar, Malta, Egypt, Jerusalem (or rather, Joppa) & other important ports. He would also lose no opportunity to promote the introduction of our Cotton stuffs into Turkey & the adjacent dens[e]ly populated Countries.

It seems to me to be the height of folly for us to keep up at this day a large fleet of U.S. ships of war in the Mediterranean. That sea is fairly swarming with British war steamers, which are furnished with long range ordnance that enables them at thier pleasure to choose thier own distance & sink our ships before our short range guns could be brought to bear on them. As a proof that it is absurd in the highest degree, I have but to refer you to a case that occurred only a short time since, when on the mere rumour that war had been declared by England against this Country, one of our ships of war came home pell-mell & the Commander gave as a reason for returning without orders, that he considered it worse than madness to remain in the Mediterranean a moment after war should be declared against us by England. It is to be hoped that new discoveries & inventions are rapidly working a complete revolution in the commercial world.

Cumberland [Maryland] Coal, entirely superior for steam purposes, we have in endless abundance. That coal, according to a late Report of Professor [Walter R.] Johnson, & to my own knowledge contains full one third more heat-generating-material (Carbon) than is found in the best New-Castle Coal used by British Steamers. As soon as the Chesapeake & Ohio Canal is completed (which will probably be next year) we shall be able to supply the world with Cumberland Coal. We can afford to sell it in New York at as low a price, notwithstanding two tons of it are equal to three of the best New Cast[l]e Coal, as that Coal is sold for in London & Liverpool. A really philosophical Propeller, has recently been invented by Capt. R.F. Loper of Philadelphia. It has already been fairly tested, in heavy gales of wind at sea & surpasses the most sanguine expectations of every one who takes an interest in the success of our commerce. If it is possible to overcome the prejudices of our old Commodores, we shall have the Loper Propeller added to all of our ships of war, & they will be rendered efficient as steamers. But, steam power will be of no avail unless we have the suitable kind of cannon. We must be able to throw shot & shells as far as can be thrown by the vessels of any other nation. A recent invention covers this point, & puts us in possession of the means of building wrought iron guns that will be much stronger than those that are cast, & which with leaden shot will range equal, if not superior to the ordnance of the English Steamers, or to those possessed by any other nation. The Loper Propeller, with the necessary machinery, Boilers, furnaces &c, can easily be put far below the water line, & the Propeller itself acts best the deeper it is immersed. The machinery will occupy no part of the ship that is absolutely of consequence, as the space half way from the mizzen mast to the stern post in the run of a merchant vessel, or on the berth deck of a line of a battle ship is ample room for the whole of it. The Propeller fits into the dead wood of the stern, without effecting the looks, or impairing the strength of the ship. When we have our ships of war put in the proper condition, with Loper Propellers, wrought iron cannon, lead shot & furnished with Cumberland Coal, we shall be able to compete with any of the English war Steamers. The Loper Propeller, requires only about half as much fuel as is required by any other Propeller, (or by the old fashioned paddle wheels) to drive a vessel at the rate of ten or twelve miles through the water. In view of the foregoing, it takes no very great stretch of the imagination to see that we are on the eve of a new era in commercial affairs. Steam is the great leveller or equalizer of prices throughout the world, & as soon as it becomes universally adopted, trade will be regular & entirely free from the baneful influence of wild speculation. The Turks & all their co-religionists are extremely averse to wearing linen. They clothe themselves almost entirely with cotton, which they purchase at high prices, principally from the English. Now could we have facilities to introduce our cheap fabrics into that part of the world, it would vastly increase the consumption of Cotton. The English, sell at high prices, we should sell at low prices, & a better article, consequently the consumption would be greatly & rapidly increased. Hoping that the present golden opportunity will not be permitted by you to pass unimproved, & again earnestly beseeching you to write a few lines as already requested, if it is only to call the favorable notice of President Polk to the merits of your old & sincere friend Judge Noah, I remain with esteem Your Ob[edien]t Ser[van]t, Saml. W. Dewey.

ALS in ScCleA.

From J[ohn] S. Barbour

Catalpa [Va.] June 26th 1845

My Dear Sir, I returned from Fauquier [County] yesterday whither I had gone a few days since & immediately after the receipt of your favour of the 7th instant.

The present aspect of our federal affairs bodes but little good to the cause of the Country & the Constitution. I believe the intentions of the President [James K. Polk] are pure—full as much so, as cou[l]d be expected. Yet he cannot master the difficulties that *enfilade* his position, & strip him of all energy & volition. He is dependent on others, *than those of sound principles,* to maintain his administration. *He must yield to those upon whom he leans.* I do not see what strong man ["there" *interlined*] is in our favour in either branch of Congress. To stand with folded arms & yield the battlement to the enemy, in the frail hope of a redeeming energy in the virtue of the people; is neither the duty nor the policy of patriotism. In the Senate the administration has to stand the brunt of a powerful combination of talent & celebrity. It is *there* that the fate of the Country is to be settled. It *must* be rescued *there if rescued at all.*

The leading champions of Democracy, are anything but champions for the true principles of our system. In all times that are past, those champions have never been so true to themselves as when most false to us. Who can confide in [Thomas H.] Benton, or [William] Allen [Senator] of Ohio & men like these? [George] McDuffie is powerless if he ever returns to the Senate. Virginia will give you nothing in the place of [William C.] Rives that will not sit [*sic*] a stigma upon her former name. Whoever fights the battles of Democracy in that Senate, will be [*one word canceled and* "rewarded" *interlined*] with the confidence of the party throughout the Country. His true principles & purposes will be masked, & public sympathy will endue him with all the attributes of an admirable patriot, & yield him its rewards. These will be fatal to all that is near to the South. For those rewards will be conferred with ["no" *canceled*] reference to no other considerations, than those belonging to the conflict in which Benton, & men like Benton, will provoke & fight out on some false issue, with the [Daniel] Websters & [John M.] Claytons of the Senate. The administration will follow the drift of the popular sympathies, & yield its confidence & favour to such men as I have indicated. How is this to be prevented? In my opinion by your coming to the Senate leading your own forces & seizing the master's position, which is now vacant, but which some man must & will take *if you do not.* You have friends enough, devoted enough, but none of them can lead ["&" *canceled*]. You remarked to me in March last that you cou[l]d not be in the Senate "without drawing the enemy's fire." That you will do in or out of Congress, when you are strong enough to provoke their anger & invite their assaults. In the Senate you will be the head of the party. Your vast moral power gives you great advantage. The Country will prefer you as her leader, as the head & champion of her cause. Your triumphs will call to your aid that passion of the multitude which follows victory, or that sympathy which attends defeat ["in a glorious cause" *interlined*] if you are overthrown by selfish & unworthy combinations.

Your retirement is ruin & annihilation to us. In the whole South we have not a man who has the elements for a commander, neither in Congress nor out. Nor is there any time to be lost. If the fact is announced tomorrow, that you will return to the Senate, the whole virtue & patriotism of the Country, will feel its elastic energy springing up from despondency to hope. The rebound from its present depth of despair will be felt at once in the centre & in all the extremities of the confederacy. The administration will drive from its favour those ["who were(?) not" *canceled*] it does not love, but on whom it may be forced to depend. You will be trusted with its whole confidence, because its *penchant* is naturally & honestly towards you, because it wou[l]d be proud & ready to lean on you, because there is instinctively a leaning on virtue[']s side, (for the greatest ["knave," *interlined*] wou[l]d be upright if he cou[l]d be so safely & selfishly) and in no other mode will the power & patronage of this Govt. ever be drawn to support our Southern principles, & without ["that" *canceled*] that support we are powerless & hopeless. With it we have fearful odds in the contest, & those odds against us; *but with it, we shall triumph*—and that triumph is the only guaranty to Constitutional freedom, for which patriotism may cherish a last[?] & cheering hope. These are my views given you very hastily & very briefly. They are frank & free, for such is the province of friendship. I entreat you to weigh these intimations with many others the subject suggests, and if you concur, crush the egg of the cockatrice before it hatches the hydra of mischief. The knowledge that you will be in the Senate—aye the expectation & hope of it, will bring down the frown of "the powers that be" on those they dare not *now* offend. You can [*one word canceled*] save the Country & no other man can do it.

I am in greatest haste, Your true & sincere friend, J.S. Barbour.

ALS in ScCleA; PEx in Boucher and Brooks, eds., *Correspondence*, pp. 297–298.

From S[HADRACH] PENN, JR., "Confidential"

St. Louis, June 26 1845

Dear Sir, I visited Washington last month, and remained there four weeks. During my stay in the city I received assurances from the

President [James K. Polk] that he would pause in the appointment of Bentonians to office in St. Louis and the State of Missouri, and that the advertising patronage of the Departments would be immediately given to the Missouri Reporter. The first of these assurances was violated by the ["appoi" *canceled*] appointment of two Bentonians to office in St. Louis, some twelve or fourteen days after I left Washington, and I suppose the other will also be violated.

Whilst at Washington I became convinced that R[obert] J. Walker [Secretary of the Treasury] is, "the power behind the throne"—and I think the following facts will lead you to the same conclusion: The Globe, in the last months of its existence openly praised Mr. Walker, and stated that he consulted its editor [Francis P. Blair] as to all his movements in reference to annexation, &c. Gov-[ernor Lewis] Cass had failed to influence appointments in his own State, and his friends were, in effect, excluded from office. In Maine only one Texas man had received office; in Ohio all the appointees ["were" *interlined*] anti-Texas men, except one; in New Hampshire, none but the enemies of Mr. [Levi] Woodbury were deemed worthy of office; in Connecticut none but anti-annexationists received appointments; in Pennsylvania Mr. [James] Buchanan's enemies had received most of the important offices, and he was complaining that he had no influence, even in reference to appointments in his own State. It was also currently reported that he would go out of the Cabinet and be placed on the bench of the Supreme Court; and from the conversations of Pennsylvanians, I learned that the [George M.] Dallas and Buchanan factions were waging a war of extermination against each other in the Keystone State—in reference to which I had no reason to suppose Mr. Walker felt like a neutral. In New York the appointments had been given almost exclusively to Hunkers, and the Plebeian, the only paper that boldly advocated annexation, had been repudiated, and ceased to exist. You know, sir, how the South has been treated. In Missouri the appointments would indicate a determination to endorse and sustain the conduct of Col. [Thomas H.] Benton, as only two petty offices have been given to annexationists. The game is, to undermine all the prominent men of the party; and the aim of Walker is to administer on the political estates of Benton and [Martin] Van Buren, force Buchanan out of the Cabinet; get his place, make a few flourishes in it, and thus secure the succession. The President has thus been made to trample on his friends and confer offices on his foes, and violate the most solemn assurances and pledges. Of course, no confidence can be reposed in an Administration thus controlled. Walker carries with him Cave Johnson and [George] Bancroft, and the trio bear sway.

What is to be done? Will not the annexation Democrats find it necessary to combine in their own defence, and, if possible, sustain an organ at Washington by giving it the printing of the House or the Senate? If they do not, they will be trampled in the dust, and the restoration of Hunkerism will be fully consummated. It is idle to suppose any change will take place in the policy of the Administration without a previous change in the Cabinet. I believe we shall annex Texas in spite of the *dodgers* and *balkers* who are receiving all the offices of Government, or nearly all. On the Oregon question timid action may be expected; indeed, the [Washington] Union has intimated that a compromise is desirable—and that disposition was manifested by others in Washington. On the Tariff, the course of Mr. Polk will be *judicious*, if he knows how to make it so; and that question cannot be settled without an understanding between the North and South, and an approximation on the part of those sections of the Union. Cannot something like [James I.] McKay's bill be agreed on and carried through Congress? We must look to men unconnected with the Administration to carry such measures as are demanded by the interests and honor of the country, and I therefore trust you will return again to the Senate, where you can aid in giving a proper direction to legislation and the main body of the Democratic party, against whom the patronage of the Administration is now wielded. Annexationists, in most of the States, are as effectually excluded from office, as if they were Whigs. With some difficulty I shall be able to sustain myself against Col. Benton and the influence of the Administration. Yours Truly, S. Penn, Jr.

P.S. I think Mr. Buchanan will be forced out of the Cabinet; and an effort may be made to prevail on Cass to take the place. Should a fair or reasonable tariff be proposed Benton will assail it. He is courting the manufacturers and Abolitionists of the North.

ALS in ScCleA; PC in Boucher and Brooks, eds., *Correspondence,* pp. 298–300.

To [JAMES BUCHANAN], Secretary of State

Fort Hill, 30th June 1845

Dear Sir, A short time before I left the State Department, [Samuel W. Dewey] a friend of Maj[o]r [Mordecai M.] Noah presented his name for the Constantinople Mission, backed by numerous letters of recommendations in support of his claims. I informed his friend, that the then existing administration was too near its close to give the subject any consideration; but at his earnest request I read over the papers by which his application was supported. I learn by a letter from him, that he left them with Mr. [John] Tyler, & that they have been lost. He requests me to acquaint you with the nature & purport of the Major's testimonials; and I now write you in compliance with his request.

They were from highly respectable sources. One was from The Trustees & managers of all the synagogues of the city of New York. There were many from respectable Hebrews from nearly all parts of the Union. There was one from Sir Moses Montefeare [*sic*; Montefiore] of London, of a very flattering character. They all bore high testimony to the character of the Maj[o]r & his qualifications for the Mission. In addition, they placed his recommendation on the ground, that they, as a people, had received but few offices from the government; that his appointment would be very gratifying to them & their brethren in this country, in Europe & the East; that they exerted great influence both in Europe & the East, which would be brought to bear in our favour at Constantinople, should he be appointed. They also suggested, that he would be a suitable person to negotiate with the Egyptian Government on the subject of the right of passage between the Mediter[rane]an & the Red seas, which already claim the attention of several of the European Governments; & that he would be backed there by the influence of his brethren, who possessed much influence in Egypt. This, as well as I can recollect, was the nature & character of the Maj[o]r's Testimonials. Yours truly, J.C. Calhoun.

ALS in DNA, RG 59 (State Department), Applications and Recommendations, 1845–1853, Noah (M-873:63, frames 295–297).

SYMBOLS

▯

The following symbols have been used in this volume as abbreviations for the forms in which documents of John C. Calhoun have been found and for the repositories in which they are preserved. (Full citations to printed sources of documents can be found in the Bibliography.)

Abs   —abstract (a summary)
ADS   —autograph document, signed
ADU   —autograph document, unsigned
AEI   —autograph endorsement, initialed
AES   —autograph endorsement, signed
AEU   —autograph endorsement, unsigned
ALI   —autograph letter, initialed
ALS   —autograph letter, signed
ALU   —autograph letter, unsigned
CC   —clerk's copy (a secondary ms. copy)
CCEx   —clerk's copy of an extract
CSt   —Stanford University Library, Stanford, Cal.
DLC   —Library of Congress, Washington
DNA   —National Archives, Washington
DS   —document, signed
DU   —document, unsigned
En   —enclosure
Ens   —enclosures
ES   —endorsement, signed
EU   —endorsement, unsigned
FC   —file copy (usually a letterbook copy retained by the sender)
IGK   —Knox College, Galesburg, Ill.
LS   —letter, signed
LU   —letter, unsigned
M-   —(followed by a number) published microcopy of the National
          Archives
MH   —Harvard University, Cambridge, Mass.
MHi   —Massachusetts Historical Society, Boston
MoSHi   —Missouri Historical Society, St. Louis
NcD   —Duke University, Durham, N.C.
NcU   —Southern Historical Collection, University of North Carolina at
          Chapel Hill
NjMD   —Drew University, Madison, N.J.
NjMoN   —Morristown National Historical Park, Morristown, N.J.
NjP   —Princeton University, Princeton, N.J.
NNPM   —Pierpont Morgan Library, New York City

PC	—printed copy
PDS	—printed document, signed
PEx	—printed extract
PHarH	—Pennsylvania Historical and Museum Commission, Harrisburg
PHi	—Historical Society of Pennsylvania, Philadelphia
PWbWHi	—Wyoming Historical and Geological Society, Wilkes-Barre, Pa.
RG	—Record Group in the National Archives
ScC	—Charleston Library Society, Charleston, S.C.
ScCleA	—Clemson University, Clemson, S.C.
ScCM	—Waring Historical Collection, Medical University of South Carolina, Charleston
ScU-SC	—South Caroliniana Library, University of South Carolina, Columbia
T-	—(followed by a number) published microfilm of the National Archives
Tx	—Texas State Library, Austin
TxGR	—Rosenberg Library, Galveston, Texas
TxU	—Barker Texas History Center, University of Texas at Austin
Vi	—Virginia State Library, Richmond
ViHi	—Virginia Historical Society, Richmond
ViU	—University of Virginia, Charlottesville

BIBLIOGRAPHY

❑

This Bibliography is limited to sources of and previous printings of documents published in this volume.

Aderman, Ralph M., and others, eds., *Letters [of Washington Irving]*. 4 vols. Boston: Twayne, 1978–1982. (Vols. 23–26 of *The Complete Works of Washington Irving*.)

Ambler, Charles Henry, ed., *Correspondence of Robert M.T. Hunter, 1826–1876*, in the *American Historical Association Annual Report* for 1916 (2 vols. Washington: U.S. Government Printing Office, 1918), vol. II.

Autograph Letters, Manuscripts, Documents. Somerville, Mass.: Kenneth W. Rendell, Inc., [1970].

Boucher, Chauncey S., and Robert P. Brooks, eds., *Correspondence Addressed to John C. Calhoun, 1837–1849*, in the *American Historical Association Annual Report* for 1929 (Washington: U.S. Government Printing Office, 1930).

British and Foreign State Papers (170 vols. London: HMSO, 1812–1968), vols. 33 and 34.

Camden, S.C., *Journal*, 1826–1891?.

Charleston, S.C., *Courier*, 1803–1852.

Charleston, S.C., *Mercury*, 1822–1868.

Columbus, Ga., *Times*, 1841–1845?.

Crallé, Richard K., ed., *The Works of John C. Calhoun*. 6 vols. Columbia, S.C.: printed by A.S. Johnston, 1851, and New York: D. Appleton & Co., 1853–1857.

Edgefield, S.C., *Advertiser*, 1836–.

Garrison, George P., ed., *Diplomatic Correspondence of the Republic of Texas*, in the *American Historical Association Annual Report* for 1907, vol. II, and for 1908, vol. II. Washington: U.S. Government Printing Office, 1908–1911.

Greenville, S.C., *Mountaineer*, 1829–1901.

Holmes, Alester G., and George R. Sherrill, *Thomas Green Clemson: His Life and Work*. Richmond: Garrett & Massie, 1937.

Jackson, Miss., *Mississippian*, 1832–1865?.

Jackson, Miss., *Southern Reformer*, 1843–1846.

Jameson, J. Franklin, ed., *Correspondence of John C. Calhoun*, in the *American Historical Association Annual Report* for 1899 (2 vols. Washington: U.S. Government Printing Office, 1900), vol. II.

[Janney, Samuel M.?] "A Virginian," *Letter Addressed to the Hon. John C. Calhoun. On the Law Relating to Slaves, Free Negroes, and Mulattoes*. Washington: J. & G.S. Gideon, 1845.

"Letters from John C. Calhoun to Francis W. Pickens," in *South Carolina Historical Magazine*, vol. VII, no. 1 (January, 1906), pp. 12–19.

Lexington, Ky., *Observer and Reporter*, 1840–?.

Liberator, The. Boston, 1831–1865.

Manning, William R., ed., *Diplomatic Correspondence of the United States: Canadian Relations, 1784–1860*. 4 vols. Washington: Carnegie Endowment for International Peace, 1940–1945.

Manning, William R., ed., *Diplomatic Correspondence of the United States: Inter-American Affairs, 1831–1860*. 12 vols. Washington: Carnegie Endowment for International Peace, 1932–1939.

Milledgeville, Ga., *Federal Union*, 1830–1872.

Mobile, Ala., *Register and Journal*, 1841?–.

Moore, Frederick W., ed., "Calhoun as Seen by His Political Friends: Letters of Duff Green, Dixon H. Lewis [and] Richard K. Crallé During the Period from 1831 to 1848," in *Publications of the Southern History Association*, vol. VII (1903).

Nashville, Tenn., *Union*, 1835–1875.

Nashville, Tenn., *Whig*, 1838–1855.

Natchez, Miss., *Mississippi Free Trader & Natchez Gazette*, 1835–1861?.

New Orleans, La., *Jeffersonian Republican*, 1844–1845.

New York, N.Y., *Herald*, 1835–1924.

New York, N.Y., *National Anti-Slavery Standard*, 1840–1872.

Niles' Register. Baltimore, 1811–1849.

Oliphant, Mary C. Simms, Alfred Taylor Odell, and T.C. Duncan Eaves, eds., *Letters of William Gilmore Simms*. 6 vols. Columbia: University of South Carolina Press, 1952–1982.

Pendleton, S.C., *Messenger*, 1807–?.

Raleigh, N.C., *North Carolina Standard*, 1834–1870.

Rayback, Joseph G., "The Presidential Ambitions of John C. Calhoun, 1844–1848," in *Journal of Southern History*, vol. XIV, no. 3 (August, 1948), pp. 331–356.

Richmond, Va., *Enquirer*, 1804–1877.

Sioussat, St. George L., ed., "Selected Letters, 1844–1845, from the Donelson Papers," in *Tennessee Historical Magazine*, vol. III (June, 1917), pp. 134–162.

Tyler, Lyon G., *The Letters and Times of the Tylers*. 3 vols. Richmond: Whittet & Shepperson, 1884–1896.

U.S. House of Representatives, *House Documents*, 28th and 29th Congresses.

U.S. House of Representatives, *House Journal*, 28th Congress.

U.S. House of Representatives, *House Reports*, 28th Congress.

U.S. Senate, *Senate Documents*, 28th, 29th, 32nd, and 41st Congresses.

U.S. Senate, *Senate Journal*, 28th Congress.

Washington, D.C., *Constitution*, 1844–1845.

Washington, D.C., *Daily National Intelligencer*, 1800–1870.

Washington, D.C., *Madisonian*, 1837–1845.

Washington, D.C., *Union*, 1845–1859.

INDEX

Ⅲ

615

53, 109–110, 113, 133, 135, 160,
165, 179, 193, 210, 221, 224, 286,
301, 326, 335, 340, 342–343, 352,
416, 463, 582, 586; from, 338;
mentioned, xiii, 3, 28, 35, 42, 44,
53, 70, 72, 92–93, 97–98, 155, 157,
161, 166–170, 175, 180, 189, 222,
231, 238, 250, 256, 258, 260,
267, 275, 280–281, 303–304,
319, 325, 335–336, 342, 348, 354,
359, 361, 372, 378, 389, 396–397,
422, 472, 497–498, 502, 552, 568,
576; messages of, 71, 78, 108,
153–154, 161–162, 234, 260, 347–
348, 364, 366; to, 45, 87, 112,
235, 236, 242, 261, 262, 266, 296,
331, 338, 390, 395, 407.
Tyler, Julia Gardiner: mentioned, 352.
Tyler, Robert: from, 495; mentioned,
352.

United States Democratic Review:
417, 500–501.
U.S. Military Academy: 102.
University of Georgia: ix, 425–426.
University of North Carolina: docu-
ments in Southern Historical
Collection of, 134, 419.
University of Pennsylvania: 460.
University of South Carolina: docu-
ments in South Caroliniana Li-
brary of, 36, 52, 106, 107, 181,
248, 289, 302, 418, 444, 445, 461,
465, 529, 532, 539, 540, 589, 594.
University of Texas: documents in
Barker Texas History Center of,
93, 282.
University of Virginia: documents in
library of, 207, 558; mentioned,
106, 248, 526, 532, 558, 569.
Unknown Person: from, 546.
Upshur, Abel P.: mentioned, 68, 93,
122, 258, 391, 570.
Uruguay: xviii–xix, 99–101, 131, 166–
167, 244, 266–268, 332, 338, 349,
367–368, 395–396, 406.
Usher, George F.: from, 13.
Utica, N.Y.: xi.

Van Buren, John: mentioned, 354.
Van Buren, Martin: mentioned, ix,
xiii, 26, 80, 81, 109–110, 114, 116,
139, 208, 209, 221, 301, 318, 319,
339, 353–354, 387, 450, 456,
463, 470, 472, 476–478, 495, 496,
498, 500, 531, 547, 553, 573,
580–581, 584, 597, 599, 608.
Van der Horst, ———: mentioned, 117.
Van Horne, B.: from, 503.
Van Ness, Cornelius P.: from, 263;
mentioned, 15, 89, 193, 253–255,
264, 405, 583–584, 599.
Van Zandt, Isaac: mentioned, 35, 108,
177, 283.
Vasquez, Santiago: mentioned, 53–55.
Vatican: 101–102, 163.
Vaucluse Mill: 525.
Vaughn, James: mentioned, 438.
Velasco, Tex.: 180–181.
Vendel, E. de: from, 47.
Venezuela: 16, 42–43, 54–56, 148,
158–159, 177, 191, 214, 336, 338,
363, 420.
Vera Cruz: 46–47, 119, 207, 210, 361.
Vergara, ———: mentioned, 54–56.
Vermont: 82, 453.
Vice-President, U.S.: 28, 496, 498,
559, 573, 599. *See also* Dallas,
George M.
Vicksburg, Miss.: 556.
Victoria, Queen: mentioned, 49–51,
123, 164, 171–173, 218, 220, 277,
280–281, 284, 327, 349, 367, 371–
372, 388, 403–404.
Vincent, Frederick: mentioned, 360–
361.
Virginia: 4–5, 9–13, 52, 97, 138–139,
141–142, 144, 155, 162, 198, 250,
280, 293, 295, 310, 320–322,
360–361, 374–376, 421–423, 427–
428, 439–440, 447–450, 454, 462–
463, 488–490, 510–513, 536,
542, 546–548, 551, 556–561, 565–
567, 581, 587, 595, 605–607.
Virginia Historical Society: documents
in, 9, 155, 493, 509.
Virginia Military Institute: 102.
"Virginian, A" (pseudonym): from, 4.

645